THE INSTITUTE FOR POLISH–JEWISH STUDIES

The Institute for Polish–Jewish Studies in Oxford and its sister organization, the American Association for Polish–Jewish Studies, which publish *Polin*, are learned societies that were established in 1984, following the International Conference on Polish–Jewish Studies, held in Oxford. The Institute is an associate institute of the Oxford Centre for Hebrew and Jewish Studies, and the American Association is linked with the Department of Near Eastern and Judaic Studies at Brandeis University.

Both the Institute and the American Association aim to promote understanding of the Polish Jewish past. They have no building or library of their own and no paid staff; they achieve their aims by encouraging scholarly research and facilitating its publication, and by creating forums for people with a scholarly interest in Polish Jewish topics, both past and present.

To this end the Institute and the American Association help organize lectures and international conferences. Venues for these activities have included Brandeis University in Waltham, Massachusetts, the Hebrew University in Jerusalem, the Institute for the Study of Human Sciences in Vienna, King's College in London, the Jagiellonian University in Kraków, the Oxford Centre for Hebrew and Jewish Studies, the University of Łódź, University College London, and the Polish Cultural Institute and the Polish embassy in London. They have encouraged academic exchanges between Israel, Poland, the United States, and western Europe. In particular they seek to help train a new generation of scholars, in Poland and elsewhere, to study the culture and history of the Jews in Poland.

Each year since 1986 the Institute has published a volume of scholarly papers in the series *Polin: Studies in Polish Jewry* under the general editorship of Professor Antony Polonsky of Brandeis University. Since 1994 the series has been published on its behalf by the Littman Library of Jewish Civilization, and since 1998 the publication has been linked with the American Association as well. In March 2000 the entire series was honoured with a National Jewish Book Award from the Jewish Book Council in the United States. More than twenty other works on Polish Jewish topics have also been published with the Institute's assistance.

Further information on the Institute for Polish–Jewish Studies can be found on its website, <www.polishjewishstudies.co.uk>. For the website of the American Association for Polish–Jewish Studies, see <www.aapjstudies.org>.

THE LITTMAN LIBRARY OF
JEWISH CIVILIZATION

Dedicated to the memory of
LOUIS THOMAS SIDNEY LITTMAN
*who founded the Littman Library for the love of God
and as an act of charity in memory of his father*
JOSEPH AARON LITTMAN
and to the memory of
ROBERT JOSEPH LITTMAN
who continued what his father Louis had begun
יהא זכרם ברוך

'*Get wisdom, get understanding:
Forsake her not and she shall preserve thee*'
PROV. 4: 5

*The Littman Library of Jewish Civilization is a registered UK charity
Registered charity no.* 1000784

POLIN
STUDIES IN POLISH JEWRY

VOLUME THIRTEEN
The Holocaust and its Aftermath

Edited by
ANTONY POLONSKY

Published for
The Institute for Polish–Jewish Studies
and
The American Association for Polish–Jewish Studies

The Littman Library of Jewish Civilization
in association with Liverpool University Press

*The Littman Library of Jewish Civilization
in association with Liverpool University Press
4 Cambridge Street, Liverpool* L69 7ZU, UK

www.liverpooluniversitypress.co.uk/littman

Managing Editor: Connie Webber

*Distributed in North America by
Oxford University Press Inc., 198 Madison Avenue,
New York,* NY 10016, USA

First published in hardback and paperback 2000

© *Institute for Polish–Jewish Studies 2000*

*All rights reserved.
No part of this publication may be reproduced,
stored in a retrieval system, or transmitted, in any form or by
any means, without the prior permission in writing of
The Littman Library of Jewish Civilization*

*The paperback edition of this book is sold subject to the condition
that it shall not, by way of trade or otherwise, be lent, re-sold, hired out
or otherwise circulated without the publisher's prior consent in any
form of binding or cover other than that in which it is published
and without a similar condition including this condition
being imposed on the subsequent purchaser*

*Catalogue records for this book are available from the
British Library and the Library of Congress*

*ISSN 0268 1056
ISBN 978-1-874774-47-1*

*Publishing co-ordinator: Janet Moth
Copy-editing: Laurien Berkeley
Proof-reading: Lindsey Taylor-Guthartz
Index: Bonnie Blackburn
Design: Pete Russell, Faringdon, Oxon.
Typesetting: Footnote Graphics, Warminster, Wilts.*

*Printed in Great Britain by
CPI Group (UK) Ltd., Croydon, CR0 4YY*

Articles appearing in this publication are abstracted and indexed in
Historical Abstracts and *America: History and Life*

To all victims of oppression in the century gone by

JOHANNA ROSS

———

The publication of this volume of POLIN *was made possible by grants from the*

DAVID AND BARBARA B. HIRSCHHORN

and

LUCIUS N. LITTAUER

foundations

Editors and Advisers

EDITORS
Monika Adamczyk-Garbowska, *Lublin*
Israel Bartal, *Jerusalem*
Antony Polonsky (Chair), *Waltham, Mass.*
Michael Steinlauf, *Philadelphia*
Jerzy Tomaszewski, *Warsaw*

REVIEW EDITORS
ChaeRan Freeze, *Waltham, Mass.*
Joshua Zimmerman, *New York*

EDITORIAL BOARD

Chimen Abramsky, *London*
Władysław T. Bartoszewski, *Warsaw*
Stanislaus Blejwas, *New Britain, Conn.*
David Engel, *New York*
David Fishman, *New York*
ChaeRan Freeze, *Waltham, Mass.*
Józef Gierowski, *Kraków*
Jacob Goldberg, *Jerusalem*
Yisrael Gutman, *Jerusalem*
Jerzy Kłoczowski, *Lublin*
Ezra Mendelsohn, *Jerusalem*
Elchanan Reiner, *Tel Aviv*

Jehuda Reinharz, *Waltham, Mass.*
Moshe Rosman, *Tel Aviv*
Henryk Samsonowicz, *Warsaw*
Rafael Scharf, *London*
Robert Shapiro, *New York*
Michael Steinlauf, *Philadelphia*
Adam Teller, *Haifa*
Piotr S. Wandycz, *New Haven*
Jonathan Webber, *Oxford*
Joshua Zimmerman, *New York*
Steven Zipperstein, *Stanford, Calif.*

ADVISORY BOARD

Władysław Bartoszewski, *Warsaw*
Jan Błoński, *Kraków*
Abraham Brumberg, *Washington*
Andrzej Chojnowski, *Warsaw*
Tadeusz Chrzanowski, *Kraków*
Andrzej Ciechanowiecki, *London*
Norman Davies, *London*
Victor Erlich, *New Haven*
Frank Golczewski, *Hamburg*
Olga Goldberg, *Jerusalem*
Feliks Gross, *New York*
Czesław Hernas, *Wrocław*
Maurycy Horn, *Warsaw*
Jerzy Jedlicki, *Warsaw*
Andrzej Kamiński, *Washington*
Hillel Levine, *Boston*
Lucjan Lewitter, *Cambridge, Mass.*

Stanisław Litak, *Lublin*
Heinz-Dietrich Löwe, *Heidelberg*
Emanuel Meltzer, *Tel Aviv*
Czesław Miłosz (Hon. Chair), *Berkeley*
Shlomo Netzer, *Tel Aviv*
David Patterson, *Oxford*
Zbigniew Pełczyński, *Oxford*
Szymon Rudnicki, *Warsaw*
Alexander Schenker, *New Haven*
David Sorkin, *Madison*
Edward Stankiewicz, *New Haven*
Norman Stone, *Ankara*
Daniel Tollet, *Paris*
Shmuel Werses, *Jerusalem*
Jacek Woźniakowski, *Lublin*
Piotr Wróbel, *Toronto*

Preface

Polin is sponsored by the Institute for Polish–Jewish Studies, Oxford and by the American Association for Polish–Jewish Studies, which is linked with the Department of Near Eastern and Judaic Studies, Brandeis University. As with earlier issues, this volume could not have appeared without the untiring assistance of many individuals. In particular, we should like to express our gratitude to Dr Jonathan Webber, Treasurer of the Institute for Polish–Jewish Studies, to Professor Jehuda Reinharz, President of Brandeis University, and Mrs Irene Pipes, President of the American Association for Polish–Jewish Studies. As was the case with earlier volumes, this one could not have been published without the constant assistance and supervision of Connie Webber, managing editor of the Littman Library, Janet Moth, publishing co-ordinator, and the tireless copy-editing of Laurien Berkeley. We also owe a debt to Gwido Zlatkes for keeping to a minimum mistakes in the Polish language.

Plans for future volumes of *Polin* are well advanced. Volume 14 will feature a cluster of articles on Jews in the borderlands of the former Polish–Lithuanian Commonwealth. We are also planning volumes on Jews in smaller Polish towns, on Jewish spirituality, on Polish–Jewish relations in the United States, on Jewish popular culture in Poland, and on Jewish women in eastern Europe. We should welcome articles for these issues, as well as for our New Views section. In particular, we should be very grateful for assistance in extending our coverage to the areas of Ukraine, Belarus, and Lithuania, both in the period in which these countries were part of the Polish–Lithuanian Commonwealth and subsequently. As always, we should also welcome any suggestions or criticisms. Finally, we are happy to announce that we are publishing a consolidated index to the first twelve volumes of *Polin*. As well as a full index of subjects covered by the volumes, this will contain complete tables of contents, indexes of contributors and of books reviewed, and maps and chronological tables, all of which will make it much easier to mine the many riches contained in past issues.

We are very honoured that *Polin* was nominated the winner of the 1999 National Jewish Book Award in the eastern European category. This is a tribute to all those who have worked so hard to produce the thirteen volumes which have appeared since the founding of the journal.

Finally, we should like to express our sadness at the passing of Jerzy Turowicz, long-time editor of *Tygodnik Powszechny*, a member of our editorial advisory board, and a man who played a crucial role in Polish–Jewish and Christian–Jewish understanding. He will be sadly missed.

POLIN

Gentle Polin (Poland), ancient land of Torah and learning
From the day Ephraim first departed from Judah

From a selihah *by Rabbi Moshe Katz Geral
of the exiles of Poland, head of the Beth Din of the
Holy Congregation of Metz*

We did not know, but our fathers told us how the exiles of Israel came to the land of Polin (Poland).

When Israel saw how its sufferings were constantly renewed, oppressions increased, persecutions multiplied, and how the evil authorities piled decree on decree and followed expulsion with expulsion, so that there was no way to escape the enemies of Israel, they went out on the road and sought an answer from the paths of the wide world: which is the correct road to traverse to find rest for the soul. Then a piece of paper fell from heaven, and on it the words:

Go to Polaniya (Poland).

So they came to the land of Polin and they gave a mountain of gold to the king, and he received them with great honour. And God had mercy on them, so that they found favour from the king and the nobles. And the king gave them permission to reside in all the lands of his kingdom, to trade over its length and breadth and to serve God according to the precepts of their religion. And the king protected them against every foe and enemy.

And Israel lived in Polin in tranquillity for a long time. They devoted themselves to trade and handicrafts. And God sent a blessing on them so that they were blessed in the land, and their name was exalted among the peoples. And they traded with the surrounding countries and they also struck coins with inscriptions in the holy language and the language of the country. These are the coins which have on them a lion rampant towards the right. And on the coins are the words 'Mieszko, King of Poland' or 'Mieszko, Król of Poland'. The Poles call their king 'Król'.

When they came from the land of the Franks, they found a wood in the land and on every tree, one tractate of the Talmud was incised. This is the forest of

Kawczyn, which is near Lublin. And every man said to his neighbour, 'We have come to the land where our ancestors dwelt before the Torah and revelation were granted.'

And those who seek for names say: 'This is why it is called Polin. For thus spoke Israel when they came to the land, "Here rest for the night [*Po lin*]." And this means that we shall rest here until we are all gathered into the Land of Israel.'

Since this is the tradition, we accept it as such.

S. Y. AGNON, 1916

Contents

Note on Names of People and Places — xvi
Note on Transliteration — xviii
List of Abbreviations — xix

PART I
THE HOLOCAUST AND ITS AFTERMATH

Introduction — 3
ANTONY POLONSKY

Anti-Jewish Violence in Poland, 1918–1939 and 1945–1947 — 34
JOANNA MICHLIC-COREN

Jewish Reaction to the Soviet Arrival in the Kresy in September 1939 — 62
ANDRZEJ ŻBIKOWSKI

Reflections on Soviet Documents Relating to Polish Prisoners of War Taken in September 1939 — 73
SIMON SCHOCHET

The Demography of Jews in Hiding in Warsaw, 1943–1945 — 78
GUNNAR S. PAULSSON

Psychological Problems of Polish Jews who Used Aryan Documents — 104
MARIA EINHORN-SUSUŁOWSKA

My Two Mothers — 112
ELŻBIETA FICOWSKA

Early Swedish Information about the Nazis' Mass Murder of the Jews — 113
JÓZEF LEWANDOWSKI

Jewish Identities in the Holocaust: Martyrdom as a Representative Category — 128
JONATHAN WEBBER

Three Essays on Jewish Education during the Nazi Occupation — 147
MARIAN MAŁOWIST

Two Coffins on Smocza Street and Śliska Street — 163
JANUSZ KORCZAK

Krzysztof Kamil Baczyński: A Poet-Hero JOANNA ROSTROPOWICZ CLARK	166
Paper Epitaphs of a Holocaust Memorial: Zofia Nałkowska's *Medallions* DIANA KUPREL	179
Letter to Father JAN RYSZARD BYCHOWSKI	188
Stereotypes of Polish–Jewish Relations after the War: The Special Commission of the Central Committee of Polish Jews JAN GROSS	194
The Bund and the Jewish Fraction of the Polish Workers' Party in Poland after 1945 BOŻENA SZAYNOK	206
Whose Nation, Whose State? Working-Class Nationalism and Antisemitism in Poland, 1945–1947 PADRAIC KENNEY	224
Poles and Jews in the Kielce Region and Radom, April 1945–February 1946 ADAM PENKALLA	236
Polish Jews during and after the Kielce Pogrom: Reports from the Communist Archives JOANNA MICHLIC-COREN	253
Bełżec RUDOLF REDER with a translator's note by M. M. RUBEL	268
The Auschwitz-Birkenau Memorial and Museum: From Commemoration to Education TERESA ŚWIEBOCKA	290

PART II
A DEBATE ABOUT ANTISEMITISM IN POLAND TODAY

Black is Black STANISŁAW MUSIAŁ	303
A Rainbow in Black WALDEMAR CHROSTOWSKI	310
The Sin of Antisemitism: A Response to Waldemar Chrostowski STANISŁAW MUSIAŁ	317

Difficult Remarks to Write STANISŁAW KRAJEWSKI	323
A Shadow over the Dialogue MONIKA ADAMCZYK-GARBOWSKA	325

PART III
AN INTERVIEW

Marian Małowist on History and Historians	331

PART IV
NEW VIEWS

The Day after the Pogrom: A Documentary Account JÓZEF BEKKER	347
Jewish Theatre in Poland before the Second World War: Its Audiences and its Critics MAYA PERETZ	356
Forbidden Fruit: Illicit Love Affairs between Jews and Gentiles in the Novels of Julian Stryjkowski REGINA GROL	366
Ludwik Rajchman: A Biographical Sketch of a Polish Jew MARTA ALEKSANDRA BALIŃSKA	373
Abraham Joshua Heschel in Poland: Hasidism Enters Modernity EDWARD K. KAPLAN	383

PART V
REVIEWS

REVIEW ESSAYS

Recent Books on the Catholic Church in Poland JOHN T. PAWLIKOWSKI	401
'You shall not bear false witness': Stanisław C. Napiórkowski (ed.), *A bliźniego swego . . . Materiały z sympozjum 'Św. Maksymilian Maria Kolbe—Żydzi—masoni'* JERZY TOMASZEWSKI	406

A Lithuanian Account of Life in the Camps: Balys Sruoga,
Forest of the Gods: Memoirs 411
NERIJUS UDRENAS

Analyses of World Antisemitism Published between 1991 and 1997 418
ALINA CAŁA

BOOK REVIEWS

Joseph Perl, *Revealer of Secrets: The First Hebrew Novel*,
trans. and ed. Dov Taylor 425
PAUL RADENSKY

Hanna Kozińska-Witt, *Die Krakauer Jüdische Reformgemeinde,
1864–1874* 427
ANDRZEJ ŻBIKOWSKI

Emanuel Melzer, *No Way Out: The Politics of Polish Jewry, 1935–1939* 431
JERZY TOMASZEWSKI

Ezra Mendelsohn (ed.), *Essential Papers on Jews and the Left* 433
JERZY TOMASZEWSKI

David Weinfeld (ed.), *Hebrew Poetry in Poland between the Two
World Wars* 434
DAVID ABERBACH

Włodzimierz Mich, *Obcy w polskim domu: nacjonalistyczne koncepcje
rozwiązania problemu mniejszości narodowych 1918–1939* 436
JOANNA MICHLIC-COREN

Natan Gross, *Toledot hakolnoa hayehudi befolin, 1910–1950* 440
YARON PELEG

Robert Liberles, *Salo Wittmayer Baron: Architect of Jewish History* 443
IRA ROBINSON

Michael C. Steinlauf, *Bondage to the Dead: Poland and the Memory of
the Holocaust* 444
JERZY TOMASZEWSKI

Agata Tuszyńska, *Lost Landscapes: In Search of the Jews of Poland*,
trans. Madeline Levine 446
RUTH ABRAMS

OBITUARY

Teresa Prekerowa (1922–1998) 450
GUNNAR S. PAULSSON

CORRESPONDENCE

Exchange between Rafał Żebrowski and Hanna Kozińska-Witt 453

Notes on the Contributors 457
Glossary 463
Index 465

Note on Names of People and Places

POLITICAL connotations accrue to words, names, and spellings with an alacrity unfortunate for those who would like to maintain neutrality. It seems reasonable to honour the choice of a people regarding their own name, and of a population regarding the name of their city or town, but what is one to do when the people have no consensus on their name, or when the town changes its name, and the name its spelling, again and again over time? The politician may always opt for the latest version, but the hapless historian must reckon with them all. This note, then, will be our brief reckoning; out of consideration for our readers we will hereafter use only one name per people and one designation for each city.

PLACE-NAMES

There is no problem with places which have accepted English names, such as Warsaw. But every other place-name in east central Europe raises serious problems. A good example is Wilno–Vilna–Vilnius. There are clear objections to all of these. Until 1944 the majority of the population was Polish. Today the city is in Lithuania. 'Vilna', though raising the least problems, is an artificial construct. In this volume we have adopted the following guidelines, although we are aware that they are not wholly consistent.

1. Towns which have a form which is acceptable in English will be given in that form. Some examples are Warsaw, Kiev, Moscow, St Petersburg.

2. Towns which in the period to 1939 were clearly part of a particular state will be given in a form which reflects that situation. Some examples are Breslau, Przemyśl, Rzeszów. In Polish Kraków has always been spelled as such. In English it has more often appeared as Cracow, but the current English trend is to follow the local language as much as possible. In keeping with this trend towards local determination, then, we shall maintain the Polish spelling.

3. Towns which are in mixed areas should take the form in which they are known today and which reflects their present situation. Examples are Poznań, Toruń, Kaunas, L'viv. This applies also to bibliographical references. We have made one exception to this rule, using the common English form for Vilna until its first incorporation into Lithuania in October 1939 and using Vilnius thereafter. We use Danzig until 1945 and Gdańsk thereafter. We refer to books published in Munich in that form, not in the German form. Galicia's most diversely named city, and one of its most important, boasts four variants: the Polish

Lwów, the German Lemberg, the Russian Lvov, and the Ukrainian L'viv. As this city currently lives under Ukrainian rule, and most of its current residents speak Ukrainian, we shall follow the Ukrainian spelling. Other towns today in Ukraine, Belarus, and Lithuania have their present-day form. There is one exception to this, which is Stanisławów, which has its present-day form mentioned only on its first appearance (Ivano-Frankovsk). This means giving the Ukrainian form for Husiatyne, Tyśmienica, etc.

4. Some place-names have different forms in Yiddish. Occasionally the subject-matter dictates that the Yiddish place-name should be the prime form, in which case the corresponding Polish (Ukrainian, Belarusian, Lithuanian) name is given in parenthesis at first mention.

ETHNIC IDENTITIES, PEOPLES, AND NATIONHOOD

When referring to various peoples living in one country, we shall use the terms 'people', 'ethnic group', 'ethnicity', 'nation', and 'nationality'. The concept of nationality as reflecting citizenship alone and not ethnicity never reached Galicia, where political rights reflected ethnicity. Nationalism and national consciousness accordingly focused on ethnicity, language, and sometimes religion, not on any sense of commonality among members of different peoples sharing a single country. 'National' may thus appear in this text in the sense of 'concerning an ethnic group united by or perceived as sharing a political consciousness'; 'multinational' and 'multi-ethnic' thereby become near synonyms, distinguished only by the connotation of political consciousness ('nationalism') implicit in the former. So as to avoid confusion, however, we shall refer to interactions among peoples within a single country as 'inter-ethnic' rather than as 'inter-national'. We hope that these decisions reflect our respect for all concerned, not only past and current members of these peoples and residents of these cities but also our readers, who deserve to find lucid and reasonably consistent prose within these pages.

Note on Transliteration

HEBREW

An attempt has been made to achieve consistency in the transliteration of Hebrew words. The following are the key distinguishing features of the system that has been adopted:

1. No distinction is made between the *aleph* and *ayin*; both are represented by an apostrophe, and only when they appear in an intervocalic position.
2. *Veit* is written *v*; *ḥet* is written *ḥ*; *yod* is written *y* when it functions as a consonant and *i* when it occurs as a vowel; *khaf* is written *kh*; *tsadi* is written *ts*; *kof* is written *k*.
3. The *dagesh ḥazak*, represented in some transliteration systems by doubling the letter, is not represented, except in words that have more or less acquired normative English spellings that include doubling, such as Hallel, kabbalah, kaddish, rabbi, Sukkot, and Yom Kippur.
4. The *sheva na* is represented by an *e*.
5. Hebrew prefixes, prepositions, and conjunctions are not followed by hyphens when they are transliterated; thus *betoledot ha'am hayehudi*.
6. Capital letters are not used in the transliteration of Hebrew except for the first word in the titles of books and the names of people, places, institutions, and generally as in the conventions of the English language.
7. The names of individuals are transliterated following the above rules unless the individual concerned followed a different usage.

YIDDISH

Transliteration follows the YIVO system except for the names of people, where the spellings they themselves used have been retained.

RUSSIAN AND UKRAINIAN

The Library of Congress system has been used, except that we are not employing character modifiers and a double prime for the hard sign.

Abbreviations

AK	Armia Krajowa (Home Army)
BCh	Bataliony Chłopskie (Peasants' Battalions)
BZIH	*Biuletyn Żydowskiego Instytutu Historycznego*
BLHG	Beit Lohamei Hagetaot (Ghetto Fighters' House)
CENTOS	Centralne Towarzystwo Opieki nad Sierot (National Society for the Care of Orphans)
CKS	Centralna Komisja Specjalna (Central Special Commission)
CKŻP	Centralny Komitet Żydów w Polsce (Central Committee of Jews in Poland)
CYSHO	Tsentrale Yidishe Shul Organizatsye (Central Yiddish Schools Organization)
EJ	*Encyclopaedia Judaica*
FOP	Front Odrodzenia Polski (Front for the Rebirth of Poland)
JDC	Joint Distribution Committee, the 'Joint'
KRN	Krajowa Rada Narodowa (National Council for the Homeland)
KS	Komisja Specjalna (special commission)
MBP	Ministerstwo Bezpieczeństwo Publicznego (Ministry of Public Security)
MO	Milicja Obywalelska (Citizens' Militia)
NSB	Nationaalsocialistieke Beweging (National Socialist Movement: Dutch Nazi party)
NSZ	Narodowe Siły Zbrojne (National Armed Forces)
ONR	Obóz Narodowo-Radykalny (National Radical Camp)
ORMO	Ochotnicza Rezerwa Milicji Obywałelskiej (Voluntary Workers' Citizens' Militia)
OWP	Obóz Wielkiej Polski (Campaign for a Greater Poland)
PKWN	Polski Komitet Wyzwolenia Narodowego (Polish Committee of National Liberation)
PPR	Polska Partia Robotnicza (Polish Workers' Party)
PPS	Polska Partia Socjalistyczna (Polish Socialist Party)
PS	Polsiy Socjaliści (Polish Socialists, later the RFPS)

PSL	Polskie Stronnictwo Ludowe (Polish Peasant Party)
PSL—Piast	Polskie Stronnictwo Ludowe—Piast (Polish Peasant Party—Piast)
PZPR	Polska Zjednoczona Partia Robotnicza (Polish United Workers' Party)
RGO	Rada Główna Opiekuńcza (Central Relief Council)
RPŻ	See Żegota
SICSA	Vidal Sassoon International Centre for the Study of Antisemitism
SOS	Społeczna Organizacja Samopomocy (Social Self-Help Organization)
TKPŻ	Tymczasowy Komitet Pomocy Żydom (Temporary Committee to Aid Jews)
UB	Urzędy Bezpieczeństwa (Security Office)
WiN	Wolność i Niepodległość (Freedom and Independence)
WRN	Wolność, Równość, Niepodległość (Workers' Party of Polish Socialists)
WSM	Warszawska Spółdzielnia Mieszkaniowa (Warsaw Housing Co-operative)
Żegota	Rada Pomocy Żydom (Council to Aid Jews)
ŻKK	Żydowski Komitet Koordynacyjny (Jewish Co-ordinating Committee)
ŻOB	Żydowska Organizacja Bojowa (Jewish Combat Organization)
ŻKN	Żydowski Komitet Narodowy (Jewish National Committee)

PART I

The Holocaust and its Aftermath

Introduction

ANTONY POLONSKY

Nas nauczono. Nie ma sumienia.
W jamach żyjemy strachem zaryci,
w grozie drążymy mroczne miłości,
własne posągi—źli troglodyci.

Nas nauczono. Nie ma miłości.
Jakże nam jeszcze uciekać w mrok
przed żaglem nozdrzy węszących nas,
przed siecią wzdętych kijów i rąk.

(We learned the lesson: conscience does not exist.
We dwell in caves, fear enfolds us,
we carve in horror our dark loves,
our own statues—evil troglodytes.

We learned the lesson: love does not exist.
How else can we hide in the darkness
while sniffing nostrils seek our scent,
while swollen sticks and fists seek to envelop us.)

KRZYSZTOF KAMIL BACZYŃSKI

POLAND was one of the principal focuses of the Second World War. It was here that the Nazis tried to impose their racial blueprint for eastern Europe, attempting to ensure the permanent eastward expansion of Germany by destroying the Polish élites and reducing the remainder of the population to disfranchised colonial serfs of the Third Reich. The partition of Poland in 1939 also saw the Soviet Union extend the Stalinist system westwards, mounting a frontal attack on bourgeois and Polish elements in what were now referred to as western Belarus and western Ukraine. This 'revolution from abroad' was followed by mass arrests, the banning of all political parties apart from the communists, and the deportation eastwards between September 1939 and June 1941 of between 1.25 and 1.5 million 'anti-Soviet' elements. The effect of Nazi and Soviet oppression on Polish society was devastating. During the war Poland lost more than 20 per cent of its population (including 3 million of its Jewish citizens, but also including at least another 3 million ethnic Poles, many of whom died as a result of the treatment they endured after deportation to the eastern areas of the Soviet Union). Forty-five per cent of Polish doctors did not survive the occupation, 40 per cent of Polish academics, 45 per cent of lawyers, 30 per cent of technicians, 20 per cent of priests, and most journalists. In the last years of the war over 100,000 Poles were incarcerated in German concentration camps and prisons.

Poland also became one of the principal bones of contention between the Allied coalition, which came into being after the Nazi invasion of the Soviet Union in June 1941. The Soviets were determined to create a 'friendly' Poland on their western border and to ensure that they would be able to reincorporate into the USSR the areas they had annexed in 1939. In the summer of 1944 a communist-dominated regime was installed in power in Chełm, the first town to be liberated by the Red Army west of the Curzon line, the new eastern border of Poland. By 1948 the regime was effectively Stalinist and its politics was controlled by the security apparatus, in which Soviet 'advisers' played a crucial role.

In addition, Poland was one of the principal areas where the Nazis attempted to carry out their planned genocide of European Jewry. It was here that the major death camps were established and that Jews were brought from all over Nazi-occupied Europe to be gassed, above all in Auschwitz, where at least 1 million lost their lives in this way. According to the records of the Central Committee of Jews in Poland (Centralny Komitet Żydów w Polsce: CKŻP), the principal Jewish body in post-war Poland, 74,000 people had registered by June 1945. Of these, 5,500 had returned from concentration camps in Germany, 13,000 had served in the army commanded by the communists, established in the USSR after the withdrawal of the Anders Army, about 30,000 had made their way back from the Soviet Union, 10,000 had been freed from concentration camps in Poland, and some 20,000 had emerged from hiding places on the 'Aryan side'. Over the next two years 137,000 Jews returned from the USSR, mostly people who had been deported or evacuated to the interior of the country. In 1956 several thousand more returned to Poland, while between 100,000 and 150,000 remained in the Soviet Union.[1] Even bearing in mind that a significant number of those who survived did not wish to register with a Jewish organization, the total number of survivors cannot have been much more than 350,000–400,000. Thus, almost 90 per cent of Polish Jewry perished in the Holocaust. Only in the Baltic states was the percentage of Jewish casualties higher.

There is no more controversial topic in the history of the Jews in Poland than the question of the degree of responsibility borne by Polish society for the fact that such a small proportion of Polish Jewry escaped the Nazi mass murderers, and this is the central issue discussed in this volume of *Polin*. The primary responsibility clearly lies with the Nazis. The genocide was carried out in three stages. Its initiation was part of the radicalization of Nazi policy which accompanied Operation Barbarossa, the planned conquest of the USSR, and its final adoption accompanied the euphoria of victory in September and October 1941. At first mobile

[1] Józef Adelson, 'W Polsce zwanej Ludową', in Jerzy Tomaszewski (ed.), *Najnowsze dzieje Żydów w Polsce* (Warsaw, 1993), 388–9.

killing squads, the Einsatzgruppen, advanced behind the Wehrmacht killing Soviet officials and Jewish men and, after a period, Jewish women and children. At least 1 million Jews were killed in this way between July and December 1941. This method of murder was for the most part abandoned because of its effect on the morale of those required to carry it out. It was replaced, in the second stage, by the creation of death camps, where assembly-line techniques were developed using first carbon monoxide and then an insecticide, Zyklon B. During this period of the genocide, which came to an end in late 1942, the Germans were operating in areas where there was no limit to their absolute freedom of action. Their power was at its height and the ability of the Allies or of populations subject to the control of the Third Reich to exercise any influence on their behaviour was minimal. Most of the actual genocide at this stage was carried out by Germans and at least another 2.7 million Jews were murdered. Most came from within the pre-1939 borders of Poland, and by the end of 1942 very few Polish Jews survived. In the third stage of the genocide, which lasted until the end of the war, the Nazis found themselves obliged to persuade or coerce their allies, satellites, and puppets in the new Europe to hand over their Jews. By this time these satellite governments, the Allies, and virtually everybody else in Nazi-occupied Europe knew that Nazi policy towards the Jews involved genocide and were obliged to articulate some sort of response.

The genocide was only possible because of the cruelty and barbarism of the Nazi regime: the Soviet regime was also cruel and sadistic, but what was unique about the Nazi anti-Jewish genocide was its use of industrial techniques to carry out mass murder. The essence of the regime is probably more easily captured in literature than by historical methods, which rest on the careful and judicious weighing of evidence. In this issue we publish an analysis of Zofia Nałkowska's *Medallions*, whose graphic portrayal of the essential nihilism of the Nazi regime has rarely been surpassed.

However, the recognition of the primary role of the Germans in the genocide has not prevented bitter arguments over Polish behaviour during the Second World War. Jews have harshly criticized what they see as Polish indifference to the fate of the Jews and the willingness of a minority to aid the Nazis or to take advantage of the new conditions to profit at Jewish expense. According to Mordekhai Tenenbaum, commander of the Jewish Fighting Organization in the Białystok ghetto, writing in his memoirs, published shortly after the war,

If it had not been for the Poles, for their aid—passive and active—in the 'solution' to the Jewish problem in Poland, the Germans would never have dared to do what they did. It was they, the Poles, who called out 'Yid' at every Jew who escaped from the train transporting him; it was they who caught the unfortunate wretches, who rejoiced at every Jewish misfortune—they were vile and contemptible.[2]

---

[2] Mordekhai Tenenbaum-Tamaroff, *Dapim min hadelekah* (Beit Lohamei Hagetaot, 1947), 49–50.

A somewhat more moderate but still strongly critical view was expressed by Emanuel Ringelblum in his *Polish–Jewish Relations during the Second World War*, written in hiding on the 'Aryan side' in 1944:

The Polish people and the Government of the Republic of Poland were incapable of deflecting the Nazi steam-roller from its anti-Jewish course. But the question is permissible whether the attitude of the Polish people befitted the enormity of the calamities that befell the country's citizens. Was it inevitable that the Jews, looking their last on this world as they rode in the death trains speeding from different parts of the country to Treblinka or other places of slaughter, should have to see indifference or even gladness on the faces of their neighbours? Last summer, when carts packed with captive Jewish men, women and children moved through the streets of the capital, did there really need to be laughter from the wild mobs resounding from the other side of the ghetto walls, did there really have to prevail such blank indifference in the face of the greatest tragedy of all time?[3]

Polish responses to these accusations have taken two forms: attempts to justify Polish behaviour and regret for the failings of the Poles in this period. The most characteristic articulation of the apologists' point of view was set out by the late Władysław Siła-Nowicki, a prominent opposition lawyer and former resistance fighter. In 1987, in his article 'A Reply to Jan Błoński', he attacked those (including the literary critic Błoński) who argued that the Polish reputation during the Second World War in relation to the Jews should be strongly contested. Błoński, and those who published his views, were, he claimed, playing into the hands of Poland's enemies and lending credibility to 'anti-Polish propaganda'. He rehearsed the familiar and not entirely inaccurate selection of facts that so many Poles have used to justify their behaviour towards Jews before, during, and after the Holocaust. For centuries, he asserted, when they had been expelled elsewhere Jews were able to settle in Poland and their numbers increased significantly. Before 1939 the Jews dominated certain professions and controlled a disproportionate share of wealth in Poland. During the war no European nation did more to assist Jews than Poland, where the risk attached to giving such assistance was the greatest, the usual penalty being death, not only for the individual but for his or her family as well. Polish suffering during the occupation was enormous, second only to that of the Jews. There were, he argued, no quislings in Poland, and the Polish underground sentenced to death those who betrayed Jews to the Nazis. It was the passivity of the Jews more than anything else that led to their destruction. Their attitude of accommodation, presumably different from that of the insurrectionary Poles, led them to go to their deaths without offering resistance. He concluded defiantly (and inconsistently):

I am proud of my nation's stance in every respect during the period of occupation and in this I include the attitude towards the tragedy of the Jewish nation. Obviously, attitudes

---

[3] Emanuel Ringelblum, *Polish–Jewish Relations during the Second World War*, ed. Joseph Kermish and Shmuel Krakowski (Evanston, Ill., 1992), 7–8.

towards the Jews during that period do not give us a particular reason to be proud, but neither are they any grounds for shame, and even less for ignominy. Simply, we could have done relatively little more than we actually did.[4]

There have been voices much more critical of the Polish response. Such views were articulated immediately after the war, but communist cultural uniformity meant that they have been largely unheard until more recent years. Thus, in his contribution to a pamphlet denouncing antisemitism published in 1947, the Catholic writer Jerzy Andrzejewski observed:

For all honest Poles, the fate of the Jews who perished was bound to be exceedingly painful, since the dying . . . were people whom our people could not look straight in the face with a clear conscience. The Polish nation could look straight in the face of Polish men and women who were dying for freedom. It could not do so in the face of the Jews dying in the burning ghetto.[5]

A similar point of view was expressed by Jan Błoński. In his article 'The Poor Poles Look at the Ghetto' Błoński observed that any attempt by Poles to discuss Polish reactions to the Nazi anti-Jewish genocide, whether with Jews or with other people, very quickly degenerates into attempts to justify Polish conduct. The reason for this, he claimed, is Polish fear, conscious or unconscious, of themselves being accused either of participation in the genocide or, at best, acquiescence. This fear cannot easily be evaded, even if it is shared by the Poles with the rest of Europe. The only way to deal with it, he asserted, is for Poles to 'stop wrangling, trying to defend and justify ourselves. To stop arguing about the things that were beyond our power to do, during the occupation and beforehand. Nor to place blame on political, social and economic conditions. But to say first of all, "Yes, we are guilty".'

This guilt does not consist, in his view, in involvement in the mass murder of the Jews, in which he claimed the Poles did not participate significantly. It has two aspects. First, there was 'insufficient effort to resist', a 'holding back' from offering help to the Jews. This was the consequence of the second aspect, that in the nineteenth and early twentieth centuries the Poles had not created conditions in which Jews could be integrated into the Polish national community.

If only we had behaved more humanely in the past, had been wiser, more generous, then genocide would perhaps have been 'less imaginable', would probably have been considerably more difficult to carry out, and almost certainly would have met with much greater resistance than it did. To put it differently, it would not have met with the indifference and moral turpitude of the society in whose full view it took place.[6]

---

[4] Władysław Siła-Nowicki, 'Jan Błoński w odpowiedzi', *Tygodnik Powszechny* (22 Feb. 1987); Eng. trans. in Antony Polonsky (ed.), *My Brother's Keeper? Recent Polish Debates on the Holocaust* (London, 1990), 59–68.

[5] Jerzy Andrzejewski, 'Zagadnienia polskiego antysemitizmu', in *Martwa fala* (Warsaw, 1947).

[6] Jan Błoński, 'Biedni Polacy patrzą na ghetto', *Tygodnik Powszechny* (11 Jan. 1987); Eng. trans. in Polonsky (ed.), *My Brother's Keeper?*, 34–52.

These 'accusations', 'apologetics', and 'apologies' are, above all, concerned with how one should respond to the past and deal with a shared but divisive memory. In effect, the two sides operate on quite different planes, one concerned with 'moral' shame, the other concerned to demonstrate the incalculable cost of greater assistance to the Jews. As the *émigré* Polish Jewish sociologist Zygmunt Bauman put it,

> Siła-Nowicki and Błoński do not argue with, but past, each other. Błoński wrote of the moral significance of the Holocaust, Siła-Nowicki responded with an investigation of the rationality of self-preservation. What he failed to notice was the ethical meaning of the very form such rationality took (or, rather, was forced to assume): the very fact that the Nazi regime set the logic of survival against the moral duty (as a value superior to ethics) was simultaneously the secret of the technical success of the mass murder, one of the most sinister horrors of the event called the 'Holocaust', and the most venomous of its consequences.[7]

It is not the primary intention in this issue of *Polin* to elucidate these moral dilemmas, which are as much philosophical and ethical as historical in character. Rather, we hope by placing the reactions of Polish society to the anti-Jewish genocide carried out by the Germans in a better-defined contextual framework to illustrate more clearly the character of these dilemmas and their relationship to the longer-term evolution of Poland and of Polish–Jewish relations. Thus along with articles on the genocide itself and on Polish and Jewish reactions to it, we have included discussions on the deteriorating situation of the Jews before the Second World War, on the implications of the territorial changes in eastern Poland in the first month of the war and of Soviet annexations, on the general consequences of Nazi rule and the wider context of the genocide, and on the relationship between the wartime and post-war situations in Poland.

In understanding the context of the genocide, it is crucial to bear in mind that on the Polish lands the great majority of Jews defined themselves and were regarded by most of the population as a separate national group. In western and central Europe the break-up of the autonomous Jewish communities, linked across frontiers by a common religion and a common set of moral and cultural values, had been followed by political and ultimately a degree of social integration, as the Jews of various countries began to define themselves and be regarded as Englishmen, Frenchmen, or Germans of the Mosaic faith. The integrationist ideology, linked with political liberalism, had enjoyed a certain amount of support from both Jews and non-Jews on the Polish lands, particularly in the period before and after the insurrection of 1863. But by the late nineteenth century the size of the Jewish community, the absence of a national system of higher education, the emergence of political antisemitism, and the development of autonomist Jewish ideologies, above all Zionism and Bundism, had reduced to an insignificant minority the number of Jews and Poles who wished the Jews to become Poles of the Mosaic

---

[7] Zygmunt Bauman, 'On Immoral Reason and Illogical Morality', *Polin*, 3 (London, 1988), 296–7.

faith. This development greatly complicated the issue of how to ensure equal rights for the Jews in Poland, since what was being demanded was not only individual equality before the law, but recognition of group separateness in a society committed to pluralism. Perhaps under happier political and social conditions a way could have been found to reconcile Polish national interests with those of the large, impoverished, diverse, and nationally conscious Jewish community. However, the conditions of the 1930s were conducive neither to political pluralism nor to interethnic toleration.

As a consequence, as is pointed out in the chapter by Joanna Michlic-Coren comparing the patterns of anti-Jewish violence in Poland between the two world wars and after 1945, the decade before the outbreak of war saw a serious deterioration in the situation of the Jews in Poland. This was partly the result of the persistence of the great depression in Poland, where attempts to maintain the overvalued zloty delayed economic recovery until 1936. Demagogic arguments that the Jews were responsible for Poland's economic difficulties and that their dispossession would alleviate the country's problems became much more widespread. The contagious effect of Nazi antisemitism was also significant. Antisemites in Poland were buoyed up by the obvious defencelessness of the Jews and the ease with which the Nazis were able to disfranchise and expropriate one of the wealthier and better-integrated Jewish communities in Europe. The death of Piłsudski in May 1935 proved extremely damaging to the stability of the regime he had established, and a section of his followers attempted to strengthen their position by making common cause with the antisemitic right. It is true that the conflict between those who wished to return to liberal-democratic norms and those who wished to establish some specifically Polish variant of the radical-right regimes which were mushrooming in Europe at this time had not yet been decided when war broke out. Nevertheless, the government, reflecting widespread popular feeling, now began to call for the emigration of a large part of the Jewish community. Anti-Jewish violence grew as attempts were made to enforce a boycott of Jewish shops and stalls and to exclude Jews from the universities. Efforts were also made to limit the number of Jews in the professions. Very few political parties (with the exception of the Socialists, the Democratic Party, and, for its own rather specific reasons until the dissolution of their party in 1938 by Stalin, the communists) resisted the antisemitic tide.

The consequence of the fact that the Jews were regarded as a separate national group and of the deterioration of Polish–Jewish relations in the 1930s was that when the Nazis established themselves in Poland, the two societies were largely separate. There were few organic ties between them and most Poles did not regard the Jews as part of what Helen Fein has called 'the universe of obligation . . . that circle of persons towards whom obligations are owed, to whom rules apply and whose injuries call for expiation by the community'.[8]

[8] Helen Fein, *Accounting for Genocide* (Chicago, 1984), 33.

A second particular feature of the genocide in Poland was that the Poles saw themselves as faced by two enemies, the Nazis and the Soviets. Polish diplomacy and underground political strategy was dominated by a desire to ensure the re-emergence of the country as an independent state within the 1939 frontiers, which could only be achieved by at least taking a very firm line with the Soviets and probably by conflict with them. The Soviets had already acted in a very brutal manner in 1939 to ensure the incorporation into the USSR of the areas they described as western Belarus and western Ukraine. The Germans did not seek Polish collaborators on an anti-Soviet basis until it was apparent that they were losing the war, by which time their own actions had created an almost insuperable wall of hatred between them and the Poles. But the fact that the Jews, by and large, did not accept Polish strategic thinking and took a basically favourable view of the Soviets, particularly after June 1941, greatly complicated Polish–Jewish relations.

Undoubtedly, Polish resentment against Jewish 'collaboration' with the Soviet authorities established after the Soviet occupation of eastern Poland in September 1939 greatly exacerbated Polish–Jewish tension. It is true that a fair number of Jews (like the overwhelming majority of Belarusians, a considerable number of Ukrainians, and even some Poles) welcomed the establishment of Soviet rule. In the Jewish case, this welcome was natural: a desire to see an end to the insecurity caused by the collapse of Polish rule in these areas, fear of the consequences of Nazi rule and a belief that the Soviets were the lesser evil, resentment at Polish anti-Jewish policies in the inter-war period, and support for the communist system. Although the Soviets did offer new opportunities to individual Jews, they acted to suppress organized Jewish life, both religious and political, dissolving *kehilot*, banning virtually all Jewish parties, and arresting their leaders. Jews made up just under a third of the nearly 1 million people deported by the Soviets from the areas they annexed (which, paradoxically, meant that many escaped the Nazi genocide). Under these conditions the overwhelming majority of the Jewish population of the area very quickly lost whatever illusions they had about the Soviet system.

This was not how most Poles saw the situation. They were affronted by Jewish behaviour in 1939, probably exaggerated Jewish participation in the new system because a Jewish presence in the apparatus of government was so unprecedented in Poland, and accused the Jews of disloyalty in a moment of national crisis.

According to General Stefan Grot-Rowecki, commander-in-chief of the Home Army (Armia Krajowa: AK), the resistance movement linked with the Polish government in exile, many Poles greeted the invading Germans in July 1941 as 'liberators from the Bolshevik oppression in which Jews had played a great part'.[9] General Anders, commander of the Polish army created in the Soviet Union after the Nazi invasion from Polish citizens deported to the USSR after September 1939, wrote: 'I was greatly disturbed when, in the beginning, large numbers from

[9] In a report to London of 8 July 1941, cited in Krystyna Kersten, *Narodziny systemu władzy: Polska, 1943–1948* (Paris, 1986), 172.

the national minorities, and first and foremost Jews, began streaming in to enlist. . . . some of the Jews had warmly welcomed the Soviet armies that invaded Poland in 1939'.[10]

It is not my intention to discuss at length here the truth of these allegations. I have done so elsewhere and have attempted to show that they are at best half-truths, reactions to national humiliation and to the sense that it would be very difficult to re-establish the Polish claim to most of the territories incorporated by the Soviets. Rather, attention should be drawn to the widespread acceptance of the stereotype of the pro-Soviet and anti-Polish Jew, which certainly widened the gulf between the two communities. This stereotype, embodied in the Polish concept of Żydokomuna (Judaeo-communism), had a long history on the Polish lands going back to Julian Ursyn Niemcewicz's dystopia *The Year 3333; or, A Nightmare* (1817), which described a Warsaw of the future renamed Moszkopolis, after its Jewish ruler, which had been taken over by a mafia of superficially modernized Jews. It was given a new lease of life by the Bolshevik revolution. Many Poles felt directly threatened both by the prospect of revolution and by Russian imperialism in a new guise, which they saw embodied in the Soviet regime. The fact that the Jews played a significant part both in the government of the USSR and in the illegal Polish Communist Party further strengthened the hold of this form of political paranoia.

This was clearly to be seen during the Polish–Soviet war of 1919–20. An official army poster during this war represented Bolshevism as the Devil with obviously Jewish characteristics, sitting on a pile of skulls. According to a letter of the Polish episcopate to the bishops of the world,

Bolshevism is truly aiming at the conquest of the world. The race which leads it previously subordinated the world to it through gold and the banks. Today, driven by the age-old imperialist drive which flows in its veins, it is undertaking the final conquest of all peoples under its yoke. All the slogans which are used—People, Workers, Freedom and so on—are only masks whose aim is to hide the true goal.[11]

As Joanna Michlic-Coren shows in her chapter 'Anti-Jewish Violence in Poland, 1918–1939 and 1945–1947', the idea of Żydokomuna was a basic feature of the political discourse of the radical right in the 1930s and now seemed to have been confirmed by the events of 1939. Different aspects of the problems of the Soviet annexations are examined in the chapters by Żbikowski and Schochet.

Resentment over the Jewish 'betrayal' in 1939 was one of the factors which led to a widening gap between Poles and Jews in the first two years of the Nazi occupation. The adoption of a policy of genocide by the Nazis can be dated to the summer of 1941. Before that date they were not sure how to proceed in relation to the Jews:

[10] Władysław Anders, *Bez ostatniego rozdziału: wspomnienia z lat 1939–1936* (Newton, Mass., 1950), 99.

[11] Quoted in A. Nossig, *Polen und Juden. Die polnisch-jüdische Verständigung. Zur Regelung der Judenfrage in Polen* (New York, 1920), 45–6.

whether they should be concentrated in some sort of reservation in eastern Europe or expelled to an African penal colony, such as Madagascar. Yet throughout this period Nazi policy was extremely harsh. The September campaign had been accompanied by sporadic anti-Jewish violence in which about 5,000 Jews lost their lives and a number of Jewish institutions were destroyed. Once the Nazi occupation had been established, Jewish property was expropriated and the Jews confined to ghettos, subject to brutal forced labour and deprived of the means of subsistence, so that in Warsaw alone nearly 85,000 died of starvation or from diseases resulting from malnutrition and overcrowding in the first eighteen months of the occupation. Yet it was in this period that the Polish–Jewish divide grew even wider, so that there was virtually no chance that Polish society could provide significant aid to the Jews once the policy of mass murder had been embarked upon. How is one to explain this widening of the already large gulf between Polish and Jewish society?

The German occupying authorities were determined to exacerbate Polish–Jewish relations. The numerous gratuitous acts of violence carried out against Jews, their seizure for forced labour, their subjection to humiliating physical punishments, and the plucking out or cutting of the beards (and often the hair) of Orthodox Jews were all intended, at least in part, to show that the Jews had no rights and could be assaulted with impunity. So too was the widespread confiscation of Jewish property by German soldiers and the fact that those who sought restitution of their goods were further punished.

Two important means of isolating the Jews were the requirement that they wear an armband displaying a Star of David, which was introduced by Hans Frank on 1 December 1939, and the regulations, operative until the creation of ghettos, that Jewish shops were to be marked with a large Star of David and that Jews were to be barred from certain streets, public parks, and trains. This isolation was further increased by propaganda spread by the extensive Polish-language 'reptile' press established by the Nazis and by the German-controlled radio, public loudspeaker systems, special antisemitic exhibitions, brochures, leaflets, and posters. The constant stigmatization of the Jews as dirty and responsible for disease also had an effect. Once the ghetto walls had been erected, which of course further isolated Jews from Poles, they were plastered with warning notices announcing 'Jews, lice, typhoid'.

Given the powerlessness of the Jews, anti-Jewish violence became widespread. Sometimes it was spontaneous, the work of antisemites or thugs, but generally it was inspired by the Nazi occupying authorities, who cynically averred that they were not responsible for the hatred aroused among the Poles by Jewish exploitation. The general Jewish assumption was that these assaults were instigated and controlled by the Nazis.

Another factor that widened the Polish–Jewish divide was the Polish belief that they were in fact more persecuted than the Jews. The Poles were certainly subject to savage repression, intended both to make permanent the incorporation of the Polish lands into the Third Reich and to deter attempts at resistance. By February 1940, for instance, over 200,000 Poles and 100,000 Jews had been expelled from the Warthegau. In accordance with German policy, over 50,000 Poles were executed in the areas annexed by the Third Reich in the first months of the occupation. As early as 6 September nearly 200 academics from the Jagiellonian University and the Mining Academy were arrested and twenty were executed. At the end of April 1940 Himmler ordered the incarceration of 20,000 Poles in concentration camps. As we have seen, Jews were also being savagely persecuted, but to many Poles the fact that Jews were allowed a degree of (spurious) autonomy and that Jewish political activity was not actively repressed seemed confirmation that at this stage the Jewish fate was not significantly worse than that of the Poles and might even be somewhat better. Some aspects of Nazi brutality and of its divisive effect are alluded to in Zofia Nałkowska's short stories as discussed by Diana Kuprel and in the poetry of Krzysztof Kamil Baczyński, discussed in the chapter by Joanna Rostropowicz Clark.

The divide was also widened because a significant part of the Polish population was benefiting from Nazi expropriation of Jewish property and the Jew's expulsion from Polish economic life. The aim of the Germans was clear—the removal of the Jews as soon as possible from all significant participation in the economy of occupied Poland. They thus, in a different and more brutal manner, accomplished what a significant portion of Polish society had seen before the war as a desirable objective. They also created in this way a large group of people who benefited from Jewish dispossession and who would obviously fight to retain what they had received at Nazi hands. According to a memorandum sent in the summer of 1943 to the Polish government in London by Roman Knoll, head of the Foreign Affairs Commission in the Office of the Government Delegate for the Homeland:

In the Homeland as a whole . . . the position is such that the return of the Jews to their jobs and workshops is completely ruled out, even if the number of Jews were greatly reduced. The non-Jewish population has filled the place of the Jews of the towns and cities: in a large part of Poland this is a fundamental change, final in character. The return of masses of Jews would be experienced by the population not as restitution but as an invasion against which they would defend themselves, even with physical means.[12]

Another important element was the fact that antisemitic attitudes and policies were not seriously compromised by the establishment of Nazi rule in Poland. The Germans had no desire for genuine collaboration in Poland. The Polish élite was to be destroyed, the remaining population forced to work for the Third Reich. In the long run the Polish lands were to be colonized on an analogy of the policy being

---

[12] Roman Knoll, head of the Foreign Affairs Commission in the Office of the Government Delegate for the Homeland, Memorandum, repr. in Ringelblum, *Polish–Jewish Relations during the Second World War*, 257.

pursued in Upper Silesia, Warthegau, and the area around Danzig. This had important consequences for the character of the Polish underground. It meant that while the socialist and democratic organizations continued to advocate full equality for the Jews in a future liberated Poland, pre-war antisemitic parties did not abandon their hostility to the Jews merely on the grounds that the Nazis were also antisemites.

The numbing effect of the brutality of Nazi occupation also inhibited the ability of ordinary people to rise above their own predicament and think altruistically. So too did the shock of the defeat and of the effects of the Nazi onslaught. In the battle and siege of Warsaw about a quarter of the city's buildings were totally destroyed or badly damaged. It has been calculated that 50,000 people were killed or seriously injured. The sense of betrayal and outrage led to strong hostility to the pre-war government. It also led to a search for scapegoats, and while this made some people rethink their views on the Jews, in others it intensified their existing antisemitism.

It is true that some pre-war antisemites did attempt (sometimes even while retaining their antisemitic beliefs) to aid Jews. But the increase in the gulf between the two societies and the growth in hostility towards the Jews seem to be beyond question and were widely commented on by political figures and taken into account in their political calculations. In a report compiled for the Polish government in Angers in February 1940 Jan Karski wrote:

With regard to the Germans, the Jews are docile, submissive, treated roughly: they live in perpetual fright, terror . . . The attitude of the Jews towards the Poles is similar to their attitude towards the Germans.

Generally one gets the feeling that it would be advisable if the prevailing attitude amongst the Poles towards 'the Jews' were one of understanding that in the end both peoples are being unjustly persecuted by the same enemy. Such an understanding does not exist among the broad masses of the Polish population.

Their attitude towards the Jews is overwhelmingly harsh, often without pity. A large percentage of them are benefiting from the rights the new situation gives them. They frequently exploit those rights and often abuse them.

This brings them, to a certain extent, nearer to the Germans . . . The solution to the 'Jewish Question' by the Germans—I state this with a full sense of responsibility for what I am saying—is a serious and quite dangerous tool in the hands of the Germans, leading towards 'moral pacification' of broad sections of Polish society.

It would certainly be wrong to suppose that this issue alone will be effective in winning for them the acceptance of the people.

However, although the nation loathes [the Germans] mortally, this question is creating something akin to a narrow bridge upon which the Germans and a large part of Polish society find themselves in agreement.

It is certain that this bridge is no less narrow than the desire of the Germans to strengthen and reinforce it is great.

Moreover, this situation threatens to demoralize broad segments of the population, and this in turn may present many problems to future authorities endeavouring to rebuild the Polish state. It is difficult: 'the lesson is not lost'.

Furthermore, the present situation is creating a schism among the inhabitants of these territories—first a schism between Jews and Poles in the struggle against the common enemy, and second a schism among the Poles, with one group despising and resenting the Germans' barbaric methods (and conscious of the danger in this), and the other regarding them (and thus the Germans, too!) with curiosity and often fascination and condemning the first group for its 'indifference towards such an important question'.[13]

A year later the situation had, if anything, deteriorated. In a dispatch from the commander of the AK, General Stefan Grot-Rowecki, to London of 30 September 1941, he wrote:

Please take it as an established fact that the overwhelming majority of the population is antisemitic. Even the socialists are no exception. There are only tactical differences about what to do. Hardly anybody advocates imitating the Germans. German methods provoke compassion, but after the merging of the occupation zones, on learning how the Jews behaved in the east, this is now considerably reduced.[14]

These attitudes were particularly painful to acculturated and assimilated Jews, as emerges clearly from Joanna Rostropowicz Clark's chapter about the Polish underground poet Krzysztof Kamil Baczyński and from the letters to his father of the young Polish airman Jan Ryszard Bychowski.

How did the political organs of Polish society react to the widening Polish–Jewish divide? The Germans were not interested until much later in the war in maintaining any form of Polish political authority or in creating a collaborationist government. But after the Polish defeat the forces which had opposed the post-Piłsudski regime had succeeded in staging a coup, which had brought to power a government under the moderate centrist and pro-Western politician General Władysław Sikorski. This government established itself in Angers, where it was recognized by the Western Allies as the legal government of Poland. After the fall of France it reconstituted itself in London. It was a coalition of the main forces, from right to left, which had opposed the Piłsudski regime, and also included a number of the less discredited followers of the marshal. It was committed to the establishment of a liberal and constitutionalist regime in liberated Poland, as was made clear in General Sikorski's numerous public pronouncements. It also held firmly to the view that though some frontier modifications should be made in Poland's favour in the west, in the east the frontier set by the Treaty of Riga in 1921 should be re-established. This, of course, would have meant incorporating areas which, although they included a substantial Polish (and Jewish) population, were, for the most part, inhabited by Ukrainians and Belarusians. In order to carry

[13] Jan Karski, 'An Early Account of Polish Jewry under Nazi and Soviet Occupation Presented to the Government-in-Exile, February 1940', ed. David Engel, repr. in Norman Davies and Antony Polonsky, *Jews in Eastern Poland and the USSR, 1939–1946* (London, 1991), 269.
[14] In the report to London of 8 July 1941, cited in Kersten, *Narodziny systemu władzy*, 172.

on the struggle for Polish independence and an allied victory, the Polish government created armed forces outside Poland, first in France and the United Kingdom and then, after the Nazi invasion made possible an agreement with the USSR, in the Soviet Union, an army which by the second half of 1942 had been withdrawn to the British-controlled Middle East. In addition, the government in London established an underground movement in occupied Poland. This was made up of a political directorate, the Government Delegation (Delegatura), composed of the political parties represented in the exile government, and a military wing, called first the League of Active Struggle (Związek Walki Czynnej) and then the Armia Krajowa, to carry on armed struggle against the invaders of Poland.

What was the attitude of these groups to the Jews in occupied Poland in the period before the Nazis embarked on the policy of genocide? The policy of the government in London has been subjected to intensive examination in two large and extremely well-researched books by David Engel.[15] He shows that in this period the Polish government, which was under strong pressure from both the Allied governments and Western Jewry, issued on 5 November 1940 a declaration guaranteeing the full equality of Jews in liberated Poland. The key paragraph reads: 'The Jews, as Polish citizens, shall in liberated Poland be equal with the Polish community, in duties and in rights. They will be able to develop their culture, religion and folkways without hindrance. Not only the laws of the state, but even more the common sufferings in this most tragic time of affliction will serve to guarantee this "pledge".'[16]

Engel argues that this declaration was issued unwillingly and that its implementation was regarded as conditional on the Jews supporting the Polish war effort, including the regaining of the Riga frontier. Under these conditions, not surprisingly, the declaration did not achieve its goal of a genuine improvement in Polish–Jewish relations. I agree that there was opposition to the adoption of the declaration and that there were both in the government and in the National Council (the government in exile) a fair number of people unfriendly to the Jews. Yet the adoption of the declaration in itself seems to me significant. More important than the strict conditionality, which Engel sees as crucial to Polish disappointment with the results of the declaration, are, in my view, the mutual suspicions created by the deterioration of the position of Jews in Poland in the 1930s. Neither side was able to rise to the very difficult occasion and the declaration was followed by no concerted propaganda effort by the Polish government in occupied Poland to stress 'the common sufferings in this most tragic time of affliction'. No pressure was brought to bear on the underground structures, whether political or military, to include Jewish groups in their activities. Very little was done to educate Polish opinion, on the lines suggested by Karski, on the dangers of Nazi antisemitism.

---

[15] David Engel, *In the Shadow of Auschwitz: The Polish Government-in-Exile and the Jews, 1939–1942* (Chapel Hill, NC, 1987); *Facing a Holocaust: The Polish Government-in-Exile and the Jews, 1943–1945* (Chapel Hill, NC, 1993).   [16] Engel, *In the Shadow of Auschwitz*, 80.

Indeed, the reaction to the declaration in the occupied country was not calculated to induce the government to take bold steps to change attitudes towards the Jews.

Something should also be said about the attitude towards Jews in the period between September 1939 and the end of 1941 of the Catholic Church, which certainly claimed a significant moral authority. The pre-war view of the Church in Poland on the Jews, which did not differ significantly from that of the Church as a whole, had been articulated by the primate, Cardinal Hlond, in a pastoral letter in 1936:

> The Jewish problem is there and will be there as long as Jews remain Jews . . . It is a fact that Jews are in opposition to the Catholic Church, that they are freethinkers, the vanguard of godlessness, bolshevism, and subversion. It is a fact that they exert a pernicious influence on public morality and that their publishing houses are spreading pornography. It is true that Jews are swindlers, usurers, and that they are engaged in fostering immoral earnings. It is true that the effect of the Jewish youth upon the Catholic is—in the religious and ethical sense—negative. This does not apply to all Jews. There are very many Jews who are believers, honest, righteous, merciful, doing good works. The family life of many Jews is healthy and edifying. And there are among Jews people morally quite outstanding, noble and honourable people.[17]

This was the Church's principal line, with its classic statement of anti-Judaism, coupled with its rejection of anti-Jewish violence and its refusal to link individual Jews with the negative behaviour of the majority. There was also within the Church a more strongly antisemitic element which adopted a near-racist position, linked with a strong populism and nationalism, best represented by the Catholic periodical *Rycerz niepokolanej* and the daily *Mały Dziennik*. In this context those circles within the Church which espoused liberal and humanistic attitudes, including the centre at Laski, near Warsaw, which published the periodical *Verbum*, and the Association of Catholic University Students (Odrodzenie), were inevitably small, isolated, and without influence. The views of the Church remained basically unchanged until the adoption of the genocide. The only initiative it took in the first years of the Nazi occupation seems to have been to intervene on behalf of converts. This intervention was not always efficacious. A list of converts was handed to the Gestapo so that they could be exempted from wearing the band with the Star of David. It was used by the Gestapo when the Warsaw ghetto was established to ensure that all those on it were confined within the ghetto walls.

This was the state of affairs when the Nazis embarked upon genocide. Virtually all the links between Polish and Jewish society had been broken and the moral authorities who claimed to speak on behalf of Polish society either felt themselves too weak to protest much against the process or did not believe that to do so would necessarily be in the Polish interest. The consequences of this situation are clear.

[17] A. Hlond, *Na straży sumienia i narodu* (Ramsay, 1951; repr. Warsaw, 1999), 164.

Moreover, by the time the genocide had begun, the Polish strategic position had deteriorated significantly. The Polish–Soviet *rapprochement* did not prove lasting and disputes over the Polish eastern frontier, the amnesty for Poles imprisoned by the Soviets, and the formation of a Polish army in the Soviet Union soon soured relations. In early 1942 the Soviets gave permission to Polish communists in the USSR to re-form the Polish Communist Party, dissolved on Stalin's orders in 1938. It was intended that the new party, called the Polish Workers' Party (Polska Partia Robotnicza: PPR), should act both to put pressure on the Polish government in London to be more amenable and also to provide the nucleus of a pro-Soviet government in Poland, should an accommodation with Sikorski prove impossible. The PPR pursued a 'popular front' policy in occupied Poland, but soon found itself in bitter conflict with the underground forces linked with the Polish government in London. It also established an underground military group, first called the People's Guard (Gwardia Ludowa) and then the People's Army (Armia Ludowa). In the summer of 1942, after a series of further conflicts, the Polish army created in the USSR left for the Middle East, and in April 1942, under the pretext that the Poles were falsely accusing the Soviets of the murder of 4,000 Polish officers found by the Nazis at Katyn in Belarus (they had in fact been murdered by the Soviets), Stalin broke off relations with the Polish government in London. Efforts by the Western Allies to heal the breach, especially after the Tehran Conference of December 1943, failed. The Soviets thus proceeded unilaterally to declare the Curzon line the eastern frontier of Poland and incorporated into the Soviet Union the areas east of it. In July 1944 they established what was in effect a Polish provisional government in Lublin, the first large town taken west of the Curzon line.

These developments totally preoccupied the government in London and dictated the strategy of the underground it controlled. The communist-controlled forces, which were quite weak, advocated immediate confrontation with the Nazi occupier, both to take pressure off the Soviet Union and in order to radicalize the situation in Poland by courting savage German reprisals. The AK wanted to avoid a major confrontation, partly to spare the civilian population, but above all because it wanted to conserve its strength for the decisive moment when German power was collapsing. Its aim was to use this moment to take power in Poland and confront the Soviets with the alternatives of negotiating with the government in London and its forces in Poland or crushing them before the eyes of the world. This was a risky strategy and, as is well known, it failed disastrously and was followed by the sovietization of Poland. It was dictated by the desperate strategic position of the country and by the realization on the part of the London Poles that they had very little chance of returning home. As a result, when the Jews of Poland were being murdered *en masse*, the minds of Polish politicians in London and in the underground in Poland were firmly concentrated on what was to them the central issue of how to regain the independence of their country.

What was the attitude of the forces which made up the Polish underground state to the implementation of the anti-Jewish genocide? The tragic fate of the Jews did arouse considerable sympathy in the central bodies of the underground. This was clearly expressed in the principal paper of the underground, *Biuletyn Informacyjny*, a weekly which appeared throughout the war and which reflected the views of the co-ordinating body of the civilian underground, the Government Delegation and its head, the Government Delegate. Its circulation reached about 45,000 copies, a considerable achievement for an underground periodical. Its principal editor was Aleksander Kamiński, a well-known Polish educator and scout leader, who before the war had become friendly with Mordekhai Anielewicz, later the leader of the Jewish Fighting Organization (Żydowska Organizacja Bojowa) in the Warsaw ghetto. On 17 September 1942 the paper wrote:

Along with the tragedy which Polish society is having to endure, being decimated by the enemy, for nearly a year now Jews have been brutally butchered in our land. This mass murder has no precedent in the history of the world and all other atrocities known to history pale alongside it. Babies, children, young people, adults, the old, cripples, invalids, men, women, Jewish Catholics, and Jews practising the Mosaic faith are murdered in cold blood, poisoned by gas, buried alive, thrown out of windows of high-rise buildings, forced to endure agonies before their death, the hell of homelessness, and the anguish of cynical ill treatment at the hands of their executioners. The number of victims killed in this way has passed a million and is growing with every day.

Not able actively to resist it, the League of Active Struggle protest in the name of the entire Polish nation against the crime being perpetrated against the Jews. All Polish political and social groups join in this protest. Just as in the case of Polish victims, the physical responsibility for this crime will fall on the executioners and their accomplices.

Among the political parties which made up the underground state, the genocide did not lead to a fundamental revision of attitudes to the 'Jewish question'. The Information and Propaganda Bureau of the AK undertook a study of the views of those parties linked with the Government Delegation at the end of 1943. They found that four groupings, the Convention of Independence Organizations, the Syndicalists, the Democratic Party, and the breakaway section of the pre-war Socialist Party, Freedom–Equality–Independence, favoured full equality for the Jews, while eight other parties, some of them very small, were still in favour of the emigration of all or most Polish Jews, and one, the Confederation of the Nation, favoured 'liquidation'.[18] Opposition to the genocide and sympathy for the Jews was also expressed by the liberal Catholic Front for the Rebirth of Poland (Front Odrodzenia Polski), though with some of the characteristic ambiguities of most Catholic thinking about the Jews before Vatican II. In August 1942 one of the group's founders, Zofia Kossak-Szczucka, published a pamphlet with the title *Protest*, which, with all its contradictions, enables us, in the words of Jan Błoński,

---

[18] For this report, see Jan Rzepecki, 'Organizacja i działanie Biura Informacji i Propagandy Komendy Głownej Armii Krajowej', *Wojskowy Przegląd Historyczny*, no. 4 (1971), 147–53.

'to penetrate the thoughts and feelings of a significant (dominant?) section of Polish society at that time'.[19] Because of its significance, we quote extensively from it:

In the Warsaw ghetto, cut off by a wall from the world, several hundred thousand condemned prisoners wait for death. There is no hope of rescue; no help comes to them. The executioners scour the streets, shooting anyone who dares to leave his house. They even shoot at those who show themselves at the windows. Unburied corpses cover the pavements.

The daily requirement of victims is between eight and ten thousand. The Jewish police is required to deliver them to the German executioners. If they do not do this, they die themselves. Children too weak to walk are loaded onto wagons. This is done in such a brutal fashion that few of them make it alive to the ramps. Mothers who witness this lose their wits. The number of those driven mad by grief and terror rivals those shot . . . What is occurring in the Warsaw ghetto has been taking place for six months in Polish villages, small towns, and cities. The total number of murdered Jews already surpasses a million, and this number is increasing every day. All are dying. Rich and poor, the old, women, men, young people, infants, Catholics dying with the Name of Jesus and Mary on their lips as well as Jewish believers. All have been declared guilty because they have been born into the Jewish nation, condemned by Hitler to be wiped out.

The world observes this crime, more terrible than any seen by history—and it remains silent. The massacre of millions of defenceless people is taking place amid a universal ominous silence. The executioners are silent; they do not boast of what they are doing. Neither England nor America raises its voice. Even international Jewry, so influential and formerly so sensitive to injuries to its own, is silent. Poles are also silent. Polish politicians sympathetic to the Jews limit themselves to writing articles in newspapers. Polish opponents of the Jews demonstrate a lack of interest in a matter to which they are indifferent. The dying are surrounded on all sides by Pilates washing their hands.

This silence can be tolerated no longer. Whatever the motives for it, they are base and ignoble. He who is silent in the face of a murder—becomes an accomplice to that murder. He who does not condemn—assists.

We therefore, Polish Catholics, raise our voice. Our feelings towards the Jews have not undergone a change. We have not stopped regarding them as the political, economic, and ideological enemies of Poland. What is more, we are well aware that they hate us more than the Germans, that they hold us responsible for their misfortune. Why, on what basis—this remains a secret of the Jewish soul, but it is a fact which is constantly confirmed. Our awareness of these feelings does not free us from *the obligation to condemn the crime*.

We do not wish to be Pilates. We do not have the means to act against the German murders, we cannot advise, we can save no one—but we *protest* from the depths of our hearts overcome with pity, indignation, and dread. This protest is demanded of us by God, God who does not permit murder. It is demanded by Christian conscience. Every being who is called human has the right to the love of his neighbour. The blood of the defenceless cries

---

[19] Jan Błoński, 'Polak-katolik i katolik-Polak', in *Biedni Polacy patrzą na ghetto* (Kraków, 1994), 40. The 'Protest' is reprinted in full in this volume, which also contains the most penetrating discussion of the issues raised by the document.

out to heaven for vengeance. He among us who does not support this protest is not a Catholic.

We also protest as Poles. We do not believe that Poland can derive any advantage from the German cruelties. On the contrary. In the stubborn silence of international Jewry, in the efforts of German propaganda attempting to shift the odium of the massacre onto the Lithuanians and . . . the Poles, we sense the planning of an action hostile to us. We know also how poisonous are the seeds of this crime. The compulsory participation of the Polish nation in the bloody spectacle which is taking place on Polish soil can easily breed indifference to crime, sadism, and above all the perilous conviction that it is possible to murder one's neighbour without punishment.

He who does not understand this, who dares to link the proud, free future of Poland to base joy at the misfortune of his neighbour—he is indeed neither a Catholic nor a Pole.

It is not clear why the author included in this otherwise moving appeal the jarring anti-Jewish sentiments. Some have argued that it was because she could not overcome her own basic dislike of the Jews; others have seen their inclusion as the result of her belief that only in this way could she persuade her Catholic audience, of whose hostility to the Jews she was well aware, to heed her appeal. Certainly, the striking combination of a call for sympathy combined with distaste for those same victims was not untypical in occupied Poland.

The Warsaw ghetto uprising provoked an upsurge of sympathy for the Jewish insurgents, partly because it seemed to negate the widespread stereotype of Jewish passivity in the face of persecution. According to Aurelia Wyleżyńska, writing in *Nowy Dziennik*, a paper which appeared daily in occupied Warsaw, on 14 May 1943,

Gloria Victis! 14 May 1943. Pockets of resistance are still holding on in the hopeless battle. I approach the front line. It is rather one great cemetery. No natural disaster has ever produced such a mass grave. Near the freshly demolished wall some German soldiers are engaged in target practice. Haven't they practised enough? The defence of Warsaw's Nalewki Street will pass into history alongside the defence of Saragossa, Alcazar, Westerplatte, and Stalingrad, every one of them held with blood. The defenders of the ghetto succumbed not only to the brutal violence and overwhelming strength of the enemy. They have gone through an inferno of suffering, through every torment that man can inflict on man. They depart, victims of a total and complete burning. The civilized world will remember them for ever.

At the same time the mass murder of the Jews did not lead to any significant rethinking in the main centre and right-wing parties, the Christian democratic Party of Labour, the Peasant Party (Stronnictwo Ludowe), and the National Democrats (Endecja), all of which were represented in the London government (although the Endeks withdrew in July 1941: one faction, headed by Marian Seyda, re-entered the government in early 1942, while the other, led by Tadeusz Bielecki, regarded itself as a 'loyal' opposition). Even the more moderate Peasant Party was for 'voluntary emigration'. On 15 August 1942 *Naród*, organ of the

Party of Labour, combined a call to provide help to Jewish fugitives with undisguised expressions of antisemitism:

> At this moment, from behind the ghetto walls, we can hear the inhuman moans and screams of the Jews who are being murdered. Ruthless cunning is falling victim to ruthless brutal power and no Cross is visible on this battlefield, since these scenes go back to pre-Christian times.
>
> If this continues, then it will not be long before Warsaw will say farewell to its last Jew. If it were possible to conduct a funeral, it would be interesting to see the reaction. Would the coffin evoke sorrow, weeping, or perhaps joy?
>
> In one of our previous issues we urged kindness, but today we are faced with the following question. For hundreds of years an alien, malevolent entity has inhabited the northern sections of our city. Malevolent and alien from the point of view of our interests, as well as our psyche and our hearts. So let us not strike false attitudes like professional weepers at funerals—let us be serious and honest . . . We pity the individual Jew, the human being, and, as far as possible, should he be lost or trying to hide, we will extend a helping hand. We must condemn those who denounce him. It is our duty to demand from those who allow themselves to sneer and mock to show dignity and respect in the face of death. But we are not going to pretend to be grief-stricken about a vanishing nation, which, after all, was never close to our hearts.

Walka, one of the papers published by the underground National Democrats, wrote shortly after the suppression of the Warsaw ghetto uprising in the spring of 1943:

> From a biological point of view the Jews have lost a great deal of their power. The decline of Israel, in which Roman Dmowski once believed, has come much closer because of the biological defeat of that nation, namely, the destruction of millions of its most racially pure representatives.

The views of the small fascist groups which were independent of the Government Delegation—the Rampart Group (Grupa Szańca), the Awakening (Pobudka), the Confederation of the Nation (Konfederacja Narodu), and the National Armed Forces (Narodowe Siły Zbrojne)—were even more hostile to the Jews. The young men who composed these groups have been accurately described by the historian Władysław Pobóg-Malinowski as

> hot-headed dynamic youths, mostly town-bred, among them many supporters of 'national radicalism', perhaps not quite a kind of Nazism, but characterized by many of its features—brutally uncompromising in striving for power and domination, devoted to hard terrorist methods, verging on banditry, utterly chauvinistic, vehemently hostile attitude to the national minorities, above all the Jews—finally a totally uncompromising, aggressive attitude to communism . . .[20]

What was the reaction to the genocide of the organizations which claimed to speak for Polish society as a whole? The government in London was well aware of

---

[20] Władysław Pobóg-Malinowski, *Najnowsza historia polityczna Polski*, iii (London, 1960), 356–7.

the divisions in Poland on the Jewish question. It was also preoccupied with regaining Polish independence and with the increasing complexities of its diplomatic position. On 24 February 1942 it reaffirmed its commitment to Jewish equality. The future Poland, it asserted, would be 'a democratic and republican state' in which 'the rights and liberties of all loyal citizens, regardless of national and religious differences' would be guaranteed. The two Jewish representatives on the National Council were not entirely satisfied with this reassurance, alarmed as they were by the return of the National Democrats to the government and by the strength of antisemitic groups in the underground state in Poland.

The government began to receive information about the anti-Jewish genocide in the summer. The slowness of its reaction seems to be less the result of its unwillingness to take up Jewish issues, as has been claimed by Engel, and more the consequence of problems of communication and the difficulty in internalizing the appalling implications of what was happening, a problem which has been extensively treated by Walter Laqueur in his book *The Terrible Secret: Suppression of the Truth about Hitler's 'Final Solution'*.[21] The difficulty of comprehending what was going on and the failure of the Swedish government to communicate information it received from its consul in the General Government, Karl Vendel, is the theme of Józef Lewandowski's chapter. By October the government understood well what was taking place, and made the news public in a protest meeting it organized at the Albert Hall on 29 October, where Polish, Jewish, and British figures all spoke and the chair was taken by the archbishop of Canterbury. General Sikorski in his address 'assured Polish Jews that, on an equal footing with all Polish citizens, they will benefit fully from the victory of the Allies'.[22]

The government set out its position in a declaration on 27 November:

The Polish government in full consciousness of its responsibility has not neglected to inform the world about the mass murders and bestialities of the Germans in Poland and has, at the same time, done everything in its power to counteract that terror.

We are well aware that the fundamental condition for effectively counteracting German activities, which in relation to Poland can be summarized as an attempt *to destroy the Polish nation and wipe out any trace of its existence*, can only be the shortening of the period of suffering and struggle of Polish citizens in the country and the speedy defeat of the enemy.

Thus, the earlier call from the country for a second front and the present appeals to speed up, at all cost, the course of the war are basic guidelines for the Polish government and its activities. The development of the military situation in recent weeks, symbolized by the movement of the Allies to the offensive and their victories, has been received with great relief and true joy—the country reacted immediately by sending congratulations to President Roosevelt and Premier Churchill.

A special page in the martyrology of Poland is constituted by the persecution of the Jewish minority in Poland.

Hitler's decision that the year 1942 is to be the year in which at least half of Polish Jews

[21] Boston, 1981. [22] *Dziennik Polski* (30 Oct. 1942).

are to be done away with is being implemented with an utter ruthlessness and barbarity the like of which is unknown in human history. The figures speak for themselves: of the approximately 400,000 Jews in the Warsaw ghetto, over 260,000 have been liquidated starting on 17 July and in a little less than three months. Mass murders are taking place over the whole country; Polish Jews are being exterminated along with Jews from other occupied countries who have been brought to Poland for this purpose.

Forceful protests are coming from the country against these murders and pillage. Protest is accompanied by fellow feeling and a cry of one's own powerlessness in the face of what is taking place. Poles in the country are fully aware, as is revealed in reports, that the accelerated pace of murder which *today is taking place in relation to the Jews will tomorrow affect those who remain*.[23]

Engel has argued that this declaration reflects both the Polish desire to subsume the Jewish tragedy within its own narrower political objectives and an unwillingness to accept the scale of what was happening. These arguments do not seem wholly convincing, since it would have been very surprising if the Polish government had not been primarily concerned with the Polish national interest as it understood it. More persuasive is the view that the declaration reflected a basic unwillingness to take any meaningful action beyond protesting. Certainly the government did protest strongly. It reissued Zofia Kossak-Szczucka's *Protest* without its anti-Jewish sections (which gave it much greater impact). The constant stress on powerlessness, even if it was largely true, did lead to a failure to act. The government may also have been unwilling to press the underground authorities on a matter on which it knew there was divided opinion in Poland. When the Polish foreign minister, Edward Raczyński, wrote to Chaim Weizman on 3 December, he stressed his 'heartfelt compassion with the martyrdom which the German barbarians have inflicted upon the Jewish nation'. As for action, he wrote: 'I can assure you that the Polish government is determined that the dehumanized perpetrators of these dreadful crimes shall receive a punishment commensurate with their guilt'.[24]

Under these circumstances, the initiative to respond to the genocide fell to the underground authorities in Poland, civilian and military. The Government Delegation and its head, the Government Delegate, were basically sympathetic to the Jews, but aware that they lacked the power to impose their will on the various groupings which made up the underground. It was only in April 1943 that the Government Delegate issued an appeal to Poles to hide Jews. Before this, at the end of 1942, the Council for Aid to the Jews (Rada Pomocy Żydom, code-named Żegota) was set up by representatives of the Front for the Rebirth of Poland and some underground socialist and left-wing groups. The council was able to obtain a degree of support from the Polish government in London and, between 1942

---

[23] *Dziennik Polski* (28 Nov. 1942).

[24] Quoted in Yisrael Gutman and Shmuel Krakowski, *Unequal Victims: Poles and Jews during World War Two* (New York, 1986), 97.

and the end of the war it was granted a total of nearly 29 million zlotys (over £1 million), which it used to provide monthly relief payments for a few thousand Jewish families in Warsaw, L'viv, and Kraków. According to one of its historians, Teresa Prekerowa, by the middle of 1944 between 3,000 and 4,000 were benefiting from its financial support. In addition, it provided Jews with the false documents they needed to survive on the 'Aryan side' and established a network of safe houses where those who had an 'unfavourable appearance' could hide.[25]

The successes of Żegota, which was able to forge false documents for 50,000 people, suggest that, had it been given a higher priority by the Government Delegation and the government in London, it could have done much more. One of its members, Władysław Bartoszewski, Polish foreign minister until December 1995, declared that the organization was regarded as a 'stepchild' by the central underground authorities. According to Yisrael Gutman, Żegota's achievements were 'very little considering the dimensions of the tragedy' but 'considerable in light of the conditions and spirit of the times'.[26] This assessment was shared by Emanuel Ringelblum, who wrote: 'A Council for Aid to the Jews was formed, consisting of people of good will, but its activity was limited by lack of funds and lack of help from the government'.[27]

How this organization functioned in Warsaw is the theme of Gunnar Paulsson's chapter, which assesses its achievements rather more highly than has been the norm in current historiography. His researches take a comparative approach, and his conclusion, which is based on an imaginative use of newly available documents, suggests that the situation of Jews hidden on the 'Aryan side' was better in Warsaw than in Berlin or Amsterdam.

Most of those who hid Jews were individuals acting on their own initiative, whether impelled by moral considerations or hopes of financial gain. How many Jews were saved on the 'Aryan side'? It is difficult to be exact, but, as I argued earlier, it is doubtful whether more than 40,000 Jews survived thanks to Polish assistance, although Paulsson's figures suggest that this estimate could be slightly increased. Not all hidden Jews survived the war, because of denunciations or because they were discovered in random searches. Teresa Prekerowa estimates that only half of those who moved onto the 'Aryan side' lived to see liberation. She has also attempted to assess how many Poles were involved in the rescue of Jews. According to her reckoning, because on average two to three Poles were involved in saving one Jew, in order to reach a figure for how many Poles were involved in the rescue of Jews one should multiply the number of survivors by two or three.

[25] Teresa Prekerowa, *Konspiracyjna Rada Pomocy Żydom w Warszawie, 1942–1945* (Warsaw, 1982); 'The Relief Council for Jews in Poland, 1939–1942', in Chimen Abramsky, Maciej Jachimczyk, and Antony Polonsky (eds.), *The Jews in Poland* (Oxford, 1986), 161–76.
[26] Yisrael Gutman, 'Polish and Jewish Historiography on the Question of Polish–Jewish Relations during World War II', in Abramsky *et al.* (eds.), *The Jews in Poland*, 186.
[27] Ringelblum, *Polish–Jewish Relations during the Second World War*, 212.

This gives us a figure of between 160,000 and 240,000 Poles who, at the risk of their own lives and those of their families, helped rescue Jews.[28] We do not know how many people died trying to save Jews. Yisrael Gutman has argued that this number is probably in the hundreds. How is one to judge these figures? Only one who was prepared to risk his life in this way is in a position to do so. Such a person is Władysław Bartoszewski. He has written: 'The moral issue remains. From a moral point of view it must be stated clearly that not enough was done either in Poland or anywhere else in occupied Europe. "Enough" was done only by those who died.'[29]

One of the main problems facing Jews attempting to hide were the *szmalcownicy* (blackmailers) who battened on Jewish misery. What did the underground attempt to do about this problem, whose moral consequences have been alluded to in a number of the newspapers cited in this chapter? The Government Delegation ordered the trial and execution of a fair number of collaborators. Yet it was only in April 1943 that it issued a warning condemning the blackmail of Jews, a threat which, as Ringelblum wrote, 'remained on paper'. From September 1943 death sentences began to be meted out to *szmalcownicy*. According to Prekerowa, in 1943–4 five blackmailers were put to death in Warsaw and a few in Kraków and its environs. Ringelblum was certainly correct when he observed that 'a larger number of death sentences for blackmailers, together with public announcements of these executions, would certainly have some effect'.[30]

One subject which we have not treated in any detail but which is of major importance is the attitude of the military underground to the genocide. This is both more complex and more controversial. Throughout the period when it was being carried out, the AK was preoccupied with preparing for Plan Storm (Burza), the strategy of confronting the Soviets with a political authority linked with the government in London at the moment of the collapse of Nazi rule in Poland. It was determined to avoid premature military action and to conserve its strength (and weapons) for the crucial confrontation which would determine the fate of Poland. Its position was clearly set out on 10 November 1942 in an order of its commander-in-chief, General Stefan 'Grot' Rowecki:

> 1. Polish society is apprehensive that in the aftermath of the current extermination of the Jews, the Germans may proceed to apply similar methods of extermination against the Poles. I call for restraint and for these apprehensions to be counteracted with reassurances. The principal German objective in relation to us could be described as the absorption of our nation. Attempts to exterminate the resistant segments of our nation by the methods applied against the Jews cannot, however, be ruled out.
>
> 2. In the event that the Germans do indeed undertake such attempts, they will encounter

---

[28] Teresa Prekerowa, ' "Sprawiedliwi" i "bierni" ', *Tygodnik Powszechny* (29 Mar. 1987).
[29] Władysław Bartoszewski, 'Polish–Jewish Relations in Occupied Poland, 1939–1945', in Abramsky et al. (eds.), *The Jews in Poland*, 160.
[30] Ringelblum, *Polish–Jewish Relations during the Second World War*, 216.

our resistance. Irrespective of the scheduled timing of our uprising, the units under my command must proceed to armed struggle in defence of the life of the nation. In the course of this struggle we shall switch from defence to attack, with the aim of undercutting the entire network of enemy lines to the eastern front. This decision is mine and will be communicated to all ranks of the clandestine forces.[31]

This document makes brutally clear the principal lines of AK strategy. It also brings out the fact that to the AK the Jews were not a part of 'our nation' and that action to defend them was not to be taken if it endangered other AK objectives. Certainly the AK was not willing to absorb the Jewish partisan groups formed in the forests by fugitives from the ghettos, regarding them as unreliable and potentially communist in sympathy. There was one exception to this. In Volhynia, which was wracked by a brutal ethnic conflict between Poles and Ukrainians, the AK was eager to co-operate with Jewish partisans to defend Polish villages. It was also not, by and large, willing to accept Jews as individuals, though here too there were exceptions, such as the Bureau of Information and Propaganda of the High Command. It should be mentioned, too, that the AK, like the civilian underground, was made up of adherents of different political orientations, some of them sympathetic and others hostile to the Jews. The AK was not sympathetic to the plight of individual Jewish fugitives, seeing them as security risks, likely to endanger its own position. Local commanders and the High Command often referred to these people (and also to communist partisans) as 'bandits', an echo of the language used by the Nazis themselves. These attitudes—the desire to avoid a premature uprising, suspicions about the Jewish sympathy for communism, and a belief that the weapons provided would not be used efficaciously—largely explain the meagre supply of arms to the Warsaw and other ghettos. In the case of Warsaw, more weapons were supplied after the confrontation with the Nazis in mid-January 1943 had demonstrated the willingness of the Jewish Fighting Organization to undertake armed action. The smaller Jewish Military Union (Żydowski Związek Wojskowy), which was controlled by the Revisionist Zionists, who had some pre-war links with the Polish military and were impeccably anti-communist, had more success initially in obtaining weapons.

The small military formations linked with the various fascist groups, the National Armed Forces (Narodowe Siły Zbrojne: NSZ) and the Rampart Group (Grupa Szańca), were openly hostile to the Jews and frequently were guilty of murders both of Jewish partisans and of Jews hiding in the villages. This situation continued even when the NSZ became more closely linked with the AK towards the end of the war.

The People's Guard (Gwardia Ludowa) and its successor, the People's Army (Armia Ludowa) were much more willing to absorb Jews, both because in their isolation they needed any support they could obtain and because their ideology

---

[31] Quoted in Gutman and Krakowski, *Unequal Victims*, 74–5.

stressed the importance of transcending national divisions. This was of course a mixed blessing, because the more Jews supported these groups, the more they seemed to confirm the belief amongst the AK (and elsewhere in Poland) that they were essentially siding with the communists.

Discussions about the role of the Polish resistance take place in a sort of time-warp. Elsewhere in Europe the myth of the powerful resistance has been subjected to harsh and largely convincing criticism. It is probably unrealistic to have expected the AK, which was neither as well armed nor as well organized as its propaganda claimed, to have been able to do much to aid the Jews. The fact remains that its leadership probably did not want to do so.

Throughout the implementation of the genocide the Catholic hierarchy in Poland made no statement on the fate of the Jews. This was partly because, persecuted as it was, the leadership of the Church feared to expose itself to additional repression. The fate of the converts, on whose behalf the Church had intervened when the question arose of wearing an armband with a Star of David, may have contributed to this caution. Certainly, nearly a fifth of Polish priests were killed by the Nazis. Many monasteries and nunneries were closed, several thousand monks and nuns were imprisoned, and nearly 900 lost their lives. Different Catholic groups did express their views of the genocide, and, as has been seen in regard to the Front for the Rebirth of Poland and the Party of Labour, often in radically divergent ways.

One area where the Church was active was in the rescue of Jews in nunneries. In all, two-thirds of the female religious communities in Poland took part in hiding Jewish children and adults. The fact that the action was on such a large scale suggests that it had the support and encouragement of the Church hierarchy. We have no accurate record of how many people were saved in this way, but it was certainly not less than 1,500. Two sisters of the Order of the Immaculate Conception and eight Sisters of Charity were shot by the Germans for assisting Jews and their children.[32]

As we have seen, by June 1945, 74,000 people had registered with the CKŻP. In the next two years 137,000 Jews returned from the USSR, mostly people who had been deported or evacuated to the interior of the country. This meant that at its height the organized post-war Jewish community in Poland numbered nearly a quarter of a million people, small by comparison with the pre-war Jewish population, but a substantial community none the less. The number of Jews was in fact significantly larger, since these figures do not include those who, for whatever reasons, did not register with the CKŻP. The community was soon faced with serious problems and was caught up in the near-civil-war conditions in post-war Poland as sections of the wartime underground movement attempted to resist the imposition on the country of an unpopular communist regime.

Moreover, it soon became clear that the war had not brought an end to anti-semitism, or seriously compromised the antisemitic ideology, since the Nazis had

---

[32] On this question, see Ewa Kurek-Lesik, *Gdy Klasztor znaczył życie* (Kraków, 1992).

persecuted the Polish radical right as fiercely as they did all other manifestations of Polish resistance to their rule. This meant that the anti-Judaic tradition of the Catholic Church emerged almost unscathed from the war. After the worst outbreak of anti-Jewish violence in post-war Poland, the pogrom in Kielce of July 1946, in which forty-two Jews were killed by a mob (some of whom believed that the Jews had abducted a Christian boy to take blood from him in order to cure anaemia resulting from the deprivations they had suffered during the war), a Jewish delegation went to see the bishop of Lublin, Stefan Wyszyński, who later, as primate, was to protest against the anti-Jewish campaign of Mieczysław Moczar. After asserting that popular hatred had been kindled by Jewish support for communism, which had also been the reason why 'the Germans murdered the Jewish nation', he went on: 'At the trial of Beilis many old and contemporary Jewish books were gathered, but the question of the use of blood by Jews was never completely clarified.'[33]

On 28 August 1946 the British ambassador to Poland, Victor Cavendish-Bentinck, cabled the Foreign Office in London:

Bishop Bieniek, Auxiliary Bishop of Upper Silesia, astonished me yesterday by stating there was some proof that the child whose alleged maltreatment by Jews had provoked the Kielce pogrom had in fact been maltreated, and that the Jews had taken blood from his arm.

If a bishop is prepared to believe this, it is not surprising that the uneducated Poles do too.

I am sending a copy of this letter to the Holy See.[34]

As is clear from Bishop Wyszyński's remarks, the war also strengthened the identification of Jews with communism. Certainly in the civil war conditions of post-war Poland the Jewish community could expect protection only from the new communist-dominated authorities. More importantly, communists of Jewish origin played a significant, though not dominant, role in the new regime. In the political apparatus Jakub Berman might be mentioned, who was responsible for ideological and security questions on the Politburo of the PPR, and Roman Zambrowski, who had been one of the principal creators of the communist-dominated Polish army in the USSR.

Jews also played a key role in the cultural policy of the new regime. Writers of Jewish origin were prominent in Kuźnica (the Forge), a group of writers who hoped to restructure Polish cultural life in the new political conditions, drawing on the traditions of the Polish Enlightenment and avoiding as much as possible the extreme versions of Marxism and social realism. Among the principal Jewish members of the Kuźnica group were the literary critic Jan Kott, Adam Ważyk,

---

[33] Quoted in Michał Borwicz, 'Polish–Jewish Relations, 1944–1947', in Abramsky *et al.* (eds.), *The Jews in Poland*, 195.

[34] Quoted in Aryeh Josef Kochavi, 'The Catholic Church and Antisemitism in Poland following World War II as Reflected in British Diplomatic Documents', *Gal-Ed: On the History of the Jews in Poland*, 11 (1989), 123.

Kazimierz Brandys, Paweł Hertz, Seweryn Pollak, Mieczysław Jastrun, and Adolf Rudnicki. The most significant figure in the group was probably Adam Ważyk. For close to ten years, in the words of the critic Artur Sandauer, 'he was the official artistic authority. He wrote dramas which were immediately produced and inevitably failed; film scripts that were immediately shot and met with a similar fate; he excoriated Norwid for his petty-noble ideology and the producers of Coca-Cola for serving atomic death. He delivered a programmatic lecture at the Fifth Conference of the Association of Polish Writers and carried over Stalin's linguistic theses to the methodology of literary studies.'[35] Although he was later to repent his Stalinist past and make an important contribution to the thaw in Poland prior to 1956, he was seen by many in the Stalinist period as the official face of communist culture.

Jews were also widely held to play a key role in the security apparatus of the new regime. In his *Europe: A History* Norman Davies writes that in Poland 'Popular knowledge ... has always insisted that the notorious communist Security Office (UB) contained a disproportionate number of Jews (or rather ex-Jews) and that their crimes were heinous.' He goes on to concede that 'few hard facts were ever published', but claims that this point of view has become 'all the more convincing' because of recent 'disclosures' that have 'broken the taboo' and are particularly credible since 'they were made by a Jewish investigator on evidence supplied by Jewish participants ... The study deals with the district of Upper Silesia, and, in particular, with the town of Gliwice (Gleiwitz).' Following the author of this study, John Sacks, Davies claims that 'in 1945 every single commander and three-quarters of the local agents of the UB were of Jewish origin; that ex-Nazi camps and prisons were refilled with totally innocent civilians, especially Germans; and that torture, starvation, sadistic beatings, and murder were routine'.[36] However, Sacks's book, *An Eye for an Eye: The Untold Story of Jewish Revenge against Germans in 1945*, is quite irresponsible and is little more than an extended interview with Lola Potok, one of the Jews in the UB. In it he produces no documentary evidence to justify his claims, which have been used to argue, in Davies's words, that 'in this light, it is difficult to justify the widespread practice whereby the murderers, the victims, and the bystanders of wartime Poland were each neatly identified with specific ethnic groups'.

Andrzej Paczkowski in Warsaw is doing pioneering research on this subject. He and Lech Głuchowski have made an assessment of the nationality of UB functionaries, making use of a confidential study prepared by the Ministry of Internal Affairs in 1978. According to this study, between 1944 and 1945 a total of 287 functionaries held leadership positions in the UB. The number of those listed as having 'Jewish nationality' totalled 75. This meant that Jews made up 26.3 per

---

[35] Artur Sandauer, *O sytuacji pisarza polskiego pochodzenia żydowskiego w XX wieku (Rzecz, którą nie ja powinienem był napisać)* (Warsaw, 1982), 50.

[36] Norman Davies, *Europe: A History* (Oxford, 1996), 1022.

cent of the UB leadership, while the figure for Poles was 66.9 per cent. The remaining 6.9 per cent were Russians, Belarusians, and Ukrainians. The proportion of Jews at lower levels of the organization was considerably less. In another document Stanisław Radkiewicz informed Bolesław Bierut that in November 1945 the UB employed 25,600 personnel and that 438 (or 1.7 per cent) of them were Jews. Furthermore, the rapid increase in the number of UB functionaries that took place in 1945 occurred in a political framework which placed the political orientation and class origins of the candidate above almost all other considerations. To quote Paczkowski and Głuchowski:

The great majority of candidates actually consisted of young—and very young—political transients, with no professional experience and mixed reasons, if not questionable motives, for joining the UB. There was a constant movement of lower-level cadres in and out of the UB between 1945 and 1946. At this time, approximately 25,000 employees left the UB: about the same number that were employed by the UB at the end of 1946. The majority had been released from the UB for drunkenness, theft, abuse, or for a lack of discipline.[37]

Different aspects of the relationship between the Jews and the new regime and the way this fed anti-communism are investigated in the chapters by Jan Gross, Bożena Szaynok, Padraic Kenney, Adam Penkalla, and Joanna Michlic-Coren.

There were other factors which intensified antisemitism in the immediate post-war period. One was resistance on the part of those who had benefited from the expropriation of Jewish property by the Nazis to attempts by its former owners to regain what they had lost, which frequently led to violence. According to the critic Kazimierz Wyka, writing in 1945:

The central psycho-economic fact of the years of the occupation remains undoubtedly the disappearance from trade and intermediary occupations of the several-million-strong Jewish masses. This disappearance, when today it is possible to number the survivors, is definitive and final . . . Shielded by the sword of the German executioner, who was carrying out a crime never before seen in history, the Polish shopkeeper took possession of the keys of the till of his Jewish competitor and believed that he was acting in the most moral manner. For the Germans are left the guilt and the crime, for us the keys and the till. The shopkeeper forgot that the 'legal' destruction of a whole nation was not staged by history so that the sign could be changed on someone's shop. The manner in which the Germans liquidated the Jews falls on their conscience. *The reaction to that liquidation, however, falls on our conscience.* A gold tooth extracted from a corpse continues to bleed even though no one remembers its origin.[38]

The conditions of Nazi occupation led to a general barbarization of society, and the massive post-war population movements, involving, above all, Germans and Ukrainians, also encouraged those who thought that Poland would be better off without Jews. Moreover, there was little serious discussion of the character of

---

[37] Letter to the *Times Literary Supplement* (*c.* Jan. 1997).
[38] Kazimierz Wyka, *Życie na niby: szkice z lat 1939–1945* (Warsaw, 1957), 197, 199.

antisemitism after 1945. The only general account in Polish of Polish antisemitism published in the post-war period was the collection *Martwa fala* ('Dead Wave'), which appeared in 1947, before the rigours of Stalinism. This was a polemical collection intended to re-educate the Polish public, but it was not followed up. The issue soon became bedevilled by communist politics as the new Stalinist regime came to argue that the entire anti-communist opposition was tainted with antisemitism and only the communists had resisted anti-Jewish prejudice and actions.

Yet, as some of our chapters demonstrate, antisemitism was not entirely absent in the PPR itself. After the relatively brief Stalinist period, the regime sought to legitimize itself by stressing its Polish character and purging communists of Jewish origin. Official government policy was to defend the Jews and to foster their economic rehabilitation, but within the party, some factions were much less sympathetic to the difficult plight of the Jews. During the war Polish communist politics had been highly factionalized. The disputes revolved around three separate but related issues: who should have priority in setting communist strategy, the party in Poland or that in Moscow; how far would the new communist Poland be able to pursue its own 'road to socialism'; and how far was it possible to pursue the Moscow strategy of a broad 'national front' made up of all anti-fascist forces in the country. In the end the PPR, established in late 1941, was forced to take power virtually on its own and dependent on Soviet support. By 1947 the communists were constructing a Soviet-style regime, and in 1948 the principal national communist, Władysław Gomułka, was forced out of office. Jewish communists were mostly to be found in the Moscow centre and in the groups which were suspicious of the Polish road to socialism. Many of these people soon repented of their flirtation with Stalinism and became among the most ardent supporters of democratization in the period of the thaw, which brought Gomułka back to power in October 1956. But at the time their position in the party aroused considerable resentment, which was to surface in 1956 and still more in 1968.

What conclusions can be drawn from what Jan Gross has described as 'the infernal decade' (*upiorna dekada*) between 1939 and 1948? Success in implementing mass murder rested on persuading both victims and bystanders that it was more sensible to co-operate than to resist, whether by false claims that what was involved was merely resettlement, by holding out the hope that some would survive, or by stressing the penalties of non-co-operation. As Zygmunt Bauman has written,

By and large the rulers can count on rationality being on their side. The Nazi rulers twisted the stakes of the game so that the rationality of survival would render all other motives of human action irrational. Inside the Nazi-made, unreal and inhuman world, reason was the enemy of morality. Logic required consent to crime. Rational defence of one's survival called for non-resistance to the other's destruction. This rationality pitched the sufferers against each other and obliterated their joint humanity. This rationality absolved them from immorality. Having reduced human life to the calculus of survival, this rationality robbed human life of humanity.[39]

This leads on to a more fundamental issue. Jan Błoński is clearly right to stress the significance of the emergence of two separate societies on the Polish lands—Polish and Jewish—and to draw attention to the way the gulf between them widened in the 1930s and in the first two years of the Nazi occupation of Poland, leading to mutual incomprehension, suspicion, and even hatred. The fact that the Jews were not part of the 'universe of obligation' of most Poles made the genocide easier for the Germans to carry out and also made much more difficult the task of those Poles who wished to assist the Jews.

The destruction of Polish Jewry was a blow from which world Jewry has not recovered. The diarist Abraham Lewin, who perished in Treblinka in January 1943, wrote at the end of 1942, after the deportation of most of the Jews from the Polish capital:

Warsaw was in fact the backbone of Polish Jewry, its heart one could say. The destruction of Warsaw would have meant the destruction of the whole of Polish Jewry, even if the provinces had been spared this evil. Now that the enemy's sword of destruction has run amok through the small towns and villages and is cutting them down with murderous blows—with the death-agony of the metropolis, the entire body is dying and plunging into the abyss. One can say that with the setting of the sun of Polish Jewry, the splendour and the glory of world Jewry has vanished. We, the Polish Jews, were after all the most vibrant nerve of our people . . . Hitler has murdered an entire people.[40]

Yet, as has been pointed out, there was a remnant left on Polish soil after 1944. The failure to create a viable post-war community was the result of a number of factors: the difficulty of living in a cemetery, where the Nazis had murdered the overwhelming majority of the pre-war community; the persistence of anti-semitism and anti-Jewish violence; and the character of the post-war communist regime, which was clearly distasteful to the majority of Jewish survivors. It may be that this failure was inevitable, given all the difficulties the community faced. Nevertheless, it makes a sad epilogue to the tragic events of the war and constitutes a posthumous victory for Hitler.

[39] Zygmunt Bauman, 'On Immoral Reason and Illogical Morality', *Polin*, iii. 296.
[40] Abraham Lewin, *A Cup of Tears: A Diary from the Warsaw Ghetto* (Oxford, 1988).

Anti-Jewish Violence in Poland, 1918–1939 and 1945–1947

JOANNA MICHLIC-COREN

VERY little comparative analysis has been done so far on the subject of anti-Jewish violence in twentieth-century Poland.[1] Historical research has tended to focus on descriptions of individual riots, such as the Przytyk pogrom of 9 March 1936 and the Kielce pogrom of 4 July 1946, or on discussion of a particular historical period.[2] There has been no attempt to explore the similarities and differences between the mechanisms of and reactions to anti-Jewish riots.[3]

In this chapter I examine the link between the myth of the Jew as the 'Threatening Other' and eruptions of anti-Jewish excesses between 1918 and 1939 and between 1945 and 1947, concentrating on the extent to which this myth influenced the initiation and evaluation of anti-Jewish violence in these two distinctive historical periods. By the term 'violence', I understand here the following types of actions: inflicting damage on Jewish properties, including private homes, shops, institutions, and synagogues; slander; physical harassment; assaults; and murder.

Before moving on to the main examination, I provide a brief outline of the socio-historical context in which the anti-Jewish violent disturbances and riots occurred in both periods.

---

[1] The subject of Polish anti-Jewish violence has not so far produced any study to match the comprehensive work on Russian anti-Jewish violence by John D. Klier and Shlomo Lambroza (eds.), *Pogroms: Anti-Jewish Violence in Modern Russian History* (Cambridge, 1982).

[2] Anti-Jewish violence in the inter-war period has been more widely researched than that of the early post-war period. The latter still awaits thorough historical investigation. Among the most significant works on Polish anti-Jewish violence of the inter-war period are Jolanta Żyndul, *Zajścia antyżydowskie w Polsce w latach, 1935–1937* (Warsaw, 1994), Ronald Modras, *The Catholic Church and Antisemitism in Poland, 1933–1939* (Chur, 1994), 301–23, and Emanuel Melzer, *No Way Out: The Politics of Polish Jewry, 1935–1939* (Cincinnati, 1997), 53–80.

[3] The need for comparative analysis was recently pointed out by Jerzy Tomaszewski. See the discussion on the problematics of research into the Kielce pogrom in 'O stanie badań nad pogromem w Kielcach', *BŻIH* 4 (1996), 13.

THE SOCIAL AND HISTORICAL BACKGROUND TO THE VIOLENCE

The Inter-War Period

It is possible to differentiate four major waves of anti-Jewish violence sweeping inter-war Poland, each of which was characterized by specific historical conditions and developments. The first wave, in 1918–1920, was rooted in the formation of the new Polish nation-state; the second, in 1930–3, was based primarily in the universities; the third, and least researched, was linked to the emergence of the National Radical Camp in 1934; and the last, in 1935–7, was the most widespread and the most severe.

The first wave of violence began in 1918 and lasted until the end of the Bolshevik War in 1920. Territories most affected were the Eastern Provinces, where heavy fighting took place between the Polish and the Ukrainian armies during the first two years of independence, and parts of Małopolska, where a peasant revolt erupted in the spring of 1919.[4]

The second major wave broke out in universities during the first term of the academic year of 1930/1 and again during the same term of the following two academic years.[5] During this phase anti-Jewish excesses were frequently associated with demonstrations against the Sanacja government, which was perceived by the Endecja as representing Jewish interests.[6] Violence against Jewish students was advocated by organizations such as the All-Polish Youth (Młodzież Wszechpolska), the youth movement of the Camp for a Greater Poland (Ruch Młodych Obozu Wielkiej Polski: OWP), and the student self-help associations (Bratnia Pomoc: Brotherly Help), which were mostly controlled by the OWP. These organizations regarded anti-Jewish action as a way to put pressure on the government to introduce a policy of *numerus clausus* in the universities.[7] In some cities the students

---

[4] See Witold Stankiewicz, *Konflikty społeczne na wsi polskiej, 1918–1920* (Warsaw, 1963), 159–69; Jerzy Tomaszewski, 'Trzeci maja 1919 roku w Rzeszowie', in *Almanach Żydowski, 1996–1997* (n.p.), 7–16.

[5] See the reports on student anti-Jewish demonstrations in *Sprawy Narodowościowe*, 6 (1931), 644–54; 6 (1932), 698–703.

[6] See e.g. Roman Rybarski, 'Polityka żydowska', *Gazeta Warszawska*, 220/19 (7 June 1931). As a result of the parliamentary election of 1930 the Sanacja gained a majority in parliament (247 seats; 46.8 per cent) and on taking government became independent of their political opponents. The National Party (Stronnictwo Narodowe: SN) became the main party of opposition (62 seats; 12.7 per cent). See Szymon Rudnicki, *Obóz Narodowo-Radykalny: geneza i działalność* (Warsaw, 1985), 58–9.

[7] The policy of *numerus clausus* was a discriminatory policy aimed at limiting the number of Polish Jewish students at Polish universities and institutions of higher education. It was in violation of the Polish constitution and as such was condemned by the Polish Jewish community, the international academic world, and a group of leading Polish intellectuals including Adam Czyczewicz, Ryszard Ganszyniec, Tadeusz Kotarbiński, and Mieczysław Michałowicz. The policy had been continually proposed by the All-Polish Youth since its establishment in 1922. The youth movement of the OWP, set up in 1927, was dissolved, along with the entire organization of the

were joined by gymnasium pupils, who were also influenced significantly by the OWP and the Endecja.

The third wave, in 1934, was initiated by the newly formed National Radical Camp (Obóz Narodowo-Radykalny: ONR); violence took place in April, May, and the first half of June.[8] Given the explicitly fascist position of the ONR, on 12 May the ministry of interior affairs had to issue special directives against the excesses. At the same time leaders of the Jewish community began talks on setting up an organization to monitor anti-Jewish events in the country.[9]

The fourth wave of anti-Jewish excesses occurred between 1935 and 1937, amid increasing popular support for the ethnic nationalization of the Polish state during the second half of the 1930s.[10] Once again violence broke out in the universities, where the All-Polish Youth and the ONR intensified the campaign for 'ghetto benches' for Jewish students. In some universities attempts were made to move Jewish students by force to segregated sections of lecture halls. Characteristically campus violence continued to take place even after ghetto benches were introduced by universities on the grounds that such a measure would bring an end to the disturbances and would guarantee the maintenance of peace on campuses.[11] A clear indication that the introduction of ghetto benches did not end anti-Jewish violence can be seen at L'viv Polytechnic, where such a regulation was imposed by the dean's council in two departments in December 1935, two years before the government officially granted universities power to regulate the seating of Polish and Jewish students.[12]

OWP, by the state administration in 1933. The student organization Bratnia Pomoc, controlled by All-Polish Youth in almost every university, numbered 30,000 students in 1930 (approximately 60 per cent of all students). Polish Jewish students were banned from membership of this organization at all universities except the Jagiellonian University in Kraków. See Szymon Rudnicki, 'From *Numerus Clausus* to *Numerus Nullus*', *Polin*, 2 (1987), 246–68, and *Obóz Narodowo-Radykalny*, 72.

[8] The ONR replaced the OWP, which had been dissolved a year earlier. In its declaration issued in Apr. 1934 the ONR posited the notion that a Jew could not be a citizen of the Polish nation-state (see 'Żydzi', *Sprawy Narodowościowe*, 4 (1934), 474). After 11 July 1934 the government made the ONR illegal. Many members of the ONR were also members of the legal SN, however.   [9] Ibid. 286.

[10] For a short and concise summary of that period, see Emanuel Melzer, 'Antisemitism in the Last Years of the Second Polish Republic', in Yisrael Gutman, Ezra Mendelsohn, Jehuda Reinharz, and Chone Shmeruk (eds.), *The Jews of Poland between Two World Wars* (Hanover, NH, 1989), 126–37.

[11] In the late 1930s the SN and the ONR started to demand *numerus nullus*, a project that aimed at the complete 'dejudaization' of all Polish institutions of higher education. In fact campus violence continued in the academic year 1938/9, becoming even more extreme as murders of Jewish students were committed. See Melzer, *No Way Out*, 71–80.

[12] This step did not put end to anti-Jewish disturbances at the polytechnic, which continued throughout Jan.–Mar. 1936. The majority of Jewish students refused to accept the new system of seating on the ground that it violated their civic rights. The ghetto benches regulation was abolished at the polytechnic the same academic year. See 'Wystąpienia żydowskie i ich echa', *Sprawy Narodowościowe*, 1–2 (1936), 107.

Outside the universities anti-Jewish excesses orchestrated by the local sections of the National Party (Stronnictwo Narodowe) occurred in 150 towns and villages. The most frequent rioting took place in central Poland, where the Jewish community was highly concentrated, but violence erupted all over the country regardless of the size of the Jewish population living in any particular area. For example, in Silesia, where the Jews constituted only 1.7 per cent of the population, attacks still took place.[13]

This widespread violence was a direct result of the newly intensified anti-Jewish campaign launched by the National Party and the ONR in 1935. These two political parties looked on violence as a viable, indeed indispensable, tool in the 'dejudaization' of the Polish nation-state (*odżydzanie Polski*).[14] The main aim of the anti-Jewish riots was to make the daily life of Polish Jews so unbearable (*obrzydzanie*) that they would be 'persuaded' to emigrate voluntarily. It was also supposed to warn Jews that the Poles were no longer willing to tolerate their presence within the Polish nation-state.

Between 1935 and 1937 an estimated 2,000 Polish Jews were injured and between twenty and thirty killed.[15] In comparison, between 1918 and 1919 the dead numbered 230. The majority in this earlier period, however, were killed not by civilians but by soldiers, members of the two armies of Józef Haller and of Wielkopolska.[16] On average the number of dead resulting from a single outbreak of anti-Jewish violence was one or two. For example: one person died in Strzyżów on 21 April 1919 and in Baranów on 5 May 1919; two died in Niebylec on 28 April 1919, in Grodno on 5 June 1936, and in Przytyk on 9 March 1936. Amongst the higher figures were five dead in the Odrzywół riots of 20 and 27 November 1935, and eight dead and 100 injured in the riot in Kolbuszowa, Rzeszów district, on 6 May 1919.[17]

The two most common forms of violence directed against Jews in inter-war Poland were smashing windows and plundering shops and private homes, and beating up the inhabitants of villages and towns, students at universities, and commuters on trains. At certain times on some of the suburban lines, such as

[13] Jolanta Żyndul, 'Zajścia antyżydowskie 1935–1937: geografia i formy', *BŻIH* 3 (1991), 69.

[14] As early as 15 Nov. 1935 the leading SN paper *Warszawski Dziennik Narodowy* called for the expulsion of the Jews from Warsaw as a step on the way to achieving complete 'dejudaization' of Poland. See 'Żydzi', *Sprawy Narodowościowe*, 5 (1935), 481. On the problem of anti-Jewish terror between 1935 and 1937, see also Włodzimierz Mich, *Obcy w polskim domu: nacjonalistyczne koncepcje rozwiązania problemu mniejszości narodowych, 1918–1939* (Lublin, 1994), 84–9.

[15] Jewish sources in Palestine presented higher figures of people killed and injured than those in Polish sources. A discussion on these statistics and the numbers quoted appears in Żyndul, *Zajścia antyżydowskie w Polsce w latach, 1935–1937*, 70. See also Ezra Mendelsohn, *The Jews of East Central Europe between the World Wars* (Hanover, NH, 1989).

[16] See e.g. Jerzy Tomaszewski, 'Polskie formacje zbrojne wobec Żydów 1918–1920', in *Żydzi w obronie Rzeczypospolitej* (Warsaw, 1996), 97–111, and Żyndul, *Zajścia antyżydowskie w Polsce w latach, 1935–1937*, 9.

[17] According to data in Stankiewicz, *Konflikty społeczne na wsi polskiej, 1918–1920*, 162.

Warsaw–Otwock, the police had to set up extra patrols in order to protect Jewish travellers.[18] Less common were the burning of Jewish shops and the bombing of Jewish institutions and synagogues, and throwing harmful chemicals at Jews in the street.[19]

The Post-War Years: 1945–1947

The years 1945 to 1947 saw a new eruption of violent attacks against both individuals and groups of Polish Jewish Holocaust survivors returning to their pre-war homes or trying to settle down in new areas. Halina Birenbaum's memoirs *Powrót do ziemi praojców* ('The Return to the Land of the Forefathers') describes the atmosphere surrounding the first encounters between Poles and the returning Jews: 'The Poles didn't show much joy at the sight of their Jewish neighbours returning home . . . Instead uncomfortable questions were asked: How come you are alive? How is it that you have survived?'[20] Accounts of hostility ranging from verbal harassment (including advice to 'leave the village otherwise something bad is going to happen to you') to robbery, beating, and murder are frequent in individual statements and diaries, and official records of the Central Committee of Jews in Poland (Centralny Komitet Żydów w Polsce: CKŻP) and of the Polish Workers' Party (Polska Partia Robotnicza: PPR). In some instances Jewish communities settling in small villages received threats against their lives and were advised to leave.

In the summer of 1945 the CKŻP became alarmed by the frequency of anti-Jewish attacks in central and eastern parts of Poland, where 100 people had been murdered in only two months. Six months later, with the repatriation of Jews from the Soviet Union that began on 8 February 1946, an anti-Jewish atmosphere had spread all over the country.[21] Even in the Western 'Recovered' Territories (Ziemie Odzyskane), where both ethnic Poles and Polish Jews were newcomers, anti-Jewish activity became noticeable in the spring of 1946.[22] Leaflets were circulated

---

[18] See Żyndul, 'Zajścia antyżydowskie 1935–1937', 58.

[19] Bombing of synagogues was objected to by a faction within the Endecja on the ground that they were not fighting against Judaism as a religion but against the judaization of Poland (ibid. 58–9). [20] Halina Birenbaum, *Powrót do ziemi praojców* (Warsaw, 1991), 7.

[21] It is estimated that of the 214,210 who returned from the Soviet Union between 8 Feb. and 31 July 1946, 136,579 were Jews. See Józef Adelson, 'W Polsce zwanej Ludową', in Jerzy Tomaszewski (ed.), *Najnowsze dzieje Żydów w Polsce: w zarysie (do 1950 roku)* (Warsaw, 1993), 397–8.

[22] According to Danuta Blus-Węgrowska, the new influx of Polish Jewish repatriates from the Soviet Union stimulated the spread of anti-Jewish propaganda in Lower Silesia and Pomerania in the spring of 1946 (Danuta Blus-Węgrowska, 'Atmosfera pogromowa', *Karta* 18 (1996), 97–8). On Polish–Jewish relations in the Western Territories, see also Stanisław Ossowski, 'Na tle wydarzeń kieleckich', *Kuźnica*, 38 (1946), 124, and Albert Stankowski, 'Emigracja Żydów z Pomorza Zachodniego w latach 1945–1960', in Jerzy Tomaszewski (ed.), *Studia z dziejów i kultury Żydów w Polsce po 1945 roku* (Warsaw, 1997), 83–102.

warning: 'Jewish hordes if you do not leave the city by 15 May we will take appropriate action!', and individuals were robbed, injured, and murdered.[23] By the end of 1947 the death toll reached an estimated 2,000 people, including 200 killed in the so-called 'train actions' (*akcje pociągowe*) orchestrated by units of the illegal National Armed Forces (Narodowe Siły Zbrojne).[24]

Anti-Jewish violence had escalated in Poland in the early post-war years. The number of people killed in individual attacks was much higher than at any time between the wars. For example, seven people, including a 14-year-old boy, were killed near Czorsztyn on 30 April 1946; out of a group of twenty men, women, and children on a road near Krościenko on 2 May 1946, twelve were shot and six seriously injured; and forty-two people were killed in the Kielce pogrom of 4 July 1946.[25] Many were also found murdered in their homes and in more secluded public areas. In addition, attacks were less discriminatory and more extreme, frequently occurring amongst the most vulnerable sections of the Jewish population, such as the elderly and women and children. For example, Jewish patients were killed in a Lublin hospital on 9 May 1945; a family with a 9-month-old were killed in Tarnogród on 20 December 1945; and two pregnant women were killed in Kielce on 4 July 1946.[26]

Amongst all this it is evident that no ethical, religious, or humanitarian issues were being discussed, while during the 1930s a debate had taken place even within the exclusivist ethno-nationalist camp on the use of violence in the context of ethical and religious considerations.[27] For example, articles condemning violence had appeared in the press associated with the National Party, such as the editorial signed by B.K. in *Kurier Warszawski* on 11 November 1931. There had also been disagreement among OWP students on the issue of attacks against female Jewish students, which could be considered unchivalrous according to the Polish code of male behaviour.

Summary

This extreme intensification of brutality was one of the chief characteristics of the anti-Jewish disturbances of the early post-war era. Important features common to both the pre-war and post-war periods can be found, however, in the vocabulary of the perpetrators and supporters of such violence, in particular their use of the myth of the Jew as the Threatening Other, with the purpose of inciting to ethnic

---

[23] Text of the leaflet quoted from Blus-Węgrowska, 'Atmosfera pogromowa', 98.

[24] The figures for the dead vary in different sources. It is estimated that between 1,500 and 2,000 people were killed. However, Yisrael Gutman gives the highest number, 3,000, in *Hayehudim befolin aḥarei milḥemet haolam hasheniyah* (Jerusalem, 1985).

[25] Cases of murder described in Blus-Węgrowska, 'Atmosfera pogromowa', 93, 95.

[26] See Alina Cała and Helena Datner-Śpiewak, *Dzieje Żydów w Polsce 1944–1968: teksty źródłowe* (Warsaw, 1997), 18, and Bożena Szaynok, *Pogrom Żydów w Kielcach 4 lipca 1946* (Wrocław, 1992), 60.

[27] This problem was pointed out by Modras, *The Catholic Church and Antisemitism in Poland, 1933–1939*, 308.

hatred and violent attack. Indeed, it can be argued that this image provided the basis for the evaluation and justification of the use of anti-Jewish violence as a necessary form of national self-defence.

THE MYTH AND ITS LANGUAGE AS DESTRUCTIVE MEANS OF COMMUNICATION

Even before Poland had regained its independence in 1918, the Endecja deployed the myth of the Jews as the enemy of the Polish nation in political propaganda, stressing that the Jews constituted a major threat to the future Polish nation-state. Contemporary newspapers reveal that the Jewish community was already concerned about the potential outcome of such accusations. For example, in Kielce, frequently visited by Roman Dmowski in 1910, the *Gazeta Kielecka* published the following statement issued by the local Jewish community: 'We are protesting against the accusation . . . that portrays a section of Polish Jewry as hostile in all aspects to the Polish nation. Such a section does not exist. All rightly thinking Jews support the development of Poland and Polish culture and will never oppose the Polish *raison d'être*.'[28]

The myth was particularly evident during the political campaigns of 1905 and 1912. In the former the Endecja accused the Jews of causing social unrest by spreading socialism, an ideology that was supposedly alien to the Poles. In 1912, the year of major political defeat for the Endecja, the party accused the Jews of being the enemy of the Polish economy and proclaimed the first economic boycott of the Jewish ethnic minority.[29] The key slogan 'Do not buy at Jewish shops' (*Nie kupujcie u Żydów*) was presented by the Endeks as a national commandment (*nakaz narodowy*). In the press supported by the party that section of the Polish population that did not approve of the economic boycott was accused of violating 'the most holy national principle', whereas Poles who supported it were praised for being truly patriotic and Catholic. Violent attacks on Jewish shopkeepers took place, although the perpetrators were limited to young activists of the Endecja.[30]

After 1918 the myth of the Jew as the enemy of the Polish nation underwent further elaboration, and eventually the obsession with Jews came to constitute the main political feature of the entire ethno-nationalist camp. The Endek line was that the Jew as the Threatening Other was chiefly responsible for all the upheavals of the newly resurrected Polish nation-state: the sharp decline in national income between 1929 and 1933, the growing social unrest, and the cultural and economic crisis. As other political parties and movements each came nearer to supporting the exclusivist ethno-nationalist model of the state, the myth of the Jew as the

---

[28] *Gazeta Kielecka*, 30 (1910); quoted in Krzysztof Urbański, *Kieleccy Żydzi* (Kielce, 1992), 59.
[29] See Rudnicki, *Obóz Narodowo-Radykalny*, 112.
[30] Stanisław Wiech, 'Polacy a Żydzi w Kielcach w latach 1911–1916', in *Społeczeństwo województwa kieleckiego wobec niepodległości 1918 roku* (Kielce, 1991), 140–1.

Threatening Other became central both to Polish–Jewish relations and to the general debate on Polish society and identity.[31]

On a national level the myth was intended to have two important functions: to raise the collective cohesiveness of the Polish ethno-national community and to provide simplistic explanations for the community's past and present failures—in essence suggesting that Poland would be a great and prosperous nation if not for the presence of the Jews. It blocked any rational enquiry into the reasons behind national upheavals and social and economic crises, offering instead an explanation of Polish national experience that was incongruent with reality.[32]

The myth of the Jew as the Threatening Other continued to have the same functions in the early post-war years, when most of a political opposition against the imposed communist regime saw in the Jew a major political threat linked to that other main enemy, the Soviet Union. The fact that a section of Polish Jews held visible and high-ranking positions within the communist party and the state apparatus intensified the myth. Jews were made responsible as a collectivity for all the ills that had befallen the Polish nation emerging from the aftermath of the Second World War. Typical messages circulating around the country informed the population thus: 'Poles! Do you know who is in charge of the trials against Poles? Jews! Do you know who is murdering Poles? Jews! Do you know who is ruling over Poland? Jews and the Bolsheviks!'[33]

As a rule, the myth of the Jew as the Threatening Other was formulated in highly emotive language. Since the myth became deployed in both political propaganda and popular culture, its vocabulary was primitive, vulgar, and aggressive. The Endecja and its supporters described the Jewish Threatening Other in words expressing a high level of animosity and hostility, such as Jewish 'menace', 'horde', 'curse', 'flood', and 'tribe of parasites'. Even the term 'Jew' itself came to have negative connotations. This was reinforced by phrases stressing struggle, battle, and even war against Jews. Examples from two inter-war monthly publications, the student *Alma Mater* and the Catholic *Pro Christo*, are typical of the way in which these expressions were used: 'the struggle against the Jews is a national duty';[34] 'the struggle against the Jews is also a struggle against the communist gangrene that is spreading in the country; it is a struggle for our true independence';[35] 'our existence is dependent on how we fight the Jews step by step'.[36]

---

[31] See Mich, *Obcy w polskim domu*, 18–89.

[32] On the functions of myth in the national context, see George Schopflin, 'The Functions of Myth and a Taxonomy of Myths', in Geoffrey Hosking and George Schopflin (eds.), *Myth and Nationhood* (London, 1997), 19–35.

[33] Message written on the back of an illegal leaflet circulated in Kielce in Aug. 1945; quoted in Blus-Węgrowska, 'Atmosfera pogromowa', 101.

[34] St.P., 'W szrankach polemiki', *Alma Mater*, 3 (1939).

[35] Zbigniew Dymecki, 'W obliczu czerwonego niebezpieczeństwa: agentury komunizmu w Polsce', *Alma Mater*, 6 (1938).

[36] Adolf Reutt's speech 'Rola Polski wśród innych narodów wielkich', *Pro Christo*, 11 (1936).

In the 1930s these phrases were overwhelmingly present in the political propaganda of the National Party, the OWP, the ONR, and the All-Polish Youth. 'The struggle against the Jews' (*walka z Żydami*) became the key slogan of the ethno-nationalist press including a whole range of student, social, Catholic, and tabloid papers. The purpose of using such expressions was to portray Polish–Jewish relations as a zero-sum conflict in which the Polish ethnic community had to take action to defend itself against control and destruction by the Jewish ethnic minority.

The extent to which this anti-Jewish vocabulary was absorbed by the wider population is difficult to establish owing to the lack of a viable methodology. However, it can be argued that it was at the very least absorbed by that section of society that actively took part in anti-Jewish violence. Here the destructive nature of this type of communication is unquestionable, since there was a high level of social mobilization. Some of the riots organized by the National Party attracted substantial crowds. The largest numbered 15,000 people, who participated in anti-Jewish excesses in Częstochowa on 19 June 1937.[37]

It can also be argued that anti-Jewish vocabulary was absorbed by the readers of the ethno-nationalist press and literature. Since this body of writing constituted a large and influential section of works published in inter-war Poland, the degree of absorption and level of popularity of such anti-Jewish propaganda is unquestionable. A look at the circulations of the antisemitic tabloid papers that constituted the most extreme part of the ethno-nationalist press shows that even these papers had a good-sized readership. In 1938 alone the total circulation of such papers exceeded 100,000 and equalled that of all weeklies dedicated to social and literary issues. Two of the anti-Jewish weeklies, *Pod pręgierz* ('Under the Ban') and *Samoobrona Narodu* ('Self-Defence of the Nation') each reached a circulation of more than 25,000 the same year.[38]

As in the ethno-nationalist press the same anti-Jewish language was employed in popular books on Jewish subjects. Prominent authors of this genre were published in the so-called 'Jewish Expert Library' (Biblioteka Żydoznawcza) series. This literature, advertised in the ethno-nationalist press, was directed at both the more sophisticated as well as the popular market. For example, the monthly *Alma Mater*, directed at Catholic university students, ran a special column entitled 'Books to Read' ('Co czytać?'), in which anti-Jewish and anti-communist works were highly recommended. Similar columns were published by the popular daily *Mały Dziennik* and in *Pro Christo*, which also published a list of recommended books entitled 'Literature on the Subject of Jews' (Literatura Żydoznawcza).

This kind of language was also deployed in lectures, seminars, and discussions organized by the National Party. These events were significant propagators of ethnic hatred, and cases of spontaneous attacks on individual Jews after such events were reported in the Jewish and Polish press. Among the more extreme

[37] Żynduo, *Zajścia antiżydowskie w Polsce w latach 1935–1937*, 67–8.
[38] See Andrzej Paczkowski, *Prasa Polska w latach 1918–1939* (Warsaw, 1990), 291–2.

examples was the knife attack by Jan Antczak on three Jewish men in Łódź in January 1937, which took place after a lecture given by the priest Stanisław Trzeciak, known as a prominent expert on Jewish matters. Two of the men were badly injured and the other died.[39]

Despite the new communist regime's official position that anti-Jewish propaganda was an aspect of sabotage against the state and its new political system, illegal anti-Jewish pamphlets circulated around the country in the early post-war years. The same vocabulary can be found in these writings as in those of the inter-war period. Jews as a collectivity are continually referred to as a 'menace', a 'plague', and a 'curse'. Expressions of hatred and hostility are extremely explicit where they arise out of the Jewish minority's having been associated with the new communist regime. An example of this is the text of a leaflet circulated in Frydland, in the Wałbrzych district, in May 1948:

> Attention! . . .
> A Jewish plague has swamped our town
> every townsman agrees . . .
> that Jewish mugs and their deceitful eyes
> look at us as if to say: We will show you Poles! . . .
> however we are not afraid
> and we are going to beat the Jews back on each and every street
> until this Jewish plague is gone.[40]

Cases such as the Kielce pogrom show that such phrases proliferated in times of anti-Jewish riots and that people were not afraid to repeat them to representatives of the communist regime during public meetings held in factories to condemn the pogrom. For example, in a report from a meeting at the Dęblin railway factory on 11 July 1947 Stefan Tomaszewski, head of the Warsaw Department of Communication, reported:

The meeting lasted 2 hours and was very stormy. Comrade Chodkiewicz and I both made our statements. During the speeches people shouted back: Get rid of the Jews! It's a disgrace that they have come to defend the Jews! . . . We had control over the meeting, but I knew that the prepared resolution would not be accepted because of the hostile atmosphere, so I didn't bother to read it out. After the meeting the workers spoke among themselves. I heard them saying: 'They are servants of the Jews, fuck them all!'[41]

Another illustration of the spread of public hostility was to be found amongst schoolchildren, a group that could not have absorbed the myth of the Jew as the

---

[39] This case was reported in *Warszawski Dziennik Narodowy*, 31 (1937); quoted in Żyndul, *Zajścia antyżydowskie w Polsce w latach 1935–1937*, 92.
[40] Blus-Węgrowska, 'Atmosfera pogromowa', 98.
[41] See Andrzej Paczkowski, 'Raporty o pogromie', *Puls*, 3 (1991), 109–10.

Threatening Other in inter-war Poland. When, in April 1947, a questionnaire was conducted in primary schools in Szczecin, 50 per cent of pupils interviewed replied 'no' when asked if they would accept a Jewish child as a friend.[42]

VIOLENCE AND NATIONAL SELF-DEFENCE

In both the inter-war and the post-war periods there was a strong tendency amongst perpetrators of violence and their supporters to rationalize anti-Jewish violence in terms of national self-defence. This concept functioned in four main ways: firstly, to mandate and justify anti-Jewish riots and disturbances; secondly, to make the participants appear to be national heroes; thirdly, to shift the guilt and responsibility for the violence onto the victim, the Jewish ethnic minority; and, finally, to minimize the unethical and criminal nature of inter-ethnic violence itself. At the root of such argumentation lay the myth of the Jew as the Threatening Other.

This tendency was first to be found in the speech and actions of officers and soldiers of the Haller and Wielkopolska armies in the eastern territories between 1918 and 1919. In general these officers and soldiers shared the conviction that Jews were the enemy of the Polish nation-state and that they collaborated with the other enemies of Poland, the Ukrainians and the Bolsheviks. The chief accusation made against Jews was of Bolshevism and these armies treated all Jews as communists, despite the political diversity within the Jewish communities. The strong belief in the myth of the Jew as the Threatening Other resulted in the murder of seventy Jews in L'viv between 22 and 24 November 1918, while thirty were killed in Pinsk on 5 April 1919. These two massacres caused an uproar in the parliament, where Ignacy Daszyński, one of the leaders of the Polska Partia Socjalistyczna (Polish Socialist Party: PPS), demanded an end to the excesses of the army, whom he referred to as hooligans in uniform. These condemnations, however, did not stop the soldiers from believing that they had acted in national self-defence. Such a view is stated in the memoirs of a lieutenant, Antoni Jakubowski, who said of the L'viv killings that 'the Jewish perfidy was even greater than the Ukrainian one . . . the Jews were rightly punished. The whole suburb had to be pacified by military action . . .'.[43]

The same arguments were used in relation to peasant anti-Jewish riots in Małopolska in April and May 1919. Records of the investigation reveal that members of the National Party justified the anti-Jewish violence on the grounds that the Jews constituted a political threat to the nation. For example, Dezydery Ostrowski, headmaster of a local gymnasium and leader of the local section of the National Democrats, stated that 'In my opinion the Jewish menace is one that is hostile to

---

[42] Stankowski, 'Emigracja Żydów z Pomorza Zachodniego', 90.

[43] Tomaszewski, 'Polskie formacje zbrojne wobec Żydów 1918–1920', 100. See also Józef Lewandowski, 'History and Myth: Pinsk, April 1919', *Polin*, 2 (1987), 50–72.

us, and socialism—also hostile to us—is supported mainly by the Jews. During the war, we saw the Jews as they betrayed us and supported the Germans . . .'.[44]

National self-defence was also used as the grounds for the anti-Jewish student riots of the 1930s. In the aftermath of the first major rioting, the Supreme Council of the National Party passed a resolution on 22 November 1931 stating that:

> The numbers of Jews in this country and their strong position in its economic life, which has only strengthened under the present government, is threatening our economic future. Their destructive influence on the population's morals and on spiritual national life, and their hostile attitude towards the Polish *raison d'être*, proves that the rightful aim of Polish national politics has to be opposition to the Jewish Threat.
>
> Therefore, the Supreme Council sees in the latest student 'events' a sign of a battle for Polishness and proof that the majority of Polish youth is highly patriotic. This for us is reassurance that the political and cultural future of our Homeland will be secured and that the State will become an ethno-national one . . .[45]

Acting in national self-defence was also the justification used by Adam Doboszyński, the chief instigator of the 'march on Myślenice' (*marsz na Myślenice*) on 22 and 23 June 1936. Under Doboszyński's command 150 people terrorized the local Jewish community and destroyed all its material goods. The Myślenice police could not stop the attack because they were disarmed by Doboszyński's men. Afterwards Doboszyński was proclaimed a national hero in the circles of the National Party and was later appointed to the position of vice-chairman of the party.

The same conviction was publicly expressed by the perpetrators of the Przytyk pogrom and their lawyers during the trial in June 1936. According to Joshua Rothenberg:

> The Endek lawyers acting for the Polish defendants repeatedly attacked not only the Jewish defendants but the Jewish people as a whole. One of their most frequent accusations was that most Jews were communists and that the Jewish defendants were either communists or were manipulated by communists. The Jewish religion was also attacked. The question of the right of Jews to remain in Poland was raised on numerous occasions.
>
> According to several Jewish newspaper correspondents, the Polish defendants, and even more so the witnesses, conducted themselves defiantly, like heroes to whom the future of Poland belonged.[46]

The sentences of the Przytyk defendants exemplified the common tendency to be more lenient to ethnic Poles participating in anti-Jewish riots than to Jewish co-defendants. Although they brought a wave of protest not only from the Jewish ethnic minority but also from Polish left-wing political and social organizations,

---

[44] Quoted in Tomaszewski, 'Trzeci maja 1919 roku w Rzeszowie', 14.

[45] From the political debate on student anti-Jewish riots in the autumn of 1931, *Sprawy Narodowościowe*, 6 (1931), 651.

[46] Żyndul, *Zajścia antyżydowskie w Polsce w latach 1935–1937*, 92. See also Joshua Rothenberg, 'The Przytyk Pogrom', *Soviet Jewish Affairs*, 16/2 (1986), 40.

chiefly the PPS, the sentences were not revised. In such cases the judicial institutions gave the strong impression of minimizing the criminal nature of inter-ethnic violence, thereby making such violence socially acceptable. Jolanta Żyndul suggests that ideological reasons such as acting in national self-defence were seen by some judges to be extenuating circumstances.[47]

According to the records of the CKŻP, the tendency to play down anti-Jewish violence continued on the part of some local governments and institutions of law and order between 1945 and 1947. In some cases, such as the murder of a couple with a baby in Tarnogród on 20 December 1945, the local government discontinued investigation into the murder despite there being sufficient testimony by witnesses.[48] The third trial of the Kielce pogrom, which took place in December 1947, also serves as an example of very lenient treatment in the case of Major Władysław Sobczyński, chief of public security in Kielce, and Colonel Wiktor Kuźnicki, chief of the provincial police. Both men were acquitted despite sufficient evidence that their actions had contributed to the development of the pogrom on 4 July 1946.[49]

The shifting of responsibility for anti-Jewish violence onto the Jewish ethnic minority was not only limited to the perpetrators and supporters of physical violence; it was also to be found among political groups and social institutions that in principle condemned the use of physical violence. The most salient example of this phenomenon is the Polish Catholic Church. In both the inter-war and early post-war periods the Church took the same stance, on the one hand condemning physical violence but on the other hand blaming Jews themselves for anti-Jewish incidents, thereby reinforcing the myth of the Jew as the Threatening Other. The only significant difference is that in the inter-war period the Church accused Jews of a variety of crimes against the Polish nation: of spreading atheism and communism, of permissiveness, and of destroying the economy and the morals of the Polish population. In the early post-war years the Church concentrated on Judaeo-communism and on Jewish responsibility for imposing the communist regime upon the Polish nation.[50]

The pattern of the Church's responses to anti-Jewish violence in the early post-war years resembles clearly that of the inter-war period: once again Jews were accused of being enemies of the Polish people and the Catholic religion, and once again similarly ambivalent condemnations of anti-Jewish violence were expressed by the clergy. The extent to which the Church's evaluation of the Jewish community remained intact can be seen in three cases.

[47] See also Rothenberg, 'The Przytyk Pogrom', 39–43.
[48] See Blus-Węgrowska, 'Atmosfera pogromowa', 88.
[49] See Bożena Szaynok, *Pogrom Żydów w Kielcach 4 lipca 1946*, 90–3.
[50] The problem of the justification of anti-Jewish violence as national self-defence in the Catholic press between the wars is discussed by Modras, *The Catholic Church and Antisemitism in Poland, 1933–1939*, 308–18.

In the first example a delegation of rabbis from the Union of Rabbis of the Polish Republic (Związek Rabinów Rzeczypospolitej) visited Cardinal Aleksander Kakowski on 7 June 1934 and asked him to influence the youth of Endecja not to orchestrate anti-Jewish disturbances. His response was full of contradictions. On the one hand he entirely condemned anti-Jewish riots; on the other hand he spoke about Jewish provocation and charged the Jewish community with the crimes of insulting Christian feelings, spreading atheism, and supporting communism.[51] Secondly, after the Przytyk pogrom of March 1936 Cardinal August Hlond and Bishop Sapieha of Kraków issued pastoral letters. These letters contained, along with a general statement condemning physical violence, approval of an economic boycott of the Jewish ethnic minority and a list of accusations of atheism, Bolshevism, corruption, and dissemination of pornography. Those parts of the letters dedicated to the condemnation of violence were short and written in vague terms, whereas the rest—concentrating on criticism of Jews—were direct and explicit. The letters were received in the Polish Jewish press as statements that could only contribute to an increase in inter-ethnic hostility.

The response of the Catholic Press Agency (Katolicka Agencja Prasowa) to the Przytyk pogrom raised even more controversy. As in the case of the pastoral letters, the statement contained a message condemning the physical attacks against Jews but at the same time demanded the cultural separation of the Polish majority from the Jewish minority and the social and economic emancipation of the ethnic Polish population.[52]

In the third example, after the Kielce pogrom of July 1946 the response of Bishop Stefan Wyszyński of the diocese of Lublin to the Jewish delegation of the Lublin district was very similar to that of Cardinal Kakowski. Kakowski's charges of atheism and religious offence become, in Wyszyński's statement, charges of Judaeo-communism and of minimal positive contribution to Poland. The report of two members of the 1946 Jewish delegation, M. Szyldkraut and S. Słuszny, states:

The delegation presented its analysis of the political situation in the country contributing to the anti-Jewish excesses. Bishop Wyszyński disagreed with this analysis; he stated that the reasons behind anti-Jewish excesses were far more complex and were based in the population's anger against Jews, who take a very active role in the present political system. The Germans murdered the Jewish nation because the Jews were the propagators of communism. . . . The bishop stressed that the Nazi [concentration] camps had their roots in the Soviet [labour] camps, which were the first school of barbarism for the Germans.

[51] Report on anti-Jewish excesses, *Sprawy Narodowościowe*, 1–2 (1936), 107–8.
[52] Reports from that visit were published by the Union of Rabbis of the Polish Republic and the Catholic Press Agency (see *Sprawy Narodowościowe*, 2–3 (1934), 285–6, 4 (1934), 474–5). The Jewish community was shocked by the cardinal's statement, while at the same time the Zionists condemned the delegation of rabbis for taking inappropriate action.

According to the bishop, the contribution of the Jewish community to Polish life was minimal . . .[53] The bishop condemned all kinds of murder from the point of Christian ethics and, regarding the Kielce incident, had nothing to add or particularly condemn as the Church [the bishop claimed] had always condemned evil . . . . In Poland [the bishop asserted] not only Jews are murdered but also Poles. Many Poles are in [communist] gaols and camps.[54]

In the aftermath of the Kielce pogrom a similar statement was issued by Cardinal Hlond to foreign journalists on 11 July. Hlond's position caused great controversy among the foreign media, which were shocked by the primate's view that anti-Jewish violence was a reaction of the frustrated Polish population against the rule of communist Jews. Hlond had said that

> The course of the highly regrettable events in Kielce shows that they did not occur for racial reasons but, rather, they developed on a totally different, painful and tragic basis . . . Numerous Jews in Poland are alive today because of the help of Poles and Polish priests. The fact that this condition is deteriorating is to a great degree due to Jews who occupy the leading positions in Poland's government and endeavour to introduce a governmental structure that a majority of their people do not desire . . .[55]

The most detailed statement of national self-defence in the context of the Kielce pogrom was found in Kielce Cathedral on 12 January 1952.[56] The document, signed by the Revd R. Zelek, calls the Kielce pogrom a 'guilt-free event', while the rightness of national self-defence is expressed throughout the document, which, like Hlond's statement, denies any racial basis for the attacks:

> General opinion in Polish society is that the Jews have taken over the state. In comparison to the number of Jews in the government, only a tiny number of Polish Jews are in opposition to the new regime. It is widely known that Jews occupying the highest positions have acquired Polish names and usurped Polish origins. Most of them come from the Soviet Union. Jews are favoured in management positions and with all sorts of aid. This situation has brought about a general anger within society and an increase in feelings of injustice.

---

[53] Bishop Wyszyński's position on anti-Jewish violence between 1945 and 1947 was raised by Michał Borwicz, 'Polish–Jewish Relations, 1944–1947', in Chimen Abramsky, Maciej Jachimczyk, and Antony Polonsky (eds.), *The Jews in Poland* (Oxford, 1987), 195. Importantly, in 1968 Wyszyński as the primate of Poland protested against the anti-Jewish campaign organized by the nationalist communists. This was part of his general condemnation of the communist regime. His earlier perception of anti-Jewish violence between 1945 and 1947 was entirely influenced by the myth of Judaeo-communism and Judaeo-sovietism.

[54] Żydowski Instytut Historyczny, Warsaw, Legal Department file 248, Sprawozdanie z audiencji u J. Eksc. ks. biskupa Wyszyńskiego delegacji wojewodzkiego Komitetu Żydów Polskich w Lublinie, 1.

[55] Quoted in W. H. Lawrence, 'Cardinal Puts Blame on Some Jews for Pogrom; 9 Poles to be Hanged', *New York Times*, 12 July 1946. See also 'Cardinal Hlond', *Manchester Guardian*, 17 July 1946.

[56] Four documents were found in Kielce Cathedral on 12 Jan. 1952. They are all in a private archive. (There is no confirmation that they are genuine, but, according to Krystyna Kersten, there is no reason to believe that they have been falsified.)

Both the workers and the intelligentsia in general say that we are under a Jewish–Bolshevik occupation and that the communist Jews are acting on behalf of the Russians. . . . Our impression of the incident [the Kielce pogrom] is that the Jews have become a symbol of the present political oppression, and of the hated government. The crowd was often heard to shout, 'Get rid of the Jewish government!' during the incident.

The actions of the Kielce population during the incident of 4 July was an unusual reaction of an oppressed nation against the new regime dominated by Jews. . . . The entire incident was not directed against Jews as a different religious or ethnic group but against Jews who rule over the country. This is the opinion of the whole of society after the Kielce incident.[57]

The most salient element of the concept of national self-defence was alleged Jewish provocation, which was used as a straight explanation for Polish counter-attack and was generally defined in the broadest sense, to suit each particular situation. It appears that any social and political actions on the part of the Jewish ethnic minority could be classified as provocation against the Polish nation. In inter-war Poland this included alleged support for foreign powers, particularly the Soviets, the Ukrainians, and the Germans; participation in communist and socialist parties; parliamentary speeches by Jewish MPs criticizing the actions of the National Party; reaction of the Polish Jewish press to anti-Jewish propaganda; and individual criminal acts committed by individual Jews. In the early post-war years provocation was defined as Jewish participation in the communist party and state apparatus, Jews taking managerial positions at work, and their receiving welfare from Jewish organizations.

To understand how anti-Jewish violence could have been justified on the ground of national self-defence, one has to look into the ethno-nationalist use of a prominent theme in Polish national mythology, the myth of victimhood and unjust treatment by the Other. For obvious historical reasons, the theme of Polish victimhood has become prominent in Polish national mythology since at least the partitions of the Polish commonwealth in the second half of the eighteenth century. The main message here is that the Poles are always the victims, whereas Others are the oppressors of the Polish nation. The ethno-nationalist version of national history intertwines the myth of Polish victimhood with the myth of the Jew as the Threatening Other. In this version the Jew constitutes the most dangerous and sinister oppressor of the Polish nation, whereas the Pole is the long-suffering victim. This interpretation stresses that Poles have been consistently marginalized and thwarted by Jews, that Poles have been relegated to the position of a minority in their own country, and that they have to fight back in order to regain their rightful position. Furthermore, it stresses that, in all their actions, Jews have been particularly ungrateful to their Polish hosts, who allowed Jews to settle in Polish territory at times when other states in Europe had expelled them.

[57] Revd R. Zelek, 'Uwagi i ostrzeżenia na temat zajść kieleckich z dnia 4 lipca' ('Comments on the Kielce Incident of 4 July 1946'), introd. and conclusion. I would like to express my gratitude to Bożena Szaynok of the University of Wrocław for giving me a copy of this document.

The myth of the Jew as the oppressor and the Pole as the victim was one of the most powerful elements of ethno-nationalist propaganda and was conducive to anti-Jewish violence in both inter-war and early post-war Poland. According to the myth, Jews were never to be seen as victims of the Poles. The extent to which this myth defined perceptions of reality in the latter period can be illustrated by an article describing the alleged murder of 160 Poles as revenge for the Kielce pogrom, published in *Honor i Ojczyzna* ('Honour and Homeland') in October 1946, three months after the pogrom.

> Public opinion all over the country is shocked by the news of a terrible crime committed by the Jews . . . on Poles. We are stressing that this savage murder committed by Jews has racist overtones. The victims of this murder were defenceless members of the Home Army (AK). Among the victims was Kazimierz Markwart, one of the most talented painters of the young generation, whose father was killed by the Gestapo. The Jews received permission from [the Ministry of] Public Security to execute one hundred Poles as 'compensation' for the Kielce pogrom . . .[58]

VIOLENCE AND NATIONAL MARTYRDOM

In both periods under discussion some Polish individuals who died as a result of active participation in anti-Jewish riots were identified by a section of society as national heroes and martyrs. The most obvious examples are the cases of Stanisław Wacławski and of the nine people who were sentenced to death in the first trial after the Kielce pogrom.

Stanisław Wacławski, a student of the law faculty at the University of Stefan Batory in Vilna, was fatally injured on the second day of the anti-Jewish excesses that began on the university campus on 9 November 1931.[59] His funeral, attended by approximately 2,000 students, turned into a national demonstration which had to be dispersed by the police.[60] In the propaganda of the All-Polish Youth Wacławski was instantly turned into a national martyr who had died for the cause of the dejudaization of Polish universities. News of his death travelled fast to other academic centres in L'viv, Poznań, and Lublin—where combined anti-Jewish and anti-government demonstrations took place. Violence also spread to the provincial cities and towns of the Białystok, Kielce, and Łódź districts, where agitated youths smashed windows of Jewish properties and propagated slogans such as 'Beat up

---

[58] Quoted in Krystyna Kersten, 'Pogrom kielecki: znaki zapytania', in *Polska—Polacy—Mniejszości Narodowe* (Wrocław, 1992), 185–6. According to Krystyna Kersten, this article illustrates the importance and potency of the stereotype of the Pole as the victim and of the Jew as the oppressor (Krystyna Kersten, *Między wyzwoleniem a zniewoleniem: Polska 1944–1956* (London, 1993), 40–1).

[59] On the Endeks and Polish Jewish students at universities, see Rudnicki, 'From *Numerus Clausus* to *Numerus Nullus*'.

[60] To prevent further fighting the rector closed the university and issued a statement condemning anti-Jewish violence ('Zajścia antyżydowskie', *Sprawy Narodowościowe*, 6 (1931), 647).

the Jews and save Poland'.⁶¹ In many places police arrested the most violent students as well as pupils of gymnasiums who had been drawn into the events by groups of older students. On 14 November the biggest mass in commemoration of Wacławski's death, attended by 7,000 students, was held in the church of St Anne, in Warsaw.⁶² One year later, on the first anniversary of his death, anti-Jewish violence of varying degrees occurred in the major universities. The following list illustrates examples from the universities of Warsaw and L'viv.⁶³

9 November 1932 University of Warsaw	Members of the OWP from the faculty of law throw their Jewish colleagues out of the lecture halls; twenty Jewish students are injured
10 November 1932 University of Warsaw	After the mass dedicated to Wacławski at St Anne's Church, 2,000 students gather in an academic hostel. Attempts to organize street demonstrations are prevented by the police
14–17 November 1932 University of Warsaw	Anti-Jewish atmosphere at the medical and law faculties; fights between Polish and Jewish students. Polish students from the Myśl Mocarstwowa and Akademicka Młodzież Państwowa⁶⁴ sign a petition condemning the anti-Jewish actions of students associated with the National Party
12 November 1932 University of L'viv	After the mass approximately 1,000 students form a march to the Dom Technika, where the plaque commemorating Wacławski's death was to be unveiled. The police break up the crowd and confiscate the plaque. Students continue on to other parts of the city, where they smash windows of 120 Jewish properties and beat up Jewish passers-by. Thirty-three students are arrested. Anti-Jewish demonstrations last the whole day
13 November 1932 University of L'viv	Anti-Jewish demonstration takes place throughout the day. The police arrest twenty-three Polish students. The mayor of L'viv, Drojankowski, issues a statement condemning the anti-Jewish excesses

Over the ensuing academic years those students who were radical ethnonationalists continued to portray Wacławski as a symbol of the national struggle against the Jews and as a martyr whose death should be avenged. One of the

---

[61] Ibid.   [62] Ibid. 646.
[63] Data based on 'Akademickie wystąpienia antyżydowskie', *Sprawy Narodowościowe*, 6 (1932), 698–700.
[64] The Myśl Mocarstwowa was a conservative student organization close to the Sanacja and the Akademicka Młodzież Państwowa was a Sanacja student organization. Both organizations opposed anti-Jewish violence.

ONR's leaflets refers to him as a hero and explicitly incites the public to anti-Jewish violence: 'On the anniversary of Wacławski's death, Jewish blood must flow. On that day Jewish homes and businesses, acquired by wrongs done to Poles, and even by their deaths, must burn.'[65]

The nine men sentenced to death at the first trial of the Kielce pogrom, which concluded on 11 July 1946, had been charged with battery and murder and with inciting the crowd to ethnic hatred.[66] They were all of peasant or working-class background and of low education. Among them were two low-ranking policemen.[67] Their execution took place on 12 July 1946 in the presence of an official from the supreme military attorney's office, a military priest, and two members of the Ministry of Public Security. Neither the families of the nine sentenced nor the press were informed of the execution.

Historians conclude that this first trial was conducted in a hasty and biased fashion with important material on the participation of the militia and the army suppressed, and that this was because of its political character. They seem reluctant, however, to analyse one crucial aspect: that of society's reaction to the trial and particularly towards the execution.[68] An examination of anonymous correspondence sent to members of the state government, and of special PPR reports prepared for internal circulation only, reveals that a segment of the population was against the decision made by the court on 11 July, and particularly against the executions that followed. Those who participated in the pogrom were identified in these communications as patriots fighting for the dejudaization of the Polish nation-state.

Such a position was not limited to the lower, uneducated classes, but extended even to members of the clergy.[69] An anonymous priest's letter sent in July 1946 to the prime minister, Edward Osóbka-Morawski, explicitly describes the people involved in the pogrom as patriots committed to the national cause and warns the government about the potentially hostile mood of the nation should executions

---

[65] Such images of Wacławski appeared in leaflets and brochures. The ONR leaflet is quoted in Rudnicki, 'From *Numerus Clausus* to *Numerus Nullus*', 266.

[66] Altogether twelve were sentenced at this trial. Three, including one woman, Antonina Biskupska, and the mentally handicapped Stanisław Rurarz, were given lesser sentences. See Stanisław Meducki and Zenon Wrona (eds.), *Antyżydowskie wydarzenia kieleckie 4 lipca 1946 roku: dokumenty i materiały* (Kielce, 1992), i. 192–205.

[67] Act of Sentence, 11 July 1946, CA MSW, sygn. SN-9/46, t.2; quoted in Meducki and Wrona (eds.), *Antyżydowskie wydarzenia kieleckie 4 lipca 1946 roku*, i. 192–205.

[68] The lack of proper historical investigation of this issue comes out of the assumption that the Kielce pogrom was not spontaneous but was orchestrated by 'some particular forces'. This was first pointed out by Andrzej Paczkowski, who stated that for some historians to accept the idea of a spontaneous pogrom would mean accepting the embarrassing fact that a substantial section of Polish society was intensely antisemitic (Paczkowski, 'Raporty o pogromie', 103). One exception is Józef Adelson's position on the spontaneous character of the Kielce pogrom ('W Polsce zwanej Ludową', 387–477).

[69] The American journalist of Polish Jewish origin Shmuel L. Shneiderman raised this issue in his popular book *Between Fear and Hope* (New York, 1947), 118.

take place. Here it appears that the execution is seen as a crime against the entire Polish nation.

> On behalf of the entire nation I warn you that the sentencing to death of these great Polish patriots in Kielce who acted only in self-defence and in despair after six years of fighting for their lives . . . will be the beginning of your ruin and will cause harm to the whole nation. Instead of getting rid of the Jews from Poland now when there is a good chance, you are instead murdering your own brothers. In any case, you should protect this eight-year-old hero [Henryk Błaszczyk, a child allegedly kidnapped by Jews], otherwise the Jews will try to poison him as an inconvenient witness . . .[70]

In big cities factory workers launched protest actions which in some cases turned into sit-down strikes against the sentences. In Radom railway workers went on strike, and similar events took place in Łódź in all the textile factories. A special communist report on the situation in Łódź after the Kielce pogrom stated:

> The social situation in Łódź is serious. The strikes have moved swiftly from one factory to another and the women are very aggressive . . . Women have been calling for revenge if the death sentences are to be carried out . . . Their antisemitic arguments were: 'a pregnant Jewess gets 60,000 zlotys and I get nothing! The Jews are running Poland!' The Jews of Łódź insist that there is an atmosphere of pogrom in the city. In trams people spread rumours that Jews killed a child in Bałuty [the poorest suburb of Łódź]. The Provincial Party Committee organized a meeting . . . It was decided to mobilize the whole party [PPR] to take counteraction against reactionary movement [the official communist interpretation was that reactionary forces were responsible for the pogrom] that is spreading anarchy in factories.[71]

The atmosphere was particularly tense in the Kielce district, where the communist authorities feared that a new wave of riots would take place.[72] Special reports reveal that the communist envoys had to put considerable pressure on the management of various factories in the area in order to pacify the mood of the workers:

> We had to use drastic measures in many towns [report from the seven towns of the Kielce district: Częstochowa, Kozienice, Ostrowiec, Pionki, Radom, Skarżysko-Kamienne, and Starachowice]; for instance, we had to put pressure on the management of the Pionki Explosive Factory: comrades Woźnicki and Mastalerz warned all the directors that they would be held personally responsible for maintaining a calm situation.[73]

In the light of such examples of the popular mood the regime's strategy in its method of conducting the executions becomes clearer. Aware of the level of public

---

[70] Quoted in Krystyna Kersten, *Polacy—Żydzi—Komunizm: anatomia półprawd, 1939–1968* (Warsaw, 1992), 113.
[71] Sixth Section AAN, Report by Comrades Doliński, Domagała, Krych, and Fir; quoted in Paczkowski, 'Raporty o pogromie', 111.   [72] See Adelson, 'W Polsce zwanej Ludową', 403.
[73] Sixth Section AAN, Report by the Brigade from the Visit to Kielce between 4 and 5 July 1946; quoted in Paczkowski, 'Raporty o pogromie', 115.

support and sympathy for the sentenced, the communist authorities wanted to minimize publicity around the executions for fear of an escalation in this popular support. According to Bożena Szaynok, news about the execution was posted only on the streets of Kielce and was not published even in the local press.[74] The suppression of this information resulted in a counter-reaction as rumour circulated in the town that the sentenced men had been sent to Siberia, historically an important place of Polish national martyrdom from the early nineteenth century.[75]

JEWS PORTRAYED AS A PHYSICAL THREAT TO THE POLISH NATION

In the context of the growing anti-Jewish propaganda in the 1930s the Jewish ethnic minority were now perceived not only as an economic, political, and cultural threat to the Polish nation, but also as a physical one. The radical ethno-nationalists interpreted individual murders of Poles by Jews as a sign of the strength and aggressiveness of the Jewish minority. And, as Emanuel Melzer observed, the real motives behind these killings, such as self-defence or individual criminality, were completely discounted by the ethno-nationalists and by that section of the public whom they influenced.[76]

Defining cases of individual murders of ethnic Poles as a conflict between the Polish and Jewish communities was to touch the 'raw ethnic sentiment'. It is not difficult to perceive how the notion of 'the Jew as the murderer of one of us' was to engender heated, spontaneous, and violent reactions against the Jewish minority. Arguably, the dissemination of this notion triggered the most brutal beatings and killings in the inter-war and post-war periods under discussion. Here are three examples of such cases from the 1930s.

On 26 November 1932 three Polish students were injured in a fight with Jewish artisans on the streets of L'viv.[77] One of them, Jan Grotkowski, a veterinary student, was mortally wounded. The next day members of the student self-help association Bratnia Pomoc and of the OWP urged their colleagues to avenge the death of Grotkowski with the slogan 'Blood for blood' (*Krew za krew*). The reaction to this was instant; several hundred students from the University of Jan Kazimierz took to the streets, mercilessly beating up Jewish passers-by and smashing windows in Jewish shops. Further anti-Jewish excesses continued for another four days, despite police attempts to stop them and despite condemnations by the rector of

[74] Szaynok, *Pogrom Żydów w Kielcach 4 lipca 1946*, 83.
[75] 'Mój ojciec nie zabił', *Gazeta Wyborcza*, 24 Mar. 1992. Bożena Szaynok also mentions the fact that Aleksandra Kuklińska, the wife of one of the executed, believed that her husband had been sent to Siberia by the Russians (Szaynok, *Pogrom Żydów w Kielcach 4 lipca 1946*, 83).
[76] Melzer, 'Antisemitism in the Last Years of the Second Polish Republic', 129.
[77] See the report on Grotkowski's death and on the student anti-Jewish demonstrations in *Sprawy Narodowościowe*, 6 (1932), 700–3.

L'viv University and by the Catholic archbishop of the L'viv diocese. News of Grotkowski's death spread to other universities in the state, and in Warsaw and Kraków Jewish students were beaten up and thrown out of the universities. Other anti-Jewish demonstrations took place at academic centres in Kraków, Lublin, Poznań, Warsaw, and Vilnius.

In Przytyk on 9 March 1936 an initial clash between Jewish youths and gangs of young Poles attacking them turned into a full-scale bloody riot after a Polish peasant, Stanisław Wieśniak, was killed by a Jew, Szolem Lesko.[78] The sight of Wieśniak's corpse being publicly carried by his weeping family to the doctor's house, along with the cries of 'They've killed one of us!', enraged the crowd. In its anger the mob launched a large-scale attack on the two Jewish neighbourhoods of Podgajek and Zachęta. According to a conclusive statement issued by the deputy public prosecutor, S. Dotkiewicz, the riot proceeded in the following way:

> Here groups, 20 to 30 strong, armed mainly with stanchions, ran along the street, forcing their way into houses. Dozens of Jewish apartments had windows and doors wrenched from their frames by metal bars, pegs, stones weighing twelve kilograms or more, and even shafts.... Inside the apartments and shops furniture and goods were destroyed; some were looted, although these cases were rare. Some of those wronged maintained that their money from the fair was lost during the sacking. Where the inhabitants were caught, they were beaten up with shouts of: 'Kill them; don't forgive them for what they have done to our brother!'[79]

As a result, one Jewish couple, the Minkowskis, were killed and their house completely wrecked. Their children, despite being seriously beaten, were saved, however, by their ethnic Polish neighbour.[80] The violence ceased after police reinforcements were brought to Przytyk from Radom.

In Mińsk Mazowiecki a riot lasting almost four days occurred on 1 June 1936, after a Jew named Judka Lejb Chaskielewicz shot a Pole, Jan Bujak, out of personal animosity. Only a few hours later a furious crowd smashed windows in all the Jewish shops and private houses. Fearing for their lives, 3,000 local Jews fled the town. Among the ones who stayed, forty-one were injured over the next two days and some Jewish houses were burned on the last day of the riot.[81]

In the National Party propaganda that followed, these two deaths became incorporated into a key slogan: 'The blood of Bujak and Wieśniak has divided Jews and Poles' (*Krew Bujaka i Wieśniaka dzieli Żyda od Polaka*).[82] Such slogans aimed to show that there was no possibility of peaceful coexistence between the two ethnic

---

[78] Rothenberg, 'The Przytyk Pogrom', 37.

[79] Conclusions of the investigation signed by the public prosecutor S. Dotkiewicz, ed. Adam Penkalla, 'The Przytyk Incidents of 9 March 1936 from Archival Documents', *Polin*, 5 (1990), 349.

[80] Adam Penkalla, 'Zajścia przytyckie 9 marca 1936 roku', *Kultura*, 9 (1989), 10.

[81] Żyndul, 'Zajścia antyżydowskie 1935–1937', 66.

[82] Rudnicki, *Obóz Narodowo-Radykalny*, 295.

groups and that ethnic hatred and violence were 'natural' elements of Polish–Jewish relations. Some of the most brutal anti-Jewish events of the early communist period also resulted from the dissemination of a similar slogan: 'We Poles are being murdered by the Jews'.

One key characteristic, however, did change in the post-war reality: the myth of ritual murder became the most prominent source of such accusations. Ritual murder was an old religious belief that was deeply rooted among the peasants, the lower classes, and sections of the Catholic Church, which had itself disseminated the belief in various pre-war publications, including the popular *Mały Dziennik*. Cases of ritual murder were alleged to have occurred in Poland during the first decade of the twentieth century and during the formative period of the Second Republic.[83] It appears, however, that the number of accusations of ritual murder reached its peak in the early post-war years, when it became the prime cause of anti-Jewish demonstrations and violence.[84]

How can one explain such a willingness to believe in an old medieval myth? Without doubt, the myth of ritual murder grew on psychologically well-prepared soil, the Polish community having been exposed to cruelty beyond any understanding of human values over five years of war. Moreover, the experiences of war had generated a profound sense of insecurity among many Poles, which was only reinforced by the terror, arrests, and murders perpetrated by the new communist regime in the early post-war years. Historians stress that during this time the population felt a deep fear not only for material goods but also for health and life itself, which sometimes manifested itself in the most incredible rumours circulating around the country.[85] Here are three examples collected by the officers of the Ministry of Public Security in 1947:

They say: 'We should not accept vaccination against typhoid, as it contains a poison which has a one-year delayed reaction. The Soviet state has given us this vaccination in order to poison us.' (9 July 1947, Olsztyn)[86]

Members of the Union of the Youth Fighting Movement (ZWM) have abandoned a course in 'industrial instruction' in Częstochowa. They tell stories about forced blood donations,

[83] The subject of ritual murder in Poland during the first three decades of the 20th c. has not been widely researched. There has been no adequate assessment of how successful the Catholic press was in disseminating accusations of ritual murder during that period. Furthermore, there is only fragmentary data on the number of anti-Jewish riots where ritual murder constituted one of the causes of violence. Ritual murder was the cause of anti-Jewish demonstrations in 1904 in Ostrowiec Świętokrzyski and of anti-Jewish riots that started on 21 Apr. 1919 in Strzyżów and then spread to other villages and towns of the Rzeszów district. See Piotr Wróbel, 'Przed odzyskaniem niepodległości', in Tomaszewski (ed.), *Najnowsze dzieje Żydów w Polsce*, 53, and Stankiewicz, *Konflikty społeczne na wsi polskiej, 1918–1920*, 159.

[84] According to Alina Cała, belief in ritual murder persisted among peasants even in the 1970s. Among the sixty peasants she interviewed during her fieldwork, only twelve firmly rejected the concept of ritual murder (Alina Cała, *The Image of the Jew in Polish Folk Culture* (Jerusalem, 1995)).

[85] Andrzej Paczkowski, *Pół wieku PRL* (Warsaw, 1996), 149.

[86] *Biuletyny Informacyjne Ministerstwa Bezpieczeństwa Publicznego 1947* (Warsaw, 1993), 134.

infertility injections, shortages of food, and Russian and Jewish female lecturers running the course. (23 July 1947, Kielce, Starachowice)[87]

We suspect that the Jews have stolen the atomic bomb from the USA and are transporting it in a coffin to the Soviet Union. (31 July 1947, Białystok)[88]

Given the Polish openness to superstition and to the myth of the Jew as the new ruler of the Polish nation-state, it becomes even clearer how the psychological fear of losing one's life could find its ultimate irrational expression in accusations of ritual murder. These allegations used in a national context reinforced the belief in a Jewish enemy who murdered Christian Poles and who plotted both world domination and Polish servitude. In this sense the Jews were perceived as a powerful ethnic group with an ability to destroy future generations of Poles.

The Catholic Church, the only institution that enjoyed real authority among various social sections of the population, did virtually nothing to counter these accusations. In fact, members of the senior clergy, with the exception of a few individuals such as Bishop Teodor Kubina of Częstochowa, themselves believed in ritual murder.[89] Records from the British embassy in Warsaw illustrate this situation well. One-and-a-half months after the Kielce pogrom Victor Cavendish-Bentinck, the British ambassador to Poland, recorded a discussion he held with Bienik, auxiliary bishop of Upper Silesia:

Dear Rubin
My telegram no. 1332 of today's date. [28th August 1946]
Bishop Bienik, auxiliary bishop of Upper Silesia, astonished me yesterday by stating that there was some proof that the child [Henryk Błaszczyk], whose alleged maltreatment by Jews had provoked the Kielce pogrom, had in fact been maltreated, and that the Jews had taken blood from his arm.
If a bishop is prepared to believe this, it is not surprising that the uneducated Poles do so too.
I am sending copy of this letter to the Holy See.[90]

There is also evidence that some Catholic churches preserved religious artefacts commemorating the alleged victims of ritual murder. For example, in the church of the Jesuits in Łęczyca a little coffin with a skeleton of a child allegedly killed by the Jews in 1639 was exhibited with a manuscript describing the event

---

[87] Ibid. 135. [88] Ibid. 144.

[89] In an appeal to his diocese Bishop Teodor Kubina adamantly rejected the idea of ritual murder: 'no Christian, either in Kielce, Częstochowa, or anywhere else in Poland has been harmed by the Jews for religious or ritual purposes . . . We therefore appeal to all citizens of Częstochowa not to believe criminal rumours, and to counteract any excesses against the Jewish population' (9 July 1946; appeal broadcast by Warsaw radio on *Poland for Abroad*, Archives of the Wiener Library, PC. 8 189. 22.A).

[90] Public Record Office, London, FO 371/57694, WR2335; quoted in Aryeh Josef Kochavi, 'The Catholic Church and Antisemitism in Poland following World War II as Reflected in British Diplomatic Documents', *'Gal-Ed': On the History of the Jews in Poland*, 11 (1989), 123.

and a painting depicting a group of religious Jews actually committing the murder of the child. In November 1946, during the relocation of the Jesuits from the church, the artefact and the painting disappeared.[91]

This theme of ritual murder was to emerge repeatedly during the many attempts to create panic and anti-Jewish pogroms before and after the Kielce pogrom. Rumour and so-called whispered propaganda published in the bulletins of the Ministry of Public Security show its extent and influence. Here are three examples:

Rumours have spread in the Brzeski district that in Silesia a Christian child has been allegedly killed by two Jews in a ritual murder. (31 March 1947, Kraków)[92]

Once again a nine-year old girl has disappeared. It may be that the Jews from Rzeszów have eaten her and have now run away from the town in fear. (7 July 1947, Rzeszów)[93]

Jews have murdered Christian children in Łódź. The police have already discovered some corpses during a one-day search. (20 September 1947, Kielce)[94]

On 11 August 1945 a rumour spread in Kraków that the bloody corpses of Polish children were lying in the Kupa synagogue at Miodowa Street. Instantly a crowd broke into the synagogue and started to beat up the Jewish congregation, who were praying at the Saturday morning service. The synagogue was demolished, and violence spread to other parts of the city. Among the many injured were four fatal casualties, including two women; in addition, two Jewish institutions were plundered.[95]

A similar situation occurred in Kielce during the infamous pogrom of 4 July 1946.[96] Mojżesz Cukier, an eyewitness who lived at 7 Planty Street, remembered it thus: 'At about nine o'clock, on 4 July, crowds started to surround the building. I heard voices from the crowd: "You Jews have killed fourteen of our children! Mothers and fathers unite and kill all the Jews!" '[97] The rumour that a 9-year-old boy, Henryk Błaszczyk, had escaped from Jewish captivity and that other Polish children had been killed led to the murder of forty-two Jews, ten of them women. The records of the CKŻP reported thirty more Jews murdered in several trains on

---

[91] In the Archives of Modern Documents, Warsaw, MAP, 787, k. 144–5, there are three documents relating to this case: a letter from the district representatives of the Jewish community to the CKŻP, statements by Maurycy Zielonka, and statements by the representative of the voivodeship (pub. in Blus-Węgrowska, 'Atmosfera pogromowa', 120).

[92] *Biuletyny Informacyjne Ministerstwa Bezpieczeństwa Publicznego 1947*, 30.

[93] Ibid. 135.   [94] Ibid. 183.

[95] The Kraków pogrom was the first major anti-Jewish riot of the post-war era. Very little has been written on this event, however (Tomasz Polański, 'Pogrom Żydów w Krakowie', *Echo Krakowa*, 10–12 Aug. 1990). The Stalin files also contain information about the Kraków pogrom (Siergiej Kriwienko, 'Raporty z Polski', *Karta*, 15 (1995), 30–2).

[96] According to Józef Adelson, the Kraków and Kielce pogroms were both spontaneous eruptions of anti-Jewish violence (Adelson, 'W Polsce zwanej Ludową', 403).

[97] Quoted in Meducki and Wrona (eds.), *Antyżydowskie wydarzenia kieleckie 4 lipca 1946 roku*, i. 113.

that day.⁹⁸ For example, in a train on the Wrocław–Lublin line, Jewish travellers were thrown out and killed in various places. A Polish eyewitness, Brunon Piątek, waiting to meet his wife at Kielce railway station, recalled that the atmosphere there reached a state of brutal hysteria:

> When the train reached the station, people were forced out; those who resisted were taken out by men standing on the platform . . . they were immediately killed . . . the crowd was extremely hysterical, shouting that Jews had killed Polish children in cellars and taken their blood for matzah . . . men in military and police uniforms took part in the murders . . . I counted about seven dead bodies lying there.⁹⁹

Among the attacked were Poles who were perceived as Jewish in appearance. Antoni Salaj, an ethnic Pole himself, witnessed such a case: 'I heard screaming in the street . . . I went outside and about twenty people were beating up a Pole . . . as they thought he was Jewish. Finally someone recognized him and they stopped the beating . . .'.¹⁰⁰ The fact that in the municipal hospital the injured Jews were in such a state of fear that they refused to be treated by the local Polish doctors also indicates the intensity of the event.¹⁰¹

The slogan 'The Jews are killing Polish children' stirred up an atmosphere of panic, with the most aggressive reactions being among women, who were often the chief disseminators of accusations of ritual murder. This has been confirmed in various recollections and in documents of the Polish Workers' Party. For example, Julia Pirotte recalls that in a conversation she had in Kielce on 5 July 1946 with the party second secretary, he stated: 'There was a rumour yesterday morning that the Jews had killed a Polish child to use his blood for matzah. The story was immediately spread by agitators, mostly women [who] were calling for revenge. Two women ran around the town shouting, "Listen to this, the Jews have been murdering Polish children!" A crowd gathered almost at once and went towards No. 7/9 Planty Street . . .'.¹⁰²

Referring to the public mood in Kalisz after the Kielce pogrom, an official report also stated: 'The rumour grew. People were talking about four, eight, and twenty-four boys being killed. One woman, who was not identified, said that she had seen fourteen boys' heads and that their flesh had been taken by Ukrainians or Soviets and their blood drunk by the Jews . . .'.¹⁰³

Those women who rejected the claim of ritual murder on 4 July were accused of

---

⁹⁸ Statement by Icchak Cukierman from the minutes of the CKŻP, 10 July 1946; quoted in Marian Turski, 'Pogrom kielecki w protokołach Centralnego Komitetu Żydów Polskich', in *Almanach Żydówski*, 1996–1997, 57.

⁹⁹ Żydowski: Instytut Historyczny, Warsaw, A051/14–10/84, Brunon Piątek, Pogrom.

¹⁰⁰ Quoted in Meducki and Wrona (eds.), *Antyżydowskie wydarzenia kieleckie 4 lipca 1946 roku*, i. 117.

¹⁰¹ Szaynok, *Pogrom Żydów w Kielcach 4 lipca*, 69–70. See also Julia Pirotte, 'Kielce 1946', *Polityka*, 25 (1991), 10.   ¹⁰² Pirotte, 'Kielce 1946', 10.

¹⁰³ Paczkowski, 'Raporty o pogromie', 107.

'not being good mothers' by their female peers. Antonina Biskupska, a suspect in the Kielce pogrom, said in her interview, 'Muchowa told me to go home, because I was very upset. She didn't want any trouble. I paid no attention to her and some women who joined us told Muchowa that she wasn't a good mother if that was her attitude . . . Then Muchowa left and we reached the building [7 Planty Street].'[104]

Women often took the lead in incitement to the most brutal actions. Andrzej Drożdżeński, a Polish eyewitness to the Kielce pogrom, recalls: 'The atmosphere in the square was dramatically different. There were already several people armed with sticks, bars and stones. Among them a group of furious and unrestrained women was the worst. When the next victim taken out of the building was a Jewess, I saw that the [male] perpetrators hesitated for a moment . . . but the women shouted cruelly, "Beat up the Jewess!"'[105]

This willingness to act violently in reaction to allegations that Polish children were being killed in ritual murder was highly evident for at least three years among the urban population. Recent research reveals that even in 1949, in cities such as Częstochowa and Kraków, there were attempts to incite anti-Jewish violence by spreading rumours that Polish children had already been killed or were being targeted by Jews. Two examples of this are: in April a female worker from the cotton factory Częstochowianka spread a rumour that bodies of children with slashed veins were lying in the ruins of the Jewish suburb of Częstochowa. This resulted in several attempts at anti-Jewish excesses in the city. They were prevented, however, by the local authorities. On 8 September in Kraków a crowd numbering 150 attacked a couple with a child. The participants in this incident were convinced that this was a Polish child that had to be saved from the Jews.[106]

In the 1950s, although society had recovered from the insecurities of the late 1940s, the Jewish minority continued to be perceived as a menace to the Polish nation. This was particularly apparent in 1956, when violent anti-Jewish attacks, mainly in the form of verbal and physical harassment, were on the increase and when any personal animosities between members of the Jewish and Polish communities were interpreted as ethno-national conflict.[107] For example, in Łódź the

---

[104] Interview with Antonina Biskupska from the Central Record Office, Ministry of Interior Affairs; quoted in Meducki and Wrona (eds.), *Antyżydowskie wydarzenia kieleckie 4 lipca 1946 roku*, i. 129–31.

[105] Andrzej Drożdżeński, 'Widziałem', *Polityka*. 14 (1990). An expanded version of this article appeared in Tadeusz Wiącek (ed.), *Zabić Żyda! Kulisy i tajemnice pogromu kieleckiego, 1946* (Kraków, 1992). The observation that women were often the prime movers in the incitement to brutal action appears in many other statements.

[106] Dariusz Jarosz, 'Problem antysemitizmu w Polsce w latach 1949–1956 w świetle akt niektórych centralnych instytucji państwowych i partyjnych', *BŻIH* 2 (1997), 49–52. Jarosz records cases of attempts to incite anti-Jewish violence by spreading accusations of ritual murder.

[107] For a description of cases of anti-Jewish disturbances in 1956, see Paweł Machcewicz, *Polski rok 1956* (Warsaw, 1993), 216–31, and Jarosz, 'Problem antysemitizmu w Polsce w latach 1949–1956 w świetle akt niektórych centralnych instytucji państwowych i partyjnych', 50.

mother of a child who had fought with his Jewish peer made an outcry on the street that 'Jewish children beat up Polish kids and no one takes any action.'[108]

CONCLUSION

My aim in this article has been to demonstrate that the ethno-nationalist perception of the Jew as Threatening Other played an important part in the outbreaks of anti-Jewish violence between 1918–39 and 1945–7. I have focused on those aspects of anti-Jewish violence that reveal the ways in which the myth was used to instigate, evaluate, and justify anti-Jewish attacks—despite major differences in historical, social, and political conditions between the two periods. Overall, I have shown that the myth of the Jew as Threatening Other constituted a salient factor in mandating and justifying all forms of anti-Jewish violence. Moreover, the myth provided a ground for the participants in anti-Jewish riots to be seen as national heroes and for shifting the guilt and responsibility for the violence onto the victim.

Of course, this is not to say there was no major variation in the nature of anti-Jewish violence between 1918–39 and 1945–7. In fact, the early post-war years were characterized by a much higher level of brutality than the inter-war period. This high level of brutality was brought about by three major factors: familiarity with Nazi treatment of the Jews, widespread anticipation that most of the Polish Jews had been killed by the Germans, and the pre-war Polish ethno-nationalist evaluation of the Jews as the enemy of the Polish nation. However, in general, in both periods examined, the myth constituted the driving force behind anti-Jewish violence.

[108] Archives of Modern Documents, Warsaw, VI, 237/VII-3835; quoted in Machcewicz, *Polski rok 1956*, 219.

Jewish Reaction to the Soviet Arrival in the Kresy in September 1939

ANDRZEJ ŻBIKOWSKI

SEVERAL studies have already been written on why the Jews welcomed the Soviet armies entering the Kresy (Polish eastern borderlands) in September 1939, and I take as my starting-point an original essay by Jan T. Gross, 'I thank them for such a liberation, and I ask that this is the last time that I have to experience it'.[1] In this article Gross deals with most of the traps besetting those who have written on the topic over nearly six decades. He disarms his potential opponents, who differ from him on the course and significance of the events of those years, by acknowledging that their most important assertion is correct: the Jews did greet the Russians with joy, and this reception was important for the future course of the Soviet occupation and especially for relations between the different ethnic groups living in the territory. Gross notes that opinion-forming circles in Polish society had good reason to see this reaction as important to all the inhabitants of the region. In addition, later Polish historians had some justification for stressing its impact on relations between the Jewish community and its neighbours during the Nazi occupation, and, most significantly, on the limited help extended to the Jews during the mass murder carried out by the Nazis.

Gross labels this commonly accepted opinion a stereotype, thus greatly diminishing its value in explaining the processes that were taking place. In this interpretation the key to understanding the Jewish response is the context in which the Russians were warmly welcomed: it is necessary to re-establish this context by reconstructing the state of mind of the protagonists in those events.[2] For them the implications of the events of September 1939 were opaque, since the intentions of the Soviets, who pretended to be allies coming to rescue their Slav brothers and to liberate the oppressed Jewish population from the yoke of antisemitic Poland,

---

[1] Jan Tomasz Gross, 'Ja za takie wyzwolenie dziękuję i proszę ich żeby to był ostatni raz', in *Upiorna dekada: trzy eseje o stereotypach na temat Żydów, Polaków, Niemców i komunistów 1939–1948* (Kraków, 1988), 61–92.

[2] Many of the elements of Gross's argument can be found elsewhere, as Gross admits. See e.g. Ben-Zion Pinchuk, *Shtetl Jews under Soviet Rule: Eastern Poland on the Eve of the Holocaust* (Oxford, 1990) and the essay by Dov Levin, 'The Response of the Jews of Eastern Poland to the Invasion of the Red Army in September 1939 (As Described by Jewish Witnesses)', in *Gal-Ed: On the History of the Jews in Poland*, 11 (1989), 87–102.

were unknown. The illusions of the Jews were shared by Ukrainians dreaming of a free Ukraine, by a section of the Polish army who were counting on help in the war against the Germans, as well as by the socialist youth, who were awaiting deliverance for the workers and peasants.

The Russians were welcomed mainly in small and medium-sized towns, and it is understandable that the composition of the welcoming crowds echoed the structure of a typical *shtetl* and differed fundamentally from the ethnic make-up of the region as a whole, which was overwhelmingly agricultural. In the small borderland towns Jews were extremely numerous, including fugitives (*bieżeńcy*) from central Poland.[3] In addition, the Jewish poor, who constituted the majority of the population in some *shtetl*s, must have been very visible, as were young people, who could not find jobs in the late 1930s and who were, accordingly, highly dissatisfied with their circumstances under Polish rule. Unfortunately, there are no statistics to show to what extent this is an accurate picture of the social structure of small towns in eastern Poland.

Gross stresses a number of factors which led the Jews to welcome the Soviet troops. Perhaps the most important phenomenon he brings to light is the fact that a wave of peasant revolts swept over the Kresy in September 1939, the principal victims of which were the landowners and the Jews, as in the revolts of Khmelnytsky and Gonta. It may be worth recalling the often expressed adage that a vacuum in state authority creates danger for any minority surrounded by hostile neighbours—a view which has been confirmed by the long history of the Jewish diaspora in Europe. Certainly, for the Jews, any kind of authority was better than anarchy. Furthermore, to all Jews it was obvious that the Soviets prevented the Germans from entering the area. The German attitude towards the Jews was widely known, and refugees arriving in the east gave graphic accounts of how the Jews were treated in central Poland. Finally, and importantly, under the new regime antisemitism was prohibited. As one memoirist noted, 'For the first time a Jew was not a second-class citizen.'

This analysis of the principal factors, as set out by Gross, seems to me to be largely correct. The average Polish Jew had no reason to be greatly enamoured of the Polish authorities after twenty years under their rule. Poland had proved to be a capricious and often harsh stepmother, and Jews had good reasons to put their personal and group interests above the abstract idea of Polish patriotism, which Endek and then Sanacja governments had done little to encourage. The question is, how much loyalty towards their former compatriots could have been expected from the Jews of the Kresy? Clearly the Poles demanded the maximum, while

---

[3] On the high number of Jews among the fugitives even before the May 1940 exchange with the Germans, see, among others, Małgorzata Giżejewska, 'Deportacje obywateli polskich z ziem północno-wschodnich II Rzeczypospolitej w latach 1939–1941', in T. Strzembosz (ed.), *Studia z dziejów okupacji sowieckiej, 1939–1941* (Warsaw, 1997). At the beginning of 1940 in Belarus out of 73,000 fugitives, 65,000 were Jews.

many Jews felt none. Under these conditions, perhaps the most that could have been expected of them was that they should observe commonly accepted rules of behaviour: not to inform on people because of their views; not to use underhand methods to take someone's job; not to take advantage of other people's hardships. There are always some who disregard general human standards, but Gross shows rather convincingly that only a few Jews crossed that limit, while the majority, contrary to the claims of their Polish accusers, remained attached to Poland. There is strong evidence for this: a large number of the fugitives soon became so disillusioned with the Soviet paradise that they tried to return to the German zone; they also rejected Soviet passports, for which they were punished by their new rulers by deportation to Siberia in June 1940.[4] In addition, few Jews rose to the upper echelons of power in the reorganized areas of what was now western Ukraine and western Belarus (although this was not their choice). As a group, they had their share of suffering under the new order, since most of them owned property, while their new rulers believed that everything should be common. While these arguments serve to absolve Jews of the accusation of disloyalty, however, they have no bearing on the issue of how many Jews welcomed the Soviets and for what reasons.

Since there are no statistical data to answer these questions, let us examine how the events were recorded in Jewish and Polish group memories. Most historians who have addressed the problem have allowed their conclusions to be coloured by their selection and evaluation of sources. It is important not only whether someone describing an event witnessed it personally, but also when, under what circumstances, and even why he or she recorded it. Also relevant are the world-view, education, and war experiences of the observer. We need to avoid the falsifiers of history, both conscious and unconscious, and the last half of the century brought forth enough of them on both the Polish and Jewish side. The simplest solution would be to exclude all reports and memoirs written after the fact, but this would not leave many sources. It is possible, however, to put aside sources written after the war. These constitute the majority of memoirs and accounts as well as the hundreds of *Yizkorbikher*, the books published in Israel and in North and South America for the purpose of honouring and remembering the dead. Of course, there will be falsifiers among those who recorded their war impressions at the time, but their number is likely to be smaller, and, in addition, the texts themselves reveal their authors' intentions. In the end we have to trust someone, though whom one should trust is always an arbitrary decision.

Recently many historians have treated as decisive the reports of the German Einsatzgruppen and the statistics of the NKVD, believing that only the perpetra-

---

[4] For data on the deportation of June 1940, verified by the NKVD archives, see A. E. Gurianov, 'Polskie spetspresedlentsy v SSSR v 1940–1941 gg', in *Repressii protiv poliakov i polskikh grazhdan*, Istoricheskie sborniki 'Memoriala', i (Moscow, 1997). From the formerly Polish areas 78,000–79,000 people were deported, of whom 82–4 per cent were Jews.

tors, when relating their crimes to their superiors, had no reason to falsify the events.[5] These are certainly excellent sources for establishing the scope and the chronology of the crimes, but they do not reveal much, from the psychological or the sociological point of view, about either the perpetrators or their victims.

We approach historical events best through the memory of those who witnessed them. The fresher these memories are, and the less blurred they are by many years of pondering over the war tragedy, the greater the chance that they will grasp the most important elements of a particular situation. There is a difference between a diary written for oneself or for posterity, and a report delivered to an organization. In order to assess an account in a memoir, the credibility of its author, and the extent to which his personal experiences may have influenced his account, must be checked.[6] With a report the problem is even more difficult, as it usually reflects the views of some group. It is not always known how large this group is and what ideology it professes, and a report is often written with its recipient in mind, so as to reinforce his preconceptions. All these problems will be encountered in analysing materials containing information on the attitudes of the population towards the entering Soviet army. Not all of them can be resolved. The majority of reports mentioning the warm reception of Soviet soldiers by the Kresy Jews comes from unnamed cells of the pro-London Polish underground. What they have in common is that they were written for the central bodies of this underground and that their authors were probably all Poles.[7] On the other hand, the rare reports written for Jewish organizations come from the pens of Zionist activists, which surely influenced their content and also their style. The reports of the German apparatus of coercion and the Soviet press releases are ideologically coloured in a

---

[5] I refer here particularly to a book by Russian historians affiliated with the Memorial Association, L. P. Eremina (ed.), *Zvenia* (Moscow, 1997), 256, and a whole array of studies by a younger generation of German historians, notably Dietrich Pohl and Christian Gerlach, for example their essays in Peter Klein (ed.), *Die Einsatzgruppen in der besetzen Sowjetunion 1941–42. Die Taetigheits- und Lageberichte des Chefs der Sicherheitspolizei und des SD* (Berlin, 1997). In his book *Nationalsozialistische Judenverfolgung in Ostgalizien 1941–1944. Organisation und Durchfuehrung eines staatlichen Massenverbechens* (Munich, 1997) Pohl of course uses sources of many kinds, but he gives the clear impression that he places only limited trust in memoirs.

[6] There are very few memoirs written by Jews hiding in the Kresy. Of particular value are the extensive notes by a Jewish physician from Tluste and later Pidhaitsi, Baruch Milch, written in hiding on the 'Aryan side'. See Milch's memoir in Baruch Milch, *Wspomnienie*, ed. Andrzej Żbikowski (Warsaw, 1998).

[7] Many of these 'Reports from Poland' and 'Depictions of the Situation in Poland' come from the documents of the Polish government in exile or the Office of the Government Delegation in Poland (Delegatura) stored in archives in Stanford, California, in London, and in Warsaw; fragments of them circulate in scholarly literature. However, neither Dariusz Stola (*Nadzieje i Zagłada. Ignacy Schwartzbart: żydowski przedstawiciel w Radzie Narodowej RP, 1940–1945* (Warsaw, 1995)) nor David Engel (*In the Shadow of Auschwitz: The Polish Government-in-Exile and the Jews, 1939–1942* (Chapel Hill, NC, 1987)), nor Krystyna Kersten (*Polacy—Żydzi—Komunizm: Anatomia półprawd* (Warsaw, 1992)), nor Marcin Kula ('Między żydowską palestyną a polskim Londynem', *Więź*, 347 (1987), 100–18) enquired into who wrote the reports from which they quote.

different way, but still very strongly. There are very few recorded observations by Western diplomats, who display the least bias.[8]

In this short chapter I will not be able to exhaust even the fairly limited subject of the welcome accorded to the Red Army by the Jewish population, so I will focus only on a few aspects which I regard as central, relating mostly to the context in which the phenomenon was recorded. First, let me quote extracts from a few sources almost contemporary with the events.

Gershon Adiv, an eyewitness to the Soviet entry into his home town, Vilna, recorded in his diary for 18–19 September:

It is difficult to describe the feeling that agitated me when in the street I saw, opposite our gate, a Russian tank carrying smiling young men with red shining from their caps. A crowd gathered around where the tanks were standing, someone shouted: 'Long live the government of the Soviets', and everyone cheered in their honour . . . It was difficult to make out non-Jews in the crowd. Mostly it was the Jews who showed enthusiasm. This aroused the anger of the Poles somewhat . . . The Jews' happiness was complete: the Russians are better than the Germans. Even those to whom the Soviet messiah brought no blessing at all thought this way . . . At least they will not suffer because they are Jews. The worst thing that will happen is that they will be sent to work.[9]

The observations of Moshe Kleinbaum, who managed to reach Palestine in 1940, are very similar: 'The residents of Stryi received the Soviet army with mixed feelings. The Poles regarded the Soviets with hatred; the Ukrainians were reserved and the Jews looked upon the new regime as the lesser of two evils.'[10]

The chronicle of kibbutz Baminharah, which belonged to the organization Hashomer Hatsa'ir, recorded on 18 September 1939:

We were all ready to leave when we were overtaken by the news that the Red Army was about to enter Rovne. Immediately, we changed our plans and remained in the city. It is difficult to describe what effect this news had on the populace. The feeling that they had been saved from Nazi barbarism swelled in everyone's breast and caused people to dance in the streets. With a feeling of gratitude, they lined the streets to greet the Red Army marching in. The welcome extended by the civil population was rather exciting. People actually kissed the soldiers and cheered them as they were passing by.[11]

The next account comes from the underground Archive of the Warsaw Ghetto; its author is an unknown young Zionist who, after arriving in Warsaw in February

---

[8] Among the documents of the Reichskommissariat für den Ukraine und Einsatzstab Rosenber (microfilms in the US Holocaust Memorial Museum, Washington, Kiev Archive, RG 31.002/1333) I found a few reports of commanders of the Einsatzgruppen der Sicherheitspolizei und des SD to their Berlin headquarters from Sept. 1939 about the participation of Jews in popular militia units in the areas taken by the Red Army.

[9] Quoted in Dov Levin, 'The Response of the Jews of Eastern Poland', 95. Unfortunately, it is not entirely clear how accurate Adiv's quote there is, and whether the author 'edited' his occupation diary after going to Palestine in the mid-1940s.   [10] Ibid. 101.

[11] *Youth Amidst the Ruin: A Chronicle of Jewish Youth in the War* (New York, 1941), 33–4.

1942, described his war experiences in south-eastern part of the Polish Kresy occupied by the Soviet army:

I arrived in Lutsk on 18 September 1939 in the afternoon. At 4 p.m. the Red Army entered. The streets were crowded. The Polish police who was still there tried to maintain order, but without success . . . A workers' militia was created at once that included the citizens of all nationalities. It needs to be emphasized that this was not exclusively workers' militia, as the representatives of different strata joined it, including politically hated elements . . .

[Question from the Oneg Shabbos member interviewing the eyewitness:] How did the Jewish population receive the Red Army?

The simple Jew received it coldly, some even with hatred. The majority of the youth expressed great enthusiasm. They kissed the soldiers, climbed the tanks, they gave an ovation. Even earlier, before the Red Army had entered the town, a part of Jewish youth organized meetings and demonstrations. For us Jews it was politically very unwise that a part of the Jewish community had a very bad attitude towards Polish society and the Polish army.[12]

Another report from the Ringelblum Archive records:

Between Yom Kippur and Sukkot of the year . . . the Germans left the town [of Zamość]. We learned about the Russians entering. The Jews were very afraid of pogroms and assaults by Poles during the entry of the Russians. They kept their shops closed, the doors barred. All the men gathered in the gateways armed with crowbars, axes, and other bits of iron to defend themselves against assault by Poles, but there was no assault.

After three days Russian tanks with many soldiers on them entered the town. Jews rejoiced and came to the market square. The army went on, and a 'city council' was established consisting of formerly arrested communists of whom the majority were Jews. The local Jewish communist Holcman was placed at the head of it. Shortly, a militia was formed that consisted of dubious individuals, both Polish and Jewish. The goods stored in the municipal warehouse were divided among the Polish and Jewish poor. Each night there were meetings at the market place. Holcman and others delivered communist speeches in Polish, Russian, and Yiddish.

After several days we learned that the Russians were to leave the town, and the Germans were coming back. A great panic and fear seized the Jewish population. Holcman called a meeting at the market square and categorically denied the rumours, but the next day we learned that he sent his mother, wife, and child away on a peasant's wagon.

The next day the retreat of the Soviet army through our town began. Because of the fear of the Germans, many Jews followed the Russians. The soldiers readily took Jews to their cars . . .[13]

---

[12] Żydowski Instytut Historyczny, Warsaw, Underground Archive of the Warsaw Ghetto (Ringelblum Archive), pt. I, no. 1042. All records of the Jewish fugitives who at the turn of the year 1941–2 clandestinely returned to Warsaw, some of which are quoted in this chapter, will be published in the complete edition of material from the Ringelblum Archive: Andrzej Żbikowski (ed.), *Relacje z Kresów Wschodnich, 1939–1941* ('Reports from the Eastern Kresy, 1939–1941'), ii.

[13] Żydowski Instytut Historyczny, Warsaw, Underground Archive of the Warsaw Ghetto (Ringelblum Archive), pt. I, no. 1042; it was probably Rachela Zilberberg who at the end of 1939 arrived in Vilna from a kibbutz in Krzeszowice, near Kraków.

What is common and what is specific to these reports? In all, there is an underlying fear of the Germans and joy that the Soviets had forestalled their arrival. However, what separates the first three reports from the other two is also important. For Adiv, Kleinbaum, and the unnamed *ḥaluts* the joy of the Jews was natural and fully justified, only the first of them remarking, *en passant*, that some Poles did not appreciate their joy. For the Jewish fugitives, perhaps accustomed to a different ethnic balance in central Poland, the joyful welcome afforded the Red Army was just part of a larger phenomenon, namely the deterioration of Polish–Jewish relations in the Kresy, with the Jews, in Polish opinion, largely responsible. Memories of the euphoria of September 1939 were apparently overshadowed by the later events.

This mood is common to the reports of fugitives. Here are two from the Ringelblum Archive. In the view of one interviewee,

Relations between the different nationalities in Ukraine should be described in short as 'mutual and bitter hatred'. The Ukrainians hate the Poles and the Jews, the Poles—the Ukrainians and the Jews, and the Jews pay the Poles and the Ukrainians back in the same currency. To maintain peace and order in these circumstances without favouring or harming one group requires great diplomatic skill on the part of the Soviet authorities, who demonstrate it only to a minimal degree.

As for Jews, they took revenge on Poles sometimes in a very nasty way; the expression 'Your time is over' was not only much used, but, by and large, overused.[14]

According to another observer,

The situation of Jews in the Polish areas seized by the Soviets was quite favourable. Owing to their natural cleverness and talents, they could make their lives most agreeable.

When the Bolsheviks entered Polish territory, they were very mistrustful of the Polish population, and they fully trusted the Jews. They deported to Russia the more influential Poles and those who before the war held important jobs, and all offices were given mostly to Jews, who everywhere were trusted with positions of power. For these reasons, the Polish population at once assumed a very hostile general attitude. Hatred became even stronger than before the war. The Poles, however, could not vent it in any way, and therefore nourished and cherished it. It needs to be mentioned that the Jews themselves stirred up this hatred because as soon as the Russian armies entered, they showed their disregard for the Poles and often humiliated them. The coming of the Bolsheviks was greeted by Jews with great joy. Now they felt proud and secure, they almost considered themselves in charge of the situation; towards the Poles they were condescending and arrogant, and they often let them feel their powerlessness and scorned them because of it. In Grodno there were numerous occurrences when a Polish woman approached a Jewish vegetable-seller who refused to sell to her: 'You Pole, go away, I don't want to deal with you'. There were many Jews who at any opportunity took special pleasure in mentioning to Poles that their time was over, that now nothing depended on them, and that they had to obey the Soviet authority.

[14] Żydowski Instytut Historyczny, Warsaw, Underground Archive of the Warsaw Ghetto (Ringelblum Archive), pt. I, no. 475.

The economic situation of Jews in the occupied territory was much better than that of the Polish population. While Poles had to earn a living with hard work, Jews took better jobs and were employed in lighter work. Poles were mostly employed in factories and *kolkhozes*, whereas Jews preferred to work as clerks in warehouses and shops, etc. Even if salaries in these positions were officially much lower than those of workers in factories, while working as clerks, salespeople, or warehouse attendants they had opportunities to make use of their skills in trading and speculation; they made various deals and in this way they earned privately a substantial amount.[15]

There are many similar accounts by fugitives, though, of course, not all recalled the atmosphere under the Soviet occupation in this way. Nevertheless, for the majority it was clear that relations between the different ethnic groups substantially worsened during these two years, and the Jews were to a large extent to blame for it. It is not my goal here to determine whether this generalization is justified, since these reports came from a very uniform and narrow group without strong roots in local Jewish communities. What seems to me more important is the agreement of their authors in this respect and the similarity of their views as regards the opinion of most Poles on the collaboration of the Jewish population with the new Soviet authority. Let me quote several representative views. In his memoir of the war Jan Zalewski recorded:

In Zbarazh and in Vishniovets revolutionary committees were established. They consist mostly of young Jews. In Polish uniforms and with red armbands, armed with rifles, they guard the buildings of their committees. They also stop soldiers and force them to enter the place. There they strip-search them, most often seeking for arms, and they humiliate them with dirty words.[16]

Władysław Chudy described an incident which he experienced on 24 September 1939 in Ruzhishche (Rzhyshchiv) when he tried to obtain a pass to Kovel:

The whole thing became complicated when we were taken before the commissar himself. He was a young Jew with a red star in his lapel. He started a regular interrogation . . . that I was surely a student, I surely belonged to the ONR, had beaten Jews, etc.[17]

Descriptions of this kind can be found in innumerable Polish occupation memoirs. According to one of the general surveys about the Soviet occupation prepared by the Historical Office of the Anders Army,

In the reports, I did not encounter a single response testifying to a favourable attitude of Jews towards the Polish population; on the contrary, from the reports it comes out that from the beginning of the Soviet occupation the Jewish population had an enthusiastic attitude towards the occupying power. Jews flocked to fill all ranks of the militia, and all

[15] Ibid., no. 934.
[16] *Stała się omyłka: wspomnienia z niewoli sowieckiej wrzesień 1939–sierpień 1941* (Warsaw, 1994), 30. It seems (though one cannot be certain) that this memoir has not been 'tidied up' prior to publication.   [17] 'W sowieckim więzieniu w Brześciu nad Bugiem', in *Zeszyty Historyczne*, 61 (1982).

offices. Accounts tell about many wrongs the Polish population suffered because of the collaboration of Jews with the Soviet authorities.[18]

Equally unfavourable towards the Kresy Jews was the opinion of General Stefan 'Grot' Rowecki, commander of the Home Army, expressed in his message to London on 25 September 1941:

> When, at the end of 1939, many witnesses from different social levels returned home, outrage and hostility towards the Jews was stirred up in Polish society. People were angered, not so much by stories about the Soviet army's behaviour as by accounts of how the Jews zealously served the Bolsheviks. It became clear that the entire Jewish population in all areas, and particularly in Podlasie, Polesie, and Volynia, even before the retreat of Polish units, had displayed red flags and built triumphal arches to welcome the Bolshevik army; they spontaneously organized *revkoms* [regional committees] and a red militia. Straight after the Bolsheviks entered, they turned with all their fury against Polish offices; they subjected the officials of the Polish state, and Polish activists, to mob law; they stigmatized them *en masse* as antisemites and delivered them into the hands of the social scum adorned with red ribbons.[19]

The young emissary Jan Karski, who personally visited L'viv at the beginning of 1940, in a report submitted to Minister Kot in Angers regarding the situation of the Jewish population under the German and the Soviet occupations, wrote:

> The attitude of the Jews towards the Bolsheviks is regarded among the Polish populace as quite positive. It is generally believed that the Jews betrayed Poland and the Poles, that they are basically communists, that they crossed over to the Bolsheviks with flags unfurled.
>   In fact, in most towns the Jews greeted the Bolsheviks with baskets of red roses, with submissive addresses, etc.
>   However, one needs to introduce here certain distinctions.
>   Certainly, Jewish communists adopted an enthusiastic stance towards the Bolsheviks, regardless of the social class from which they came. The Jewish proletariat, small merchants, artisans, and all those whose position has at present been improved *structurally* and who had formerly been exposed primarily to oppression, indignities, excesses, and so on from the Polish element—they too responded positively, if not enthusiastically, to the new regime . . . On the other hand, as for the intelligentsia, and the richer and more cultured Jewish circles, I have the impression that they think about the Poles rather warmly (of course with many exceptions and allowing for outward appearances), and they would welcome with joy a change in the present situation [leading to] the independence of Poland . . . Generally, however, *en masse*, the Jews have created the situation in which the Poles regard them as devoted to the Bolsheviks, and—one can safely say—wait for the moment when they will be able simply to take revenge on the Jews. Virtually all Poles are resentful and disappointed in relation to the Jews, and the vast majority (first among them, of course, the youth) literally look forward to an opportunity of 'repayment in blood' . . . An attempt to

---

[18] 'Województwo lwowskie pod okupacją sowiecką'; quoted in Krystyna Kersten, *Polacy—Żydzi—Komunizm: Anatomia półprawd, 1939–1968*.

[19] Quoted in Kula, 'Między żydowską Palestyną a polskim Londynem'.

create any common front would encounter very large difficulties on the part of the broad layers of Polish society in which antisemitism has by no means decreased.[20]

Stanisław Kot, now the Polish ambassador in Moscow, wrote on 8 September 1941 to the foreign ministry in London:

The Poles are, in general, very bitter towards the Jews because of their behaviour during the occupation, their joyful welcome for the Red Army, cursing Polish officers and soldiers led under guard, servility to the Soviets, informing on Poles . . . These charges are laid almost exclusively on the Jews from the Eastern Lands [*Ziemie Wschodnie*], who even before the war gravitated towards Russia, especially the Jewish proletariat [*plebs żydowski*] . . . On the other hand, there are many positive accounts about the behaviour of the Jewish intelligentsia and the 'bourgeoisie'. The majority came out openly as Poles and remained connected to the whole Polish population. The Jewish masses [*drobny element*] aroused hostility also because they constantly indulged in speculation, bought up goods, and raised prices without consideration for the needs of their neighbours.[21]

Karski's evaluation deserves special attention; it seems that the Jewish intelligentsia, favourably mentioned by him, had a similar opinion of the Kresy Jews. It seems that 'the Jews . . . created the situation in which the Poles regard them as devoted to the Bolsheviks'. Karski cannot be suspected of hostility towards the Jews: his whole life testifies to his sympathy for them and there is no reason simply to pass over his judgement. Unfortunately, most historians discussing this problem do so.

Of course, it must be remembered that we are dealing with a stereotype, a generalization that is probably not entirely without some basis, since we find it in such diverse sources. It was to a large extent a continuation of the pre-war Polish phobia of 'Judaeo-communists' (Żydokomuna), that Jews were particularly susceptible to leftist ideologies. This leaning on the part of a substantial section of Jewish youth was also noticed by many Jews, especially from the Polonized intelligentsia. The testimonies also show something more important: that in September 1939 it was absolutely clear to the entire Jewish population in the Kresy that the Soviets saved the Jews from the Germans; moreover, they provided them with the opportunity to get even with their former oppressors, the Polish, Ukrainian, and Lithuanian antisemites. However, the widespread nature and the strength of Polish antisemitism is also a stereotype which is not entirely justified.

---

[20] Copy of a report in the Hoover Archive, Stanford, Calif., courtesy of Prof. Karski; pub. in Artur Eisenbach, 'Raport Jana Karskiego o sytuacji Żydów na okupowanych ziemiach polskich na początku 1940 r.', *Dzieje Najnowsze*, 2 (1989). The report was 'discovered' and introduced to scholarly circulation by David Engel, 'An Early Account of Polish Jews under Nazi and Soviet Occupation Presented to the Polish Government-in-Exile, February 1940', *Jewish Social Studies*, 45 (1983). Thanks to him we know that four of the report's pages have two versions, one originally written by Karski, and the other, more favourable to the Poles, the work of a clerk in Minister Stronski's office. Interestingly, the paragraphs about the Soviet occupation were altered. Prof. Karski acknowledged that he personally agreed to rework the text for 'propaganda purposes'. He himself marked the original: 'Caution: pages 6–9–10–11 have dual texts'.

[21] Stanisław Kot, *Listy z Rosji do Generała Sikorskiego* (London, 1956), 63.

For Polish–Jewish relations under the Soviet occupation, the crucial issue was not primarily the festive welcoming of the invader. It is clear that not all Jews welcomed the Soviets and that many non-Jews were among those who welcomed them. In addition, the reasons for the Jewish response were quite clear, at least to some Poles. The key factor was rather the collaboration of a substantial section of the Jewish community. That this collaboration was for the most part forced and rarely openly directed against the Poles was of little interest to those who formed public opinion in occupied Poland. In the unwritten code universally rejecting the occupation, and the call for at least passive resistance (which was so close to the tradition of Polish society under the partitions), there was no room for exceptions: who is not with us is against us. Given this attitude, every Jewish doctor, clerk, agronomist, or bookkeeper who accepted a job in a Soviet office took upon himself the odium of a collaborator. He placed himself in the same position as a young communist starting his career in the local party committee or in the local NKVD office. Polish opinion classed with such people those who, unable to provide for themselves legally, engaged in black-market trade. In Polish memoirs we find no words of approval for their resourcefulness, but accusations of making money out of Polish misery. We also will not find a positive word about the young people who sought to escape the *shtetl* for a school in the cities of Białystok, Vilna, or L'viv. As one might expect, in Jewish memoirs there are many favourable judgements of the Soviet authorities who put an end to the *numerus clausus*, which was universal in Polish universities before 1939.

Even if we regard the accusations directed against the Jews by Polish society as completely unjustified,[22] we have to accept that the two communities chose different strategies for surviving the Soviet occupation. The Jewish strategy was surely more rational from the beginning, relying on the need to prepare thoroughly for a long winter. It was Moshe Kleinbaum, whose testimony we have already cited, who noted: 'Typical of the facts is that straight away a saying began to circulate among the Jews who evaluated their position following the arrival of the Soviets as follows: Until now we have been sentenced to death, but now our sentence has been converted to life imprisonment.'

Translated from Polish by Gwido Zlatkes

---

[22] In one of his essays ('The Jewish Community in the Soviet-Annexed Territories on the Eve of the Holocaust', in L. Dobroszycki and J. S. Gurock (eds.), *The Holocaust in the Soviet Union: Studies and Sources on the Destruction of the Jews in the Nazi-Occupied Territories of the USSR, 1941–1945* (New York, 1993)) Gross included a surprising, and in my opinion unconvincing, suggestion: 'What about the shared memory of Jews lending a helping hand to the Soviet invader? . . . But that they were remembered so vividly and with such scorn does not tell us necessarily that Jews were massively involved in collaboration. Rather, I think, it is a reflection of how unseemly, how jarring, how offensive it was to see a Jew in a position of authority. That is why this remembrance is so deeply engraved.'

Reflections on Soviet Documents Relating to Polish Prisoners of War Taken in September 1939

SIMON SCHOCHET

THE recent opening of the Soviet archives and sudden availability of thousands of documents is a major opportunity for Western scholars. It enhances the understanding of the workings of the communist regime in the USSR and in many cases provides some enlightenment regarding the sources of political decisions made by the Soviet leaders. It clarifies the internal functioning and defines the allocation of responsibilities within the NKVD, and finally, after nearly fifty years of denials and fabrications, the USSR has accepted responsibility for the Katyn massacre. The Katyn death lists of Polish prisoners of war seized by the Soviets in September 1939 have at long last been released.

The Soviet archival documents that I have been able to study, which I obtained from Russian and Polish historical sources as well as from books and articles, show considerable statistical variations in the description of single facts and events. In order to obtain a clear view of these events it is necessary, therefore, to carry out a careful study and verify the documents so as to ascertain the reason for these contradictions. It is also helpful to keep in mind that these documents were written primarily by NKVD personnel, who, as members of the most notorious and ruthless arm of the Soviet regime, must have had their own reasons for reporting certain information designated 'top secret'. The skill with which Soviet propagandists were able to fabricate their innocence in the Katyn murder is well known, and the possibility that some documents, although archival, may contain erroneous or dubious information is very high. It seems to me that in order to establish the fate of these prisoners of war one must first determine precisely the total number of Polish prisoners taken by the Soviet forces in 1939, but the available Polish and Russian documents defy the historian's ability to do so.

Vladimir Abarinov, a correspondent for the weekly paper *Literaturnaia Gazeta*, was one of the first Russian writers to report the truth about the Soviet mass murder of 15,000 Polish officers. In his book *The Murderers of Katyn* he lists the total number of Polish prisoners of war as 226,391.[1] As he states, this figure is

[1] (New York, 1993), 25–7.

closest to the 250,000 estimated by the Polish historians Janusz Zawodny and Jerzy Łojek.[2] Natalia Lebedeva, a senior researcher at the Institute of General History in Moscow, states that, according to NKVD archives, 130,242 Polish servicemen fell into Soviet hands.[3]

I recently studied a document originating in the Soviet Central Archives and dated 19 November 1939. It was entitled 'Report on Prisoners of War who were Interned, Deported, and Remain in NKVD Camps'.[4] This document, designated 'top secret', was signed by Major Soprunienko, chief of the NKVD directorate for the affairs of prisoners of war, which was set up in September 1939.[5] (The rank of major in the NKVD was equivalent to that of brigadier-general in the Soviet army.) The document states that the total number of prisoners of war was 125,000: 42,400 were sent to western Belarus and western Ukraine; 43,000 were handed over to the German authorities; 15,000 were held in Kozielsk, Ostashkov, and Starobielsk; 24,600 were held in the Rovno camp and in work camps connected to iron and steel industrial plants. The final figure, which lists the total number of prisoners of war still in the NKVD camps, is 39,600. This is the most puzzling figure as it is impossible to correlate it with figures given in a report of 22 September 1939 stating that there were eight prison camps and 138 transit camps for Polish prisoners of war, and that these camps, all located in European Russia, were designed to accommodate 10,000 prisoners each.[6]

My research among the Soviet documents, which still continues, is prompted by a wish to find documentation concerning the Polish Jewish officers who were killed in Katyn. Although they were murdered not because they were Jews, but rather because they were Polish officers serving their country, they nevertheless belong to and are a definitive part of the history of Polish Jewry as well as of the Polish nation. For almost two decades I have pursued this research and sought to identify these officers, and I have published works on the subject in both English and Polish.[7] These initial publications dealt with the officers from the camp of Kozielsk. At a later date, after the Soviet transport lists became available, I also included the prisoners of Starobielsk. Having established definite proof that Jews served not only in the Polish armed forces but also in the police force as well as in border guard units, I also included the victims of the Ostashkov camp. The

---

[2] Janusz K. Zawodny, *Katyn* (London, 1989), 18; Jerzy Łojek (Leopold Jerzewski), *Dzieje sprawy Katynia* (Białystok, 1989), 12. Dr. Łojek, an eminent Polish writer and historian of the political history of Poland and Europe from the 18th to the 20th c., worked as an historian for the outlawed Solidarity movement. He has also published under the pseudonyms of Antoni Jałowiecki, Leopold Jerzewski, and Łukasz Jodko.

[3] Natalia Lebedeva, 'The Katyn Tragedy', *International Affairs* (Moscow) (June 1990), 100–9.

[4] Soviet Central Archives, Moscow, CAHDK, F1. OP OLE, 2, 228.

[5] Lebedeva, 'The Katyn Tragedy', 100.   [6] Abarinov, *The Murderers of Katyn*, 28.

[7] Simon Schochet, *Polscy oficerowie pochodzenia żydowskiego-jeńcy Katynia na tle walk o niepodległość* (New York, 1988), 152–65; *An Attempt to Identify the Polish Jewish Officers who were Killed in Katyn*, Working Papers in Holocaust Studies, no. 2 (New York, 1988).

empirical bases of my research included interviewing families, analysing the names of the murdered, reading all available officers' files, and checking official Soviet transport lists, which indicated the name of the father of each prisoner. Using these data, I estimated the total number of Polish Jewish officers who perished in all three camps. This number is about 700, and I still consider it to be as close as possible to the true figure.

My subsequent findings were published after I had obtained opinions from eminent historians to whom I had explained my research and methodology.[8] Janusz Zawodny was a soldier in the Warsaw uprising and is known as the foremost scholar and expert on the subject of Katyn. He is the author of *Death in the Forest*, considered the seminal work on the subject.[9] Professor Zawodny estimated, based on the statistics of university graduates in Poland prior to 1939 and on the percentage of Jews living in Poland, that at least 800 Jews may have been killed in Katyn.

In Warsaw the head of the Independent Historical Committee to Investigate the Crime of Katyn, Jędrzej Tucholski, who cross-referenced the names of the murdered prisoners of war with the names of the Soviet transport lists in his book *Mord w Katyniu*,[10] estimates that at least 600 Jews were murdered in the three camps at Katyn.

Second Lieutenant Salomon W. Slowes, a medical doctor from Vilna, left the Soviet Union with the army unit led by General Władysław Anders. During the Italian campaign he was decorated with the Cross of Monte Cassino. He had been a prisoner in Kozielsk and was transferred from there to Griazoviets, and he became one of the 432 survivors from the three camps. In his memoir *The Road to Katyn* he writes, 'Among the victims were about 1,000 Jewish officers who had been inducted into the Polish Army when the war broke out. These were men in their prime. Most were university trained experts in various fields: medicine, engineering, law. Others were prominent in public and economic life.'[11]

Władysław Bartoszewski, a member of the Polish Armia Krajowa (Home Army), was a co-founder of the underground Council to Aid Jews (Żegota) and is the author of various documentary works on the Nazi occupation of Poland, among them a unique chronicle of the Nazi terror in Warsaw from 1939 to 1945. He states: 'Among them were about 1,000 Jewish officers, including Major Baruch Steinberg, the Chief Rabbi of the Polish Army . . .'.[12]

---

[8] Simon Schochet, 'Próba określenia tożsamości polskich oficerów pochodzenia żydowskiego-jeńców obozów sowieckich (dalsze badania w świetle niedawno udostępnionych dokumentów sowieckich)', *Przegląd Polski*, 29 Nov. 1990, 2–3; id., 'Polish Jewish Officers who were Killed in Katyn: An Ongoing Investigation in Light of Documents Recently Released by the USSR', in *The Holocaust in the Soviet Union* (New York, 1993).

[9] *Death in the Forest: The Story of the Katyn Forest Massacre* (Notre Dame, Ind., 1962). The significance of Professor Zawodny's work may be gauged by the many subsequent editions and translations which have appeared in many languages and countries.   [10] Warsaw, 1991.

[11] Salomon W. Slowes, *The Road to Katyn* (Oxford, 1992), 3.

[12] Foreword to Slowes, *The Road to Katyn*, p. xiv.

Polish and Russian historians who have had access to the Russian archives and who are aware of the subject of my research were able to provide me with only one copy of a single NKVD document, which deals with the nationalities of the Polish army prisoners of war who were in the camps of Starobielsk and Kozielsk.[13] The report, dated February 1940, is also signed by Major Soprunienko. It states that in the Starobielsk camp the total number of prisoners was 3,908, of which seventy-one were Jews. In the Kozielsk camp the total listed is 4,486, of which eighty-nine were Jews. Based on my estimate as previously described, the number of Jewish officers as given in this document is only a fraction of the correct number. To disprove the validity of these numbers I had to examine the procedures used by the NKVD to manipulate these statistics.

Stanisław Swianiewicz, former professor at the University of Vilna, was a lieutenant serving in the Anders Army and worked for the Polish government in London. He was an inmate of Kozielsk and was one of the survivors of Katyn who was sent to Griazoviets. In his memoir *W cieniu Katynia* he describes and analyses how the Polish prisoners were interrogated in order to classify them according to the political directives of the NKVD.[14] In order to appraise this information and to verify the methods of interrogation used in the Katyn camps, I sent a copy of the NKVD document to Salomon Slowes, asking him for his comments and recollections about how the interrogations were conducted in Kozielsk. In his answer of 14 April 1994 Dr Slowes writes,

From the moment that the prisoner arrived in the camp, interrogations conducted by the NKVD got under way. These were called 'doprosy'. Statements were taken about personal data, family, profession, and political activity and orientation. There never were any questions relating to *religion*—only to nationality. These statements were then signed by the prisoner. The overwhelming majority of Jews gave their nationality as Polish. Only a very small number gave their nationality as *Jewish*.

Dr Slowes adds:

For the most part, those who identified themselves as Jews came from the border areas of Eastern Poland (Kresy), Vilna, Grodno, and Volynia and its environs. Therefore, the number of Jews given in this document is smaller and does not reflect the true figure. The number of Jews as estimated by Professor Zawodny and Engineer Tucholski is very near to the actual numbers. One should note that the Soviet transport lists *do not* indicate the religion of the prisoner. According to the listing I estimate that 800–1,000 Jews were in the three camps. I have sent the list of the names to Mrs Janina Ziemian.[15] Her response was that, basically, to prepare a list of Jews who were killed in Katyn without making mistakes is not possible.

[13] General State Soviet Army Archives, Moscow, CGOA, F. fin, le, D.3, D/98.
[14] (Paris, 1986), 96–8.
[15] Janina Ziemian is the head of the 'Katyn family in Israel'. She is the daughter of Second Lieutenant Heronim Brandwajn, a medical doctor from Warsaw held prisoner at Kozielsk and subsequently murdered.

As I write this I think of an essay by George Steiner.[16] In it he contemplates historical events such as Katyn which because of their nature are unimaginable, incomprehensible, and thus impossible to speak of. The proper manner in which to honour the countless dead who were victims of these unimaginable horrors would be through prayer or silence. The documents that have survived and that attest to the atrocities are for 'review' only if 'review' means 'seeing again'—over and over: pausing at the names of the dead to be able to repeat a few and to remind ourselves that we live on.

[16] *Language and Silence* (New York, 1974), 155–68.

The Demography of Jews in Hiding in Warsaw, 1943–1945

GUNNAR S. PAULSSON

NUMEROUS questions that have been a matter of speculation and controversy concerning the Jewish fugitives in Warsaw during the Holocaust can be answered with the aid of a hitherto overlooked archival resource, the Berman Archive. This archive, described in more detail in the Appendix to this chapter, contains the records of the Jewish National Committee (Żydowski Komitet Narodowy: ŻKN) and the personal papers of its chairman, Dr Adolf Berman. It was in the personal possession of Dr Berman until his death in 1979, when it was bequeathed by his widow, Basia Temkin-Berman, to the Ghetto Fighters' House (Beit Lohamei Hagetaot: BLHG), near Nahariya, Israel.

The documents from the Berman Archive that are of greatest interest to this chapter are lists of people who were receiving financial assistance from the committee (BLHG 357 and 358). These lists contain, all told, some 7,500 individual entries, each consisting of some of the following information: name (of an individual or family group); number of people in the group; receipt number and amount received; age, or date, and place of birth; other identifying information such as occupation and place of origin; name of the responsible activist; and comments of various kinds. The individual list entries are now being compiled into a computer database. See the section 'Methodological Problems and Approaches', below, for a more detailed discussion of this process.

To date 6,989 entries have been computerized, of which 4,764 have been subjected to detailed analysis. Of the latter, 119 were judged not to be relevant to this study (for example, because they pertained to people outside the Warsaw area) or to contain insufficient information to permit further analysis (for example, entries that were illegible or written using cryptic abbreviations that could not be deciphered). The remaining 4,645 records were assigned 2,460 distinct identifying numbers representing 2,356 named individuals or family groups and 104 groups of entries which contained no surname but sufficient other information to distinguish individual cases. These are calculated to represent between 3,200 and 3,700 distinct individuals. It is expected that when the tabulation process is complete, this number will reach between 5,000 and 5,800.

The interpretation of these documents requires some knowledge of the structure and functions of ŻKN and, indeed, of the whole organized effort to bring relief to Jews in hiding. A considerable amount has been written about the Council to Aid Jews (Żegota), much less about Jewish self-help. Indeed, apart from scattered references in memoirs and books on related topics, the only systematic published description of ŻKN and its work is an article by Dr Berman himself which appeared in 1953.[1]

Berman was the director of CENTOS, the organization which cared for orphans in the Warsaw ghetto. He was a prominent Left Labour Zionist and edited the left-wing underground newspaper *Der Ruf*. In the course of the great deportation in 1942 the ghetto's child welfare institutions were liquidated, rendering CENTOS superfluous. Berman then, having himself been rescued three times from the Umschlagplatz, escaped from the ghetto on 5 September 1942.

ŻKN was formed within the ghetto about 20 October 1942 as an umbrella group uniting the Zionist parties and youth groups (except for the Revisionists and their youth group, Betar). Shortly afterwards the Jewish Co-ordinating Committee (Żydowski Komitet Koordynacyjny: ŻKK) was established, with representation from the Bund as well as ŻKN. The impulse for the formation of ŻKN and ŻKK was the decision by the underground political parties in the ghetto to prepare for armed resistance: ŻKK was meant to present a united front in negotiations with the Polish underground and to provide political leadership for the Jewish Combat Organization (Żydowska Organizacja Bojowa: ŻOB), which had been formed in July by Zionist youth groups.

Berman was named the representative of ŻKN, and its representative on ŻKK, on the 'Aryan side'. Dr Leon Feiner, long established on the 'Aryan side', represented the Bund. Berman, a psychologist, had extensive pre-war professional contacts with the Polish intelligentsia, and as director of CENTOS had also maintained sporadic contact during the ghetto period with the Polish above-ground relief organization the Main Welfare Council (Rada Główna Opiekuńcza: RGO). Through these contacts, Berman became drawn into the Temporary Committee to Aid Jews (Tymczasowy Komitet Pomocy Żydom), founded about the same time as ŻKN on the initiative of the Catholic activist Zofia Kossak-Szczucka. When this body was reorganized in December 1942 into the Council to Aid Jews (Rada Pomocy Żydom: RPŻ or Żegota), under the umbrella of the Polish civil underground, he became the representative of ŻKN on its governing council. After the defeat of the ghetto uprising and the final liquidation of the ghetto Berman became the chairman of ŻKN. From this point on the committee's chief focus was relief work to help Jewish fugitives.

---

[1] Adolf Berman, 'Hayehudim betsad ha'ari', in *Entsiklopediyah shel galuyot*, vol. vii/8: *Varshe* (Jerusalem, 1953), 685–731. See also Adolf Berman, 'Rozwój działalności ŻKN po stronie aryjskiej', Yad Vashem Archive, Jerusalem, O33/238; Yitzhak Zuckerman, *A Surplus of Memory: Chronicle of the Warsaw Ghetto Uprising* (Oxford, 1993); Simcha Rotem, *Wspomnienia bojowca: ŻOB* (Warsaw, 1993); Yisrael Gutman, *The Jews of Warsaw, 1939–1943* (Bloomington, Ind., 1989).

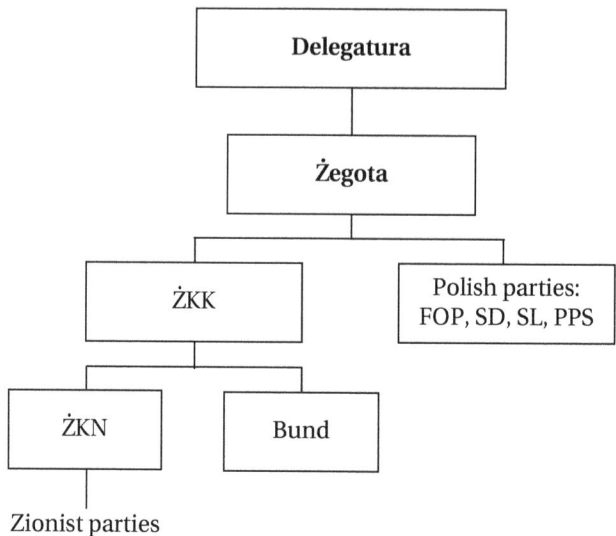

Figure 1. Structure of aid organizations on the 'Aryan side'. SD: Stronnictwo Demokratyczne (Democratic Party); SL: Stronnictwo Ludowe (Peasant's Party)

The aid organizations clustered under the financial umbrella of Żegota comprised a multi-tiered federal structure, with Żegota at the top (Figure 1). Polish parties and ŻKK formed the next tier, with the Bund and ŻKN below ŻKK. Below that were ŻKN's member organizations, the Left and Right Labour Zionists, the General Zionists, the youth groups Hashomer Hatsa'ir, Dror Hehaluts, Akiba, and Gordonia, and the Joint Distribution Committee (JDC, or the 'Joint'). ŻKN also channelled funds to the religious party Agudas Yisroel and the Revisionist Zionists, and maintained fraternal contacts with the (communist) Polish Workers' Party (Polska Partia Robotnicza: PPR) and its associated organizations. In addition, ŻOB continued to exist on the 'Aryan side', supported by the Bund and ŻKN through ŻKK. A few ŻOB activists lived in hiding in Warsaw; others operated as partisans in nearby forests.

On the Polish side Żegota was supported by its member organizations, political parties of the left and centre, as well as the Catholic Front for the Rebirth of Poland (Front Odrodzenia Polski: FOP). Many of the Żegota activists were also active in Polish relief organizations—above ground: RGO, the Catholic welfare organization Caritas, and the Polish Red Cross; underground: the Social Self-Help Organization (Społeczna Organizacja Samopomocy: SOS), formed in 1942 by the Democratic Party. Kossak-Szczucka declined to work with Żegota and formed a Jewish branch within SOS instead; this served principally as a liaison with convents and Catholic orphanages caring for Jewish children. PPR looked after its

Jewish members directly, as did the two branches of the Polish Socialist Party (Polska Partia Socjalistyczna: PPS), the right-wing Freedom, Equality, Independence (Wolność, Równość, Niepodległość), and particularly the left-wing Polish Socialists (Polscy Socjaliści), later the Revolutionary Party of Polish Socialists, (Rewolucyjna Partia Polskich Socjalistów), who maintained fraternal contacts with the Bund. The underground military arm of the Polish Scouts, Szare Szeregi, co-operated with Hashomer Hatsa'ir. Individual members of these organizations provided the bulk of the manpower on which ŻKN and the Bund relied. The Warsaw Housing Co-operative (Warszawska Spółdzielnia Mieszkaniowa: WSM), associated with the PPS, provided some hiding-places and occasionally jobs as well. Forged documents were provided by the Paszportówka, a cell of the civil underground, and by the 'legalization' cell of Żegota. This activity was also supported by parish priests, who provided forged birth and baptismal certificates, and by municipal employees working with the underground, who falsified entries in city housing files. Several Polish political parties were represented by delegates to the Żegota board and contributed activists to cells of the Jewish organizations at the lower levels.

On the Jewish side each organization provided financial support, as required, for its own members, and also to whatever Jews came to its attention. In time the distinction between ŻKN and its member organizations became blurred, the latter becoming in effect cells of ŻKN.

ŻKN's work expanded rapidly in 1943 and 1944 (Figure 2), as the committee and the Jewish fugitives managed to find each other and as the latter's own resources ran out. Though most of the recipient lists in the Berman Archive are undated, it can be inferred (see the section 'Dating the Lists', below) that these records pertain mainly if not exclusively to the period from October 1943 onwards and especially to the spring and summer of 1944.

By this time the number of cells had grown to fifty or 100, according to Berman, each employing a group of activists and communicating through a single contact person with the central organization.[2] It can be inferred that the average cell had some fifty people under its wing. As it finally evolved, ŻKN had a three-tiered structure. At the top was a central committee, consisting of Berman and his wife, the committee's secretary, Hirsch Wasser, and representatives of member groups.[3]

---

[2] In his report to the Delegatura of 20 Mar. 1944 (BLHG 313) Berman claimed that the organization had fifty cells, while in his report 'Rozwój działalności ŻKN po stronie aryjskiej' of 24 May he claims 100 cells.

[3] Daniel Kaftor (David Guzik) for the 'Joint'; Szymon Gottesmann for the General Zionists (in Kraków); Avram Warman for Hashomer Hatsa'ir (in L'viv); and a number of others who were unable to participate actively in the ŻKN's activities because they were forced to hide 'under the surface', but who took part in its internal work. These included Zivia Lubetkin, Józef Zak, Stefan Grajek, Lejzer Lewin, Pola Elster, Dr Emanuel Ringelblum, and Hersch Berlinski (Berman, 'Hayehudim betsad ha'ari', 711).

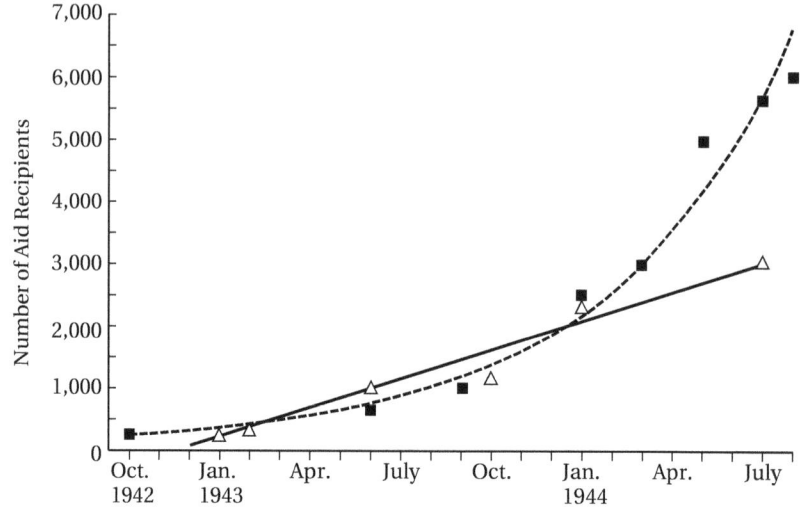

Figure 2. The growth of Żegota and ŻKN, 1942–1944

At the next level Berman names twenty individuals as the 'central team'.[4] Below that were the local cells. It follows that each member of the central team served as the contact for several different cells.

Information flowed upwards through the organization, and money flowed downwards. A person in need would in some way establish contact with one of the cells and thereby with one of the committee's activists. Sometimes she or he would submit a written plea for assistance (some of these have been preserved; list 33). This, or simply the activist's recommendation, would be transmitted to the central cell, which upon getting it would allocate appropriate additional funds to the activist. Each activist would then receive a monthly sum to distribute, normally 500 zlotys per recipient, at times reduced to 400 or even 300 zlotys.

On receiving money from a ŻKN activist, each recipient was asked to sign a receipt: these were written on small pieces of paper, which the activist concealed, typically under his or her watchstrap. A few of these receipts are preserved in the archive (list 21).

Individual activists were asked to tabulate the receipts (e.g. list 1, signed by

---

[4] Basia or Batya Berman, Symcha Rathajzer (Simcha Rotem—'Kazik'), Bela Elster, Klima Fuswerk, Anna Gotesman, Irena Gelblum, Helena Merenholc, Dr Lota Wegmajster, Jakub Roth, Joseph Zysman, Dr Nina Asserodobraj, Anatol Matywiecki, Halina Gertner, Pola Bugajska, Riva Moszkowicz, Zofia Kimelman, Joanna Tykocinska, Jakub Wiernik, Emilka Kossower, and the mother of Mark Folman (Yad Vashem Archive, Jerusalem, O33/238).

'Helena'), and these individual lists would filter up to the leadership. Not all activists kept such lists, however, some feeling it to be too dangerous.[5] Attempts by the central committee to keep central records seem to have been sporadic and incomplete, probably also for security reasons. No central register was kept, but activist lists were used for a time to prepare monthly statements to the financial review committee of Żegota (list 5, consisting of monthly sublists 5.1 (October 1943) to 5.6 (March 1944)). In addition, several members of the central committee seem to have tried to collate activists' lists into an alphabetical register (lists 4 and 6, kept by Wasser; list 3, by Basia Berman; list 2, typed and unsigned, consisting of sublists 2.1–2.9). In addition to the monthly registers of list 5, there is another, similar, but much rougher monthly tabulation (list 7, with sublists 7.1 (January 1944) to 7.6 (June 1944)). Both list 5 and list 7 are incomplete. In the case of list 5, entries were written up neatly on slips of paper and signed and dated by 'Borowski' (Berman), 'for the presidium of ŻKN'. They are countersigned, all on 14 June 1944, by three members of the financial review committee of Żegota, 'Lasocki' (Feiner), 'Łukowski' (Marek Arczyński), and 'Różycki' (Tadeusz Rek). In the case of list 7, the lists take the form of rough notes with liberal use of abbreviations and cryptic notations. To date, of list 7 only the register for March 1944 has been tabulated (list 7.3) sufficiently to demonstrate that it differs significantly from list 5.6, also dated March 1944.

The function of the individual lists is in some cases identified explicitly, while in other cases it has to be inferred. List 7.4 is identified as individual subsidies (*subwencje indywidualne*), that is, people under the care of ŻKN directly rather than of one of its member organizations. Another list (list 14) is marked 'Podopieczni ŻKK', that is, people under the direct care of ŻKK. In general, the lists fall into the following categories:

1. Letters requesting assistance (82 letters, mostly dated June–July 1944).
2. Individual receipts (30 receipts, mostly dated, but most signatures illegible).
3. Monthly registers of receipts (lists 5 and 7). Cf. the published list for Żegota cell 'Felicja', dated December 1943–May 1944, with partial receipts for November 1943 and June 1944.[6]
4. Reports from individual activists, some dated. The average number of cases in each such list is roughly consistent with the number of cases calculated to be under the care of each low-level cell.
5. Comprehensive registers of recipients, each probably for a high-level cell (ŻKN: lists 2, 3, 4, 6; ŻKK: list 14).
6. Notes and jottings of various kinds.

[5] Author's interview with the late Helena Merenholc. Dr Merenholc denied being the 'Helena' of list 1.
[6] Teresa Prekerowa, 'Komórka "Felicji": Nieznane archiwum działaczy Rady Pomocy Żydom w Warszawie', *Rocznik Warszawski*, 15 (1979).

DEVELOPMENT AND FINANCES OF ŻKN

ŻKN received money from Żegota, which in turn received it from the Polish government in exile. Starting in mid-1943, however, sums of money raised in the United States were channelled to ŻKN through the government in exile: a payment of $10,000 was received each month from June until September. (As a benchmark both of the value of the zloty at the time and of the rate of inflation, it is worth noting that Berman was able to convert this money on the black market at the rate of 66.15 zlotys to the dollar in June and 90.34 by September. At these rates the standard monthly relief payment of 500 zlotys was worth $7.55 in June and $5.53 in September.)

It offers some insight into both the structure of ŻKN and the scale of its operations to examine the disposition of the $40,000 received in June to September 1943. The total sum obtained on the black market was 3,030,550 zlotys. Its distribution is shown in Table 1.

On this basis, it can be calculated that at this point ŻKN and its member organizations were providing financial support for some 800 people, exclusive of camps and ghettos. But Berman complained that towards the end of this period individual grants had to be cut to 300–400 zlotys monthly, at the very time that favourable black-market rates were effectively increasing the sums at the committee's disposal. Therefore a more realistic picture would be that the number of recipients during this four-month period grew from about 600 to 1,000 or more. This comprised about 600 activists of the member organizations (judging from the amounts disbursed to them), a number which no doubt gradually dwindled, and

Table 1. Distribution of funds acquired by the Jewish National Committee (ŻKN), June–September 1943

Recipient	Amount (zlotys)
Camps and ghettos	585,000
Right Labour Zionists	355,000
Individual grants (includes small allowances for Agudas Yisroel and Revisionists)	350,000
General Zionists	335,000
Dror Hehaluts and other youth organizations	335,000
Left Labour Zionists	285,000
Donations to Żegota	250,000
Administrative expenses	30,550
[Unaccounted for[a]	505,000]
TOTAL	3,030,550

[a] The body of the report from which this table is produced mentions subsidies to ŻOB for the purchase of weapons, upkeep of fighters (in forests near Warsaw), and travel expenses. These are said to amount to a 'significant portion of the ŻKN budget' and probably account for the missing sum, which seems to have been omitted through a clerical error.

Source: Financial report of ŻKN, 1 Jan.–31 Oct. 1943, Yad Vashem Archives, Jerusalem, collection O6 [Ob/48].

an ever-increasing number of individual recipients who had 'succeeded in making contact' with one of the cells of ŻKN. According to a note in the Berman Archive (BLHG 357, list 7.1), the number of recipients had grown to 2,500 by January 1944. In a letter to the plenipotentiary of the government in exile dated 20 March 1944 (BLHG 310) Berman estimated the number at just under 3,000. In a report on the committee's activities on 24 May his estimate has risen to 5,000 (BLHG 309), and at a meeting with the plenipotentiary on 17 July to 5,600 (BLHG 313). (See Figure 2.)

As we have seen, the evidence from the recipient lists supports Berman's claims, which have met with strong scepticism in some quarters.[7] Since there is no guarantee that the records we have are complete—indeed, there is good reason to think the opposite—they may even be too low. After the war Berman claimed further that Żegota had had an additional 4,000 people in its care in the Warsaw area and the Bund 1,500–2,000, making a total of 11,000–12,000 receiving aid in the Warsaw area alone.[8] But this claim does not stand up. As to Żegota, Teresa Prekerowa has put forward in conversation the more modest figure of 3,000: the higher figure, apparently, should refer to the whole of Żegota's sphere of activity, not just the Warsaw area. What is more important, a preliminary survey of the one surviving set of Żegota receipt lists (for cell 'Felicja', see above) indicates that there was considerable overlap between its operation and ŻKN's–that is, that there were substantial numbers of people who drew money from both sources, either at the same time or first from one and then from the other. It does not seem that there was widespread welfare fraud; the reason is rather that Żegota took on only as many people as it could handle financially (hence its linear growth, observed in Figure 2), transferring any surplus to ŻKN and the Bund. Żegota specialized in children, who made up 2,500 of the 4,000 people under its care.[9]

What appear to be complete Bund recipient lists have also turned up and will be the subject of a subsequent report.[10] These lists support Berman's estimate for the Bund, comprising some 1,500 individual cases. The Bund records are dated March–June 1944; by the outbreak of the uprising in August the number of recipients may have grown by several hundred. There is an overlap of about 10 per cent between the Bund and ŻKN lists.

Revising Berman's claims in this light, we are obliged to conclude that ŻKN could well have had 5,600 or so people under its care, but that Żegota was paying money to only some 1,500 additional people, while the Bund had perhaps a further

---

[7] For example, Yisrael Gutman and Shmuel Krakowski describe this and related estimates as 'greatly exaggerated' (*Unequal Victims: Poles and Jews during World War II* (New York, 1986), 266). Gutman (in conversation with the author) has theorized that Berman exaggerated the ŻKN's activities in reports to London so as to justify requests for increased funds. After the war, he thinks, Berman was too embarrassed to admit his deceit, so that these exaggerated estimates 'just stuck'.

[8] Berman, 'Hayehudim betsad ha'ari', 685.

[9] Teresa Prekerowa, *Zarys dziejów Żydów w Polsce w latach 1939–1945* (Warsaw, 1992), 165.

[10] Archiwum Akt Nowych, Warsaw, 30/III t. 5, 18–46.

1,000 additional people under its care. Small numbers of people also received aid from other organizations such as the PPR, PPS, RGO, WSM, and SOS. This would mean that Jewish recipients of financial assistance in Warsaw in the summer of 1944 numbered about 8,500 rather than 11,000–12,000 as claimed.

Another investigation tested some 300 names of Jews in hiding, gleaned from memoirs, against the database. The names were those of people mentioned by memoirists, omitting the names of the memoirists themselves in order to avoid creating a bias in favour of survivors. The object was to estimate what proportion of all Jews in hiding were represented by those whose names have been tabulated. Though comparison of names is naturally subject to some uncertainty, the investigation suggested that the 2,356 names tabulated represent about 10–15 per cent of the total, which would bring the total number of Jews in hiding in Warsaw in the spring and summer of 1944 to between 15,000 and 24,000—in good agreement with published estimates of 15,000–20,000.

METHODOLOGICAL PROBLEMS AND APPROACHES

The principle used in constructing the database is to preserve all the information in the original entries so that there is one database record per entry containing the unaltered original information. To this is added identification of the source (list and line or receipt number) and an identifying number, assigned in such a way that entries judged to represent the same individual or family group receive the same number. When it has been judged that two apparently different names represent the same person (as in the case of variant spellings or 'Jewish' versus 'Christian' given names), then the surname has been standardized, with the variant form preserved as a comment.

Computerizing the recipient lists is a time-consuming process: many of the lists are written in pencil on poor-quality wartime paper which has yellowed and is now barely legible; some have been scrawled hastily on random scraps of paper; and they are written in various hands which the researcher has to master individually. Once deciphered, entries from various lists have to be correlated, a process which often entails considerable detective work. To take one example: there are in the source lists entries for Julian Adelberg, Juliusz Adelberg, Helena Adelberg, Zdzisław Adelberg, and a Julian and Helena Achalberg. Comparison of various lists and of activists' comments shows that Zdzisław is the son of Helena and that his wife's name is also Helena: there are two Helena Adelbergs. Julian Adelberg and Juliusz Adelberg are the same person, the husband of the elder Helena and father of Zdzisław. The Achalbergs appear in only one list (list 3, compiled by Basia Berman), but this is not unusual. Mrs Berman usually lists family groups together, and she has listed the Achalbergs separately from the Adelbergs. So she believed them to be distinct, and therefore—with some trepidation—they have been given separate identifying numbers. In other cases the principle of parsimony has been invoked to conflate entries with similar names when there was no information which allowed them to be clearly distinguished. In this way, two entries for 'Dr Borenstein', with no given name, were initially conflated; but it turns out that there were two Dr Borensteins, one a professor of medicine and the other of logic. (The medical Borenstein sat on the board of ŻKK.)

An additional difficulty arises because some lists will group a family under a single entry while others will provide an individual entry for each family member. Therefore, there is some uncertainty, especially in the case of common surnames, as to which individual records belong with which family records. Again, appropriate detective work can often—but by no means always—resolve these problems. It is because of these uncertainties that the number of individuals represented by these lists can be given only approximately. The ranges stated above represent the estimates arrived at by using the most exclusive and inclusive criteria, respectively. Two kinds of identification error are possible: identifying two entries as the same when they should be different, and as different when they should be the same. Since both kinds of error are likely to be present, the estimates most likely to be correct are those approximately at the mid-point of the range. Thus 3,450 individuals ± 250 have been identified so far, with the number expected to reach 5,400 ± 400.

DATING THE LISTS

Some of the lists are dated explicitly, while others can be dated inferentially. None of the explicitly dated lists bears a date earlier than October 1943, and most pertain to June or July 1944. Inferential dates can be established by comparing undated lists with dated ones. For example, list 4 (1,059 names) contains all but sixty-four of the names in list 6 (507 names), and an additional 616 besides; both were compiled by Hirsch Wasser. Probable inference: list 4 is a later version of list 6, reflecting attrition (the names which have been dropped) and the organization's growth. If list 6 were a reduced version of list 4, it would have been simpler to cross off the names that were dropped and add the few new names in the spaces which have been left blank (presumably for this purpose) at the end of each alphabetical section. List 2.9 (100 people) is headed 'I request assistance for June for:'. List 2 as a whole was therefore presumably typed in May or June—certainly 1944 rather than 1943, since otherwise at least some of these names which were new for June would have found their way onto at least some of the subsequent lists, including those which are dated. But there is no significant overlap between list 2.9 and any other list, except for a 70 per cent overlap with list 3 and a 7 per cent overlap with list 4. Inference: list 3 was compiled in June or July 1944. Some of the other sub-lists of list 2 overlap significantly with list 4, but there is no overlap at all between any part of list 2 and list 6. Inference: list 2 consists of people who came to the organization's attention during the interval between list 6 and list 4; again it is confirmed that list 6 is earlier. The 7 per cent overlap between list 4 and list 2.9 is small but significant. Possible inference: most of the people who were new for June were assigned to the cell represented by list 3, a few to the cell represented by list 4, and both lists were compiled in June or July.

The degree of overlap between list 4 and the dated monthly registers of list 5 is month by month virtually the same as the overlap between list 6 and list 5. Inference: the additional cases in list 4 did not come to the organization's attention during the period covered by list 5; therefore lists 4 and 6 were both compiled no earlier than March 1944.

There are a number of other lists dated June and July 1944; almost none of the names in these lists is to be found in either list 4 or list 6. Particularly telling: list 21, headed 'New for July', contains no names which are in either list 4 or list 6. Inference: both lists are earlier than July and probably earlier than June 1944. Therefore, we can tentatively place list 6 in April or more likely March 1944, and list 4 in about June (since the number of entries is about doubled, it is reasonable to assume that the difference between the two is greater than a single month).

Further analysis of the same sort reveals that list 3 probably pertains to June or July 1944. Thus tentative dates can be assigned to the largest lists: lists 2, 3, and 4 all seem to date from June or July 1944, and list 6 from March 1944. Many of the other lists were inferentially dated in a similar manner (see Appendix).

DEMOGRAPHIC CHARACTERISTICS

Table 2 shows the age and sex distribution of those people for whom these characteristics could be determined. For comparison, Table 3 shows figures for the final period of the ghetto. See also Figures 3 and 4.

Table 2. Age and sex distribution of Jews on the 'Aryan side' in Warsaw, 1943–1944

Age group	Male		Female	
	No.	%	No.	%
0–9	8	9.5	15	11.5
10–19	14	16.7	17	13.0
20–29	20	23.8	34	26.0
30–39	18	21.4	34	26.0
40–49	11	13.1	11	8.4
50–59	4	4.8	9	6.9
60–69	6	7.1	6	4.6
70+	3	3.6	5	3.8
TOTAL	84	100.0	131	100.2

Note: Male–female ratio: 39.1 : 60.9

Source: Developed from the Berman Archive database. Percentages do not add up to 100 because of rounding errors.

The Demography of Jews in Hiding

Table 3. Age and sex distribution of Jews in the ghetto before and after the main deportations (July–Sept. 1942) and in hiding on the 'Aryan side' (1943–1944) (%)

Age group	In the ghetto				In hiding	
	Early 1942		End October 1942		1943–4	
	Male	Female	Male	Female	Male	Female
0–9	16.3	12.2	1.3	1.6	9.5	11.5
10–19	22.4	18.8	11.0	14.6	16.7	13.0
20–29	12.5	17.1	19.5	29.5	23.8	26.0
30–39	18.5	19.4	34.2	30.8	21.4	26.0
40–49	13.4	14.5	21.9	16.5	13.1	8.4
50–59	9.4	9.9	10.2	6.1	4.8	6.9
60–69	5.6	5.8	1.8	1.0	7.1	4.6
70+	1.8	2.4	0.2	0.1	3.6	3.8
TOTAL	99.9	100.1	100.1	100.2	100.0	100.2

Source: For ghetto figures, 'Materialn tsu demografishe forshungen vegn der yidishe bafolkerung in Varshe beys der hitleristisher okupatsye', *Bleter far geshichte*, 8/3–4 (1955), 206–8.

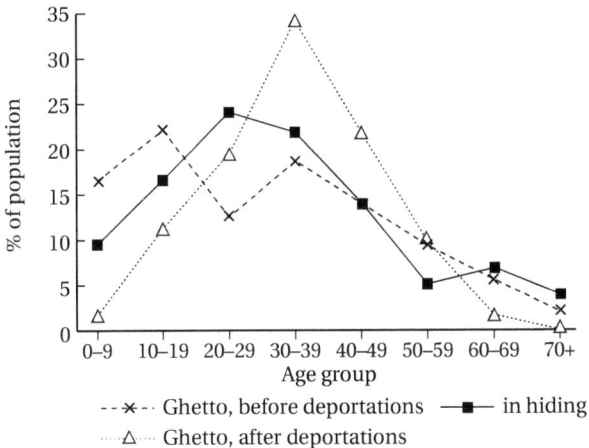

Figure 3. Age distribution of the Jewish population in Warsaw (male)

It should be noted that the figures derived from the Berman Archive are likely to underrepresent women and especially children. This is because an entry in the recipient registers often represents a family rather than an individual and will thus tend to represent the paterfamilias or, failing that, the mother. Consideration was also given to the possibility that there are other biases—for example, that activists were especially apt to note the ages of children and old people, or of men rather than women. To the extent that this possibility could be evaluated it seems not to

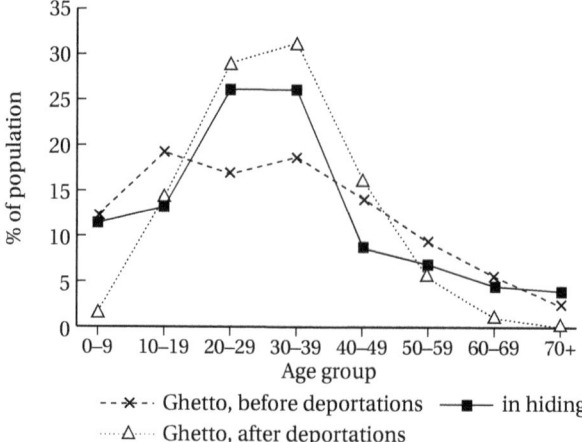

Figure 4. Age distribution of the Jewish population in Warsaw (female)

be the case, however. For example, list 13 systematically notes the ages or dates of birth of all those listed, and within this admittedly small sample the age distributions do not differ significantly from those given above. Nor does the gender distribution of those whose ages are listed differ significantly from the overall gender distribution. Finally, as will shortly be shown, the age distributions, with certain exceptions, conform to expectations. In short, it seems that age information was kept either as a form of identification or with an eye to documentation, but in any case is fairly unbiased.

The age distribution pattern can perhaps be seen more clearly if ages are grouped into broader bands (see Table 4). The method of computing the 'expected' distribution in this table is explained below. The figures for October 1942 reflect the terrible effects of the first liquidation on the Jews of the ghetto, striking hardest at those least able to defend themselves. Among the very young and the very old, losses approached 100 per cent. None of the ghetto's 890 octogenarians survived, and only 498 out of 51,458 children under 10. Out of 7,804 persons over 70, there were forty-five survivors. Women were more vulnerable than men: overall, 92 per

Table 4. The impact of the deportations: broad-band age and sex distribution

	Male			Female			Overall	
	0–19	20–59	60+	0–19	20–59	60+	Male	Female
Ghetto before deportations	38.7	54.8	7.4	31.0	60.9	8.2	42.7	57.3
Ghetto after deportations	12.3	87.8	2.0	16.2	76.8	1.1	56.0	44.0
In hiding, actual	26.2	63.1	10.7	24.5	67.3	8.4	39.1	60.9
In hiding, expected	22.9	74.6	4.2	22.1	70.4	3.9	50.7	49.3

cent of the ghetto's women were taken, compared with 87 per cent of the men. The difference between the sexes was greatest among the middle-aged: 20 per cent of men aged 30–59 survived, and only 9 per cent of women.

An analysis of a sample of memoirs and testimonies on file at Yad Vashem and the Jewish Historical Institute in Warsaw[11] shows that some 60 per cent of escapes from the ghetto took place after the end of the first *Aktion*, and the distribution of the population in hiding—intermediate between those before and after the *Aktion*, but more closely resembling the latter—reflects this fact. However, comparison of the actual distribution of Jews in hiding with the expected distribution computed according to this proportion shows clearly that the population in hiding favours the young and the old over the middle-aged, and women over men. The prevalence of women was no doubt due to the fact that men, being circumcised, were thought less likely to escape detection, particularly 'on the surface'. An analysis of fifty-three memoirs shows that nearly three-quarters of those who risked life on the surface were women, whilst among those hiding 'under the surface', the numbers of men and women were approximately equal. Since for the same reason Christian families were less willing to take in Jewish boys than girls, girls probably outnumbered boys in hiding. Children under the care of ŻKN were mainly hiding with their own families, however, and in the Berman Archive there are only slightly more girls than boys.

Men and women between 20 and 39 make up nearly half the Jews on the 'Aryan side', compared with a third in the pre-deportation ghetto. Families often sent young adults, particularly young men, out of the ghetto with the idea that they would establish themselves and then help their relatives to escape; but such plans were often overtaken by events, leaving young men and women stranded on the 'Aryan side'. Children of both sexes were over-represented, as were men over 60: children and older people made up a large proportion of those who were smuggled out of the ghetto during the deportation, when there were relatively many Jews still alive. On the other hand, the middle-aged of both sexes and, for some reason, teenage girls were the least likely either to be saved or to save themselves.

The sample is no doubt biased, since the relief organizations made a special effort to rescue just such people; for example, as is well known, Żegota activists managed to arrange the escape of the historian Emanuel Ringelblum from the Trawniki labour camp. Also ŻKN activists were themselves members of the intelligentsia; that was where their contacts were and where they began their activities. There can be little doubt, however, that the Jews in hiding were indeed largely drawn from these classes, since these were the Jews in Poland who spoke Polish well, and who had contacts with the Polish side, through whom the necessary arrangements could be made.

[11] G. S. Paulsson, 'Hiding in Warsaw: The Jews on the "Aryan Side" in the Polish Capital, 1940–1945', University of Oxford D.Phil. thesis, 1998.

The survival of the elderly also reflects the prevalence of the intelligentsia; here is a complete list from the database of people known to be over 65:

Idalia Bejlin (70)	teacher
Felicja Bloch (70)	teacher
Ignacy Bruner (73)	lawyer
Mrs Fajgenbaum (72)	profession unknown
Leopold Hausner (68)	engineer
Janina Lipszyc (70)	lawyer's widow
Kazimierz Majzel (83)	history teacher
Marta Pfefferberg (72)	merchant's widow
Michał Piszczakowski (71)	profession unknown
Helena Sołowicz (66)	profession unknown
Leokadia Szenwic (70)	profession unknown
Ludwika Zelcer (80)	profession unknown

While hardly the leading lights of Jewish Warsaw, most are among its respected elders, with seven out of twelve known to be members of the intelligentsia and middle class. Thus there is a still heavier predominance of these classes among the elderly than is observed in the fugitive population as a whole.

DISTRIBUTION BY OCCUPATIONAL CATEGORY

Among the papers in BLHG 358 is a tabulation in Basia Berman's hand of Jews in hiding according to pre-war profession. The counts are shown in Table 5. The last category in the table ('unknown or unclassified') no doubt includes housewives and reflects the prevalence of women among the sample. Apart from that, the overwhelming predominance of the intelligentsia is apparent. ('Trade and industry'

Table 5.   Pre-war occupations of Jews in hiding

Occupation	No.
Blue-collar trades	8
Clerical workers	25
Doctors and related professions	14
Engineers and technicians	15
Journalists	4
Lawyers	11
Literature, arts, and science	16
Military	2
Teachers	26
Trade and industry	45
School-age children	17
Unknown or unclassified	103
TOTAL	286

ATTRITION

On the basis of memoir evidence and post-war records, about 16,000 of the 27,000 Jews on the 'Aryan side' in Warsaw failed to survive the war. Of these, about 3,500 gave themselves up at the Hotel Polski and another 6,800 died before the 1944 uprising.[12] Choosing 1 May 1943 as a base date, when the number of Jews in hiding reached its peak of about 25,000, and supposing for convenience that 800 of the deaths had occurred before that date, then some 6,000 people died on the 'Aryan side' in the fifteen months that followed. After the Hotel Polski affair, which unfolded in the summer of 1943, 21,500 of the 25,000 remained exposed to capture or denunciation. A figure of 6,000 deaths out of 21,500 represents an average rate of attrition of 2.2 per cent per month: assuming the rate remained constant, 473 per month or 18 per day in mid-1943, and 341 and 11, respectively, a year later. There were, of course, better and worse days and months.

Contemporary testimony points to roughly similar numbers. Ringelblum maintained that 150 Jews had been caught on the 'other side' during the great *Aktion*, which lasted fifty-two days;[13] later, he estimated that 'tens' (*kilkadziesiąt*) were being caught each day.[14] Probably more soundly based is the testimony of Julien Hirshaut, who spent a year in the Pawiak prison after having been caught on the 'Aryan side' in the summer of 1943. Hirshaut was kept in cell 258, where people suspected of being Jews were held while their cases were investigated. Cell 258 had some 28 inmates, he tells us, with 'a few' arriving and leaving each day, and the neighbouring cell 257, where condemned Jews were kept prior to execution, housed 'several' Jews at any one time. Hirshaut estimates that on average 500 Jews per month passed through the Pawiak, and that 8,000 Jews died there in all.[15]

These estimates do not quite add up: 500 Jews a month would mean 17 each day, about 8–9 from each cell. As to cell 258, this would be rather too large a fraction of 28 to be described as 'a few', and on this scale of things, certainly the largest number in cell 257 that could be described as 'several'. We know from the memoirs of the relatives and friends of prisoners that investigations could be quite thorough and time-consuming, so that people could spend weeks or even months in the prison before their cases were disposed of. If we suppose that an average stay was one week, then the number removed from cell 258 would have been on the

---

[12] Paulsson, 'Hiding in Warsaw', 248.

[13] Emmanuel Ringelblum, *Kronika getta warszawskiego* (Warsaw, 1983), 419.

[14] Emmanuel Ringelblum, *Polish–Jewish Relations during the Second World War*, ed. Joseph Kermish and Shmuel Krakowski (New York, 1976); id., *Stosunki polsko-żydowskie w czasie drugiej wojny światowej*, ed. Artur Eisenbach (Warsaw, 1988), 81.

[15] Julien Hirshaut, *Jewish Martyrs of Pawiak* (New York, 1982), 36–40.

order of four per day, or half as many as Hirshaut implies. Not all of this number, furthermore, were taken to be shot: some were released, because their documents had stood the test, or after the payment of a bribe, or after someone had vouched for them. Those who were to be killed were normally first transferred to cell 257, so that simply adding the numbers taken from the two cells would involve some double counting. All things considered, it is therefore doubtful that the total number of Jews killed in the prison reached even half of the total claimed by Hirshaut.

Of course not all Jews who were caught came to the Pawiak, but most did. Many people suspected as Jews were interned pending investigation in local stations of the 'Blue' police, at Kripo headquarters at Ujazdowska 8, or at the Daniłowiczowska Street prison, or were taken for questioning to Gestapo headquarters in Aleje Szucha. Normally, such people were eventually either released or transferred to the Pawiak. There were other possibilities, however. During the ghetto period Jews caught on the 'Aryan side' were held in the Gęsia Street prison or Werterfassung headquarters, or else they were taken directly to the Umschlagplatz. Children returned from the 'Aryan side' were placed in a special orphanage in Dzika Street, and thence were eventually sent to the Umschlagplatz. Other Jews were simply shot on the spot. Reliable estimates of the number of people killed in these various ways are very hard to come by.

Not all of those caught on the 'Aryan side' were true fugitives from the ghetto. Many who were captured while the ghetto was still in existence were food smugglers, and probably a few were Christians who had been falsely accused. On the other hand, there were Jews who were killed for political or other reasons, without their identities having been discovered. Such cases are difficult to identify, let alone count.

Another method of calculating attrition rates is available through the analysis of monthly receipt registers. The published register of Żegota receipts, referred to above, spans the period from December 1943 to May 1944, with fragmentary records for November 1943 and June 1944. Of the 84 people on this list who received money in November or December, 79 also received money in May or June. On the most unfavourable assumption, that all those who dropped off the list had been captured, this represents a six-month attrition of about 6 per cent, or just over 1 per cent monthly. This group, at any rate, evidently had a considerably better than average survival rate.

An attempt was made to analyse the ŻKN monthly receipt registers (lists 5 and 7) in the same manner as the Żegota receipts, but this proved infeasible. The purpose of list 5 was to provide an accounting for funds received by ŻKN through Żegota. But these funds represented only a fraction of the ŻKN's income, most of which came independently from Jewish sources. In this context, only numbers mattered and not individual names. These lists therefore do not track a fixed set of individuals from month to month, but appear to be drawn at random from the

ŻKN pool. Therefore, no conclusions about attrition rates can be drawn from them.

The question of attrition is therefore complex and difficult to answer on the basis of direct evidence, but certainly these partial estimates are not inconsistent with the claim that some 6,000 Jews died after being caught or betrayed: half of them, let us say, at the Pawiak, and half in other ways.

Data on attrition within the ghetto are readily available, and a comparison with the attrition rates calculated above allows an assessment on the objective rationality of the decision to leave or remain within the ghetto prior to the liquidation action. Thus in 1941 there were 42,239 recorded deaths in the ghetto, out of a peak population estimated at 460,000—an attrition rate of 0.83 per cent monthly. Of the approximately 490,000 people who passed through the ghetto all told, 350,000 were still in the ghetto on the eve of the liquidation action, twenty months after the ghetto was closed. This represents a rate of loss due to all factors, including deportation to labour camps, of 1.7 per cent monthly. Thus even with the benefit of hindsight, and with calculator in hand, there is little reason to recommend flight from the ghetto before the liquidation started. Indeed, since those who had the best chances of escaping from the ghetto were also those who had the best means of surviving within it, it must be said that remaining outside the ghetto in 1940, or escaping from it before 22 July 1942, was for the great majority of Jews not a rationally supportable option. It is therefore not surprising that the great majority of escapes took place only after the start of the Great Deportation on 22 July 1942, but particularly after the second *Aktion* in January 1943, when fewer than 60,000 remained in the ghetto. About one-fifth to one-quarter of this remnant managed to flee.[16]

SUMMARY AND CONCLUSIONS

The Berman Archive and other sources (Bund and fragmentary Żegota lists) lend concrete support to post-war estimates of the number of Jews in hiding in Warsaw, against scepticism from some sources. On the basis of the data analysed so far, it would appear that the aid organizations had between them some 8,000–8,500 people under their care in the Warsaw area in the spring and summer of 1944, and that the total number of Jews in hiding during that period was between 15,000 and 20,000. This was the remnant of a larger number, estimated at 27,000, who had managed to hide at one time or another.

Demographic analysis of this population shows that it was drawn largely from the intelligentsia, and that a distinct majority (61 per cent) were women. The age distribution of the population was intermediate between those in the ghetto before and after the 1942 deportation, more closely resembling the latter. This reflects the fact that about 60 per cent of all escapes from the ghetto took place after the

[16] Paulsson, 'Hiding in Warsaw', 66.

deportation, that is, when the number of Jews in the ghetto was already severely depleted. However, there were more children and old people in hiding than these proportions would suggest, more women, and more young men. Conversely, there were fewer middle-aged people and teenage girls. These discrepancies reflect the fact that families tried to save their most vulnerable members; but they also tended to send young adults to the other side, as the most resourceful and often the most assimilated, hoping that they could establish a foothold and then help the rest of the family escape. Such plans often could not be realized in time.

It is estimated that about 6,800 Jews perished on the 'Aryan side' in Warsaw before the 1944 uprising, not counting those who gave themselves up at the Hotel Polski, for an overall rate of attrition of 2.2 per cent per month. On this basis, it can be calculated that but for the Warsaw uprising of 1944, about 88 per cent of those in hiding on 1 August 1944 would have survived to see liberation in January 1945. This would have yielded between 13,000 and 17,500 survivors: 48–65 per cent of the 27,000 in hiding, or 55–75 per cent of the 23,500 who did not go to the Hotel Polski.

For the sake of comparison, the case of the Netherlands might be examined. There, 20,000–25,000 Jews are estimated to have gone into hiding, mainly in Amsterdam, of whom 10,000–15,000 survived the war.[17] The overall survival rate in Holland was thus 40–60 per cent, and in Warsaw, after levelling the playing field, notionally 55–75 per cent. Thus the attrition rate among Jews in hiding in Warsaw was relatively low, contrary to expectation and contemporary perceptions.[18] The main obstacles to Jewish survival in Warsaw are seen to have been the Hotel Polski trap and the 1944 uprising and its aftermath, rather than the possibility of discovery or betrayal.

Despite frequent house searches and the prevailing Nazi terror in Warsaw (conditions absent in the Netherlands), and despite extortionists, blackmailers, and antisemitic traditions (much less widespread in the Netherlands), the chance that a Jew in hiding would be betrayed seems to have been lower in Warsaw than in the Netherlands.

To some extent, this extraordinary fact can be ascribed to circumstances specific to Poland and Warsaw. The German policy of terror in Poland backfired

---

[17] Various estimates are cited by Jacob Presser, *Ashes in the Wind: The Destruction of Dutch Jewry* (Detroit, 1988), 383. The one used here is the most favourable to the Dutch, for which Presser cites 'K.P.L. Berkley *op. cit.* 94', but the full citation for Berkley is never given. Bob Moore cites an estimate of 16,000–17,000 out of 24,000–25,000 (64–70 per cent), but describes it as 'problematical' (Moore, *Victims and Survivors: The Nazi Persecution of the Jews in the Netherlands 1940–1945* (London, 1997), 146). Among other things these figures appear to include people who were exempted from deportation, of whom there were 15,632 in April 1943 (ibid. 103). Most but not all of these exemptions were eventually cancelled, and some holders of exemptions went into hiding expecting that they would lose theirs as well. Both Moore and Presser state that the majority of those in hiding were concentrated in Amsterdam, but neither ventures an estimate.

[18] Thus Emmanuel Ringelblum writes: 'In Western Europe, especially in Holland, the Aryan population has hidden Jews on a mass scale', and later that 'Poland has not taken an equal place alongside the Western European countries in rescuing Jews' (*Polish–Jewish Relations*, 246–7).

because of its crude and brutal nature. It was so extreme that there could be no significant native collaboration, thanks to which the Germans, despite a large occupation force, did not in practice have the manpower or the roots among the population to enforce their policies consistently. Nazi rule in Poland therefore degenerated into a state of chaos, in which corruption, criminality, and profiteering flourished. Low wages and meagre rations forced Poles to rely on black marketeering and other illegal activities for survival, while draconian penalties indiscriminately applied made hiding Jews for money no riskier than many other ways of earning a living. Blackmailing Jews, too, was relatively risk-free and more profitable than turning them over for the paltry rewards that were offered. Blackmailers, unless they were themselves police agents, were criminals who preferred not to have dealings with the police; therefore, the threat of denunciation, used to extract money from Jews, was rarely carried out in practice. The betrayal of Jews was also inhibited by the Nazi policy of collective reprisals: Poles who betrayed Jews could also bring down severe penalties on their fellow Poles, often members of their own families, so that even rabid antisemites thought twice about it. Similarly, the Polish 'Blue' police were reluctant to carry out German orders to shoot Jews on sight, since there had been cases of Poles being mistaken for Jews, hence suspects were arrested and subjected to lengthy investigations, with some possibility of being released. In the generally chaotic atmosphere, both Polish and German police could readily be bribed. This not only allowed many Jews to buy their freedom if they were betrayed, but also made mass escape from the ghetto possible. The reclamation of homes from the shrinking ghetto also provided the Jewish fugitives with places to live—unfortunately in a district which would become one of the hardest hit in the 1944 Warsaw uprising.

Apart from Żegota, the Polish underground did little that was directly aimed at helping Jews. Many of its activities, however, benefited the Jews indirectly. Most notably, civil officials working for the underground managed to delay the introduction of German identity documents, the *Kennkarte*, until 1942, and then dragged out the process of issuing them well into 1943. Thus the mass flight of Jews from the ghetto coincided with, and was camouflaged by, the mass registration of the whole Warsaw population. Tens of thousands of forged identity documents could be introduced, for Jews and members of the underground, without arousing suspicion. By contrast, in the Netherlands a collaborationist civil servant devised identity documents that were very difficult to forge, causing the Dutch underground a good deal of trouble and making it hard for Dutch Jews to live 'on the surface'. The 'legalization' branch of the Polish underground, well practised in creating false identities for its own members, made its expertise freely available to those Jews who managed to find it, usually through the aid organizations. The contacts of the Polish underground with London also made possible the transfer of money from the government in exile and Jewish groups abroad, to support the aid effort.

Warsaw's success in hiding such a large number of Jews owes a great deal to the city's role as the centre of Jewish assimilationism in Poland, thanks to which there existed a bridging community of converts and assimilants, especially among the intelligentsia. The assimilated Jews and their Christian friends and family members formed the core group around which the 'secret city' of the Jews on the 'Aryan side' crystallized, with its own underground organizations, networks, and financial resources. This core group, before the war forced into a posture of exceptional solidarity in the face of opposition from antisemites and anti-assimilationist Jews, extended its networks deep into both Polish and Jewish milieux. It was thus able to mobilize a larger group of helpers, as well as to help less assimilated Jews to escape in the last days of the ghetto's existence. It is possible that had the ghetto not been liquidated when it was, some tens of thousands more 'Jewish Jews' might have been able to join their more assimilated relatives in hiding.

If a more general conclusion can be drawn, it is that the fate of Jews in hiding was determined less by the force of native antisemitism in a given country than by the degree of local collaboration with the German authorities and the strength of the local anti-Nazi underground. The programme of native antisemites rarely extended to murder, certainly not systematic murder, unless they were organized for that purpose by the German Nazis. On the other hand, people who collaborated with the Nazis for careerist or other reasons might well be drawn into the killing process, even if they were not antisemites. In the Netherlands there were relatively many collaborators, mostly members of the Dutch Nazi party (Nationaal-socialistise Beweging: NSB) which had some 8 per cent of the vote in pre-war elections. The NSB was not antisemitic and even had some Jewish members before the war. Nevertheless, its members became actively involved in anti-Jewish actions, including the hunt for Jews in hiding. Knowing the language and local conditions, such people were much more adept at ferreting out Jews than the Germans themselves.

In Poland, however, the parties of the extreme right, though they pursued an active anti-Jewish programme of their own, did not co-operate with the Germans. The authorities were forced to rely on the uncertain co-operation of the Polish 'Blue' police, a conscript rather than a volunteer force, and a small number of informers. Blackmailers—with whom corrupt members of the 'Blue' police not infrequently collaborated for their own profit—were a serious hardship for Jews in hiding, but in practice were usually content to extract money from the Jews and rarely made good on threats to denounce them. Neighbours who threatened to denounce Jews also rarely carried out their threats: fearing collective reprisals, they meant only to induce Jews to leave, rather than to cause their deaths. Politically motivated murders of Jews did occur in Warsaw—among the prominent victims were Ludwik Landau and the historian Marceli Handelsman—after the rightist National Armed Forces (Narodowe Siły Zbrojne: NSZ) split in 1944, with the more extreme wing carrying out a vendetta against communists, socialists, liberals, Jewish intellectuals, and their own former leaders. The victims of this campaign were numbered in the dozens rather than the thousands, however. A far larger number of Jews fell victim to antisemitic partisans and peasants in the countryside, but they are not part of this study.

In conclusion, the absence of an organized collaborationist movement in Poland worked in the Jews' favour, at least in Warsaw, to a greater extent than the presence of native antisemitism worked against them; and the powerful political underground worked on balance in the Jews' favour, even as it continued to be perfused with antisemitism and unwilling to accept Jewish members.

Antisemitism was not without its effects, however. The most important effect was psychological. By adding to the terror faced by Jews in hiding and creating an impression of general hostility and great danger, Polish antisemites drove some Jews who had escaped back into the ghetto, dissuaded others from making the attempt, and caused still others to decide upon the desperate gamble of the Hotel Polski. By contributing to the anxiety felt by Jews in hiding, readily betrayed by gesture, face, and voice, antisemites made Jews easy prey for extortionists, blackmailers, Gestapo agents, and informers. Antisemitism clearly cannot be discounted as a negative factor, directly or indirectly costing thousands or even tens of thousands of lives. Whether hundreds of thousands could have been saved, as Ringelblum maintains, is debatable. That would have required mass escapes from the ghettos at a time when they still held large reservoirs of Jewish population, and escape from the ghettos at such an early stage was (as has been shown) not rationally supportable.

Whatever might have been, in the event it is clear that Warsaw was the most important centre of rescue activity, certainly in Poland and probably in the whole of occupied Europe. The city accounted for perhaps a quarter of all Jews in hiding in Poland, whereas it held only one-tenth of the country's pre-war Jewish population. The 27,000 Jews in hiding there also constituted undoubtedly the largest group of its kind in Europe, although reliable studies of other centres have yet to be performed. On the basis of the rough knowledge presently available, Amsterdam was probably second, with perhaps 15,000. In Berlin the number of Jews in hiding is estimated at 5,000.[19]

The most important factors accounting for the city's prominence in relation to the rest of Poland were, first, its role as the centre of the Polish underground, and, secondly, the large size of the city's intelligentsia: it was from this milieu that the bulk of Żegota activists were drawn. Another factor was the presence of a relatively large assimilated Jewish intelligentsia, with good contacts among the Poles. This was the milieu of Dr Berman and many of the ŻKN activists. Those who were rescued,

---

[19] Leonard Gross, *The Last Jews in Berlin* (London, 1982), 147. Gross cites estimates ranging from 2,000 to 9,000 for the number of Jews living illegally in Berlin when it was declared *judenrein* on 19 May 1943. Himmler's estimate was 4,000; the figure cited here is attributed to post-war estimates by the Berlin Jewish community.

however, were also drawn largely from the Jewish intelligentsia and assimilated middle and upper classes. As Helena Merenholc observed: 'The Jewish proletariat was lost'.[20]

Whatever final assessment one makes of the life and death of the Jews on the Aryan side in Warsaw, there can be no doubt that it was a substantial and remarkable phenomenon. It deserves to be better known.

APPENDIX

THE BERMAN ARCHIVE

The Berman Archive consists of the papers of Dr Adolf Berman, chairman of the ŻKN from 1942 to 1945, which were in his personal possession until his death in 1979 and were then donated to the Ghetto Fighters' House (Beit Lohamei Hagetaot: BLHG), near Nahariya, Israel, by his widow, Basia Temkin-Berman.

The archive consists of some eighty file folders, most of which are Dr Berman's personal papers from after the war. There are twelve folders of relevance to the present study of the ŻKN and other wartime matters; these are listed here according to their BLHG file numbers at Beit Lohamei Hagetaot:

301 Letters to Dr Berman from 'Antek' Zuckerman

308 Letters to Dr and Mrs Berman from Emanuel Ringelblum, his wife Judyta, and Marek Passenstein

309 Copies of reports from 'Wacław' (Henryk Woliński) to the Delegatura. Rough notes and typed reports

310 Letters from ŻKN and the Bund to the Delegate. Żegota reports

313 Minutes of meetings of the presidium of Żegota with the Delegate. Pamphlets and leaflets

315 Files on blackmailers: accusatory letters, lists of accused people, notices of sentences carried out against blackmailers clipped from the underground press

324 Two ghetto memoirs by Ber Warm

328 Two memoirs from the ghetto and Pawiak prison by Dr Leon Polisiuk

331 Reports by members of the Polish underground: Captain Grom-Potyka about action at the ghetto walls during the uprising; testimony concerning the rescue of Jews by Father Kazimierz Ptaszek

357 Records of people receiving money from ŻKN: lists of names with amounts received and other information; receipts; partial accounts; copies of letters asking for help; lists of names classified by profession

358 Continuation of BLHG 357

592 Two draft chapters of a book by Berman about the 'Aryan side' (Yiddish, 10 pp.)

All the materials except the last are in Polish.

[20] In conversation with the author.

The Demography of Jews in Hiding

Because these materials are not organized within their file folders, an internal classification scheme was developed for the lists which make up BLHG 357–8, as follows:

List	Description
1	43 entries, undated, signed 'Helena'. Inferentially dated June or July 1944. Entitled 'new'; no significant overlaps
2	Typed register, 329 entries (601 people), with carbon copies. Inferentially dated May–June 1944. Divided into sections with section numbers in roman numerals and numbered entries in each section, as follows:

Sublist (assigned)	Section no.	No. of entries	Marginalia on original	Marginalia on carbon
2.1	—	47	Sm I	Sm IX
2.2	III	14	IV 09	V 09
2.3	IV	27	III Kw	VI Kw
2.4	V	13	01, VI	V 01
2.5	VI	25	T., VI	VII T
2.6	VII	35	X	
2.7	I	42	V	X K
2.8	—	13	IV	IX
		5	III	IX
		22	II	XI
2.9	none	56	VIII	I

The significance of the section numbers and marginal notes is unknown. List 2.9 is headed: 'I request payment for June for:' and is signed 'Edward'

3	1,182 entries (1,388 people). Undated, alphabetical register. Handwriting of Basia Berman. Name and number of people only. Overlap of 300 entries with list 4. Inferentially dated April–June 1944
4	1,059 entries (1,783 people). Undated, alphabetical register. Name, number of people, name of activist, frequently other identifying information (place of origin, age, occupation). Handwriting of Hirsch Wasser. Appears to be a list of people under the care of activists 'Antek', 'Basia', 'Bogusia', 'Danusia'. Inferentially dated April–June 1944
5	Monthly registers of receipts for October 1943–March 1944. Six separate sets of slips (here numbered 5.1–5.6), each signed 'For the presidium of ŻKN, Borowski' (Dr Berman) and dated 14.VI.44; countersigned 'checked by the review committee' with three signatures, also 14.VI.44

5.1   90 entries (171 people), dated October '1933'
5.2   246 entries (436 people), dated November '1933'
5.3   182 entries (254 people), dated December '1933'
5.4   257 entries (459 people), dated January '1934'
5.5   185 entries (330 people), dated February '1934'
5.6   184 entries (329 people), dated March '1934'

To deflect suspicion, dates on receipts and registers were often given as ten years earlier, and amounts were divided by 100 to give the appearance of pre-war (hence pre-inflation) figures. The same system was used by Żegota and the Bund (except that the Bund divided by 10 rather than 100). The system was not always adhered to, as when these lists were signed and dated by the financial review committee. This 'code' of course could not stand even casual scrutiny, but it was hoped that the Germans would not be interested in scraps of paper with Jewish names and appearing to be pre-war records of some kind

6   507 entries (842 people). Undated, alphabetical register. Handwriting of Hirsch Wasser. All but sixty-four entries are also found in list 4

7   Monthly registers of receipts, dated January–June 1944. Only 7.3 has been entered into the database so far. Numbers of entries in other cases are approximate

    7.1   240 entries, dated January 1944
    7.2   160 entries, dated February 1944
    7.3   155 entries, dated March 1944
    7.4   440 entries, dated April 1944
    7.5   200 entries, dated May 1944
    7.6   660 entries, dated June 1944

There is an overlap of sixty-two entries between lists 5.6 and 7.3, both dated March 1944. List 7 is written in pencil on slips of poor-quality paper which has yellowed severely, and has the character of rough notes, with frequent use of abbreviations. Entries are consequently very difficult to decipher and unambiguous identifications often cannot be made

8   Slips with names of recipients arranged according to activist

9   (unassigned)

10   14 entries. Handwriting of 'Antek' Zuckerman, marked 'new'. (Obverse of list 11)

11   97 entries. Handwriting of 'Antek' Zuckerman. Sixty-one overlap with list 2.1, fifty with list 3, twenty-nine with list 4; no other overlaps (reverse of list 10)

12   35 entries. For each: date and place of birth, address, profession, amount received

13   113 entries (201 persons), subdivided into lists numbered I, VI, and VII

    13.1   47 entries. Thirty-one overlap with list 2.7, thirty-two with list 3, fourteen with list 4; no other overlaps

    13.6   32 entries. Nineteen overlap with list 2.5, twenty with list 3; no other significant overlaps

    13.7   34 entries. Twenty-six overlap with list 2.6, thirty with list 3; no other significant overlaps

14   Register of people under the direct care of ŻKK, 145 entries

15–20   Assorted individual activists' lists

21	30 individual receipts
22–32	Assorted notes and jottings
33	Letters asking for assistance

Psychological Problems of Polish Jews who Used Aryan Documents

MARIA EINHORN-SUSUŁOWSKA

No ONE knows exactly how many Jews survived the Nazi occupation of Poland. In comparison to the number murdered, the number who survived is insignificant. Of those Jews who were imprisoned in labour and concentration camps, found temporary refuge in various hiding-places (cellars, attics, etc.), or used false Aryan identification papers, a small percentage survived. This chapter will focus on the last group.

I began my study with an examination of the 1966 Jagiellonian University doctoral dissertation of Krystyna Epstein. From there I moved to interviews with people who had themselves used Aryan identification papers. Here I will draw upon my own experiences, interviews with people who lived through similar experiences, recently published diaries, and Epstein's case-study of twenty-five survivors. As this kind of material does not lend itself to a quantitative examination, my analysis will be more qualitative in nature.

Many towns and cities in occupied Poland were divided into crowded ghettos of displaced Jews and the more fortunate Aryan districts. The Aryan district, the world outside the wall, contained the only 'normal' world in the eyes of the inhabitants of the cramped ghettos. We now know that even this outside world was neither 'normal' nor safe. However, it was at least possible for those living on the outside to 'save lives' within the ghettos. To do this, it was necessary to acquire help from Poles living outside the ghetto. During the occupation help took many forms. Early on it consisted of protecting valuables (furniture, carpets, pictures). With the establishment of the ghettos Poles who were in contact with imprisoned friends provided food and medicine, usually on a voluntary basis.

When it became obvious what was to happen to the ghetto inhabitants, Jews began to flee to Aryan districts. Some Poles provided security and housing to both known and unknown Jews. This kind of help became extremely dangerous to give. A decree of 10 December 1941 prescribed the death penalty for Jews and non-Jews alike who were caught aiding ghetto inhabitants. Despite the danger, this help continued in 1942, aided and encouraged by the establishment of the underground Council to Aid Jews (Żegota). Żegota introduced organized and planned action, from finding housing to providing forged Aryan documents. The number of Jews rescued by the organization and by individual Poles is unknown.

While some Polish Jews survived on forged documents, others remained in hiding without identification papers, unable to leave their hiding-places. These survivors may be divided into two subgroups: first, those living in towns and cities in which they were well known (such as Anne Frank and her family in Amsterdam); and secondly, those who were unfortunate enough to have 'bad appearances' (Semitic features) and little working knowledge of the Polish language. The general conditions of life in hiding may be summed up in the following words: lack of room, poor food, and lack of privacy, or else its opposite—stifling loneliness, constant fear of discovery, awareness of danger to the protectors, and the inevitable horror of 'not knowing'. First-hand accounts are available describing these conditions.

My major objective here concerns the use of Aryan identification papers by Jews. The writer Michał Borwicz, a Polish Jew who had such Aryan documents, wrote in 1968 that 'being in possession of Aryan identification papers became a mania, a dream of all Jews. It meant escaping death.'[1]

Out of the group of twenty-five survivors whom Epstein interviewed, fifteen obtained some sort of documentation, either birth or marriage certificates acquired from friends. Seven survivors bought documentation, two acquired documents from underground Jewish organizations in the ghettos, and one survivor married a Catholic and changed residence. With identification papers such as birth certificates, which Jews could acquire from Catholic priests, one could get an authentic German *Kennkarte*. The card was a valuable identification document because it contained a photograph. It was a prerequisite for registration and employment. It did not guarantee survival, however.

Using Aryan documents successfully meant assuming another identity. This was no easy task. It required not only knowledge of the personal data of the new identity but familiarity with that person's complete biography as well. Sometimes a situation called for the creation of fictitious but plausible biographies. Whichever method was used, it meant the denial of one's own name and life history and the abandonment of one's affiliations, plans, and aspirations. However, as the Israeli writer Aharon Appelfeld has put it, it is impossible to create a new personality or to obliterate the past.[2]

The physical appearance of the person who assumed a new identity was also critical. As already mentioned, almost anyone using false Aryan documentation had to overcome a so-called 'bad' or Semitic appearance. Bleaching one's hair in an attempt to hide its natural colour was commonplace. Dress was also an important issue. Although during the occupation dressing up became rare, the majority

---

[1] Michał Borwicz, *Vies interdits* (Paris, 1969), 8.
[2] Aharon Appelfeld, 'The Plight of the Survivor', in Berel Lang, *Writers and the Holocaust* (New York, 1988), 17.

of survivors interviewed indicated that they focused on remaining 'clean and tidy' for the sake of their protectors.

In addition to appearance, language was a central concern. It was an especially difficult problem for educated people who took on working-class identities. A young woman with a degree in law who worked on a farm describes such a situation. She milked cows, cooked, cleaned, and helped in the fields.

I tried to change myself as much as possible, taking on the personality of a primitive person. I walked hunched over and wore a scarf to hide my black curly hair. When speaking, I used Ukrainian dialects. I attempted, and succeeded, in forgetting my higher education, and imitated peasant behaviour. I was careful not to say anything that would betray my new identity. I expressed general lack of interest and spoke mostly in monosyllables. I was afraid of neither hard work nor death; my only fear was disclosure—that fear, however, helped me survive.[3]

An essential element of successful assimilation was mastering Catholic rituals: prayers and church behaviour. This was especially important in small towns, because membership and participation in the Catholic Church was used as a test of Aryan background. Jack Eisner mentions the advice given: 'You have to learn Catholic prayers by heart, and when you talk to people use expressions such as "Oh Jesus!" and learn everything about our church.'[4] To save lives, this participation was necessary, but it caused moral difficulties for Orthodox Jews.

The use of false Aryan documents created many complicated psychological problems. What happened to human beings who took on the appearance, lifestyle, language, and general behaviour of other human beings? The Jews who used false documentation had no opportunity to be themselves. They had to assume a role day in and day out, never knowing for how long. The audience was ever present. Forgetting the script meant death, not just for the actor but often for friends, protectors, and family as well.

It is impossible to overestimate the mental and psychological damage caused by such a situation. Evidence drawn from occupation diaries supports the notion that many Jews who had Aryan documents voluntarily gave up and returned to the ghettos, knowing this meant death. Among the twenty-five interviewed survivors, there were some who did not return to ghettos only because of family members in hiding.

Assuming a false identity strongly influences one's own sense of identity, which is necessary for retaining one's sense of individuality, continuity, and mental fitness. Specific forms of identity crisis appeared among those living under aliases. The comments of some of the survivors attest to these mental difficulties. 'Sometimes I lost a sense of reality. I couldn't understand why I had to remain in hiding.' 'Sometimes I lost my sense of identity—I wasn't sure who I was.' At times, this identity crisis created lasting 'split personalities'. One of the women said she tried

[3] Interview with unnamed source.   [4] Jack Eisner, *The Survivor* (New York, 1980), 18.

hard to blend into the Aryan group. 'Externally I succeeded. I was, however, always aware of my distinct character'. Erich Fromm wrote in 1966: 'The problem of identity is not, as is commonly thought, only a philosophical problem concerning our mental and sensory mechanism. The necessity of identity stems from the very essence of existence and constitutes the sources of our strongest aspirations.'[5]

The subjects of my own study were people whose central aim was survival. They often risked their own psychological identities in trying to achieve that goal. There is not enough material or evidence to let us clearly understand how such Jews solved this problem. It is important, however, to point it out. Aharon Appelfeld concluded his observations about Holocaust survivors with the view that 'the whole generation has no identity, only the necessity to escape, but you cannot escape from yourself'.[6] The conditions under which the people with false Aryan documents lived destroyed their world-order. 'Illegal life was, for those of us who were used to observing the law, incomprehensible, surpassing our experiences,' writes Stefan Chaskielewicz.[7] Fear of recognition became an element of every day life.

Blackmailing Jews who had false Aryan documents was commonplace. Jews were forced either to pay off the blackmailers or, if that were not possible, to change apartments, towns, or documents and identities. Underground organizations took on these blackmailers, often imposing the ultimate punishment: death. But punishment and identification were impeded by a lack of information.

Another danger was the possibility of being accidentally identified by an acquaintance from before the war. One woman recalled meeting a former maid of her parents, who luckily walked by as if she had not recognized her former employers' daughter. When they met again after the war, the maid explained: 'I pretended not to know Miss ——, because I didn't want her to be afraid. I was so glad she was alive. One of my schoolfriends was upset, because when encountering him in the street I did not stop. "How could you be afraid of me?" he said.'[8]

Of course, there were acquaintances who, in such situations, behaved quite naturally, as if nothing out of the ordinary had happened. Nevertheless, meeting someone who knew you were using a false identity was always a danger that aroused great fear. Living in fear of this risk had psychological effects that became easily discernible. Chaskielewicz said: 'I soon realized, walking around the city, that Jewish people were identifiable not because of appearance but by the uncertainty of their look. Even people with typical Semitic features were not conspicuous if their behaviour remained calm. Self-confidence was indispensable. Existence under a false identity also required masking normal fears caused by everyday occurrences.'[9]

---

[5] Erich Fromm, *The Art of Loving* (New York, 1956), p. x.
[6] Appelfeld, 'The Plight of the Survivor', 31.
[7] Stefan Chaskielewicz, *Ukrywałem się w Warszawie* (Warsaw, 1988), 38.
[8] Interview with unnamed source.
[9] Chaskielewicz, *Ukrywałem się w Warszawie*, 187.

Jews on the 'Aryan side' lived with constant stress and fear. This was influenced by factors such as whether they lived alone or with relatives and what their financial status was. The majority took employment for which they were unqualified, and traded. Often women worked in German homes as maids in exchange for being introduced as wives of Polish officers—officers who were in captivity, abroad, or in the underground army.

Jews who were not required to work and were sometimes part of the underground would spend mornings walking around the city appearing to work or participating in some underground activity. The focus of their efforts was on blending into the environment, not drawing attention to themselves. At times this meant active imitation of the assumed identity. One woman, a doctor, who received identification papers from a nurse she had worked with before the war, took on the characteristics of her former friend while working as a ward attendant and later as a nurse in a different hospital. She lived alone and, apart from getting to and from work, made no other contacts. She did occasionally attend church on Sundays but did not pray. She was calm and diligent at work and learned to consume vodka as her co-workers did. She never read or wrote, in order to conceal her education.

Jews, especially women, used a wide variety of strategies to survive the horrors of hiding and war. The strong will to live was enough for some. Others became so well integrated into their new environment as to remove some of the danger. Some Jews got involved in the care and aid of others to the point that they were able to forget about their own situation and overcome the fear. Others created an imaginary dream world in which they escaped from an incomprehensible reality. They lived under the threat of being recognized; interviewed survivors said the fear was ever present. One woman said she had always been 'conscious that she could die at any moment'. Others reported that they had been sure of their survival, but not how or why this was so. Such attitudes aided morale, but there is no proof that they aided survival. Perhaps they helped create more confidence, which in turn decreased the risk of drawing attention and being recognized.

As already mentioned, there are no data on the number of Jews who survived by using forged documents. No information is available about how many returned to the ghetto, were recognized by the Nazis, or could not handle their false identities. We know, however, that a certain number did survive, so it is worth touching on their lives after the war.

Some survivors reinstated their true identities after 1945, while others kept their false identities. It is difficult to guess whether the latter did so because of the degree of identification (assimilation) or because of the new, post-war conditions. All of the survivors were preoccupied with searching for lost relatives at the end of the war. Another personal tragedy often followed when it became obvious that no other family members had survived. For many interviewed survivors who had been accustomed to large, extended families, their new-found loneliness constituted a major psychological setback. Additional stress was raised by the question 'Why did I survive and they didn't?' Survivors also had tormenting doubts about whether they had done enough to save others, or had done too much to save themselves.

During my interviews, I employed the incomplete sentence technique. Interviewed survivors often formed sentences such as 'My biggest mistake was . . . not to force my family to escape in 1941', or 'The worst thing that happened to me was . . . to outlive my relatives'.

Eysenck's Personal Inventory, which I employed, contains the question 'Do you feel a sense of guilt?'[10] Without knowing why, many respondents answered 'yes'. We might suppose that they referred to their own undeserved luck in surviving. For example, one interviewed woman felt guilty because she survived despite her Semitic appearance while her Aryan-looking siblings died. As Miriam Mariańska and Mordecai Peleg have testified, meeting hungry, ragged, armbanded Jews returning from work also evoked much guilt in Jews using Aryan documents at the time.[11] As the full extent of the Holocaust became apparent, survivors began imagining their relatives in those situations: the transports to the camps, the Nazi liquidation of those who lived through the transports. These pictures, like all pictures of human suffering, increased the sense of guilt and fear. In my opinion, those who survived will never completely eliminate the feeling of guilt. Under examination this feeling is irrational: survivors had been powerless to save relatives. Still, it is among the most lasting damage caused by war, because the death of a family member challenges one's own right to live.

Another specific problem is the survivors' debt of gratitude owed to the people who risked their lives and others' to help hide Jews. Survivors have solved this problem in different ways. Some stayed in close contact with those who helped them; some gave financial support; and some disappeared abroad. The last group has been tormented the most. While shopping in New York once I met a Polish Jewish woman, a shop owner, who was sending a wedding gift to the daughter of the Polish man who had helped her survive by providing her with Aryan documents. She wanted to send the best, most expensive gift, and asked my advice. I learned that she had been assisting her former helpers from the moment she had settled in the United States. Hers was one of the most effective ways of dealing with the debt of gratitude. Yad Vashem's awards to 'righteous gentiles' are a beautiful way of showing gratitude to those who risked so much to help the Jews. Poles who are given this award are very proud and appreciative, and moved to have received it in Israel.

Some of the interviewed survivors, mostly the younger ones, indicated a loss of motivation immediately after the war, a feeling of powerlessness, and a lack of

---

[10] Personal Inventory, in Hans Eysenck, *The Scientific Study of Personality* (London, 1952), 36.
[11] Miriam Peleg-Mariańska and Mordecai Peleg, *Witnesses: Life in Occupied Kraków* (London, 1991).

concern about education or work. The majority, however, returned to work with energy and enthusiasm. Their attempt to re-create a normal life might be described as too passionate. The sudden absence of the various compulsory limitations imposed by being in hiding was the major reason for starting an active life, although we should not forget the desire to escape accompanying feelings of guilt and loneliness. Between three and five years after the war many survivors still experienced intense exhaustion and assorted other maladies. This may have been a deferred psychological reaction to their experiences.

One important question is whether the period of 'being someone else' had a lasting influence on the personalities of those assuming false identities. Many data exist on this issue. All interviewees answered this question: there was indeed a lasting change in their attitudes towards other people as well as a change in their moods, aims, and hierarchy of values. A change in attitude towards others was mentioned most frequently. 'I became mistrustful; I counted only on myself; I became reserved,' said one. Another said she lost all illusions of the goodness of people and relied only on herself: 'When there is danger, there are no friends.' Some survivors expressed deep distrust, caution, reserve, and bitterness, while others showed extreme forbearance, tolerance, gentleness, willingness to help others, and a sense of connectedness. A few survivors acquired milder, more tolerant attitudes, but the majority became distrustful and closed. The number of interviewees was insufficient to establish a pattern for these changes. It was noticeable, however, that bitterness and preference for isolation was characteristic primarily of those who had encountered blackmailers (*szmalcownicy*).

One of the interviewed survivors told of her strong emotional reaction to hearing the word 'Jew'. Another pointed out that after the war she had become reserved and quick-tempered at the same time. She was very unhappy and wondered if a secure place in the world existed for her. She journeyed to Israel and then back to Poland, but everywhere she felt the same. Some interviewed survivors were tormented by an obsession with war and were overcome by a desire to achieve financial security, to live without having to do humiliating work, or by a constant wish to escape for the sake of their children.

The care of children became very important in the survivor value system. Some survivors indicated desires to save children from the poverty and hardships they had experienced. Others concentrated on their own children's well-being. The fear that survivors had felt during the war was now focused on their children. One wanted to avoid having children so that they would not have to experience what she had been through. Another woman hid from her son the fact that he was Jewish.

Although rare, positive influences can also be found. One interviewee claimed that war experiences, hardening him, had made him strong and unafraid. He constructed his own value system. Life became the most important thing, not material goods or money. He tried not to take anything from anyone—an attempt to eliminate debts of gratitude—and learned to count on himself.

It is worth stressing that even the most reserved, bitter survivors spoke with kindness and appreciation about those who helped them. It is also significant that the survivors talked of their helpers as individuals, always separating them from the rest of humanity, whom they viewed with suspicion. In evaluating other people, survivors learned to value kindheartedness, generosity, and straightforwardness. Most of all, they valued people who were reliable in difficult situations, placing less value on intellect.

I would like to conclude by mentioning the nightmares experienced by all interviewed survivors. Just as the concentration camp survivors dreamed of camp scenes that symbolized fear, survivors who had remained in hiding using Aryan documents also dreamed scenes symbolizing subconscious feelings of dangers (bunkers, escapes, shootings).

My own nightmares, which first appeared during the war, are characteristic. I constantly dreamed that I had lost my purse, which contained my identity documents. This caused great despair—how to get new documents? The purses always changed: sometimes the dream bag was like one I had actually owned, sometimes not, although the content of the dream and the accompanying fear were the same. This recurring dream stayed with me for several years after the war, then ended. It reappeared again in 1969, a period of discrimination against Jews in Poland. Today, the dream represents moments of extreme stress in my life, returning with new problems that generate fear.

With the acceptance of Freud's thesis regarding the relationship between the subconscious and dreams, we also accept the deep and lasting effect of war experiences on Jews who hid with Aryan documents. I think these survivors are similar to people who suffer the so-called K-2 syndrome, with the concomitant changes in personality and nightmares.

Does the analysis of the material presented here allow us to make some generalizations about the examined group? I think not. Everyone coped with their problems and organized their lives differently. They shared the external situation, a state of permanent danger, with lasting effects—not all the same, but impossible to ignore.

My Two Mothers

ELŻBIETA FICOWSKA

I BELONG to the youngest generation of survivors. I was one of those who was born only to die, one of those from whom the right to live was taken away in earliest infancy. I am here today, so many years later, through an act of love. It was a goodness that knew no fear, a goodness that dared to be itself at a time when evil was triumphant and bestiality went unpunished.

Every one of us who was spared—so few among the countless masses of the murdered—owes his or her life to someone else's help, to someone else's self-sacrifice, to an active refusal to countenance the death of innocents to which we were condemned.

I did not know then, I could not know, how much self-denial, how much heroism, was needed just to provide a roof over my head. I did not know then, but I have since learned, that there are two ways to extend a hand: one is as a fist and the other as an open palm offering help. My mothers chose the second way, my Jewish mother, who gave me life, and my Polish mother, who saved that life.

Both accomplished something that went beyond ordinary humanity. To save me in the nightmarish days of July 1942 my Jewish mother endured the pain of giving up her only child to Żegota, a Polish organization that provided help to dying Jews. Through this organization I was placed in less threatening hands, hands that at first had seemed alien but did not turn out so. My Polish mother fulfilled the deepest desires of my Jewish mother. She conquered her own fear to save me, showering great love on me to take the place of the one who brought me into the world and who was soon to leave it.

Although I was too small to remember her clearly, I will never forget my Jewish mother. I cannot even recognize her face in a photograph, but I see her in my dreams. Both my dead mothers are with me and will remain with me to the end. Their presence reminds me that there is nothing more destructive than hatred and nothing more blessed than human goodness. As far as my limited strength allows, I have tried to be faithful to this truth, never accepting enmity between people and nations, never acquiescing in that contempt that sometimes is manifested through clenched fists.

This is what both my mothers taught me: my Jewish and Polish mothers. It is this deep faith, this mission, which I feel bold enough to pass on to the compatriots of both my life-giving mothers.

Translated from Polish by Gwido Zlatkes

Early Swedish Information about the Nazis' Mass Murder of the Jews

JÓZEF LEWANDOWSKI

EVERY state tries to keep information secret that, if revealed, could harm it or reduce the advantage it receives from having exclusive access to such information. In totalitarian states the blocking of information is a working principle. The totalitarian system and the free exchange of information are fundamentally contradictory. The actions of totalitarian states are of a criminal nature; therefore, such states try to prevent information about their activities from becoming public knowledge. In such systems information is blocked off both externally, from other countries, and internally, from their own societies. Various means can be employed to achieve this end, such as censoring the press and correspondence, making citizens' contact with foreigners difficult or impossible, and sealing the borders—all of these enforced by a police endowed with extraordinary power and a cruel penal system. That is why a substantial part of the study of Nazi Germany is preoccupied with the problem of information, of what the world knew and didn't know. Researchers have sought to examine to what extent knowledge informed not only official structures but also individuals and societies. These enquiries have not led to common conclusions. It appears that the meaning of 'being informed' is flexible. In many cases, perhaps even in general, people knew exactly as much as they wanted: only some facts were recognized and internalized; others were rejected. Knowledge depended on the questions asked and on sensitivity towards key issues.

In Hitler's Germany the blocking of information increased gradually. During the first years of the totalitarian regime the world was relatively well informed about what was going on under the rule of Hitler and the Gestapo. In fact, before 1939 the Nazis were unable to introduce an information barrier. They persecuted people for describing the facts and for propaganda that they claimed to be slanderous, but they themselves acted in a fairly open manner, even boldly, and they publicized their actions. Only matters concerning decision-making by the Third Reich were hidden from the world (although certain materials indicate that some shrewd observers could precisely predict Hitler's successive moves on the basis of their knowledge of Nazi ideology and its execution). At that time it was also hard

The first draft of this chapter was published in *Biuletyn Żydowskiego Instytutu Historycznego*, 164/4 (1992).

to hide knowledge of goings-on in Germany. Until the war started, all countries maintained diplomatic agencies there. There was also a network of consular offices, and among the foreign press correspondents were outstanding journalists. If they failed to know, it was because they did not ask questions in the face of reality. Another factor impeding an early blocking out of information was the permeability of the borders. Exiles were an important source of information about the Third Reich. In addition, the inherited German state apparatus worked according to old legalistic habits, and it absorbed the Nazi philosophy of state slowly and not without resistance.

The principal change came with the outbreak of the Second World War. Diplomatic and consular agencies and journalists from the Allied countries disappeared from Germany, although the many neutral agencies remained in place. More importantly, the representatives of foreign countries were prohibited from remaining in the territory of conquered Poland, which was where the Nazis first applied on a large scale their plans for the genetic reorganization of the lands they had conquered. It was here that the Nazis intensified their persecution of the Jewish population they found under their control. From the summer of 1941 they began to implement their genocidal programmes, which had been planned as part of their invasion of the Soviet Union.

A fair amount of research has been devoted to the question of when and how the outside world came to know about this genocide. In Sweden there has been considerable public and private debate on this question centred on a document from August 1942, known as the Vendel Report, which contains a description of the situation in Germany and in German-occupied Poland.

Karl Yngve Vendel, a 45-year-old officer of the Swedish consular corps, was transferred in January 1940 from Holland and appointed as consul in Stettin. The consulate was only partly intended to take care of Swedes in the area and deal with trade relations, for, as Vendel wrote several years later, 'There were hardly any strictly consular matters.'[1] Vendel's principal assignment was to gather intelligence. Sweden feared German aggression, a justified fear, for only several months later Germany was to attack Denmark and Norway and conquer them easily.

Vendel's tasks and methods were fairly simple: he watched ports and roads to see if the Germans were regrouping their military force in a way that endangered Sweden. Such work was a standard part of consular work. Vendel's activity was effective, as was acknowledged years later in Swedish specialist publications.[2] The consul had been informed in time of the preparations for the attack against Norway in the spring of 1940, and, a year later, about the invasion of the USSR. (That this information was not used is a completely different matter.) Vendel asked many different questions, and was extremely well informed. In addition,

---

[1] Karl Yngve Vendel, legatory councillor emeritus, 'Var Sverige hotat under andra världskriget?', *Effektivt Försvar: Fritt Militärt Forum*, 5 (1965), 386.

[2] Editorial, 'Undensk personalpolitik', *Effektivt Försvar: Fritt Militärt Forum*, 6 (1965), 441.

although the German police probably were aware of the nature of his activity, he made many acquaintances and friends in Nazi official circles, as well as outside them. The Vendel Report is the result of one of these friendships.

On 9 August 1942 Vendel went to visit some German friends at their estate in east Prussia. He stayed there until 13 or 14 August, and then he returned, not to Stettin but to the embassy in Berlin. There he wrote a report of what he had seen and heard during his trip. The top-secret report, dated 20 August, consists of seven large pages. Two days after its writing it was sent to Stockholm. The councillor of the legation, Erik von Post, provided a covering letter:

> I respectfully send this *pro memoria*, in which Vendel summarizes his impressions from his conversations with various people met by him primarily during his trip to eastern Germany undertaken with the permission of Richert.[3] Enclosed in this memorandum is the description, which is based on the conversation [with a person] close to the former minister of agriculture, Mr Darré, about the conflict between Himmler and Darré. This conflict was the primary cause of the latter's fall. I stress that the version depicted there corresponds exactly to the information acquired by the embassy earlier from the circles of the SS (compare Richert's letter to Söderblom of 8 July). Vendel relates also what he learned about the conditions in the General Government; about statements by Ribbentrop; about the situation on large estates in the east, etc.
>
> Yours,
> ERIK VON POST[4]

The first two pages are indeed devoted to 'dirty politics' among the Nazi dignitaries. But Vendel did not stop there. As the narration progresses, the report deals with more and more important matters. Vendel writes:

> The above record gives a frightening picture of the relations within the government of the Reich; it confirms the past year's fear among wide military circles, also shared in the industrial ones: that the leadership of Great Germany is slipping more and more into the hands of Mr Himmler and his horrific organization, the SS.

He continues:

> It is well known that Mr Himmler has publicly stated that the new policy of settlement in the east is ruled by *new* principles; the old German settlement policy based on imposing German customs on the indigenous population has failed. In accordance with the new methods of settlement, cultivation of the land would be entrusted only to the German race. In other words, through Himmler's settlement project the theory of the master race and its slaves would be implemented. In this respect, Mr Himmler serves as a tool for Hitler. I bring to your attention the speech by Foreign Minister von Ribbentrop that I referred you to about a year ago. Answering the question about German cruelties in Poland, and whether such conduct could be excused, Ribbentrop said that it was impossible to evaluate Hitler's projects at this time. Only in fifty years would the first fruits of his actions appear, and in some hundred years there would not be any Polish problem at all! *Ausrotten* [uproot] and

---

[3] Arvid Richert was the Swedish ambassador in Berlin.
[4] Riksarkivet Stockholm, HP 324–84.

vernichten [annihilate]: these two words belonging to the National Socialist terminology are used particularly often, and put into practice with ruthlessness and brutality that is unheard of. Mr Himmler's activity on Polish territories provides us with the most terrifying examples of his settlement methods.

The conditions in the General Government are much worse than in any other occupied territory. The most obvious question one must constantly ask oneself is on what and how the population manages to live, especially in the towns. On the one hand, the rations received by Poles (640 calories a day, i.e. one-fourth the needs of an adult) are so small that, with the passage of time, people would have to die of hunger. But on the other hand, symptoms of mass malnutrition cannot be seen, although from time to time one sees hungry people, especially children. Apparently, the majority of the population can still procure the food necessary to live. It is possible partially because everybody participates in secret trade, and partially because of the selling of all goods and things to get food. As in Germany after the last war, there are in Poland clear symptoms of inflation. There is extreme poverty on one side, and on the other there are war profiteers with large funds. Clerks with fixed incomes must take bribes in order to survive. According to the person to whom I spoke, and who studied the conditions in the General Government for several months, the opinion 'Die Juden haben alles' is often heard.[5] If we consider the immense poverty in the Jewish quarters of different towns, we have to say that this statement applies only to a handful of the Jews who are still well off. As a matter of fact, the statement should say, 'Durch die Juden kann man alle haben, die Juden beschaffen alles.'[6] Owing to the old connections with producers and farmers who are accustomed to doing business with the Jews, there still are possibilities for acquiring otherwise unobtainable goods.

There was an attempt to put the entire distribution of produce in the General Government under control and to organize a system of coupons to provide for the needs of the population at a minimum level, but despite many efforts this project completely failed. Lack of transportation makes distributing even the stored stocks difficult, not to say impossible.

Supplying the cities, particularly Warsaw, with fats, milk, and eggs is carried out exclusively by illegal trade. Prices have risen excessively. For example, the person to whom I spoke presented me with data from spring 1942 in Kraków:

Bread, 1 kilogram: 16–19 zlotys
One egg: 1.10 zlotys
Butter, 1 kilogram: 50 zlotys
Milk, 1 litre: 4 zlotys
Pork, 1 kilogram: 50 zlotys
Coffee, 1 kilogram: 625 zlotys
Sugar, 1 kilogram: 55 zlotys (before the war: 1 zloty)

The exchange rate has not changed for the Germans: 1 German mark equals 2 zlotys. As for salaries, for example, in Kraków and Warsaw a German office clerk earns 1,500–2,000 zlotys monthly, and a typist 800–1,000 zlotys. The salaries of Poles are completely different. A typist gets only 120–400 zlotys. To provide his food needs, a Pole has at his disposal mainly the 'black market'. The prices are determined by bread: for example, in Kraków a

---

[5] 'The Jews have everything.'
[6] 'Through the Jews you can get everything, the Jews can obtain everything.'

kilogram costs 16–18 zlotys. These data portray how terrible the situation of the Polish population is, especially in towns. To overcome the scarcity of food, a system of bonuses has been introduced, by which the Germans try to encourage the farmers to produce more, and to deliver their produce to purchasing centres. Whether this can generate improvements the person to whom I spoke was unable to say.

This account of the situation of the Polish population in the General Government is equally objective and frightening, even if limited to only one aspect of the economic situation, the food supply. Vendel does not mention murder, violence, terror, or robbery; nor is the Polish resistance discussed, either civil or military. The account is by someone who is sympathetic to the Poles but has not had real contact with them, and therefore perceives the reality as though through glass, without actual contact. He does not describe how the Poles live; he cannot imagine it. He only expresses his amazement at how they can be subjected to the organized hunger and survive at all. We can see that he takes at face value the information about attempts to take precautions against hunger. It is possible that whoever served as the author's source of information wanted to appear to him as a decent person. Let us also note as important for our purposes the use of such terms as 'inflation', a word which at that time was not at all current among the Poles, and the comparison between the situation in Poland and the situation in post-First World War Germany, which would hardly have been likely to cross the mind of a Pole.

The account that Vendel had passed on is true and honest. It speaks well for the German who portrayed the situation to him. This German undoubtedly opposed Nazism. Moreover, in the conflict between the Nazis and the Poles he took the side of the persecuted and hunger-plagued Poles. Still, the information is hardly a revelation: Polish organized resistance had accurate data (even more accurate than Vendel's) and had been sending it through its network to the government in exile of the republic of Poland in London. In other words, the part of the report quoted above is an important source for the history of Germany; however, it was not a discovery that could have inspired international discussion at the time. Such discussion could have been evoked by the following paragraph:

The treatment of the Jews, as described by the person to whom I spoke, is of the kind that is impossible to express in writing. That is why I limit myself to a few brief pieces of information. The treatment differs in different locations, depending on the number of Jews. In some cities there are Jewish quarters; in others there are ghettos surrounded by high walls, which Jews can trespass only at the risk of being shot; finally, in some others Jews enjoy some freedom of movement. Nevertheless, the aim is the extinction of them all. The number of Jews murdered in Lublin is estimated at 40,000. The Jews over fifty years of age and children under ten are especially subjected to extermination. The rest are left alive in order to fill the gap in the workforce; they will be exterminated as soon as they are no longer useful. Their property is confiscated; it mostly falls into the hands of SS men. In the cities all Jews are gathered; they are officially informed that it is for the purpose of 'delousing'. At the entrance they have to leave their clothes, which are immediately sent to a 'central warehouse of textile materials'. Delousing is in practice gassing, after which all are packed into previously prepared mass graves. The source from whom I received all the information about the conditions in the General Government is such that there can be no shadow of a doubt that his description is true.

This account was one of the first revelations of the scale of the Nazi genocide to be sent to the West. It was sent three months before the arrival in the West of Jan Kozielecki-Karski, the courier of the Polish resistance, and also pre-dated the dispatches of Gerhart Riegner from Geneva. The account was truthful, yet it was incomplete. For example, the source knew about burying the corpses of people who had been gassed as in Bełżec, but not about burning them, as in Treblinka or Auschwitz. But even more important than the information about murdering the Jews is the statement, which Vendel did not doubt, that the murder of Jews did not have the casual character of ordinary war cruelties but that its goal was to kill all Jews who fell into German hands.

Let us note Vendel's emotional attitude towards the information he transmitted. In the last sentence of the paragraph quoted above he states that the person who gave the account deserved complete trust and was undoubtedly competent. Vendel does not mention the name in his report, as that would have been too dangerous. But he would not have refused to reveal his source if his superiors had asked. Besides, the head of the Berlin post, Ambassador Arvid Richert, knew whom Vendel visited in eastern Prussia, and why. In other words, Vendel demanded that his report be treated seriously in this principal point.

We can summarize the rest of Vendel's report. It contains information of a more 'routine' character, if such a word can apply to news concerning the Third Reich. In it we read about the expulsion of Poles from the 'former Polish Corridor'[7] and the resettlement there of Germans from Bessarabia, and about conscription into the Wehrmacht of the Poles who declared themselves ethnic Germans and their deployment to the front.[8] This last fact cooled the readiness of Poles to sign the *Volksliste*: 'The Poles prefer to bear their national sign "P", a bond that in the present time ties all Polish elements more strongly than ever, rather than allow themselves to be naturalized.' Then we read this: 'During my week-long stay in the region of the Mazurian lakes in eastern Prussia, where in the very same neighbourhood as the headquarters there are the quarters of the foreign minister and his staff, I again had the opportunity to meet the people who have intimate contacts with the headquarters.' We do not know who these were, but they certainly could not have been unimportant from the point of view of intelligence, since Vendel repeated Ribbentrop's outpourings about the planned Japanese attack against Vladivostok, the future location of Hitler's headquarters, the

---

[7] Germany's demand for a corridor linking Germany proper with eastern Prussia was one of its pretexts for starting the war.

[8] In the territories incorporated into Germany in 1939 the Poles were forced to declare their German nationality by signing the so-called *Volksliste*.

prospects and premises of the German summer offensive, and the condition of supplies in Germany, including oil and rubber. Then details follow about the situation in agriculture, the living conditions of forced labourers (i.e. the Poles and the Soviet prisoners of war), the supplying of German cities, etc. The last page presents Vendel's observations made in Sopot and Gdynia. He noticed the testing of new raiding ships capable of transporting tanks and trucks. We know that for Vendel's superiors this was important information because Sweden still feared aggression. In the summer of 1942 Germany was at the height of its success, and it could afford to attack vulnerable Sweden, which was surrounded by German armies, stationed also in Finland.

In the last paragraph of his report Vendel describes his meeting with an industrialist (recall that Vendel mentions contacts in both military and industrial circles) from the Ruhr, who informed him of the mood there. The industrialist was anti-Nazi. He assured Vendel emphatically, although not necessarily in full accord with the truth, that 'in the entire Ruhr region there is no one who believes in German victory'.

Vendel's report was brought to light by Steven Koblik, an American scholar of Swedish history and the author of a study of the attitude of Sweden towards the Jewish problem in the years 1933–45.[9] The Vendel document had been in the hands of historians before, especially those who worked during the 1970s on the huge project 'Sweden during the Second World War', but they did not pay attention to it. Incidentally, Vendel himself, even before it was brought to light, had described his report in his article mentioned earlier, accurately evaluating the hierarchy of facts and events; he emphasized the paragraph about the Holocaust, and quoted the whole of it.

Koblik's monograph excited much discussion in Sweden, but generally not in the public forum. Vendel's had been one of the first reports not of Nazi cruelties and crimes (such details had been available even earlier) but of the Holocaust, which was in progress not far from Sweden. It should have sounded the alarm, as everybody would agree now. But it did not. Vendel's report was understood in Stockholm, and it was made known to the leaders in the ministry and to the prime minister, whose signatures appear on one copy of it. Nevertheless, it remained hidden from the world. In the discussion started by Koblik the focal point was the responsibility of respected, humanitarian Swedish politicians and diplomats for their silence in the face of the crime, or even more for the way they hid it. This was not the first such discussion in Sweden. Others like it had surfaced from time to time ever since the end of the war. And they had cited not only Vendel's report but also the 1942 conversation between Kurt Gerstein and Swedish attaché von Otter.[10]

---

[9] Steven Koblik, *The Stones Cry Out* (New York, 1987); pub. in Swedish as *Om vi teg, skulle stenarna ropa* (Stockholm, 1987).

[10] After receiving some unspecified signals, Kurt Gerstein, a chemist, joined the SS in order to uncover the crime. He obtained direct evidence of genocide. He tried to alert the world, but in vain. The

Investigating the document, Koblik asked the question: Why, in spite of their high-flown phrases, did Swedish leadership, aware of the Nazi crime of genocide, conceal Vendel's report as well as other reliable testimonies? His answer, well balanced and based on almost every possible consideration, including Sweden's strategic situation, is devastating from an ethical point of view. However, he did not ask such questions as how the report came into existence, who spoke with Vendel, and why they gave him their information.

These questions are intriguing. Who were the people with whom Vendel spoke, and why would they talk to a representative of a foreign country? Did they only pour out their emotions, or did they have some aim, and if so, what? Where in eastern Prussia, close to Hitler's headquarters, did this conversation take place, and why there and not in Berlin or Stettin? Did the people realize that Vendel was in Germany on a confidential mission? Did they talk to him despite their awareness that he would write a report, or was it rather precisely because they knew that he would pass on their information?

Some conclusions can be drawn on the basis of the report itself, especially if we compare it with the earlier ones he wrote. It appears that Vendel was friendly with a Prussian junker (a big landowner), who possessed a large property in eastern Prussia. That was why agriculture and the connections in the ministry of agriculture come up so often in his reports. Vendel spent that particular week with the man's family somewhere near Hitler's quarters in Rastenburg. Certainly, the junker families of eastern Prussia were not lacking in outstanding personalities, and the names of more than one individual among them who opposed Nazism spring to mind.

I set out to learn whom Vendel visited that week and to whom he talked. My search followed two paths. First I tried to find Vendel or his descendants. Regretfully, I learned that Vendel himself had died in 1980 at the age of 85. In the registry of the inheritance court I discovered that he left no direct descendants, and his more distant relatives could probably not tell me much. Thus the first path reached a dead end.

So I turned, as a second possibility, to the archives of the foreign ministry in Stockholm. The archivist, Sven Johansson, granted me help far beyond my limited expectations. Not only did he tell me everything he knew about the report and its author, but he also found out that the name of the estate visited by Vendel was (until the end of the war) Gross Steinort. Its owner was Count Heinrich von Lehndorff, a reserve lieutenant, at that time in the Heeresgruppe Mitte. This

papal nuncio in Berlin, Archbishop Orsenigo, simply showed him the door when he tried to relate what was going on in extermination camps. On 22 Aug. 1942, two days after the date of Vendel's report, Gerstein met the attaché of the Swedish embassy, Otter, in the train from Warsaw to Berlin. He not only presented him with a detailed account but also showed documents proving the crime. It has been claimed that Otter made a report of this but somehow it got lost. Scholars and archivists doubt whether such a report was presented at all. See Walter Laqueur, *The Terrible Secret* (London, 1980).

information is reliable and concrete: Johansson found an official letter from 1951 in which Vendel openly wrote about 'the tragic fate of my contact in the German headquarters, Count Lehndorff'.

Lehndorff and Gross Steinort played well-known roles in the history of the war. Heinrich von Lehndorff was one of the leading figures in the anti-Nazi conspiracy known as the Generals' Plot. It was also from here, from Gross Steinort, that Count Claus von Stauffenberg was delegated to perform the failed attempt to assassinate Hitler on 20 July 1944. Moreover, Lehndorff was instrumental in the last contact between Stauffenberg and the leader of the conspiracy, General Henning von Tresckow. In Gross Steinort Lehndorff passed on to Stauffenberg the words of Tresckow that 'the assassination must be carried out no matter what. The attempt must be undertaken even if it fails. Now the point is not so much the practical goal as in showing the world that the German resistance has the courage to risk the life [of its people]. Compared to this, everything else is less important.'

The available literature expresses high regard for Lehndorff, but it did not introduce anything new into my investigation. Fabian von Schlabrendorff, one of the few participants in the assassination conspiracy who survived and whose memoirs constitute the canon of knowledge about the organization and its people, apparently met Lehndorff late, only after August 1942.[11] There may also be other reasons why Lehndorff remained in the shade. It seems he was especially trusted by Tresckow and acted out a double conspiracy: first, because he lived near Hitler's headquarters and his estate had been considered the base for the assassination all along, and secondly, because he had contacts with the outside world—that is, contacts with Vendel.

Vendel mentioned Lehndorff as his contact in the headquarters. This description is naturally given in the language of intelligence, with a certain rationale behind it. However, investigating Vendel's reports more closely may yield the opposite conclusion: that, in fact, it was the conspirators who tried, through Vendel, to establish contacts abroad and overcome the information barrier. Very few Germans maintained contacts with the outside world in 1942, and that was why even isolated citizens of foreign countries, or the rare official representatives of these countries, would have been especially valued.

Whether it was Lehndorff who found Vendel or vice versa is unclear, but it is not very important: they needed each other. The reports indicate that for a certain time Lehndorff tested Vendel, probing whether he could be trusted and to what extent. At first he told him things that were attractive from an intelligence standpoint and risky for anyone who revealed them, but that still fell within the framework of glorified gossip. In the case of Vendel's possible indiscretion or disloyalty

---

[11] Above all, see the memoir documentary book by a participant in the conspiracy: Fabian von Schlabrendorff, *Offiziere gegen Hitler*, ed. Gero von Gaevernitz (Zurich, 1946). Also see Peter Hoffmann, *Widerstand, Staatsstreich, Attentat. Der Kampf der Opposition gegen Hitler* (Munich, 1969).

(which undoubtedly was Lehndorff's concern), such items would not have caused the unmasking of the conspiracy.

Another question arises. Why did Lehndorff, who had frequent meetings with the Swedish consul in Stettin, not divulge his knowledge during one of them, and why did Vendel have to go all the way to the Rastenburg area? The neighbourhood of Hitler's field quarters and command post was heavily guarded. Access was difficult, and the area was under special police protection. It would have been practically impossible for Vendel to go there by train or in his own car. He was probably delivered in the car of one of the generals, a vehicle that would not have aroused the inquisitiveness of the police. If such steps were undertaken, it was probably not just for theatrical effect. Then why?

Everything seems to indicate that during this week-long stay close to Hitler's 'Wolf's Lair', Vendel met not only Lehndorff. Erik von Post alludes to this in his covering letter. But the names of those whom Vendel met were buried with him, and all we have left is deduction. Nevertheless, an attempt can be made to establish their names. Sven Johansson holds that the people from both military and civilian circles who were involved in the plot and visited Gross Steinort should be considered: the host's father-in-law, Colonel von Mellenthin; Fabian von Schlabrendorff; General Henning von Tresckow; diplomat Hasso von Etzdorf; and General Hans Oster.

Are these the individuals Vendel met, and did the information he received come from them? We can rule out Schlabrendorff. If he had given Vendel the information about the Holocaust, or if he had known that such information was given, he would undoubtedly have written about it in his book, especially as he was sensitive to the issue of the murder of Jews. For different reasons, we should also exclude General Oster, who was a deputy of Admiral Canaris, the head of military intelligence. He had his own channels for sending information to the West; they were at a higher level and therefore probably more efficient. Was it then one of the remaining ones?

The information that Vendel passed on to Stockholm undoubtedly came from a *German* source. This is clear not only because Vendel himself said so, but also because both Polish and Jewish tragedies were portrayed through the eyes of an outside observer. In all of Vendel's reports I have found no trace of a Polish or Jewish contact. If he had information from Polish or Jewish sources, he would probably have considered it too partial and only credible to a limited extent. He would not have characterized Polish or Jewish sources as trustworthy in every respect.

Vendel had a lot of confidence in his host, but probably not enough for him to write about Lehndorff that 'the source from which I received all the information about the conditions in the General Government is such that there cannot be a shadow of a doubt that his description is true'. Besides, Lehndorff did not have to drag him to Gross Steinort. He had contacted Vendel earlier and they had had meetings in both Stettin and Berlin.

Until new data should undermine my hypothesis, I think that the mysterious person for whom Vendel undertook his adventurous and risky trip to the Rastenburg area, the trip that required approval from the head of the Swedish diplomatic agency, was the first officer in the staff of the Heeresgruppe Mitte: General Henning von Tresckow.

According to the opinion of both his contemporaries and historians of today, Tresckow was the spiritual father of the conspiracy. He was an outstanding general, one of the best in the German army, which abounded with extraordinarily talented officers. This factor, together with Tresckow's personal charm and persuasive skills, made generals who were even higher ranked than he in the army hierarchy willingly admit his intellectual and organizational leadership.

Tresckow was Lehndorff's superior, both in the army and in the conspiracy. It is impossible to believe that Lehndorff, his most trusted and loyal collaborator, would maintain risky contacts with Vendel without Tresckow's knowledge and approval. Therefore, Tresckow was almost certainly involved in passing on the information about the Holocaust.

Why do I think it was he who talked to Vendel? First of all, because Vendel's report is so sophisticated in its presentation. Everything indicates that the report follows the structure of the information he received in Gross Steinort. The source did not want to estrange the recipients with the harsh and off-putting facts. The world was not yet prepared for the bare truth of the Holocaust. Recall the reserve that greeted Jan Karski, a courier from Warsaw and a witness to the Holocaust, when he told the leaders of the anti-Nazi coalition what he had seen and heard.

Whoever spoke to Vendel understood this. Most likely for this reason, the communication starts with gossip. What could attract a diplomatic reader more than gossip? Posterity might disregard it as banal, but contemporaries never would! After the gossip comes the statement that Himmler has more and more power. He had probably always had tremendous power, but this statement prepares the listener for further information. Until now the world could tolerate Nazism, suggests the speaker, but it is now becoming ever more dangerous. While neutrality has its justifications, from this point on it is impossible. Then follow the details about hunger in the General Government, almost obvious and consistent with what had already been known in Stockholm; none the less, this information was formulated very cautiously: no hungry people could be seen on the streets, the German authorities were trying their best. Only after this is the crucial fact revealed, the one for which the trip of the Swedish consul and the meeting had been arranged: the information about the Holocaust. Vendel's document displays, in fact, a high-quality art of dialectics and great understanding of the reluctance to accept such horrifying news.

One further argument supports the Tresckow hypothesis: a surprising number of stock-exchange terms are employed in the report's descriptions of the economic conditions. Such terms were hardly applicable to the situation in the General

Government. And for some years after the end of the First World War Henning von Tresckow had been a stockbroker in Berlin.

The whole course of the report testifies to a sense of logic and a good knowledge of the faulty human psyche. Tresckow's contemporaries agreed that unlike other German high officers, preoccupied only with military matters, he was a man of broad horizons. It has been claimed that his way of thinking more resembled a philosopher's than a simple staff officer's. He was made aware of the murder of the Jews even earlier: in the autumn of 1941 he had been a witness when the specially dispatched SS men murdered the Jews of the German-captured town Borysov in Belarus. Breaking the rules of conspiracy, Tresckow then led a protest, almost a mutiny, of the staff officers in the group of the Heeresgruppe Mitte.

Whatever the judgement of history will be regarding the problem of identifying who spoke to Vendel—or who gathered these materials, for these did not have to be the same individuals—the more important task seems to be to find out the purpose for which they did it. Certainly, the information would not have been relayed just so that Swedish intelligence would know. That would not have justified dragging Vendel to Gross Steinort and having him meet the leaders of the conspiracy. The aim was different—it was clearly to alert the world.

I will not attempt to present the attitude of the conspirators towards the Jewish question. The materials indicate that there were diverse opinions within this circle. There had to be differences between Dietrich Bonhöffer and Karl Goerdeler, not to mention the generals. Most of the conspirators came from aristocratic families embodying the caste system. It is thus more to their credit that they felt obliged to alarm the world in defence of people who seemed alien to them.

Let us turn now to the fate of the report. The covering letter by Erik von Post was already unpromising. It treated Vendel with contempt, mentioning him without his title and first name, which violated etiquette generally accepted in Sweden. Maybe this lapse expressed a then frequent disrespect for the consular staff on the part of even lower-ranking diplomats, but it seems that the purpose was different. Expressing disrespect for the author probably served the purpose of diminishing the importance of the report. When listing the problems addressed in the document, Post skipped over its most essential content, the data about the extermination of the Jews. It was a clear hint to Stockholm not to get involved in that problem. Obviously, various hypotheses can be put forward, but it seems doubtful that Post would have omitted this crucial part by oversight. There are no grounds for accusing Erik von Post or Arvid Richert of being Nazis, but there are even fewer grounds for regarding them as anti-Nazis. More cautiously, we can conclude that they were both convinced that remaining on good terms with the Third Reich was in the best interests of Sweden, and they acted accordingly. They prevented, or tried to prevent, anything that would loosen Sweden's dependence on Germany and avoided engendering discontent in Berlin. They refused to act even in such obvious cases as possible intervention in defence of the Swedish industrialists in Warsaw whom the Gestapo had arrested and sentenced to death.[12] It is no wonder that in November 1942 (three months after Vendel wrote his report), when the foreign ministry asked Richert, in regard to some incidental information from an embassy report, if it was true that the Germans deported the Jews from Polish towns, Richert answered: 'The truthfulness of this information cannot be determined; therefore, it needs to be treated with maximum reservation.' About reports of the evacuation of the Warsaw ghetto, he added: 'I do not have access to any credible information about this.' In his next letter he thanked the ministry for not having made such details known to Rabbi Ehrenpreis of Stockholm, and he demanded that 'information about the treatment of the Jews, etc., whose source is the embassy, should not reach people on the outside'.[13] What more did he need? Yet already by the spring of 1942 the most credible witnesses, the Swedes Sven Norrman, Sigge Haggberg, and Carl Wilhelm Herslow, had told him about deportations.

In spite of Post's efforts, Vendel's report excited interest in the Swedish foreign ministry, albeit not at once. After two weeks, on 8 September 1942, the director of the political department, Staffan Söderblom, had copies of the report sent to the offices in Helsinki, Rome, and Copenhagen; to the general staff; and to the deputy governor of Stockholm. Söderblom's copy was signed by several people to whom the report was presented. Among others, the signatures of Deputy Foreign Minister Eric Boheman and Prime Minister Per Albin Hanson can be deciphered on his copy of Post's covering letter. However, those men did not receive their own copies. It is therefore unclear whether they actually read the report or were only informed about its content, most likely in a manner determined by the covering letter. (I suggest this not without reason. Söderblom was a man of low calibre who owed his career to family connections. His father, an archbishop, was head of the Church in Sweden. At the time of Hitler's victories Söderblom ingratiated himself with the Germans, and later he did the same towards the Soviets. The failure to demand the release of Swedish citizen Raoul Wallenberg, who had been kidnapped by the Soviets in Budapest, has been attributed at least in part to Söderblom's lack of character.) As a result, the information from the German anti-Nazi officer was sunk so effectively that even the publication in the 1960s of Vendel's essay did not arouse interest.

Steven Koblik thoroughly analyses all the factors that contributed to Sweden's undertaking its particular course of action.[14] There was a fear of provoking Germany. Sweden was not able to fight a war against Germany, certainly not for the purpose of saving the Jews. The politicians and diplomats we have mentioned were not antisemites, but they had to think of the interests of their own country.

---

[12] Richert and Post are treated extensively in the diary of Sven Grafström, *Anteckningar* (Stockholm, 1989).

[13] For more on this, see Ivarsson Martin, 'Att kunna men inte vilja' (1989), manuscript in the possession of the author.   [14] Koblik, *The Stones Cry Out*.

On the one hand, on the threshold of the war, Swedish authorities had issued a series of instructions directed against German (and also Polish) Jews seeking help, but later they displayed exemplary behaviour, saving the Jews from Denmark who faced extermination. The Swedish public willingly recalls the truly heroic efforts of Raoul Wallenberg, who towards the end of the war rescued Jews in Hungary, and the mission of Folke Bernadotte, who in the war's last weeks saved thousands of concentration camp prisoners of many nationalities. In the end Koblik condemns the behaviour of Swedish authorities. At the same time he finds circumstantial excuses, asking what Sweden could have done.

Sweden could have done one thing that Koblik did not consider. It could have used its channel to pass Vendel's information on to the West, to the countries of the anti-Nazi alliance. Such action was not unheard of in diplomatic practice. But it was not done. Moreover, the report was not made known to the director of the information bureau in the Swedish foreign ministry, Sven Grafström, who was anti-Nazi. He had proved in the past that he would not refuse to take unconventional steps if they were necessary.

Instead, a copy of the report was made for the deputy governor of Stockholm, Hellgren, who after the war was accused of having abused his power by collaborating with the German police authorities. It seems that he also disregarded Vendel's report. There is in addition the possibility that a report originating from Stockholm denounced the German anti-Nazis, but was suppressed, possibly by Admiral Canaris or one of his collaborators.

After all the years that have passed, a reading of Vendel's report evokes mostly sadness. Nothing can now help save the people who were murdered, even if there had been a substantial chance that the Nazi death machine could have been stopped then. Such was the aim of the leaders of the German officers who conferred with Vendel in Gross Steinort in August of 1942. Their anxiety and sincerity impressed Vendel, but their united efforts were in vain. Two years later Lehndorff was to die, murdered by the Nazis, and Tresckow would commit suicide when their assassination plot failed. Many of their comrades, the élite of the nation, would share the fate assigned earlier to the Jews.

Examining the materials to write this study, I felt, with a clarity very rare in my forty years' experience as a historian, how greatness and loftiness exist side by side with ignominy, mediocrity, and pettiness. On one side there is Tresckow, on the other Söderblom; Lehndorff and Richert can likewise be opposed. And the one only briefly mentioned here, but nevertheless hard to forget, a member of the conspiracy, the great Dietrich Bonhöffer, presents a striking contrast to the petty archbishop of Uppsala, Eidem, who, even when absolutely no doubt remained about the goals and actions of the Nazis, refused to sign a letter to the Hungarian bishops in defence of the murdered Jews. Also at fault was the Jewish congregation in Stockholm, worried about an influx of Jews from Poland and eager to prevent this 'danger'. It is painful to study documents that show how sacrifice and generosity can be annihilated by small-mindedness. But let us do what we can and should do: pay respect and bow our heads to those who, at a time when the wolves roamed freely, upheld the honour of humanity.

Translated from Polish by Gwido Zlatkes

Jewish Identities in the Holocaust: Martyrdom as a Representative Category

JONATHAN WEBBER

INTRODUCTION

THE immense scale of the genocide that was perpetrated against the Jews during the Second World War makes it difficult for the ordinary person today to have any strong sense of how best to represent the identity of the victims. Genocide—by definition—includes the murder of both men and women, the elderly and the very young, the rich and the poor, the educated and the uneducated, townsfolk and country folk, the strong and the weak, the healthy and those too ill to move. It was not that there was any particular group of Jews who were specifically singled out for murder; on the contrary, as is well known and well understood by all, the central fact of the Holocaust was that all types of Jews, without exception, became the object of the German state policy of extermination. Some kinds of Jews, it is true, seemed at certain stages of the war to be treated differently from others—those, for example, who could take on a leadership role in the local Judenrat and Jewish Police, or those who could be used as slave labour for the German war effort—but even such Jews, once it became clear that they had outlived their 'usefulness', were then herded off to their doom along with the rest. Certainly any detailed internal history of the Holocaust will need to take into account such factors as the age, occupation, or wealth of the Jews in order to grasp the unfolding of the atrocities in their specific local conditions, since from time to time during the war they indeed may have been relevant to German policy decisions for a brief period. But looking back at the Holocaust today, such differences of social identity would probably seem to many to miss the central fact of the attempted German annihilation of an entire people. If so, how then to represent just who the victims actually were as real people? Even in the Polish lands, they were not all Polish Jews—or (for example) all believing, practising Jews.

This problem, of finding a suitable way of encapsulating the identity of all those who suffered and died because they were Jews, has commonly been solved by dubbing them all as martyrs; and it is the purpose of this chapter to explore this usage. But before turning to examine it in detail it is worth pausing for a moment to consider the alternatives. In some sense the idea that all the Jews who were murdered in the Holocaust were martyrs is of course a remarkable simplification of an exceedingly complex and nuanced set of realities. But it is precisely the need to simplify that underlies ordinary social memory. We actually know comparatively little about the pre-war social life of all the individuals who were murdered. There is not even a complete record of all their names, with at least their dates and places of birth (although certain segments of such a record have been available for some time, and in recent years substantial efforts are finally being made to retrieve these basic details for the entire catastrophe). Relatively speaking, we know much more about the identity of the perpetrators and their mode of operation—such things as why Auschwitz was located where it was, how it was constructed, how it was managed, how much it cost to run—although, to be sure, none of those issues is without controversy. But as far as the victims are concerned, much less of such detail is known and less still is remembered. What has commonly been taken as the most effective and clear-cut representation of the Holocaust, as far as Jewish victimhood is concerned, is the numbers involved: 6 million.

The figure of 6 million is so immense and incomprehensible that as a symbol of Jewish victimhood in the Holocaust it does encapsulate very effectively the impossibility of grasping the vast scale of the tragedy as well as the impossibility of understanding any ordinary meaning it might encompass. For decades this figure has been used by Jews as a simplified, shorthand way into the identity of those who were murdered. Hence the common Jewish phrase 'the 6 million'; and hence, for example, Holocaust commemoration ceremonies at which six candles are lit, or commemorative sculptures using a six-branched candelabrum (traditional Jewish candelabra have seven or nine branches), or memorial gardens with six evergreen trees. The notion of 6 million—a figure which is of course not really supposed to be taken absolutely literally—has become well established as a totally acceptable ritual simplification among Jews throughout the world. After all, even a list of the place-names of the destroyed Jewish communities would be too long for the ordinary person to remember, too long for the ordinary synagogue to inscribe on its walls or embed in its liturgy; and in any case the unpronounceability of obscure east European place-names would detract from the sanctity of the memory that they would otherwise be expected to embody. Hence the Holocaust reality has been condensed down to something more culturally manageable—in particular the use of numbers to represent Holocaust victims. Interestingly enough, it is probably the same type of thinking that underlies the recollection of only a small number of the main death camps—Auschwitz, Majdanek, Treblinka—where it supposedly 'all happened'.[1] In the ordinary public Jewish memory today, vast

[1] Inasmuch as Auschwitz has come to be treated as the common Jewish symbol of the Holocaust, it is common to find ordinary Jews who merge the figure of 6 million with the total number of those Jews who were murdered there—that is, they notionally imagine that 6 million Jews were murdered in

elements of the Holocaust have disappeared from view: not only the names of the death camps from where there were very few survivors—most notably Bełżec, from where only three people are said to have survived, out of total Jewish losses there of 600,000; not only the hundreds of place-names of the small towns and villages in eastern Europe where Jews were murdered by shooting; but also the names of the individual Jews themselves. With this immense scale of human catastrophe, how could the names of these people be remembered? In practice, highly simplified forms of representation have established themselves as the basis for commemorative activity; it would seem that there is no other way. Certainly the ordinary Jewish schoolboy in London or New York would be hard-pressed to name even ten Jewish victims of Auschwitz (outside his own family circle), and might well see no particularly good reason for doing so.

Under these circumstances, then, ordinary Jewish attempts at representing the Holocaust have taken several forms. Apart from visual representations such as photography (notably pictures of the entry gates at Auschwitz I and Auschwitz-Birkenau), one of the most commonly encountered is the use of memoirs and diaries, and the oral accounts of survivors. Whether in films, books, or commemorative synagogue liturgies, excerpts from such diaries or survivor testimonies have come to form a particularly poignant mode of the attempt to recapture the essence of the Holocaust past. But by definition they are simplifications in the sense that they can be no more than isolated details and fragments—the part standing for the whole—and even the totality of these diaries and testimonies are themselves no more than a very partial representation of the realities they describe. 'Everything I am telling you now', as one survivor from Prague told her interviewer in 1955, 'is like a grain of sand by the sea—absolutely nothing compared to what happened'.[2] We are thus today at least at a double remove, relying on fragments of fragments.

What I wish to discuss in this chapter—the issue of Jewish martyrdom in the Holocaust—is in one sense no more than another such isolated detail. But like other such fragments of the Holocaust, the notion of martyrdom—in its own way like the use of the term 'the 6 million'—seems to be helpful to people in their attempt to condense the Holocaust down, simplify it, make it somehow more manageable in order to understand the totality. The use of the term 'martyrs' to describe the 6 million Jews who were murdered in the Holocaust is very common. But were they really martyrs? Did all the Jews who died see themselves as martyrs? Were those Jews who consciously went to their deaths as martyrs somehow 'typical' of all Holocaust victims? Or is the notion of Jewish martyrdom yet another

Auschwitz. The total figure for the number of Jews who in fact died in Auschwitz is a subject of disagreement among historians; according to a recent view of the historical research department of the Auschwitz State Museum, it is about 1 million (Franciszek Piper, 'Estimating the Number of Deportees to and Victims of the Auschwitz-Birkenau Camp', *Yad Vashem Studies*, 21 (1991), 49–103).

[2] Isaiah Trunk, *Jewish Responses to Nazi Persecution: Collective and Individual Behavior in Extremis* (New York, 1982), 72.

representation—a contemporary simplification that is merely presumed to do justice to the totality of the catastrophe?[3]

WHERE DOES THE NOTION OF JEWISH MARTYRDOM IN THE HOLOCAUST COME FROM?

The English word 'martyr' has been used for a long time as a term to represent Jewish Holocaust victims, and indeed it was used during the war itself. A book published in 1943 by the American Federation for Polish Jews that gave a series of detailed reports about the murder of Jews in Poland, including the camps at Chełmno, Treblinka, and Bełżec, appeared under the title *The Black Book of Polish Jewry: An Account of the Martyrdom of Polish Jewry under the Nazi Occupation*.[4] Despite this reference in the title to the 'martyrdom' of Polish Jews, the book does not contain any discussion of theological matters that would justify the use of this term. It seems that the word entered English usage in this context without a significant declaration of principles; and indeed it is still a common term used in English today. Thus, for example, the official English name for Yad Vashem in Jerusalem is the Holocaust Martyrs' and Heroes' Remembrance Authority. This secular Israeli usage, referring to both 'martyrs' and 'heroes', is doubtless intended to draw attention to those 'heroic' Jews who fought the Germans or became involved in underground activities, of which perhaps the prototype was that of the Jews who participated in the Warsaw ghetto uprising in 1943. It seems to suggest that all those Jews who died in the Holocaust were martyrs, but some were heroes as well. In this view, martyrdom was thus achieved by ordinary Jews simply for having passively accepted being murdered because of their identity as Jews—a passivity that was indeed later derided by many Zionists as characteristic of Holocaust victims having gone 'like sheep to the slaughter'. But is this adequate as a representation of the facts? Does the term 'martyrdom' in effect convey the idea of a non-heroic death and thereby conceal within it a very specific understanding of the nature of Jewish victimhood in the Holocaust? It is important to recognize that there is no single Jewish view regarding the history and meaning of the Holocaust: different kinds of Jews, whether secular or religious, Zionist or non-Zionist, see the Holocaust according to different moral perspectives and therefore present the

---

[3] A preliminary version of the ideas put forward in this chapter was first presented at a seminar at the Evangelical Academy in Loccum, Germany, in 1995, later published as Jonathan Webber, 'Jewish Martyrdom in the Holocaust: A Representative Category?', in Yasmin Doosry (ed.), *Representations of Auschwitz* (Oświęcim, 1995); repr. in Kulturwissenschaftliches Institut im Wissenschaftszentrum Nordrhein-Westfalen, *Jahrbuch 1994* (Essen, 1995); and 'Do Jews See their Holocaust Victims as Martyrs?', in Detlef Hoffmann (ed.), *Das Opfer des Lebens: Bildliche Erinnerung an Märtyrer*, Loccumer Protokolle 12/95 (Rehburg-Loccum, 1996). I am grateful to Prof. Detlef Hoffmann of the University of Oldenburg for first suggesting that I research this topic, and to Prof. Jörn Rüsen of the Kulturwissenschaftliches Institut, Essen, for encouraging me to continue with it.

[4] Jacob Apenszlak (ed.), *The Black Book of Polish Jewry* (n.p., 1943).

facts of the Holocaust differently. The case of Yad Vashem could thus be interpreted in different ways.⁵ Here, however, I wish to pursue the specifically religious character of martyrdom in the Jewish tradition—not only because martyrdom has a long history in that tradition but also because religious Jewish accounts are relatively seldom represented in wider discussions of the problem, and to ignore them is to misrepresent the past.⁶

Only a handful of Holocaust memoirs and diaries from a traditionally Orthodox Jewish perspective have been published, but it is clear even from this relatively small body of literature that it represents the Holocaust quite differently from ordinary secular accounts. Central to this Orthodox Jewish representation is the notion of martyrdom—or, to use the correct Hebrew term, *kidush hashem*, which is not quite the same thing as martyrdom. Jews do not have martyr-saints as there are in Christian traditions, with the result that to use the term 'martyr' in respect of the Jewish victims of the Holocaust is something of a cultural distortion (or alternatively, for secular Jews, an attempt to fix Jewish victimhood within a broader category meaningful within the non-Jewish world). *Kidush hashem* means the sanctification of the name of God—to bring God into the world, and thereby achieve the divine purpose for which humanity was created.

Although the general duty to practise *kidush hashem* is first mentioned in the Hebrew Bible (e.g. at Lev. 18: 3–5, 22: 31–2), finding the most appropriate way to fulfil this in practice was only really developed in the Talmud and later commentaries, largely in the light of Jewish historical experience. The Bible indicates two basic concepts. First, Jews should consecrate their lives to God, and should indeed do everything they can to preserve their lives for this purpose; they should not put their lives in unnecessary danger in order to observe their religion. On the other hand, there comes a point beyond which it makes no moral or theological sense for

---

⁵ James Young, for example, notes that it links specifically with nationalist Israeli approaches to the Holocaust, mapping a dialectic relationship between martyrdom and heroism on to key aspects of Israeli identity (*The Texture of Memory: Holocaust Memorials and Meaning* (New Haven, 1993), 209–82)). It may also be, however, that Yad Vashem here drew on political ideas current during the wartime itself: Isaiah Trunk (*Jewish Responses to Nazi Persecution*, 34) refers to an underground pamphlet published in the Warsaw ghetto (1940–Apr. 1943) under the title 'Martyrdom and Heroism'.

⁶ The dominance of secularist accounts of Holocaust-related Jewish history is well described (although somewhat overstated) by N. M. Gelber: 'As a native of Lvov I was invited to participate in the writing of the Book of Lvov ... [At] a meeting of the writers' panel for this volume, I met some thirty people: doctors, lawyers, poets, writers and journalists and among these were to be found only two observant Jews ... During the discussions and arguments that followed, the nature and contents [of the proposed volume] became evident. I realized that they would falsify completely the traditional Jewish image of Lvov and would describe it as a secular-nationalist, proletarian and socialist city devoid of its most important source—that of authentic traditional Judaism. I have seen this time and again in the hundreds of memorial volumes which ignore the truth, that the great majority of Jews in the destroyed communities were believing Jews' (Pesach Schindler, *Hasidic Responses to the Holocaust in the Light of Hasidic Thought* (Hoboken, NJ, 1990), 140 n. 3). A similar point is made by the hasidic authors Shlomo Zalman Lehrer and Leizer Strassman (*The Vanished City of Tsanz* (Southfield, Mich., 1997), 18), in commenting on the memorial book of Nowy Sącz.

Jews to preserve their lives if they are being forced to abandon their religion altogether—such as during a period of religious persecution. What the Talmud was concerned to establish was the definition of the latter situation: under precisely which circumstances should Jews choose to die for their religion?[7] What *kidush hashem* came to mean in the talmudic literature was an injunction to make the right decision, taking into account all the relevant facts and circumstances. For example, under 'normal' circumstances it was felt to be morally and theologically wrong for Jews to allow themselves to be put to death rather than break the sabbath, but in 'abnormal' circumstances such a course of action was to be preferred. Of course, the Jewish authorities could not force a Jew to die for his or her religion, but the existence of these talmudic guidelines did make it possible for the ordinary pious Jew to develop a sense of the role models that he or she should try to follow, particularly in situations of religious persecution. Some of the relevant texts even slowly found their way into the liturgy, thereby reinforcing the common awareness and historical consciousness of Jews that death at the hands of non-Jews (a frequent enough occurrence, particularly in medieval Europe) was more than just a theoretical possibility. It could involve the individual, and it could involve the entire local Jewish community. It was a part of the love of God, an acceptance of God's justice even though man would never be able to understand it. But it needs to be emphasized that *kidush hashem* did not necessarily mean death: in some circumstances the duty of *kidush hashem*—correct moral and ethical behaviour, undertaken in praise of God—could be better achieved by trying to stay alive.

The rabbis of each generation of massacres had the unfortunate duty of having to interpret and apply these guidelines. Before the Holocaust, probably the most important shift in thinking took place after the massacre of whole Jewish communities in the Rhineland in the year 1096, at the hands of the Crusaders. Many Jews then committed suicide rather than fall into the hands of the Christians who had threatened them with forced conversion. Suicide is clearly forbidden in Jewish law—but in recognition of the courage and devotion shown by these Jews, the rabbis in the following generations came to accept that what they had done was indeed *kidush hashem*, an act of glorification rather than one of desperation. To cite the poetic imagery that subsequently found its way into the folk tales and liturgical elegies: these Jews had somehow 'sacrificed' themselves to God.[8] It is worth recall-

---

[7] The relevant references are scattered, and the arguments subtle, but *Sanhedrin* 74a–b is the *locus classicus*.

[8] This sacrifice imagery, deriving biblically from the story of the binding of Isaac (Gen. 22), thereafter remained a dominant motif in Jewish allusions to losses incurred during pogroms. The Hebrew word *korban* (also used in Yiddish), meaning 'sacrifice', can be found in Holocaust memoirs written by pious Jews and on early Holocaust monuments erected shortly after the war in eastern Europe. It is likely that the adoption of the term 'Holocaust' (deriving from the Greek for a 'whole burnt offering'), drew both on this imagery as well as on Christian notions of sacrifice, which by definition is something which is total, and where nothing is held back (I am grateful to Ivan Strenski for clarification of this point). The theological implications of this usage are today seen, especially by more secular Jews, as an

ing this medieval precedent in order to grasp that the rabbis who were responsible for their congregations during the Holocaust period similarly drew on ancient Jewish tradition in the way they expressed their leadership, but at the same time made innovations. Innovations were inevitable: although the rabbis who functioned in the major ghettos (Warsaw, Kaunas, Drohobych, etc.) in the earlier part of the war could have had no idea that the Germans intended to murder every single Jew they could lay their hands on, without any exception, nevertheless they were aware that the Nazi persecution was without historical parallel in the Jewish memory—in terms of its ruthlessness of scale, brutality, and apparent absence of any viable mode of escape. How could Jews practise *kidush hashem* under these circumstances? From the limited information that is available (i.e. from the memoirs of the handful of distinguished rabbinical scholars who happened to survive the war), we know that this question evidently absorbed the minds of Orthodox rabbis, particularly in eastern Europe, and, by extension, of the countless masses of Orthodox Jews who looked to these rabbis for leadership and spiritual encouragement at the time of their greatest need.

KIDUSH HASHEM DURING THE HOLOCAUST

The character of Holocaust literature written from this kind of Orthodox Jewish perspective is thus not 'history' in the usual academic sense. Rather the Holocaust is seen as a set of human problems that should be studied and contemplated as morally instructive, within the framework of Jewish law. It is a Holocaust representation in which the names of the chief German perpetrators and the details of their respective careers largely fade into the background, and where instead the names of pious Jews and the details of their moral traumas emerge prominently into light. In this approach problems of ritual and other enquiries about the demands of Jewish law form the true representation of the Holocaust, and accordingly I should like now to give a few examples—or isolated fragments, as they should perhaps be called.

Perhaps the most important question that was raised, and one which constitutes the best way into this complicated subject, was whether the Nazi persecution was a religious persecution or not. Once again, with the benefit of the hindsight that we possess today, it seems an absurd question; but during the time before Jews actually found themselves in front of the firing-squad or inside the gas chamber, the question was very real. If the Nazi persecution was to be understood as a

---

unacceptable way of categorizing Jewish losses at the hands of the Nazis—hence the increasing popularity of the alternative Hebrew term 'Shoah' (a biblical word meaning 'total destruction'). In the effort, perhaps, to distance themselves from the secular Jewish world, some Orthodox Jewish usage today is tending towards the Hebrew term *ḥurban*—a word also meaning 'total destruction', but self-consciously evoking earlier Jewish catastrophes of major significance as this is the classical term used to refer to the destruction of the Temple in Jerusalem by the Romans in AD 70.

situation where Jews were being forced to give up their religion, then according to talmudic law (and as later restated by Maimonides) Jews should not obey any order of the SS that conflicted with their religion; if they were then shot for disobeying such orders they would automatically be said to have died as martyrs for *kidush hashem*.

It seems that the situation in Germany was rather different, in this perspective, from how things looked in German-occupied eastern Europe.[9] The German rabbis concluded that the Nazis had no especially *religious* motive in their actions against Jews: after all, they were not interested in Jews giving up their religion, and persecuted even those Jews who had converted to Christianity. Moreover, as these rabbis noted, the prohibition introduced by the National Socialist government in 1933 on the kosher slaughtering of animals according to Jewish religious law was not expressed as part of an anti-religious campaign but was issued (so it was claimed) to avoid cruelty to animals; it applied to all inhabitants, not just to Jews. A synagogue functioned in Vienna throughout the war; there was a *mikveh* (ritual bath) in Berlin and Hamburg during the war, and even in 1943 a new *mikveh* was built in Hamburg after the existing one had been bombed. So most rabbis in Germany did not define what was happening as a *religious* persecution.

But in German-occupied eastern Europe the persecution was much more anti-religious in character. Perhaps one of the most detailed Orthodox memoirs to come out of the war was put together by Rabbi Ephraim Oshry, the responsible rabbi in the ghetto established by the Germans in Kaunas (the capital of pre-war Lithuania, known in Yiddish as Kovne); one of the cases he cites makes this point clear. A German decree was issued in August 1942 in the Kaunas ghetto stating that praying or studying Talmud was now a crime punishable by death. Rabbi Oshry, whose community was famous before the war for its piety and talmudic learning, was immediately asked whether a Jew could be permitted to put his life in danger by praying or studying Talmud. His answer is interesting and important. Reviewing the evidence, he pointed out that the Germans deliberately wanted to undermine the teaching of children, took away Torah scrolls and holy books by force, closed down houses of learning and prayer, and often imposed special forced labour specifically on the sabbath and Jewish holidays so as to cause Jews to desecrate the holiness of those days. Rabbi Oshry concluded that the enemy's main intention was not merely to destroy the Jews but also to destroy their faith and religion. What the Germans were doing amounted in talmudic terms to the explicit denial of the perfection of the one God—and in such a situation the law of submitting to death for *kidush hashem* unquestionably applied. What this meant was that Jews should disobey the German order, even if it meant putting their lives in danger. Oshry said he did not wish to force Jews to pray or learn Talmud, but that this would be his recommendation—they should do these things for *kidush hashem*—and he personally conducted daily lectures on Talmud. In accordance

[9] H. J. Zimmels, *The Echo of the Nazi Holocaust in Rabbinic Literature* (n.p., 1977), 244–50.

with his wishes, a couple of weeks later, in September 1942, the Jews in the Kaunas ghetto assembled for prayer on the Jewish New Year and followed the New Year's Day ritual of blowing the *shofar* (ram's horn), even though the noise would undoubtedly have attracted the attention of the SS. Unfortunately we do not know from Oshry's account if the SS made any specific retaliation for this infringement of the order.[10]

I have cited Rabbi Oshry's decision in order to give a preliminary indication of the kinds of problems that Orthodox Jews faced during the Holocaust period (and the kinds of Holocaust histories, built up out of such representative problems, that are still disseminated amongst Orthodox Jewish circles). It should be noted, however, that not all Orthodox rabbis would necessarily have shared his legal opinion, on this or any other issue. On the contrary, during the Holocaust there were substantial differences of opinion between rabbinic leaders about precisely how religious Jews ought to behave; the examples that follow are thus intended to illustrate these issues rather than offer generalizations on all rabbinic decisions reached during the war.

Oshry records a case where he decided that under no circumstances may Jews commit suicide, whatever the suffering they had to endure,[11] and the same subject was also discussed at length in other ghettos, especially by various rabbis in the Warsaw ghetto. Rabbi Yitzhak Nissenbaum is recorded as having made an important speech there in which he explained that the suicides committed in the Middle Ages took place in a situation where the enemy wanted to convert Jews to Christianity—but that the Nazis were different as they simply wanted to have the pleasure of killing Jews physically. Suicide, he explained, was an acceptable solution in the Middle Ages because that way the Jews frustrated the wishes of the

---

[10] For an account of this episode, see Ephraim Oshry, *Responsa from the Holocaust*, trans. Y. Leiman (New York, 1983), 78–80; Zimmels, *The Echo of the Nazi Holocaust*, 248–50; Irving J. Rosenbaum, *The Holocaust and Halakhah* (n.p., 1976), 50–2, 165 n. 11. Rabbi Oshry survived the war and was later appointed to a rabbinic post in New York City. He published a three-volume work in Hebrew (1949–69) describing his wartime decisions, under the title *Mima'amakim* ('Out of the depths [I cried out unto thee]', based on Ps. 130: 1); Oshry's *Responsa from the Holocaust* is an abridged one-volume English edition which appeared later. The latter is very terse, however, and does not reproduce the argumentation underlying the decisions reached. Readers without specialist knowledge of talmudic literature are therefore referred in this article to scholarly secondary sources which have analysed in detail both Oshry's work and the memoirs of other rabbinic scholars published after the war; these sources give full bibliographic references for cases cited.

[11] Oshry, *Responsa from the Holocaust*, 34–5. Rosenbaum (*The Holocaust and Halakhah*, 35–9) discusses the complex technicalities of this case at some length; what Oshry also took into account in reaching his decision was that suicide had to be avoided at all costs, since it would engender a spirit of despair and so play into the hands of the Germans. In fact the suicide rate was surprisingly low in the east European ghettos (apart from certain famous cases such as the suicide of Adam Czerniaków, president of the Judenrat of Warsaw), in contrast with its comparatively high incidence amongst assimilated Jews in Germany and Austria; but certainly there were no Masada-like mass suicides during the Holocaust (Zimmels, *The Echo of the Nazi Holocaust*, 82–6; Trunk, *Jewish Responses to Nazi Persecution*, 15).

enemy, and in doing so practised *kidush hashem*. The only way for the Jews to frustrate the wishes of the *Nazi* enemy was for them to survive: thus the very act of *survival* would in these circumstances constitute *kidush hashem*. Here, in this speech of Yitzhak Nissenbaum, one can see how the concept of *kidush hashem* is rendered historical and consciously adapted to the circumstances. Rabbi Nissenbaum told his listeners that they must therefore do everything they could in order to survive—for example, by escape or by bribery. All this represents a clear movement away from the practice and the imagery of sacrifice that had largely dominated thinking about *kidush hashem* since the Crusader massacres of 1096; and Nissenbaum coined the term *kidush haḥayim* (the sanctification of life) to convey the point. Other rabbis expressed similar opinions during the war, thereby clearly offering the evidence that *kidush hashem* does not necessarily mean death, as I mentioned above. Rabbi Menahem Ziemba of Warsaw, who also argued specifically that *kidush hashem* expresses itself differently in different times, took the view that Jews ought physically to resist the Germans, and 'fight to the very end'.[12]

If survival, according to these opinions, was now to take precedence in formulating an attitude to *kidush hashem*, the question soon arose whether Jews could try to save their lives by escaping from the ghetto and disguising themselves as Christians. My impression is that this was one of the questions most commonly asked of rabbis during the Holocaust. The rabbis agonized over it: on the one hand, for a Jew actually to get himself or herself a certificate of baptism amounted to the very opposite of *kidush hashem*, and therefore could not be encouraged; on the other hand, in the opinion of Jacob Avigdor, chief rabbi of Drohobych and Boryslav in south-eastern Poland, how could a rabbi in effect support and strengthen the decrees of the Germans, who regularly shot Jews for acquiring false papers or otherwise going into hiding? So, for this latter reason, which he justified on the grounds that Jews were in all these cases disobeying the enemy and thus in effect acting under duress—a talmudic principle that separates action from intention, thereby in effect acknowledging the appalling realities facing Jews during times of persecution, which during the Holocaust enabled many rabbis to be lenient on a variety of issues—Rabbi Avigdor decided to allow it.[13]

A similarly lenient attitude was displayed by Rabbi Oshry following an order made by the Germans in the Kaunas ghetto in May 1942 that any Jewish woman found to be pregnant would immediately be put to death (such a decree was rare during the war, and in fact is known only from Kaunas and Theresienstadt). Given that the primary purpose of marriage, in Jewish tradition, is procreation, Rabbi Oshry was asked whether, in consequence of this German order, married

---

[12] Zimmels, *The Echo of the Nazi Holocaust*, 63–4; Schindler, *Hasidic Responses to the Holocaust*, 61, 65; Trunk, *Jewish Responses to Nazi Persecution*, 15. Both Rabbi Nissenbaum and Rabbi Ziemba died in the Warsaw ghetto in 1943.

[13] Zimmels, *The Echo of the Nazi Holocaust*, 78–9. Rabbi Avigdor survived the war and later took up a rabbinic post in Mexico City.

women could use a contraceptive (normally forbidden), and whether a pregnant woman could or should undergo an abortion (also normally forbidden). His decision on both these questions was in the affirmative; and marriages continued to be consecrated.[14]

A particularly moving case is reported from Auschwitz on the eve of the Jewish New Year in 1944: the SS made one of their routine 'selections' in the concentration camp, weeding out those 'surplus' labour camp prisoners whom they regarded as no longer *arbeitsfähig* (capable of work) to be sent to the gas chamber. One thousand four hundred male teenagers were thus 'selected' and confined to a barrack, to await execution the following day. In the meantime relatives of these young men began to plead and bargain with the *kapos* guarding the barrack to release some of them. The *kapos* had to be bribed: since an exact count had been taken of the internees, the *kapos* would release someone only if somebody else would replace that person. To replace one life with another is expressly forbidden in the Talmud (who can say that one life is more precious to God than another?), but it so happened that a distinguished rabbi and Talmud scholar Zvi Hirsch Meisels of Vac in Hungary, who was himself in Auschwitz at the time, was asked by a religious Jew whether he could under these circumstances try to save the life of his only son. Meisels writes in his memoirs that he found it difficult to give a straight answer, knowing that he could not in fact permit it, but that once this Jew had understood that the answer was no, he displayed a sense of great relief that the moral issue (as far as he was concerned) was settled, and also some spiritual satisfaction in the knowledge that according to Jewish values he could accept God's decree regarding the death of his son 'with love and joy'.[15]

It should by now be clear from the theological and sociological background underlying the notion of *kidush hashem* that pious Jews could draw on countless ritual contexts to express their faith at the last. Yet again it should be recalled that although the idea of Jews risking their lives during the Holocaust period in order to fulfil some religious precept may seem to us absurd, given our historical hindsight and our knowledge that all Jews within the Nazi domain had been condemned to death anyway, nevertheless both within the ghettos prior to deportation and also within the labour camps, even inside Auschwitz, Jews would often have felt that they had somehow been spared from immediate death; many perhaps believed that they would somehow survive the war altogether. For pious Jews to risk their lives in such situations was technically quite unnecessary and, in the opinions of the rabbis cited above, probably wrong. And yet Holocaust stories told

---

[14] Oshry, *Responsa from the Holocaust*, 71 ff.; see also Zimmels, *The Echo of the Nazi Holocaust*, 212–14; Rosenbaum, *The Holocaust and Halakhah*, 40–4.

[15] Rosenbaum, *The Holocaust and Halakhah*, 3–5, 109–11; Zimmels, *The Echo of the Nazi Holocaust*, 113. Significantly, Rabbi Meisels's memoirs bear the title *Mekadeshei hashem* ('They who Practise *Kidush Hashem*'), published in 1955 in Chicago, where Meisels held a post after the war, after first having been chief rabbi of Bergen-Belsen and of the British sector in Germany.

by Orthodox Jewish survivors emphasize not only the divine 'miracles' they witnessed that kept them alive but also the utterly remarkable performance of Jewish ritual obligations in the most difficult circumstances. According to eyewitness accounts, the ceremonial lighting of a candle on the first night of the festival of Hanukah, the distribution of Hebrew prayer-books, the wearing of tefillin (phylacteries), even the construction of a sukkah (temporary ritual dwelling) on the festival of Sukkot (Tabernacles) in 1943—all of these things, taking the form of snatched and hurried attempts to enact fragments of religious Jewish ritual, are recorded from Auschwitz.[16] Knowledge of the correct date in the Jewish calendar, regularly confirmed by newly arriving transports of deportees, constantly provided religious prisoners with an anchorage in their own cultural world.[17] On the festival of Sukkot in 1944 a sukkah was again erected in Auschwitz, this time by Rabbi Meisels, who encouraged the performance of many religious Jewish customs in the camp: for the same festival he managed to obtain a set of *arba'ah minim*.[18] He also blew the ram's horn on New Year's Day on twenty different occasions, including a visit (at great personal risk) to the block where the 1,400 boys were incarcerated prior to being gassed later that day.[19]

In all these cases—of which indeed many other similar examples are cited in the literature from Buchenwald, Płaszów, Stutthof, Mauthausen, and other camps—mention is routinely made of the enormous psychological consolation and encouragement that the practice of such rituals conveyed to the participants and onlookers. Given the substantial risks involved (being found out would normally have meant at least a flogging if not immediate death by shooting), such practice can at one level be regarded as a form of preparation prior to altruistic suicide, comparable perhaps to the stirring emotions engendered in modern times for the notion of dying for one's country; but what it certainly succeeded in doing was

---

[16] For sources documenting the four examples cited, see, respectively, Rosenbaum, *The Holocaust and Halakhah*, 118, 53, 78–9, 115–16; Schindler (*Hasidic Responses to the Holocaust*, 100) and Lehrer and Strassman (*The Vanished City of Tsanz*, 361) also cite a case of tefillin worn in Auschwitz. Sometimes these fragments of religious Jewish life consisted only of representations of the fragments—as, for instance, the emotional humming by Jewish girls, in their barrack in Birkenau on the eve of the Day of Atonement, of the well-known solemn melody of 'Kol Nidrei' (an account I heard *in situ* in 1995, at the fiftieth-anniversary commemoration of the liberation, from one of the women involved, now Mrs Miles Lerman). Trunk (*Jewish Responses to Nazi Persecution*, 24) cites a somewhat macabre version of something similar, when on the eve of the Day of Atonement a female Jewish *kapo* ordered a violinist in her block to play this melody and then suddenly interrupted her, shouting 'Enough! You've had enough pleasure!'

[17] I am indebted to Rabbi Shlomo Zalman Lehrer (co-author of *The Vanished City of Tsanz*), a former Auschwitz prisoner now living in Antwerp, for this observation (personal communication).

[18] Rosenbaum, *The Holocaust and the Halakhah*, 113–15. The *arba'ah minim* (which normally comprise a palm branch, a citron, and sprigs of myrtle and willow—an especially challenging combination to put together in Auschwitz) were in fact incomplete (no myrtle was to be found), and in the absence of any reference books Rabbi Meisels had to rely on his memory of the talmudic commentaries to reach a decision whether this incomplete set could in fact be used to satisfy the ritual requirements.

[19] Ibid. 110–11.

granting to many Jews the opportunity— under the most appalling conditions—
to learn how to die as a Jew, and to face the end with dignity and probably also
scorn towards the murderers:

> Rabbi Mendele Alter, the brother of the Gerer Rebbe, was among a group of Jews in
> Treblinka during the [hot] summer of 1942 who were ordered to undress. Realizing that
> these were his last moments the Rebbe pleaded desperately for a glass of water. A Jewish
> guard, usually noted for his cruelty to fellow Jews, was touched by the plea. He provided
> the water under the impression that the Rebbe wished to quench his thirst before dying.
> Instead, the Rebbe used the water to cleanse his hands as an act of purification prior to
> *kidush hashem*, urging, 'Fellow Jews, let us say the *vidui* [confession] before dying.'[20]

JEWISH MARTYRDOM IN THE HOLOCAUST AND THE PROBLEM OF GENERALIZATION

Martyrdom in general, and *kidush hashem* in particular, undoubtedly form a genre
of historical reflection and glorification that is especially prone to mythologization.
The storytelling is often dehistoricized; narratives of the heroes and their exploits
merge anachronistically into each other; the isolated fragments become framed in
a new representational setting. I have cited sources for the examples I have given,
but these (I am sure) will be thought by some to be indeed of no more importance
than as mere footnotes to the history: there may in fact have been many Jews, perhaps even a majority of Orthodox Jews, who cried out 'Shema Yisroel' or some
other appropriate biblical verse as they were led out to be shot or gassed. But
would this entitle Jews today to characterize all Jewish losses during the Holocaust
under the rubric of *kidush hashem*, or gloss them in English as martyrs?

In brief, the emphasis on *kidush hashem* in this kind of Holocaust representation
simplifies the Holocaust by essentially reducing it to two agendas: there was the

---

[20] As reported by an eyewitness (Schindler, *Hasidic Responses to the Holocaust*, 62). There are many
such stories in the literature, describing rabbis who encouraged their followers on the way to execution by singing, reciting psalms, even dancing, so as to prepare themselves spiritually for the great
honour and privilege that God had given them—to die for *kidush hashem*. Yaffa Eliach (*Hasidic Tales
of the Holocaust* (New York, 1988), 160–1) cites a case of pious Jewish women in the ghetto in Bochnia,
southern Poland, who, having been 'selected' for execution, obtained the agreement of the SS to prepare themselves for death by taking a ritual bath in a *mikveh*; the building had to be specially
reopened, heated, and cleaned for the purpose—after the bath the women were shot. Stories on these
themes also include the idea that this type of devotion occasionally inspired non-observant or secular
Jews to adopt Jewish ritual practices both to identify themselves with these Orthodox Jews and to
learn from them how to die with dignity: see e.g. Zimmels, *The Echo of the Nazi Holocaust*, 62–3 (an
assimilated Jew who begged to be circumcised) or Eliach, *Hasidic Tales of the Holocaust*, 155–9 (an
assimilated Jewish *kapo* who in solidarity with a group of hasidim in his barrack refused to eat on the
fast of the Day of Atonement, and for this was shot in front of them by an SS officer). A good example
of scorn towards the murderers is cited by Eliach (ibid. 159–60): a hasidic Jew about to be shot
received permission from the German officer in charge to recite a short prayer. Quoting from the daily
liturgy, what he recited (first in Hebrew, then in German) was: 'Blessed are You, O Lord our God,
King of the Universe, who has not made me a heathen.'

German agenda (the 'unquenchable lust for Jewish blood', as it is described) and there was a Jewish agenda (a long history of a relationship with the divine, in which there is one unbroken tradition of giving up one's life according to God's will). 'Let them proceed with their business, and we shall proceed with ours', to cite a classic formulation of the idea, uttered by a young hasidic Jew in a cellar in Kraków whilst the Germans paced overhead.[21]

In this perspective the problem of isolated fragments disappears from view: individual events, whether adequately attested or not, become redefined as examples of predetermined categories; there is no longer any particular need to deliver a full account or full narration of the totality of the facts. It is, of course, this latter problem of an appropriate historical emplotment of the Holocaust that inevitably absorbs the energies of the professional secular historian—whence the questions surrounding its representation.[22] Martyrdom, or *kidush hashem*, is clearly far from 'typical' of Jewish responses during the Holocaust: the whole thing is infinitely more complicated. It is not only that some Jews chose to fast before their deportation, while other Jews lost their faith; there is a much wider range of issues. Economic life in the ghettos was to a large extent taken over by a new Jewish underworld, consisting of extortionists, blackmailers, informers, bribers of all kinds; the cruelty of many Jewish *kapos* in the concentration camps is well attested by countless survivors; most Orthodox Jewish males did follow German orders to cut off their beards and sidelocks (i.e. rather than try and preserve them as a form of resistance), and in general seem to have followed those rabbinical rulings that enabled them to ignore standard forms of ritual on the grounds of preserving life—eating non-kosher meat, for example.[23] For the person interested in a generalized historical picture—as opposed to a mythologized view of martyrdom and heroism—it is necessary to look further afield. A good example is provided by Isaiah Trunk in his reference to the huge quantities of mail, mainly postcards, that were sent in from provincial towns to friends and relatives in the Warsaw ghetto (and now preserved in the Ringelblum Archive). They form an excellent source for gaining an insight into the state of mind of a good cross-section of the Jewish population:

---

[21] Schindler, *Hasidic Responses to the Holocaust*, 187 n. 29. Interestingly enough, a very similar remark is also reported from a town in Lithuania (cited in Trunk, *Jewish Responses to Nazi Persecution*, 57) and from another town in the Ukraine (Eliach, *Hasidic Tales of the Holocaust*, 159–60).

[22] See e.g. Saul Friedlander (ed.), *Probing the Limits of Representation: Nazism and the 'Final Solution'* (Cambridge, Mass., 1992) and discussions cited there.

[23] Trunk, *Jewish Responses to Nazi Persecution*, 10–38. There are, of course, attested cases of rabbis who refused to cut off their beards or wear other than hasidic dress (Schindler, *Hasidic Responses to the Holocaust*, 99), although Zimmels (*The Echo of the Nazi Holocaust*, 40) implies that most rabbis did shave off their beards, specifically in order to conceal their status as leaders from the eyes of the Germans. This meant that once they were deported to a concentration camp none but their followers from their home town would necessarily know who they were (see e.g. Eliach, *Hasidic Tales of the Holocaust*, 155).

adults and children, men and women, simple people and educated people, religious and non-religious, people of different professions and political affiliations. These documents record resignation and desperate calls for help, faith in divine providence and utter atheism, apathy and feverish efforts to find some kind of rescue, natural optimism and unlimited despair, a clear sense of what was in store and completely unfounded illusions. The letters tell us how diversely different people reacted to the same events.[24]

A similar diversity of reactions was noted by Rudolf Höss, commandant of Auschwitz, in his autobiography: he describes a mother who managed to joke with her children despite the terror in her eyes; a young woman in front of a gas chamber who helped the small children and elderly women undress and keep calm; women who shrieked, tore their hair, and became totally hysterical; children who refused to enter the gas chamber and had to be dragged in; a man who hissed at him 'Germany will pay a heavy penalty for the mass murder of the Jews'; and (curiously) a Dutch Jew who gave him a list of Dutch families hiding Jews.[25]

It needs to be recalled, moreover, that Jews were murdered in large numbers in eastern Europe by an array of local nationalists and fascists whose political programme, while coinciding in this respect with that of the Nazis, derived from sources substantially different from German state theories regarding the objective need for the genocide of the Jews. East European fascists, particularly in Lithuania and the Ukraine, often took the initiative in undertaking pogroms of Jews after the German attack on the Soviet Union in 1941 because of their anger at Jewish collaboration (both real and imagined) with the Soviet authorities prior to that date. In each country it was a different story: in Belarus, by contrast, the Germans found it comparatively difficult to find local recruits for their auxiliary police to undertake actions against Jews; and in Poland there were numerous shifts and adjustments of position among the various underground political parties, especially in their attitudes towards the German murder of Jews—although towards the end of the war Polish fascists joined the Home Army and often murdered Jewish partisans hiding out in the woods. 'The Poles were worse than the Germans,' as many a Polish Holocaust survivor will today confidently recount.

Given the totality and complexity of all these circumstances (on which, of course, much more could be said), the very notion here of a 'Holocaust' as a unitary category—or at least a meaningful category supplied *ex post facto*—speaks clearly of the Jewish need for a retrospective simplification of the past. Technically, the 'Holocaust' as a single event or category can be faulted on many grounds, but the usage should alert us to the widespread apperception—largely, although not exclusively within the Jewish world alone—that there is indeed a single issue here. And it is in relation to that single issue that the reaching out for martyrdom, or *kidush hashem*, as the all-embracing category to account for the totality of the victims would seem ostensibly to be addressing itself, even despite the observed

[24] Trunk, *Jewish Responses to Nazi Persecution*, 56.   [25] Ibid. 56–7.

CONCLUSION: MARTYRDOM AS A REPRESENTATION OF THE HOLOCAUST

'Every man and woman who died in the Holocaust is a holy martyr,' declared the Lubavitcher *rebbe* in a speech in 1990.[26] With this statement the *rebbe* echoed rabbinic opinions articulated in the Warsaw ghetto, where, for example, Rabbi Shimon Huberband (in a work bearing the title *Kidush Hashem*) applied the term *kidush hashem* to every victim of the Holocaust: 'As Maimonides ruled, "A Jew who is killed, though it may be for reasons other than conversion but simply because he is a Jew, is called *kadosh* [holy, i.e. a martyr]." '[27] From such a perspective there is no moral need to make the historical distinction between (say) Jews murdered in the gas chambers at Auschwitz and Jews murdered by Polish partisans in the forests, or for that matter between Jews who expressed their faith in divine providence and Jews who were atheists—they are all martyrs. Martyrdom here does not necessarily involve self-sacrifice, that is, a conscious decision to die specifically for *kidush hashem*. It is this latter which appears to be an innovation within Jewish theological responses during the Holocaust (that is, despite Huberband's supposed reference to a classical source): the category has been extended to embrace all those who went to their deaths, regardless of their state of mind or religious belief—and it would presumably even include Jews (such as Edith Stein) who had converted to Christianity, as well as the children of such people, who were murdered by the Germans because of their Jewish ancestry.

This is clearly all rather different from the notion of *kidush hashem* as it was developed by pious Jews in the early Middle Ages; this is necessarily so in the twentieth century, when, as a reflection of the widespread assimilation and secularization in the Jewish world, much of the force of the classical Jewish concept of living a life and dying a death to sanctify God has ceased to have the socially accepted meaning it once had. Whether or not the majority of Jews who were murdered in the Holocaust would have thought of themselves as religious rather than as secular (although the dividing-line is not self-evident), to settle on a single category to account for them all is by no means straightforward. But the extension, by leading rabbis, of *kidush hashem* to cover all the Jewish victims seems to solve the problem: amongst other things, it nicely coincides with the inclusive approach

---

[26] Shmuel Boteach, *Wrestling with the Divine: A Jewish Response to Suffering* (Northvale, NJ, 1995), 190. The Lubavitcher *rebbe*, who lived in Brooklyn and died in 1994, was a saintly figure with a substantial international following, who led a powerful hasidic movement of Jewish outreach.

[27] Schindler, *Hasidic Responses to the Holocaust*, 60. It is not clear, however, whether Maimonides in fact ever made such a statement (ibid. 164 n. 7).

embedded in secular notions of Jewish martyrdom. Martyrdom, in today's Jewish world, thus comes as a sort of ecumenical compromise, especially in English-language usage: in addition to the implicit reference to the classical religious imagery, it evokes the innocence of the victims (best exemplified by the 1 million or so children who were murdered), and it also links Jewish victimhood in the Holocaust with wider notions of national sacrifice (ironically secular in their usual connotations today) common in a variety of non-Jewish national European traditions.

This vagueness, double-sidedness, and sense of compromise surrounding the use of the term 'martyr' is conveniently illustrated in the text of a Holocaust memorial service proposed by the Rabbinical Council of America.[28] Six candles are lit (for 'the 6 million'), each dedicated liturgically to a particular subgroup of Holocaust victims, and as such offering an interesting insight into how these are to be characterized. With one candle to be lit for each of them, the six subgroups proposed in this liturgy are:

1. the helpless infants, children, and teenagers;
2. mothers who died with their children in their arms;
3. mothers and fathers who were separated from their families;
4. scholars, teachers, and rabbis;
5. heroes of the resistance who fought the Nazis; and
6. the martyrs who gave their lives to help their brothers.

In this part of the memorial service 'martyrs' thus appear here as a subgroup, characterized by their specific form of behaviour in contrast with the others, and indeed given a very specific definition (dying by helping others). However, immediately after the candle-lighting comes a memorial prayer, which begins as follows: 'We remember this day the nameless millions of martyrs of the children of Israel ... offered up by the Nazis on altars of savagery and demonic brutality.'

Note the shift: the ceremony is having it both ways as far as martyrdom is concerned. In the memorial prayer the 'martyrs'—in their nameless millions—represent the *entire* collectivity of victims, not just one subgroup of them as during the candle-lighting. And here we begin to see a more generalized approach to Holocaust martyrdom showing through. First, the victims have not sacrificed themselves (as the Jews of 1096 would have said about themselves), but rather are sacrificed by the enemy, i.e. according to the enemy's set of values. But, nevertheless, their deaths in some unknown (or at least unspecified) way add something to Jewish history and Jewish destiny. The memorial prayer continues: 'We must sanctify the names of the *kedoshim* [martyrs, the plural of *kadosh*] whose deaths deepened the holiness of Your chosen people. We must dedicate ourselves to the perpetuation of Your saving remnant through greater devotion to Your holy Torah

---

[28] Bernhard H. Rosenberg and Fred Heuman (eds.), *Theological and Halakhic Reflections on the Holocaust* (Hoboken, NJ, 1992), 347–63.

and through dedication to the creation of a holy land in the State of Israel.' Just how Jewish deaths in the Holocaust can be deemed to have deepened the holiness of the Jewish people, though the natural corollary to any theory of martyrdom, remains unclear; it is the subject of much controversy (and much misunderstanding), and also much passion. There is a long tradition in Judaism of arguing with God, and complaining that the death of the righteous is not the best way for God to achieve His purpose in the world.[29] One of the main founders of the United States Holocaust Memorial Museum in Washington, which opened in 1993, himself gave an impassioned impromptu performance in the last functioning synagogue in Kraków in 1979: 'Where were You', he called out, 'when all over Europe Your sons and daughters were burning . . . ?'[30] But not all rabbis have agreed on the need to question God. We cannot 'explain' the Holocaust, the Lubavitcher *rebbe* declared in his 1990 speech, for we are limited by the earthbound perspective of mortal understanding; as it is written in the book of the prophet Isaiah (55: 8), 'For My thoughts are not your thoughts'.[31] Both during the Holocaust and also today, the proverb of the Hafets Hayim (Rabbi Israel Meir Hakohen, an outstanding Lithuanian Jewish scholar who died before the war) is often quoted: 'For the believer there are no questions; for the unbeliever there are no answers.'[32]

In short, theories of martyrdom and their associated ideas represent the Holocaust in different ways to different kinds of Jews today. In addition to the existence of highly specific definitions, martyrdom seems principally to be used as an overarching, inclusive symbol to show respect for the identity of the dead, a cover-term to conceal the shame, the nagging doubts and debates over Jewish passivity, and the complexity and sheer incomprehensibility of what happened—and, at the same time, it offers the opportunity for pious Jews to elaborate this theologically based term and elevate it through the allusion to the re-enactment of ancient Jewish styles of *kidush hashem*. The notion of Jewish martyrdom in the Holocaust thus in practice has more than one meaning; its different meanings unselfconsciously coexist, even side by side within a single liturgy. So it is necessary to end here on a note of caution: there is no view of the Holocaust, whether simplified or otherwise, that will appeal unambiguously to all. It is both true and untrue to say that Jews today really do regard all the victims of the Holocaust as martyrs in any literal sense, for it may be in the long run that the sense of certainty embedded in the notion of martyrdom can never really encompass or override a sense of the ultimate incomprehensibility of the Holocaust, even though technically it ought to be able to do so. Although there are signs, particularly in the United States, that perpetuating Holocaust memory (in some representation or

---

[29] See e.g. Anson Laytner, *Arguing with God: A Jewish Tradition* (Northvale, NJ, 1990).
[30] Eliach, *Hasidic Tales of the Holocaust*, 212–13.
[31] Boteach, *Wrestling with the Divine*, 190.
[32] For the attribution of this widely quoted proverb to the Hafets Hayim, see Rosenbaum, *The Holocaust and Halakhah*, 5–6.

another) has itself become a focus of Jewish ethnic identity, there are those Jews who deeply object to the recurrent sound of its demonic voice and would rather leave the dead in peace—and in silence. Why should they serve the living as a pretext for their own belief or unbelief in God? Why should they, in fact, be taken as 'representing' anything at all? Perhaps indeed, to paraphrase Jacob Neusner, 'Auschwitz', or any representation thereof, profanes Auschwitz.[33]

[33] Jacob Neusner, *Stranger at Home: 'The Holocaust', Zionism, and American Judaism* (Chicago, 1981), 80.

Three Essays on Jewish Education during the Nazi Occupation

MARIAN MAŁOWIST

The Spiritual Attitude of Jewish Youth in the Period before the Second World War and in the Ghetto

INTRODUCTION

MY remarks regarding Jewish youth and its spiritual attitude in the pre-war period and during the war are based on observations made primarily during six years as a teacher in high schools from 1934 until 1939, and then in clandestine study groups in the years 1939–42. I had contacts with a fairly diverse group. Between 1934 and 1937 I was a history teacher, and at the same time I was successively head teacher of the seventh, sixth, and upper-second grades in a well-known Warsaw school catering for Polish and Jewish students. The school had initially been established to assimilate the children of the Jewish bourgeoisie and intelligentsia, but that objective was later abandoned, and the school worked towards becoming simply a Polish state secondary school. From the beginning of 1937 I taught at two Jewish schools for girls, with students from the better-off *petite bourgeoisie*, which was, on the whole, little assimilated. I also gave classes at one of the better Jewish schools for boys where students were the sons of the rich bourgeoisie who, however, wanted to maintain Jewish national traditions. With all of these groups of students I have at present close contacts through clandestine teaching.

The problem of the spiritual attitudes of young people has interested me for a long time. In order to base my views on a deeper understanding of this group, I tried to establish contacts outside school with my students, both boys and girls, and in most cases I succeeded. However, I cannot conceal that at times I ran into great difficulties, and in certain cases there was mutual animosity, which I will describe later and which is related to the problems which I want to discuss in this chapter.

These three essays are to be found in the Ringelblum Archive in the Żydowski Instytut Historyczny, Warsaw, 1941 Warsaw R-I no. 72; prepared by a collaborator of the Ringelblum Archive, the historian Dr Małowist.

I

For me, it was relatively easy to earn the trust of my students in the Polish school where I worked. I was then very young, and very excited about my job as class teacher; the young people I encountered there were also relatively close to me in their social environment and culture. I should like to address the question of their attitude towards the principal issues in their lives.

The boys attending the school were mostly the sons of well-to-do parents who wished to secure for their children either an appropriate position in society or social advancement. High-school and university education were seen as the way to achieve this, and the vast majority of my Jewish students expected to go on to university. They regarded knowledge as a step towards securing a comfortable place in life, towards becoming a well-placed lawyer, engineer, or businessman. Lower-paid jobs held no appeal for them. Only a few considered studying the humanities or natural sciences, which did not guarantee a high income. This attitude undoubtedly reflected a lack of deeper intellectual interests, which was also easily discernible in the school's everyday work. The students' theoretical interests were almost non-existent. Characteristically, their readiness to participate in extracurricular workshops diminished greatly in the last years before the war. As a result, schools were compelled to maintain these interests artificially to satisfy the school inspectorate. This state of affairs existed everywhere I worked. At best the student organizations which were established evolved into low-level political clubs. In humanistic workshops, only lectures on current political topics evoked any response. However, even in this area genuine interest was lacking, as was any attempt at a deeper understanding of the issues. Very little good literature was read. During discussions both lecturers and participants competed to bandy about the most radical slogans, with Stalinist and revisionist demagoguery having the greatest appeal. This was not confined to Jews: the same phenomenon could be observed among Polish students, who professed an exclusively antisemitic–fascist ideology. In some schools science workshops were more or less able to continue as their topics could sometimes raise curiosity, whereas humanistic workshops had no reason at all to exist. In recent years a diminishing interest could be observed even in sport. I am positive, in addition, that in my schools no private unsupervised forums existed where students could take part in free discussions.

How is this to be explained? Recently the authority of learning has widely diminished, especially in fascist countries. These countries aim to develop an uncritical personality; they seek to influence primarily the emotions and not the intellect. This was one of the principal features of the school syllabus and it negatively influenced teaching, especially in the 'four-year' high school. The subject-matter of the curriculum was covered very superficially and there was pressure to politicize instruction, of course in line with the interests of the regime. As a result, the school accustomed its students to superficial thinking and demagoguery and was unable to provide them with a proper basic education or to excite intellectual interests. If the influence of the press and the radio are taken into account, there can be little surprise that in the last years before the war the intellectual development of young people left so much to be desired. Of course, other factors were important, such as economic difficulties, which strongly affected the Jewish *petite bourgeoisie*. Parents were preoccupied and unable to maintain close contact with their children. This contact was especially limited in the purely Jewish schools. The majority of parents here spent their entire time in their shops and had no time to take care of their children. Besides, with the passage of time the cultural distance between the older and younger generations grew, to the exclusion of any closer contact. In the Polish school where I worked this was less acute. The Jewish intelligentsia and bourgeoisie which sent its children there were excessively preoccupied with them. However, even this group was losing touch with the young generation, especially in the higher grades. To the older generation, their children were completely alien and often incomprehensible. It seemed to me that young people were approaching the ideal set by the Sanacja regime: a generation had emerged that was vacuous and which lacked any principles, intellectual or even moral.

The question arises: where and in what way did these young people find outlets to discharge their energy? The truth is that it was firstly in the sphere of sexual relations. I was struck, in both the boys' and the girls' schools, by the extremely early sexual awakening of my students, and it is my impression that this too had a bad influence on their intellectual development. By 11 and 12 years old, girls and boys devoted a large part of their free time to sexual encounters. The absence of any proper guidance on these issues by the school or by parents led to spontaneous discussions among themselves. What emerged was a clearly brutish attitude towards the issues of sexual life, and the lack of idealism and the overly realistic attitude of young people in this area were very striking.

This lack of idealism was characteristic of a very large number of the young people from the intelligentsia and from bourgeois circles with whom I had direct and indirect contact. If they let themselves be drawn into political organizations, they did not feel deeply about their involvement, and because of that they came and went with ease. They readily joined the school sections of university corporations, whose basic appeal was their showiness: both boys and girls liked the hats and bands, the swords and other gadgets. In addition, these forums provided another opportunity to meet the opposite sex.

Jewish youth reacted strongly to the commonplace instances of the brutal antisemitic policy of the Sanacja, and in general to the political events of recent years. Although revisionism and Stalinism were widespread, they were only vague sentiments, and almost nobody tried to develop his or her *Weltanschauung* by extensive intellectual work. They were not prepared for this kind of work, and they avoided any unnecessary effort. If some problem aroused their interest, they asked for an explanation, but did not want to find out for themselves. The causes of this were beyond young people themselves, as I have already explained. Anti-Jewish incidents put the problem of their national identity strongly on the agenda, and some reaction arose even among the largely assimilated youth. Following the inclination towards radicalism which is natural in youth, boys who had been assimilated for a long period and who were detached from the Jewish masses turned in many cases to fascist nationalism. They thought that employing fascist methods in the Jewish community would bring the same 'excellent' results as in Germany and Italy. This section wanted fascism in Palestine, hated the Arabs, and approved of Hitler's methods, rejecting only his antisemitism. Interestingly, they made no moral evaluation of political activity. Again, this can be explained by the political climate in pre-war Poland.

Young people attending Jewish schools had less contact with antisemitism than those who were assimilated. The ghetto which had just started to emerge for the latter, had existed for the former for a long time. Perhaps because of this, fascism found less fertile ground here; instead, one might encounter Stalinism. Political activity, however, was relatively infrequent, though sometimes sentiments were expressed in the form of an interest in economic problems. In recent years, however, Stalinism diminished because of events in Russia, such as the trials of the anti-Stalinist opposition.

This was how, in my opinion, the situation looked for Jewish youth before the outbreak of the war. Young people were spiritually completely unprepared for the hardships of the times. They lacked the minimum intellectual and moral skills. Their basic qualities were a narrow pragmatism and an obscurantist realistic attitude towards life, bordering on spiritual and behavioural boorishness. Any idealistic drives were alien to them. Again I stress that the reasons for that situation were beyond their control: they had absorbed all the negative qualities of social life before the war. Of course, there were small groups and individuals who proved resistant to this intellectual and moral decay, but they were all too rare and they have demonstrated their merits during the war.

II

The outbreak of war, with the traumatic bombing of Warsaw and the occupation, greatly affected the young. A substantial section went to the Russian-occupied territories in the hope of finding further education or work, and in any case to find protection from German persecution. By and large the best element from among the youth, and the most self-sufficient, left Warsaw at that time. Often they sympathized with Stalinism and imagined that they would be creating a new life. Correspondence with them gave the impression that they were happy with their lot and that they had found a place for themselves. Jewish youth felt free from the monster of antisemitism, and, being unaccustomed to political freedom, they imagined that they were truly free: hence their enthusiasm, often naïve and sometimes even disgusting, for the Bolsheviks. They forgot in what circumstances, and allied with whom, the Soviets took over the eastern part of the Polish republic. The great majority of young people, especially the well-to-do, remained in Warsaw. They had nothing to do. The schools were closed, and entire days had to be filled. They did not want to go out on the streets, where they could be caught and taken for forced labour. They were completely disorientated. They were in no hurry to return to school, and many counted on the war to end in the spring of 1940. Thus, clandestine instruction organized in 1939-40 catered mainly for younger students sent to classes by their parents. The older students, especially boys, assumed a waiting posture. Girls gradually started to return to their studies. The autumn of 1940 brought a major change: everybody understood that the war would last for some time; the ghetto was established, and a great number of the young intelligentsia and bourgeoisie were gathered in the Jewish quarter and were seeking guidance. The newly opened vocational schools became very popular; boys especially wanted to learn any kind of trade, and as soon as possible, and they enrolled in these schools in great numbers. Many of them went to school in order to protect themselves from the threat of forced-labour camps. This was especially important, and it is probably why the participation of girls in vocational schools was on a smaller scale. Girls preferred to join clandestine classes.

What has prompted young people to study during the war? There are various reasons. They fear degeneration, and want to do something useful. They expect the war to end well, after which, having participated in clandestine study groups, they can relatively easily get school certificates. Pure interest in learning plays a minor role in the increasing drive of the young towards education. At clandestine courses they study diligently because they want to get through the material as fast as possible, and studying is expensive. They bargain fiercely with the teachers, criticize them, suspect them of holding them back. Characteristically, even the well-off do it, although to their parents 40 to 45 zlotys cannot be significant. Students work harder than before the war, particularly those who had studied in Jewish schools, and classes are attended mainly by those talented and diligent students who showed good progress before the war. The less committed are far less in evidence on the courses. Students from assimilated families initially displayed slower progress in work. Their lives underwent greater changes as they suffered expulsion from Polish schools and eviction from their apartments. They found themselves in completely new circumstances, in surroundings that were essentially alien to them and towards which they felt distrust or even contempt. In their eyes less assimilated Jews were always inferior to themselves. Interestingly, many of them do not even want to enrol on courses; they study at home and now and again go to the 'Aryan side' to take tests. This shows their distrust towards Jewish teachers, and they also think that in the future their certificates from Jewish schools will have no value. However, I believe that the most important reason for the withdrawal of this small group is their snobbery. Many of the most valuable among the assimilated youth gradually join our groups, and, after overcoming initial difficulties, keep pace with their peers from Jewish schools. Recently, the composition of classes has somehow changed. Many boys come; the vocational courses have lost some of their attraction, and people think that we are approaching the end of the war. There can be no doubt that participation in clandestine learning has a very positive impact on the youth. They say themselves that hard work saves them from decline and moral breakdown. Unfortunately, the great majority remain outside clandestine education. This is obviously the result of economic hardship, but there are also other factors. Many boys and girls, once free of the restrictive framework of school life, want fully to use their freedom, which they understand in a specific way. Again the darker side of pre-war life comes to light, of course greatly intensified. In the first place, one may observe sexual licence; then the drive to entertainment. In many cases, young people take relatively little notice of their present degradation and accept the situation surprisingly easily, wanting only to accommodate themselves to it. Most noticeable is their low moral resistance. Young people readily join suspect organizations like the Thirteen or Pogotowie (the Vigil) with no regard to the nature of these organisations.[1] Their purpose is to acquire goods, income, and protection from the labour camps. These organizations are joined mostly by the better-off, i.e. by those not forced by their circumstances to seek a living. They join in order to get the 'joys of life'. I noticed that one of the plagues demoralizing the young is their participation in commerce. In many cases parents, forced by the hardship, employ their sons and daughters to help them in petty trade. I know very talented young boys of 14 who are so involved in their businesses that they have completely lost interest in other things and have stalled in their development. Their moral level is significantly lower, and in dealings with adults they have learned to cheat. It is a dangerous state of affairs, for which there is no cure in the present tragic situation. The war deepened even more the moral and intellectual crisis that existed before. The boys and girls whom I know from pre-war times by and large lowered their morals. This often concerns individuals who before were very promising. In the best cases the level of morals has not changed.

Another question is, to what extent has the present situation affected the national identity of the youth? Of course, the views of groups that before the war regarded themselves as belonging to the Jewish community have not significantly changed; however, many illusions about the supposedly special values of the Jews have disappeared.

---

[1] The Thirteen was a group of suspect individuals headed by Abraham Gancwajch who had their headquarters at 13 Leszno Street and who, with Nazi support, established a small police unit parallel to the Jewish police subordinated to the Judenrat. On this group, see Yisrael Gutman, *The Jews of Warsaw, 1939–1943: Ghetto, Underground, Revolt* (Bloomington, Ind., 1989), 90–3. Pogotowie was another suspect organization in the ghetto.

As for the assimilated youth, I think that in general they have not come closer to the Jewish community. At the present time they encounter the darkest sides of Jewish life, and in many cases they extend their disapproval of it to the whole Jewish community. In my view many people from this circle will be baptized after the war in order to make a definite break with their Jewishness. Cohabitation in the ghetto of assimilated groups with others will not bring the former closer to the Jewish community, but, on the contrary, it will accelerate the breach of this part of the Jewish intelligentsia and bourgeoisie with the Jewish masses.

To an outside reader these conclusions may seem very pessimistic, and he may accuse me of an exceptionally hostile attitude towards the young. However, I maintain very close contacts with my students, both boys and girls, and in general we are very friendly towards each other. My views result from many years of observation. They were formed before the war, and what I see now confirms these earlier notions. Moreover, other teachers have come to similar conclusions.

Finally, I should like to note that corruption has affected not only Jewish but also Polish youth, especially the intelligentsia and the bourgeoisie. Lack of idealism and hooliganism among them were even more striking than among the Jews. Of course, the causes of this lay in economic hardship and fascist methods of government and propaganda. A prominent democratic Polish teacher justly condemned the new system of teaching and its 'emotional approach', seeing it as encouraging brutishness and thoughtlessness amongst the young. Therefore, I think that if this war ends well, there must be a general change in pedagogical methods. The emotionalism which is in fact a continual encouragement to chauvinism must be replaced by a sane, rationalistic attitude towards knowledge and the world. Schools must again become places of learning, and their aim must be to provide wide-ranging and honest support for the intellectual and moral development of individuals.

Jewish High Schools in Warsaw during the War

In this essay I shall try to describe in general outlines the education of young people during the war. I shall deal only with the high-school (*gimnazjum* and *liceum*) levels, since it is only them that I have observed directly and it is only about them that I have reliable information. At the end of September 1939, when the occupiers took power, neither teachers nor parents realized what the situation would be for education. Everyone expected restrictions in certain subjects, for example in history and geography, but the general view was that the Germans would allow schools to stay open. The Jewish community expected the situation to be similar to that in Germany and the Czech Protectorate, i.e. that Jewish youth would be able to attend Jewish schools.

In the meantime, in the field of education there was much confusion. A great many teachers and a section of the older Jewish students escaped to the Soviet-occupied territories, many buildings were damaged by bombs, and so on. For some time the German authorities issued no regulations regarding schools. In this context the headmasters in tacit agreement with the still-existing inspectorate decided to begin classes in October. The beginning of the school year was declared, but without posters or public proclamations so as not to attract the attention of the authorities. The students began to arrive, but they were mainly the younger boys and girls; for a while the older ones kept away. By the end of October, however, classes were being held in an atmosphere of widespread uncertainty. This feeling proved justified since, a few days after classes began, the authorities ordered them to be stopped throughout Warsaw. The official German explanation was that this was because of the danger of epidemic, but in fact they wanted a delay in order to get Polish schools reorganized; they had probably already decided to disband Jewish schools completely.

Indeed, after a few weeks Polish schools were permitted to open as vocational institutions. According to the new regulations, young people of Jewish origin were barred from these schools, and it became clear that the new educational policy was only part of a general policy to destroy the intelligentsia in the occupied country. Jewish teachers entertained hopes that it would still be possible to do something, but it soon became clear that this was out of the question. In the meantime their situation became tragic. The majority of teachers had no financial reserves and were starving. The small amount of relief (about 20 zlotys per person) from the funds of the former teachers' union failed to improve matters, while a large number of Jewish youth, deprived of school, wandered around aimlessly. Of course, in this situation the idea of creating clandestine teaching emerged spontaneously, and a similar development was already taking place in Polish society as a supplement to the existing schools. Undoubtedly the tradition, still vivid, of clandestine education under Russian partition had prompted our decision. Still, we were encountering great difficulties. Many headmasters and students feared repression, for it was the time of the Kott case, the Nalewki Street massacre, and so on.[2]

Parents and students also did not know how to respond. Many expected a favourable end to the war by the spring of 1940. Older boys especially did not evince any particular desire to return to school. This was largely a consequence of trauma caused by the war and bombings. However, we should not forget that the lack of a willingness to learn and of genuine intellectual interest had become severe

[2] On 22 Nov. 1939 fifty-three Jews in an apartment block at 9 Nalewki Street were executed by the Germans, allegedly in reprisal for the murder of a Polish policeman and the wounding of another by a Jewish criminal who resided in the block. In mid-January over 100 members of the Jewish intelligentsia were taken hostages, allegedly in order to compel the Judenrat to hand over a member of a Polish underground group, Andrzej Kott. Kott had been converted to Christianity as an infant and had no links with the Jewish community. Most of those who were taken hostage were subsequently executed.

many years before the war. Other factors that slowed the development of clandestine teaching were the general hardships of the autumn of 1939, such as the scarcity of food and the constant hunting of Jewish men on the streets.

The problem of schools had somehow to be solved, especially since a great number of Jewish youth expelled from the countryside had arrived in Warsaw. Around December 1939 a new chapter began. The teachers, prompted by poverty, started energetically to organize the young people, in most cases without the knowledge of their headmasters. Establishing contacts with former students was relatively easy. The only possible form of education was in study groups of approximately four, or occasionally as many as six, students. They met for twelve hours a week, on average. Many teachers also did individual tutoring, but in this area we suffered from competition from less qualified people who asked low salaries. In general, competition was detrimental for the teachers, and our salaries proved to be very low. In Jewish study groups students paid 30–40 zlotys per month, about 20 per cent less than in Polish study groups. However, the cause of this lay not only in the market economy, but also in the traditional Jewish view of teachers as pariahs. Our study groups were mostly composed of students and teachers from the same school, so that coeducation was exceptional, although it was not ruled out in principle. Young people from outside Warsaw created separate groups led by their own teachers, especially in Łódź, although some of them joined Warsaw study groups. In general, we aimed to follow the curriculum fully. Some organizers, however, had the unfortunate idea of excluding history and geography, which were seen as particularly dangerous. These gaps were later filled, though the results of it are felt even today.

In general it was the better section among the young that started learning, that is the more talented and diligent students; the less dedicated individuals soon gave up. Their standard of living was in most cases irrelevant as the fees were very low. Many students had their tuition fees reduced, and a few were taught free of charge. Girls proved more willing to learn than boys. By the winter of 1939–40 work was going on quite satisfactorily. The students showed perhaps even greater interest in studying than before the war. One obstacle was the lack of study rooms and libraries, but there were still sufficient schoolbooks at that time.

At the beginning of 1940 a regulation was promulgated prohibiting teachers from holding classes without previously submitting an application for a teaching permit. This caused some anxiety among teachers, but did not prompt panic, and the work was not interrupted. The position which has been taken towards the new act is that to obey it will be taken as disloyalty on the part of teachers as Polish citizens. As a result, Jewish teachers decided to follow the example of the teachers in Polish schools, and not to submit applications. For safety reasons, some study groups were divided into groups of two to three people; this, however, did not last, as it would have been financially disastrous for the teachers. Students also did not react to the German threats and continued to learn as usual. As a precaution we told our students not to carry too many books on the streets so as not to draw attention to themselves.

Soon it became apparent that the concern on the part of Jewish teachers was without foundation. Apparently the school act was among the broad group of regulations intended not for implementation but to terrorize the population. There were a few arrests among Polish teachers, but the arrested were soon released. The Germans took the view that the act did not cover Jews, for whom the issue of education has not yet been regulated. They realized that large groups of young people participated in learning, but they decided to look the other way; the issue did not interest them, and they would not waste time and people dealing with it. They knew that the great majority of young people did not go to school at all, and their objective was to demoralize the masses in order to destroy Jewish culture, so perilous for humankind. In the long run such a policy could bring very dangerous results. The German indifference was evident from numerous instances when the police entered apartments where classes were being held but took no action. One incident went as follows:

During a class with a study group of six girls the police entered the apartment so suddenly that there was no time to hide exercise books. One of the Germans turned to the confused teacher and ironically stated: 'Well, a clandestine class. Schadet nicht, lehren Sie weiter, es ist doch erlaubt' ('It does no harm. Go on learning. It is permitted'). The Germans did not even check documents. They confiscated a bundle of linen and left the apartment.

The establishment in 1940 of many vocational courses had no significant impact on the situation in study groups. A great number of young men enrolled in these courses in order to free themselves of the threat of labour camps, but the participation of boys in study groups was limited anyway, and in many instances the students who enrolled on vocational courses did not stop attending our classes.

During the summer and autumn of 1940 the work continued; the political catastrophes had no major impact on it. The establishment of the enclosed ghetto created a new era in the life of study groups. A large number of young people from assimilated families arrived in the Jewish quarter. Until then, they usually studied in their own study groups under the guidance of Christian teachers. This group of young people was affected by the war and oppression perhaps worse than their less assimilated peers. Having been completely uprooted from their previous lifestyle, they proved more demoralized. Thus, teaching them initially had worse results. After contacts were established between them and the teachers, separate study groups were organized for them which consisted of close friends or individuals originally from the same school. Uniting this new element with old students created difficulties because of cultural differences, different patterns of behaviour, tradition, and so on. But gradually a fusion became more and more apparent.

During the winter of 1940–1 the number of study groups and of young people attending them had increased significantly. The same is true of the quality of instruction. The study groups established themselves well, and the teachers raised their demands on students. Because the study groups of the second grade of the *liceum* and the fourth grade of the *gimnazjum* had completed their curricula, it became necessary to organize final exams. They were held entirely *lege artis*. Of course, for safety considerations no certificates were issued; however, we believed that after the defeat of the Germans the Polish authorities would recognize these exams. Characteristically, the students' attitude towards the exams was the same as before the war. Girls especially were anxious, but students were generally extremely preoccupied with grades.

The attitude of parents towards education was a different matter. They willingly sent the younger children to study so that they would not wander around aimlessly. At the same time they were indifferent to the education of the older ones, even if the cost was relatively lower than before the war. Parents were not interested in their childrens' progress, often even making it more difficult for them to study. This was caused not only by the hardships of life, but also by the low cultural level of the Jewish *petit bourgeoisie*. It had a very negative impact on the circumstances of teachers, whose earnings had increased only slightly in 1941 despite wild rises in prices. The general rise in tuition fees introduced in the spring of 1942 brought with it ridiculous consequences. At present in the highest-paying study groups a teacher can earn 4 or more zlotys per hour; at two hours per week this brings their monthly income to about 34 zlotys. On average, however, the fee for an hour is about 3 zlotys, and in many cases only 2 zlotys. Competition from less qualified teachers greatly contributes to this situation.

I think, however, that, in spite of its many shortcomings, the work of teachers is of great importance to society. When this war has reached a favourable conclusion, the Jewish community will have a group of well-educated young people able to produce in a short time a nucleus of professionals. The minds of these young people will not be clouded by the stupid fascist demagoguery that teachers were obliged to propagate before the war. Only now can they say in class what they think. Also, study groups are indubitably a kind of dam against the demoralization spreading so rapidly among young people. Boredom, inactivity, and, above all, general corruption and the work of the Thirteen that preys on the poverty and weakened moral resistance of the masses—these factors endanger young people especially. It needs to be added that pre-war times had already negatively influenced their psychological condition. Clandestine education can prevent demoralization only in a very limited way since it encompasses a relatively small group, but at least we create a core with a good intellectual and a reasonable moral level. After the horrible debasement of the war such a healthy element will be greatly needed. Interestingly enough, young people themselves are highly aware of this aspect of the work in study groups, and they often express it in conversation. The brighter individuals see the dangers and try to avoid them; and they really want to learn.

The final question to be answered concerns the attitude of study group students towards work. While they study very diligently and often exhibit great interest, it would be a mistake to attribute the intensity of the work merely to diligence and interest. Very important, especially among the older students, is a quite practical factor, namely the need to conclude their studies as soon as possible so as to limit the expense. This is fully understandable in the difficult times of war; however, students and their parents often emphasize it so strongly that it stirs up conflict with teachers. Dishonest tutors take advantage of it and promise to go over the material in a very short time. The low cultural level and lack of understanding on the part of parents and students make teachers' work even more difficult. The latter make every effort to maintain high standards in their study groups, and in general they succeed. The requirements of the old curriculum and the genuine honesty of teachers prove to be perfectly adequate weapons against external temptations and pressures. Teachers work very hard and with exceptional honesty even if their material circumstances are extremely difficult, and they are badly affected by the prevailing indifference in our society. Even if we have to admit that at the root of teachers' work today there are less idealistic motives than was the case in Poland at the end of the last century, the results will be no worse, either for the society or for scholarship.

Teaching Jewish Youth in the Warsaw Ghetto during the War, 1939–1941

INTRODUCTION

In this essay I should like to describe the situation of Jewish secondary education during the Second World War. It is a task that presents serious difficulties because the clandestine character of this type of education makes it very difficult to gather accurate statistical data, and as a result it is difficult to compare the present situation with pre-war times. Such a comparison would provide interesting sociological material. It should be noted that before the war quite a large group of Jewish youth did not attend Jewish schools, but instead were enrolled in Polish schools. This group has been incorporated at least in part into the clandestine educational network. More or less the same applies to many young people from outside Warsaw.

A comparison of the numbers attending Jewish schools in the pre-war period and the participants in clandestine education is not possible, since such an investigation would encounter problems which are insoluble at the present time. Because of this I have chosen a different approach here. In Section 1 I shall try to describe the general characteristics of Jewish education in the period directly before the

---

The original manuscript of this essay is partly illegible, and fragments, including the last section, are missing.—Ed.

outbreak of the war, in the years 1935–9. In Section 2 I shall describe the present situation. I shall try to trace in which way the circumstances of the war have influenced forms of teaching, pedagogical conditions, and relations between teachers and young people, as well as [the attitude?] of society towards education.

I

[. . .] the so-called lease of the school to its personnel. The owner secured a profit for himself while making his employees bear all the risk and expenses. All these phenomena were also present on the Polish side, although not in such acute form.

The small group of privileged schools for boys and girls which I have described catered mostly for well-to-do young people from the bourgeoisie or rich intelligentsia. These circles could afford to pay higher tuition fees in order to place their children in first-class schools. The less wealthy sectors of the population sent their children to the lower-ranking schools. It needs to be stated that the Jewish *petite bourgeoisie* made great efforts to enable their sons and daughters to attend school, but, as I have mentioned elsewhere, their goal was advancement in society rather than the acquisition of knowledge. It is my impression that in recent years the interest of young people in learning has diminished very substantially. This has been caused by a number of factors, such as economic problems and badly formulated curricula. In addition, the generally lower prestige of learning has had its impact. It was rare to encounter genuine interest in a subject, and if it happened, it was almost exclusively in the areas of the natural or technical sciences. Humanistic problems interested almost nobody. Characteristically, school workshops, which were once so popular, had now withered completely [. . .]

[. . .] In the 1920s numerous organizations, both legal and illegal, worked in this area [among Jewish youth?]. In recent times the drive to join them diminished, as did any deeper interest in them. Self-education groups, once so popular, disappeared. Young people took the easy way out, turning for explanations to older, trusted people. On the other hand, they expressed their views outspokenly, choosing extreme positions to impress those around them. School sections of university corporations relied on a whole array of props such as caps and foils to impress their members, and became highly attractive in the upper grades. The general shallowness of opinions led to frequent changes of ideology.

The attitude of young people towards school was generally less favourable than it had been. The blame lay to a large extent with the school itself. It compromised itself by using nasty competitive tricks and pro-government propaganda, while overworked teachers were unable to take care of the students properly. There was also an additional factor. Uncultured Jewish society still saw in a teacher the *melamed* of old, and the poor economic circumstances of school employees aroused in rich merchants only feelings of contempt and superiority; young people were affected by these sentiments and treated teachers accordingly. The latter often reacted strongly to this negative assessment, and it is no wonder that relations were strained.

In this situation serious pedagogical work was hardly possible [...]

[... Government reforms had] a deep impact on Jewish education [...] which was faced with the need to increase teaching aids substantially, to improve the state of classrooms, and so on. Given that these changes occurred in a time of significant worsening in the economic crisis and the rapid pauperization of the Jewish masses, it is easy to understand that the reforms had a negative impact on the situation in Jewish schools. In Warsaw these problems emerged more sharply, since the situation of Jewish schools was very difficult even before the reforms. There were a large number of these schools, and a disproportionately large number of these were attended by very few students. Only three boys' and three girls' schools had a reasonable number of students. Otherwise there were dozens with a ridiculously low number of children, sometimes as low as 200, and extremely low tuition fees. The tragedy was that even these institutions had to be maintained because of the teachers who were employed in them, since when a school was closed the teachers faced starvation. At the same time this scattering led to unhealthy and unethical competition. This involved lowering fees, a largely fictitious system of tuition breaks, the notorious phenomenon of bribing teachers [...]

[...] of the young people who, as I have already mentioned, were already not disposed to respect their teachers. But the most important difficulty for Jewish teachers was their catastrophic material situation. A young teacher, even with a full workload of thirty-six hours a week, earned at most 300–350 zlotys before the war; an older one, with more than ten years' experience, could earn up to 600 zlotys, which included special bonuses for being head of a class, for running workshops, marking exercise books, and so on. And only a few worked as many hours as that. In addition, only a few Warsaw schools paid twelve monthly salaries per year; the majority paid ten or eleven, and even these were paid irregularly. There were continual conflicts, and the role of the teachers' union in them was unfortunately minor. Thus, teachers had to look for numerous additional jobs at summer camps, on evening courses, and so on. As a result, they were overworked. Besides classes, they had endless other duties. If they were head of a class, they had to be in the school hall for the most of the breaks, and to lead workshops or sports clubs, which was difficult and unrewarding. Natural sciences teachers spent long afternoons in school supervising laboratories; humanities teachers had to work in the library. In addition, there were some sessions lasting often late into the night, as well as a lot of report-writing, in regard to which each school wanted to be more conscientious than the next. A very irritating part of school life was the so-called work for the country (*praca państwowa*) which involved innumerable celebrations of patriotic anniversaries [...]

An extremely important element in the situation was the attitude of the school authorities towards Jewish education. I believe it is true to say that in the Warsaw school district the attitude of the superintendent's office towards Jewish schools was wholly loyal. The inspectors tried to act properly. Of course, they created annoyance with their close supervision, and often bad treatment of teachers, but similar things were happening on the Polish side. The incidents of an antisemitic character which sometimes occurred were caused rather by Polish teachers who were sent to us to run the matriculation examinations. In addition, the state education authorities conducted a policy which was hostile to Jewish schools in that they very rarely listed them in the higher categories of school. At one time a large number of Jewish schools were suddenly downgraded. This was often tantamount to the closing of the school. Although the representatives of the authorities often indicated the proliferation of schools as the cause of the poor situation and claimed that this needed to be corrected, it is doubtful whether this factor played a significant role in their policy. Even if teachers in Jewish schools could be held partially responsible for the negative aspects of life in their schools, the fundamental causes lay much deeper. The standard of teachers varied greatly. Their average level of education was higher than on the Polish side, with no less diligence and scrupulousness, but, a significant problem was the frequent lack of inner culture, for example [. . .]

II

AUTUMN 1939

The outbreak of war with its disastrous results, and the bombing and surrender of Warsaw, were events that put an end to the previous way of life. Secondary schools in the capital found themselves in a highly ambiguous situation. Although Polish school authorities still existed, they had no influence on the situation. The increasingly frequent arrests of teachers by the Gestapo scared many people. In the Jewish community the situation was particularly difficult. Many teachers and older students had fled to the areas of Soviet occupation; in general, those who stayed were passive. In addition, many people were afraid to go out on the streets, where German catchers roamed around abducting people for forced labour or simply 'confiscating' money. Many classrooms in Jewish schools were destroyed by bombing. These circumstances produced a state of apathy among the majority of Jewish teachers, which was the more dangerous because almost everyone was exhausting his or her modest financial reserves and many people suffered from hunger. Since the Germans completely ignored the problem of education, the teachers, together with the still existing superintendent's office, decided to see whether it was possible to organize the work of schools. Nobody was aware that the Germans were aiming to wipe out secondary education completely in order to stop the growth of the intelligentsia; at the same time they tried to destroy the intelligentsia physically, and to suppress it economically. Probably by then their plans for the occupied territories already included the existence only of vocational schools. According to these plans, such schools were to prepare technicians to be used in industry who, at the same time, would be entirely dependent on the German leadership. Besides, creating a sizeable semi-intelligentsia would create [. . .]

[. . .] beginning of the classes. In Jewish schools this was done discreetly, so as not to attract the attention of the authorities. In the second half of November work began. At once we encountered great problems. First of all, only a small number of students reported for school. There were not enough classrooms. Because of that many schools had to borrow classrooms from others, which caused confusion. But all this lasted for a very short time. The German authorities prohibited classes, claiming as a pretext the danger of spreading typhus. Of course, no one took this bureaucratic excuse seriously. Although some still hoped to restart the schools, the threat of the establishment of the ghetto, which hung over the Warsaw Jews for the first time in November 1939, distracted attention towards other problems. In the meantime Polish schools partially returned to work either as vocational or as elementary establishments. At once the idea emerged among them to organize clandestine teaching; given the indifference of the occupation authorities, it was quickly organized without great difficulties.

On the Jewish side, too, at the end of 1939, we came to realize that in the new circumstances the only forms of education could be study groups or individual instruction; however, fear of the Germans was too strong to start work immediately. Although some teachers and even certain groups began to establish contacts with students, at the beginning this proceeded very slowly. This was the result of many different factors. Above all, fear of the Germans stopped many teachers from working and parents from sending their children to study groups. As for older students, the better ones had fled . . .

Translated from Polish by Gwido Zlatkes

Two Coffins on Smocza Street and Śliska Street

JANUSZ KORCZAK

WHEN I walk on the street I always look ahead so as not to fall, not hurt myself: the broken bones of the old do not easily grow back together—so I didn't see him, or maybe I did notice him and thought for a moment, 'What a beautiful boy.' Maybe that was what I had thought and forgotten at once.

He's 15, or maybe 14 or 16. People say, 'He has lived for fifteen springs.' They say it because young years are sunny, and the colourful flowers of dreams bloom even if it's going badly at home and it's going badly for people in general. Warm spring years, fifteen blooming springs, sunny, joyful, young—and full of dreams that are colourful like spring butterflies.

Many such boys and girls walk on the streets, beautiful and shining, and even if in dirty rags—clean.

Even if I noticed this boy in passing, I knew nothing about him. Not even if his mother was alive, or if he had a mother—or a father. Where could his father and mother be? Here or there? Nowadays people part—one goes here, another goes there—even little children, not only such a big boy in the fifteenth spring of his life.

And you know what? Recently, on a very cold day, on Smocza Street, I saw him again. This, I can say, was not the first time.

You know Smocza Street. It was as always. Full of people—jostling—hurrying—quarrelling and bargaining. And all at once, yelling: one has potatoes, another cigarettes, another clothing, another sweets.

The beautiful boy—quietly, very quietly—lay on the snow, he lay on the white, he lay on the clean white snow.

His mother stood by him and repeated over and over:

Help him, people help him.

Naturally. She was his mother. Only these three words. And she wasn't crying, just repeating it in a clear whisper, only this and nothing more.

People help him, people help him.

This chapter was first published, as 'Dwie trumme na Smoczej i na Śliskiej', in *Odra* (June 1995). It was written in the winter of 1941/2.

People were passing by. Nobody was helping him. But they weren't at fault. He didn't need help any more.

Here he lies, so quiet and so bright, on the white snow.

His mouth is half open, as if in a smile. I haven't noticed the colour of his lips, probably pink. And white teeth.

His eyes are half-open, and in one eye—right in its pupil—a tiny sparkle, perhaps the littlest of stars. A star is shining.

Now the second coffin: I think it was on Saturday. I'm sure it was Saturday. Everyone who went on the left side of our good Śliska Steet to the fam[ily] must have seen that coffin.

It was a child—a little child—maybe 3 years old. A little foot, little toes.

By the wall, wrapped in paper. Also on the snow. I didn't notice, I don't remember if the paper was grey or black. I only know that this grey or black paper was very carefully, very lovingly, very tenderly, very neatly and evenly—from the bottom, from the sides, and from the top—tied with string.

Only toes on a little foot.

Before bringing it out and placing it on the snow, somebody carefully tied this little bundle, this child's package.

Certainly the mother.

Certainly she didn't have the paper or the string at home. She went to the store and bought them.

That's how much I know, nothing more. Unless I should tell you how that mother bore this child, how she was in labour, how she was bleeding red blood, and then fed it with white milk. With her breast she fed it—with white milk, sweet and warm, from her breast.

You probably want to know. Why do I write about this little child? There are so many others younger and older, adults, women and men. And I saw them, too. In the doorways and by the walls on many different streets, where living people wear on their forearms bands with the yellow Star of David.

So, that mother, slowly, evenly, carefully, lovingly, and elaborately tied her package with a string, preparing for expedition.

It was thick paper, good for wrapping.

How could it happen that she left these five little toes and the foot up to the ankle to stick out, to protrude? She couldn't overlook them.

On purpose, then. Perhaps.

Yes.

Why?

It wasn't easy to wrap that little cottonball in paper in such a way that everything was even and neat—except this one thing.

I will tell you if you want.

The mother was afraid that a passer-by could think that somebody had dropped, or put down, something dark, or that he forgot it, or lost it, or left it for a moment in worried haste so he could come back later to take it under his arm and carry it wherever it was supposed to go. It could happen. It's hard now for people to think reasonably, hurried because the kitchen serves soup only for a short time, and in the offices one has to wait a long time.

It could happen. That's what a passer-by could think. And, unaware, in passing, carelessly, without actually thinking at all, just to make sure there was nothing valuable in the paper, nothing of use—and in order not to bend down needlessly—he might kick it. Just to check whether it was firm, whether there wasn't something to pick up.

And that she did not want. Which is why she left that naked foot: so people would know. There were no shoes, no stockings, nothing to take.

That's why she did it to her dead child, her little one.

For it is sad when someone kicks something that you love. And people nowadays are impatient and distracted, and often they don't say what they want to say and often do not do what they want to do. Just whatever occurs to them at the moment.

Even dreams, sometimes they make no sense either: they are weird and twisted.

Translated from Polish by Gwido Zlatkes

Krzysztof Kamil Baczyński: A Poet-Hero

JOANNA ROSTROPOWICZ CLARK

> Po co, matko, taki skrzydeł pokrój?
> Taka walka, ojcze, po co—takiej winie?
> Why, mother, do the wings take such a shape?
> Father, why does this guilt need such a fight?
> KRZYSZTOF KAMIL BACZYŃSKI

IN his book *Poeci i Szoa* ('Poets and the Shoah')[1] Natan Gross, a critic, translator, and film director who has lived in Israel since 1950, writes about Baczyński:

Krzysztof Kamil Baczyński was a Pole, considered himself a Pole, and expressed this with his whole heart and work. However, Hitler had a different view of the matter. Hence, when in Warsaw they started building the ghetto wall, Krzysztof, together with his mother, Stefania, and the family of her brother Adam Zieleńczyk, decided to stay on the 'Aryan side' with 'Aryan documents'. Krzysztof's father, Stanisław Baczyński (Bittner), a member of Piłsudski's Legions who could speak and write Yiddish, died before the war. Baczyński's mother was converted; she fell into a religious devotion which drew people's attention. Baczyński's mother's brother was a Piłsudski-ite, and his daughter 'Dziula' (Krzysztof many times warmly recalled her) had rather left-wing convictions.

After this brief introduction Gross quotes extensively from several poems in which Baczyński either directly linked himself in suffering with the fate of Polish Jews, or by an always scrupulously recorded date indicated the specific context, thus highlighting this suffering for the poem's meaning. One of the examples offered by Gross is the poem 'Pokolenie' ('A Generation'), written on 21 July 1943, a day after the arrest of the Zieleńczyks, who had been denounced to the Germans:

> Nas nauczono. Nie ma sumienia.
> W jamach żyjemy strachem zaryci,
> w grozie drążymy mroczne miłości,
> własne posągi—źli troglodyci.
>
> Nas nauczono. Nie ma miłości.
> Jakże nam jeszcze uciekać w mrok
> przed żaglem nozdrzy węszących nas,
> przed siecią wzdętych kijów i rąk.

[1] Sosnowiec, 1993.

> (We learned the lesson: conscience does not exist.
> We dwell in caves, fear enfolds us,
> we carve in horror our dark loves,
> our own statues—evil troglodytes.
>
> We learned the lesson: love does not exist.
> How else can we hide in the darkness
> while sniffing nostrils seek our scent,
> while swollen sticks and fists seek to envelop us.)

Perhaps I am wrong in thinking that my feelings of shock, and then of sadness and depression, after reading these eight stark and yet so dense lines, do not require explanation. So, this was another burden which he carried, during his short and tragic life—a burden he probably could not, and did not, want to share with his friends, perhaps with the exception of a handful of those closest to him, who some twenty years later alluded to it extremely cautiously in a volume of memoirs collected by Zbigniew Wasilewski.[2] Why have the critics—including Kazimierz Wyka, one of the first admirers of Baczyński's poetry and the author of an important introduction to his *Collected Poems*—constantly omitted this part of the life of one of the most prominent twentieth-century Polish poets? Even if this part was imposed on him by history, it is undoubtedly present in his work, especially during its greatest period from the autumn of 1941 to the summer of 1943. I say 'undoubtedly' with self-reproach, since my youthful reading of Baczyński was also hasty and superficial. Would it have been different had I known about his Jewish origins?

'Jewish origins' is not an appropriate phrase, I was told by Professor Henryk Hiż, whom I called to share my doubts. For years I have regarded highly his wisdom and *amor patriae* (without his spiritual help I would not have completed my doctorate). Another reason why I called him was that I knew that he had personally known the poet and his family situation. Professor Hiż was quite dismissive of my doubts, and even rather annoyed by the revelations of Natan Gross, previously unknown to him. 'So what?', he said (I quote from memory).

Nobody in our circle, which was absolutely free of antisemitism, cared about these divisions. *They* wanted to divide us. The Endeks and the Zionists. The Germans! Was Baczyński in hiding? He was in the underground. We were all in hiding, moving, changing addresses, helping each other. And all of us reacted in the same way to the ghetto, the deportations, Auschwitz. We talked about it all the time. The influence of Baczyński's parents, his mother, was at the beginning of the war much less important than his break with Ania, who was a devout Catholic. Then there was his love for and marriage to Basia. And the matter that was most important for all of us—the struggle with the occupier. Would talk of his ethnic origins have diminished Baczyński's legend? That is nonsense. In whose eyes? I would advise against such simple-minded argumentation. It is like speaking to the poetry instead of listening to it . . .

---

[2] *Żołnierz, poeta, czasu kurz* ('A Soldier, a Poet, Dust of the Time') (Kraków, 1967).

I agreed. I always feel reassured when talking about attitudes in the Warsaw underground circle of that time, which was also my family environment—not to divide, not to search for 'genealogies', to resist 'the flood of hatred'. However, that resistance and the sense of its common cause and brotherhood, as well as the awareness, even if imposed, of the link with those who wanted or had to remain separate and because of that suffered hell, were the source of a painful struggle and were recorded in an outstanding artistic work by Baczyński himself. Can one, therefore, in the name of the noble idea of transcending narrow ethnic divisions, regard this recording as of less significance or simply unimportant? Great art often expresses what its creator pushes away from himself in his rational thought and action; it is a palimpsest of his conscience, an open symptom of a concealed sickness of his soul, a sickness of the epoch. Yet one cannot even claim this with Baczyński. Too much testifies that he was extremely conscious of the thoughts and feelings contained in his work.

Let us return to the poems; I quote from Wyka's introduction: 'There is an obvious similarity to Słowacki's family situation . . .'; this is agreeable nonsense. And later the rhetorical question, which puzzles him: why did 'this shock at the horror of the occupation' occur to Baczyński earlier than to his peers, already in the autumn of 1941, when the greatest period of the poet's creativity had already begun and was to last for several months? 'In the autumn of 1941', the critic writes in regard to the poem 'Bez imienia' ('Nameless'), 'the Germans had not yet resorted to public executions on the streets as a means of terror.' This is not quite correct. In the fall of 1941 the Warsaw ghetto was finally sealed and a terrible hunt had started on the streets of the city. Emanuel Ringelblum noted in his *Diary*: '11.10. An order was issued threatening all Jews leaving the ghetto without a pass with the death penalty . . . On November 8 two Jews were shot in the street, without even a summary trial (so it is reported): Lejman, the well-known owner of a cinema (on Teatralny Square), and another at the Main Station.' Several days later, eight Jews were executed, including six women in the Jewish prison on Zamenhof Street. The Polish underground press, writing about this crime, revealed the name of the policeman in navy blue responsible for the shooting, Wiktor Załek. In the late autumn and winter of that year Baczyński wrote, along with 'Bez imienia':

> Wtedy krzyk krótki zza ściany;
> wtedy w podłogę—skałą
> (Then, a short cry behind the wall;
> then a rock—against the floor).

He also wrote poems expressing paralysing pain and internal torment, such as 'Jesień 41 r.' ('Autumn 1941'):

> Żeśmy po schodach szli z czarnych ciał braci
> (We walked on the steps of our brothers' blackened bodies).

'Krzyż' ('The Cross'), 'Z szopką' ('Carolling'), 'Śnieg' ('The Snow'), 'Psalm 4'—read them! Kazimierz Wyka has suggested that in that period Baczyński reacted to the horror of the war, '. . . not so much reaching for the facts, and their lyrical illustrations, but anticipating these facts by his innate moral imagination'. Thus Wyka identified Baczyński as a representative and forerunner of 'generational catastrophism', as opposed to the 'historiosophic catastrophism' represented, for example, by Czesław Miłosz and Władysław Sebyła. Baczyński—a synthesis and a monument of a representative. And as always, the higher the pedestal, the deeper the shadow.

Before the cycle of the trauma of the occupation's horror, correctly delineated by Wyka, already in the spring of 1941 Baczyński had written a few remarkable poems testifying to his shock at what everybody had seen. In his memoir about Baczyński, Tadeusz Sołtan writes about a few weeks spent together with his friend from the pre-war organization Spartakus in the hospital on Solec Street in March and April 1941.[3] 'The reason for that hospitalization was, in my case, not so much illness, even if my heart was giving me trouble already then, as a desire, dictated by the considerations of safety, to disappear from home for some time,' he explains, adding that Krzysztof, too, who always suffered from asthma, wanted 'temporarily to change his environment'. We know that in March 1941 the establishment of a ghetto in Warsaw had essentially been completed, with the simultaneous influx to the city of the enormous masses of deportees and escapees. Mass round-ups of men for deportation to labour camps began, including two large ones, on 15 April and at Easter, 20–1 April, in which the navy-blue police actively participated. Adam Czerniakow was arrested and severely beaten in prison. Suicides multiplied and the plague of informers began. About the poems written by Baczyński in hospital, Sołtan writes: 'I connect them with our conversations there, where you could see "the farthest shore of grief" (*najdalszy brzeg żalu*) and where at nights you dreamt of "eyes of bitter, oblong almonds" (*oczy z gorzkich podłużnych migdałów*) that you had seen during the day'. Joanna Weintraub, together with her husband, Jerzy Kamil Weintraub, a poet, translator of Rilke, and Baczyński's close friend, waited through that period in a village near Warsaw. Prompted by a letter from Stefania Baczyńska, she paid Baczyński a visit in the hospital. This is how Joanna Weintraub remembers the event:

His neighbour was a large man, about whom Baczyński whispered to me that he had come out of gaol, was all swollen, and was hiding there in the hospital. I can't remember today whether Baczyński said 'he was hiding there' or 'he too was hiding there'. It is hard, after so many years, to recall what was the actual truth and what was the conclusion which I drew from the circumstances. It seems that the truth was that Krzysztof was already involved in the conspiracy and the situation required him to hide in the hospital. Perhaps that was why his mother didn't want to visit him, not to draw attention to him.

[3] *Trudne rachunki pamięci* ('Difficult Accounts of the Memory') (Warsaw, 1988).

Those were times in which nobody asked any questions.

We should admire the great sensitivity of Joanna Weintraub and Tadeusz Sołtan, perhaps, consisting of an appropriate sense of what questions should not be asked openly and what conclusions should not be drawn for the public. However, a critic is duty-bound to the work of art; he is first obliged to explain, and only then, if his temperament is such, to construct syntheses. Especially in poetry there are certain codes, images, and metaphors, and, in the case of Baczyński and his peers, particularly important dates, for which the references are facts and things incomprehensible without a certain knowledge of them. How is a contemporary reader supposed to know what to understand by what Baczyński had seen from the window of the Solec hospital, what was the 'current' against which he was wading, 'athwart the coughing and death' (*na ukos kaszlu i śmierci*)? Kazimierz Wyka somehow disregarded these real references to the years from 1941 to 1943; he blurred the sense of the poems written then by speaking of their 'prophetic' vision, meaning the foreseeing of the later 'Columbian' events. A much younger critic, the author of the introduction to the recent (1992) selection of Baczyński's poems,[4] Jerzy Święch, offers a critical approach free from 'historical contexts' (apart from a general overview):

If we compile the darkest and most incomprehensible fragments of Baczyński's poems possibly it is here that this mysterious fate, impossible to name, of the community on behalf of which he spoke thickens and accumulates. There are many such fragments, since the whole of Baczyński's work overflows with metaphors, allusions, ellipses, symbols, silences (an important means of expression which the poet learned from Norwid). The 'impenetrability' and 'incomprehensibility' of Baczyński's language is what he has derived from the Truth he has touched.

Translated into plain English this means that the critic advises us not to try too hard to understand many unclear fragments, and 'above all enjoy' the fragments where 'the universal dimension appears strongly enough'. Is it not more enjoyable, in the serious sense of that word, to know from what concrete thing that universal value has emerged?

Poets writing and publishing their booklets of poems during the occupation in clandestine publishing houses used allusion and silence not just as a means of expression, but also as a precaution. The circle of their readers, a few thousand strong, who every day were in contact with the same truths, understood every metaphor and every ellipse. The poems that were closest to these truths–facts were most often copied, recited among friends and in prison cells. At the same time their authors wanted to hope that 'the song would survive' (*pieśń ujdzie cało*), even if they themselves would not. They believed that the future reader, not compelled to hide his body and soul, would invest a little effort to look into his knowledge and imagination for a proper key to a metaphor, that he or she would think about

[4] Krzysztof Kamil Baczyński, *Poezje* (Lublin, 1992).

the date and the place. And they counted on an enlightened critic to help the reader.

Let us go on reading, carefully, like Miłosz's mole with the lantern. It is summer 1941; the wall is being erected around the ghetto. From the poem 'Ci ludzie' ('These People'):

> Głowa przy głowie—taki to mur?
> Twarze jak orzech twardych czaszek.
> Pięści spęczniałe jak garby gór—
> —nasze. . . .
>
> W dróg poszarpanych linach
> motyw jak zasiek się rwie:
> nasze, nie nasze, nasze, nie nasze.
> To coś przypomina . . . Już wiem:
> Pęknięte serca skrzypiec.
>
> (Head by head—is this a wall?
> Their faces are like nuts of firm skulls.
> Their fists are swollen like the mountains' humps—
> —they're ours.
>
> On the roads' ropes torn to pieces
> a motif like barbed wire breaks:
> Ours, not ours, ours, not ours:
> It reminds of something . . . I know:
> Violins' broken hearts.)
>
> (July 1941)

After that autumn, with the closing of the wall and the first cycle of Baczyński's unrestrained laments, which I have already mentioned (in the collection *Poezje*, edited by Święch, these poems are in the chapter entitled 'Bohater': 'A Hero'), came the winter with his fulfilled love for Barbara Drapczyńska, beautiful erotic poems (among them 'Biała magia': 'White Magic'), and religious poetry: dialogues of faith, doubt, and hope. Cold weather always made Baczyński's asthma worse, so, through Jerzy Andrzejewski's intervention, the poet was invited to spend the week of Easter and a few extra days in the Iwaszkiewiczs' manor at Stawiska. Again, during the exceptionally cold March, with the rumours of deportations to Treblinka, and *szmalcownicy* circling Warsaw streets, Baczyński was overwhelmed by depression. He wrote in 'Milczenie' ('Silence'):

> . . . Znowu dym spowija
> i snem przybity, leżąc umieram. Wiek mija.
>
> O, zatrzymać! Milczenie. Widzę jeszcze ludy
> i naród pod kopułą, gdzie szalone wozy
> wypruwają z obłoków deszcze krwawych nożyć.
> I pada mór, i ludzie wypłoszeni
> do bram łomoczą, a bramy z kamieni.

> Więc przypadają do stóp drżącej ziemi,
> a ta otwiera paszcze, całuje i wchłania,
> i niebo drga, nie woła żaden głos.
>
> (... Again, the smoke takes over,
> I'm dying nailed by a dream. The century's passing.
> Stop it! Stop it! A silence. I still see the nations,
> and the people in the dome where the wild carriages
> tear from the clouds the rains of bloody scissors.
> And the plague falls down, and the frightened people
> are banging at the doors, the doors of stone.
> So they squat close to the trembling ground
> that opens its mouth, kisses, and swallows them
> the sky is shaking and no voice is calling.)
>
> (16 March 1942)

In 'Martwa pieśń' ('Dead Song'):

> A sen wieczny upiory zabitych unosi,
> których—krzyżów ognistych i krzyż nie uprosi,
> i płacz wzniesiony późno nie przywróci bieli
> i nie zetrze znamienia z śmiertelnej pościeli.
>
> (The eternal dream carries away the murdered people's ghosts
> whom—even the cross won't pledge out their fiery crosses
> and the lament too late won't restore the whites,
> and won't bleach the stigma from their death sheets.)
>
> (April 1942)

In 'Samotność' ('Solitude'):

> Nie ma ludzi. To tylko tragiczność tak krzepnie
> w pomniki fantastyczne rosnące beze mnie
> i poza mną rosnące. Wzrok ich jak zasłona
> i za grzech pierworodny odjęte ramiona.
> O, daj mi ten grzech poznać. Nikt na mnie nie woła.
>
> (There are no people. That's just the tragedy freezing
> into fantastic monuments growing by themselves
> and beyond me. Their sight's like a veil
> and the original sin took their arms away.
> Oh, let me know that sin. Here nobody calls me.)
>
> (28 June 1942)

In 'Noc wiary' ('Night of Faith'):

> Ręce jak żuki węgli
> popieleją u okien.
> Wiatry czarną posokę
> i gwiazdy sypią w głąb.

(Hands like coal beetles
grow grey in the window.
Winds sow into the deep
black gore and the stars.)

(28 June 1942)

On 3 June 1942 the wedding ceremony of Krzysztof and Barbara took place in the presence of perhaps the largest gathering of poets in one place at the same time. Jarosław Iwaszkiewicz has recalled that the newly-weds appeared to him like a couple of adolescents taking their First Communion and that he gave them a huge 'bundle' of lilacs, well remembered also by others who were present in the Church of the Holy Trinity on Solec Street. Tadeusz Sołtan writes:

Perhaps a new chapter in Baczyński's life started then. Different matters and threads were strangely mixed in it. Yet I can't help feeling that even what is called the most intimate happiness could not save the poet from being torn apart internally. Nothing could suffice— neither the warmest tenderness of those closest to him, nor the youthful friendships of fellow soldiers in the underground, nor even poetry—poetry for its own sake, and not to judge the world justly.

An important event in the summer of 1942 was the mimeograph publication of Baczyński's first 'volume' of poems, his first appearance in book form, preceded by the inclusion of several of his poems in two underground anthologies. These volumes sold out immediately, and circulated among friends, who borrowed them for brief periods; yet the criticism offered by Baczyński's peers (among them, Tadeusz Gajcy) was rather harsh and painful to the author. A few months later Andrzej Obornicki (Stanisław Marczak) published a review in the magazine *Sztuka i Naród* which concluded 'Alien coachman, with a whip of decadent moods you drive the horse.' Although extremely encouraged by the enthusiastic letter-essay about his work by Kazimierz Wyka, and grateful to the 'elders', above all Jerzy Andrzejewski, who extended his patronage with great tact and care, Baczyński wanted to be understood—even if not applauded or idolized—by the young, by his own and by the succeeding generation. Important though they might have been for the budding poet, the praise and criticism he received did not reach into his poetic workshop. He continued to write from that place unique to each artist where, in continuous flame, reality is forged with consciousness into forms more durable than life. In the midst of the summer of 1942, on the third anniversary of his father's death, he wrote the poem 'Wigilia' ('Christmas Eve'), dedicated to his mother: it described the search of a widow's apartment (*Ciemni, trzej, schyleni, długo szukali w szafie*: 'The three, dark, bent, searched the closet for a long time') in which a black cross on a wall frightens the agents away. In September, day after day, Baczyński wrote from the deepest despair, unilluminated by love, faith, or hope. In 'Ten czas' ('This Time'):

'Znowu jesień' ('Autumn Again'):

> I płynie mrok. Jest cisza. Łamanych czaszek trzask;
> i wiatr zahuczy czasem, i wiek przywali głazem.
>
> (The darkness floats in. The silence. The cracking of broken skulls;
> And the wind sometimes storms, the century crushes it with a rock)
>
> (10 September 1942)

'Znowu jesień' ('Autumn Again'):

> A oto już i jesień. Drzewa są na nowo
> żaglami martwym domom, skrzydłami martwym snom,
> jakby nie powstawały nad rozrąbaną głową,
> jakby nie było kolumn roztratowanych rąk.
>
> (Autumn is here already. Trees are again
> the sails for dead houses, the wings for dead dreams,
> as if they didn't appear above the hacked head
> as if there were no columns of hands trampled into the ground)
>
> (12 September 1942)

'Modlitwa II' ('Prayer II'):

> Nikt z nas nie jest bez winy. Kiedy noc opada
> wasze twarze i moja ociekają krwią
> i własne ciało jest jak duszy zdrada
> i nienawistne ćwieki własnych rąk
>
> (None of us is without guilt. When the night descends
> your faces and my face are all dripping with blood
> and my own body feels as if it has betrayed its soul,
> and hateful are the hobnails of my hands.)
>
> (17 September 1942)

'Modlitwa III' ('Prayer III'):

> Jeśli skrzydła dzieci maleńkich
> pobcinają, zamienią w kamień,
> odbierz nam ziemię spod stóp przeklętych,
> w glinę nas zamień.
>
> (If little children's wings
> can be cut off and turned into stone,
> then take away the ground from under our accursed feet,
> turn us into clay.)
>
> (September 1942)

'Tren II' ('Lament II'):

> Nie ma, nie ma ucieczki. Na rozdartej ziemi
> ten milion serc kalekich z mojej piersi krwawi.
> Byli żywi, odeszli z słowami prostemi,
> tych Bóg milczeniem zbawił.

> (There's no escape. Upon the broken earth
> this million of wounded hearts spills blood from my chest.
> They were alive, they've gone with a few simple words,
> they are redeemed by the silence of God.)

The reality? Between July and the second half of September more than a quarter of a million Jews were deported from the Warsaw ghetto, mainly to Treblinka. The last transport of 2,196 people caught in hiding left the Umschlagplatz on the Day of Atonement, 21 September 1942. From the poems that Baczyński wrote unceasingly during those accursed months I have cited merely a few fragments, although each of them deserves separate attention, since in each there is a different leitmotiv, a different part of the same wound. Yet, it seems to me, they do constitute a discrete cycle of poems, the only one in wartime Polish poetry directly reacting to the Gehenna of Polish Jews. This was, without doubt, an extremely difficult topic. Joanna Weintraub explains that her husband could not 'write about it while it was hot . . . The burden of the experience was too heavy, the blow too hard'. Without entering too obtrusively into psychological complications and half-tones, we can assume that Baczyński's distance from his Jewish connections, greater than Weintraub's, helped him to break the silence. He may have been plagued by qualms of guilt; he may have possessed the degree of control necessary to express this pain. Certainly he could not write openly about the Jewish fate without endangering his relatives. But it is not necessary to speculate on what made it possible for him to treat this subject as he did.

Again, after his Job-like lament in the autumn of 1942 the poet's voice falls still for a few months. He studies at the clandestine Warsaw University and, above all, gets involved more and more deeply in the underground. His less numerous poems written during the long and extremely cold winter of 1942–3 are filled with a tone of painful pensiveness, religious humility (which was perceived even at that time by Wyka in his famous letter), and faith that something could be salvaged, even if in the distant future. Hence the view that 'no coffin is in vain' (*żadna trumna nadaremno*). Yet immediately after Basia's name-day, 4 December, Baczyński wrote in a poem without a title:

> I gdzie postąpię pęknie mi pod stopą
> ostatni kamień, a dalej już ciemność,
> i jestem jak ten pierwszy człowiek po potopie,
> który zawinił.
>
> (Wherever I go, under my foot
> the last stone breaks and the darkness opens,
> and I am like the first one after the flood
> who sinned.)
>
>   (6 December 1942)

He also expressed at this time the need for struggle and revenge, stemming from the city's dark mass, from its 'collapsed ruins' (*z zawalonych ruder*) in another untitled poem:

> Stań się krzywdą i zemstą, miłością i ludem.
> O, chwyć za miecz historii i uderz! i uderz!
>
> (Become the wrong and the vengeance, the people and the love
> Take in your hands the sword of history and strike! and strike again!)
>
> (February 1943)

In the third week of January the first armed resistance in the Warsaw ghetto organized by the Żydowska Organizacja Bojowa (Jewish Combat Organization: ŻOB) was bloodily suppressed. It seemed at the time, although we now know that this understanding was false, to have halted German plans to deport the remaining Jews in the ghetto. Contacts also began to develop with the Polish underground regarding the supplying of arms to the ghetto. On 19 April at dawn, faced with a new German attempt to begin deportations, an uprising broke out in the ghetto. In April Baczyński wrote a poem without a date or title which begins:

> Byłeś jak wielkie stare drzewo,
> narodzie mój jak dąb zuchwały,
> wezbrany ogniem soków źrałych
> jak drzewo wiary, mocy, gniewu.
>
> (Like a grand old tree you were,
> my people, bold as an oak,
> heavy with burning juices of old,
> like a tree of faith, of might, of rage.)

It concludes:

> Lecz kręci się niebiosów zegar
> i czas o tarczę mieczem bije,
> i wstrząśniesz się z poblaskiem nieba
> posłuchasz głosu serca: żyje.
>
> I zmartwychwstaniesz jak Bóg z grobu
> z huraganowym tchem u skroni
> ramiona ziemi sie przed tobą
> otworzą. Ludu mój! Do broni!
>
> (The clock of heaven moves on,
> time bangs a sword against a shield,
> you'll shudder with the dawn's first glow,
> you'll hear your heart's voice: it's alive.
>
> You'll rise like God from the dead
> with the breath of hurricane
> for you the earth's embrace
> will open. My people! to arms!)

The song concludes, 'runął na nas grzmiąć ognisty strop' ('The fiery ceiling has fallen onto us with thunder'), but Baczyński has now finally decided to undertake what he has long contemplated. In June he enters the ranks of the Zośka battalion of the underground organization Szare Szeregi. In his poem 'Pokolenie' ('A Generation') he links the common wrong and the common fate of the whole nation:

> Nas nauczono. Nie ma litości.
> Po nocach śni się brat który zginął,
> któremu oczy żywcem wykłuto,
> któremu kości kijem złamano;
> i drąży ciężko bolesne dłuto,
> nadyma oczy jak bąble—krew.
>
> (We learned the lesson. Pity does not exist.
> In dreams we see our brother dead.
> Alive, they poked out his eyes,
> alive, they broke his bones with a club;
> the chisel of pain works hard,
> the eyes are bubbles swollen with blood.)

One last year was left to Baczyński. A year of fighting with the resistance, of love trembling for every hour (*i jedno mi dane małe ciało kobiece*—'one small woman's body was given to me'), a year of consciously bidding farewell to life. In these poems by a Home Army soldier, with a fragile body but with a great soul, there is, in equal measure, patriotic zeal and last testament. On the basis of several memoirs from that period it seems that Baczyński, a delicate and dreaming asthmatic, was doing well both physically and psychologically in the role that required from him neither explanations nor to keep silent. Perhaps for the first time in his life he was not 'someone different', since for his teenage subordinates his seriousness and reserve meant nothing more than the advantage of age and rank. In the very intense military training, and in several field actions, he tried to keep pace with stronger yet equally determined boys. He studied diligently to be a good officer, although he had some problems with topography. When one of the superiors offered Baczyński a transfer to the press division, he refused. In the apartment where he had lived with his wife on 3 Hołówko Street, classes were held and arms were stored. His wife, against all the rules of conspiracy, knew everything about what he was doing.

He wrote less, and even this last chapter in one of the greatest achievements in Polish poetry is by no means monolithic. New contradictions and splits can be seen in it: the clearly determined choice of the Home Army soldier, together with anxiety over the future of Poland stemming from his left-wing inclinations; readiness for death, combined with love of life and great sadness at the prospect of leaving it. Many of his friends tried to plead with him not to go to the barricades. Others accepted that, in the words of Zbigniew Wasilewski, Baczyński 'had to choose to fight'. His friend from the academic courses organized in the underground, Michał Jaworski, would write that 'Krzysztof's decision to give himself unconditionally to the struggle is clearly enough explained in his poems.' The poems 'tell about the things that we all witnessed, yet we neither felt them so strongly nor understood and evaluated them so deeply'. This simple sentence encompasses all that the reader of Baczyński's poetry should know to understand it fully and, even more, to appreciate it.

Officer Cadet 'Krzysztof' (Baczyński's underground pseudonym) died a soldier's death defending the Blank Palace on 4 August 1944, a few days after the outbreak of the Warsaw uprising. He aimed well, and before a bullet shattered his skull, he managed to lay low a few Germans.

Paper Epitaphs of a Holocaust Memorial: Zofia Nałkowska's *Medallions*

DIANA KUPREL

THE final entry in Zofia Nałkowska's *Dzienniki czasu wojny* ('Wartime Diaries', 1970) is dated 10 February 1945: 'Borejsza proposes that I become the president of the Commission for the Investigation of War Crimes in Auschwitz.'[1] This conclusion to the diaries, and the writer's acceptance of a position on the commission, mark the genesis of Nałkowska's literary Holocaust memorial *Medaliony* ('Medallions').[2] The commission was established immediately after the war to investigate Nazi war crimes committed on Polish soil, and Nałkowska's work in this area, together with her own experience of living in occupied Warsaw, influenced her profoundly.

A novelist, playwright, short-story writer, and essayist, Zofia Nałkowska (1884–1954) was the daughter of Anna and Wacław Nałkowski, a prominent Warsaw scholar and publicist. In her youth she belonged to the Young Poland (Młoda Polska) movement, which symbolized that country's *fin-de-siècle* artistic world.[3] During the inter-war period she served as an active member of the Polish PEN Club, and in 1937 she became the first female member of the Polish Academy of Literature, was the patron of a popular Warsaw literary salon (Zespół Literacki Przedmieście), and helped to publish the first short stories of Bruno Schulz, an avant-garde Polish Jewish writer living in the Galician town of Drohobycz.[4]

A series of historic upheavals—the 1905 Russian Revolution, the First and Second World Wars—shattered Nałkowska's world of learning and high culture. In a 1929 article she describes how her view of reality was changing: 'Ever since I was a child, I've been surrounded by books. The adults around me talked about

This article is published by kind permission of Northwestern University Press.

[1] Zofia Nałkowska, *Dzienniki czasu wojny* (Warsaw, 1970), 399. All translations from Polish texts are mine.   [2] Trans. Diana Kuprel (Evanston, Ill., 2000).
[3] The Young Poland movement (1890–1918) was flanked by positivism in the 19th c. and the twenty-year inter-war period in the 20th c. It had three major centres: Kraków, Warsaw, and Lwów.
[4] Drohobycz was occupied by the Germans in 1941. The Polish underground procured false documents for Schulz, but he postponed using them. He was shot by a Gestapo officer on 19 Nov. 1942 during an action in the ghetto known as Black Thursday.

scholarship. Our friends were scholars or writers. I thought it was like this everywhere, that the world of thoughts and ideas constituted the only reality. Later, I was shocked to learn that it was otherwise.'[5]

The definitive break came with the burning of the Warsaw ghetto during the Second World War: 'Nothing of the former world holds true any more. Nothing has remained' (7 May 1943).[6] In her *Wartime Diaries* Nałkowska expresses the impact that ubiquitous death has had on her during this critical period: 'The dead. The dead. The solemn march-pasts of the resigned. The leaps into the flames. The leaps into the abyss. The woman in the garden listening to the trickling droplets. The boy at the window. The children clung onto. I cannot bear these thoughts. I am changing because of them' (28 April 1943).[7]

This change, which can be charted in the *Diaries*, involved a developing consciousness of her obligation as a writer to bear witness to what was around her and to fix in words all that was being wiped off the earth to prevent it from vanishing without a trace. Before the Warsaw ghetto uprising, in a diary entry dated 15 January 1943, Nałkowska verbalizes her task as writer in strictly personal terms: 'The only reason I've ever had to write has been the desire to preserve life, to keep it from being lost or destroyed. I always find it hardest to write about events, to talk about someone else's affairs. It turns out in the end that I preserve only myself. [The thought of] passing without a trace fills me with fear.'[8] Even *Medallions* incorporates passages from Nałkowska's *Wartime Diaries*. Already in 1936 the Polish avant-garde writer Witold Gombrowicz noted this tendency towards self-reference as he commented glowingly on her elegant style, which he equated with her self:

There is good reason why her style is the most valuable attribute of her art and one of the very few exportables in our national literature. Nałkowska herself is style and there is no difference between the style of her books and her life. Even though she is widely regarded as an intellectual, no puzzles really exist for her. In the final analysis, what is essential to her is only the attitude taken towards the puzzle, the particular feeling that a problem evokes when it comes up against her person. In spite of appearances to the contrary, she is a great egoist for whom the whole matter comes down to this—namely, how to rescue her own humanity from the snares of contemporary civilization.[9]

Another diary entry, written a year after the Warsaw ghetto uprising and the razing of the ghetto district, shows a radical alteration in Nałkowska's realization of the depth of her responsibility to the broader human drama going on around her, and affirms the ethical task of representing the occupation and the Holocaust. At the same time, she acknowledges the impossibility of portraying the whole, and that, as a consequence, aspects are consigned for ever to the realm of silence: 'Air

---

[5] Nałkowska, 'O sobie', *Wiadomości Literackie*, 47 (1929).
[6] Nałkowska, *Dzienniki czasu wojny*, 280.   [7] Ibid. 279.   [8] Ibid. 267.
[9] Witold Gombrowicz, 'O stylu Zofii Nałkowskiej', *Proza (Fragmenty), Reportaże, Krytyka, 1933–1939* (Kraków, 1995), 207.

raids wipe out towns. People die in various ways, in every possible circumstance. Nothing remains. And the whole thing for me can be encapsulated in this. Namely, that I write. And on this it ends. This is everything. And yet it is. By writing, I salvage that which is. The rest is beyond my reach. The rest is relegated to silence' (May 1944).[10] This tension between writing and silence reappears in *Medallions* and becomes transfigured into the ethical issue of speaking versus remaining silent.

In 1945, having survived five years of Nazi occupation in Warsaw, Nałkowska joined the editorial staff of the literary weekly *Kuźnica* ('Forge'), became a member of the Commission for the Investigation of Nazi War Crimes, and served as a member of the Krajowa Rada Narodowa (National Council), the Sejm Ustawodawczy (Legislature) from 1947, and the Sejm PRL (Diet of the Polish People's Republic) from 1952.[11] The commission was based in Łódź and was established, partly for self-interested reasons, by the communists, who had seized power in Poland while they carried on a savage political struggle with the Armia Krajowa (Polish Home Army).[12] Its work took her to Oświęcim-Brzezinka (Auschwitz-Birkenau), Sztutowo (Stutthof, near Gdańsk), Majdanek (near Lublin), Treblinka, and numerous other extermination sites.

Considered a masterpiece in anti-fascist world literature, *Medallions* (written in 1945 and first published in 1946) is the literary offspring of Nałkowska's wartime and commission experiences. It also stands as the culmination of her stylistic, formal, and thematic literary evolution from flowery description and a concern with aesthetic concepts of personality in *Kobiety* ('Women', 1906), *Książę* ('The Prince', 1907), and *Lustra* ('Mirrors', 1913); through a concern with the fate of nations and peoples in *Tajemnica krwi* ('The Secret of Blood', 1917); to the simple narration of facts, everyday reality, and the lives of ordinary people in *Dom nad łąkami* ('A House in the Meadows', 1925), and the re-evaluation of the fact-based and documentary genres in *Choucas* (1927).[13] Her work in the 1930s proved especially significant as a background to her post-war concerns. *Granica* ('The Boundary Line', 1935), judged by herself and others as her masterpiece, focuses on how character is determined externally by social roles and cultural patterns. *Ściany świata* ('The Walls of the World', 1931), a series of prison stories contemplating the social and existential causes of criminality, *Dzień jego powrotu* ('The Day of his Return', 1931), a play about the potential for criminal behaviour latent in everyone, and *Niecierpliwi* ('The Impatient Ones', 1939), a philosophical novel presenting her attitudes towards evil, suffering, and death, lead directly to *Medallions*.

[10] Nałkowska, *Dzienniki czasu wojny*, 337.
[11] Biographical details are taken from 'Nota biograficzna', in Nałkowska, *Medaliony* (Warsaw, 1994), 73-4.
[12] Jerzy Andrzejewski's novel *Popiół i diament* (1948) portrays this period of civil war in Polish history; trans. as *Ashes and Diamonds* by D. F. Welsh (New York, 1980).
[13] For an overview of Nałkowska's literary development, see Helena Zaworska, *'Medaliony' Zofii Nałkowskiej* (Warsaw, 1969); Włodzimierz Wójcik, *Zofia Nałkowska* (Warsaw, 1973).

Despite the obvious evolution in subject-matter towards her anti-fascist work, the raw material that confronted her during the hearings required that Nałkowska take an innovative approach to representation and adopt a perspective distinct from her usual one.[14] Commenting on the intimate relation between theme and form, she discusses the demand placed on her to find a new means of expression by which to represent the unique event called the Holocaust:

I maintain that it is the theme . . . that determines the appropriate manner of representation. I didn't work for the Commission for the Investigation of Nazi War Crimes right after the war in order to find material for a new book. When I wrote *Medallions*, I wasn't conscious of creating a new technique, a different literary mode from my other books. The theme alone, which is so difficult to grasp, so impossible to deal with emotionally, demanded that I use this realistic form of expression.[15]

Medallions is one of the first, and most important, in the flow of literary accounts to take up the challenge to represent the Nazi machinery of genocide. Comparable to it in significance is the work of her compatriot Tadeusz Borowski, whose slender but powerful collection of short stories, *This Way for the Gas, Ladies and Gentlemen*, was born from his personal experiences as a prisoner in Auschwitz and Dachau. Włodzimierz Wójcik evaluates the importance of *Medallions* in the context of Polish Holocaust literature: 'Despite the obvious fact that none of the writers [e.g. Andrzejewski, Putrament, Rudnicki] was in a position to tell the whole truth about the Nazi crimes, it must be emphasized that perhaps two people, Borowski and Nałkowska, did succeed in showing the most important aspects [of these crimes].'[16]

Avoiding the tendency to mythologize the victims as either heroes or martyrs,[17]

[14] Kazimierz Brandys, in '*Medaliony* Zofii Nałkowskiej', *Kuźnica*, 4 (1947), comments on this change: Nałkowska, 'the discoverer of vast regions in human psychology, stands helpless before humanity in *Medallions*, as though she understood that explicating this world's secrets *vis-à-vis* the psychology of the individual was just not appropriate. This is her first book in which the human being is not penetrated by the writer, but only described—like the wall against which one perishes, or the instrument of death. Bound to the world of realists, she fulfils one of the demands of composing the universal drama before which the author acknowledges the powerlessness of her methods up to this time . . .'; cited in Nałkowska, *Medaliony*, 12.
[15] Nałkowska, 'Pisarze wobec dziesięciolecia', *Nowa Kultura*, 2 (1954).
[16] Wójcik, *Zofia Nałkowska*, 373. These writers' works, which touch on different aspects of the war experience and are of varying degrees of artistic merit, all (with the exception of Borowski's) speak about the tragic fates of individuals faced with an unusual test of character, endurance, and courage. *Medallions*, by contrast, Wójcik argues, is one of the few to represent 'the commonness of the occupation experience' (p. 372). See also Kazimierz Wyka's similar conclusion in 'Sprawy prozy', *Szkice literackie i artystyczne*, ii (Kraków, 1956); cited in Nałkowska, *Medaliony*, 7–8.
[17] Piotr Kuhiwczak comments on popular representations of the concentration camps, to which he contrasts Tadeusz Borowski's *Pożegnanie z Marią* and *Kamienny świat* (both trans. into English as *This Way for the Gas, Ladies and Gentlemen*) and Primo Levi's *Survival in Auschwitz* and *The Reawakening*: 'To circumvent such uncomfortable questions, some prefer to suppose that all inmates of Nazi concentration camps were people of outstanding character, either national heroes or born martyrs. Popular fictitious representations of prison camps peddle the same mythology. Almost invariably they

Medallions offers instead a concise, severely elegant witness to what people experienced in Poland during the war as distilled from the mass of facts gathered while Nałkowska served as a member of the commission. In reference and deference to the writer's accomplishment here, Jarosław Iwaszkiewicz comments, 'Only from deep wisdom and great feeling are such works, superficially cool and restrained but in reality burning and passionate, born.'[18]

The book consists of seven short reportages, each merely a few pages long, and one summation, 'The Adults and Children of Auschwitz'. In the latter Nałkowska gathers the various threads together, drawing on the facts to emphasize the enormity of the crime and suffering, and the ultimate compromise of humanity. In the process Poland is portrayed as a land where every site has become as good a place as any for the bloody task of disposing of the 'undesirable' element. Her terse, sometimes fragmented, eyewitness reports appear as formal testimonials, private interviews, and chance conversations, and are sparingly interjected with objective authorial commentary. The protagonists speak for themselves, from their own limited understanding of the human drama; at the same time they speak on behalf of millions, for each 'medallion' becomes a permutation on the principal theme that 'People dealt this fate to people.'[19] Ewa Pieńkowska sums up:

Zofia Nałkowska's 'economical booklet', written directly after the war in the spring and summer of 1945, holds a special place in the abundant and varied canon of so-called camp literature. By preserving the authenticity of facts and the deeply personal character of individual experiences, and remaining true to documentary prose and the memoir . . . she goes beyond ordinary reportage. However, she does import intellectual and literary frameworks that allow her to generalize from individual experiences and bestow an objectivity on them. The moral theme of vigilance and protest against the psychological devastation by fascism, together with . . . the conviction—and how early on!—that there are experiences that time does not erase, that memory preserves, [these features of her writing] set the line of inquiry followed by writers of the younger generation, [such as] Tadeusz Borowski and Tadeusz Różewicz.[20]

centre on successful escapes, like that presented in the recent American film about Sobibor, for example, well-organized resistance networks, and numerous acts of individual heroism. It seems that a hero dying for a noble cause is still preferable to a survivor who manages to preserve a minimum of human integrity; that a prisoner who declares his/her trust in the goodness of the human heart against all odds, scores more points than a prisoner who is skeptical about human nature and manages to stick to just one of the commandments Pawelczynska found prevailing at Auschwitz—"Do not harm your neighbour and, if at all possible, save him" ' ('Beyond Self: A Lesson from the Concentration Camps', *Canadian Review of Comparative Literature* (Sept. 1992), 398). Although Nałkowska is not speaking from personal experience of the concentration camps, her *Medallions* falls into the same category as Borowski's and Levi's works.

[18] Jarosław Iwaszkiewicz, 'Do Zofii Nałkowskiej', in *Cztery szkice literackie* (Warsaw, 1953); cited in Nałkowska, *Medaliony*, 13.
[19] The initial formulation of the theme is found in the *Wartime Diaries*, 28 July 1944.
[20] Ewa Pieńkowska, 'Zofii Nałkowskiej życie i twórczość' (Warsaw); cited in Nałkowska, *Medaliony*, 5.

Using this documentary form, Nałkowska seeks to restore to the victims and witnesses of genocide a voice that had been almost silenced by the Nazis. She asserts the adequacy and reliability of the survivors' own words. And she engages in the painstaking work of preserving what remains from intentional or inevitable oblivion caused by overgrown graves, natural decomposition, or orders from the top (undermined by the soap 'recipe' left hanging on the wall in 'Professor Spanner'). Lore Shelley explains the ethical appropriateness of using the literary strategy of the eyewitness account to represent the Holocaust:

Abandoning the general view of the anyway too gigantic whole in favour of an essential detail establishes the right of the individual not to be overlooked and conforms to John Ruskin's view of obtaining the facts right from the source: 'The only history worth reading is that written at the time of which it treats, the history of what was done and seen, heard out of the mouths of the men who did and saw.'[21]

Medallions, then, presents the reader with more than a mere historical record. It presents not only the words but also the voices, intonations, silences, gestures, postures, and actions of the witnesses as they struggle to relate their experiences. Nałkowska offers a startlingly immediate performance that repeats the past event in the testimonial present, demonstrating how it persists in the consciousness and conscience of these individuals:

'What's wrong? Are you ill?'
  Her naturally round, pale face was flushed and drawn, her forehead wrinkled as if from constant exertion, her eyes, feverishly bright.
  'No, no, nothing like that,' she responded blackly. 'It's just . . . people just can't live here any more.'
  Even her voice was unsteady, muted and tremulous.
  'We all live right by the wall, you see, so we can hear what goes on there. Now we all know. They shoot people in the streets. Burn them in their homes. And at night, such cries and shrieks. No one can eat or sleep. We can't stand it. You think it's pleasant listening to all that?'
  She glanced around warily as if the graves in the empty cemetery were listening. ('The Cemetery Lady')

The book thus preserves for its readers the traces of the original experiences by inscribing human suffering in epitaphs.

Medallions portrays a terror-filled time ruled by chance, when one could never tell when, where, or under what circumstances one would die ('The Cemetery Lady' and 'Dwojra Zielona'). 'By the Railway Track', the story of a Jewish woman who chose uncertain over certain death by escaping through a hole in a moving train, reverses this narratively by establishing the fact of her death with the opening line: 'Yet another person now belongs to the dead: the young woman by the

---

[21] Lore Shelley, comp., trans., and ed., *Experiments on Human Beings in Auschwitz and War Research Laboratories: Twenty Women Prisoners' Accounts* (San Francisco, 1991), 3.

railway track whose escape attempt failed.' The account transposes the dying woman's feelings of terror, pain, and solitude onto the landscape, which is described as desolate, empty, and menacing to both the wounded woman and the villagers, who can only stand by and watch: 'The situation was clear. Her curly black hair was clearly dishevelled, her too dark eyes were visible under her lowered lids. No one uttered a word to her . . . It was a time of terror. Whoever offered help or shelter was marked for death.' (It is important to note that such a refusal to help was not simply a sign of antisemitism. During the German occupation, in Poland, alone among the occupied European countries, giving aid to a Jew was punishable by death. Not only the individual who helped, but his or her entire family, risked this sentence. Yet despite this, according to the Yad Vashem Institute in Jerusalem, the greatest number among those honoured for saving Jews during the war were Poles.)

Accounts in 'The Hole', 'The Visa', and 'The Adults and Children of Auschwitz' show how humanity can be reduced to committing acts of cannibalism, to behaving like animals, and to playing a vicious game of hunter and hunted. The survivor in 'The Hole', for example, divulges a secret about women sent without food to a bunker as punishment for some small offence: 'They did eat, though . . . Once, one of them moved her jaw. Another had bloodied fingernails. Please, madame, that was severely punished! But at night, they would eat the flesh of those corpses!'

Nałkowska reveals how a human being's sense of morality can be strangled. In 'Professor Spanner' the young man from Gdańsk who is being questioned by the tribunal about activities in the Anatomy Institute is considered not so much a criminal as someone who has been desensitized to the moral reprehensibility of his actions. He speaks earnestly and unsensationally about the executions and the requisitioning and preparation of corpses, and refers to the production of soap from human fat in terms of German enterprise—of being able to 'make something from nothing'.

Medallions exposes the victory of fascism over the German intelligentsia. Again, in 'Professor Spanner' the lack of surprise on the part of the visiting German professors when confronted with Professor Spanner's activities at the Anatomy Institute, and their measured explanations of his motives as stemming from either obedience to party orders or the wish to aid the German economy, suggest that they, too, could easily have been co-opted by the fascist genocidal machinery.

Nałkowska captures the critical moment when death is no longer an individually experienced event but has become collective and widespread. 'The Cemetery Lady' opens by contrasting two instances of death by leaping from a window (suicide and escape) and two types of cemetery: the traditional site where the burial ritual is enacted, and the burning ghetto in which people die *en masse*. She thereby establishes a breach between two spatial realities delimited by the wall, and two temporal realities, before and during the war. The reach of the genocidal action comes across vividly in 'The Visa' as the narrator compares the fortitude of the Yugoslav, French,

Dutch, Belgian, Greek, Polish, Gypsy, and Russian women in the camp. And in 'The Man is Strong' the graveside uncovering of a child's knuckle, a Greek matchbox, and papers from some unspecified foreign pharmacy signifies the indiscriminateness of the murder of people of all ages and nationalities.

But the stories also express the persistence of the belief that life has value in and of itself, and that people must bear witness to history, even in the face of certain death and mounting loss. 'Dwojra Zielona', for example, paints a portrait of a woman who fought tenaciously to stay alive in order to tell, but who could not bear to go on alone, and who voluntarily followed the others to the concentration camp at Majdanek:

I wanted to live. I don't know why. Because I didn't have a husband or family, no one, but I wanted to live. I was missing an eye, I was hungry and cold, but I wanted to live. Why? I'll tell you why: to tell everything just like I'm telling you now. To let the world know what they did. I thought, 'I'm the only one who's going to survive.' I thought, 'There won't be a single Jew left on the face of this earth.'

Yet, even more telling than what is stated outright is what is relegated to silence; trapped in the interstices of partially enunciated truths and fragmented testimonials; broken by emotion, shame, ignorance, fear, shock; noted by the narrator only in the lines drawn across the forehead, the outpouring of tears, or the sagging of shoulders—that is, in the physical traces of an event as it is relived mentally ('The Hole' and 'The Man is Strong'). Henryk Vogler aptly remarks that *Medallions* 'speaks with silence. Silence has value there where even the most powerful words prove too weak.'[22]

Through its objective, multifaceted witnessing, *Medallions* consciously and thematically engages the reader's intellect, emotions, imagination, and judgement in the critical detection of 'distortions, assumptions, discrepancies, and misperceptions',[23] so that he or she may begin to fill in the unsaid and the unsayable, and thereby render it real and present once again. This makes the book unusual for its time and interesting for ours, over fifty years after the fact and the book's first publication, and even with our by now abundant knowledge about the Holocaust. To quote from 'The Cemetery Lady': 'reality is endurable because it is selective. It draws near in fragmented events and tattered reports, in echoing shots, in the distant smoke-drifts, in the fires which, history cryptically says, "turn to ashes". This

---

[22] Henryk Vogler, 'Medaliony ryte w słowie', *Z notatek przemytnika* (Warsaw, 1957); cited in Nałkowska, *Medaliony*, 10.

[23] James Wilkinson ('A Choice of Fictions: Historians, Memory, and Evidence', *PMLA* 3/1 (Jan. 1996)) discusses this critical tendency to read beyond what is expressly stated with respect to the work of the historian: ' "Even in the most resolutely intentional evidence," [Marc] Bloch notes . . . "what the text tells us expressly has today ceased to be the primary object of our attention. We ordinarily show much more interest in what it reveals without meaning to." . . . The gap between the witness's initial intent and the historian's final discovery lies in the historian's ability to detect distortions, assumptions, discrepancies, and misperceptions through a critical reading of the evidence' (p. 85).

reality, at once distant and played out against the wall, is not real—that is, until the mind struggles to gather it up, arrest, and understand it.'

The reader, then, is put in the same position as the narrator in 'The Visa', who is faced with the witness's deliberately provocative equation of Jews and vermin. Nałkowska does not make moral judgements; she leaves that to the reader. She lets the witnesses, survivors, and participants implicate themselves—as do Professor Spanner's soap-making assistant, the visiting German professors, or the cemetery lady, who turns murder into an act of self-preservation: 'if the Germans lose the war, the Jews will kill us all. You don't believe me? Listen, even the Germans say so . . . and the radio, it says so too.' In effect, each of Nałkowska's medallions confronts us with what Harold Kaplan, in *Conscience and Memory*, refers to as our own 'consciousness struggling for comprehension', with the awareness that 'It may be that only questions are possible, interrupted answers, abortive explanations, and yet, one hopes, there may be judgment, something that touches conscience as well as memory, but with sharpness, unclouded by abstraction and generalizing formulae.'[24]

[24] Harold Kaplan, *Conscience and Memory: Meditations in a Museum of the Holocaust* (Chicago, 1994), p. xi.

Letter to Father

JAN RYSZARD BYCHOWSKI

THE 'new boy', which I was, was immediately taken up by the 12-year-old (born like me in 1922), lively, likeable, freckled, pug-nosed, blond Ryszard Bychowski, son of Gustaw, a well-known psychoanalyst, author of a once famous book, *Psychoanalyzing Hitler*. I recall how the next day we 'paid off' a big boy to whose two-person bench I had been assigned, Rysiek took his place, and from that time we practically never separated, making our way home together, seeing each other continually outside school, sharing reading, cinema, swimming, tennis. Bychowski was a Jew—he himself told me about it, but perhaps no one other than me in the class knew about it. Besides, it was hard to find a less Jewish physical type, yet not Slavic. I discovered the type only later, during the war in England among Irishmen. . . .

Towards the end of the next year (1934–5) the proverbial thunderbolt struck us from the sky, already dark although we did not truly realize it. It was in the mathematics class that Mr Jumborski taught. . . . He summoned Rysiek Bychowski to the blackboard (both he and I did worst in mathematics) and Rysiek answered very poorly. From somewhere in the back of the class, someone sang out, *Jew-ew-ew*, . . . and soon it was taken up by *almost the entire class*! Until then, we had *never* had *any* unpleasantness on that theme! Mr Jumborski (who, nicknamed Jumbo, was big, heavy, a bit elephantine) got up, pale with rage (we found out later that he himself was a Jew), and started to shout something like 'Barbarians, villainous barbarians!' Then he left the classroom, slamming the door, in order to fetch the director. I then pounced on my nearest classmate, who had belonged to the 'choir'. Rysiek joined in and there began a literally bloody scuffle, in which out of *over thirty* only five classmates fought on our side. . . .

A year later I left Batory [High School] (my father was posted abroad, and my grandmother, Stefan Czarnowski's sister, with whom I was then living, died). I corresponded with Rysiek Bychowski for a long time. I met him later in England during the war. He was in the air force and died, shot down in his bomber, in a raid over Cologne. . . .

KONSTANTY A. JELEŃSKI[1]

---

[1] Excerpt from a letter from Konstanty A. Jeleński to Józef Lewandowski, *Zeszyty Literackie*, 21 (1987), 128–9.

Letter to Father 189

Bircotes, near Doncaster 5 December 1943

My dear Father,[2]

This is the second of a series of unsent letters. I wrote the first one in June and it is at Max's. I am writing this one today because there are matters about which I must speak with you. I want you to know my point of view on certain fundamental problems. On the night of 2–3 October I had a serious crash landing, from which I walked away only by a miracle, and now I have again returned to flying. This letter has to be insurance: in the event of a repeat accident with less fortunate results, you will know what I would have wanted to tell you if we could talk with each other today.

After that over-long preface I shall go immediately to the heart of the matter.

After a year's stay in England I have come to the conclusion that Poles are not yet up to independence and sovereignty and that we Jews have nothing in, and must not return to, Poland (*do Kraju*). I shall attempt to explain to you below how I came to these two conclusions.

First point: Poles are not yet up to independence of the sort that they had before the war. Now, governing a state is a certain art, requiring such characteristics as, above all, organizational ability, ability to compromise, a sense of realism, besides, of course, intelligence and knowledge of the principles of administration, economics, etc. All of these traits are lacking, not only among the mass of our fellow countrymen, which would be understandable (we stand to that extent behind the West) and would not in itself be fatal to the possibility of Poland's independent existence, but their lack is strikingly apparent among the so-called intelligentsia.

The political life of the Polish emigrant community on England's soil, the government's foreign 'policy', relations in the army all confirm my conviction that it is much worse with these people, and thus with Poland, than we had thought. Lack of organizational ability is what is really deadly, and it cannot be seen by people who are themselves caught up in it, but at every step it occurs to those who have lived for a few months or years in one of the countries of the West, at a distance from ministries or the army.

I tried to persuade myself for a long time that this picture that I see is distorted, that each *émigré* group is sick, derailed, and not at all characteristic of the nation. Under the influence of our political friends in Stockholm and New York, who are sincere but naïve, I thought: 'It's different back home.' Unfortunately, it is not different. I saw people who had just arrived from there and I read reports of the situation at home, issued here as a secret document for the use of ministers and members of the National Council. Back home there really is taking place a heroic

---

[2] This text is Jan Ryszard Bychowski's 'List do ojca' ('Letter to Father'), *Zeszyty Literackie*, 34 (1991), 112–17. English translation published by permission.

underground struggle, but the manner of thinking, regardless of party affiliation, has remained narrow, 'national', romantic, and devoid of any sense of reality. Underground struggle is not a good school, nor is it good preparation for normal government of a state. Just the opposite. If in the underground they still dream of plans for a protectorate over Lithuania and an anti-Bolshevik crusade into the bargain (see *Reports from the Country* issued by the Ministry of Internal Affairs, the volume for May–June 1943), then things must not have changed much there, in spite of the cataclysm that the fall of the state was, and in spite of the German terror.

A word on Polish–Soviet relations. We all know how Russia appears and what methods it employs (although possibly we did not look at it through very objective lenses). But if I were today the most democratic Russian, one who knew what I know about Polish feelings, and I were deciding on the development of relations between the two governments, I would do absolutely the same as Stalin did.

Hatred, contempt, desire for vengeance on Russia are assuming downright bestial forms. The Germans are not spoken of or thought about at all (unless from abroad). Russia is the eternal and hated foe. War with it is only a question of time. Each Soviet victory is greeted with tightened fists and an execration; each German counter-attack and retrieval of even a single town, with a smile of contentment and satisfaction.

That is the feeling from generals to privates and from the nationalist to the socialist. I do not know what the rightist parties think, but it is sufficient to read their press. Alas, I have learned what Polish Socialist Party members think, at an hours-long gathering to which I listened. Great socialist figures, ministers, and members of the National Council unanimously recited about national unity against 'Soviet tricks'; they cried that we will not give up even an inch of soil; they voiced the hope that the German counter-offensive will succeed. Pragier assailed Minister Romer for conducting a too-weak foreign policy, for having said to journalists, 'We cannot talk about borders, *especially* in time of war.' Professor Pragier declared, 'We will not talk about borders or a plebiscite, neither now nor after the war.' Ciołkosz sharply criticized Singer for some comment about Petliura in *Dziennik Polski*. 'Petliura is our ally,' said Ciołkosz, reportedly the most intelligent person of the Left.

No, my dear father, these people are sick and also have cataracts on their eyes. In my opinion all of them are driving themselves into a blind alley, into the situation of the White Russian emigrants after the last war. It could well be that Russia does not want compromise at all. If it did, there would not be anyone to compromise with. In these conditions there is no question of any government other than on an anti-Soviet basis, or of a different army than one disposed for war with Russia.

I will now move to the second issue, which is for me much more essential, of much closer concern, and much more painful.

Attitudes towards Jews have become a gauge of morality: of the morality of the individual, of liberalism, and of the democracy of societies.

I know that it is difficult to wipe out twenty years of antisemitic propaganda in a short time. But it seemed to me that if not even a war against Hitler, if not even the common misfortune, then certainly the immense tragedy of the Jews in Poland in 1942 and 1943 would lead to a revolution in Polish views. Nothing of the sort.

A great black book could be written about what happened during the formation of the Polish army in Russia and during the departures to Persia. Savage antisemitism was the first reaction to regained freedom, to leaving prisons, to uniforms with a [Polish] eagle. I have buddies who were beaten bloody, who were thrown out after weeks' and months' service in the army. I know some who in camp in Persia still wore bands on the right shoulder (thus!). It was not the Russian who did not want to let out Jews. A Soviet circular on this theme came out after the conclusion of recruitment, just before the departure. General Zhukov told Kot, who intervened with him, 'We need this regulation for political considerations. Interpretation is up to you. Did we reject even one Jewish name from your departure lists?'

Polish delegates refused financial or food aid to Polish Jewish citizens. Current vice-premier of the Polish government and 'socialist' Kwapiński was notorious in this regard. After arriving in London, at a welcoming reception at the embassy, asked about the number of those left in Russia, he declared, 'About a million, because I do not count the Jews, after all.'

It seems to me that the silence covering this chapter of war history, the departure from Russia, is only momentary. We will hear more about it from our friends, when we see them, and from Soviet propaganda, which industriously collected materials and will surely exploit it at a suitable moment.

Not much news reaches here from the Polish army in the Near East. But in one respect observers agree with each other: if that army ever enters Poland, its first act, like that of Haller's army after the last war, will be an anti-Jewish pogrom.

We also know about General Anders's secret order to officers on the theme of antisemitism (I saw a copy of this order). He asked them to refrain from excesses, for thus he termed it, for we are allies of England and America and it harms us propagandistically. So 'temporarily' it is necessary to let things quiet down. 'After the return to Poland, we ourselves will mete out justice for the fact that Jews welcomed the Soviet army in September.' 'We ourselves will mete out justice in the Christian spirit, [but] for the time being we must refrain from antisemitic acts.'

In July 1942 the emptying of the Warsaw ghetto commenced. Today, after a year of systematic murder in the capital and in the provinces, the Jewish community in Poland has virtually ceased to exist. How did the Polish nation react to this unprecedented crime by the hand of the common enemy?

My colleagues in the air force and the army either were indifferent or openly rejoiced. For an entire week I saw fellows smiling scornfully on seeing the headlines of the *Dziennik Polski* about murders of Jews. They did not want to buy the *Dziennik* because it was 'continually only about those Jews'. Surely you understand how painful it was, but I can assure you that I was aware the whole time that it was partly a pose, partly ignorance of the true state of affairs, the great distance, both factual and psychological, from the place in which it all happened. Again I consoled myself with the thought that back home it is different, again I nourished myself with the propaganda stories, that someone there hid someone at risk of his own life.

Today I know that the homeland ('kraj') also did not pass the test. The Germans chose Poland as the execution site for the Jews of all Europe not only because that was where most of those whom they wanted to liquidate were. The Germans were aware that in Poland they would not meet with the massive protest of the population, that there would not be such a spontaneous reaction as in Denmark or Holland, that they would not have to fear such effective protest on the part of the Church as in France (the appeals of the archbishops of Toulon, Marseilles, etc.).

Sometime, unfortunately, we will hear the whole truth from one of our relatives who nevertheless survived. But already at this moment I see that there was only indifference around the Jewish people going to their death: scorn, that they did not fight; satisfaction, that 'it's not us'. I sense that there was not the atmosphere in which today every downed Allied airman finds himself in France, Belgium, or Holland, an atmosphere giving a Jew who had escaped from the ghetto certainty of aid. Jews could not flee in masses because they did not have anywhere to go. Beyond the walls of the ghettos was an alien state, an alien populace, and this is, it seems, a terrible truth.

Polish circles jeered at the Jews' passivity towards massacre. When defence of the Warsaw ghetto was resolved, there began the tragic negotiations for weapons with the Polish (government) military organization. They lasted months, when each day was decisive. The Poles evaded, [claiming] that they themselves had none, that it was difficult for them to give. The first weapons and ammunition arrived from—Bolsheviks.

A few thousand managed to extricate themselves and escape Treblinka, Majdanek, or Sobibor. They live unsure of the moment, not only because a surprise German search could uncover them. There are Poles who are regularly involved in blackmailing Jews and who extort from them the last of their money under the threat of delivery to the Germans. I know that there were many instances of denunciation and deaths of the denounced, and the monetary reward (500 zlotys) for the informer was large. The latest book of reports on the home situation, written in Warsaw and issued here by the Ministry of Internal Affairs, turns to the already concluded epic of the Warsaw ghetto in connection with discussion of activity of the 'Soviet agencies'. 'It is difficult to refrain from the observation', writes this book, 'that liquidation of the Warsaw ghetto was a significant blow for the communist cells. The Soviets lost at one stroke printers, presses, readers, and followers. Liquidation of the ghetto distinctly weakened the activity of the eastern enemy.'

In another place, discussing the future of Lithuania (under Poland's protectorate, of course), Warsaw politicians ask the government and the *émigrés* to underscore and publicize the role of Lithuanians in the extermination of Jews. 'This will divert the sharp propaganda of international Jewry, which will accuse Poland of collaboration in the murder of Jews, into a proper direction and will enable us simultaneously to win our political aims.'

Characterizing Lithuanian attitudes and feelings, the 'soldiers of Underground Poland' write: 'Lithuanians yielded little to Jews in servility and glorification of the Soviets.'

That's the way it is. I tremble at the thought of what I write to you here, and there would not be a person happier than I if it all turned out to be untrue. Unfortunately, these are facts to which we are not free to close our eyes. I want you to have open eyes; you especially cannot be free not to see reality, [for] you can have a chance of return to a high position. But you were not born a politician, ideological like some underground soldier. What is important for you is scientific work and good luck, but above all your own peace and satisfaction (i.e. those of family and friends). Returning would be a great wrong to yourself. Returning would be a wrong towards those of ours who will escape and who will be able to live and even partially forget only when we draw them out from within those walls and from among those people where every moment will remind them of what they survived.

I hope that I will come out of the war whole. I have already decided that I will not return to Poland. I do not ever again want to be a second-class citizen and I do not want my son not to have equal chances with others. But above all I fear knowledge of the whole truth about the reaction of Polish society to the extermination of the Jews. I cannot live, consequently I am unable to work, with people who could have turned their backs on Jews in need of aid, people who managed to brush aside the Jews' liquidation, to occupy their homes, and to denounce or blackmail the saved remnants.

This much I had to tell you, my dear father.

Maybe someday, years from now, I will go back there in order to gather material for a book on the Jewish tragedy which I would like to write.

I kiss you warmly.

>Your son,

>Jan Ryszard Bychowski

Translated from Polish by Robert Moses Shapiro

Stereotypes of Polish–Jewish Relations after the War: The Special Commission of the Central Committee of Polish Jews

JAN GROSS

EVEN though most Polish Jews were killed during the German occupation, the stereotype of Judaeo-communism survived the war. If anything, it was reinforced by a widespread consensus that Jews assisted the Soviets in the subjugation of the Polish Kresy in 1939–41.[1] The establishment of the Lublin government in the aftermath of the war served to perpetuate this stereotype still further. Popular sentiment attributed a nefarious role to the Jews and portrayed them as particularly zealous collaborators with the security police serving the new regime. Was it indeed the case that the dominant post-war Jewish experience in Poland was imposing scientific socialism on reluctant fellow citizens and persecuting ethnic Poles? I do not think so. Rather, I would argue that the dominant Jewish experience in Poland after the Second World War was fear.[2]

The Special Commission (Komisja Specjalna) established by the Centralny Komitet Żydów w Polsce (Central Committee of Jews in Poland: CKŻP) was an ephemeral institution that existed for a mere eight months, from July 1946 to

---

This chapter was first published in S. Kapralski (ed.), *Zydzi polscy* (Kraków, 1999).

[1] A critical study of this stereotype can be found in my article 'Jewish Community in the Soviet Annexed Territories on the Eve of the Holocaust: A Social Scientist's View', in *East European Politics and Societies*, 6 (1992), 191–206.

[2] Let me state immediately that I do not consider it particularly fruitful to count the number of Jews in the Communist Party's apparatus of repression. Even if one were to find an inordinately high number of Jewish-born party members, this does not lend itself to a simple interpretation. Communists of Jewish extraction, like people of other nationalities in various countries where communist regimes were installed, worked in the security apparatus as communists and not as Jews—or Poles, or Georgians—and they were enforcing not 'Jewish interests' but rather 'interests of the people' on the reluctant population. And, on the other hand, it is very well known to students of totalitarianism that communists had an instrumental attitude to all values and institutions, and that they also exploited ethnic prejudices to gain and establish themselves in power. Hence, it seems to me that the most sensible, perhaps the only, answer to the question why Jewish communists worked in the security apparatus of their respective countries at all is simply 'And why not?'

March 1947. Its name was also rather enigmatic. Thus, we should not be surprised that the two boxes containing its files have thus far attracted little attention from scholars perusing the archives of the Jewish Historical Institute in Warsaw. Yet its records tell a fascinating story. Here is a fragment of the commission's final report dated 30 May 1947:

The main task of the Central Special Commission [Centralna Komisja Specjalna: CKS] was to organize an adequate protection and defence of Jewish institutions and thereby assist the authorities in their defence of the lives of the Jewish population in the country, to prevent panic, and to facilitate the peaceful, constructive efforts of Jewish society in trying to rebuild its existence. The first measure of the CKS was to establish close contacts with the Security Services of Democratic Poland. These services approved of our efforts and offered us comprehensive assistance. . . . Contacts between the special commissions (KS) and the Ministry of Public Security (MBP), the Citizens' Militia (MO), and the Voluntary Workers' Citizens' Militia (ORMO) were established all over the country and collaboration proved fruitful. . . . During its existence the KS made over 2000 *interventions with the authorities* in the country. . . . The work of our information network was comprehensive. We had our people in factories, in open markets, at schools, at universities, etc. Our people went to church services . . .[3]

Thus, under the enigmatic label of 'Central Special Commission' we find *a Jewish organization that collaborated with the secret police in defence of Jewish interests*. In this manner the stereotype pointing to a close association between Jews and the security police in post-war Poland finds a concrete embodiment. It behoves us to ask what this collaboration entailed and how it came about.

The CKS was established in the aftermath of the July 1946 Kielce pogrom, which caused panic among the Jews residing in Poland at the time and prompted their massive flight from the country. Jews had already started to leave Poland some months before, but after Kielce the wave of departures swelled. Still, tens of thousands of people, exhausted by the horrors of their wartime experiences, could not leave their country at a moment's notice, and many did not even contemplate departure. So, as one consequence of the tragic events in Kielce, the Jewish community decided to establish a self-defence organization. The presidium of the CKŻP broached the idea of reactivating the Żydowska Organizacja Bojowa (Jewish Combat Organization: ŻOB), as the wartime underground organization had been called. When the CKS was finally established, Yitzhak Zuckerman, 'Antek', the last ŻOB commander, was designated its chairman in a highly symbolic gesture. It was no coincidence that the very evening when news of the Kielce pogrom reached the committee, Zuckerman set out for Kielce with Marek Edelman to bring the remaining Jews to safety.[4]

[3] Żydowski Instytut Historyczny, Warsaw, Centralny Komitet Żydów w Polsce, Komisja Specjalna, box no. 3–7, 'Sprawozdanie z działalności CKS przy CKŻP' 1, 3, 4. The CKS files are deposited in two boxes numbered 1–2 and 3–7.

[4] The episode is described in Yitzhak Zuckerman's *A Surplus of Memory: Chronicle of the Warsaw Ghetto Uprising* (Berkeley, Calif., 1993), ch. 15. Zuckerman does not mention Edelman in this context, but Edelman recollects that they both went to Kielce (personal communication).

The Jewish community interpreted the Kielce pogrom as a sign of pending ultimate danger. We have no precise statistics enumerating all the Jews murdered in Poland after the war, and even if we had, they would be difficult to interpret. The post-war period was a time of banditry and rampant violence almost on the scale of civil war. Tens of thousands of people lost their lives. Dr Lucjan Dobroszycki, who studied this period and always paid meticulous attention to statistical evidence, counted some 1,500 Jewish victims. Given the general level of disorder at the time, and that many victims were killed not as Jews but as targets of political violence or armed robbery, only a fraction of these deaths can be attributed to antisemitism. Still, one must be aware of the circumstances of each episode: robbers often chose their targets on the basis of ethnicity. For this reason, the railways became an especially dangerous place for Jews:

On 3 October [1946] at 7 in the evening I boarded a train from Warsaw to Kraków. I was accompanied by my husband, Henryk Liberfreund, and Amalia Schenker. We rode in a compartment with a couple of other passengers, including a nun. A candle was burning. We travelled peacefully until we reached the Kamińsk station, near Radomsko. In the meantime, the candle burned out and the passengers were sleeping in darkness. At the stop in Kamińsk a man in civilian clothes, wearing a cap with an eagle sign and toting a submachine-gun, entered the compartment. He checked the passengers one by one with a flashlight. When he reached my sleeping husband, he pulled off the coat that was covering him and said, 'I got you, kike, heraus, heraus, aussteigen.' My husband drew back, unwilling to get off the train, and the man pulled him by the arm but could not budge him. Then he whistled and immediately another man appeared, whom I could not see very well, accompanied by the conductor. I started screaming terribly, and then the first assailant started to push me and pull me using the words 'heraus, aussteigen'. I pulled myself away, and in the meantime the train started, and the assailant pushed my husband off the train and jumped after him. I continued to scream and I don't know what happened afterwards. I wish to add that nobody's documents were checked, not even my husband's. The other passengers and the conductor did not pay much attention to the whole episode; on the contrary, they laughed and behaved rather improperly. One man sitting next to my husband was accosted by the assailant with the words 'you Jew'. But he stated that he could show documents [to prove] that he was not a Jew, and he was left alone.

This unusually detailed description—for the most part murders on the railway leave little trace in the archives—is supplemented by an unsigned memorandum entitled 'Information' dated three days after the event:

On the Kraków–Warsaw line trains go through Kamińsk, about fifteen minutes beyond Radomsko. The railway line cuts through this village, which is situated in a wood, with houses built along the tracks. The inhabitants of these houses before the war, during the war, and now, for the most part, live off the passing trains. This applied especially to coal transports which pass by there. Almost all the people in the vicinity made a living from coal pushed off these trains, especially at night. In two of these houses, one right next to the station and the other a one-storey house further down, there lives a gang, whose central figure is a woman of dubious reputation. . . . They party at night and drink, and from time to time they stake a passing train in expectation of some spoils. Jewish passengers are now victimized by these bands, for they can easily be scared with a gun, taken off the train, robbed of their cash and possessions in the forest, where all of this takes place, and then they can be made to disappear, and thus one gains an easy living for oneself and one's companions. This area should be carefully watched and put under observation.[5]

Whether anything noteworthy was observed I cannot tell, but the circumstances of Liberfreund's disappearance were not discovered. In all likelihood he was the victim of robbers who deliberately targeted Jews.

In addition to such assaults, we come across aggression specifically directed against Jews during pogroms, when crowds of assailants acted, motivated by the belief that Jews had committed the ritual murder of a Christian child. Finally, Jews returning to their pre-war homes were sometimes murdered in an effort to pre-empt their claims on property that had been taken over by the local population in the meantime. However, no more than a few dozen people were killed in the pogroms. And since many, perhaps most, could not return to their places of origin, which had been incorporated into the Soviet Union after the war, the number of returnees killed in their homes was also limited. Hence, it was perhaps not so much the murder of Jews as Jews that evoked such a panic reaction among the Jewish population as the widespread antisemitism that they encountered after the war ended. For even though antisemitism was nothing new in their interaction with Polish society, after the Holocaust no one could be oblivious to the realization that antisemitism opens up the gates to ultimate catastrophe. Let us ascertain, therefore, how widespread anti-Jewish sentiments were in Poland fifty years ago.

The state administration acts rather slowly, as we know, and it does not send circulars in response to individual complaints. Thus, it is fair to assume that the Ministry of Public Administration must have received a good number of them before circulating a memorandum entitled 'Concerning Attitudes towards Citizens of Jewish Nationality' to all the voivodes (i.e. chief administrators of the largest territorial units, voivodeships), district plenipotentiaries, and presidents of Warsaw and Łódź. Dated 5 June 1945, the memorandum was issued scarcely a month after the capitulation of Nazi Germany:

The Ministry of Public Administration has been apprised that the voivodeship and county authorities, as well as the offices of general administration, do not always apply the necessary objectivity when dealing with individuals of Jewish nationality. In the unjustifiably negative attitude of the said authorities and offices when handling such cases, and especially when making it difficult for Jewish returnees to take apartments that are due to them, a highly undemocratic antisemitic tendency comes to the surface rather clearly. The Ministry of Public Administration calls attention to this undesirable phenomenon and emphasizes that all loyal citizens of the Polish republic, irrespective of nationality and religious denomination, should be treated equally, and ought to be helped within the boundaries

---

[5] Żydowski Instytut Historyczny, Warsaw, Centralny Komitet Żydów w Polsce, Komisja Specjalna, box 1–2, 156–8.

of existing law. Therefore the Ministry of Public Administration implores you to ensure that the authorities and offices within your jurisdiction abide by the recommendations of this memorandum.[6]

In the archives of the voivodeship office in Kraków can be found several complaints not unlike those that must have come to the attention of the writers of the memorandum. They were frequently passed on to the authorities through the Jewish committees.[7] A thorough study of this would require a search for evidence in over a dozen voivodeship archival collections, but even a few examples from the Kraków office can give us a sense for what was at issue. Thus, at the beginning of July of 1945 in Chrzanów,

> a registration clerk at the Citizens' Militia office requested that Citizen Schnitzer Gusta, who returned from a camp, prove her identity by bringing a witness who would testify to her identity, and that she had lived in Chrzanów before the war. When Citizen Gusta presented the chairman of the county Jewish committee in Chrzanów, Citizen Bachner Lesser, to the clerk at the said office as her witness, the said clerk stated in the presence of the witness that he had no confidence in the witness presented and that he would trust only a witness of non-Jewish extraction and that he would register the citizen [Schnitzer] only when she presented such a witness.[8]

Admittedly this is a trivial matter when compared with the robberies and murders described above, but for this very reason also meaningful. For we cannot justify the awkward, offensive language of the militia clerk even as an attempt on the part of the administration to stem the tide of Jewish property claims. Soon after the liberation there were altogether 105 Jews left in Chrzanów county.[9]

Jewish committees all over Poland complained about the antisemitic attitudes of Citizens' Militia personnel. Interestingly, the attitude of the security offices (*urzędy bezpieczeństwa*), the most politicized organs of the administration, also made the Jews uneasy. In documents from Kraków's special commission we find a memorandum on a theatrical revue put on by the sports club Siła in Auschwitz, of all places, on 24 and 25 January 1947. 'The themes and content of this show made fun of Jews in various sketches and songs. We want to stress that most of these anti-Jewish gimmicks were performed by the commander of the security police in Auschwitz.'[10] We likewise find the following demonstration of poor judgement

---

[6] The phrasing of this document is somewhat oblique and awkward in Polish as well; State Archive, Kraków, Urząd Wojewódzki II, file 1073.

[7] i.e. local chapters of the CKŻP established in several localities with sizeable Jewish populations. For a recent study of the CKŻP and its politics, see David Engel, *East European Politics and Societies*, 10 (1996).

[8] State Archive, Kraków, Urząd Wojewódzki II, file 1073, memo from the county Jewish committee in Chrzanów to the socio-political department of the Kraków voivodeship, dated 11 July 1945.

[9] State Archive, Kraków, Urząd Wojewódzki; II, file 1071, card 183, 'Stan liczebny poszczególnych narodowości w chwili obecnej'.

[10] Żydowski Instytut Historyczny, Warsaw, Centralny Komitet Żydów w Polsce, Komisja Specjalna, box 1–2, Oświęcim, 27 Jan. 1947.

and lack of sensibility, again in Chrzanów, where the town office began sending daily request for labourers to the Jewish committee. On 5 July, for example, the town office demanded that 'Twelve persons of the female sex be designated to wash the dirty linen of Red Army soldiers.' In the eyes of the Jewish committee, which filed the complaint, it mattered less that the town office did not honour its promise to pay the honorarium than that it issued the request in a form 'emulating the methods of the occupiers by making the Jewish committee responsible if the labour contingent did not appear at the designated time and place. Such requests are issued solely to the Jewish population through the committee. In this manner the town office in Chrzanów perpetuates traditions established by the occupiers, who communicated with the Jewish population with the help of Judenrat.'[11]

Of course the state administration at the time of reconstruction had other issues more pressing than pestering the Jews. And the central administration—as demonstrated, for example, by the previously quoted memorandum of the Ministry of Public Administration—was sensitive to issues of discrimination against Jews. But ordinary citizens dealt with officials mostly at the local level, and here they very often encountered hostile treatment. Even though they could complain and get higher levels of the state bureaucracy to intervene on their behalf, such repeated difficulties had a shocking cumulative impact.

Jews encountered hostility not only in governmental offices and places of employment, but also in the streets. One hears numerous stories from provincial towns about physical assaults, break-ins in Jewish houses, offensive graffiti, and verbal threats. 'It is an undeniable fact', wrote Jan Kowalczyk, the Kraków voivodeship commissar for productivization of the Jewish population, in a note to the presidium of the district commission of the labour unions, 'that the living conditions of the Jewish population in county towns are extremely difficult. Because of terrorizing reactionary elements [a phrase often encountered in the official language of the time], the Jewish population is running away from these locations in order to save their lives, and [so] they concentrate in larger towns.'[12] Indeed, the Jewish committees in small counties and voivodeships urged the Jewish population to move to larger towns, where the committees tried to provide support in finding adequate housing and employment. But even in larger towns, such as Kraków, Jews were not safe.

On Friday evenings after dark, according to Jewish religious custom, the Shabbat service takes place. Services are held in a synagogue at 27 Miodowa Street, which also has an entrance from 8 Warszauer Street. After the service begins, a crowd of hoodlums and teenagers assembles and attacks the synagogue, primarily from the direction of 8 Warszauer, throwing stones, and using special bottles to ruin the roof and break the windows. And so it goes on every Friday, each time from a different side. These acts of public violence are accompanied by frightening screams, verbal abuse, laughter, and often attempts to enter

[11] State Archive, Kraków, Urząd Wojewódzki II, file 1073.
[12] State Archive, Kraków, Komitet Wojewódzki Żydowski, file 14, 87.

the synagogue. These attacks take place every Friday and twice the rabbi was hit with a stone when he was praying at the altar, so, no longer able to take this in stride, we call this to your attention, Citizen Voivode, as well as to the attention of the Public Security Office, with a request for immediate order so as to permit the Jewish population to finally worship in peace.[13]

One might attempt to pass over these episodes on the grounds that a sort of *demi-monde* and lumpenproletariat had resided for many decades in Kazimierz, the old Jewish section of Kraków. But this was far from an isolated case: Jewish orphanages, old people's homes, summer camps, and buildings housing Jewish returnees were frequently the targets of similar attacks. Only three weeks after this complaint had been sent to the voivode's office, on 11 August 1945, a pogrom took place in Kraków, this time in other parts of the city as well. One of the badly beaten victims reported later on the attitudes of soldiers, militiamen, railway workers, and health service personnel who witnessed these events—in other words, people whose opinions could not be dismissed as socially marginal.

I was carried to the second precinct of the militia, where they called for an ambulance. There were five more people over there, including a badly wounded Polish woman. In the ambulance I heard the comments of the escorting soldier and the nurse, who spoke about us as Jewish scum whom they had to save, and that they shouldn't be doing this because we murdered children, that all of us should be shot. We were taken to the hospital of St Lazarus at Kopernik Street. I was first taken to the operating room. After the operation a soldier appeared, who said that he would take everybody to gaol after the operation. He beat up one of the wounded Jews waiting for an operation. He held us under a cocked gun and did not allow us to take a drink of water. A moment later two railway workers appeared and one said, 'It's a scandal that a Pole does not have the civil courage to hit a defenceless person,' and he hit a wounded Jew. One of the hospital inmates hit me with a crutch. Women, including nurses, stood behind the doors threatening that they were only waiting for the operation to be over in order to rip us apart.[14]

From today's perspective one would not consider it an extenuating circumstance that the invalid using his crutch as a weapon, the nurse, the soldier, or the railway workers were all speaking and acting blinded by passion, as they were firmly convinced that Jews had murdered Christian children in order to use their blood for matzah.

This medieval prejudice brought people into the streets in post-war Poland on many occasions and in many different towns—in Kraków, Kielce, Bytom, Białystok, Szczecin, Bielawa, Otwock, and Legnica. One is tempted to say that the whole matter was treated with disarming simplicity: on 19 October 1946 a few drunken men were looking for a child in a building where Jewish returnees lived in

---

[13] State Archive, Kraków, Urząd Wojewódzki II, file 1073, Pismo Żydowskiego Zrzeszenia Religijnego w Krakowie do Obywatela Wojewody Krakowskiego, 25 July 1945.

[14] Żydowski Instytut Historyczny, Warsaw, individual statements, collection 301, doc. 1582, Hania Zajdman.

Kraków, at 10 Stradom Street. A small crowd began to assemble in the street, and when the guards of the building proceeded to disperse it the head of the militia patrol, which had been summoned in the meantime by the alarmed residents, simply told one of the guards that 'if your child got lost, citizen, you would also be searching around' (*gdyby obywatelowi zginęło dziecko, to obywatel też by szukał*).¹⁵ This allows us perhaps to understand better what was on the mind of Kraków's voivode when he wrote his June 1945 'situational report': 'There were no serious anti-Jewish demonstrations of any kind in the Kraków voivodeship last month. Despite this, however, there are no indications that attitudes towards Jews in society have changed. They are still of such a kind that the smallest incident is sufficient to generate the most outrageous rumours, and to provoke a serious outburst.'¹⁶

So much for attitudes of the general public. And what were the views of the local élites on this matter? Thanks to the record of a meeting held on 19 August 1945 in the Raj cinema in Bochnia, some light may be shed on this issue. According to the anonymous reporter who submitted this account to the voivodeship office, about 1,000 delegates of the Peasant Party (Stronnictwo Ludowe) assembled at the cinema for a county meeting. The gathering, which people could attend by invitation only (*za zaproszeniami imiennymi*) brought together local activists, i.e. the leaders of Mikołajczyk's opposition party.

The third speaker (his name unknown) took the rostrum in his turn, and, by analogy to the thesis from Kiernik's speech that Poland must be a monoethnic state [the matter previously discussed concerned the expulsion of the German population from the newly incorporated territories], put up a resolution that the Jews should also be expelled from Poland, and he also remarked that Hitler ought to be thanked for destroying the Jews (tumultuous ovation and applause). Citizen Ryncarz Władysław, who was presiding at the time, immediately reacted to this speech by cutting it short and condemning what was said.¹⁷

In line with the tradition of Jewish humour one might comment on this episode by pointing out that it contained both good news and bad news for the Jews.

To summarize the prevailing mood among the Jewish population, and the circumstances in which Jews found themselves at the time, I should like to quote extensively from a letter by the chairman of the Jewish committee in Częstochowa and a member of the central committee of the Bund Party, Brenner, which was published in the first issue of *Głos Bundu* in August 1946. The letter provides a concise history of one Jewish community in post-war Poland:

Częstochowa was the only city in Congress Poland where 5,200 Jews were freed from camps. . . . We were freed on 16 January 1945. The local Polish population was friendly

---

¹⁵ Żydowski Instytut Historyczny, Warsaw, Centralny Komitet Żydów w Polsce, Komisja Specjalna, box 1–2, 114, memo to MBP, 6 Nov. 1946.
¹⁶ State Archive, Kraków, Urząd Wojewódzki II, file 905, 26.
¹⁷ State Archive, Kraków, Urząd Wojewódzki II, file 914, 'Sprawozdanie z powiatu bocheńskiego', 21 Aug. 1945.

towards us: some genuinely so, others because it was becoming, still others, because they were afraid. But after a few days there was a change. We discovered that in order to live one must eat, find somewhere to live, and above all, work. The problem of apartments became urgent. Various unsavoury types, who joined the militia and state administration during the early days, showed their teeth. We concluded that one may not wait passively. On my initiative a Jewish committee got established. . . . Our community was gripped by tension. Jews started to leave Częstochowa. Of the 5,200 who left the camps in January, only 3,000 remained in March. By May we were less than 2,000. Soon, however, Jews from Częstochowa began to return from the camps and by July the community grew to 6,000. . . . The situation slowly began to deteriorate. Killings of Jews in various cities and villages impacted on the state of mind of our Jews and an exodus from Częstochowa began. The Jewish community was dwindling. News of the pogrom in Kraków came as a shock. Larger groups started to leave Częstochowa. Chaotic mass flight followed. Shops and prospering businesses were closing, institutions coming to a standstill. The number of Jews fell daily. By the end of 1945 about 3,000 Jews remained. Then emigration from Częstochowa stopped for a few months. But in March 1946 it resumed for much the same reasons. The number of Jews fell to 1,200. . . . Then came the repatriation of Jews from the Soviet Union. The number of Jews grew rapidly. Once again we got to work energetically to anchor the Jewish community in Częstochowa. Institutions started expanding. In May 1946 there were already 2,500 Jews. Faith in permanent settlement grew and we had renewed enthusiasm for work. But in late June rumours started circulating among the Polish population of Częstochowa that the Jews kill Polish children for ritual purposes. The few Jews of Częstochowa got mobilized. The leaders of the Jewish committee immediately established contacts with local security organs. . . . On 4 July the news of the pogrom in Kielce struck us like a thunderbolt. . . . Lately an 11-year-old Christian child walked with his mother along Garibaldi Street, where many Jews were living, pointing to a building where Jews had allegedly held him for two days. This time the Christian neighbours laughed the boy off, and chased him away . . . Even though the threat is almost gone, and the atmosphere is calming down, this episode had a terrible impact on our community. People quickly started to close down their apartments and businesses, leaving what they were doing, and started to flee. But where can they go? Nobody knows, or even has a clear idea . . .[18]

This was the context in which the CKS was established. After the Kielce pogrom it became clear that not only isolated individuals in secluded villages, in the privacy of their apartments, or travelling on night trains, but entire Jewish communities were imperilled with potential loss of life. In July, after the decision to establish the CKS had been made in Warsaw, the voivodeship Jewish committees and their local branches set up special commissions. All political parties collaborating on the Jewish committees participated in this endeavour. Lists were drawn up of all the apartment buildings housing refugees, old people's homes, Jewish party headquarters, orphanages, and other Jewish institutions that needed protection, and they were all put under guard.

About half of the personnel worked voluntarily; the remainder received

[18] *Głos Bundu*, 1 (Aug. 1946).

payment from the budget of the CKS. Over 3 million zlotys (a substantial sum at the time) were paid out each month in salaries for security guards. Weapons were issued to some 2,500 people.

In theory, the special commissions were subordinate to the ORMO, but in practice they functioned under the authority of the Jewish committees and the CKS in Warsaw. Their principal tasks in the field were twofold: to post armed guards at designated locations, and to establish a system of communication whereby they could alert the nearest outpost of the militia or the security service to any impending danger. Telephones were installed wherever possible, supplemented by a network of messengers for keeping in contact. Building plans were drawn for all buildings under the protection of the special commissions, and maps of neighbouring streets were sketched, including the closest outpost of the security services or the militia. These sketches are to be found amongst the CKŻP documents deposited at the Jewish Historical Museum in Warsaw.

One should not exaggerate the professionalism of the special commissions' personnel or procedures. The armed organs of the Jewish committees were hardly awe-inspiring.

In reality these were doormen, caretakers, and other workers used for various menial tasks. . . . The heads of various Jewish institutions and departments claimed the right to use these guards, since it was not clear who was in charge of them, the committee or the special commission. . . . Their condition was pitiful. They were dirty, unshaven, unkempt, and altogether pretty disgusting to look at.[19]

But at least someone with a weapon was patrolling the premises.

Fortunately, they had only rare opportunities to use their weapons. The final report of the CKS notes two such episodes, in Robka and in Białystok, without mentioning details. The list of 108 employees of the special commissions presented for a special award after the commissions were abolished on 1 April 1947 includes two names of individuals who had lost their lives in the line of duty—in Ząbkowice and in Łódź. We know of one episode when 'self-defence units' were used for other purposes than what has been described here—namely, when members of special commissions were detailed to provide security for meetings during the January 1947 national elections. Later this led to complications when the guards could not get the committee to pay their supplementary wages for overtime. 'We feel that such matters should not be brought before an outside public forum. We appeal to you, therefore, for the last time to pay what you owe us within two days, or else we will file a complaint with the labour court,' a group of guards wrote to the voivodeship Jewish committee in Łódź on 1 April 1947.[20]

As to denunciations filed by members and employees of the special commis-

---

[19] Żydowski Instytut Historyczny, Warsaw, Centralny Komitet Żydów w Polsce, Komisja Specjalna, box 3–7, 107, 'Sprawozdanie KS przy WKS w Warszawie'.

[20] Żydowski Instytut Historyczny, Warsaw, Centralny Komitet Żydów w Polsce, Komisja Specjalna, box 3–7, 70.

sions, for the most part they concerned circumstances or developments that could endanger Jews or buildings in their custody. But this mandate could be interpreted broadly. Thus, for instance, after a meeting to elect a workers' council in a knitting factory in Nowa Ruda, a denunciation was sent to the local security service office about a speaker (a member of the Communist Party, as was duly noted) who requested that no Jews be allowed on the council after a Jewish female worker received a nomination from the floor. The chairman of the meeting, we read in the denunciation filed by the Jewish committee in the town, assured those assembled that he would certainly see to that, and his assurances met with wild cheering.[21]

There were other instances of denunciations, with dire consequences. The final report of the CKS, quoted above, includes the statement, 'On the basis of our information, the *authorities* have liquidated four gangs of NSZ [Narodowe Siły Zbrojne: National Armed Forces, a nationalist underground organization] and WiN [Wolność i Niepodległość: Freedom and Independence, an illegal underground branch of the Home Army] in Wrocław and Szczecin.' Perhaps if we had access to the archives of the Ministry of Public Security, we could tell what human tragedies lay behind these few words; the CKŻP documents contain no further details. One can only hope that the designation 'four gangs' was self-congratulatory report-padding, as was another 'success' described in glowing terms in the final report: 'The special commission in Włocławek has discovered a centre of propaganda and agitation that was distributing antisemitic literature. The centre was liquidated.' A memo preserved in the archives gives us a closer insight into what actually happened:

To the county UBP [security office] in Włocławek, Włocławek, 1 February 1947. In the middle of December 1946 or thereabouts, when I was in a certain establishment in a company, I found out that in the town library in Włocławek there are books with anti-democratic content. We decided to clarify this matter by sending members of our committee, citizens LEPEK ICEK and LEPEK HELCZE, as patrons of the library. Our members, after looking through the catalogue, spotted a book with especially anti-Jewish content entitled *The Jewish Danger*, which we enclose with the above. We want to add that our members also noticed that there are books with anti-Soviet content in the above-mentioned library.[22]

Unfortunately, in those days books could be denounced by semi-literates with dire consequences, and as a result of the Lepek siblings' report, the Włocławek town library was closed and its librarian arrested.

Energetic activists from Włocławek urged the CKS to assign the task of cleansing public libraries and reading rooms to special commissions all over Poland. Thankfully, there are no traces in the archives that their advice was heeded. This, in a nutshell, is the balance sheet summarizing the activities of the only Jewish

---

[21] Żydowski Instytut Historyczny, Warsaw, Centralny Komitet Żydów w Polsce, Komisja Specjalna, box 1–2, 282, 'Komitet Żydowski w Nowej Rudzie do Urzędu Bezpieczeństwa w Nowej Rudzie, Doniesienie; 8 Dec. 1946'.

[22] Żydowski Instytut Historyczny, Warsaw, Centralny Komitet Żydów w Polsce, box 1–2, 317.

institution in post-war Poland to collaborate with the secret police in defence of Jewish interests.

The history of the Central Special Commission established by the CKŻP is but a small episode in the long history of Polish–Jewish relations. It stands, however, at the focal point of an extraordinary phenomenon: the massive emigration of Jews from Poland *after* the Second World War. Because, after all, the exodus of a quarter of a million people from their mother country (this is the approximate number of Jews who had left Poland by the end of 1948) when they were not compelled to do so by government order or by administrative pressure presents a real challenge and intellectual puzzle, which has not thus far been taken up by either Polish historiography or public-interest journalism. The Jews left everything behind—the graves of their ancestors, their belongings, and the material culture they had accumulated over centuries. Barely alive, literally, they left for a devastated Europe, not knowing where they would end up. And what they knew makes the whole matter even more of a mystery—for they went to camps for displaced persons in Germany. Was this another wave of emigration in search of better material living conditions? If not, if it was a flight of a whole people from the threat of persecution, how do we come to terms with it? How is this to be fitted into the narrative of post-war Polish history? In a frequently quoted phrase Theodor Adorno declared the impossibility of writing poetry after Auschwitz. This leaves us with a staggering research problem—how was antisemitism possible in Poland after the war?

The Bund and the Jewish Fraction of the Polish Workers' Party in Poland after 1945

BOŻENA SZAYNOK

THE General Jewish Workers' Union, the Bund (Ogólno-żydowski Związek Robotniczy) was established in Vilna in 1897. After the Bolshevik Revolution the Bund in the USSR was forcibly united with the Communist Party of the Soviet Union. In independent Poland the Bund by the 1930s moved to a less revolutionary and more social-democratic position and established itself as one of the principal parties on the 'Jewish street'. It retained its basic programme of establishing 'national-cultural' autonomy for the Jews in Poland, once a democratic socialist state had been achieved. After the Second World War it was also active in countries other than Poland. Although the activists of Bund chapters outside Poland supported the Polish Bund with funds, the Polish Bund remained fully independent in its work in Poland.

The Bund in post-war Poland began its activity in the autumn of 1944. Its leaders, who were in Lublin at the time, decided to accede to the National Council for the Homeland (Krajowa Rada Narodowa: KRN), the *de facto* parliament of the new authorities, and fully accepted the programme of the *de facto* government, the Polish Committee of National Liberation (Polski Komitet Wyzwolenia Narodowego: PKWN), and its manifesto of 22 July 1944. At this stage both these bodies were already effectively dominated by the communists, although they ostensibly pursued a popular-front policy and allowed other 'democratic' parties to function. The activists of the Bund joined the Jewish institutions which were emerging in Lublin to provide help to Jews. A member of the Bund, Szlomo Hirszenhorn, became the head of the Referat Pomocy Ludności Żydowskiej (Department of Assistance to the Jewish Population). In November 1944 the first party convention following Polish liberation was held. In the convention's principal resolution the Bund responded to the new conditions:

The convention is convinced that at the present time the only effective way to break Hitlerism and establish democracy is to realize the principles of the [PKWN] manifesto and

This chapter was first published as 'Bund i komuniści żydowscy w Polsce po 1945 roku', in *Midrasz*, 7–8/15–16 (1998), 57–65.

uphold a policy of a sincere and genuine fighting alliance with the USSR, the common struggle of the Red Army and the Polish army, and the close collaboration of democratic parties on the platform of the July manifesto. The convention maintains . . . that the Bund as an organization should fully collaborate with the block of democratic parties and participate in its activities . . . The convention recognizes the necessity to strive to unite the workers' movement in Poland. Towards that end, the Bund endorses the establishment of . . . closer contact with the PPS [Polska Partia Socjalistyczna: Polish Socialist Party] . . . as well as the entering into an agreement with the PPR [Polska Partia Robotnicza: Polish Workers' Party] regarding co-operation on work amongst the Jewish population.[1]

In February 1945, after the liberation of central Poland by the Red Army, Bund activists who had spent the war there arrived in Lublin, among them Marek Edelman, Leon Feiner, and Salomon Fiszgrunt, and a new temporary leadership of the Bund was established. Yitzhak Zuckerman in his memoirs recalls his meeting with Marek Edelman after the war:

Marek went off to study medicine and was no longer with us. He told me of the gathering of the Bundists to restore their movement. Marek was an extraordinarily brave man, but not a contemplative or articulate man. He told me his speech at that gathering. He got up and said, 'Comrades, enough splashing around in piss!' That is, the Bund had nothing more to do. That was his whole speech.[2]

Zuckerman's memoir also mentions Salomon Fiszgrunt, one of the post-war leaders of the Bund. He writes:

We were always friendly, and he also participated in the underground. He wasn't a fighter, but was one of their politicians, since because of his age he wasn't suitable for the Jewish Combat Organization . . . In the Jewish Central Committee's public struggles, we maintained good relations, even though the hardest attacks against us came from the Bund. We can say of the Bund that they not only didn't learn anything, they didn't know anything either. The Jewish communists at least knew what their Polish comrades would allow them to do now. Fiszgrunt set his course according to pre-war Bundist ideology, whereas the communists received practical instructions on how to behave.[3]

In June 1945 the first post-war congress of the Bund took place in Łódź. A new leadership was elected, which included Szuldenfrei, Fiszgrunt, Hirszenhorn, Jaszuński, and Lejb Putowski. Beside Polish and Jewish problems concerning which the party's position had not changed much since the November 1944 convention, the congress also dealt with the problem of the Bundist activists who had remained outside the country, for whose programme disapproval was expressed. The resolution on this matter read: 'The political line of our comrades [abroad] is the result of their separation from the home country and their connections with London *émigrés* who are grouped around antisemitic and reactionary ideologies.'

---

[1] Archiwum Akt Nowych, Warsaw, KRN, Prezydium Rady Ministrów, sig. 23, 86.
[2] Yitzhak Zuckerman, *A Surplus of Memory: Chronicle of the Warsaw Ghetto Uprising* (Berkeley, 1993), 577.   [3] Ibid. 577–8.

Despite the declaration's assurances that the Bund in Poland did not intend to deepen the differences, and wanted to maintain the unity of the movement, there was no chance of agreement. The adherence to 'a steadfast implementation of our political line—without deviations', and opposition against the 'London orientation' left no room for compromise despite the declaration that 'we see no reason for a split in our ranks which has left our ranks so appallingly decimated'.[4]

Like other parties, the Bund started its work in Poland by searching for its pre-war members and taking care of Jewish youth regardless of orientation. One of my sources in Israel, a member of Dror, having returned to Poland, found herself in Częstochowa. The Bund cell there helped her to enrol in a school. For those who survived, the Bund promised a continuation of the life that had been lived by those who perished, of the preservation of the Yiddish language and Jewish culture. At first, my source very strongly endorsed the Bund's programme, until she learned about Palestine and the option to leave Poland. In her recollections she emphasized that, despite her enthusiasm to work in Poland, it was very difficult for her to live in a place where her family and friends had lived. The Zionists' proposal was for her a rescue—an escape from the memories which, despite her efforts to transcend them, would not allow her to remain in Poland.[5] This case seems to illustrate well the reasons why after the war the Bund's ideology did not find widespread support among the Jewish population. It recruited mostly pre-war activists and young people from families with Bundist links.

The Bund was active in the Centralny Komitet Żydów w Polsce (Central Committee of Jews in Poland: CKŻP), in the KRN, and in the Bund's youth organization, Tsukunft. The Bund representatives in the CKŻP were Hirszenhorn, Fiszgrunt, and Szuldenfrei. During meetings of the presidium they were the fiercest opponents of Jewish emigration from Poland, on various occasions attacking 'propaganda in favour of emigration, harmful to the Jews', and supporting very strongly all ideas related to the settlement of Jews in Poland, especially in Lower Silesia. An article by Eugene Duschinsky cites the view of Yaacov Zerubavel that it was only the Bundist leaders who strongly opposed emigration, while the middle-level activists wanted to leave for Palestine.[6] My interviewee, who initially had been involved with the Bund, told me that when she switched to the Zionists, only old pre-war communists remained in the Bund centre; within a year they too left Poland.[7]

In the CKŻP the main opponents of the Bund were the delegates of Zionist groups, but there were also encounters between the Bund and the representatives of the Jewish fraction of the PPR. However, while the fraction conceded that

---

[4] Eugenio Reale, *Raporty: Polska, 1945–1946* (Warsaw, 1991), 243.

[5] Interview with Dora Sz., Israel, 1995.

[6] P. Meyer, N. Sylvian, B. Weinryb, and E. Duschinsky, *The Jews in Soviet Satellites* (Syracuse, NY, 1953).

[7] In 1950 in Israel my source met the director of that Bund centre.

'co-operation with the Bund was necessary', relations were far from smooth. At meetings of the committee fraction delegates attacked the Bundists, mainly for organizing co-operatives linked to the party. Before 1 May 1945 the fraction suggested that all Jewish parties march together in the May Day parade, as a part of the trade unions linked with the Jewish committee. It was obvious that such an arrangement best served the fraction, and, not surprisingly, some of the Zionist parties and the Bund decided to march separately. The members of the PPR fraction regarded this as 'an act of premeditated sabotage', which, in their opinion deserved 'a definite response'.[8]

In addition, the existence of Bund-affiliated work organizations (workshops and co-operatives) excited considerable hostility among the activists of the PPR fraction. The Bund intended to implement the idea of productivization (which it shared with the fraction) only in co-operatives, which were also seen by them as a means of creating a sense of community. According to Marek Bitter, the creation by the political parties of branches in co-operatives and workshops was an unhealthy symptom: 'party propaganda is being conducted under the cover of productivization. These workshops are turning to the CKŻP for money, which, however, is not spent in a proper way, but for recruiting new members and followers for the Zionist parties.'[9] One of the activists of the PPR Jewish fraction argued, 'If the parties want to create workshops, we should absolutely support these aims, reserving for ourselves, however, the right of leadership.'[10] The opposition of the PPR fraction to party connections with workplaces and propaganda among young people applied only to Zionist parties or the Bund. The activists of the fraction themselves organized the communist-dominated League for Fighting Youth (Związek Walk; Młodych) within the Jewish community.

The Bund regarded its representation in the KRN as an important part of its work. It felt it was extremely important for the party to be able to present to Polish comrades its vision of the future of the Jews in post-war Poland, which differed from that of the Zionists. Szuldenfrei, the Bund delegate to the KRN, often spoke on Polish issues. At one of the first sessions of the KRN in 1945 he affirmed: 'The five-month-long period in which the PKWN has governed . . . has accomplished the principal goals indicated in the July manifesto. This fact gives the Bund a basis to endorse fully and without restrictions the request of all Polish democratic parties for the establishment of a provisional government.'[11]

At the KRN the Bund delegate often spoke against Sommerstein, the representative of the Zionists, and did not support his initiatives concerning the Jewish population—thus acting in concert with Polish delegates. After a statement by

---

[8] Archiwum Żydowskiego Instytutu Historycznego, Warsaw, Wydział Organizacyjny, sig. 15, *Sprawozdania, Protokoły Centralnej . . . Posiedzenie z maja i czerwca 1945 roku*.
[9] Ibid.   [10] Ibid.
[11] Archiwum Akt Nowych, Warsaw, KRN, *Sprawozdania stenograficzne z posiedzeń Krajowej Rady Narodowej, Warszawa 1946, sprawozdanie z VI sesji 31.XII.1944 r.–2/3.I.1945 r.*

Edward Osóbka-Morawski, the chairman of the KRN, that a set of motions proposed by Sommerstein were 'unnecessary and meretricious; accepting them would confirm that the reality is as Sommerstein portrays it, whereas it is otherwise', Szuldenfrei voted against the Zionist proposals.[12] In July 1945, after a speech by Sommerstein on Jewish emigration, Szuldenfrei responded:

I do not want to leave the impression that the opinion and the position represented by Citizen Sommerstein are of the opinion and the position of the whole Jewish community. Jewish workers, socialist workers, Jewish intelligentsia do not have their eyes turned towards the roads of emigration [applause]; they don't have their eyes turned towards the roads of emigration, whether they lead to America or to Palestine. Jewish workers and Jewish intelligentsia saved from the Nazi Gehenna, returning from the underground, or coming back from the camps all share one aim: to return to their homeland, to struggle in their homeland for its well-being, to find solidarity with the Polish working class.[13]

The way the Jewish population was represented in the KRN also excited opposition from the representatives of the PPR Jewish fraction. In their memorandum to the PPR central committee the members of the fraction complained that the Jewish delegation to the KRN 'proceeds as if it represents the attitude of all Jews, ignoring completely the alternative approach to Jewish problems by the PPR Jewish fraction, which is the strongest group in the CKŻP'.[14]

Although it was better able than other parties to publicize its programme, and despite its having a strong group of leaders, the Bund found it difficult to maintain its position in post-war Poland. According to Italian ambassador Eugenio Reale: 'Despite its close ties with the PPS and unconditional allegiance to the government, the Bund is heading towards its doom.'[15] Yitzhak Zuckerman thought that the Bund's anti-Zionist policy was also directed unwittingly against the Bund itself:

I must say that the official position of the Bund was the sharpest and silliest position opposed to Zionism. Their words and actions were not only against Zionism, but also against themselves. It was self-destruction, but they didn't understand it. Most others had no choice, since they were Poles and Poland was their homeland; but the Bundists could have been Bundists in any free place in the world, and they didn't understand there wouldn't be room for the Bund in Poland.[16]

This evaluation of the Bund by Zuckerman, along with those of other Jewish activists, is very bitter. An Israeli source, formerly a Bund member, explained in a conversation with me why he joined the Bund after the war:

[12] Archiwum Akt Nowych, Warsaw, KRN, *Sprawozdania stenograficzne z posiedzeń Krajowej Rady Narodowej, Warszawa 1946, sprawozdanie z VI sesji 31.XII.1944 r.–2/3.I.1945 r.*   [13] Ibid.
[14] Diaspora Museum Archive, Tel Aviv, *Memoriał grupy PPR do KC PPR w Warszawie, 15 V 1945*, sig. J.N.V.153/24.
[15] Reale, *Raporty Polska*.   [16] Zuckerman, *A Surplus of Memory*, 652.

We wanted to develop further our relation to Jewish culture, to help it survive, to help it develop so that the youth would learn Yiddish and speak Yiddish. It was our ideology. We were socialists; we saw no contradiction with socialism. We were democrats and we believed that everyone had a right to belong wherever he wanted. We saw no conflict with the Polish reality. That's why I was a Bundist.[17]

In the first half of 1946 the issue of the repatriation of Jews from the USSR to Poland dominated the activity of Jewish parties. For the activists of the Bund, the most important task was to keep the returning Jews in Poland. They strongly opposed the actions of the Zionists. The records of the meetings of the presidium of the CKŻP from that time are full of protests, mostly by Bund activists and to a lesser extent by the PPR fraction, against the agitation conducted by the Zionists at railway stations. Ignacy Falk, a Bundist representative, spoke in the CKŻP about 'the Zionist agitation against Jews' staying in Poland, in light of pogroms that are taking place here'.[18]

The Bund's position in regard to emigration was also presented during the CKŻP meeting in February devoted to preparation of a memorandum on behalf of Polish Jews for the Anglo-American Commission on Palestine. The visit of the commission was seen by the majority of Jewish activists as an important event. The principal subject of the memorandum was Jewish emigration from Poland after the Second World War, but it also set before the commission other important demands of Polish Jews, including the abrogation of the Palestine White paper of 1939, free Jewish immigration to Palestine, and the creation of an independent Jewish national entity in Palestine.

It might seem that the memorandum itself, as well as the work of the commission in Poland, would be of no great importance for the Bund—that they were essentially issues of concern for Zionist parties only. But when it was prepared, the memorandum claimed to be representative of the position of Polish Jewry as a whole. This caused severe conflict among the representatives of Jewish parties. On 20 February, at the meeting of the CKŻP, the text of the memorandum was submitted to a vote. The Bund representatives—Falk, Hirszenhorn, and Falkensztajn—spoke against it because it did not include their demands. They argued that the fraction, by endorsing the memorandum, had betrayed the interests of the Jewish nation. In response, Szymon Zachariasz, a leading figure in the PPR fraction in Warsaw, reminded them that Hirszenhorn had signed the document on behalf of the Bund and that he had not thought it expedient to participate in the delegation's work. Zachariasz admitted that not bringing a working version of the document to the CKŻP was a procedural error, but there had been no time for it. The Bund's action was incomprehensible since they had known all along what had been going on, and they also knew that at a certain point the fraction had changed

[17] Interview with I. Sz., Israel, 1995.
[18] Archiwum Żydowskiego Instytutu Historycznego, Warsaw, Prezydium Centralnego Komitetu Żydów w Polsce 1946, sig. 303/2, 47.

its position and signed the document. The delegates of the Bund had withdrawn from working on the preparation of the document and had only waited for an appropriate moment to make their opposition public.[19] It should be mentioned, however, that in January 1946, when the issue of the memorandum was first raised at the meeting of the presidium of the CKŻP, the delegates from the Bund had declared that they would not sign the memorandum if it did not contain clauses on free emigration not only to Palestine but to all countries.

The principal goal of the Bund's programme, to reconstruct Jewish life in Poland, determined its actions at that time. The position closest to its own on the future of Polish Jewry was of course that of the PPR fraction. But the Bund's slogans did not find many adherents among Jewish repatriates coming to Poland, and although it maintained many party centres and branches, the number of people connected with these institutions was limited.

Members of the Bund encountered many problems in their work, especially in relations with local authorities. These must have been rather serious, since, as a result of the Bund's complaints, the Ministry of Public Administration issued a special instruction regarding 'obstacles encountered by the Bund in Lower Silesia and Szczecin'.[20]

On Polish issues the Bund was close to the PPS; on Jewish issues it collaborated on many occasions with the PPR fraction. Yet the programme of Jewish communists aimed, above all, at gaining influence in the Jewish community. Thus the fraction could not be the Bund's permanent partner in implementing its programme, despite the similarities between assumptions regarding the future of the Jews in Poland. The fraction based its policy on strengthening its influence among the 'Jewish masses'; the Bund could not endorse such a policy. To a great extent the latter consisted of pre-war idealistic activists attached to Bundist ideology who were not receptive to any modifications in its basic principles.

Having chosen to reconstruct Jewish life in Poland, the Bund had to accept the slogan of 'productivization', which meant changing the professional structure of the Jewish population. Unlike the fraction, the Bund aimed to implement the policy of productivization primarily through co-operatives, but for Bund activists, more important than productivization itself was the creation of communities grouped around co-operatives. In June 1946 a decree of the Council of Ministers established the office of the government commissioner for the productivization of the Jewish population in Poland. The delegates of the Bund and some activists of the Zionist parties protested against this decision, objecting not only to the way the office had been established without consultation with Jewish circles, but also to the extremely broad range of its duties: 'The Commission for the Productivization of the Jewish Population should not have been established, especially without its

[19] Interview with Hana Szlomi, Israel, Sept. 1995.
[20] Wojewódzkie Archiwum Państwowe, Wrocław, Bund, sig. 78/5, n. p., Pismo MZO Departamentu Administracji Publicznej do Bundu w Warszawie, 20 Aug. 1946.

first having consulted Jewish social organizations . . . If, in spite of the name of this commission, its activities were also to encompass other areas of Jewish social and cultural life, it would constitute a breach of the basic principles of a democratic, self-governing Jewish community.'[21] The Bund saw the possibility of collaborating with the commissioner only on issues of antisemitism. In contrast, the PPR fraction welcomed 'the news of the establishment of the commission . . . It is a duty . . . of PPR comrades to popularize the commission among the Jewish population as proof of a policy of active support for productive Jewish groups in Poland'.[22]

At that time, in regard to Polish issues the Bund perceived itself as closest to the PPS, which was sympathetic towards its Jewish counterpart. In an article about the Jews Julian Hochfeld wrote, 'Naturally, the PPS is most closely tied to this Jewish party, which for decades has maintained a programme of being connected to the Polish land, i.e. the Bund . . . The scope of PPS co-operation with each of the two Jewish socialist parties is determined precisely by . . . their two different modes of development, towards a firm allegiance to Palestine by the Po'alei Zion and to Poland by the Bund.'[23]

After the Kielce pogrom in June 1946 the activity of the Bund was halted. The situation of Polish Jews had now radically changed. The news coming from Kielce to other cities had a horrifying effect—not only because of the number of victims killed and wounded, but also because of the passivity of the city authorities, the militia, and the army. Directly after the pogrom the Jewish population started to move, migrating from smaller localities to larger cities. Those previously undecided over whether they should leave Poland were looking for contacts with the representatives of the Berihah, the organization helping with illegal immigration, and the number leaving greatly increased.

A few days after the pogrom, on 13 and 14 July, in Warsaw, an extraordinary meeting of the heads of regional and local Jewish committees was held. Participants acknowledged that the pogrom was a turning-point in the history of Polish Jewry. In the CKŻP the main dividing-line was between the Zionists on one side and the PPR fraction and the Bund on the other. The Kielce pogrom and the feelings of exposure and panic among the Jewish population set the backdrop for discussion. The Bund delegate Salomon Fiszgrunt stated that his party

is obliged to act against the detrimental phenomenon of panic escapes from the country . . . This is being orchestrated; someone is responsible. Comrades, Zionists won't be offended if I blame them for the panic. No one should be surprised: [emigration] is the goal of Polish Zionism . . . They are undeniably guilty of creating this panic . . . The situation is very difficult. The Zionist camp is pursuing a very risky policy. According to them, all who leave intend to go to Palestine. But there are objective problems, the difficulties of emigration. The Jews are being cheated . . . Without question, the psychosis has seized the broad

[21] *Głos Bundu*, 2–3 (1946), 6.
[22] Archiwum Akt Nowych, Warsaw, PPR, sig. 295-VII-149, 3.
[23] Julian Hochfeld, 'PPS wobec kwestii żydowskiej', *Głos Bundu*, 2–3 (1946), 4.

masses, including even party members (the Bundists, members of the PPR) who have succumbed to the panic. I propose that we issue a proclamation on the situation, about the panic, that there are perils in leaving for the unknown.[24]

In their speeches the activists of the PPR fraction, Kameraz and Zelicki, emphasized the same things as Fiszgrunt: 'the artificial character of the panic' and the situation in camps for displaced persons.

The Zionists in their speeches rebutted the accusations of the Bundists and the communists. The Zionist representative Rozenberg asserted:

the reasoning of comrade Fiszgrunt . . . arouses surprise and it only shows that he and his comrades have learned nothing. They are motivated by the malice and blind hatred traditional in their party towards [Zionism]. This old argument is now irrelevant. Only com. Zachariasz presented the issue in a serious way, but he started from false premises and thus his conclusions are also false. He talked about stabilization. This idea is little more than wishful thinking. In fact we are misplacing the blame. It is convenient to find a scapegoat. It is easy to blame the Zionists for what is going on. But this is not the answer. It does not solve the problem. We are not even on the path towards stabilization. Every shooting, every murder, makes its achievement more difficult. The facts could not be denied before, and they cannot be denied now . . . In Polish society we encounter a poisoned atmosphere. There is nothing enabling a psychological or actual stabilization. Jews are threatened everywhere. A Jew cannot go to a barber or to a restaurant . . . The people who survived six hard years cannot endure being tormented any more.[25]

Despite the Bund's rejection of strong pro-emigration sentiments, Jews were leaving Poland: in just three months from July to September 1946 more than 60,000 people left. At the beginning of 1947 the border was sealed. From then on, leaving Poland was possible only through official institutions.

In autumn 1946 about 90,000 Jews lived in the territory of Poland, and a period of stabilization in the life of the Jewish community began. The calming of the mood in favour of emigration opened up a period of intense activity within Jewish political parties. Events of 1947–8 in Poland and in Palestine had an enormous impact on the work of these parties, and the political and social changes that saw the establishment of the Polish version of Stalinism also influenced them. While the situation in Palestine determined the programmes and attitudes primarily of the Jews with links to Zionist parties, parties that did not tie their future to the Jewish state also had to take a stand in regard to events in Palestine. A third factor that affected the thinking of the Jewish parties was the international situation, in particular Stalin's Jewish policy.

The most important political effort in that period was undoubtedly preparation for the parliamentary elections. In the CKŻP the members of the PPR fraction proposed joining the Blok Demokratyczny (Bloc of Democratic Parties) and that

[24] Archiwum Żydowskiego Instytutu Historycznego, Warsaw, Prezydium Centralnego Komitetu Żydów w Polsce, sig. 25b, n. p.: Protokół Nadzwyczajnej Narady Przewodniczących Wojewódzkich i Lokalnych Komitetów, 13–14 July 1946. [25] Ibid.

the CKŻP select Jewish candidates. The Bund rejected this idea, and its objection was strong enough to ensure that Jewish candidates were proposed by the respective political parties. Szuldenfrei was elected from the PPS list as a Bundist.

During the election the Bund campaigned independently of other Jewish parties, despite inter-party agreements. The PPR fraction resented this, informing the authorities of the publication and distribution of separate Bund leaflets, for example, in Wałbrzych, 'where the Jewish population of that city, together and without regard to their party allegiance, marched in the general parade, whereas members of the Bund withdrew from the column, put on the armbands prepared in advance with the word 'Bund', and formed a separate group at the end of the parade'.[26]

The period of the election created new coalitions amongst the Jewish parties in Poland. The programmatic allies (the PPR fraction and the Bund) split because of different electoral strategies. The PPR fraction now made new allies within the Zionist parties. The regional secretary of the PPR fraction in Lower Silesia, Jakub Wasersztrum, in his report stressed 'the positive attitude of the organizations Ihud and Hashomer Hatsa'ir, which cannot be said of the Bund'.[27] All realized, however, that these alliances were temporary. The differences between the basic positions of these parties were too great. Also, the desire of Jewish communists to predominate over the Jewish population made any real co-operation impossible. In the CKŻP the communist–Zionist coalition did act jointly during the voting for the new president of the CKŻP, when, despite the Bund's protests, Adolf Berman of Po'alei Zion-Left was elected.

Jewish youth occupied an important place in the Bund's activity. At this time, beside Jewish committees, numerous Jewish organizations, institutions, and schools were established and worked all over Poland. The issue of the language of instruction in schools divided Jewish parties into two main groups. On one side there were the Zionists and the religious parties, on the other, the PPR fraction and the Bund. Like the fraction, the Bund supported the schools organized by the CKŻP. In April 1948 *Głos Bundu* reprinted a fragment of an article entitled 'Yiddish or Hebrew?' by one of its activists, Mendelson, from 1930: 'The aim of the bourgeoisie is either assimilation or aristocratic Hebrew culture. . . . The only active force that raised the banner of culture for the masses . . . is the Jewish proletariat. In a few decades, under its direct or indirect influence, Yiddish literature has grown . . . Therefore, the struggle for Yiddish or Hebrew means a struggle between two cultures: the culture of aristocrats and the workers' culture.'[28] The Bund, like the fraction, supported a uniform system of Jewish education. However, the September 1947 resolution of the secretariat of the central committee of the PPR, addressed to the members of the party working within the Jewish community, included a directive that called for 'fighting against the detrimental work

[26] Archiwum Akt Nowych, Warsaw, Papers of Szymon Zachariasz, sig. 476/26, 181.
[27] Ibid. [28] *Głos Bundu*, 2–3/15–16 (1948), 8.

of the Bund and the Zionists, which undermines a uniform system of education, and putting emphasis on Jewish children's acquisition of as much Polish language, history, and culture as possible'.[29]

The youth organizations affiliated with Jewish political parties conducted their work among Jewish children and teenagers. One of the points of contention at that time was the question of establishing Jewish scouting organizations in Lower Silesia; however, this issue had much broader ramifications. In January 1947 the regional Jewish committee in Lower Silesia issued a circular concerning the creation of a scouting organization. This resolution was soon retracted after it was reviewed by the CKŻP. The retraction was a consequence of objections from various political parties to creating this type of Jewish children's organization. The Bund expressed its objections very sharply. At the May meeting of the presidium of the CKŻP its delegate Ignacy Falk stated, 'No institution had in its agenda the issue of scouting. This happened only in Lower Silesia ... Scouting is a political issue. We cannot imitate everything that occurs in Polish life. Until this issue is discussed among ourselves, and endorsed by our organizations, I appeal to the supporters of scouting not to introduce it.'[30] In May the CKŻP issued a pamphlet in which the children's scouting organization was proclaimed non-existent. The problem persisted, however, because even after the January decision of the Lower Silesia regional Jewish committee, scout troops were organized in several towns by fraction activists. Members of other Jewish parties which created their own children's organizations opposed scouting. The Bund in Lower Silesia issued a special proclamation on the issue, stating, 'We believe that the problem of creating a scouts' organization is a matter of principle in regard to which all parties represented in the committee must agree ... The above-mentioned resolution [concerning scouting] was accepted in the absence of our delegates at the presidium of the regional Jewish committee, and therefore we consider it invalid.'[31] The issue excited strong emotions. One of the reports mentions the case of 'a teacher, Altman, from the Bund who struck a child for coming to school in a scout's uniform'.[32] But despite protests, the PPR fraction did not stop its activities.

The Bund's youth organizations—the children's Skif and the teenagers' Tsukunft—were active in larger centres. Like other parties, they organized summer camps for Jewish children and young people. Co-operatives also occupied an important place in the Bund's work. These co-operatives, as we have noted, were one

[29] Archiwum Akt Nowych, Warsaw, PPR, sig. 195-VII-5, 138b, 139.

[30] Archiwum Żydowskiego Instytutu Historycznego, Warsaw, Prezydium Centralnego Komitetu Żydów w Polsce 1946, sig. 303/7, 23.

[31] Archiwum Żydowskiego Instytutu Historycznego, Warsaw, Wydział Organizacyjny Centralnego Komitetu Żydów w Polsce, 61.

[32] Archiwum Żydowskiego Instytutu Historycznego, Warsaw, Wydział Organizacyjny Centralnego Komitetu Żydow w Polsce, sig. 85, n. p., *Sprawozdanie z działalności WKŻ (Wojewódzki Komitet Żydowski) na Dolnym Śląsku za 1947 rok* ('Report on the Activity of the Regional Jewish Committee in Lower Silesia in 1947').

of the issues of contention between the Bund and the activists of the PPR fraction as well as with representatives of other Jewish parties and delegates of these parties.

A month after the elections, in February 1947, the eighth congress of the Polish Bund was held in Wrocław. Bundist organizations from all over Poland were represented by over eighty delegates. Szuldenfrei's report to the congress presented the central directive of the Bund: 'The Bund should renounce all pro-emigration work and demand all working activists to remain steadfastly in this country, Poland.'[33] In the period of heated discussions among Jewish parties about Palestine the Bund signed the CKŻP resolution on the subject, at the same time declaring its unchanging attitude towards Zionism. In December 1947 it issued its own resolution reaffirming its position on Zionism and, like the PPR fraction, questioning treating the UN resolution as an accomplishment of the Zionists. The Bund's unwillingness to change its position on the matter echoed its pre-war political inclinations. During its congress in November 1947, held in commemoration of the Bund's fiftieth anniversary, declarations in favour of socialism and national-cultural autonomy were repeated. According to fraction activists, the Bund's attitude made any agreement to unify the two parties difficult to realize.

The idea of unification originated within fraction circles, and it mirrored what was happening at that time on the Polish political scene, where the now dominant PPR was determined to take over the PPS and end any vestige of its independent activity. In May 1948 Szymon Zachariasz gave Roman Zambrowski, a leading Jewish member of the PPR politbureau and at the time deputy speaker in the Sejm, a programmatic statement concerning the PPR fraction and the Bund. Referring to the joint declaration of the central committee of the PPR and the central executive committee of the PPS of March 1948 concerning activity on a united front in the period of preparation for the unification of the workers' movement, the statement instructed the two Jewish parties to organize jointly meetings, consultations with activists, and the unification of party co-operatives, children's and cultural organizations, and clubs, or to incorporate them into the structure of Jewish committees. The statement also suggested conducting joint ideological work within the youth and children's organizations. The expectations of the fraction were made clear in the speeches of Szymon Zachariasz and Grzegorz Smolar at the council of top party executives of the fraction and the Bund on 20 May 1948. According to Zachariasz,

We want a unified front leading to the organic unity of the working class, that is to one ideology for the whole working class based on the doctrine of Marxism–Leninism. The necessary condition for this unity is the Bund's 're-evaluation of values', a review of its own ideological and tactical precepts over the course of its history. Presently, the comrades from the Bund deny necessity for this or try to avoid it.

[33] *Głos Bundu*, 3 (15 Mar. 1947), 2.

Smolar stated bluntly,

We reject in advance any idea of autonomy within the party. It was due to our unified party line that such a Jewish community and settlement as exists now has emerged.[34]

One of the council's resolutions was to convene meetings of the delegates of both parties in Wrocław and Łódź. On 30 May 1948 in Wrocław over 200 activists from both parties attended the meeting. The speeches of fraction activists from Warsaw were this time much more radical. One of the Bundists stated that 'the address by comrade Zachariasz was an unpleasant surprise'.[35] In general, however, the PPR reiterated its earlier position on the Bund. PPR fraction activists from Lower Silesia, who hosted the conference, described the situation in their region. According to Jakub Wasersztrum, 'In regard to the actual work in Lower Silesia, both sides indicated enough good will . . . To our remarks about the necessity of revision of their views, the comrades from the Bund responded that there was nothing to be revised because they had always been, and still were, a Marxist party.'[36]

It is interesting to trace how bringing the parties closer to each other was implemented in the country as a whole. After March 1948, when attempts at merging had started, there were several meetings of Bund and fraction delegates in Lower Silesia, which was inhabited by the largest number of Jews. At consecutive regional Jewish committee meetings on 25 and 30 March 1948 the representatives of the Bund and the fraction presented their expectations and proposals. According to Bund delegate Szafir, from Lower Silesia,

The question of structural unity is also present amongst the Jewish population, which is naturally the case: there are too few of us Jews in Poland to have any decisive influence in the future united party. The Bund would cease to exist as a separate Jewish party. We should think of creating a purely Jewish movement that would work within the Jewish community; otherwise the Jewish community is left to the exclusive influence of Zionism.[37]

The proposals of the Lower Silesia Bundists concerned also the question of autonomy in the future party, and the problem of the 'revision' of the Bund's history. The Lower Silesia activists stated during the discussion that

not all that is in Polish society must be in Jewish society. Those whom the PPR-ists think of as rightists very often prove to be leftists, and vice versa. Also, we must take into consideration the psychology of our comrades in the Bund. The Bund was for forty years a separate party. The structural form of the PPR's work within the Jewish community is unhealthy. Too much depends on the whims of local secretaries.[38]

[34] Archiwum Akt Nowych, Warsaw, Papers of Szymon Zachariasz, sig. 476/28, 170.
[35] Ibid. 151.   [36] Ibid. 155.
[37] Archiwum Akt Nowych, Warsaw, Papers of Szymon Zachariasz, sig. 476/29, 103.
[38] Ibid. 104.

The Bund members in Lower Silesia, as in the rest of Poland, disagreed with the fraction's suggestions. One of the Wrocław delegates of the latter, Intrator, stated, 'For us the issue is the Bund's past, about which the comrades from the Bund have a completely uncritical approach. Because of its fifty years of existence, hymns of praise are sung.'[39] But the members of the Bund firmly repeated: 'We cannot make ideological revision; we cannot revise Marxism. There is no ideological difference between the PPR and the Bund.'[40]

The first stage of merging the Jewish parties did not end in success. Many issues were left unresolved until after the meeting of the Krajowa Rada Bundu (the Bund's All-Poland Council), convened in Wrocław at the beginning of April. The meeting was closely watched by members of the fraction. Szymon Zachariasz sent direct reports to his Polish supervisors from the Wrocław meeting. He described the attitudes of particular activists of the Bund, pointing out the most radical supporters and opponents of unification with the PPR fraction. According to information supplied by one delegate from Dzierżoniów, 'Szuldenfrei said nothing about organic unity . . . Fiszgrunt spoke at length about the situation in the country and organic unity . . . during his speech he was interrupted and could not make himself heard. Most visible in this was Marek Edelman, who even jumped up to beat Fiszgrunt, accusing him of being a PPR flunky who does whatever he's told by the PPR.'[41] In the council's resolution the advocates of unification with the PPR regarded the Polish Bund as not radical enough; in turn, the Polish Bund affirmed its resignation from the international Bundist Co-ordination and the Socialist International.

In May 1948 new meetings took place between the Bund and PPR fraction activists. On 20 May in Warsaw, during an inter-party meeting of the representatives of the Bund and the fraction, the Bund presented its position. It declared:

for a quicker and fuller realization of the united workers' front in the Jewish community . . . we are ready to do anything . . . to create the real basis for unidirectional collaboration in all areas of Jewish life. . . . For the Bund, the question of how to continue Jewish cultural life is crucial. Our position is to support full autonomy of the Jewish population in the areas of culture and education.[42]

This position was upheld during the Wrocław meeting of 30 May 1948. Krenenberg from Legnica stated, 'Organic unity must necessarily come. . . . I am disappointed still to see such large differences in opinions.'[43] On the other hand, Szafir, one of the Bund leaders in Lower Silesia, said, 'The Bundists need to have the inner conviction that they enter organic unity voluntarily, and not forced by

---

[39] Ibid. 116. [40] Ibid.
[41] Archiwum Akt Nowych, Warsaw, Papers of Szymon Zachariasz, sig. 476/28, 115.
[42] Wojewódzkie Archiwum Państwowe, Wrocław, Bund, sig. 79/5, 74–5.
[43] Archiwum Akt Nowych, Warsaw, Papers of Szymon Zachariasz, sig. 476/28, 155.

anybody.'⁴⁴ Similar in tone was the speech of another Bund leader from Wrocław, Solar, who expressed hope that 'Comrade Zachariasz's report will not be an obstacle to achieving organic unity. In reality, the PPR showed more willingness to collaborate with the Zionists than with the Bund.'⁴⁵ The May meetings demonstrated that the road to unification was still full of conflict and misunderstanding. The Bund activists were divided into supporters of four groups within the party: Szuldenfrei's group, for merger with the PPS; Pudlowski's group, for collaboration with the PPR; Fiszgrunt's group, advocating continuation of the Bund in Poland; and Pat and Falk's group, pushing for dissolution of the Bund in Poland and emigration.

To understand the activity of the Bund in Poland in the first half of 1948 we must consider its reaction to the founding of the state of Israel. Concerning this event, the party declared:

Steadfast in our Bundist belief that the existence and the future of the Jewish nation is above all and in the firmest way connected with the struggle for and the victory of progressive socialist ideals of the worker and peasant masses in all countries where Jews live, we believe that Jews should rely, as they do now, on their laws: personal, citizens', social, and national rights. Firm in our conviction that Zionism as a political concept cannot be a complete solution to the Jewish question, that the liberation of the Jewish nation is part of the general struggle for a world of social justice, progress, and socialism—the Bundist group in the CKZP, responding to the decision of the Palestine Yishuv on 15 May 1948 to proclaim the Jewish state in a part of Palestine, declares the following:

1. The proclamation of Jewish statehood ... should be recognized as a reality, politically and legally justified, despite the fact that because of machinations of British and American imperialism, encouraging the Arab reaction, the UN resolution has not been implemented by the UN itself, which was justly demanded by the Soviet Union and the popular-democratic countries...

2. The Bund in reborn democratic people's Poland has recognized the importance of the Yishuv in Palestine after our great national tragedy, and together with the whole Jewish community here has expressed many times its deep understanding of the needs of the Yishuv in Palestine; we declare our readiness to support it in its struggle for existence and political independence...

3. At the same time we regard it as our right and duty to emphasize our sincere wish and our striving for the newly established Jewish state to overcome all difficulties and perils, with the support of the progressive and democratic forces of the Jewish nation at large and the whole world. The Jewish state should do so through a policy of dialogue with the Arab worker and peasant masses and by joining the struggle against imperialism and chauvinism, whether native or foreign, for a world of freedom, a brotherhood of nations, peace, and socialism.⁴⁶

⁴⁴ Archiwum Akt Nowych, Warsaw, Papers of Szymon Zachariasz, sig. 476/28, 156.
⁴⁵ Ibid.
⁴⁶ Archiwum Żydowskiego Instytutu Historycznego, Warsaw, Prezydium Centralnego Komitetu Żydów w Polsce, sig. 303/10, 122.

In the period from autumn 1946 to summer 1948 the Bund was active in almost all Jewish centres, and the CKŻP occupied an important place in its work. The Bund opposed the unification of the CKŻP with the religious parties. In the first half of 1948 representatives of the PPR fraction and the Bund started negotiations about organic unity. They did not reach a consensus, and only the cultural and educational agencies of these parties became united. In October 1948 the Bund met in Łódź and discussed the political situation and related issues. Unlike earlier Bund meetings, the supporters of the unity advocated by the PPR fraction set the tone. Only a few delegates criticized the Bund's new political line, which regarded 'unification with the movement that marches towards socialism'[47] as necessary. These delegates were excluded from the party, and Tsukunft was disbanded.

The supporters of the new policy presented very critically in their speeches the previous activity of their party. Szafir, a delegate from Wrocław, in his address, which one reporter called 'beautiful', 'clearly pointed to the sins of the party's present leadership . . . we must clearly and unambiguously tell ourselves that only deep and broad analysis of past mistakes will enable us to join the united party . . . The right-wingers cannot stay in the party.'[48] Liquidation of the opposition in the Bund allowed for inclusion of the pro-unification group in the (Polish United Workers' Party: Polska Zjednoczona Partia Robotnicza PZPR).

In January 1949, in Wrocław, an extraordinary congress of the Bund took place. It resolved:

We solemnly declare that the revolutionary and internationalist Polish United Workers' Party . . . is the sole exponent of the interests and aspirations of the whole working class in our country . . . The coming of our party to the position of Marxism–Leninism has prepared the ground for the Bundists to join the PZPR. . . . The extraordinary congress of the Bund in Poland resolves: to disband the party and to call on its members to join the PZPR in order to participate in its ranks in the struggle for socialism, which is the loftiest ideal of the whole of working humanity and which is also the ideal of the Jewish working masses.[49]

The transfer of Bund members to the PZPR was on an individual basis, with the agreement of the proper regional committee of the PZPR being necessary for acceptance. Quite often the crucial issue was one's declared attitude towards the USSR. Most Bund members decided to join the PZPR. The applications sent by Bundists to the party regional committees gave different explanations why entry to the PZPR was desired. The Legnica cell wrote about the Bund's not being interested in the workers' movement in Poland, and about its 'lacking proper insight and its unsatisfactory preparation of the masses for the process of unification, from the beginning not showing any self-criticism . . . Unable to stand on the sidelines at this historical moment, we have decided to ask the PZPR to accept us in the ranks of its members. Recognizing all mistakes of the Bund, we pledge to

[47] Archiwum Akt Nowych, Warsaw, PPR, sig. 295-IX-408, 124. [48] Ibid. 247.
[49] Archiwum Akt Nowych, Warsaw, Papers of Szymon Zachariasz, sig. 476/28, 227.

fulfil all tasks assigned to us and to be faithful to the ideals of Marxism–Leninism. The worker-stockholders of the Co-operative "Model" in Legnica.'[50]

Knecht Dreszer from Dzierżoniów wrote in his application: 'The Bund was a Menshevik and reformist party, and for these there can be no place in the united party. Therefore, I definitely break with the Bund's leadership.'[51] Kajta Upfal, also from Dzierżoniów, felt disappointed as a worker because the Bund had betrayed the interests of the working class. Because of that, 'I cease all contacts with the Bundist clique.'[52] Other Bund activists declared that, despite their membership of the party, they had always supported communism. Światycki from Wrocław even claimed that 'It was my only dream at the end of my life (I'm almost 70) to be in the ranks of the party.'[53] In December 1948, before the resolution of the Bund's central committee dissolving the party, a 'purification' action took place within Bundist ranks. The most frequent reasons for expulsion from the party were either rightist–nationalistic deviation or lack of party discipline. Those who at that time remained in the party were directed to the PZPR in accord with the Bund's resolution.

PZPR activists laid down criteria for all Bundists applying to the party. Of interest among them are not only those that were rejected, but also those that were accepted. In Ząbkowice-Ziębice those Bundists were accepted who, in the opinion of the town committee of the PZPR,

1. Did not revise the past of the Bund . . . a little demoralized in private life . . .
4. Jakub Sztajer—belonged to the Zionists. Paid money to join the Bund in 1947.
5. Igiel Izrael . . . Joined the Bund for material benefits. Politically dull . . . In Ziębice . . .
4. Tajtelbaum Wolf . . . Held an anti-Soviet attitude. . . . Subscribed to the foreign newspapers of the Bund.
7. Liberman Gecel . . . For two years wanted to join the PPR and on the instructions of St. of the PPR remained in the Bund.
22. Mielnik Chaja, a simple-minded cleaning woman. She won't bring anything to the party, but she won't do any harm either.[54]

According to the same criteria in Ząbkowice and Ziębice, party rejections included

> Golfarb Hersh— . . . a troublemaker; he sticks to the parties where he can get some profit for himself. After the dissolution of the Bund he'd probably stick to Zionism.
>
> Kon Lejb . . . was a sworn opponent of the Soviet Union. He said that he opposed the PPR because it was based in the USSR, and that the Bund should never be dissolved . . .
>
> Glikman Anya—a pedlar type. Conclusion: Definitely reject . . .
>
> Szmulak Chaim . . . antisocial type . . . Interested only in girls, coffee, nice clothing, and nothing more.[55]

---

[50] Archiwum Akt Nowych, Warsaw, Papers of Szymon Zachariasz, sig. 476/28, 181.
[51] Ibid. 184.   [52] Ibid. 185.
[53] Wojewódzkie Archiwum Państwowe, PZPR, sig. 74-V-48, 31.   [54] Ibid. 64.
[55] Ibid. 64, 65.

It is hard to tell how large a group of the Bundists decided to join the PZPR. Statistics from a few regions of Poland suggest that it was a majority. On the other hand, the members of that part of the Bund that did not accept inclusion in the PZPR quickly emigrated to France.

In 1949 the over fifty-year-long history of the Bund in Poland came to an end. There is no doubt that its activity in post-war Poland marked the decline of the party, but it earned a place in post-war Jewish history in Poland by trying through its programme to revive a reality that was for ever destroyed by the Holocaust.

Translated from Polish by Gwido Zlatkes

Whose Nation, Whose State? Working-Class Nationalism and Antisemitism in Poland, 1945–1947

PADRAIC KENNEY

THE ideas of citizenship and nationalism have rarely coexisted more uneasily than in communist eastern Europe. While identification with the nation has been strongly developed in the region since the nineteenth century, identification with the state has been erratic at best. Indeed, a primary purpose of forty-five years of communist governance was to convince the population to confer legitimacy upon the state; failing that, the regime sought legitimacy in its leadership of the nation. Those who succeeded, however briefly, generally found that they had to retreat from communist doctrine in one of two directions. Like Ceaușescu, emulating Stalin before him, some embraced nationalism in its most chauvinist forms, vituperating against the West, the Jews, neighbours, or even the Soviets. Others, like Poland's Gierek or Hungary's Kadar, sought peace and sometimes acceptance through a rising standard of living, often financed by the West. In the end, of course, both these cynical strategies failed.

In this chapter I shall argue that in early post-war Poland (and to some extent throughout the communist era) citizen–state relations expressed themselves in part through national identity. In this context antisemitism took on new meaning in Poland because it became not only an expression of fears about national identity and cultural vulnerability, but also a means of defining the state and citizenship. Thus, national identity paradoxically sharpened as Poland approached homoethnicity.

The most fundamental difference between the first rebuilding years and the rest of communist rule in Poland was this: for much of society, the former was a time of great promise, during which one could believe that the war, having wrought social, economic, political, and cultural destruction on the old Poland, might afford the opportunity for a new Poland, in which those groups underprivileged in pre-war

---

An earlier version of this chapter was presented at the fifteenth North American Labor History Conference, Detroit, 15 Oct. 1993. This chapter draws upon my *Rebuilding Poland: Workers and Communists, 1945–1950* (Ithaca, NY, 1997). I thank Cornell University Press for permission to use that material here.

Poland might find justice and power. This was true for much of the intelligentsia, of course; for a worker, choices of allegiance appeared more ambiguous than for intellectuals. Workers' parameters for acceptance of the regime were different: naturally enough, material concerns and community concerns took precedence over those of party doctrine. Before and during the war Polish workers had expressed a strong national consciousness, and post-war reconstruction invoked national themes. The professed class nature of the new state, however, and the practical concerns of the workers eventually made allegiance to the state a central issue. That allegiance was potentially based not just upon prosperity or nationalism, but upon agreement with certain programmes and policies of the communist regime.

Thus, in the communist era apparently 'national' conflicts often concealed class antagonisms, and vice versa.[1] I shall use examples from the great textile centre of Łódź to outline this relationship between citizenship, nationalism, and anti-semitism. Pre-war Łódź was as much Jewish or German as it was Polish. It had the second-largest Jewish community in Poland, totalling one-third of the city's population in 1931. While most Jews in inter-war Poland were workers, in roughly the same percentages as were Poles, the latter remembered only the Jewish factory owners. After the Holocaust it was easier to forget the thousands of Jewish workers and artisans, who in Łódź generally lived in the Bałuty district on the north side of the city. The German population, in turn, declined greatly after 1918: they were 21 per cent of the city's population in 1897 (and had still been a plurality a few decades earlier), compared to the Jews' 29 per cent and the Poles' 46 per cent. In 1931 nearly 9 per cent—over 53,000—of the city's residents still claimed German as their first language. This community quickly revived and expanded during the Nazi occupation; many of these Polish citizens signed the *Volksliste*, which essentially required everyone to choose a nationality and offered many Poles of German extraction the chance to declare themselves German—for which they would pay dearly after 1945.[2]

By 1946 there were only 24,300 Germans and 11,500 other nationalities (including Jews) out of almost 500,000 Łódź residents.[3] The Polish paradox of national antagonisms in a nearly homogeneous country has been noted by many scholars.[4] The reasons for this paradox are not hard to understand. In decimating

[1] See Norman Naimark, 'Revolution and Counterrevolution in Eastern Europe', in Christiane Lemke and Gary Marks (eds.), *The Crisis of Socialism in Europe* (Durham, NC, 1992), 68.
[2] Julian K. Janczak, 'Ludność', in Bohdan Baranowski and Jan Fijałek (eds.), *Łódź: dzieje miasta*, i: *Do 1918r.* (Warsaw, 1980), 219; *Drugi powszechny spis ludności z dn 9.XII.1931 r. miasto Łódź*, Statystyka Polski, seria c, zeszyt 67 (Warsaw, 1937), 14; Ludwik Mroczka, 'Skład wyznaniowy i narodowościowy robotników łódzkich w latach 1918–1939', in *Polska klasa robotnicza: Studia historyczne*, vii (Warsaw, 1976), 396–416; Szyja Bronsztejn, *Ludność żydowska w Polsce w okresie międzywojennym Studium statystyczne* (Wrocław, 1963). [3] *Rocznik Statystyczny, 1948* (Warsaw, 1949), 21.
[4] e.g. Michael Chęcinski, *Poland: Communism, Nationalism, Anti-Semitism* (New York, 1982); Krystyna Kersten, *Polacy—Żydzi—Komunizm: Anatomia półprawd, 1939–1968* (Warsaw, 1992).

Polish society, the Second World War also truncated its relationships, removing long-time political and economic foes. Such antagonisms were a familiar part of social identity, necessitating their reinvention. Although by 1945 a Polish national consciousness could perhaps be taken for granted, at least among urban residents, the new state challenged the nation in a new way. Could workers accept the new republic of Poland and its élites—chiefly the Polska Partia Robotnicza (Polish Workers' Party: PPR)—as Polish, and part of the same nation as they? We will see how the division between the two grew over the first three years of communist rule. As workers came into conflict with the state, they also began to define the state and its élites as foreign.[5]

Yet it must be emphasized at the outset that, while there was never any doubt that communist domination had been imposed from the outside, without the consent of the Polish people, some members of the working class—in particular, older, skilled, politically conscious urban workers—might have been disposed to accord it legitimacy. This could be the case as long as such workers perceived the government to be advocating and pursuing policies that these workers wanted to achieve. Chief among these was the nationalization of factories.

During and immediately after the war everyone in Poland from right to left supported the takeover of industry. Part of its appeal was in fact nationalist. The severe unemployment of the 1930s had etched on the Polish mind an image of the heartless capitalist throwing workers into the street; most believed their jobs would be safer in their own hands or in those of the state. Pre-war capital had often been perceived as foreign (German) or non-Polish (Jewish). The country's economic élite, whether foreign, non-Polish, or Polish, was decimated by the war. Those who were not murdered by the Nazis or driven out as the Germans retreated had likely spent the war abroad—a damning fact in a country that placed a high value on patriotic heroism and suffering. 'German' and 'Jew' had been shorthand for the bosses of industry, the causes of the Polish worker's misery. After the war the system of social relations, with the disappearance of the old factory owners (soon to be followed by a war on shopkeepers), became quite unclear.

In Łódź nationalism was central to the politics of liberation: a city where the Polish language had been outlawed now became the heart of Poland. At the moment of liberation, a Łódź union activist claimed, even a political rally could have symbolic value as a vehicle of Polish culture, where one could 'listen, enraptured, to the melody of a Polish word'.[6] In the post-war confusion national identity could seem a beacon of clarity, and the actions of the state only helped

---

[5] Note that 'foreign' could have two meanings for the Pole in the post-war republic: 'Soviet' or 'Jewish'. While this is a problem that deserves further exploration, it seems safe to say that the two identifications were the same in the Polish mind.

[6] Feliks Tomaszewski, Centralna Rada Związków Zawodowych library, Warsaw, memoir 33, 21–3.

to confirm this. Though the Polish terms for nationalization (*upaństwowienie*—'statization', the process of absorbing into the state; and *uspołecznienie*—socialization) do not convey it, 'nationalization' in 1945 had an unintended double meaning, as factories that had belonged to Germans or Jews now landed in the hands of the Polish state.

While the government never made such an explicit reference to the economy as Polish, the drive of workers to possess their factories did contain a nationalist element. Groups of workers began to protect, liberate, rebuild, and activate their factories in late 1944 in the eastern third of present-day Poland, even before its liberation by the Soviet army. This activity continued in central Poland in early 1945. Nationalization thus began in the absence of an extant skeleton of administration. As workers reclaimed their factories from German state or military administration, they asserted their own Polish identity; they prided themselves on the ability of Poles to outwit the Germans and to run the factories themselves. Some took up arms to defend their factories against looters from the Russian army.[7]

But to whom would the factories belong? Nationalization could be understood in different ways. While the communists came to favour state control of the means of production,[8] the experience of the war, in which many Poles had learned to make do without state and economic structures, had fostered among workers a syndicalist perspective, a general idea that factories belonged in the hands of the workers or the nation. The enormity of the rebuilding process gave workers and their factory committees or councils great latitude. Those who took part in reconstruction did not suppose that after securing and rebuilding their factories they would hand them over to the Soviets, the government, or a private employer.[9]

Still, it was always clear that their movement enjoyed the official support of the state and party. For the authorities, factory councils formed the symbolic cornerstone of a popular government, linking the working class and Polish society to the leading role of the workers' representatives, the PPR, in government. Nevertheless, they moved quickly to contain them. Factory councils chosen by workers frequently defended their factories against outside intervention, or attempted to restructure the factory themselves. They attempted to 'nationalize' small factories not yet targeted by the state, or to choose their own director from among themselves or from among respected pre-war technicians. Thus a factory might be restored to the Polish nation: a former worker at a hosiery factory recalled, 'there was a proposal that we choose someone from among those who worked there to serve as the head of the factory, as an elected director . . . There was even a suggestion that I serve as the factory's head, but I was a young man, and I didn't agree to

---

[7] Interview with Stanisław S., 9 May 1990; on Soviet attempts to confiscate factories, see Janusz Gołębiowski, *Walka PPR o nacjonalizację przemysłu* (Warsaw, 1961), 140.

[8] See documents in Hanna Jędruszczak (ed.), *Upaństwowienie i odbudowa przemysłu w Polsce, 1944–1948: materiały źródłowe*, 2 vols. (Warsaw, 1967–9).

[9] On the workers' control movement, see Kazimierz Kloc, *Historia samorządu robotniczego w PRL, 1944–1989* (Warsaw, 1992).

this. So we chose a former supervisor, a Pole of course.'[10] A metalworker described the workers who organized his factory in the first days as 'a workers' government'. A postal workers' representative explained in September 1945 that since the workers themselves had rebuilt their trucks and workplaces, 'Everything . . . trucks, tools, everything is [the workers']; they are co-owners, and will not allow the wasting of their common property.'[11]

While the state's attack on worker control began already in 1945, the symbolism of workers in power lingered for years after. Workers' exploits in the first days were recalled frequently in pamphlets and articles. Even under Stalinism Poland's hero workers used the language of ownership; as one was made to say to bureaucrats in a fictionalized account published in 1950, at the height of Stalinism: 'I've had enough of all this bureaucratizing. Mine is the factory, the weaving room, the loom, and all Poland, and yours is the office where you officiate, and where I was in over my head.'[12]

This speaker and those quoted earlier are citizens of a workers' Poland and, at least initially, believed themselves to be acting in a state-approved way. In a communist state, to be a worker was to be a citizen, more so than if one were a bureaucrat. But as the state advanced into the factory, the gap between the two sides grew, and the worker lost trust in the state.

As these quotations indicate, workers found terrain on which to counterattack the party in the Polish nation. They did not, however, do so by joining partisan groups; workers as workers were generally underrepresented in nationalist underground organizations under the communists, and such organizations rarely spoke on behalf of workers or addressed workers' concerns.[13] Instead, the workers of Łódź fought to defend their workplaces from the authorities. If the workers could not own the factories, at least they could keep control over work traditions. The struggle for control of the factory involved economic, social, and political concerns—and was never resolved, as the revolts throughout the communist era would show. In this chapter I want to concentrate on the ways in which this struggle served to sharpen imagined ethnic differences in the first years of the People's Poland. The nature of the post-war era requires consideration of imagined ethnic conflict with both 'Germans' and 'Jews', two groups of people that often seemed inseparable in the imagination of Polish workers.

'German' obviously had a meaning different than in 1939, as not just an 'other' but a traitor as well. Resentment of the Volksdeutsch, Polish citizens who had

[10] Interview with Stanisław S.
[11] Wincenty Wysocki [factory committee representative], Centralna Rada Związków Zawodowych library, memoir 644, 3–4. In the latter case a government representative reminded those present that the state was in fact the owner and the workers were not. Protocol of the conference of workers from the Łódź postal transport office, Wojewódzkie Archiwum Państwowe, Łódź, Wojewódzka Rada Związkow Zawodowych, 253.
[12] Kazimierz Koźniewski, 'Extry i primy', *Most: wybór reportaży* (Warsaw, 1951), 131–2.
[13] See Kenney, *Rebuilding Poland: Workers and Communists, 1945–1950*, 41–2.

during the war signed papers affirming their German heritage and thus won certain privileges, was pervasive throughout Poland in the first year after the war.[14] Most of these Volksdeutsch subsequently emigrated, leaving Germans behind only in the workers' imagination. Workers used the popular fear of Germans to their advantage. They accused factory management of collaboration with the Nazis, of hiding a German background or a Gestapo or capitalist past. Authorities took these charges seriously and investigated them, although the accused was not always removed. For example, workers at State Cotton Factory No. 9 wrote to the district Polska Partia Socjalistyczna (Polish Socialist Party: PPS) committee to report on a supervisor who had threatened to turn them over to the Gestapo for laziness:

So we the undersigned would like to know whether he is back in the occupation [period], when he smacked Poles in the face and sent them to Sikawa? No. We don't want such people, who strike at the interests of the working class, here in our society . . . This matter should be examined to uncover whether citizen Bilecki carries out such work consciously and purposefully, and whether he is a tool of the reaction.[15]

These workers had learned the new language of political conflict, and sought to use it to resolve labour disputes. Strikers at the Hirszberg & Wilczyński garment factory struck successfully for the removal of a supervisor who, they said, had speeded up the machines during the occupation, thus forcing workers to sew faster. Management agreed to replace him with a candidate proposed by the workers themselves.[16] In this case, the workers used two resources—information about wartime activities, and the ability to manipulate such information—to gain a difficult concession. A city-wide strike in Pabianice (near Łódź) in late October 1945 showed how nationalism could substitute for other tensions. By applying new labels to their opponents, workers at the Krusche & Ender and Kindler mills gave wage and benefit demands greater force. Workers' statements revealed many varieties of class, sectional, and ethnic injustice. But the Kindler strikers were most vehement in their attacks on factory director Herman, whom they claimed was a German and should be removed for the harm he had inflicted on Polish workers. At open meetings they charged him with numerous irregularities and malicious wrongdoing: they claimed that he had personally swindled them out of coal and stolen the socks and sweaters intended as bonuses for workers who had defended the factory in the last days of the occupation, and that his son-in-law was served

---

[14] On Łódź, see Wojewódzki Urząd Informacji i Propagandy, Łódź, Reports, June–Aug. 1945, Archiwum Akt Nowych, Warsaw, Ministerstwo Informacji i Propagandy, 298.

[15] Sikawa, near Łódź, was the site of a small labour camp during the war. Wojewódzkie Archiwum Państwowe, Łódź, Dzielnicowy Komitet, Śródmieście-Prawa, 29/XII/1, n. p. Other examples: Archiwum Ruchu Zawodowego, Warsaw, Komisja Centralna Związków Zawodowych, Wydział Organizacyjny, 141, kk. 41, 53; 125, k. 19; Archiwum Akt Nowych, Warsaw, Centralny Komitet Wykonawczy, PPS 235/XXVI/5, k. 29; Komitet Centralny, PPR 295/X/5, k. 33.

[16] Cited in Władysław Stefaniuk, *Łódzka organizacja PPS, 1945–1948* (Łódź, 1980), 82.

meat cutlets from the factory kitchen. They claimed that Herman favoured Germans and Jews over Polish workers. 'How can you say things are OK,' shouted a glazier, 'when that Jew Bork was sold 2,400 metres of [cloth], on which he made over 3 million zlotys, and a Pole isn't even sold 100 metres?' Another worker complained: 'Poles must push carts, while Germans are taught to work the looms.'[17]

The language of this strike reflects tensions specific to 1945 in Poland. First, workers had suddenly regained their voices after five-and-a-half years of Nazi repression. The voices now emerging in worker conflicts were chaotic, directed on every side—against the Germans, against the Jews (the two sometimes equated), but most of all against management. Management, then, was cheating workers both as workers and as Poles. This was both a national and an intensely local conflict, in which defence of rights to fair norms and bonuses, and to food and coal, reflected pre-war and wartime relations.

Jews served as a much more potent scapegoat for economic and political problems in Łódź, one of the strongest centres of Polish antisemitism. A frequent theme was the supposed privileged position of Jews in society. This view was common, for example, among PPR worker–activists in Łódź. While such activists claimed not to be taken in by 'reactionary antisemites', they nevertheless blamed the Jews themselves for any incidents, claiming that of 20,000 Jews in Łódź, not one worked in a factory except in management. Other young Jews, they said, were content to collect welfare rather than go to work. Still others had taken shops away from Poles. Finally, they claimed that half of the Urząd Bezpieczeństwa (Security Office: UB) consisted of Jews who sat behind desks while Polish party members—the 'real' party members—did the hard work 'with machine-gun in hand'.[18]

In the factory itself workers portrayed the Jews as both shirkers and oppressors. At the Scheibler & Grohman mill workers claimed that they had welcomed Jewish workers as colleagues in May 1945, but that only three of 120 remained a year later. According to the party's sympathetic report, 'The worker wants to see the Jew around him, but as a worker, not as a director. [The worker] says that there are still plenty of Poles to be made directors. The worker is outraged that all higher

---

[17] Report of the Findings of the Commission on the Strike at Kindler, Krusche & Endler, and Biederman, Wojewódzki Archiwum Państwowe, Łódź, Dyrekcja Przemysłu Bawelnianego, 20; Factory council meeting at Kindler, 1 Dec. 1945, Wojewódzkie Archiwum Państwowe, Łódź, Wojewódzki Komitet, PPS 22/XIV/37; personnel department, Kindler mill, Report, 27 Oct. 1945, Archiwum Akt Nowych, Ministerstwo Przemysłu i Handlu, 41, kk. 435–43. Herman, in response to the last charge, noted that the Germans were being trained for the night shift, on which no Poles were willing to work. German workers at the related Biederman strike played a different role: they were the first to return to work from the strike: ibid., k. 446.

[18] Central Committee Inspector, Report from Łódź, Aug. 1945, Archiwum Akt Nowych, Warsaw, Komitet Centralny, PPR 295/IX/29, k. 27; Labour Section, Komitet Wojewódzki, PPR Łódź, Report, June 1945, Wojewódzkie Archiwum Państwowe, Łódź, Komitet Wojewódzki, PPR 1/XI/2. See also reports in Archiwum Akt Nowych, Warsaw, Ministerstwo Informacji i Propagandy, 82, kk. 5 (30 Feb. 1945) and 10 (15 Sept. 1945).

positions are taken by Jews, who steal and then escape abroad with the money.'[19] At the Biederman mill, a factory known before the war for its strongly religious, 'backward' workforce, workers responded to the appointment of an engineer of Jewish background as factory director in June by going on strike. The strike lasted for two-and-a-half days, with the only demand being: 'we don't want a Jew director'. When a trade union official called on party members at least to return to work, he was branded a 'Jewish Wojtek' (a lackey of the Jews).[20]

It seems rather significant that party members apparently took an active part in these conflicts and in spreading these rumours, as much as or even more than the workers. In 1945 antisemitic incidents or statements had not yet become a substitute for anti-state or anti-party expression. Workers envisioned Jews (or Germans) primarily as economic exploiters—management or shopkeepers. They were not yet expressing hatred of the communists in the form of antisemitism; attacks on Jews in 1945 at no time referred to the PPR, which for some would soon be synonymous with a Jewish conspiracy to control Poland. Neither the labour parties nor the state was cast as an opponent in these strikes, nor in the Pabianice strikes in October (although the PPR leadership opposed and organized against the strikes). This was in part because old party activists, particularly socialists, were prominent strikers themselves. Those who had joined the party before 1945 still dominated party organizations in the factories, and thus they played roles based on the pre-war labour culture of the city.

But as the strikers redefined their community, they also strove to define their opponents. Beginning in mid-1946, the party initiated a series of political conflicts which effectively excluded it from the Łódź labour community and broke open the limits imposed by working-class community traditions. Over the next two years the apparent consensus on the nation began to erode, as had the consensus on state policy earlier. This was in large part a response to the Polish communists' greater aggressiveness against their political opponents, in particular to the campaigns surrounding the national referendum of June 1946 and the parliamentary election of January 1947. Both campaigns focused on visions of Poland's future; the referendum, which asked Poles to support the abolition of the senate, the nationalization of industry and redistribution of land, and the new western border, provoked especially strong ferment.

Łódź saw its first political disturbances as the referendum campaign intensified. The first of May 1946—the first peacetime celebration of the labour holiday—became an important occasion for the state and PPR to agitate in support of the referendum. Some 200,000 in Łódź took part in or watched the May Day

[19] Inspection Report, Scheibler mill, 29–30 July 1946, Archiwum Akt Nowych, Warsaw, Komitet Centralny, PPR 295/IX/32, k. 17.
[20] Labour Section, Komitet Wojewódzki, PPR Łódź, Report, June 1945, Wojewódzkie Archiwum Państwowe, Łódź, PPR 1/XI/2.

parade, which stretched 6 kilometres and took four hours.[21] This impressive symbol of the importance of the worker in the new Poland—and also of the money and supplies the state and the factories really did have at their disposal when they chose—was followed two days later by an opposite political message. On 3 May, the anniversary of the 1791 constitution, students (mostly PPS members) of Łódź University, which had opened for the first time that year, organized an unofficial parade. A 'counter-demonstration' denouncing the marchers as 'fascists' quickly greeted their slogans. The efforts of the police to break up the demonstration resulted in two wounded and seventeen arrested.[22]

While this protest may have been confined to students, the tension in the city—and throughout the country—was not. Protesting workers never mentioned the referendum campaign, nor the arrests of opposition activists. But the regime's worst fears were confirmed by a city-wide strike which began that same week. Groups of students gathered at factory gates to agitate for the strike and issued leaflets calling for strikes at high schools and the university; three-quarters of the high schools struck. Partisan political conflict appeared for the first—and last—time in the factory. The opposition Polskie Stronnictwo Ludowe (Polish Peasant Party: PSL) made an unsuccessful attempt to register a party circle at the Łódź electric plant. Tramworkers applauded PSL leader Mikołajczyk's name and whistled down the communists. At Scheibler & Grohman a courier was intercepted smuggling a strike fund into the factory; strikers sent a letter to the PSL. This strike was considered so threatening that three top PPR leaders—Władysław Gomułka, Hilary Minc, and Kazimierz Witaszewski—came to speak at the factory shortly before the referendum.[23]

After the 30 June referendum, with the parliamentary elections next on the political horizon, tensions only increased. The flames of nationalism in Łódź were fanned hottest by the pogrom of 4 July 1946, in which a crowd murdered forty-two Jewish residents of one building in the city of Kielce.[24] The politics of the pogrom, which some claim was a PPR–UB provocation intended to direct attention away from the fraudulent results of the referendum, were complicated indeed, and may never be fully unravelled; the reaction of Łódź workers to the event showed how political tensions had changed their characterization of the authorities.

If the PPR had in fact encouraged something of the sort, it was also quick to condemn it, and, as was standard practice for the time, organized worker demonstrations to condemn the pogrom as the work of 'reactionary forces'. Between 8 and 11 July labour organizers called such meetings in many factories and invited

---

[21] Archiwum Akt Nowych, Warsaw, Ministerstwo Informacji i Propagandy, 804, kk. 74–5. 1 May did not become an official holiday until 1950. [22] Ibid., k. 80.
[23] Archiwum Akt Nowych, Warsaw, Ministerstwo Informacji i Propagandy, 927, kk. 37–8, 42; Ministerstwo Pracy i Opieki Społecznej, 803, k. 11; Komitet Centralny, PPR 295/IX/32, kk. 10, 12, 22.
[24] On the pogrom, see Bożena Szaynok, *Pogrom Żydów w Kielcach 4 lipca 1946* (Warsaw, 1992); Kersten, *Polacy—Żydzi—Komunizm*, 89–142.

workers to sign prepared resolutions. The meetings themselves passed without incident, but few workers co-operated. In the Łódź Thread Factory, for example, 'the assembly accepted the proposed resolution indifferently and calmly, but supposedly [only] a small number of workers signed it.' In Scheibler & Grohman only one shop agreed to the resolution, and only some party members signed it. The next day, however, the daily PPR organ reported 'in large type' that the workers of these and other factories had approved the resolutions and demanded the death penalty for those found guilty of the pogrom. This attempt to propagandize the incident backfired, arousing the workers' antisemitism and politicizing it by turning it against the government and the PPR. Workers began to perceive the PPR and the government as 'Jewish' in their opposition to the workers. Fierce strikes broke out at nearly a dozen factories—mostly cotton mills and sewing shops—when workers saw this report. Their connection to the Kielce tragedy was clear; in one factory there was even a spurious phone call informing workers that all of Kielce was on strike and asking for Łódź's support.[25] While these protests lasted no more than an hour or so, PPR observers were taken by surprise at their vehemence. In one factory a PPR secretary who attempted to oppose the strikers was beaten up. A report prepared for the central committee warned:

The situation in Łódź is serious, as evidenced by the mood among strikers and the strikes' swift leaps from factory to factory, and the aggression of striking women in all factories; they clawed and screamed ferociously. Slogans of revenge and terror from the moment of the execution of the convicted killers of Kielce were heard in the shops. [They] compare the alacrity of the Kielce trial with that of [Artur] Greiser [commander of the Polish lands annexed to the Reich during the occupation], who is still alive, though he is guilty of [killing] so many millions of victims. Striking workers use such antisemitic arguments as 'A pregnant Jew gets 60,000 zlotys, and what do I have?' [or] . . . 'Why don't Jews work in factory shops? Poland is ruled by Jews.'[26]

Łódź Jews described a 'pogrom atmosphere' in the city; there were rumours, for example, that Jews in the Bałuty district had murdered a Polish child.[27] While the strikes themselves were easily broken up once the workers had made their demands—usually that a retraction be printed in the newspaper—the atmosphere of hostility lingered long after.

More protests occurred upon the sentencing of the pogrom leaders. Hard on the heels of the communists' political offensive during the referendum campaign the Kielce pogrom became a turning-point in popular perception of the govern-

---

[25] The Kielce strikes are mentioned in Report on Trip to Łódź, 11–13 July 1946, Archiwum Akt Nowych, Warsaw, Komitet Centralny, PPR 295/IX/32, kk. 13–15; Inspection Report, Scheibler mill, Komitet Centralny, PPR 295/IX/32, kk. 23; Miejski Urząd Informacji i Propagandy, Łódź, Report, 13 July 1946, Archiwum Akt Nowych, Warsaw, Ministerstwo Informacji i Propagandy, 927, k. 48; Social-Labour Section, Wojewódzki Komitet, PPS Łódź, Report, July 1946, Wojewódzkie Archiwum Państwowe, Łódź, Wojewódzki Komitet, PPS 22/XII/2.

[26] Archiwum Akt Nowych, Warsaw, Komitet Centralny, PPR 295/IX/32, kk. 13–15.

[27] Ibid.

ment and the PPR among workers—at least among the Łódź textile industry women, who led the protests. Workers could now make connections, for example, between the pogrom and the lowering of their wages in the recent collective agreement. At the John metalworks, which did not strike, agitation was reported against engineer Jung, a 'Semite' and a PPR member, and the director of bookkeeping—in this way, workers linked the party, the Jews, and low wages. But national association was indiscriminate; workers could equally well also call PPR members 'Gestapo' and 'Volksdeutsche'—appellations unlikely a few months before.[28] In 1945, then, Jews (and Germans) appeared in the Polish imagination in their wartime and pre-war guises, as capitalists and foreign agents. By 1947 such images were being pushed out by a new image of the Jews as communists, implicated in the repression of workers in the new system as they had been accused in the old. Workers, meanwhile, had become purely Polish in their own imagination, with national barriers dividing them from the government and even from other classes. A complaint recorded in a workers' vacation home in 1949, noted by a sociologist investigating the reasons why workers on vacation refused to consort with white-collar workers at the same resort, evoked just such a class-based nationalism:

Here we are [considered] inferior. Supposedly we eat together at dinner, but we talk little with others. . . . What can one talk about with them? They play bridge, and we play *zechcyk* or *szkot*. 'Bridge' is in English, and *zechcyk* and *szkot* in German [the speaker is a Silesian] . . . and are the same in Polish. We are people just the same, just at different work, and taught differently.[29]

The days of attacks on 'rootless cosmopolitans'—which would often be supported by workers—were not far off.

It is tempting to blame the communists for the shift in national image described here. Certainly the labour historian cannot but be disappointed in the conduct of the workers. If the fifty-five years of communist rule were just an aberration imposed from without, one could breathe a bit easier. Attention to the changing concepts of nation and state during these years yields a more appropriate explanation. Workers tried to assert their concept of the state in 1945, and were rebuffed. In short, they discovered that the state was not theirs, despite rhetoric to the contrary. In 1945 any state on Polish territory was welcome, especially if it espoused such promising policies; by 1947 workers were searching for ways to categorize the state as alien.

The nation, in contrast, was overwhelmingly the workers', though it was strangely deformed. Missing were nearly all the elements against which Poles had

[28] PPR secretaries' meeting, 13 July 1946, Wojewódzkie Archiwum Państwowe, Łódź, Komitet Dzielnicowy, PPR Górna-Prawa 1/VI/65, kk. 32–3; Archiwum Akt Nowych, Warsaw, Komitet Centralny, PPR 295/IX/32, kk. 44–6.

[29] Miner, Wieczorek-Janów mine, quoted in Barbara Bazińska and Danuta Dobrowolska, 'Kształtowanie się społeczności wczasowej', in Danuta Dobrowolska (ed.), *Robotnicy na wczasach w pierwszych latach Polski Ludowej: studia i materiały* (Wrocław, 1963), 116–17.

defined themselves. In the absence of Jews, and of Germans, Polish workers felt it necessary to reinvent them, thus re-creating a context in which they could reassert themselves as Poles. Listening to workers express national sentiments, one has the impression of people searching to re-create pre-war national relations, as if feeling for an amputated limb. They seemed to erase from memory all that came after 1939. To the consternation of the PPR political bureau, the people of Łódź even removed the physical evidence of the Holocaust as well: in the summer of 1945 worker families took apart the empty houses of the Bałuty ghetto for fuel.[30]

The means for re-creating such relations were ersatz national conflicts, expressions of Polish nationalism based on opposition rather than solidarity and evoking a multi-ethnic past as much as they demanded a de-ethnicized future. That nationalism might have a specifically working-class component became clear to most of us from the Solidarity movement of 1980–1. Thirty-five years earlier Polish workers created national conflict specifically as workers; they labelled management, officials, and workers who would not work as Germans and Jews. Very soon, they moved the communists out of the Polish nation, too. Denied a workers' state, they sought to create a workers' nation.

[30] Archiwum Akt Nowych, Warsaw, Komitet Centralny PPR 295/V/5, kk. 33–5.

Poles and Jews in the Kielce Region and Radom, April 1945–February 1946

ADAM PENKALLA

THE relations between Poles and Jews and the situation of the Jewish population directly after the end of the Second World War on Polish territory are topics which have only recently been addressed in Polish historiography.[1] The Kielce region is particularly important in any discussion of this problem, because of the importance of the pogrom in Kielce on 4 July 1946 in any evaluation of Polish–Jewish relations at that time. The documents presented here pre-date that event and come mostly from Jewish sources. They reveal the complexity of the political, economic, and social situation in post-war Poland, which determined Polish–Jewish relations, and shed light on the situation within the Jewish community, whose fate had been drastically transformed by the events of the war.

The first document is the minutes of a conference of Jewish committees active in what was then the Kielce voivodeship, which took place on 14 and 15 March 1945 in Kielce, and provides information about the meeting of the representatives of Jewish communities in different localities of the region with the representatives of the Centralny Komitet Żydów w Polsce (Central Committee of Jews in Poland: CKŻP). This committee was established on 4 November 1944 at the initiative of the Komitet Organizacyjny Żydów Polskich (Organizing Committee of Polish Jews: KOŻP) and the department for Jewish affairs of the Krajowa Rada Narodowa (National Council for the Homeland: KRN), which from 1944 played the role of *de facto* parliament. The committee's primary task was to assist local Jewish committees in providing material and financial assistance to Jews saved from the

---

[1] Krystyna Kersten, *Polacy—Żydzi—Komunizm: Anatomia półprawd, 1939–1968* (Warsaw, 1992); B. Szaynok, *Pogrom Żydów w Kielcach, 4 lipca 1946* (Warsaw, 1992); Zenon Wrona (ed.), *Antyżydowskie wydarzenia kieleckie 4 lipca 1946 roku: dokumenty i materiały. Akta procesów uczestników wydarzeń oraz funkcjonariuszy Milicji Obywatelskiej i Wojewódzkiego Urzędu Bezpieczeństwa Publicznego* (Kielce, 1992), i; Jerzy Tomaszewski (ed.), *Najnowsze dzieje Żydów w Polsce, do 1950 roku* (Warsaw, 1993); Stanisław Meducki (ed.), *Antyżydowskie wydarzenia kieleckie 4 lipca 1946 roku: dokumenty i materiały. Dokumenty władz państwowych, stanowiska organizacji politycznych, władz kościelnych, środowisk społecznych, wspomnienia, relacje* (Kielce, 1994), vol. ii.

Nazi Holocaust. In addition, it provided legal assistance in reclaiming property taken from Jews and helped Jews to find jobs, mainly through organizing artisan co-operatives and creating individual craft shops. In addition, it helped them confront the many death threats they faced.

At the meeting representatives of the CKŻP provided information about the situation of Jews in Poland, the policy of the government towards the Jewish community, and the forms of help available. Representatives of regional and local committees described the fate of Jews in particular localities in the voivodeship, their individual and group expectations, and the attitudes towards Jews encountered among the Polish population in general and, in particular, among officials in the state administration and government.

The documents illuminate various aspects of Jewish life shortly after the end of the war in Europe. From the testimony of Dr Seweryn Kahane, the president of the Jewish regional committee, it appears that the committee was responsible for 2,707 Jews. It is difficult to evaluate today the accuracy of this figure, since on 15 April 1945 the statistics of the CKŻP show that there were altogether 5,085 Jews in the Kielce voivodeship.[2] So significant a discrepancy could have been the result of a number of factors, above all the transient character of the Jewish population in the voivodeship. In addition, many people failed to register because of concern for their personal safety. This concern was fully justified, since fear of violent death appears frequently in these documents. According to data prepared by the political department of the Ministry of Public Administration for the Ministry of Public Safety, between March and August 1945 in the Kielce region there were fourteen assaults against Jews; among them four were robberies connected with the return of houses and property taken from Jews during the German occupation and directly after the war. During these assaults thirty-two people were killed and eight were wounded.[3]

The subsequent documents describe the situation of Jews in the area of the district Jewish committee in Radom, which was active in the city of Radom and throughout the Radom district (*powiat*). On 16 January 1945, after two days of fighting, soldiers of the Red Army took Radom. At the end of that month there were 300 Jews in the city, among whom 180 were originally from Radom.[4] During the period from April 1945 to February 1946 the number of permanent and temporary Jewish residents of Radom often changed. According to the data of the district Jewish committee, on 12 May 1945 there were 402 Jews, including 158 women, 194 men, and fifty children, in Radom. Six of the children were living with Poles, who had probably hidden them during the occupation; eighteen were

---

[2] Meducki (ed.), *Antyżydowskie wydarzenia*, ii. 36.
[3] Ibid. 55–61; the data based on the document are given below and dated 29 Nov. 1945.
[4] Adam Penkalla, *Żydowskie ślady w województwie kieleckim i radomskim* (Radom, 1992), 148.

orphans, fifteen had lost one parent, and eleven lived with their parents.[5] At that time the Jewish community in Radom was the largest in the Kielce voivodeship.[6]

Shortly after the liberation of the city the district Jewish committee, headed by the engineer Mojżesz Bojm, started its work. It was subordinated to the regional committee in Kielce. The Radom committee took responsibility, not only for the city itself, but also for the entire district of Radom. Thus Jews living in Szydłowiec, Białobrzegi, Gniewoszów, Kozienice, Zwoleń, and Jedlińsk (where on 12 March 1945 twelve people were living) also fell under its jurisdiction.[7]

The size of the Jewish population changed substantially over time. Some people moved from smaller to larger localities, where they felt safer and could find better living conditions. Jews freed from concentration camps also moved into the area. In mid-June of 1945, 193 former camp inmates were registered by the committee as permanent residents of Radom.[8] Part of the Jewish population saw their stay in Radom as a temporary refuge on the road to other destinations. According to the list of 25 July 1945, 152 Jews temporarily remaining in Radom were given food supplies by the committee.[9] Some planned to leave Radom for western Poland, and in June 1946, 116 Jews left the town in order to settle in Lower Silesia.[10]

For those remaining in the city, the district Jewish committee aimed to establish safe and relatively normal conditions of life, given post-war circumstances. From the documents we learn how difficult conditions were. In general, a picture emerges of widespread poverty among the Jewish population. This was true not only in the localities within the area of activity of the Radom committee, but throughout the whole region, wherever Jews had survived the war.[11] Thus, for example, a telegram sent on 24 August 1945 from the Radom committee to the regional Jewish committee in Kielce stated: 'We have no more money. We face the danger of having to close down the kitchen and cease aid to the children.'[12] Twelve Jews from Jedlińsk, who had returned to their pre-war homes, asked for help on 12 March 1945, writing to the CKŻP: 'We are in a critical situation: all of us are almost naked and barefoot, and we have no possibility of getting anything to wear. The food situation is even worse; the local authority has no income, since it has

---

[5] Archiwum Państwowe w Radomiu, Okręgowy Komitet Żydowski w Radomiu, 1944–1948, vol. 2, p. 2: document from the Radom regional committee in Kielce dated 12 May 1945.

[6] As stated in document 1, presented below, which was published by A. Penkalla, 'Sytuacja ludności żydowskiej na terenie województwa kieleckiego w maju 1945 roku', *Kieleckie Studia Historyczne*, 13 (1995), 241–2.

[7] Ibid. 242–3. Archiwum Państwowe w Radomiu, Okręgowy Komitet Żydowski w Radomiu, 1944–1948, vol. 5, pp. 1–2.

[8] Archiwum Państwowe w Radomiu, Okręgowy Komitet Żydowski w Radomiu, 1944–1948, vol. 19, pp. 20–3: list dated 16 June 1945.   [9] Ibid. 24–46.

[10] Ibid. 49–51: list of the people from Radom settled in Lower Silesia dated 27 June 1946.

[11] Document 1 presented here gives information about this.

[12] Archiwum Państwowe w Radomiu, Okręgowy Komitet Żydowski w Radomiu, 1944–1948, vol. 19, p. 36.

been completely destroyed as it was in the front line and cannot provide us with any help.'[13] Equally tragic was the situation of 106 Jews in Szydłowiec. The report from the first organizational meeting of the Szydłowiec committee on 24 February 1945 stated that 'Jews came to Szydłowiec from labour camps or from the woods, and they are in a completely destitute state. They lack clothing, and even more, shoes. Also, there is lack of underwear and bedding. Most important of all is the lack of machines and tools for productive work, and until they get these, they will all be a burden to the committee.'[14] The Radom committee also provided material help for Jews from Radom living in Łódź. More than a year after the war had ended, on 20 November 1946, these Jews in Łódź wrote, 'we have so little to distribute, while there are so many people in need of immediate and substantial help. Most of us in Łódź are factory workers who live in hardship, and cannot even dream about buying clothing or shoes.'[15] In the light of these statements, one must cast a very critical eye on the notion that in that period the Jews were better off than Poles, and showed off their wealth, which is sometimes claimed to be one of the causes of Polish anti-Jewish violence.[16]

Despite the difficult material conditions and personal danger, the Radom committee organized many aspects of life for those Jews who remained in the town. They arranged housing and food, both for former residents and for newcomers, and they established a hostel, which served as temporary accommodation. Another problem was reclaiming Jewish apartments which had been appropriated by the Polish population during the occupation or shortly thereafter. The committee established a kitchen and a dining-hall, and intervened with the authorities to obtain equipment for it.[17] It encouraged people to read the Jewish press.[18] It organized a

[13] Archiwum Państwowe w Radomiu, Okręgowy Komitet Żydowski w Radomiu, 1944–1948, vol. 5, pp. 1–2.

[14] Archiwum Państwowe w Radomiu, Okręgowy Komitet Żydowski w Radomiu, 1944–1948, vol. 6, pp. 1–2.

[15] Archiwum Państwowe w Radomiu, Okręgowy Komitet Żydowski w Radomiu, 1944–1948, vol. 7, p. 3.

[16] Compare Krzysztof Urbański, 'Casus Lejzorka Rojtszwańca: Uwagi w związku z wydawnictwem', in Stanisław Meducki and Zenon Wrona (eds.), *Antyżydowskie wydarzenia kieleckie 4 lipca 1946 roku: dokumenty i materiały*, i (Kielce, 1992), 68. The author writes, 'Starved and exhausted from the war, Polish workers were sometimes offended by the lifestyle of some Jews'; he also quotes the opinion of Eugeniusz Wiślicz-Iwańczyk, then the voivode of Kielce, about inhabitants of the Jewish hostel in Kielce at 7–9 Planty Street, the place of the Kielce anti-Jewish events of 4 July 1946.

[17] Archiwum Państwowe w Radomiu, Okręgowy Komitet Żydowski w Radomiu, 1944–1948, vol. 2, p. 11: a request dated 4 June 1945 from the committee of the city industrial department regarding delivery of fuel to this dining-hall, which provided food to Jews who had returned from concentration camps: it stated that they remained without any means; p. 17: a request dated 26 June 1945 to the same recipient, for cast-iron cooking-pots for the same dining-hall; p. 20: a request dated 12 July 1945 to the same recipient for delivery to artisans of abandoned property, including beds, bedding, tables, chairs, and sewing-machines, some of which had originally belonged to Jews; p. 55: a request dated 14 Sept. 1945 to the same recipient for material help to people returning from the Soviet Union.

[18] Archiwum Państwowe w Radomiu, Okręgowy Komitet Żydowski w Radomiu, 1944–1948, vol.

library and attempted to retrieve 1,500 books written in Polish that before the war had belonged to the Radom Jewish library and had been taken to the city library during the war.[19] The committee appealed to the mayor of Radom for the return of the Jewish hospital, in which it wanted to place patients returning from concentration camps, but the mayor turned down the request on the grounds that the building had already been taken over by the municipality for a hospital.[20]

The committee also attempted to organize religious life. Although, along with the religious congregation, it was unsuccessful in its attempt to save the historic Radom synagogue,[21] it was able to erect a commemorative monument to Radom Jews in the same place, using bricks from the demolished building. This monument was unveiled on 17 August 1950.[22] Efforts were also made to protect the Jewish cemetery from further devastation, and a ceremonial burial of the people who died or were murdered in the gunpowder factory in Pionki in the years 1942–4 was organized.[23]

One of the committee's major achievements consisted of finding a livelihood for the Radom Jews under the new post-war circumstances. This 'productivization; (*produktywizacja*) of the Jewish population constituted one of its principal goals.[24]

3, p. 1; in a letter dated 2 May 1945 the Radom committee informs the editors of *Dos naye lebn* that out of 150 copies of the first issue of the paper that were delivered, fifty were sold among the Jewish population; the remaining copies were sent back to the editors. Fifty subscriptions were ordered.

[19] Archiwum Państwowe w Radomiu, Okręgowy Komitet Żydowski w Radomiu, 1944–1948, vol. 10, p. 6; letter dated 17 May 1945 from the Radom committee to the president of the city of Radom.

[20] Archiwum Państwowe w Radomiu, Okręgowy Komitet Żydowski w Radomiu, 1944–1948, vol. 15, pp. 1–2; correspondence on matter dated 9 June 1945 and 21 Aug. 1945. The Jewish community of Radom used its own resources to erect the hospital building in the first half of the 19th c.; it served as a Jewish hospital during the Second World War.

[21] Archiwum Państwowe w Radomiu, Okręgowy Komitet Żydowski w Radomiu, 1944–1948, vol. 16, p. 6: a fragment of a letter dated 2 Dec. 1947 from the Radom committee and the religious congregation: 'The synagogue and the house of prayer of architectural value on Pereca and Bożnicza Streets in Radom had survived the Nazi occupation. After the occupying forces left, the buildings were taken down by the decision of the city board, without having informed the Jewish population beforehand that these buildings needed to be fixed'. The building of the Radom synagogue was erected in 1844 with the support of Jews from abroad (Penkalla, *Żydowskie ślady*, 148).

[22] The monument was designed and constructed by Jakub Zajdenszir, a Radom sculptor.

[23] See document 5, quoted here. In response, the president of the city stated on 16 Aug. 1945 that the city could not fence off the cemetery because of lack of funds (Archiwum Państwowe w Radomiu, Okręgowy Komitet Żydowski w Radomiu, 1944–1948, vol. 15, p. 3). Therefore, the Radom committee asked the city to post a signboard at the cemetery with information about the nature of the place, and to prohibit traffic from driving through the cemetery (ibid. 5: letter from the Jewish committee dated 28 June 1947). The cemetery was established in 1831 for victims of the epidemics; from 1837 to 1951 it served as a burial-ground for Radom Jews. In 1990 about 300 gravestones in varying states of preservation were transferred to it from Wacyn, near Radom, where they had been used to pave a square. During its restoration the cemetery was finally fenced and the gate was reconstructed. The gravestones have not yet been turned into a memorial wall (Penkalla, *Żydowskie ślady*, 148–9). The Pionki Jews were exhumed and reburied on 9 May 1949.

[24] See the statement of the general secretary of the CKŻP on the Kielce conference, quoted in document 1.

Already at the beginning of May 1945 two independent tailors' shops, a leather workshop, a jeweller, and three watchmakers were operating in Radom. In addition, a shoemaker, a hairdresser, a hat-maker, a butcher, an upholstery shop, a dental technician's laboratory, and two co-operatives, one for tailoring, and one for leather work, began work.[25] The committee managed to create jobs for Jewish artisans in Szydłowiec and Jedlińsk.

Unfortunately, while working towards normalization of life for Radom Jews, the committee faced many obstacles, as is confirmed by these documents. In addition to everyday relationships among citizens, which influenced Polish–Jewish relations, an important factor was the attitude towards Jewish problems of officials in various parts of the administration and government. Their administrative decisions played a crucial role in realizing or dashing hopes and expectations for stabilizing the lives of Jews returning from concentration camps, labour camps, the Soviet Union, the woods, or places where they had been hidden by Poles. In a letter to heads of the districts and to the offices of the provincial towns, the administrative department of the office of the Kielce voivodeship stated, apparently not without reason, that 'citizens of Jewish origin in the area of our voivodeship are not being properly received and treated by authorities and in offices'. Accordingly, the office of the voivodeship requested that personnel be instructed 'that all clients coming to its offices are to be properly received and treated, and their requests are to receive pertinent responses with all due speed'.[26] During the Kielce conference of 14–15 May 1945 delegates testified to the poor treatment of Jews by clerks in most of the towns of the region.[27]

The most important factor in Polish–Jewish relations was threats to the lives of Jews. The committee informed the institutions and authorities responsible for the security of citizens about these problems, including assaults against Jews outside Radom, in Kozienice, and in Zwoleń,[28] where people were wounded. The mass relocation of Jews from smaller localities to Radom was due primarily to death threats against the Jews. Living in fear for their lives, Jews moved from there to other places, and the committee informed the Radom authorities of this. From the

---

[25] Archiwum Państwowe w Radomiu, Okręgowy Komitet Żydowski w Radomiu, 1944–1948, vol. 3, p. 4. The statute of the Praca Jewish co-operative of leatherworkers stated that 'The goal of the co-operative is the paid employment of its members in the shoemaker's and leather-worker's professions in the way most useful for them and for society, without exploitation, humiliation, and injustice at work' (Archiwum Państwowe w Radomiu, Okręgowy Komitet Żydowski w Radomiu, 1944–1948, vol. 20, pp. 1–2).

[26] Archiwum Państwowe w Radomiu, Okręgowy Komitet Żydowski w Radomiu, 1944–1948, vol. 1, p. 2.

[27] See statements of the representatives of Jewish committees from different towns in the region, quoted in document 1.

[28] Archiwum Państwowe w Radomiu, Okręgowy Komitet Żydowski w Radomiu, 1944–1948, vol. 23, p. 3, the protocol of 1 Aug. 1945 of the assault in Kozienice on 29 July 1945. The witnesses stated that the assailants claimed to be security officers.

remaining documents about the committee's activities it appears that anti-Jewish violence had both political and criminal motives.

These documents have a relevance wider than the immediate area around Radom in illuminating little-known, overlooked, or often misinterpreted aspects of the Jewish position in Poland immediately after the end of the war and before the anti-Jewish events in Kielce on 4 July 1946. These documents reflect the attitudes of the administration and the government, as well as the Polish population, towards Jews. They come from the archival collection Okręgowy Komitet Żydowski (Local Jewish Committee) in the State Archives in Radom.[29] The documents presented below are the only ones that were catalogued in that grouping. Considering that this group of papers was transferred to the State Archives from the Citizens' Militia (the post-war police force), one assumes that there would be more documents. Thus, to present fully the problem of Polish–Jewish relations, one would need to do research in the archives of the office of the voivodeship in Kielce, the Radom municipality in Radom, the offices of the Citizens' Militia, and the security office. These institutions received the letters and documents published here. One might also gather interesting material from the surviving descendants and relations of the Jews who lived in Radom at the time, and from the officials responsible for the matters described here. The dates of the documents determined the time frame selected for this chapter. It seems significant that the last of these documents is dated 25 February 1946. Its content and recipient are also characteristic of the worsening situation of the Jews. Death threats led many of Radom's Jewish inhabitants to leave. The breaking-point came, however, with the events that took place in Kielce on 4 July 1946. Then, almost the entire Jewish population left Radom, Kielce, and other towns in the Kielce region.

The documents published here are typewritten copies of originals sent to the recipients on the date indicated. They are most often signed by the president of the Radom committee, and sometimes by his secretary. I quote them in their entirety; in a few places I have explained abbreviations or the meanings of certain terms in square brackets; I have also provided appropriate footnotes.

1. *Copy of the minutes of the first conference of delegates of the Jewish committees from seventeen towns of the Kielce voivodeship, held in Kielce on 14–15 May 1945. (Archiwum Państwowe w Radomiu: APR, Okręgowy Komitet Żydowski w Radomiu: OKŻ, vol. 2, pp. 11–14)*

Minutes of the Meeting of Jewish Committees of the Kielce Voivodeship, held on 14 May 1945.

Present: the representatives of the Central Jewish Committee: vice-president Maj. Dr [Szlomo] Herszenhorn, general secretary Mr [Paweł] Zelicki, inspector of the Central Committee Mr H. Zeliwski; the presidium of the Voivodeship Committee, Dr S[eweryn]

---

[29] Adam Penkalla, 'Unikatowe archiwalia do dziejów radomskich Żydów po II wojnie światowej', *BŻIH* 3–4 (1993), 147–9.

Kahane, Dr B[ronisław] Mandel. M[ordka] Goldberg, Eng[ineer Mojżesz] Bojm and [Chil] Leszcz (Radom), and the delegates from Kielce, Radom, Jędrzejow, Sandomierz, Kozienice, Szydłowiec, Działoszyce, Zwoleń, Ołkusz, Gniewoszów, Skarżysko, Ostrowiec, Chmielnik, Chęciny, Bodzentyn, Włoszczowa, and Starachowice.

The conference was opened by the President of the Voivodeship Committee Dr Kahane, who greets the guests, who proposed the following agenda:

1. Opening.
2. Elections for the presidium of the meeting.
3. Information from the representatives of the Central Committee.
4. Information from the Voidodeship Committee.
5. Information from the delegates from the local committees.
6. Discussion.
7. Conclusions and possible further steps.
8. Elections for the Voivodeship Committee.

Ad. 2: The president of the Ostrowiec Committee, cit[izen] Friedental, was elected president of the conference; the president of the Ołkusz Committee, cit. Parasol, and the president of the Działoszyce committee, cit. Lewkowicz, were elected assessors. Cit. J. Blasbalgowa took minutes.

Ad. 3. The General Secretary, cit. Zelicki, speaks on behalf of the Central Committee; he honours the memory of the murdered Jews in Poland by [two] minutes of silence, and he states that the present democratic government truly understands the principle of equal rights, like no other, and it has an extremely sympathetic attitude towards the handful of Jews saved from the pogrom. The Central Committee remains in close contact with the Polish Government, which as of now is single-handedly subsidizing the Central Jewish Committee. Last month the subsidy was 5 million zlotys, but this amount does not suffice for our needs; thus financial help needs to be limited exclusively to the sick, those unable to work, and children. Healthy people must start working. The fund for productivization will enable artisans to reorganize their workplaces and people of the free professions to start working. The Central Committee is preoccupied with the safety of Jews and has intervened with the respective authorities in all cases. Jews should leave small towns that are dangerous [for them] and where there is no work for them, either for bigger cities or for the West [i.e. the post-German areas annexed to Poland]. The Central Committee will provide assistance for them in leaving. Particular concern is being exercised in relation to children. The Central Committee has assigned special funds for additional nutrition for children, children's homes have been set up in Lublin, Przemyśl, Białystok, Otwock, and for sick children in Falenica, as well as in Chorzów and Częstochowa. These are all in the process of being organized. There are approximately 3,000 children. In the most immediate future we need to prepare to receive people freed from concentration camps from the West, and repatriates from the other side of the River Bug [Jews from the territory of the Soviet Union; the River Bug was then the new Polish–Soviet border]. Finally, the speaker reports that a promise has been received that co-operatives will be registered and emigration will be permitted.

Ad. 4: The president of the Voivodeship Committee, Dr Kahane, presents statistics [on Jews] as of 1 May of the present year. There are 48 distribution points (*punkty*) for 2,707 people [including] 219 children, 46 elderly, 144 sick. The subsidies which have been received have been divided proportionately among all distribution points in the Kielce voivodeship. There were 87 petitions submitted, of which the Productivization Fund approved 19. A tannery was established and also a tailoring co-operative; so far, however, the Revisory Union (Związek Rewizyjny) has not accepted the statute and has not allowed them [to begin] operation. At the moment, starting up the co-operative is difficult because a number of the partners have left.

In regard to safety in the area of the voivodeship, interventions have been made to the relevant authorities in each particular case, and the Central Committee is [routinely] notified.

Ad. 5: Jędrzejów. There are 48 people, 8 children, 6 unable to work, including 4 seriously ill; food cards [after the war food was rationed, and different cards could be redeemed for different amounts of food] of the 1st category, a subsidy of 55,000 zlotys; of that sum, 21,450 zlotys in cash was spent on help, 6,200 zlotys for children, 1,850 for the sick, and 7,000 for administrative expenses; with the remainder, food was bought and distributed. The balance as of the 10th of the present month was 4,130 zlotys. Received in kind: 4 pairs of men's shoes, one pair of women's shoes, 8 blankets, 10 caps, 7 kilograms of milk, 6 kilograms of fat, 126 kilograms of flour, which was distributed. Security is poor, one person is seriously wounded; Felus, the *starosta* [the head official of the district], has a bad attitude. There was an organized assault in Wodzisław, [in which] one family was robbed and one person was shot. Petitions to the Productivization Fund sit in Warsaw for weeks without being answered.

Skarżysko. There are 55 people, 3 [of them] children [living] with Poles [most likely hidden there during the war], the health situation is bad, 80 per cent [of them] are sick, [and] 2 [of them are] elderly people; there is no help from the local authorities. The subsidy is 6,800 zlotys. One person on the Committee is on the payroll, the administrative expenses are 650 zlotys; there are 11 artisans, and a co-operative cannot be established.

Bodzentyn. There are 16 people, no children, [and] all are ill. The surplus of expenses is 23,000 zlotys. The sum was spent on kitchen supplies.

Sandomierz. There are 41 people, plus 18 people who arrived most recently, 4 children plus one more [living] with Aryans [i.e. with Poles]. Food cards of the 1st category; security is not bad, due to the able handling of Jewish affairs by the Committee. The possibilities of generating money are limited because the department of productivization is not responding to petitions. For example, the request of Judka Tenenbaum, a farmer from Sandomierz, for a loan to stock his farm and sow [crops], submitted on 21 March 1945 as urgent, returned to the Voivodeship Committee on 23 May with a note asking whether the matter was still current. Obviously, considering the further course of the work, a matter of stocking and sowing is not current during the harvest. That case, as well as many similar [cases], compromises the trust of the population in regard to [any real] assistance (material evidence [may be found] in the actions of the Voivodeship Committee). The Committee has opened a kitchen, but this was not included in the budget; it also submitted requests for a necessary exhumation, [but] no sum has been allotted. The subsidy of 30,000 zlotys is by no means sufficient for the Committee to carry out its activities.

Kozienice. 13 people unable to work, the state of security is poor, the attitude of the authorities is bad; there are 106 people, 4 children, 13 sick, 14 working; the subsidy is 66,000 zlotys.

Szydłowiec. There are 100 people, 4 children, one child [living] with Aryans; artisans: 22 tailors, 8 seamstresses, 4 embroiderers, 4 shoemakers, 2 leather-stitchers, 6 corset-makers; 3 sick; the subsidy is 62,000 zlotys. The state of security is poor; [the committee needs to create] a permanent position for an administrative worker.

Zwoleń. There are 47 people, the subsidy is 36,000 [and there are] no food cards. The people would like to leave the town; the petitions regarding productivization were not answered.

Działoszyce. There are 121 people, 122 children, 4 sick; the subsidy is 66,000; 47,000 was spent on direct help, 4,000 on health care, [and] 11,966 on transportation.

Radom. There are 402 people, 50 [of them] children. The mood among the Jewish population is depressed and anxious, and the attitude of the Polish population is unfriendly and occasions concern.

Chmielnik-Busko. There are 150 people, 10 children; the subsidy is 18,000 zlotys; the attitude of the authorities is not good; that of the population is bad. Security is bearable. Only 20 people work; all the people receive help; most of them came from bunkers [where they were hiding during the war]. The productivization fund has decided about only one petition; the rest [of the petitions] are waiting.

Ostrowiec. One of the biggest Jewish centres: 193 people, 26 sick, 16 children, including 4 seriously [ill]; the material situation of the parents is very difficult; 45 artisans, of whom 25 are without employment; the subsidy from the Central Committee is 80,000 zlotys, and 29,000 was obtained from a private source. All of that is not enough to sustain the children, the sick, and those unable to work. The state of security is such that we have heard of assaults and killings. Not long ago the officials were saying that in regard to Jews, German laws [i.e. those in effect during the occupation] were still valid. The Jewish campers [those who returned from concentration and labour camps] are barefoot and naked, without apartments, and they have found places [to stay] in the ruins of houses. There have been cases of ordinary hooliganism, Jews were beaten, and the militiamen [officers of Milicja Obywatelska, roughly equivalent to police officers] said, 'You may beat him, I see nothing.' Jews are being arrested for illegal trade; murderers who killed 4 people were arrested, but they are to be freed. Before the Red Army entered, one Polish family had murdered one Jewish family; they were arrested but shortly after they were released. Near Ostrowiec, leaflets are being distributed [saying] 'Death to the remaining Jews'. The authorities do not react.

The Olkusz district. 148 people, 25 children, 7 elderly, 44 sick, only 44 people work. The subsidy and help is very small, and the population is hostile.

Kielce. 250 people, 28 children, many sick. 90 per cent get meals from the kitchen and receive food. Security is good, the attitude of the authorities is good, [and] the food supply is good. There is an open shelter [a kind of hostel for Jews arriving in the city]. A co-operative has not been organized because of the position of the Revisory Union. Requests for individual loans remain in the hands of the Fund for Productivization in Warsaw.

Włoszczowa. There are 64 people, 2 children, one child [living] with Aryans, 5 sick, and 1 elderly. The attitude of the authorities is unsympathetic. 6 people are sick and unable to work. The subsidy is 46,000 zlotys. 4,018 zlotys have been spent on travel expenses.

Białobrzegi. 29 people, security very poor, no provisions have been received from the *gmina* [local administrative unit]. Out of 50 people drafted to work in the mines [these were forcibly employed], 7 are Jews; the president [of the local Jewish committee] was arrested. The subsidy is 28,000, of which 11,000 have been spent on travel expenses; the remaining balance is 13 zlotys.

Gniewoszów. There are around 68 people, 9 children; the subsidy is 45,000, and travel expenses come to 8,000; the productivization has not been accomplished, the petitions that were submitted remain in Warsaw.

Starachowice. 56 people, 10 children; 5 people work in tailoring, one person in carpentry, one shoemaker, 2 leather-stitchers, one child [living] with Aryans, 5 sick, 7 unable to work, 3 elderly, one disabled veteran. 35,000 zlotys have been received, also 5 pairs of men's shoes, 1 pair of children's shoes, 10 blankets, 6 kilograms of fat, 7 kilograms of milk, 10 caps, [and] 150 kilograms of flour. No help [has come] from the [administrative] authorities. 5,490 was spent on travel expenses.

Ad. 6. Gniewoszów complains that the department of productivization does not resolve the cases [brought to it].

Chmielnik states that the Central Committee does nothing for Jews, and proposes not to accept the budget for the Kielce Voivodeship in the amount of 300,000 zlotys.

Sandomierz requests to establish a paid position on the Committee, because he argues that no one can work without pay for the whole day, and the Committee needs one [full-time] person.

Gniewoszów and Włoszczowa demand exhumation [of the corpses of Jews murdered during the German occupation]!

Kozienice demands medicine, discretionary funds, and money for official representation. The number of women unable to work predominates in that town.

Radom. Citizen Leszcz argues in a broad perspective for the need of exhumation. He cites the holiness of the dead among Jews. The Poles honour the dead, and the broad masses of Jews care about that matter. The position of the Central Committee does not reflect the position of the broad Jewish masses. The position of the Central Committee is wrong, and is impossible to accept. Our attitude towards our dead should be dignified and in accordance with Jewish tradition, for we bear responsibility in the eyes of future generations. He makes a motion to conduct official burials with the participation of representatives of the Central Committee. He thinks that children who are with Aryans should be taken back and given a Jewish upbringing. Regarding the budget, he states that a budget in the amount of 300,000 is unacceptable.

In the further discussion, other speakers take stands; they demand:
1. To increase the subsidy for the Kielce Voivodeship.
2. Improvement in the work of the Productivization Fund.
3. Assignment of one paid position in the office of each *District* Committee.
4. To conduct exhumations in necessary cases.
5. To take the children back from the Aryans immediately, and to increase help for the sick.

Major Herszenhorn responds to the participants in the discussion; he states that for financial reasons the subsidies cannot be increased; only the aid that is coming from abroad will possibly solve the problem. He thinks that demands should be made regarding the living rather than the dead. In necessary cases exhumation will be conducted; there is no money for discretionary funds. If medicine is distributed, a full treatment should be given.

Citizen Zelicki states that monetary subsidies will not solve the economic problem of the Jews. They absolutely should start working. Those who do not find work here should go to the West [the German territory incorporated by Poland after the war]; the Central Committee will provide means for them. Children cannot be bailed out. There will be a state decree regarding that matter. When aid arrives from abroad, there will be an increase in subsidies, for at the present time the budget of the Central Committee cannot keep up with the needs of increasing numbers of Jews. He is pleased with his personal contacts with the Jewish representatives from each town, which provided him with a better knowledge of all the problems and needs of the Jews.

Ad. 7. Following the motion by cit. Leszcz, the conference of the Kielce Voivodeship requests from the Central Committee: 1. Greater subsidizing; 2. To look abroad for quicker and more effective help.

Ad. 8. The conference of the Committee of the Kielce Voivodeship elected [the following individuals] to the Voivodeship Committee:
1. Dr Seweryn Kahane—President of the Committee,
2. Dr Bronisław Mandel—Secretary-General,
3. Mordka Goldberg—Treasurer,
4. Eng. Mojżesz Bojm (Radom),
5. Chil Leszcz (Radom),
6. Wajnsztok (Kozienice),
7. Murer (Jędrzejow),
8. Friedental (Ostrowiec),
9. Parasol (Olkusz).

Then, Citizen Friedental closed the conference.

2. *Letter from the Radom chapter of the regional Jewish committee to the city housing authority. 18 April 1945, Radom. (APR, OKŻ, vol. 15, p. 5)*

Re: the assignment of locations for dining-halls and shelters. We kindly request a considerate allotment, namely the place at Kiliński St., for a dining-hall and a shelter for our patients. The place is completely in accordance with all conditions required for this type of institution. The place assigned to us at 52 Traugutt St. is inappropriate because it requires a big investment, for which we have no funds. That is why we have not taken up the offer of that place for now. Because this case concerns feeding people who have returned from concentration camps and are completely exhausted, we ask that you allow us to organize a dining-hall and a shelter, and for a considerate response to the present petition, especially as the requested building is not at present being used.

3. *Response of the Radom chapter of the regional Jewish committee to the survey in circulating paper no. 3 of the Central Committee of Jews in Poland in Lublin, 2 May 1945. 12 May 1945, Radom. (APR, OKŻ, vol. 3, p. 2)*

... up until now, no incident meriting attention has been noticed; the mood among the Jewish population is depressed and anxious. The attitude of the local Polish population towards Jews is unfriendly and it occasions concern ... the attitude of the local authorities that decide on housing[30] towards the Jewish Committee and Jewish population is unfriendly, therefore a substantial part of Jewish population remains without a roof until this day, and they have to use the shelter.

4. *Letter from the Radom chapter of the regional Jewish committee to the president of the city housing commission. 17 May 1945, Radom. (APR, OKŻ, vol. 11, p. 8)*

Re: living accommodation for the people [returning] from camps. The housing problem in respect to the Jewish population in Radom, despite our numerous interventions, has not yet been resolved, and a major part of our charges have no roof of their own, and they have to stay in the shelter that is meant as a temporary place for people returning from camps. In recent days 78 women have returned to Radom from concentration camps in Germany. Further transports are on the way. We find ourselves in a situation that is just impossible, for we have no room to accommodate these people from the camps, most of whom are originally from Radom. In this situation we ask you, Citizen President, to kindly consider these extraordinary circumstances and to reserve at least 50 rooms in apartments (*izba mieszkalna*) for the people [returning] from camps who are registered with our committee.

5. *Petition from the Radom chapter of the regional Jewish committee to the city security office. 26 May 1945, Radom. (APR, OKŻ, vol. 20, p. 6)*

Petition. We request your kind permission for the people who guard the premises of the Jewish Committee in Radom at 45 Traugutt St. and the 'Praca' Co-operative in Radom at 50 Żeromski St. to possess and carry arms. On the premises of the Jewish Committee there are various articles of food and clothing, which are public property and which are intended for

---

[30] As it appears from the documents presented here, it was the city housing commission (*miejska komisja mieszkaniowa*).

distribution among people who need help, first of all among those returning from various concentration camps. On the premises of the 'Praca' Co-operative there are workstations and sewing machines as well as various materials that are the property of the co-operative or of private individuals. It is necessary for the people who guard these premises to have guns, both [to ensure] the safety of the public property entrusted to them, and [to ensure] their own personal safety. The people guarding these premises should have the capability to defend themselves in case of an assault by antisocial people and the scum of society. We humbly request a quick and favourable response to our request, and the allotment of two rifles from the office.

6. *Letter from the Radom regional Jewish committee to the president of the city of Radom. 25 June 1945, Radom. (APR, OKŻ, vol. 15, p. 2)*

Re: fencing of the Jewish cemetery. At the road, approximately 4 kilometres from Radom, near woods, there is a Jewish cemetery[31] that was destroyed by Nazi vandalism [entailing the] removal of all tombstones. Separately, the brick fence of the cemetery was taken apart, and the bricks were used for the construction of a marmalade factory. In this state of affairs we turn to you, Cit. President, with a humble request to issue a directive to fence the cemetery in order to protect it from further destruction and from trampling by the cattle that cross it.[32]

7. *Letter, probably from an underground organization, signed with the initials D.O.W.S. and passed to the Jewish inhabitants of Jedlińsk. Its content concerns both the Jews of Radom and those who live in the* powiat *of Radom. 29 July 1945, no place. (APR, OKŻ, vol. 5, p. 11)*

To the Jewish [population] in Jedlińsk. It has been stated that Jews, one and all, work for the intelligence services of the present government, which was brutally imposed upon us, [and] thus they act to the detriment of Polish society. On behalf of the voice of Polish society I order all Jews to leave the borders of the District of Radom and the city of Radom by 15 August 1945. I warn that trespasses beyond that term, or pledges for help directed to the present authorities, will be unconditionally punished. D.O.W.S. M.p. [place or residence] 29 July 1945.

8. *Fragment of circular no. 40 of the Central Committee of Jews in Poland directed to the voivodeship Jewish committees, regarding 'anti-Jewish excesses'. In addition to the Radom cases presented below, it listed assaults on 11 August 1945 on a synagogue in Kraków (the building was set on fire and the Torah scrolls were burned), and on a sanatorium in Rabka where Jewish children were undergoing treatment. 17 August 1945. (APR, OKŻ, vol. 1, p. 24)*

... In Radom, a reactionary group spread leaflets in which the Jewish population was ordered to leave the District of Radom by 15 August. On the night of 10 August there was

---

[31] See n. 23.
[32] Now within Radom city borders. The Jewish cemetery is located at Towarowa Street, which extends to Kozienicka Street.

an assault on the Jewish Co-operative, where the Co-operative workers lived; 4 people who were there at the time were killed. After that murder, no other cases were recorded.... A few army platoons were dispatched to Radom to protect the Jews.

9. *Letter from the Radom chapter of the regional Jewish committee to the Kielce voivode. Similar letters were sent by the committee to the elder of the town (*starosta grodzki*) of Radom, and to the president of Radom. 25 August 1945. (APR, OKŻ, vol. 9, p. 6)*

Because of leaflets published by various dark reactionary Nazi elements, which order the Jewish population, under the threat of repression, to leave the borders of the District of Radom, some part of the Jewish population, fearing for their lives, have temporarily left Radom, leaving their apartments. Various people take advantage of this, and they file requests with the Housing Commission in Radom to assign them these temporarily abandoned Jewish apartments. The Housing Commission accepts these requests and sends its officers, which creates an impression among the Jewish population that the whole society sympathizes with these actions of the dark elements; this increases the panic in the Jewish community even more. Since this panic, which is spread through improper actions by officers of lower rank, surely does not correspond with the intentions of the central authorities, and since now, after the situation has become less tense and calmed down, the Jews [are] gradually [returning?] to their apartments, we humbly request that you issue a directive to the Housing Commission not to accept such petitions. We request a speedy and favourable resolution of the matter.

10. *Letter, probably from the Radom chapter of the regional Jewish committee to the city office of public security, directed to the attention of Captain Brzoza. 31 August 1945, Radom. (APR, OKŻ, vol. 20, p. 13; also 14; vol. 23, p. 4)*

... After the assault on the 'Praca' Co-operative in Radom, at 50 Żeromski St. on 1 August of this year, when 4 Jews were murdered, and until the 27th of this month, it was relatively calm in Radom. On the evening of the 27th of this month, between 5 and 6 p.m., there was an assault on the Jewish shelter in Radom, as a result of which there are people wounded and battered. As a *corpus delicti* [material evidence], one of the assailants left behind a cap, which we enclose. On the 29th of this month between 5–8 p.m., there was an assault on the apartment of [Mr] Lewental at Słowacki St. On the 30th of this month, at 3 p.m., in the 'Prędocinek' sawmill, located in Glinice,[33] there was again an assault on a Jewish worker from that sawmill, Aron Łęga, who was severely beaten and robbed, and the assailants took even the clothes he had on him. Reporting this, we request that you initiate proper steps to arrest the perpetrators of these assaults, and to prevent a repetition of further such assaults, and to issue proper directives so as to guarantee the safety of the Jewish population. Enclosed, a cap.

---

[33] Now a part of Radom.

11. *Letter from the Radom chapter of the regional Jewish committee to the commandant of the Citizens' Militia directed to the attention of Citizen Lieutenant Mazur. 25 August 1945, Radom. (APR, OKŻ, vol. 23, p. 5). In response, on 3 September 1945, the commandant informed the committee that he had issued an appropriate order, and that the neighbourhood of the shelter would be patrolled by the militia.*

The Regional Jewish Committee in Radom turns to you, Citizen Commandant, with a request to dispatch a patrol to the front of the Jewish shelter located at 52 Traugutt St. for the evening hours. We wish to bring to your attention that almost every evening individuals break the windows in the shelter, and even organize assaults. In order to ensure the safety of our charges, we ask you not to turn down our request, for it is a question of life. We ask for an immediate response to our request.

12. *Letter from the Radom chapter of the regional Jewish committee to the district administrator (starosta powiatowy) in Radom. 21 January 1946, Radom. (APR, OKŻ, vol. 23, p. 7)*

Responding, Citizen Administrator, to your request of 19 January 1946, number 0.473/46, we declare that because anti-Jewish leaflets appeared at the beginning of August 1945 on walls in the towns and villages of the Radom district and in the town of Radom, a delegation of the Radom Regional Jewish Committee has turned to you, Citizen Administrator, with a petition stating that the matter concerns safety. After two hours of waiting the delegation was told that the reception time was over, and asked to come the next day. The delegation arranged an appointment for 10 a.m., and was assured that it would be received. The next day, in spite of the fact that the delegation came on time and asked to be received, it was told in the secretary's office that the Administrator was gone and he could not meet the delegation. Other than that, no delegation of the Regional Jewish Committee has appeared at the Senior Citizens' Administrator's, or sought support in any matter.

13. *Letter, probably from the inhabitants of the shelter for Jews in Radom, to the Radom chapter of the regional Jewish committee. 15 February 1946, Radom. (APR, OKŻ, vol. 23, p. 8)*

On the night of 15 February 1946, at 1 a.m., an unknown individual started to bang on the shelter and attempt to force the door. Asked who he was, he said that he was sent by the security office[34] to check passports [*dowody*: probably internal passports, i.e. identity papers.] The inhabitants of the shelter escaped in panic through the windows to the neighbouring fire station, and they called the militia in the 1st Station (*komisariat*). After almost an hour the militia came and arrested the intruder. We take this opportunity to stress that as a community of Jews the shelter is often subject to the excesses of hoodlums, and because of this we request that you dispense one *pepesha*[35] and ten hand-grenades to our shelter. [The signatures of eight people.]

---

[34] i.e. from the Urząd Bezpieczeństwa (Security Office), a common name for a unit of the Ministry of Public Security, which included political police. One of its goals was to combat groups in society that opposed communist rule.

[35] *Pepesha*, a popular name for a Soviet 1940 automatic gun designed by G. Shpagin, used in the Red Army during the Second World War.

14. *Letter from the Radom chapter of the regional Jewish committee to the City Militia headquarters in Radom, and to the voivodeship headquarters of the militia in Kielce. 22 February 1946, Radom. (APR, OKŻ, vol. 23, p. 9)*

On the nights of the 14th and 21st of this month unknown individuals organized an assault on the shelter of the Regional Jewish Committee in Radom at 52 Traugutt St. and tried to break in. Owing to the intervention of the fire brigade, the assault was defeated. I request that a guard be placed in front of the shelter in order to protect its inhabitants against assaults.

15. *Letter from the Radom chapter of the regional Jewish committee to the headquarters of the militia in Radom. 25 February 1946, Radom. (APR, OKŻ, vol. 23, p. 10)*

Because of the frequently recurring assaults on our shelter located in Radom at 52 Traugutt St., we request that you kindly issue a permit for one rifle and one *pepesha* for the shelter, and 10 hand-grenades for the office of the Committee located in Radom at 45 Traugutt St. Because it is difficult for us to be sure who are the permanent residents of the shelter at any one time, we humbly request that you issue the permit in such a way that each time when dispensing the arms we would know into whose hands they should go.

Translated from Polish by Gwido Zlatkes

Polish Jews during and after the Kielce Pogrom: Reports from the Communist Archives

JOANNA MICHLIC-COREN

ON 4 July 1946 the most horrifying outbreak of anti-Jewish violence in post-war Poland took place in Kielce. On that day ordinary citizens of this central Polish town, together with soldiers and militiamen, murdered forty Polish Jews and injured more than a hundred. The total number of dead reached forty-two, with two injured people dying two days later in hospital in Łódź, where most of the surviving Jews in fear of their lives had been transported by the Red Cross trains.[1] Both women and children were among the dead and wounded. This was not an isolated act of anti-Jewish violence in this early post-war period, but one of many such events which took place between 1945 and 1947. Nevertheless, it was striking because of its dimensions, because of the brutality with which it was accompanied, and because of the participation of local forces representing the new communist authority. The Kielce pogrom was the most powerful indicator that Jews were not to be welcomed to restore their lives among the ethnic Polish population.

A substantial body of both popular and scholarly works has been written about the Kielce pogrom, especially in the last two decades.[2] Yet looking closely at the ways the subject has been discussed in scholarly literature, particularly in Poland, it seems unsatisfactory that the debate has been limited to only two areas: description of the event itself, and investigation into the forces responsible for masterminding the pogrom, with this latter aspect standing out as the central and most controversial issue in the historiography of the subject. This has somehow hindered a proper examination of the salient problem, that is to say, the spread of anti-Jewish attitudes within Polish society at the time of the pogrom. This was

[1] The most detailed description of the Kielce pogrom is given by Bożena Szaynok in *Pogrom Żydów w Kielcach 4 lipca 1946* (Wrocław, 1992).

[2] In Poland a rise in interest in this event has been particularly noticeable during this period. Three major factors can be identified as contributing to this development: first, the influence of the Solidarity movement of the early 1980s, committed as it was to facing dark aspects of Polish–Jewish relations; secondly, the fiftieth anniversary of the event itself, and thirdly, the growing accessibility of Polish archives that hold salient data on anti-Jewish violence between 1945 and 1947.

first pointed out by Andrzej Paczkowski, who stated that for some historians a rejection of the theory of 'forces behind the pogrom' would mean the acceptance of the morally embarrassing fact that a substantial section of Polish society was marked by an intense antisemitism.[3]

A study of the anti-Jewish attitudes present within different segments of the Polish community of that time is a challenging task as primary sources are scattered in various archives. Yet such a study is essential if a more accurate explanation of anti-Jewish violence and responses to it are to be provided. It will also contribute to a proper examination of the general situation of the Jewish minority vis-à-vis the Polish majority. So far, perhaps the most discerning discussion of these issues has been provided by Jan Gross in his essay 'Stereotypes of Polish–Jewish Relations after the War' and David Engel in his article 'Patterns of Anti-Jewish Violence in Poland, 1944–1946'.[4] In both cases, however, the authors based their analysis on limited and scattered documents.

The intention behind the publication of the documents below is to provide further insight into the extent to which anti-Jewish attitudes were prevalent among Polish society during and after the Kielce pogrom. The five documents were first published in Polish by Andrzej Paczkowski in the journal *Puls*, no. 50, in 1991.[5] The fifth document has also been published by Bożena Szaynok and Zenon Wrona.[6] None of these authors attempted to analyse their content. However, Paczkowski insisted that, despite their communist propagandist language, the documents constitute a reliable source of information about the nature of Polish antisemitism and the social consciousness of the early post-war era.

These documents are located in one particular collection of Section 6 of the Archiwum Akt Nowych, which houses the files of the former archives of the central committee of the Polska Zjednoczona Partia Robotnicza (Polish United Workers' Party: PZPR). They comprise five special reports written by members of the central committee of the Polska Partia Robotnicza (Polish Workers' Party: PPR), who were formed into special brigades and sent to Kielce and other urban locations to monitor the tense social situation that arose during and after the pogrom.[7]

---

[3] Andrzej Paczkowski, Introduction to 'Raporty o Pogromie', *Puls*, 50/3 (1991), 103.

[4] Jan Gross's essay is included in this volume. David Engel, 'Patterns of Anti-Jewish Violence in Poland, 1944–1946', *Yad Vashem Studies*, 26 (1998), 43–86.

[5] Andrzej Paczkowski's publication consists of six reports. The sixth report, not included here in English translation, primarily discusses anti-Jewish attitudes within the Polish army, as well as this army's relations with the civilian population and with the illegal military groups of the Narodowe Siły Zbrojne (National Armed Forces: NSZ). The report describes the widespread hostility towards Jews among the lower ranks of the army and the exodus of Jewish officers as a consequence.

[6] Bożena Szaynok and Zenon Wrona, 'Pogrom kielecki w dokumentach', *Dzieje Najnowsze*, 3 (1991), 75–117.

[7] The PPR was formed on 5 Jan. 1942 and in 1948 absorbed one faction of the Polska Partia Socjalistyczna (Polish Socialist Party: PPS) to form the PZPR.

It is important to note that the reports were prepared in only three or four copies for a very limited circulation among the most highly ranked leaders of the PPR, including Władysław Gomułka, the secretary-general of the PPR, and Roman Zambrowski and Marian Spychalski, secretaries of the central committee of the PPR. Such a limited number of copies indicates that the reports were to be regarded as secret.

Furthermore, they contain information that clearly opposed the official communist line of the period that it was only the reactionary and fascist forces that were antisemitic and responsible for anti-Jewish violence. In fact the reports confirm embarrassing facts carefully hushed up by the communist authorities, that both the local army and militia forces participated in the Kielce pogrom (documents 1 and 5) and that railway workers, the major representative of the working classes, were also engaged in inciting hatred against and the killing of Jews in the Kielce district on 4 July (document 5). This indicates the importance of these reports as a historical source, although they should still be treated with caution.

The main objective of the authors of the reports was to assess the spread of antisemitism in the population and to describe counteracting measures that they had taken to curb this phenomenon on behalf of the central committee of the PPR. This does not mean that some authors themselves did not have negative stereotypes of Jews, a very clear example here being Hilary Chełkowski, who perceived the Jewish community of Kielce in populist left-wing terms as a wealthy, non-productive, and corrupt group (document 1). It is worth noting that some years later, in 1956, Chełkowski was to become one of the most influential members of the Natolin group, a faction within the PZPR known for its anti-Jewish stance.[8]

The reports discuss the following issues: development of events in Kielce on 4 July 1946 (documents 1 and 5); public reaction towards the first trial after the Kielce pogrom in which nine Poles were sentenced to death (document 4); the attempts to spread anti-Jewish violence in other urban locations and official communist propaganda and actions aimed at suppressing anti-Jewish events (documents 3 and 4).

The documents reveal that a high level of hostility towards Jews was not confined to Kielce and its district but was also present in other urban locations in different parts of Poland including Kalisz and Łódź (documents 2–4). In addition, hostility was not only expressed in various forms by the adult population but also affected the youth (documents 3 and 5).[9] Hostile behaviour was justified on the grounds that Jews were the chief threat to the Polish nation. This belief, fully developed already in pre-1939 Poland, only intensified after 1945 as a result of the

---

[8] Jerzy Eisler, *Marzec 1968: geneza, przebieg, konsekwencje* (Warsaw, 1991), 23.

[9] The existence of negative and hostile attitudes towards Jews on the part of young people is discussed by Albert Stańkowski, 'Emigracja Żydów z Pomorza Zachodniego', in Jerzy Tomaszewski (ed.), *Studia z dziejów i kultury Żydów po 1945* (Warsaw, 1997), 90.

involvement of people of Jewish origin in the construction of the new communist state. Yet the violent tendency towards getting rid of the Jewish population cannot be interpreted as a political act as the data shows that most of the Jewish victims of the Kielce pogrom and of similar violent incidents were not communist.[10]

On the whole, it is evident that the negative image of the Jewish community was of a multifarious nature: Jews were perceived as a political enemy of the Polish nation and responsible for introducing the Soviet-style regime, as a socially privileged group occupying the best positions within the state, and as economically privileged people who were wealthy, corrupt, and non-productive. Simultaneously, they were perceived as killers of Polish children according to the old medieval belief in ritual murder. In the early post-war years rumours of ritual murder acted as an effective tool in inciting ordinary citizens to anti-Jewish demonstrations and violence, of which the Kielce pogrom is the major example (document 5). Interestingly, accusations of ritual murder were sometimes expressed in modified versions to suit the present social and political situation, with the Jews keeping the blood of the slain Polish victims and giving their bodies to the Soviets and Ukrainians (document 3).

The reports also provide important clues to the study of the problem of anti-Jewish prejudice within the PPR. The subject of the presence of negative attitudes towards the Jewish community on the part of members of the communist party in Poland in the early post-war years has been given little attention, one of the reasons being the widely shared assumption that the communist authorities of that period were committed to fighting antisemitism and giving the Jewish ethnic minority equal rights with the rest of society.[11] It has therefore been suggested that there was in fact no anti-Jewish prejudice within the PPR. This type of interpretation does not take into account the fact that the party began to undergo dynamic structural changes between 1945 and 1948 as the membership of the PPR substantially increased from 230,000 in late 1945 to 400,000 in the autumn of the following year. The new members, who mostly came from ethnic Polish working-class and peasant backgrounds, filled in the lower and middle positions within the party and aimed at getting to the higher echelons. The reports clearly indicate that among this group many shared the same negative stereotypes as the Polish population in general of Jews as socially and economically privileged (documents 1 and 5). Furthermore, they resented the presence of people of Jewish origin within the party and competed with them for prominent positions (document 5). On the

---

[10] David Engel provides detailed evidence of the difference between the killings of Polish Jews and Polish communists between 1944 and 1946. See Engel, 'Patterns of Anti-Jewish Violence in Poland, 1944–1946'.

[11] With the exception of the following articles where the problem of anti-Jewish attitudes within the party and among local communist authorities is discussed: the chapter by Jan Gross in this issue of *Polin*; Danuta Błus-Węgrowska, 'Atmosfera pogromowa', *Karta*, 18 (1996), 87–106; and Maciej Pisarski, 'W nowej Polsce', *Karta*, 18 (1996), 108–19.

whole, the reports give a very disturbing picture of Polish society emerging from the Second World War—a society that was uncertain of its future as a nation and as a state, and as a result tended to blame the Jewish ethnic minority for the ensuing economic hardship and social ills, as well as for the political changes over which Poles as a nation and as individuals had no control.

1. *Report by Comrades Chełkowski and Buczyński: visit to Kielce and the anti-Jewish riots of 4 and 5 July 1946*

After arriving at Kielce we had a meeting with Comrade Wiślicz, during which Comrades Kalinowski,[12] the First Secretary of the Provincial Committee of the Polish Workers' Party (KW PPR), and Sobczyński,[13] the director of the Provincial Public Security Office (UB), were present.

After discussing the riots, we decided to issue a declaration that would be signed by all six Democratic parties. The declaration was printed during the night and posted around Kielce the following morning.

The active body of the PPR and the PPS was assembled at 9 a.m. to organize mass meetings in factories in order to condemn the anti-Jewish riots. After Comrade Kalinowski, Secretary of the Provincial Committee of the PPS, had read his report, it was decided that the factory party committees should be assembled for the purpose of assessing public opinion and that mass meetings should take place at 11 a.m. on 7 July 1946. The meeting was then closed.

The two of us and one group went to the Ludwików steelworks, where we spoke to the factory committee. They reported an atmosphere of excitement and confusion among the majority of workers. They also insisted that a mass meeting was needed to calm people down, so the two of us persuaded comrades from the PPS and the Polish Army to organize it in the factory's biggest hall at 12 noon. During the meeting factory workers, representatives

[12] Kalinowski was dismissed from his post in Aug. 1956.

[13] There are many questions concerning Major Władysław Sobczyński, the chief of the public security office in Kielce. He joined public security in 1944, when its whole apparatus was completely under Soviet control. According to Polish underground sources, he was responsible for pacification of the Rzeszów region in 1945. In the book *Dramatyczny rok 1945* the historian Tadeusz Żenczykowski argues that Sobczyński organized the Kielce pogrom, since he had been responsible for the anti-Jewish events in Rzeszów in 1945 and for the murder of Władysław Kojder, a member of the PPS. Sobczyński was appointed to his post in Kielce a few weeks before the pogrom, when his predecessor, a person of Jewish origin, was transferred to Poznań. Sobczyński's trial took place in Warsaw on 13–16 Dec. 1946. He was charged with failing to take action against criminal acts committed by the crowd. Two other men went on trial: Colonel Wiktor Kuźnicki and Major Kazimierz Gwiazdowicz, respectively commandant and vice-commandant of the provincial police office. Sobczyński and Gwiazdowicz were acquitted and Kuźnicki was sentenced to a year's imprisonment. It is a well-known fact that there was strong animosity between the heads of police and public security in Kielce and that, as a result, they did not co-operate with each other during the pogrom. Sobczyński was in close contact with the Soviet Colonel Shpilevoy, adviser to the public security office in Kielce. Shpilevoy's involvement in the pogrom is also highly controversial and unclear. According to the testimony of Jechiel Alpert, an eyewitness, Sobczyński refused to send troops to Planty Street; Shpilevoy explained that his soldiers did not have any Polish uniforms and that their appearance in Russian uniforms might lead to the misinterpretation that Poles were being murdered by Russians.

of the Polish Army and the PPS, and the two of us all criticized the action of the NSZ bands who had been incited by the London-based Polish government in exile to murder Jewish workers. We also criticized the way these bands misled the workers about the murder of eleven Polish children by Jews. Furthermore, the workers condemned the terrible actions of anti-democrats. The workers promised to search the factory for them and to hand them over to be punished. After the assembly had adopted the resolution and sung 'The Red Flag' ('Czerwony Sztandar'), people went back to work. Another mass assembly took place in the Społem factory.

The background information:

... The rumour about the murder of eleven Polish children had been spread by the reactionary movement for some time. On 4 July a boy went to the police with a story that he had escaped from the Jews. A few policemen under the command of Sedek were sent to investigate the place of the boy's detention, but the boy was not able to find it. His father then appeared and confirmed that it was true that his son had been captured by Jews. Fifty people from NSZ shouted, 'It's true! We must kill the Jews!' Then members of the Public Security dressed in civilian clothes appeared on the scene after the alarm had been raised by the Chairman of the Jewish Committee. The crowd entered the building, killed the Jewish Chairman[14] and six other Jews, and injured fifteen more.

Meanwhile, in shops and factories around Kielce the reactionary forces were inciting people to murder Jews. A short time later the crowd attacked the Jewish building again at 11 a.m. Thirty-five more people were killed and thirty were wounded. Other Jews were also murdered in different parts of Kielce and on trains. Altogether thirty-six people were injured. The Jews were moved out of the dangerous zone only when Captain Bednarz intervened.

At about 12 p.m. we ourselves observed that soldiers and policemen were mixing with the crowd and talking with drunk youngsters. We reported this to Comrade Wiślicz and suggested he contact military headquarters so that the army and police could be withdrawn—since they had been involved in that riot—and replaced with new forces and the ORMO.[15]

We state that the Kielce region is strongly antisemitic.[16] Even within our party, and especially among the lower ranks, there are cases of antisemitism.

In our opinion, the following points show what caused the incidents.

1. Lack of organization within Public Security (UB).

---

[14] Dr Seweryn Kahane was killed as he called for help at about 10 a.m.

[15] ORMO (Ochotnicze Rezerwy Milicji Obywatelskiej) was the Voluntary Reserve of the Civic Militia.

[16] People were still ill disposed towards Jews after the pogrom. A widely distributed leaflet claimed that, in retaliation for the Kielce pogrom, Jews took revenge on Polish prisoners in Radom. Further anti-Jewish provocations occurred in various towns in Poland (Częstochowa, Kalisz, Kłodzko, Kraków, Bytom, and Białystok). The Jewish committees of Kielce, Radom, and Bielsko-Biała were disbanded as a result of a decision made by the Central Committee of Jews in Poland in July, which also advised Jews to move to larger towns. The Zionist parties urged people to emigrate, whereas the Jewish section of the PPR opposed emigration. The Bund supported the idea of free emigration, but stressed that it was not a solution to the Jewish question and that the goal should be to fight reactionary forces and establish democracy in Poland. The communist government organized propaganda on a huge scale, covering the whole of Poland.

2. Lack of organization in the police (MO), its strong antisemitic and anti-government feelings, and its weak leadership.[17]
3. Lack of action by the local Party leadership.
4. Lack of discipline in the army. The officers were lazy and some of them were antisemitic, as were many soldiers.

Regarding the Jewish problem: in the future, we should aim to avoid a situation where they live in one big group and are not engaged in productive work. The Jews achieve wealth by engaging in various shady businesses with impunity, and their business activities are directed against the government. These facts are used by hostile political elements.

H. Chełkowski
Buczyński
6 July 1946

2. Report of the Brigade to Examine and Counteract Antisemitic Incidents

Comrade Zapecki, Comrade Najdrowicz, and I arrived at Kalisz on 10 July 1946. We immediately interviewed the police, Public Security, Party members, and civilians.

We called a conference at 9 a.m. the following day. The following people were present: Adamus (First Secretary of the Town Committee), representatives from the police (MO) and Public Security (UB), Party instructors, and Comrades Musiał, Perz, and Borucki from the police office in Poznań. The situation was outlined by Adamus, then by the First Secretary of the Kalisz District Committee, and then by the Vice-Commander of the Police and the Chief of Public Security. According to their reports and our interviews, the situation is as follows:

There are about 500 Jews in Kalisz, who are not concentrated in one part of the city. They behave in a peaceful and proper manner. A rumour spread that a boy went missing and later was allegedly found in Ostrów Wielkopolski, during the time of the pogrom in Kielce. This boy was supposedly murdered by a Ukrainian, for sausage meat. People started to gather in a street and to mill around. The rumour grew. People were talking about four, eight, and twenty-four boys. One woman, who has not been identified, said that she had seen fourteen boys' heads and that their flesh was taken by Ukrainians or Soviets and that their blood was drunk by Jews. But because of a generally calm atmosphere and the predominance of sober-minded citizens, riots have not occurred. However, antisemitic writing has appeared on walls, and there have been incidents of Polish children throwing gravel at Jewish children in the parks. Another rumour spread that Poles from Łódzka Street would have to leave their flats, which would then be taken over by thousands of Jews.

... Under these circumstances, the situation was regarded as critical. Quick preventative action was need. The conference decided:

---

[17] The state of public safety and security was unstable in post-war Kielce. Wiktor Kuźnicki, chief of the provincial police office, was frequently accused by public security of employing ex-soldiers from General Anders's army and members of the PPS. Many policemen believed that Public Security represented an alien, hostile, and Soviet force. The conflict between police and Public Security intensified when seventeen soldiers of the NSZ escaped with rifles from their police prison. According to sources, Major Gwiazdowicz, vice-commander of the provincial police office, took part in an antiJewish demonstration on the afternoon of 4 July in Kielce.

1. to issue an appeal to the people of Kalisz calling for calm. The appeal should be signed by all political parties and the Church.
2. to arrange seven mass meetings in all factories and at railway stations, with the slogan: 'Vicious attempts of reactionary forces to undermine the democratic victory in the referendum.'
3. to organize meetings of all the Factories' and Trade Unions' Committees under this same slogan.
4. to organize a meeting for the entire Kalisz intelligentsia.
5. to organize a big demonstration in Kalisz under the above slogan.
6. to have talks with the town's clergy.
7. to organize a conference with the chairman of the local Jewish organization.

The appeal was immediately presented to the Joint Committee and was unanimously accepted and signed by all the parties and by other Kalisz organizations. Seven mass meetings attended by between 200 and 800 workers were organized. The atmosphere of these meetings was good . . . and there was little hostility towards the Jews. The factory committees met at 3.30 p.m. on 12 July. The big meeting of the intelligentsia, in which Perko, the Second Lieutenant, and Dr Koszucki, the President of Kalisz, delivered their statements, occurred at 7 p.m. on 12 July. The demonstration will take place at 6 p.m. on 13 July. At 10.30 a.m. on 12 July we met Revd Martuzalski, the parish priest of Saint Mikołaj Parish Church. . . . We asked him to sign the appeal and to influence the clergy to preach calming sermons. Martuzalski did not refuse to sign the appeal but stated that he had to contact the Bishops' Council before doing so. He condemned the Kielce pogrom but stated that the loathsome Jews were not needed, that these vile rats headed by Minc and Borejsza had taken over our lives.[18] He went on to say that this rabble ruled over Szczecin, and everywhere people were rebelling against it. In the USA, which he had visited twice, people were also taking action against them because of their feeding on other nations. . . . When Lieutenant Perko attacked him for making such statements, the Revd became unclear and stated that all Jews wanted to run to Palestine because the ground was giving way beneath them and that we should follow Czechoslovakia in its policy to get rid of Jews . . . he continued to talk.

I and comrades Musiał and Zapecki left Kalisz, whereas comrades Perz and Majchrowicz remained to control the rest of the programme.

Czesław Olejniczak

3. *Report by Stefan Tomaszewski, head of the Warsaw Department of Communication: visit to Dęblin, 10 and 11 July 1946*

I arrived at Lublin at 8 a.m. on 11 July. After contacting an instructor from the Provincial Railway Department and . . . Comrade Chodkiewicz from the PPS, we all attended a mass meeting of Dęblin's railway workers.

The meeting was organized very well; 1,500 workers assembled in a mechanical depart-

---

[18] Jerzy Borejsza and Hilary Minc, both Jewish, were powerful members of the communist government. Borejsza was the organizer of the press and publishing; Minc was the economic overlord. In popular Polish belief they epitomized Jewish rule over the Polish people.

ment's hall. The workers were informed about it by telegram and knew that in the Dęblin area there were traces of the PPS and none of the PPR. The NSZ forces have prevailed over the region.

The meeting lasted two hours and was very stormy. Comrade Chodkiewicz and I both made our statements. During the speeches people shouted back, 'Get rid of the Jews! It's a disgrace that they came to defend the Jews! . . . The Jews murdered thirteen Polish children and they (meaning us) are defending them! Bierut won't have the guts to sentence them to death!'[19] Those shouting received a big round of applause from the workers. At one point a woman, the widow of an engine-driver, came up to the director, Chodkiewicz, and caught hold of the lapel of his jacket and started to shout hysterically, 'You are talking only about politics and defending the Jews! You don't say anything about the poverty of the railway workers! How can I live on 900 zlotys per month, which is the price of a hundredweight of potatoes? We don't even have enough money to buy salt!' The people clapped their hands and whistled. The woman was made silent by the commandant of the SKP[20] and then the meeting proceeded. People asked about the eastern borders and shouted, 'Wilno (Vilnius) and Lwów (L'viv) should be ours; why haven't the Soviets left them? In Poland the Soviets drive tanks and terrorize us with their rifles! Is this freedom?!!! Why are so many Poles held in prisons and why are the military barracks full of those arrested?! The Jews are the heads of Public Security!! We want democracy!!!'

As a member of the PPS, Comrade Chodkiewicz gave excellent answers. We had control over the meeting, but I knew that the prepared resolution would not be accepted because of the hostile atmosphere, so I didn't bother to read it out. After the meeting the workers spoke among themselves. I heard them saying, 'Jewish servants, fuck them all!'

Stefan Tomaszewski, Head of the Warsaw Department of Communication

4. *Report by Comrades Doliński, Domagała, Krych, and Fir: business trip to Łódź, 11–13 July 1946*

Workers from the sewing factory (Niciarnia) and from the Scheibler and Grohman factories organized a strike in protest against the sentences of the Kielce pogrom trial[21] on Thursday 11 July. Comrade Sikorska, the secretary of the PPR, was severely beaten by women in Niciarnia when the strike started. We have to admit that no Party members tried to defend Comrade Sikorska. The strike in Niciarnia was put down after an hour, and the women went back to work. It must be stressed that the workers of Niciarnia accepted a resolution condemning the Kielce pogrom on 8 July but, three days later, strongly opposed the sentences in the Kielce trial.

Workers at the Scheibler's factory from both shifts also went on strike. The first shift

---

[19] Bolesław Bierut, 1892–1956, a communist activist. He was appointed president of the Krajowa Rada Narodowa (National Council for the Homeland: KRN) in Jan. 1944, during the German occupation. He was President of the Polish Republic from Feb. 1947 to Nov. 1952.

[20] A special military unit brought into Kielce.

[21] It is worth mentioning that neither the press nor the families were informed about the carrying out of the nine death sentences, which occurred at 9.45 p.m. on 12 July 1946 in the presence of an attorney from the chief military attorney's office, Dr Balicki; a priest, Major Zawadzki; and members of Public Security, Albert Grynbaum and Kwaśniewski. Information about the executions was posted in Kielce.

stopped work for half an hour and the second for forty-five minutes. The workers used as their reason the fact that false information about their accepting the resolution against pogroms had been published in *Głos Robotniczy* ('The Workers' Voice'). According to the paper, all the workers supported the resolution; in reality, only one department did.

The following factories organized protest strikes on 12 July: Scheibler at Księży Młyn, the sewing departments of Dietzel . . . Buhle, Cimerman, Kinderman, Warta, Tempo, 'Rasik'.

The strikes of 13 July took place in Wejrach—the ribbon factory, Hofnichter, Gampe and Albrecht, and Gutman . . .

Other industries have not gone on strike. The strikes have occurred in cotton and sewing factories, where the majority of workers are women, in contrast to the wool factories, where men form most of the workforce and where strikes have not happened.

The social situation of Łódź is serious. The strikes have moved swiftly from one factory to another and the women are very aggressive. . . . Women were calling for revenge if the death sentences of the Kielce trial were to be carried out . . . They used arguments such as: 'A pregnant Jewess gets 60,000 zlotys and I get nothing!! . . . Why are no Jews working here? The Jews are running Poland!'

The Jews of Łódź insist that there is a pogrom atmosphere in the city. People spread rumours in trams that Jews killed a child in Bałuty.[22] The Provincial Committee organized a meeting attended by Comrades Sowiński, Moczar, Burski, Mijał, Kozłowski, . . . and Doliński, Domagała, and Fir. The meeting decided to mobilize the whole party to take action against the reactionary movement, which is spreading anarchy in the factories.[23]

. . . The Provincial Security Office called in the foremen from Scheibler and Niciarnia. They signed a document making them responsible for any new strikes.

The Provincial PPR Committee decided to prepare a list of strike ringleaders and to take the following action against them:

1. make some of them jobless with no right to further employment.
2. arrest the most aggressive.
3. take away bonuses from all participants in the strike.

The strikes were easily suppressed because the workers' main aim was to protest. We should add that the workers lost their will to strike when they were told about the goals of reactionary ringleaders. It is noticeable that administrations, factory committees, and even members of the PPR are indifferent to the strikes.

Stefan Tomaszewski
12 July 1946

5. *Report by the Brigade: visit to the Kielce district, 4–5 July 1946*

Head of the Brigade: Comrade Buczyński, Department of Administration
Members: Comrade Legomski, Dept. of Administration
Comrade Karubin, Dept. of Administration
Comrade Deparasiński, Dept. of Administration
Comrade Faruga, Dept. of Administration

---

[22] Bałuty: one of the poorest suburbs of Łódź.   [23] This is obviously a propaganda slogan.

Comrade Woźnicki, Dept. of Propaganda
Comrade Gościński, Dept. of Propaganda
Comrade Banach, Dept. of Propaganda
Comrade Mastalerz, Dept. of Agriculture
Comrade Angierstejn, Dept. of Railway Communication
Comrade Stachacz, Dept. of Railway Communication
Comrade Buzd, Dept. of Railway Communication

1. *The Course of the Event*

The press has given wide coverage to the Kielce pogrom, so we are concerned only with information which has not been released by the press. It is necessary to make the following facts known:

The crowd increased gradually from ten people in the morning to 15,000 in the afternoon. Security forces initially ignored the event and as a result they could not maintain control of it later on. In order to defend themselves, the Jews fired at the crowd—which aggravated the situation. The police and army lacked discipline and, instead of suppressing the crowd's actions, came under its influence. It must be stressed that the police took part in the pogrom. The police and army were the first to enter the Jewish house.[24] Policemen dragged the Jewish victims out of the building and exposed them to the crowd. Regrettably, workers also participated in the pogrom. The tub-thumpers found good ground for their propaganda in Ludwilów steelworkers; the former created an atmosphere of excitement and succeeded in leading the workers to the Jewish house during working hours. The excited crowd shouted anti-Jewish, anti-PPR, and anti-Public Security slogans.

2. *The Attitude of the Population of Kielce*

The attitude of the masses is usually negative. Antisemitism is present to a higher degree among the *petit bourgeois*, i.e. shopkeepers, craftsmen, owners of property, and small traders. Antisemitism is traditionally ascribed to these groups. It should be mentioned that most of the property in Kielce had belonged to the Jews in the past. Thus the new possessors of Jewish property fear the return of the original owners.

The workers still suffer severe poverty and have also carried the burden of rebuilding Poland. They are not aware of the essential reasons for their poverty, since they are unable to understand the complexity of economic issues. As a result, their views are deeply subjective and lacking in logic. Furthermore, the enemy's propaganda is spreading widely. It is easy to incite hatred towards Jews and at the same time towards the Party. According to the hostile propaganda, Jews are privileged.

---

[24] The police and the army's active part in the pogrom was suppressed immediately after the event. According to Jechiel Alpert, even the representatives of the Central Committee of the Polish Jews in Poland, who arrived at Kielce on 5 July, discouraged the Jews of Kielce from accusing the Polish army and suggested that it was General Anders's army and not the Polish army that was responsible for the pogrom. Albert Grynbaum, vice-director of the provincial security office in Kielce, also insisted in a conversation with American journalists (among whom was S. L. Shneiderman, an American journalist of Polish Jewish origin who was in Kielce in July 1946): 'Tell them that they were from General Anders's army; under no circumstances mention the Polish army. You cannot blame the government because of a few hooligans in the Polish army' (recollections of Jechiel Alpert, in *Sefer kielts: toledot kehilat kielts* (Tel Aviv, 1957), quoted by Bożena Szaynok in her book *Pogrom Żydów w Kielcach 4 lipca 1946*, 69.

One hundred and eighty Jews[25] lived on Planty Street in Kielce. They did not work and only two of them were members of the PPR. Also, in Ostrowiec many Jews are out of work.[26] Rich Jews and people from the reactionary movement were usually the visitors of the state's health resorts. Among 1,000 visitors at a health resort in Busk, 400 voted 'No' in the referendum.[27]

The masses feel dissatisfied and unjustly treated; needing to vent their anger, they look for someone to blame for their situation. Thus they have been easily manipulated by the reactionary movement, which pointed out the injustices of the system (the lives of some Jews with no jobs, the corruption among the PPR and members of the government). This was enough to turn the masses against the Jews, the PPR, and the government, e.g. the Radom Brewery and the State Co-operative workers' opposition to the anti-pogrom resolutions.

Railway workers have been responsible to a great extent for the anti-Jewish atmosphere because they are aware of the Jewish transports from the East. Many Polish families have suffered harsh conditions and have awaited the return of their families from the Soviet Union. So they become embittered by the fact that the Jews are entering Poland instead of their families. The Jews from the East are characterized as backward, with a tendency to isolate themselves from the rest of Polish society. The Polish population is unaware of the Jews' good points and undervalues many who have made great social contributions. Railway workers spread antisemitic slogans in the Kielce district. It must be said that the railway guards from the Kielce–Częstochowa line help the perpetrators to find the Jews by pointing at them and encouraging the perpetrators to beat up the Jews.

Peasants have few reasons to turn antisemitic, thus their antisemitism is the weakest. They are dissatisfied with the government, however, because they are not given enough protection against bandits. The enormous bureaucracy of the state apparatus, as well as the

---

[25] 25,000 Jews lived in Kielce before the Second World War. According to the Kielce Public Archives, there were seventy-nine Jews in Kielce on 25 Jan. 1945, about 304 at the beginning of 1946, and 163 in May 1946. Many of them came from the Soviet Union or from other parts of Poland. Most of them lived at 7 Planty Street.

[26] There were anti-Jewish demonstrations in Ostrowiec Świętokrzyski (Kielecki) after the Kielce pogrom.

[27] The referendum, which was regarded as the pivotal event of 1946, took place on Sunday 30 June 1946. In the referendum Polish society was supposed to decide on three key issues: agrarian reform, the Polish–German border on the Oder–Neisse line (Odra and Nysa Łużycka), and a single-chamber parliament. Polish political opposition insisted on voting 'no' three times, whereas the communists organized a propaganda campaign under the slogan 'three yes votes'. In general, the opposition predicted that the results would be rigged by the communist authorities. This is exactly what happened. The official results of the referendum, which were published on 12 July, were falsified (the 'no' votes were simply thrown away and exchanged for 'yes' votes by the PPR people). Political opposition linked the corruption and the date of these results with the Kielce pogrom, insisting that the communist government masterminded the pogrom in order to distract Polish and foreign public opinion from the referendum. This politically driven and one-sided explanation of the Kielce pogrom contributed to the development of a historical conspiracy theory claiming that the Soviet secret forces or Polish communist regime were primarily responsible for masterminding the pogrom. The communist historiography has also constructed an equivalent conspiracy theory claiming that the reactionary Polish opposition was behind the pogrom. Recent research on Polish–Jewish relations during that period clearly points to the limitations of both these conspiracy theories.

growing corruption of the Party leadership and of Public Security, have resulted in an antigovernment atmosphere.

The common ground for expressions of dissatisfaction is antisemitism, which has also infiltrated the Party, especially its lower and middle ranks. These groups have come across many corrupt practices among Party members and among Public Security's leadership.

Jewish Party members have also engaged in corrupt practices. As a result, many Polish comrades seem to think that the KC (the Central Committee) favours Jews and tolerates corruption among them, e.g. Zarecki, the president of Kielce, who got away with many corrupt practices.[28] This resulted in an increase in the antisemitic atmosphere in Party ranks.

In the atmosphere of growing antisemitism Polish comrades pay more attention to corrupt practices of the Jews than they do to any other corruption. Another matter is that of career competition within the Party. Jews are regarded as rivals by the Polish comrades.

Antisemitism caused by the above-mentioned factors can be illustrated by the following:

Comrade Józef Kosior, who has completed the district and central Party's training, during the demonstration in Ostrowiec stated, 'What is going on? In Ostrowiec, we work like slaves and the Jews feather their own nests! They can afford butter and chicken!!! Where were they when we fought in the partisan war?!' Another comrade in Ostrowiec said, 'Launch an offensive at the Jews and you will receive an enormous round of applause!' An activist from Pinczów asked, 'Why has the Jew got the flour mill? He doesn't work there; he only leases it out!' The Pinczów district secretary criticized Comrade Woźnicki for his strong defence of the Jews. When Comrade Buczyński advised Pinczów activists organizing an anti-pogrom demonstration, he was met with the answer, 'How could we talk to peasants about defending the Jews, when a Jewess receives 40,000 zlotys for giving birth?!' Buczyński immediately discredited such slander.

The clergy has also played its role in spreading antisemitism. For example, a priest from St Mary's Church in Radom preached, 'Take brooms in your hands and get rid of the rascals! The sooner you sweep the Jews away, the better! They are our enemy!'

Antisemitism has infiltrated the souls of the young. Many scouts in Kielce are both antiJewish and anti-democratic. Comrades have seen them shouting during the riots for shops to be closed. In addition, one of the scouts buried his knife in a dead Jewish body. The young organized in the working troops created by Wiślicz are also indifferent to the democratic process. The reactionary bands exploited that and tried to come close to Kielce. There are reports about their movements: from Daleszyce, a band of fifty, from Cisów, a band of fifteen, and from Dymina, a band of 200. Yet because the Party was alert and because of Public Security's actions, the reactionary bands were thwarted in their intentions.

3. *The Behaviour of Public Security and of the Provincial Kielce PPR Committee*

The governor lost his head and Public Security was powerless when the pogrom broke out. Chaos could be observed everywhere. When Comrades Buczyński and Chełkowski came to Kielce, it looked as though the Provincial Committee was ready to run away. There was no co-operation between the UB, MO, KBW,[29] and ORMO.

---

[28] As a matter of fact, he was expelled by his local constituency, but the central committee allowed him to rejoin the party.

[29] Korpus Bezpieczeństwa Wewnętrznego (Internal Security Force).

The Committee was shocked by the course of the riots and unaware of the atmosphere among the masses. Its surprise led to further exaggeration of the problem. When Comrade Buczyński suggested organizing mass meetings as quickly as possible in order to suppress the antisemitic atmosphere, local comrades disagreed. They were afraid of the masses and suggested meeting only the Party's activists from factories. Yet Buczyński went to the Ludwików steelworks, where a mass meeting attended by 1,000 workers took place. Speeches made by Buczyński, members of the PPS and the army, and a few workers brought in an atmosphere of embarrassment and shame. Workers stated that not all of them left the factory and that they condemned the tub-thumpers and perpetrators. In their resolution, they demanded the death penalty for the criminals and promised to seek them out in the factory and to release their names. Workers came forward with such a list to the committee the next day, when other mass meetings were also organized around the whole district.

4. *The Preventative Measures*
After their arrival at Kielce Comrades Buczyński and Chełkowski met with Comrade Wiślicz, the Governor. Comrades Kalinowski (the First Secretary of the Provincial Committee of the Polish Workers' Party (KW PPR)) and Sobczyński (the Director of the Provincial Public Security Office) were also present. There was a decision to release an appeal signed by all political parties. The appeal was posted the next day.

According to Buczyński's statement, instructions were issued for the District and Municipal Committees. These gave the order to mobilize all Party members, introduce emergency service in factories and committees, and report every three hours on the situation . . .

It was demanded that the police and the army, which had become too friendly with the excited crowd, be exchanged for the reserve from Warsaw.

Another executive meeting met with Wiślicz on 8 July. It was attended by Comrades Kliszko, Kalinowski, Kozłowski, Lewin, Kwiecień, and Buczyński. Comrade Kliszko severely condemned the Party's and Public Security's leadership for their lack of action.

A PPR and PPS meeting took place on 11 July. It was decided to make some arrests of troublemakers, to close down places of popular entertainment, and to allocate vacated properties to the workers. During demonstrations both our and the PPS's comrades have disseminated the idea that swindlers and restaurant owners are responsible for the misery of the common people. This was successful propaganda: the focus of the people's anger has begun to shift from the Jews to the parasites of society. And thus we have succeeded in convincing people that the party properly punishes those who hurt the masses.

Eight other members of the brigade arrived at Kielce on 10 July. Comrade Buczyński informed them of the situation and sent them to work in the district. Comrades Gościński and Stachacz went to Skarżysko; Mastalerz and Woźnicki to Kozienice and Pionki; Karubin and Grzywnowicz to Radom; Angierstejn and Gordon to Częstochowa; Deparasiński and Faruga to Ostrowiec; and Banach to Starachowice. All comrades were responsible for organizing many demonstrations and Party meetings. They condemned antisemitism and introduced anti-pogrom resolutions, which demanded death sentences for perpetrators and the detection of those who masterminded the pogrom. We had to use drastic methods in many towns; for instance, we had to put pressure on the management of the Pionki Gunpowder Factory: Comrades Woźnicki and Mastalerz warned all the directors that they would be personally responsible for maintaining a calm situation. Seven hundred people, employed in the factory for many years, support the pre-war government (Sanacja). Workers know each other very well. NSZ is active and has not been betrayed by any employees. We suspect that the local NSZ headquarters and its illegal printing office are based in the factory.

The whole action had very positive results. Riots have not occurred anywhere else. The calm situation has been maintained. It could be said that the Party, after momentary negligence, has overcome difficulties and risen to the occasion. The Party organized the funeral for the victims in a very efficient way, and masses of workers took part in it.

Conclusions

1. Ideological standards must be raised in the Party's ranks. Traces of antisemitism must not be neglected. The young should be given special attention.
2. It is necessary to fight more efficiently against corrupt practices of both Jews and Poles.
3. With the help of Jewish comrades, it is necessary to make the Jews productive in Polish society.
4. People who failed their duties in the district and municipal committees must be dismissed.
5. Party committees should be aware of hostile propaganda and oppose it quickly.
6. Party activists should meet more often.
7. In order to improve organization, instructors should be sent to any districts where the Party's structures are weak.

Bełżec

RUDOLF REDER

TRANSLATOR'S NOTE

IN 1946 a slim volume entitled *Bełżec* came out in Kraków. It was published by the Jewish Regional Historical Commission, which collected the testimonies of Holocaust survivors. The booklet included an introduction by Nella Rost, who was on the committee's editorial board, and Rudolf Reder, a former soap manufacturer from Lemberg who managed to escape from the camp and lived long enough to tell his story. He was one of only two known survivors of Bełżec death camp. The other, Chaim Hirszman, was murdered in Lublin in 1946 by two youth members of a Polish underground organization the day he began to testify about the camp to the Lublin branch of the Jewish Historical Commission. Thus, Reder's booklet remains to this day the only document written by a victim concerning this most obscure murder camp.[1]

Bełżec murder camp was the first camp set up by Aktion Reinhard, an operation whose purpose was to dispose, in the least obtrusive manner, of the Jewish population of the General Government and adjacent countries under Nazi rule. The other two camps were Treblinka and Sobibór. The building of Bełżec started towards the end of November 1941, and at the beginning of March 1942 the camp was ready. On 17 March the first transport arrived; about 10 December that year saw the last. Between those two dates, with a break for 'modernization' which lasted six weeks, Bełżec murder camp claimed between 500,000 and 650,000 victims, of whom over three-quarters came from the provinces of Kraków and Lublin, and the Distrikt Galizien.[2] The remaining 150,000 or so consisted of Jews expelled from those parts of pre-war Poland which had been incorporated into the Third Reich, Austria, and Czechoslovakia.

Like the other two camps of Aktion Reinhard, Bełżec had no attached labour camp and no ordinary prisoners. It consisted of rudimentary murder facilities: an undressing barracks for men, another for women to have their hair cut, and yet another with the gas chambers,

---

[1] There are two other documents written by eyewitnesses. Both were SS visitors to the camp. The first was Kurt Gerstein, a disinfection expert. Deeply shaken by what he saw, he tried unsuccessfully to pass his knowledge on to the neutral parties, the Swedish and Vatican legations in Berlin. In French custody after the war he wrote a harrowing account of his visit, which included a 'show gassing'. The other was Wilhelm Pfannenstiel, a professor of hygiene. He went to Bełżec with Gerstein and also accompanied Himmler on a visit in Nov. 1942. He did not come forward voluntarily to testify about Bełżec, but was interrogated about it after the war, first by the Allies and then twice by German legal authorities.

[2] The name Distrikt Galizien refers to a fifth province of the General Government created by the Nazis in July 1941 with Lemberg (Lwów/L'viv) as its provincial capital. It consisted of three pre-war voivodeships situated in south-eastern Poland: Lemberg, Tarnopol, and Stanisławów.

about thirty pits of different sizes for burying corpses, a couple of barracks for the Jewish death brigade, and living quarters for the Ukrainian guards, or *askers*, who numbered about 100. Its SS garrison was small: about twenty all told.

Into this camp Rudolf Reder was brought with one of the first transports of Jews from Lemberg caught during the great *Aktion*, which lasted for two weeks in August 1942 and which netted about 50,000 victims. He came alone: his son, Bronisław, had been apprehended in Lemberg on 10 August and was never seen again. His daughter, Sophia, managed to survive the war in Kraków; she emigrated to England, where she married. It is not known what happened to his wife. Although Reder was then 61, he was one of the lucky few to be selected on arrival at the unloading ramp to join the Jewish death brigade and to become the camp's odd-job man. He remained in the camp for a little over three months. Towards the end of November he was taken to Lemberg, where he managed to escape. He survived the war in Lemberg, hidden by his former housekeeper.

Reder arrived in Bełżec at the height of the camp's activity. Because of his position as odd-job man he was allowed considerable freedom of movement. He was used as a spare pair of hands to dig pits, he was called upon to help repair the machinery which produced the carbon monoxide pumped into the gas chambers, and he also worked as a bricklayer. He was therefore able to describe the camp, its installations, and its functioning in considerable detail. But his story is also the deeply harrowing account of someone who witnessed with horror the slaughter of innocents which went on day after day. And this, together with the relevant details which, without his description, might have remained for ever obscure, make Reder's booklet a unique document of this terrible but little-known chapter in the history of the Holocaust.

Reder was born on 4 April 1881 in Dębica, in the voivodeship of Kraków. From the 1910s he lived in Lemberg. Soon after the end of the war he must have left the town (which was then incorporated into the Soviet Union) for Kraków, where he testified about the camp three times in 1945, twice for the Jewish Historical Commission, and the third time for Jan Sehn, a district attorney who collected evidence on behalf of the regional commission investigating German crimes in Poland. In 1946 Reder collaborated with Nella Rost on the booklet about Bełżec, which appeared under his name, but was probably written by her. He emigrated to Canada perhaps in the early 1950s under the assumed name of Roman Robak, the name of his former housekeeper, whom he married. In August 1960 he was in Munich, where he made a deposition at the office of the public prosecutor concerning Bełżec ('The Case against Josef Oberhauser *et al.*') in preparation for the Bełżec trial, which took place in Munich in January 1965. He died in the late 1960s or early 1970s in Canada.

M. M. RUBEL

BEŁŻEC

I

IN August 1942 there still wasn't a walled ghetto in Lemberg. Instead there were several streets where we were forced to live: nowhere else. These together became known as the Jewish quarter. It consisted of the following streets: Panieńska, Wąska, Ogrodnicka, Słoneczna, and a few others, which had once been a part of the third quarter of Lemberg. There we lived in constant anxiety and torment.

Nearly two weeks before deportation everyone was talking about it as an imminent disaster. We were in despair, since we all already knew well what the word *Aussiedlung* [Jewish resettlement] meant. We were being told the story of a worker who had once belonged to a death commando in Bełżec, but then eventually managed to escape. While still there he was employed in building chambers disguised as baths which in fact were intended for gassing people. He forecast that none of those who had gone there would ever return. We had also heard the story of a Ukrainian guard employed there in murdering Jews recounting his experiences to his Polish girlfriend. The woman was so terrified by what she had heard that she decided to pass the news round in order to forewarn prospective victims. That is how we got to know about Bełżec.

Bełżec's legend thus became a reality, which we all knew and dreaded. That is why, for several days before 10 August, the streets of the Jewish quarter were filled with frightened and helpless people repeatedly asking each other the same question: what should they do and where should they go? Early in the morning of 10 August all exits leading out of the Jewish quarter were sealed by German patrols. The Gestapo, SS, and *Sonderdienst* in groups of five or six patrolled the streets a few paces apart. They were enthusiastically assisted by the Ukrainian police.

Two weeks earlier Generalmajor Katzman, the chief butcher of Lemberg and eastern Galicia, had distributed permits among some of the ghetto workshops. Other workshops got theirs from a police station at Smolka Square. The lucky ones were not very numerous. The vast majority of Jews, overcome by mortal fear, tried all sorts of rescues or escapes, but no one really knew what to do or how to save himself.

Meanwhile, for a few consecutive days, German patrols combed one house after another, looking into every nook and cranny. Some of those caught by the Gestapo had their permits honoured, others did not. All those without permits, or whose permits the Germans did not honour, were driven out of their houses without food or clothing. Next the Germans herded people into large groups. Those who resisted were shot on the spot. I myself was in my workshop working. I did not have a permit. I locked the front door and did not open up, even though I heard them banging outside. Eventually the Gestapo forced their way in. They found me hiding in a corner, beat me on the head with a stick, and took me away.³ They squeezed us like sardines into trams and transported us to the Janowska camp. We could neither move nor breathe.

Night was already falling. All 6,000 of us were squeezed into a meadow. We were ordered to sit down, and forbidden to move, raise an arm, stretch a leg, or get up. A watchtower directed its blinding light at us. It became as light as if it were day. We sat there, packed tightly together, young and old, women and children alike. A few well-aimed shots were fired in our direction. Someone got up and was shot on the spot. Perhaps he wished to die a quick death.

And so we passed the night. The crowd was deathly silent. Not even women or children dared to cry. At six o'clock in the morning we were told to get up off the wet grass, on which we had been sitting all night, and to arrange ourselves in a column, four in a row. The long line of condemned was then made to march in the direction of Kleparowski railway station. Our column was guarded on both sides by the Gestapo and Ukrainian police. There was not the slightest chance of escape. Our column was driven to the railway station and onto a ramp, where a long train of cattle-trucks was waiting. The Germans began to load the train. They opened the doors to each truck. On both sides of the doors stood the Gestapo men, two on each side, whips in hand, slashing each of us on our faces and heads. All the Gestapo men were alike. They all beat us so badly that each of us had marks on our faces or bumps on our heads. Women sobbed; children in arms cried. Thus driven along and beaten mercilessly, we climbed on top of one another. The doors to the trucks were high above the ground. In the general scramble we trampled those who were below. We were all in a hurry, wanting to have all this behind us. On the roof of each truck sat a Gestapo man with a machine-gun. Others beat us while counting 100 people to each car. It all went so fast that loading a few thousand people took no more than an hour. Our transport contained many men, including some who had the so-called 'secure' work permits, young girls, and women. Finally they sealed all the trucks. Squeezed into one trembling mass we stood so close to each other that we were almost on top of one another. Stifling heat was driving us mad. We had not a drop of water or a crumb of bread. The train started to move at eight o'clock. I knew that the train-driver and fire-stoker were Germans. The train went fast, although it seemed to us that it moved at a snail's pace. It stopped three times, at Kulikowo, Żółkiew, and Rawa Ruska. I suppose it was giving way to other railway traffic. During those stops Gestapo thugs got down from the roofs in order to stop anyone coming near the trucks. They were there to prevent anyone from the outside from showing us a little mercy and giving

---

³ In a deposition taken down in Kraków in 1945 by the Regional Jewish Historical Commission (Collection of Testimonies of Jewish Survivors, Żydowski Instytut Historyczny, Warsaw, file 302/162) Reder says that he was betrayed to the Germans by two Ukrainians: Edward and Marjan Kobzdej. The information was omitted from the book. (All notes in this chapter are mine—M. M. Rubel.)

water through the small window secured by barbed wire to those who were dying of thirst inside.

We went on and nobody spoke—completely apathetic and silent. We knew that we were being taken to our deaths and that we couldn't do anything about it. Although all our thoughts were occupied with escape, we saw no possibility of success. Our truck was a new one; its windows were so narrow that I would not have been able to squeeze through. In other trucks it was possible to smash doors. Every few minutes we heard shots being fired after breakaways. No one said a word to anyone else; no one tried to console lamenting women or to calm crying children. We all knew one thing: that we were going towards a certain and terrible death. What we all wished for was that it would be quick. Perhaps somebody managed to escape, but I do not know . . . Escape was possible only from the train.

About midday the train pulled into Bełżec. It was a small station surrounded by little houses occupied by the Gestapo.[4] Next to the station stood a post office and the lodgings of the Ukrainian railwaymen. Bełżec is on the line between Lublin and Tomaszów, 15 kilometres from Rawa Ruska. At Bełżec our train left the main line and moved onto sidings about a kilometre long, which led directly into the camp. At the main station in Bełżec an old German with a thick black moustache mounted the engine. I do not know his name, but I would recognize him at a glance. He looked like a butcher. He took charge of the train, bringing it into the camp. The journey lasted no more than two minutes. During my four months in Bełżec I saw no one but this thug doing the job.[5]

The sidings led through empty fields: not one habitable building in sight. The German who brought the train climbed down from the engine in order to 'help'.

[4] Wherever Reder uses the word Gestapo in reference to the German garrison at the murder camp in Bełżec, read SS men. No member of the Gestapo was ever employed in any of the murder camps of Aktion Reinhard, which were run by SS men aided by Ukrainian guards and a Jewish death brigade.

[5] The German in question was a German career railway official by the name of Rudolf Göckel (1883? – 21 Aug. 1960). In 1941 he was posted to Bełżec as a station-master. When Jewish transports began to arrive at Bełżec in the middle of Mar. 1942, he was relieved of his post and became a liaison officer between the station and the camp. In 1946 Göckel was arrested in Berlin and in May 1947 deported to Poland, where he was kept in protective custody in Zamość. There, on 19 Nov. 1948, he was interrogated by Hieronim Rolle, the district attorney. In the course of the inquiry Göckel stated that: 'I stayed in Bełżec from July 1941 until January 1943. During that period I worked as a station-master. If I remember well, transports with Jews were coming to Bełżec from about Pentecost 1942 until September that year. I cannot be sure, but not all trucks were always full: only five to six trucks on average. I was not allowed to look inside the trucks, nor had I the right to inspect them in any way. Trucks that were empty were open. I did not count Jewish transports arriving in Bełżec. Therefore, I cannot say how many came. I also do not know the number of victims, but I could see that most of them were already dead on arrival. . . . I did not have permission to enter the camp, and therefore know nothing about what was going on inside. But, on the basis of hearsay and talks with the locals, I imagined the camp in Bełżec to be like other concentration camps of isolation which received and dispatched transports. I believed that only bodies of those already dead were burnt there, and not of those who had arrived alive.' In 1950 Rudolf Göckel was released from protective custody without charge. He returned to Germany a free man. (See Coll. OB, 2 pt. 11, Archiwum Głównej Komisji Badania Zbrodni przeciwko Narodowi Polskiemu, Warsaw.)

With shouts and kicks he drove people out of the trucks. Then he went to inspect each truck personally, in case someone was trying to hide. He took care of everything. When the whole train was empty and checked, he signalled with a flag and moved the train away from the camp.

The camp was under the total control of the SS. No one was allowed to come near. Those who found themselves in the area by mistake were shot at. The train would come into a courtyard 1 square kilometre in size enclosed on all sides by barbed wire and wire netting to a height of 2 metres. This fencing was not electrified. The entrance to the courtyard was through a large wooden gate covered with barbed wire. Beside this gate was a guardhouse with a telephone. By the guardhouse stood a few SS men with dogs. When the train had been brought into the courtyard, one of the men would come out of the guardhouse, shut the gate, and then go back in. At this moment the reception of the transport began. Several dozen SS men yelling 'Los' opened the trucks, chasing people out with whips and rifle-butts. The doors were about a metre from the ground, and the people, young and old alike, had to jump down, often breaking arms or legs. Children were injured and all tumbled down exhausted, terrified, and filthy. The SS men were assisted by the so-called *Zugsführers*,[6] who supervised the Jewish death commando. They were dressed in everyday clothing without any distinctive marking. The sick, the old, and small children—in other words, all those who could not walk on their own—were thrown onto stretchers and taken to pits. There they were made to sit on the edge, while Irrmann—one of the Gestapo—shot them and pushed their bodies into the pit with a rifle-butt.

This Irrmann, who specialized in murdering old men and small children, was a tall, dark, handsome man—quite normal-looking.[7] Like the others, he lived in a small house next to the railway station in Bełżec. Alone like the rest, without women or family. He used to turn up at the camp early in the morning and stay the whole day receiving death transports. As soon as the train was empty, all the victims were assembled in the courtyard and surrounded by the *askers*. It was then that Irrmann would give a speech. There was deathly silence. Irrmann stood close to the crowd. Everybody wanted to hear him. We all suddenly hoped that, if we were spoken to, then perhaps it meant that there would be work to do, that we would live after all . . . Irrmann spoke loudly and clearly: 'Ihr geht jetzt baden, nachher werden Ihr zur Arbeit geschickt.'[8] That was all.

[6] In normal circumstances *Zugsführer* meant 'train master'. In the camp's usage the term referred to fifteen or so Jews selected from the death brigade, led by an *Oberzugsführer*, with the task of being present at the ramp to meet each transport as it arrived.

[7] SS Hauptscharführer Fritz Irrmann (11 Oct. 1914 – 1942) was in charge of a platoon of Ukrainian guards. He was accidentally shot dead in Bełżec some time in the autumn of 1942 by his colleague Heinrich Gley in a scuffle during an escape attempt by two Ukrainian guards. (See Dr Janusz Peter 'Kordian', *W Bełżcu podczas Okupacji*, Diaries, no. 221, Żydowski Instytut Historyczny, Warsaw.)

[8] 'You are going to take a bath now. Afterwards you will be sent to work.' The text of the speech varied, according to different testimonies. But it contained two basic elements: an instruction to undress in order to take a bath, and a vague promise of work. It was not always delivered by Irrmann, but by any member of the SS garrison who was at the ramp on duty.

The crowd rejoiced; the people were relieved that they would be going to work. They applauded. I remember his words, repeated day after day—three times a day on average, during the time I was there. It was a moment of hope, of illusion. The crowd was peaceful. And in silence they all went forward: men straight across the courtyard to a building bearing the inscription 'Bade und Inhalationsräume' in large letters, the women, some 20 metres further on to a large barracks, 15 by 30 metres. They were led there not knowing why. For a few minutes more there was peace and quiet. I saw that when they were handed wooden stools and ordered first to stand in a line and then to sit down, and when eight Jewish barbers, silent as death, came in to shave their hair to the bare skin, it was at this moment that they were struck by the terrible truth. It was then that neither the women nor the men—already on their way to the gas—could have had any illusions about their fate.

With the exception of a few men chosen for their trade, which could be handy in the camp, all the rest—young and old, women and children—went to certain death. Little girls with long hair had it shaved; others with short hair went to the gas chambers directly, together with the men. And all of a sudden, without any transition from hope, they were overcome by despair. There were cries and shrieking. Some women went mad. Others, however, went to their death calmly, young girls in particular. Our transport consisted largely of the intelligentsia. There were also many young men, but, as in every other transport I saw, women were in the majority.

I stood to one side with others left to dig pits, watching my brothers, sisters, friends, and acquaintances being driven to their deaths. While the women, naked and shaved, were rounded up with whips like cattle to the slaughter, without even being counted—'Faster, faster'—the men were already dying. Shaving the women took approximately two hours. Two hours was the time it took to prepare for murder and for the murder itself.

A dozen or so SS men drove the women along with whips and fixed bayonets all the way to the building and from there up three steps to a hall. There the *askers* counted 750 people for each gas chamber.[9] Those women who tried to resist were bayoneted until the blood was running. Eventually all the women were forced into the chambers. I heard the doors being shut; I heard shrieks and cries; I heard desperate calls for help in Polish and in Yiddish. I heard the blood-curdling wails of women and the squeals of children, which after a short time became one long, horrifying scream . . . This went on for fifteen minutes. The engine worked for twenty minutes. Afterwards there was total silence. Then the *askers* pushed open

---

[9] The building with the gas chambers had six cubicles, each about 25 sq. m. It is almost impossible to squeeze such a large crowd into such a small space. The figure of 750 people was provided by Christian Wirth, the camp's first commandant, to a company of high-ranking SS officers who visited the camp in the middle of Aug. 1942. Wirth's purpose was to impress them with the efficiency of his methods of murder, which they had come to improve. The figure must then have become official, although highly unrealistic, and the source of the wild overestimate made by Reder after the war of 2.5 million victims. See n. 32.

the doors that led outside. It was then that those of us who had been selected from different transports, in unmarked clothing and without tattoos, began our work.

We pulled out the corpses of the people so recently alive. We dragged them to pits with the help of leather straps while an orchestra played . . . from morning until night.

II

After a while I came to know the whole area well. The camp was surrounded by dense forest of young pine. Although the forestation was thick, extra branches were cut and interwoven with the existing ones over the gas chambers to allow a minimum of light to penetrate. Behind the gas chambers was a sandy lane along which we dragged the corpses. Overhead the Germans had put wire netting interwoven with more branches. This part of the camp was covered by a sort of roof of greenery and was darker than elsewhere. I suppose the Germans wanted to conceal the area from aerial observation. The main gate led to a sizeable courtyard. There was a substantial shed where the women had their hair shaved. Next to the shed was another small courtyard, surrounded on all sides by a fence 3 metres high. It was made of close-fitting wooden boards, greyish in colour. The courtyard led directly to the gas chambers. Thus no one on the outside would have been able to see what was happening within. The building containing the gas chambers was not high, but long and wide. It was made of grey cement blocks, and was covered by a flat roof made of asbestos sheets. Immediately above it stretched wire netting covered with branches. The door to the building was approached by three steps a metre wide and without railings. In front stood a large flower-pot filled with plants. There was an inscription in large letters on the front: 'Bade und Inhalationsräume'. The steps led to a completely empty and unlit corridor: just four cement walls. It was very long, though only about a metre and a half wide. On both sides of it were doors to the gas chambers. These were sliding doors made of wood, with wooden handles. The gas chambers had no windows. They were dark and empty. In each gas chamber there was a round hole the size of an electric socket.[10] All the walls and floors were made of cement. Both the corridor and the gas chambers were no more than 2 metres high. On a wall opposite the entrance to each gas chamber were more sliding doors 2 metres wide. Through these the corpses of the gassed were thrown outside. On one side of the building was an adjoining shed no bigger than 2 metres square. This housed the engine, which was petrol-driven. The gas chambers were about a metre and a half above ground level. The doors leading to the ramp, onto which the bodies of the victims were thrown, were on a level with the gas chambers.[11]

[10] This was the outlet of a gas pipe.
[11] The first building housing the gas chambers, which was constructed some time towards the end of 1941, was made of double wooden planks with the spaces in between filled with sand. It was only half the size of the second gassing installation. described by Reder, and had only three gas chambers. This building was taken down some time in June or July 1942, during the camp's extensive modernization.

There were also barracks for the camp's death commando. The first served the workers doing miscellaneous jobs; the other was for the so-called 'professionals'. They were identical. Each had space for 250 people. There were bunks on two levels, consisting of bare wooden boards with one small angled board as a headrest. Not far from the barracks was a kitchen, the camp's store, an office, a laundry, a tailor's shop, and, finally, comfortable barracks for the *askers*.

There were mass graves on both sides of the building housing gas chambers. Some were already full; others were still empty. I saw many graves filled to capacity and covered high with sand. It took quite a while for them to level down. There always had to be one empty pit, just in case . . .

III

I stayed in Bełżec death camp from August until the end of November. This was a period which saw the gassing of Jews on a massive scale. I was told by some of the inmates who had managed to survive from earlier transports that the vast majority of the death convoys came during this precise period.[12] They were coming each and every day without respite. Usually they arrived three times a day. Each convoy was composed of fifty cattle-trucks, each truck containing 100 people. If a transport happened to come during the night, the victims were kept in locked cars until six in the morning. The average death toll was 10,000 people a day. Some days the transports were not only larger, but even more frequent. Jews were brought in from everywhere: no one else, only Jews. I never saw anybody else. Bełżec served no other purpose but that of murdering Jews. All the transports were unloaded by the Gestapo, *askers*, and *Zugführers*. Further on, in the courtyard where the people undressed, there were also Jewish workers. We would ask in a whisper, 'Where are you from?' In a whisper they would answer, 'From Lemberg', 'From Kraków', 'From Zamość', 'Wieliczka', 'Jasło', 'Tarnów', and so on. I witnessed this once, twice, even three times every day.

Each transport received the same treatment. People were ordered to undress and to leave their belongings in the courtyard. Each time there was the same deceptive speech. And each time people rejoiced. I saw the spark of hope in their eyes—hope that they may be going to work. But a minute later, and with extreme brutality, babies were torn from their mothers, old and sick were thrown on stretchers, while men and little girls were driven with rifle-butts further on to a fenced path leading directly to the gas chambers. At the same time, and with the same brutality, the already naked women were ordered to the barracks, where they had their hair shaved. I knew exactly the moment when they all suddenly realized what was in store. Cries of fear and anguish, terrible moans, mingled with the

---

[12] Between 20 July, the date when the camp was reopened after modernization, and 11 Dec. 1942, the date of arrival of the last transport from Rawa Ruska, no fewer than *c*.520,000 Jews were murdered in Bełżec, of which *c*.38,000 died between 20 and 31 July, *c*.172,000 in Aug., *c*.132,000 in Sept., *c*.110,000 in Oct., *c*.61,000 in Nov., and *c*.10,000 in Dec.

music played by the orchestra. Hustled along and wounded by bayonets, first the men were made to run to the gas chambers. The *askers* counted 750 people to each chamber. Before all six chambers were filled to capacity, those in the first had already been suffering for nearly two hours. It was only when all six chambers were packed with people, when the doors were locked into position, that the engine was set in motion.

The engine was large, about a metre by a metre and a half. It consisted of a motor and wheels. The engine whirred at intervals and worked so fast that one could not see the spokes turning. It worked for twenty minutes. Afterwards it was turned off. The doors leading from the gas chambers onto the ramp were then opened. Bodies were thrown out onto the ground in one enormous pile a few metres high. The *askers* who opened the doors took no precautionary measures. We did not smell any particular odour; I saw no balloons filled with gas, or any powder thrown in. What I saw were petrol canisters. The machine was manned by two *askers*.[13] But once, when the engine went wrong, I was called in to put it right. In the camp they called me an *Ofenkünstler* [stove-setter]. That's why they selected me. I looked it over and saw glass tubes connected to metal pipes, which led to each gas chamber. We thought that the engine worked either by producing high pressure, or by sucking air away, or that the petrol produced exhaust fumes, which suffocated the people. The calls for help, shrieks, and terrible moans of people locked in and slowly asphyxiated lasted between ten and fifteen minutes. Horribly loud at first, they grew weaker and weaker, until there was complete silence. I heard desperate cries in many different languages. Apart from Polish Jews there were also transports of Jews from other countries. The majority of foreign transports came from France. There were also Jews from Holland, Greece, and even Norway. I do not recall seeing German Jews.[14] On the other hand, I do remember Jews from Czechoslovakia. They were brought in in cattle-trucks like the Polish Jews, although they were permitted to take their personal luggage and food. Transports from Poland were full of women and children. In contrast, transports from abroad consisted mostly of men. Children were few. Evidently their parents were able to leave them in the care of *goyim* in their respective countries, so they were able to save them from a terrible fate. The foreign Jews had no idea of their

---

[13] The engine, said to have come from a captured Russian tank, was installed and supervised by SS Scharführer Lorenz Hackenholt (b. 25 June 1914), a mechanic responsible for the gassing installations constructed first in Bełżec and then in Sobibór and Treblinka. Apart from the two *askers*, the engine was switched on and off by a Jew called Moniek, a taxi-driver from Kraków. This incriminating information comes from Reder's interrogation by Jan Sehn. The interrogation took place in Kraków on 29 Dec. 1945 (Collection of Testimonies of Jewish Survivors, Żydowski Instytut Historyczny, Warsaw, file no. 102/46). The information was omitted from the printed edition of Reder's booklet.

[14] Reder is wrong. No French Jews were deported to Bełżec. Some Dutch Jews were deported to Sobibór. Some Greek Jews were taken to Treblinka. But there were German Jews in Bełżec; most came from different ghettos in Lublin district, where they had been taken after deportation from Germany some time in the early months of 1941.

future. They were sure that they were being brought to Bełżec to work: they were well dressed and carefully prepared for the journey. Once there, they were treated by the German thugs in the same way as the Jews from other transports. And they were murdered by the same method, perishing in an equally horrible manner. About 100,000 foreign Jews might have been brought to the camp while I was there. They were all gassed.

When, after twenty minutes of gassing, the *askers* pushed open the tightly shut doors, the dead were in an upright position. Their faces were not blue. They looked almost unchanged, as if asleep. There was a bit of blood here and there from bayonet wounds. Their mouths were slightly open, hands rigid, often pressed against their chests. Those who were nearest to the now wide-open doors fell out by themselves. Like marionettes.

IV

Before they were murdered, all the women were shaved. While the first group was rushed to the barracks, others waited their turn, naked and barefoot even in winter and snow. Lamenting and nearly mad mothers pressed their children close. Each time I watched them with a bleeding heart. I could not really stand the sight of them. A group of women already shaved was hustled along, while those who followed waded through the hair of many shades which covered the entire floor of the barracks like some soft and silky carpet. When all the women had been shaved, four workers using brooms made from the branches of lime trees swept the floor and collected the hair into a large pile the size of nearly half a room. Then with bare hands they put this multicoloured pile into jute sacks, which they carried to a store.

The store where the hair, undergarments, and outer clothing of the victims were collected was in a small barracks not larger than 7 by 8 metres. Hair and personal possessions were kept there for ten days. After this time the hair in sacks was put on one side and personal possessions on the other, both ready to be loaded onto a goods train, which came to take away the spoils. Those who worked in the camp's offices told us that the hair went to Budapest. One Jew in particular told us all he knew. His name was Schreiber, a lawyer from the Sudetenland. Schreiber was an honest man. Irrmann had promised to take him on holiday. One day Irrmann took a short break. I heard Schreiber asking, 'Nehmen Sie mich mit?' ['Are you going to take me with you?'] Irrmann answered, 'Noch nicht' ['Not yet']. And so he kept Schreiber hoping. But I am sure that he perished, just like all others. It was he who told me that every few days a railway truck full of hair went to Budapest.

Apart from hair, the Germans also sent away baskets filled with gold teeth. In those few hundred metres separating the gas chambers from the pits stood some dentists with pliers. They stopped everyone as they dragged the corpses away.

They opened the mouths of the dead and yanked out the gold teeth, which they then threw into baskets ready for the purpose. There were eight dentists, usually young men specially selected to do the work.[15] I knew one of them well. He was called Zucker and came from Rzeszów. The dentists occupied a small separate barracks, which they shared with a doctor and a chemist. At dusk they went back to the barracks with baskets full of teeth, gold crowns, and bridges. There they separated the gold, which they melted into ingots. They were supervised by a Gestapo man called Schmidt, who beat them when he thought they were not working fast enough.[16] The gold was turned into ingots 1 centimetre thick, 50 millimetres wide, and 20 centimetres long.

Every day the SS men collected jewellery, money, and dollars from the store. They loaded them into suitcases, which a Jewish worker carried to the camp's main office in Bełżec. A Gestapo man went ahead, while the suitcases were carried by Jewish workers. The main office was a short distance away, no more than twenty minutes on foot. Bełżec murder camp was run from this office. Jews who worked in the administration told us that a whole transport of gold and precious objects was dispatched to the headquarters in Lublin, of which the camp in Bełżec was a branch.[17]

Clothing torn from the Jewish victims was carried by workers to the store, where another ten workers took each garment apart in search of gold and money. These workers were supervised by SS men, who beat them frequently. The SS men divided the money found in clothing between themselves. These SS supervisors were specially chosen for the job; they never changed. The Jews who worked there never took anything for themselves. Nor did they want to. For what could we do with money or jewellery? We could not buy anything. We had no

---

[15] A Jew named Sanio Ferber employed in one of the SS workshops in Lemberg testified after the war that 'Towards the end of December 1942 there came to our workshop once a young dentist whose name I do not recall.... He told us that he escaped from Bełżec.... This dentist was in Bełżec for three months. Because of his profession he was detailed to a dentist brigade, which numbered, if I remember correctly, fifteen men. Their job was to pull out gold teeth and bridges from corpses yanked out from the gas chambers.' What happened to this dentist afterwards is not known. (See Collection of Testimonies of Jewish Survivors, Żydowski Instytut Historyczny, Warsaw, file no. 4732.)

[16] See n. 18.

[17] Lublin was the headquarters of Aktion Reinhard, the operation consisting of the organized murder and plunder of the Jews in the specially designated murder camps of Bełżec, Sobibór, and Treblinka. In charge of Aktion Reinhard was Brigadeführer Odilo Globocnik, SS- und Polizeiführer for Lublin district. From 1 Aug. 1942 the responsibility for economic plunder was entrusted into the most capable hands of Christian Wirth (24 Nov. 1885 – 26 May 1944), *Kriminalrat* from the criminal police in Stuttgart, who became an inspector of SS garrisons in all three camps of Aktion Reinhard after relinquishing the post of first commandant of Bełżec. Part of his new job consisted in preparing for further use the mountains of clothing and personal items belonging to victims murdered in the Aktion Reinhard camps. The spoils were collected in hangars at a disused airport in Lublin, where 500 Jewish workers did the job of sorting, checking, and preparing items for dispatch. Money and precious metals were sent to Hitler's chancellery via Globocnik's headquarters. A final report of the financial gains of Aktion Reinhard was submitted to Himmler by Globocnik in 1944 for approval. It was approved.

hope of staying alive. No one believed in miracles. But although each worker was searched very thoroughly, it often happened that we trod on dollar bills which nobody had noticed. But we did not even try to pick them up. They served no useful purpose. One day a shoemaker took a five-dollar note. He did it deliberately and openly. He was shot together with his son. He went to his death quite obviously glad of the fact that soon he would leave all this behind him. Death was a certainty, anyway. There was no reason to prolong this agony ... In Bełżec dollars helped us to die an easier death ...

V

I was a member of the permanent death commando. We were 500 men all told. The 'professionals' accounted for half of the total, but even they were employed where no special skills were required, like digging pits and dragging corpses. We dug pits, enormous mass graves, and pulled bodies along. After they had done their own work, all the professionals had to take part in this job. We dug with spades, but there was also a machine which loaded sand, brought it to the surface, and emptied it beside the pits. There was a mountain of sand which we used to cover the pits when they were filled to overflowing. On average 450 people worked round the pits on a daily basis. What I found most horrible was that we were ordered to pile bodies to a height of about a metre above ground-level, and only then to cover them with sand. Thick, black blood ran from the mounds and covered the whole area like a sea. In order to get to the next empty grave we had to cross from one side of an already full pit to another. Ankle deep we waded through the blood of our brothers. We walked over mounds of bodies. And this was most dreadful, most horrible ...

We were supervised on this job by Schmidt,[18] a complete thug, who punched and kicked. If somebody was not working fast enough in his opinion, he ordered the man to lie on the ground to receive twenty-five lashes with a riding-crop. The poor fellow had to count the lashes. If he made a mistake, he was given fifty. The mangled victim had no chance of survival. He was hardly able to crawl back to the barracks, where he was usually found dead the next morning. The same thing went on several times a day.

No fewer than thirty or forty workers were shot each day. Usually it was a camp doctor who prepared a list of those too weak to work, but sometimes it was a *kapo* with the function of *Oberzugsführer* who submitted names of so-called criminals. At least thirty to forty men from the death commando were shot daily. They were

---

[18] Heni, or Christian, Schmidt was a *Volksdeutsch* from Latvia with the rank of *Zugwachtmann*. He was one of the former Soviet prisoners of war trained in the camp at Trawniki for service in the murder camps of Aktion Reinhard. These people were known to the Poles who lived in the vicinity of the camp as Ukrainian guards (prisoners of war of Ukrainian origin were in the majority), or *askers*. In German they were called either *Trawniki Männer* or *Hilfswillige*, *Hiwis* for short.

taken to the pits during the lunch break and shot. The death commando was supplemented daily by other men from the incoming transports. One of the jobs of the camp's administration was to keep records of all the workers of the death commando, both past and present, in order to make sure that the figure of 500 was always kept up. But there were no records concerning the number of transports or victims.[19] We knew, for example, that Jews built this camp and set the death machine in motion. Not one of those who worked on the original installations survived until my arrival there. It was a miracle if anyone survived for longer than five or six months at the most.

The gassing machine was serviced by two *askers*—always the same two murderers. When I came to Bełżec they were on the job, and they were still at it when I left. The Jewish workers had no contact with either of those two, or with any other *askers* for that matter.[20] When the people in the transports begged for a drop of water, the *askers* shot those Jewish workers who tried to bring some.

Besides digging graves the commando was also employed in emptying the gas chambers, piling the bodies on a ramp, and dragging them all the way to the pits. The ground was sandy. Two workers dragged one body. We had leather straps with metal braces, which we put round the hands of a corpse. Then we pulled, while the head of the dead man often dug deep into the sand . . . As regards small children, we were ordered to carry them in pairs on our backs. If we dragged the dead, we did not dig graves. When we dug graves we knew that thousands of our brothers were being murdered at the same time. And on those jobs we spent our days, from morning until night. Dusk signalled the end of a day. This 'work' was done only in full daylight.

At half past three in the morning an *asker-posten* [guard on duty] who kept watch of our barracks during the night would bang at the door shouting 'Auf! Heraus!' ['Up! Out!']. We were barely up when this thug Schmidt would burst in, chasing us outside with his riding-crop. We would run out, often barefoot, holding our shoes in our hands. We seldom undressed for the night. Often we also lay

---

[19] Reder is wrong. Bills of lading were delivered to the German station-master. They contained not personal names, but average numbers and the names of the localities where the *Judenzüge* (Jewish deportation trains) originated. Bełżec railway station was set on fire by a bomb dropped from a Soviet plane in 1944, and the documents did not survive. Documents from the other murder camps of Aktion Reinhard were destroyed on Himmler's specific orders after the termination of the murder operations, to obliterate all traces—written and material—of the massacre.

[20] Reder contradicts here his earlier and later testimonies. During an interrogation by Jan Sehn (see n. 13) he gave a list of four names of *askers* (Schmidt, Schneiner, Kunz, and Trottwein) and only three names of the members of the SS garrison (Irrmann, Schwarz, and Feix), which suggests that members of the Jewish death brigade had at least *some* contact with the Ukrainian guards and very limited contact with the Germans. This is confirmed by the fact that, during an interrogation in the office of a public prosecutor in Munich in Aug. 1960, Reder stated that he had never heard the names of Oberhauser, Fichtner, Floss, Hering, Schwarz, Dubois, Girtzig, Dachsel, Barbel, Groh (Groth), Kamm, Schluch, Zirke (Zierke), and Gley, although most of them had been members of the SS garrison in Bełżec murder camp. (The name of Schwarz crops up in Reder's booklet on numerous occasions.)

down in our shoes, since we rarely had enough time in the morning to put them on ... It was still dark when we were woken up. Schmidt would run through the barracks like a madman, slashing his riding-crop left and right. We got up as exhausted and desperate as we had been the night before. We were given one thin blanket, either to lie down on or to use as a cover. They always chose for us old and worn rags to dress in. If anyone so much as sighed, he was hit about the face. We were allowed a light on for half an hour in the evening; then it was switched off. An *Oberzugsführer* went round the barracks, whip in hand. He did not allow us to talk. We communicated in whispers with our neighbours.

The death commando consisted mostly of men who had seen their wives, children, and parents gassed. Many of us managed to smuggle a tallit and tefillin from the store. After our barracks had been secured for the night, a murmur of kaddish could be heard from the bunks. We prayed for our dead. Later there was silence. We were so benumbed that we never complained. Perhaps those fifteen *Zugsführers* still cherished some hope. We didn't.

We moved around like people without a will of their own: like one body. I remember some names, but not too many. It was of no importance in the camp who was who before, or what name he bore. I recall that one camp medic was a young doctor called Jakubowicz. He came from the vicinity of Rzeszów. I also knew a merchant and his son, both from Kraków. Their name was Schlüssl. Also a Czech Jew called Ellbogen. He said he had once owned a bicycle shop. There was also a Goldschmidt, once a well-known cook from the Brüder Hanicka restaurant in Carlsbad. No one was really interested in anyone else. We were just carrying on this dreadful existence mechanically.

We got our lunch at midday. At the first window we got a bowl, at the other a pint of watery soup with a potato thrown in if we were lucky. Before lunch and also before the evening meal we were forced to sing songs. At the same time we heard the moans of those who were being gassed, an orchestra played, and opposite the kitchen stood the gallows ...

VI

The SS men lived without women both in Bełżec and in the camp. Even their drinking parties took place in male company only. All the work in the camp was done by men alone. But this changed in October.[21] In that month a transport came from Zamość carrying Jewish women from Czechoslovakia. Among them were several dozen women whose husbands worked in the death commando. We decided to save some. Forty were assigned jobs in the kitchen, laundry, and tailor's shop. They were forbidden to communicate with their husbands. In the kitchen they peeled potatoes, washed up pots and pans, and carried water from a well. I do

---

[21] Between 16 and 19 Oct. three transports came to Bełżec from Zamość via the transit camp in Izbica carrying between 12,000 and 16,000 victims, the majority of whom were foreign Jews.

not know what happened to them. Presumably they went the same way as the others. These were educated women, belonging to the intelligentsia. They brought their personal possessions to Bełżec. Some even carried butter. They gave us all they had. They also helped those who worked either in the kitchen itself or in the vicinity. They lived in a small separate barracks supervised by a female *Zugsführer*. I often saw them talking (my job of stove-repairer gave me an opportunity to move around freely). They did not seem to have been as maltreated as we were. They finished their work at dusk and stood in pairs waiting for their portion of soup and coffee. Like us, they had kept their original clothing: no striped uniforms in Bełżec. I suppose it did not pay the Germans to introduce uniforms for a crew which was to stay alive for a very short period.

Straight from a transport, dressed in their own clothes and with their hair intact, these women were sent to workshops and the kitchen. Through the windows of their workplaces they could see the death convoys arriving daily . . .

VII

The camp heaved with mass murder. The days were full of mortal fear and death. But there were also cases of individual butchery. I saw some of those. There was no roll-call in Bełżec. Nor was it needed. Spectacles of horror were played out to a gallery without any special announcement. I must tell you about a transport from Zamość. It arrived some time about 15 November.[22] It was already cold. Snow and mud covered the ground. The transport from Zamość came in a snowstorm. It was one of many. It carried the entire Judenrat. When, in accordance with the usual procedure, the victims were all naked, the men driven to the gas chambers and the women into the barracks to have their hair shaved, the president of the Judenrat was ordered to stay back in the courtyard. Then, while they were driving everybody to their deaths, the SS men paraded round the man. No, I do not know his name. I saw a middle-aged man, deathly white and very still. The SS men ordered an orchestra to come to the courtyard and await further orders. The orchestra, composed of six musicians, was in its usual place on the path between the gas chambers and the pits. The musicians played on instruments which had belonged to the victims. I was working in the vicinity, doing some brickwork, and so I saw it all. The SS men ordered the orchestra to play 'Es geht alles vorüber, es geht alles vorbei' and 'Drei Lilien, kommt ein Reiter, gefahren, bringt die Lilien' ['Everything passes, everything goes by' and 'Three lilies, comes a rider bringing lilies']. And the orchestra played those tunes on violins, flutes, and an accordion. This went on for quite a while. Afterwards they ordered the man to stand against a wall and lashed him about the head and face with riding-crops tipped with lead

---

[22] The transport, which went via the transit camp in Izbica, carried 4,000 victims, among whom were the last Jews of Zamość.

until the blood ran. Irrmann participated in this savagery, and also that fat pig Schwarz,[23] and Schmidt and some *askers*. While he was being beaten, the victim was ordered to dance and jump to the rhythm of the music. After a few hours he was given a chunk of bread and beaten again in order to force him to eat it. Covered in blood he stood there, indifferent and solemn, without so much as a moan. For seven hours he was tortured. The SS men stood there laughing. 'Das ist eine höhere Person, Präsident des Judenrates' ['What a distinguished person, the president of the Judenrat'], they called in harsh voices. It was not until six o'clock in the evening that Schmidt drove the man to a pit, shot him in the head, and kicked the body onto a pile of other corpses.

There were other singular events. Soon after my arrival at Bełżec the Germans picked out from a transport (we did not always know the name of the locality a transport came from) several young men, including a young boy. He was the picture of youth, health, and strength. He also amazed us by his good humour. He looked round and asked almost playfully, 'Did anyone ever sneak out of here?' And that was that. He was overheard by some Germans. As a result this young boy, practically a child, was tortured to death. They stripped him naked and hung him upside-down on the gallows. He was there for three hours—and he was still alive. So they took him down, threw him onto the ground, and pushed sand down his throat with sticks. He died.

From time to time a transport larger than usual arrived. Instead of fifty cattle-trucks, there could be sixty or more. Not long before my escape one such transport arrived. The Germans calculated that they had to keep aside 100 men—already naked—to help with burying the murdered, who were too numerous for the death commando to manage in one day. They chose young boys only. Whipped and bludgeoned, the boys dragged corpses to the pits, naked in the snow and cold, without even a drop of water. In the evening Schmidt took them to the pits and shot them one by one with a pistol. He ran short of bullets for the last few, so he killed them with the handle of a pickaxe. I did not hear them moaning, but I saw them trying desperately to jump the death queue, tragic and helpless relics of youth and life.

VIII

The camp was under the constant surveillance of armed *askers* and several dozen SS men, but only a few were particularly active. Some of them stood out for their cruelty. They were real animals. Few murdered in cold blood. Others clearly enjoyed it. I saw their happy and contented faces at the sight of naked and wounded people driven to the gas chambers at bayonet point. They took evident

---

[23] SS Oberscharführer Gottfried Schwarz (3 May 1913 – 19 June 1944) held the post of deputy commandant of Bełżec from the end of 1941 until May 1943, when the camp was dismantled under his supervision. In 1943 he was promoted by Himmler to the rank of SS *Untersturmführer*.

pleasure in the sight of the resignation and despair of the young people, who were shadows of their former selves.

We knew that the nicest house next to the railway station in Bełżec was occupied by the commandant of the camp. He held the rank of *Obersturmführer*.[24] No matter how hard I try, I cannot remember his name. It was short. He did not come often to the camp, except on special occasions. He was tall and thick-set, over 40 years old, and with a boorish air—a real bully and a complete pig. One day the death-machine went out of order.[25] When he was informed, he came on horseback and ordered an immediate repair. He did not allow the gas chambers to be opened to let the people out: let them asphyxiate slowly and die in agony for a few hours longer. He crouched beside the engine, yelling and shaking with fury. Although he seldom came to the camp, for the other SS men he was a terror. He lived alone, attended by an *asker* who did all sorts of work and brought daily records from the camp.

Neither the commandant nor the other Gestapo had personal daily contact with the camp. They had their own canteen and a cook from Germany, who prepared meals for all the Germans. No family ever came on a visit. None of them lived with a woman. They kept large flocks of ducks and geese. People said that early in the summer they received whole baskets of cherries. Deliveries of wine and other alcohol arrived daily. I repaired an oven there once and saw two young Jewish women plucking geese. They threw me an onion and some beetroot. I also saw a village girl working there. There was no one else besides them, except orderlies. Every Sunday they took an orchestra from the camp and had a drinking orgy. The Gestapo drank and stuffed themselves like pigs. No one else was there. They threw scraps of food to the musicians. When the commandant visited the camp, I saw the Gestapo and *askers* shake with fear and apprehension.

Besides them, the Bełżec slaughterhouse was run and controlled by four other thugs. It is difficult to imagine anyone more depraved than those four criminals. The first was Franz Irrmann. About 30 years old, with the rank of *Stabscharführer*, he was responsible for the camp's supplies.[26] His little sideline was shooting old people and small children. He performed his murderous tasks coolly. Not talkative, he liked to give the impression of inscrutability. Every day he reassured people

---

[24] Neither the first nor the second commandant of the camp held the rank of *Obersturmführer*. Christian Wirth (see n. 15) was responsible for the construction of Bełżec; he held the rank of SS *Sturmbannführer* after promotion by Himmler in 1943. From 1 Aug. 1942 he was replaced by Gottlieb Hering (2 June 1887 – 9 Oct. 1945), *Kriminalkommissar* in the criminal police in Stuttgart, promoted to the rank of SS *Hauptsturmführer* by Himmler in 1943. The description by Reder fits both Wirth and Hering. Both were known and feared for their extreme brutality.

[25] As is known from other sources, the gassing engine broke down on numerous occasions. One such breakdown occurred in the middle of Aug. 1942 during the 'show' gassing witnessed by Kurt Gerstein and Wilhelm Pfannenstiel, two SS experts on disinfection (see n. 1). The breakdown, timed by Gerstein, lasted for over two hours, with the victims locked inside.

[26] Not SS *Stabscharführer* but SS *Hauptscharführer*; see n. 5.

about to be murdered that they were going to work, having bathed first. A conscientious murderer.

An altogether different sort of murderer was Oberscharführer Reinhold Feix.[27] It was said that he came from Gablonz, on the Nissa, and was married and the father of two children. He spoke like an educated man, but fast. If someone failed to get his meaning first time, he punched and yelled like mad. One day he ordered the repainting of a kitchen. The person doing the job was a Jew with a degree in chemistry. He was high up a ladder when Feix came in. Every few minutes he ordered him to come down and beat him about the face with a riding-crop until the man was covered with blood and swollen all over. This is how Reinhold did his work. He gave the impression of being abnormal. Feix played the violin and ordered the orchestra to pay endlessly the tune 'Góralu czy ci nie żal?' ('Mountaineer, do you not feel sad? [that you have to leave your own land]'), forcing people to dance and sing while he laughed and beat them. A mad dog.

I do not know which of them was more diabolical and cruel: Feix or the fat, squat, dark-haired Schwarz.[28] He came from somewhere deep in Germany. He took care that the *askers* did not show us any sympathy. He also supervised us when we were digging pits. Whipping and yelling he drove us to the gas chambers, where piles of bodies awaited their final journey to the mass graves. Once he had driven us to the gas chambers, he ran back to the pits again. There, staring blankly into the depths, with a lunatic gaze in their eyes, stood old people, children and the sick, all waiting to be shot. They had been given plenty of time to see the corpses, to breathe the smell of blood and putrefaction, before they were shot by Irrmann. Schwarz beat everyone constantly. He did not allow anyone to protect his face against the blows. 'Hände ab' ['Take your hands away'], he yelled. Tormenting was his pleasure and joy.

Even more beastly was a young *Volksdeutsch* called Heni Schmidt.[29] Probably a Latvian, Schmidt spoke German with a strange accent. He pronounced 's' as 't' (not 'was' but 'wat'). With *askers* he spoke Russian. He was in the camp every day. Agile, thin, and quick—looking like a real cut-throat and constantly drunk—Schmidt rushed around the camp from four o'clock in the morning until night. He beat whomever he could find with evident pleasure. 'This one is the worst,' we whispered among ourselves, adding immediately: 'They are all equally bestial.' Schmidt always turned up where harassment was at its worst. He never missed an opportunity to see victims being driven to the gas chambers. He stood there listening to the terrible piercing cries of women being gassed. He was the real soul of the camp, bloodthirsty, monstrous, and degenerate. It gave him real pleasure to observe the expressionless features of the death commando returning exhausted

---

[27] SS Scharführer (not Oberscharführer) Reinhold Feix (3 July 1909 – 30 May 1969) was a supervisor of the Jewish death brigade (those who emptied gas chambers, dragged bodies, and dug pits). Reder spelt his name wrongly as 'Faix'.

[28] See n. 23.   [29] See n. 18.

to the barracks at night. On the way back each one of us received a blow on the head from his riding-crop. If anyone tried to evade it Schmidt would run after him.

There were also others—perhaps less memorable, but they were all inhuman monsters. Not for a moment did any of them show any human feelings. They tormented and tortured thousands of people from morning until night. At dusk they went back to their little houses by the railway station in Bełżec. During the night the camp was guarded by the *askers*, who manned the machine-guns. During the day it was the Gestapo who 'welcomed' the death transports.

The biggest event for those thugs was Himmler's visit. It took place some time towards the middle of October.[30] That day we knew that something unusual was afoot. There was an air of secrecy all around. Everything was done with great speed. Even the process of murder took a much shorter time that day. Irrmann announced that because 'Es kommt eine höhere Person, Ordnung muss sein' ['A distinguished guest is coming; everything must be in order']. He did not elaborate, but we all knew from the whispered exchanges of the *askers*.

About three o'clock in the afternoon Himmler arrived, escorted by Generalmajor Katzman (the butcher of Lemberg and eastern Galicia), an aide-de-camp, and ten Gestapo. Irrmann and others conducted him to the gas chambers just in time for him to see corpses falling out: a terrible pile of bodies of very young people, small children, and babies. The Jewish death commando dragged the corpses along while Himmler stood there watching. He stayed and watched for half an hour and then left the camp. I saw how pleased and uplifted the Gestapo felt. I saw their joy and I heard them laughing. I also heard them talking of promotions.

IX

Words are inadequate to describe our state of mind and what we felt when we heard the terrible moans of those people and the cries of the children being murdered. Three times a day we saw people going nearly mad. Nor were we far from madness either. How we survived from one day to the next I cannot say, for we had no illusions. Little by little we too were dying, together with those thousands of people who, for a short while, went through an agony of hope. Apathetic and resigned to our fate, we felt neither hunger nor cold. We all waited our turn to die an inhuman death. Only when we heard the heart-rending cries of small children—'Mummy, mummy, but I have been a good boy' and 'Dark, dark'—did we feel something. And then nothing again.

---

[30] According to Yitzhak Arad (*Belzec, Sobibor, Treblinka: The Operation Reinhard Death Camps* (Bloomington, Ind., 1987), 165–9), Himmler never went to Bełżec but visited Sobibór and Treblinka in 1943. However, according to the post-war testimonies of Polish inhabitants of Bełżec and Tomaszów Lubelski, Himmler visited Bełżec twice: once in Aug. then in Oct. or Nov. 1942.

I had been in this nightmare for nearly four months[31] when, towards the end of November, Irrmann told me that the camp would need metal sheets, and a lot of them. I was swollen and blue all over. Pus ran from open wounds. Schmidt bludgeoned me about the face with a truncheon. With an ironic smile Irrmann told me that I would go to Lemberg under escort to fetch the sheets, adding 'Sollst nicht durchgehen' ['Don't try to escape']. Off I went in a lorry with one guard and four Gestapo. After loading the whole day, I stayed in the lorry guarded by one of the thugs, while the others went away looking for fun. I sat there for a few hours without moving or thinking. Then, quite by chance, I noticed that my guard was asleep and snoring. Instinctively and without a thought, I slipped down from the lorry and stood on the pavement pretending to adjust the load. Then I slowly backed away. Legionowa Street was full of people. There was a blackout. I pushed my cap down lower and no one noticed me. I remembered the address of my Polish housekeeper and went straight to her flat. She hid me. It took twenty months for the physical injuries to heal. But what of the mental wounds? I was haunted by images of past horror, hearing the moans of the murdered and the children crying, and the throb of a running engine. Nor could I wipe from my memory the faces of those German thugs. And in such a state of continuous nightmare I survived until the liberation.

When the Red Army expelled the Germans from Lemberg and I was finally able to come out of hiding without fear, to breathe fresh air and to begin to feel and think again, I was seized by a desire to go back to this place where two and a half million of our people met their terrible death.[32] I went there soon and spoke at length with the locals. They told me that in 1943 a much smaller number of transports came to the camp.[33] The murder centre for the Jews moved further west, to the gas chambers of Auschwitz. In 1944 the Germans opened up the pits and burned the bodies with petrol.[34] Dark, heavy smoke rising from the enormous open-air pyres hung over an area of several dozen square miles. The wind carried the stench still further, for many long days, nights, and weeks.

And later, the locals told me, the Germans pounded the remaining bones to

---

[31] Reder was brought to the camp on either 18 or 19 Aug. 1942. He escaped towards the end of Nov. that year, which makes it a little over three months—not four months, as he wrote earlier.

[32] The figure given by Reder is a gross overestimate. Post-war estimates by Polish railway workers from Bełżec give a figure of about 1 million. Polish commissions investigating Nazi crimes cut this figure by half. Arad (*Belzec, Sobibor, Treblinka*) estimates *c.*518,000 victims. My own estimate comes close to Arad's: *c.*520,000 (see n. 12). Latest estimates based on digs carried out on the site of the camp during 1997–8 raise the figure to 550,000 and even 650,000.

[33] No transports arrived at the camp after 11 Dec. 1942, but it is quite possible that Jews caught during the so-called *Judenjagd* (Jew hunt) were brought to the camp and shot there.

[34] The opening of pits and burning of bodies began immediately after the transports stopped. The burning continued for three months. By May 1943 the camp had been dismantled, the buildings taken down, and the ground levelled and planted with young conifers. Members of the Jewish brigade were loaded onto a train, which took them straight to Sobibór, where they were murdered on arrival after refusing to disembark.

powder, which the wind blew away over the fields and forests. The machine for pounding the bones had been put together by someone named Spilke, a prisoner from Janowska camp brought to Bełżec for the purpose. He told me that he found nothing in the camp except mounds of bones. All the buildings had already gone. (Spilke managed to escape, and survived the war. He now lives in Hungary. He told me all this in Lemberg, where we met after the liberation.) When the production of 'artificial fertilizer' from human bones came to a halt, the open pits were filled with soil and the blood-soaked earth scrupulously levelled. The German murderers covered this graveyard for millions of murdered Jews with fresh greenery.

I said goodbye to my informants and went along the familiar siding. The railway line was gone. Through a field I reached a young and sweet-smelling pine forest. It was very still. In the middle of it was a large, sunny clearing . . .

The Auschwitz-Birkenau Memorial and Museum: From Commemoration to Education

TERESA ŚWIEBOCKA

THE Nazi death camp Auschwitz is one of the most well known sites of genocide in human history and the largest cemetery in the world. In this place, from 1940 to 1945, the Nazis murdered between 1.1 and 1.5 million people, primarily Jews, from all over occupied Europe, as well as Poles, Gypsies, Soviet prisoners of war, and people of other nationalities. Never before in human history, in such a short time and in such a small area, were so many people murdered in such a planned and bureaucratic way.

More than fifty-nine years have passed since the arrival of the first prisoners at Auschwitz and almost fifty-four since its liberation. As the years have passed, interest in what happened there has not diminished; on the contrary it has increased. Nowadays it is obvious that when we look at the camp we do so on several levels.

The first is the history of the camp *sensu stricto*. The liberation of the camp did not close its history. Events that took place at Auschwitz still have a huge influence not only on survivors, but also on the following generations, on the lives of many individuals as well as on whole nations, even on international relations and policy. Some questions have never received a full and rational explanation. Historians, theologians, psychologists, sociologists, and jurists, and also doctors and scholars of other disciplines, try to understand and explain the origin and functioning of the camp, and human behaviour within it, and to evaluate the impact of the Holocaust on present generations. Even now new sources are still being discovered, such as the large collection of documents that had been kept in Moscow. New questions are raised and old data verified, for example those relating to the number of deportees and victims.

Some people believe that what happened in Auschwitz cannot be understood, no matter how many books we read, or how many survivors we listen to. We cannot understand the Auschwitz experience, because nothing in human history gives us reference-points to guide our imaginations. Auschwitz is inconceivable: it is beyond our cognitive capability. Although we try to learn and teach the meaning of this horrifying event, for all those who have not been there it will always remain an abstract concept, a metaphor for the ultimate evil. With all this in mind, we have, however, to continue to do research, because it is the best way to commemorate the victims, to return to them their identity, their names and biographies, and to prepare materials for the future, for education.

The second level is the symbolic meaning of Auschwitz. Auschwitz is a symbol even to those unfamiliar with the details of its history, who did not lose anybody there, who do not know what is preserved on the site, or who—for whatever reason—do not intend to study the topic or to go there.

The history of the camp was very complicated and changed at various stages of its existence, so that Auschwitz has become a symbol that holds different meanings for different people. It serves as such both in an intellectual and in an emotional sense. Its symbolic meaning started during the war, is still relevant today, and will certainly remain in the future.

For Jews, who constituted 90 per cent of the victims of Auschwitz, the camp has become the symbol of the Holocaust. Why Auschwitz, and not other camps like Bełżec or Sobibór? There are many reasons, among them the hugeness of the camp, the number of victims, and the fact that it was the place where many Jews from western Europe died. Another important factor is that a relatively large number of prisoners, including well-known writers and scholars, survived the camp and reached the Western world, where, with other Holocaust survivors, they could speak freely of it after the war.

But Auschwitz has symbolic meaning not only for Jews. For Poles it is a symbol too, but with a different meaning. It is a symbol of the Nazi occupation of their country, terror, slave labour, and the systematic destruction of intellectuals, culture, and resistance. Its life as such a symbol started during the war. The camp was established in 1940, almost two years before the first mass deportations of Jews to Auschwitz, and the killings in the gas chambers. The Nazis sent to the camp about 140,000 to 150,000 Poles, primarily political prisoners and members of the resistance, including prominent figures in cultural, scientific, political, and social life. Unlike the Jewish people, who were deported to the camp with their entire families and were mostly killed immediately on arrival, Poles on the whole were sent to Auschwitz individually. This means that relatives or friends and neighbours knew everything. Poles who were camp inmates could send them illegal or sometimes official letters. More than half, at least 75,000, died in the camp. They were usually registered prisoners, so the commandant's office would send their families official telegrams informing them of their death. Such events were spread across the Polish population, and during the war hundreds of thousands of people from Polish towns and villages knew somebody who was sent to Auschwitz or who lost a family member in the camp.

Later, when the camp atrocities in Nazi-occupied Poland became widely known, Auschwitz became a symbol of the evil that can be done by men acting, within a totalitarian system, out of racism, antisemitism, and the will to dominate—a symbol of man's inhumanity to man. Auschwitz became proof of the destructive, barbaric potential inherent in civilized society, in human nature. It is not by chance that mankind sees Auschwitz today as a symbol of the worst that can happen. There are people who call that epoch the age of Auschwitz. It became a codeword for the downfall of human culture, human thought, human behaviour, and human relations during that particular period.

Auschwitz also has significance for other people, such as Gypsies, who, like the Jews, but not on such a scale, were deported there and killed in accordance with the racist principles of Nazi ideology. We should also remember the meaning of Auschwitz for other groups, such as Soviet prisoners of war and even minorities such as the Jehovah's Witnesses and homosexuals who were deported there. It also has a very specific meaning for Germans.

So Auschwitz is a place in which different symbols and different memories support different national identities and histories. It sometimes leads to all kinds of conflict and misunderstanding, resulting from the complexity of the issue. That is why, in order to avoid new misunderstandings and prejudices, it is so important to learn, to give people appropriate knowledge about the place and its meaning to the world.

But Auschwitz is also a real, physical place, where hundreds of thousands of visitors from almost all countries of the world go every year. Not everything has survived on the site. As the Germans retreated on the eastern front, the SS began to obliterate the traces of their crimes in the camp. Some buildings were dismantled, others (notably the gas chambers and crematoria) were blown up, documents were burnt, and storehouses containing victims' belongings were set on fire. Nevertheless, they did not manage to destroy everything. Many buildings and objects, records and personal effects, survived almost intact.

In 1945, a few months after the liberation of the camp and the end of the war, a group of Polish former political prisoners who had managed to survive began to spread the idea of commemorating the victims of Auschwitz. It was on their motion that the Sejm passed a bill to preserve the grounds and buildings of the former camp as a memorial to the international martyrdom of nations.

Two parts of the Auschwitz complex were incorporated into the State Museum established for this purpose. They were the main camp in Oświęcim, the so-called Auschwitz I, and the Birkenau camp in Brzezinka (Auschwitz II). The third part of the camp, together with subcamps, was destroyed. Throughout the grounds the Polish people have placed memorial plaques and monuments.

The museum covers about 200 hectares. It includes 150 buildings of the former camp and the ruins of nearly 300 more, destroyed in the last period of the camp's existence or during and after liberation; kilometres of barbed-wire fencing around both camps; dozens of SS watchtowers; the special railway siding and unloading ramp where SS doctors carried out selections among Jewish arrivals; and the main gates leading to the camps. Buildings containing gas chambers and crematoria were partly destroyed by the SS (except one that was burnt down during the unique armed revolt organized by Jewish prisoners in 1944). But parts of such buildings survived, such as the walls of the basement of the gas chambers, together with the remnants of rooms where Jews had to undress before death.

The barracks that were saved contained remains of the belongings of the murdered, such as, for example, suitcases—sometimes with the names and addresses of the victims, shoes, spectacles, Jewish prayer-shawls, artificial limbs, even human hair, used as a raw material by German factories. All these items are essential museum exhibits and are for the most part held in the blocks of the former camp where exhibitions concerning the history of Auschwitz are located.

In the museum's collection are thousands of Nazi documents, material concerning the resistance, photographs, and works of art made illegally by the prisoners in the camp or after liberation. The museum has post-war accounts and memoirs by ex-prisoners and also depositions from the trials of Nazis conducted in various countries after the war. The collection also includes original documents and photographs hidden by prisoners during the war and discovered after liberation. All of these materials are available to scholars and students who come to the Auschwitz museum from many countries. They are also used for the museum's own educational purposes. The site, together with original buildings, relics, and documents, is the best tool for education.

The great majority of those who began to create the museum in 1947 were former prisoners of Auschwitz and other camps. Their work was pioneering. They had no models and no points of reference. They recognized intuitively that it was their duty and responsibility to protect all remaining traces of these crimes so as to preserve not only the buildings but also the memory of Auschwitz and to pass this on to future generations. Unlike most monuments in the world, Auschwitz was never intended to last. Almost everything was poorly made—the barracks, the camp uniforms, the paper used for documents. Many buildings were erected by the Nazis only for temporary purposes. The museum has to preserve even ruins, and it is a continuing, very difficult, and expensive process to halt time and to save the site with all its objects.

Such work demands a lot of money. For forty-five years maintenance and conservation costs were borne exclusively by the Polish Ministry of Art and Culture. In 1979 the museum was added to the Unesco world cultural heritage list. But the only government that committed itself to maintaining this 'tragic heritage' was still that of Poland, a country that had nothing to do with the establishment of the camp and whose citizens had been its first victims.

Then the situation changed considerably. Thanks to the activity of the Ronald Lauder Foundation the problem of maintenance became an international one.

Lauder sent to Auschwitz a special commission of conservationists to analyse the needs of the museum and to get international help, enabling more complicated and comprehensive work to be carried out.

But preservation is only a part of the problem. It is also important to decide what the place is supposed to be. Is it a memorial, a museum, a cemetery, or a place of education? Or is it all of these?

The museum tries to be diverse in its activities. It conserves and safeguards the relics and the former camp buildings; it collects, describes, and presents documents and other historical items; and it collects works of art that relate to Auschwitz. Over 200 people are employed in different departments of the museum, in the archive, the museum collections, the conservation department, the library, the historical and educational departments, the publishing house, administrative departments, and elsewhere. The museum conducts research, organizes exhibitions in Poland and abroad, and issues its own publications. In the archive there is a special section providing written information on prisoners based on surviving documents.

The museum has often been criticized. Sometimes these criticisms have not been directly connected with its activities, but they have nevertheless influenced public opinion (for example, the controversy over the Carmelite convent or the so-called supermarket). Some criticisms have arisen out of the differing expectations of the different kinds of visitor. Many people, before they arrive at the museum, have read a great deal about Auschwitz and have their own picture of the camp. Some come to commemorate lost families, to pay homage to the victims, or to pray; others want to learn, first of all, and to understand why it happened; some want to listen to guides; others want to be alone, in complete silence. Today the vast majority of visitors are from recent generations, for whom Auschwitz belongs to the history of fifty years ago, almost as remote as the Middle Ages. Also, the number of foreign visitors is constantly increasing, including those who know neither the facts of the Nazi occupation nor its reality.

The present exhibition, which was created in 1955, has therefore often been criticized partly for its lack of information, but primarily because it failed to distinguish the nationalities of the victims or to explain Auschwitz in relation to the plans for the total extermination of Jewry. In other words, it did not point up the predominant place of the Jews among the victims of Auschwitz. (Nobody can argue that Jews were not mentioned, but the scale did not correspond to their number and suffering.) Criticism came also from Polish visitors, complaining that the exhibition did not show that the camp was originally created for Poles, who among non-Jewish victims suffered the greatest losses.

In a new atmosphere the museum is considering many changes to bring Auschwitz into the twenty-first century. The most tragic paradox is that, instead of bringing people together, Auschwitz sometimes leads to misunderstanding. It is hoped that in the future an atmosphere can be created to cope with such situations in a better way and to avoid misleading interpretations. The memorial of Auschwitz-Birkenau must respond to the needs and sensitivities of different groups, which may complement one another or may conflict. Whatever is done must therefore be done with sensitivity and understanding, and with total and unmitigated dignity, in order not to transgress the sanctity of the place.

How can this be achieved? Only with help from experts from all over the world, because, although it is on Polish territory, Auschwitz has such enormous importance in and for the history of mankind that it belongs to the whole world. In an effort to answer this need, in 1990 the Polish Ministry of Art and Culture set up the International Council of the museum. It consists of many distinguished personalities: historians, theologians, and ex-prisoners, as well as specialists from various other Holocaust memorials (for example, Yad Vashem and the US Holocaust Memorial Museum in Washington). It is the task of the members of the council to give their opinions on the museum's most important projects. They are consulted on the museum's plans, and, although the council is a consultative body, its opinions are always important to the museum, which has benefited from its aid on numerous occasions.

The first important issue that the council had to resolve was the content of the texts on the international Monument to the Victims situated at the end of the unloading ramp between the ruins of the gas chambers and crematoria in Birkenau. The decision to remove the previous text was taken by the Polish Ministry of Art and Culture because of a change in the estimate of the number of victims of the camp. The opportunity to consult a wide range of specialists is essential to the proper functioning of the museum, and the work of the International Council provides such an opportunity.

Over the 1990s many improvements were introduced in the old main exhibition. Some captions were enlarged; new panels with information on the nature of the Holocaust and the specific nationalities of the victims were added. Because of the central importance of Birkenau in the Auschwitz complex, that is where the museum started work connected to the new methods of commemoration and explanation.

Anyone who first visited Birkenau in the 1970s and who returns today will be struck by enormous changes in its appearance. At great expense and with much hard work everything has been tidied up. The buildings have been preserved and the whole area has been mapped and memorialized. The designers of the new presentation of Birkenau have incorporated two basic functions into the new system: commemoration and information. Artists have devised a system of profoundly symbolic signs consisting of granite blocks in the form of black slabs that serve as mini-monuments referring to the traditional slabs that cover graves. On these, information is displayed on plates bearing text, maps, or photographs. They are located at strategic points throughout the camp, beginning at the entrance gates and ending at the places of execution. On these slabs three kinds of information are displayed:

1. textual information concerning the history of a given place;
2. plans of buildings and sections of Birkenau camp, with places remembered for specific events marked;
3. printed photographs taken during the camp's existence.

On the plates set up near the ramp and the ruins of the gas chambers there are scenes connected with the arrival of Jewish transports, selection for the gas chambers, and the road to death. These scenes make it easier to grasp the mass character of the crime committed in Birkenau. Other photographs show the faces of Jewish men, women, and children, so that we can identify with them and see, not the abstract numbers of victims, but the real people. All such plates are discreetly displayed. This discretion, which was the principal aim of the designers, is to prevent artificial signs and symbols from concealing the reality of the site, to avoid disturbing the silence and uniqueness of this area. Its commemorative function is also fulfilled by marking the spots where there are still human ashes. Here stone plaques have been placed bearing inscriptions in English, Hebrew, Yiddish, and Polish, calling for commemoration, homage, and prayer.

The new system of commemorative and informative signs in Birkenau brings visitors closer to the vastness of the site and satisfies the varying needs of people coming from different parts of the world who, alone or in small groups, wish to encounter and contemplate the place without a guide. A similar system is being prepared for Auschwitz I and the areas between the two sites.

Every year the Auschwitz-Birkenau memorial and museum is visited by hundreds of thousands of people of various ages and nationalities. From 1946 to 1997 the museum was visited by a total of nearly 24 million people, 18 million from Poland and 6 million from abroad. Young people constitute a large proportion of the visitors and their share in the total number of visitors is constantly increasing: from 1960 to 1965 they accounted for 15 per cent, in the following five years for 20 per cent, and in the 1990s for 50 per cent. Amongst Polish visitors the proportion who are of school age is even higher. For example:

in 1995 of 560,000 visitors, 290,000 were from Poland, including 210,000 school students;

in 1996 of 520,000 visitors, 290,000 were from Poland, including 203,000 school students;

in 1997 of 505,000 visitors, 266,000 were from Poland, including 200,000 school students.

School visits to Auschwitz were most commonly organized in order to deepen students' knowledge of the Second World War.

From the very beginning of the museum's existence there have been educational activities addressed to the future, to guide young people so that the tragic past of Auschwitz should not be repeated. The museum co-operates in various ways with teachers and students, arranging conferences for teachers, academic seminars, museum lessons, lectures, frequent surveys and questionnaires in various types of school, temporary and travelling exhibitions, film shows, painting sessions, and competitions. Some of these activities are very widespread and reach thousands of people; for example, between 1947 and 1997 the museum organized 100 temporary exhibitions on its own grounds and 200 travelling exhibitions outside Poland, in England, Belgium, the former Czechoslovakia, Germany, Hungary, Italy, Israel, Japan, the Netherlands, the United States, and other countries. Approximately 15 million people visited them. In the same period 5,657 lectures were delivered to a total audience of 565,000 at the museum itself, in Poland, and abroad.

Students encounter the subjects of Nazism and the Second World War mainly in history and Polish language and literature, but the Holocaust was never treated separately in Polish textbooks until Andrzej Garlicki's book *Historia 1939–1997/ 98: Polska i świat* appeared in 1997. There is no special Holocaust department in any Polish university. Many Polish teachers have tried to focus on the subject in their lessons, but they have had great difficulty in communicating the tragedy of it, in translating the unimaginable into a language and images that can be understood by young people. The Auschwitz museum has always tried to help them, and museum guides concentrate on presenting the place, original objects, and selected events from its history. But a single visit to the memorial site is not enough, and it is crucial to prepare students before a visit and to summarize it later.

In order to create special studies on the Holocaust, in 1997 an agreement was signed between the museum and the Pedagogical College in Kraków, as a result of which a two-term postgraduate course for humanities teachers began at the museum in February 1998 entitled 'Totalitarianism, Nazism, the Holocaust'. The course aroused enormous interest on the part of teachers, who felt that it filled a gap in their preparation for these subjects in their lessons at school.

The museum has also prepared a list of suggested reading for Polish teachers and students from amongst the books it has published or co-operated in publishing. They contain more than forty publications, among them the reminiscences of Jewish and Polish survivors and historical works.

The museum also tries to encourage more Polish historians and students to do research and write books and articles on the history of the camp. It also organized a competition amongst Polish universities and teacher training colleges for the best master's thesis related to the history of the Auschwitz concentration and death camp, in particular the deportations to Auschwitz of residents of a given region, and the fate of those deported. The deadline for the competition was June 1999.

In 1997 the museum's education section prepared and conducted many film symposia and seminars within its educational programme. History and Polish-language teachers, senior instructors from the Polish Scouting Association, Catholic Church and lay catechists, German pastors, and Israeli youth leaders participated in specialized tours of the grounds of the former camp. They attended talks on the history of Auschwitz, viewed films on the Second World War, and were given information packs of historical and methodological materials developed by museum staff and intended to prepare schoolchildren for visits to the former camp. Museum staff and students taking part in international study tours organized among others by the Beth Shalom Holocaust Education Centre and the International Youth Meeting House in Oświęcim heard education section staff speak on the symbolism of the Auschwitz museum and memorial, on research opportunities at the museum, and its educational role.

The majority of works published in Poland on the history of Auschwitz are written by historians from the Auschwitz museum and are published in Oświęcim by the museum's own publishing house. Since 1956 it has produced more than 400 publications, including historical works, prisoners' reminiscences, accounts by SS officers, manuscripts and reports written illegally by prisoners in the camp or after their escape, albums, guidebooks, videos, posters, slides, and photographs. The museum also publishes a series of periodicals entitled Zeszyty Oświęcimskie. This chiefly consists of historical works analysing aspects of the history of the camp. Over the 1990s the museum also issued a few especially notable publications, including Danuta Czech's *Auschwitz Chronicle*—1,000 pages giving a day-by-day account of virtually all deportations to Auschwitz and events from the camp's life, correlated with the German political and military situation at that time; and *Auschwitz, 1940–1945: Central Issues of the Camp History*, a set of historical studies on the creation and functioning of the camp from various aspects, including 1,400 pages in five volumes containing documentary material, bibliographies, and indexes. Its English edition is in preparation.

If we want to make the reality of the Holocaust more comprehensible to new generations, we need new exhibitions on the site of the camp and a new, improved educational programme. To that end the museum has set up an educational centre to co-ordinate and intensify various kinds of educational activity. Auschwitz as a historical fact should be a moral lesson to the world. It should shape the attitudes of the young generation, and teach tolerance and mutual understanding between people of different races, faiths, and ethnic and national origins.

Can Auschwitz, can a Holocaust, happen again? Many people think that it can, and that is why it has become a moral imperative to ensure that post-Auschwitz generations are told the facts of the most terrible crime in the history of humanity. Together with teachers we must try to disseminate methods of resisting and combating racial hatred, xenophobia, prejudice, and stereotypes. Young people should know that Auschwitz was the creation of ordinary people, often like us—that under certain conditions people will follow immoral orders and inhuman goals, and will acquiesce in insane ideologies.

PART II

A Debate about Antisemitism in Poland Today

Black is Black

STANISŁAW MUSIAŁ

AT the beginning of the 1880s in Berlin the Revd Adolf Stoecker—the emperor's court preacher, an activist in the Christian social movement and a well-known personality in German Protestantism of the time—thundered in one of his sermons: 'We will not rest . . . until our German nation . . . rises up to cast off Jewish rule. My German country, Christian nation, I admonish you, wake up!' The record of Stoecker's sermon shows that the preacher's call for national reawakening was received with 'unceasing and stormy applause'. Today we know that demons were awakened in Germany and in Europe, in part because of Catholic and Protestant preachers such as the Revd Stoecker. This reawakening of hatred was paid for with the lives of 6 million Jews, the number of victims who fell to Nazi antisemitism.

A NEW TABOO?

On Sunday 26 October 1997 the parish priest at St Brygida's church in Gdańsk, Prelate Henryk Jankowski, stated: 'A Jewish minority in the Polish government cannot be tolerated, because the nation is afraid of it.' This was not his first antisemitic statement: he had already apologized for others in a letter to his bishop dated 4 July 1995.

The case of the Revd Jankowski soon reached beyond the borders of Poland, for Gdańsk was apparently already too small for him. Press agencies quoted Jankowski's comment, made on 5 November [1997] in Rome, the capital of Western Christendom: 'What the Polish nation thinks, I have said out loud. Not by accident, but with conviction.'

There is every sign that in the West interest in the Jankowski affair is not only undiminished but is growing. Sadly, added to the list of names and events in recent history through which Poland is perceived is 'the Polish prelate from Gdańsk' (some have problems even saying his name) because of his antisemitic proclamations. If the Revd Jankowski, however, should think that the interest of the world media starts and ends with him, so that he has become a genuine celebrity, I must disappoint him. Antisemitic statements, by themselves, belong to

This article was first published in *Tygodnik Powszechny*, 16 Nov. 1997.

the genre of the ideological bore (a bore that is, of course, extremely dangerous). By their nature, they are intellectually impoverished and worn out from over-use, like all other fanatical views.

Why then is the international media so interested in the Revd Jankowski's case? At this point what interests world opinion is not these or others of Jankowski's antisemitic views and statements, but the question of *how the Poles react* to them. To the world, that is what is important and interesting. And we cannot hold this against the world, especially the Western media: they have a legitimate right to their interest. Poland wants to join the family of European nations, and for the west European nations it is a matter of concern with whom they associate. They have many problems, but the problem of antisemitism does not appear in such acute form. These countries know from their own experience the social disease called 'antisemitism'. Some of them have paid a heavy price for it. At their safe, rich table, do they need a sick partner?

How, then do Poles react to the Revd Jankowski's antisemitic statements? How do they respond to this problem?

If in any Western country a cleric, a Catholic priest as well known as the Revd Jankowski (he owes this fame, I think, to his fidelity to Solidarity at a time when few dared show it publicly), presented such antisemitic opinions, I think many people of good will would protest in the streets. Here it is still impossible. Though in our society sensitivity and solidarity seem to be awakening today, they express themselves in only one context: where an exceptionally hideous murder has been committed. I think that in our country it will be a long time before antisemitic excesses or statements will get people moving. After all that happened in our land at the hands of the Nazis, there is still no social awareness that antisemitism is deadly by its nature, and in every form, even if often not directly or immediately. In this regard our past is taking its toll: not long ago the subject of antisemitism was taboo, and to be a patriot meant, in the interpretation of the ruling Communist Party, to be anti-Zionist (which in practice equalled being an antisemite).

How can we be surprised that Poles do not perceive antisemitism as a dangerous evil if, in the case of Jankowski, all bodies influencing public opinion, and all moral authorities, have completely failed? By such bodies and authorities I mean politicians, intellectuals, and, unfortunately, the Church.

THE IGNOMINY OF SILENCE

Politicians appear uninterested in the Revd Jankowski. Certainly his case does not prevent them from sleeping well. Their hands are full: the new Sejm, the new senate, the new government, the new provincial governors and their deputies . . . A history lesson would be timely. That in the twentieth century young European democracies fell because they had not paid attention to the spread of fascism is, to the minds of new politicians, as strange and remote as Napoleon's wars.

Particularly surprising is the passivity of the political forces born in Gdańsk. They seem not to register that the symbolism of Gdańsk is slowly changing in the mind of the world: from the city that launched the liberation of Poland and eastern Europe from the communist yoke to the capital of Polish antisemitism or even European antisemitism. The passivity of Gdańsk's citizens is also strange; apparently 1945 marks a complete break in their cultivation of the city's thousand-year-old great traditions.

As for those we call intellectuals, they too have been seized by a great impotence. Yes, antisemitic statements by the Revd Jankowski are received with indignation, but this is a far cry from the power intellectuals once demonstrated in this arena—recall the good old days when *Tygodnik Powszechny* signed some public protest almost every week, ignoring threats from the secret police. Apparently, intellectuals take fright at the sight of a cassock. Of course, it would be quite wrong if they considered the Jankowski affair an 'internal' concern of the Church: they would be severely mistaken. The Jankowski case casts shame on Poland, on every Polish man and woman, both religious and atheist. It shames us in the eyes of the world; but, even more importantly, it brutalizes us.

How does the Church respond to the case of the Revd Jankowski? Frankly, I would gladly leave this question to future historians, who will examine the matter in detail. For how can one write about the bishops' reaction—and it is necessary to write about it—and not offend some of our clergy? Yet Jesus admonished us: 'Simply let your "yes" be "yes", and your "no", "no".' This principle will guide me. I shall not name names; but I apologize in advance, because the audience of the mass media will probably not resist the temptation to tie a particular statement to a particular person.

The clergy's reactions to the Revd Jankowski's antisemitic statements can be divided into four attitudes. The first is unlimited leniency, which stems from not seeing the problem. How else can we evaluate one clergyman's statement of 4 November: 'The Revd Jankowski is a man of a particular temperament and he preaches in his own style, and not for the first time. . . . He is a talented man, he loves his motherland, maybe in a slightly different way from others, but apart from his temperament he has a great many values.'

The second approach is to circle round the problem, not calling things by their names, resorting to phrases that are hard to understand within Aristotelian logic. How are we to understand the statement that Jankowski 'falls into the traps of antisemitism'? What traps are these? Who sets these traps? How are we to understand the argument that Jankowski is not an antisemite because 'he meets, and has friends among, Jews in the United States and in Poland, and maintains good relations with the Jewish community in the Gdańsk region'?[1] And the greatest sophists claim: 'If he did not deal in politics, he surely would not be accused of

---

[1] Cardinal Józef Glemp, speaking to journalists after the decision of Archbishop Tadeusz Gocłowski of Gdańsk concerning Prelate Jankowski; Catholic Information Agency (KAI), 4 Nov. 1997.

antisemitism.' Politics and antisemitism are two different things. In the teaching of the Church antisemitism is a sin against God and humanity. Politics is not: it is the art of self-government by human society. It *can* be a dirty thing, but it does not have to be. Dealing in politics, even by a priest, although it is prohibited to the clergy, does not necessarily expose the person to suspicions of antisemitism. Fortunately (a fortune in the misfortune), not all over-politicized priests in Poland are antisemites.

The third, and most comfortable, attitude is the perspective of the outside observer. It can take different forms, at one moment forthright evaluation (manic views), at another, grim humour. The latter was the case when a journalist from the Warsaw daily Życie asked what penalties the canonical code specified for Jankowski's statements: ' "From a reprimand to quartering," jokes Bishop ——. "We don't perform quartering anymore, but the archbishop of Gdańsk has at his disposal a whole array of means provided by Church law" ' (I have chosen to omit the bishop's name). Another time it happened in a tone on which I prefer not to comment (in an interview from the Belgian daily *Le Soir*). I quote from the Polish press: 'Asked why the Episcopate tolerates Reverend Jankowski's antisemitic statements, which do so much harm to Poland abroad, he answered: "My dear sir, I am not a psychiatrist." ' What can that journalist think of the Polish Church? (Note that the commotion around the convent in Auschwitz began with an article in the same publication, *Le Soir*, in October 1985.)

Finally, the fourth approach can be gleaned only from vague accounts here and there in the media: 'Great suffering because of the existing situation, prayer, repentance. But these matters are known only to God.'

How can we evaluate the first three attitudes? They cannot be termed anything but a trivialization of evil. And such a trivialization can be worse than evil itself, because it soothes the conscience and blurs the distinction between good and evil. A surprising answer was given by one of the episcopate's delegates to a meeting with representatives of the European Union. Before his departure for Brussels journalists from the Catholic Information Agency asked him if the subject of Jankowski was to be raised in the talks, and he answered: 'I see no point in discussing it. Why should we create an international affair because of a statement by one out of 25,000 Polish priests? It is a gross exaggeration; the subject itself does not deserve such treatment.' It is hard to agree with his assessment that the subject does not merit high-level discussion, if by 'the subject itself' the delegate meant antisemitism. It is also difficult to accept his downplaying of the role of the individual. All that is good and all that is bad in this world came from and comes from the individual soul. To take an example from Church history: in the fourth century Arius was 'just one' among many thousands of priests in Egypt, but still his views, namely 'Arianism', shook the Church throughout the Roman empire.

The crux of the Jankowski affair (as far as the Church is concerned) is that Polish bishops are not all convinced of the antisemitic character of the prelate's statement of 26 October. (Let us not even mention here his other, similar statements.) Indeed, they are willing to regard it as 'political', not 'antisemitic': one of them has 'emphasized . . . that the statement of the parish priest of St Brygida's was not antisemitic but political.'[2]

TRAGIC NONSENSE

Was Jankowski's statement really just 'political'? Let me quote it again: 'A Jewish minority in the Polish government cannot be tolerated, because the nation is afraid of it.' Let us put aside the problem of whether in the Polish government there is a 'Jewish minority' or not. Personally, I must confess to knowing nothing about this. In addition, the meaning of the word 'minority' is unclear: given that there are twenty-three individuals in the Polish government, how many people is this 'minority' supposed to be? Also unclear is the meaning of the adjective 'Jewish'. Perhaps these people were parachuted onto the roof of the office of the Council of Ministers by a foreign commando?

Jankowski's statement is not simply an antisemitic statement without further qualification; it is in fact an antisemitic statement of the worst possible, Hitlerian, kind. Just a few days after taking office, which he had done legitimately, Hitler began to introduce a programme of 'non-toleration' of Jews. The programme aimed first at judges and lawyers of Jewish descent. Since there were not yet relevant 'laws', this action was conducted in a relatively 'humanitarian' way: stormtroopers were sent to interrupt judges and attorneys during their work, to force them to leave. Hitler personally supervised the legislative work intended to remove people of Jewish extraction from all offices. The law was introduced on 7 April 1933 and included a cynical clause excluding war veterans. Soon after, other professional groups were targeted: doctors, professors, businessmen, workers. The Nazi bureaucracy got entangled in sometimes bizarre situations, naturally extremely burdensome to those affected by the limitations. For example, from August 1941 people of Jewish descent were not allowed to use 'roads, water routes, and railways'. In commuting to work, Jews could use public transport only if the distance exceeded 7 kilometres (and for schoolchildren, 10 kilometres), and they had to give up their seats to 'Aryans'. All these forms of 'non-toleration' of Jews by descent have their inner iron logic. For if someone cannot be tolerated in government, why should he be accepted as a teacher, doctor, or even a bootblack? At the end of this logical sequence only one thing remains: to liquidate physically the 'non-tolerated' person.

It is a great pity that the religious authorities, and the moral authorities in our country, are so persistent in trying to demonstrate that black is white. Just repeating it, even with a righteous stubbornness, will convince no one. There is not the

[2] KAI, 4 Nov. 1997.

slightest doubt that the quoted statement by the Revd Jankowski comes directly from Nazi antisemitism, whether or not its speaker knows or realizes it.

'Non-toleration' of others on account of their biological origins is a dark alley of thinking. There one enters a territory where all reasoning ends, all lights in the human mind go out—indeed, the domain of absurdity and death. To hold against Napoleon, for example, that he was born in Corsica of those and no other parents is completely absurd: he could not help it. He may be judged for his words and actions, but not for his origins.

To make this even clearer, let us use another example, this time with a Polish slant. (My example is completely fictitious, of course.) In the year 2050 a conclave convenes to elect a new pope. Among the prescribed number of electors is a 'Polish minority' of eight cardinals. There is a custom that the pope be elected from among the cardinals participating in the conclave. Just before the first vote the cardinal–speaker rises from his seat and states that, in the interest of the Church, no representative of the 'Polish minority' can be voted for. Asked whether Polish cardinals lack the proper qualifications to hold the office of pope, he answers no, all of them have the necessary skills and qualities in great degree; there is only one obstacle—they are 'biologically' Poles. The news of the cardinals' veto reaches the Poles. Everybody is shocked.

While on this subject. I wish to mention that there has been, in Church history, a case of a Jew occupying the pope's throne (quite apart from St Peter, of course). This man was Anacletus II (1130–8). His grandfather was a convert to Christianity. He is listed among the anti-popes only because his competitor, elected the same day, survived him by a few years (Innocent II; 1130–43). St Bernard of Clairvaux, who enjoys a reputation as one of the medieval figures most sympathetic towards the Jews, reacted to Anacletus' election in a 'racist way', stating that 'to elect a Jewish offspring to Peter's capital offends Christ'.

All Polish citizens are equal before the law, no matter what their other circumstances: whether possessed of six fingers on the right hand, whether a pygmy by origin, or a worshipper of crocodiles. Besides, no contemporary Poles can prove their pure Polish 'race'; such a thing does not exist. No Pole can even reconstruct a family tree back to, say, the eleventh century.

SIN

One more important issue remains here: How does the Church identify antisemitism? In the autumn of 1997 antisemitism was addressed in Pope John Paul II's speech at a Vatican symposium on the roots of Christian antisemitism. And I should like to quote two further Church statements. The first dates from before the Holocaust, the Nazi destruction of the Jews. On 28 March 1928 the congregation of the Holy Office in Rome issued a statement that read (in a single sentence, like all its statements): 'The Holy See . . . reproaches and particularly condemns hatred towards the people formerly chosen by God which in common language is called "antisemitism".' The second statement—for me the most important in this regard—is the one made by Pope John Paul II on 16 November 1990: 'Antisemitism, like all forms of racism, is a sin against God and humanity, and as such must be rejected and condemned.'

If antisemitism is a sin, then for a religious person the matter assumes a different dimension. It is no joking matter, as we say. For a Christian, to commit 'a sin against God and humanity' means to break the bond with God—as if one cut a live branch off a tree (though this comparison may be a little weak), and cut off the network of relations with other people. Thus it is a serious matter.

If publicly, in the eyes of the whole world, the sin of antisemitism has been committed—for the statement by the Revd Jankowski of 26 October was antisemitism of the worst kind—then it is a historical misunderstanding to try to place this act in the category of 'politics', as was done, for example, in the decree suspending Jankowski for a year from his post as parish priest. Things must be called by their names. Otherwise the Church in Poland loses its credibility, not only in the eyes of the world but also amongst its own flock. Jesus said: 'Simply let your "yes" be "yes", and your "no", "no"; anything beyond this comes from the evil one.' Let it be clearly stated that the Revd Jankowski himself is merely the backdrop to this issue. Nobody is anxious to oppress, trample into the dust, and destroy this priest, who has great achievements to his name. Even the punishment meted out to him (for his 'politics') could have been lighter, for example to study ecclesiastical writings on the subject of mutual relations between the Church and Judaism (with an examination before a specially assigned commission of experts). Our first concern should be to enlighten the minds of the faithful and properly shape their consciences in regard to the sin of antisemitism.

Should not the Church in Poland, with its universities, seminars for the clergy, and highly qualified body of experts, put out a letter, or longer clerical admonition, devoted to the subject? 'What is the Sin of Antisemitism?'—naturally written in plain, comprehensible language, and 'calling a spade a spade'. Who else can assume the Church's role in this? We must recall that it is not only Hitler who has killed Jews (including over a million children, which is often forgotten). With him it was in the name of his racist, pagan antisemitism; but Jews were also killed through the sin of antisemitism in previous centuries, in physical violence committed by Christians in spite of the teaching of the Church, and in spite of many papal decrees protecting Jewish people and property. Were such a letter or admonition now issued, we could walk towards the third millennium of Christianity with lighter hearts. Maybe we could even enter it hand in hand with our 'elder brethren in faith'—for they would no longer have to fear us.

Translated from Polish by Gwido Zlatkes

A Rainbow in Black

WALDEMAR CHROSTOWSKI

IN mid-November 1997 *Tygodnik Powszechny* and *Gazeta Wyborcza* published a long article by the Revd Stanisław Musiał entitled 'Black is Black'. I did not follow the reactions to it in *Gazeta Wyborcza*, if there were any. But in three consecutive issues of *Tygodnik Powszechny* only enthusiastic letters of thanks appeared. If the editors received no other letters, it is bad. If they did, and did not publish them, it is even worse.

DEMONIZING THE CHURCH

The opening thesis of the Revd Musiał's article is clear. In the early 1880s the Revd Adolf Stoecker, the emperor's court preacher in Berlin, called the Germans to 'awake' and 'cast off Jewish rule'. In this way, because of preachers, 'demons were awakened' in Germany and Europe, and that 'reawakening of hatred was paid for with the lives of 6 million Jews'. On 26 October 1997 in Gdańsk Prelate Henryk Jankowski said in his homily: 'A Jewish minority in the Polish government cannot be tolerated.' What will this 'reawakening of hatred' bring?

This outrageous conception has many facets, and I cannot deal with all of them. I shall touch on a few, hoping that I shall be properly understood, since the complex matter of Christian–Jewish relations is often vulnerable to manipulation. At the outset, to be quite clear, I declare that I do not excuse the Revd Jankowski's statement, nor that it took place in a church. But demagoguery of the sort of which the Revd Musiał has given us a sample brings no good either. I consider the uneasiness and outrage that his article evoked to be fully justified. Since *Gazeta Wyborcza* listed the author's credentials, probably to enhance the authority and glory of his views, it must be clarified that the Revd Musiał was indeed the secretary of the Commission for Dialogue with Judaism at the episcopate of Poland; however, he participated in its sessions only sporadically, and the records of those he attended show no input on his part. Also, the role he played in the matter of the

---

This article was published in *Tygodnik Powszechny*, 11 Jan. 1998, as well as in: Serwis Prasowy Katolickiej Agencji Informacyjnej, 3 Dec. 1997; *Biuletyn Prasowy Katolickiej Agencji Informacyjnej*, 97 (5 Dec. 1997), 50–1 (16–23 Dec. 1997); *Głos*, 5–7 Dec. 1997; *Wiadomości Archidiecezjalne Warszawskie*, 87/12 (1997); Peter Raina, *Ks. Jankowski znów atakuje: spór o kazanie prałata* (Warsaw, 1998), 85–93; *Gość Niedzielny*, 11 Jan. 1998; *Gazeta Niedzielna*, 25 Jan. 1998 (pt. 1), 1 Feb. 1998 (pt. 2).

A Rainbow in Black 311

Carmelite convent in Auschwitz, together with Jerzy Turowicz, the editor of *Tygodnik Powszechny*, was not as unequivocally positive as the *Gazeta Wyborcza* journalist portrayed it. When he and I worked together on the commission we differed on many issues, including the Carmelites. These differences can be reduced to one common denominator: there were no discussions as to *whether* a dialogue should take place, but only about *what kind* of dialogue. I think the piece 'Black is Black' underlines this dilemma.

It is most demagogic to equate a Protestant priest's statement with Hitler's antisemitic obsession, and thereby to equate anti-Jewish motifs in church sermons with criminal hatred by the National Socialists. Such an equation is prevalent in statements by the representatives of the Jewish side who are most hostile towards the Church. They participate in no dialogue, nor do they wish to. Their strategy is to present the Church as an almost criminal institution whose only possible reason to exist would be to continually apologize to Jews for all past evil perpetrated against them. It is surprising and shocking that an accusation springing from such ground should be uncritically repeated by a priest, and in a Catholic weekly. Some of its elements deserve particular attention.

The principal element is closely bound up with historical realities. The last quarter of the nineteenth century was the period of the birth and burgeoning of the communist movement. Its effects have been most clearly seen in Russia, but this ideology shook the societies of western Europe as well. A rise in tensions in Germany occurred at the turn of the 1880s, when the stir caused by proponents of the new doctrine grew stronger and stronger. Also, financial catastrophes of varying proportions were frequent, causing frustration and a sense of threat. We can assume that the reason the Revd Stoecker's speech was received with 'unceasing and stormy applause' was that it reflected more general moods and anxieties. There were enough adherents of the communist utopia (and the facts from a later period, when the bloody revolution in Russia began, show how much strength and influence they were able to gain). There are gloomy legends about characters such as Rosa Luxemburg. The overrepresentation of Jews in creating the new 'order' was obvious. In those circumstances the stereotype of Judaeo-communism emerged, followed by a significant increase in anti-Jewish attitudes. It was these factors, and not Christian teachings, that constituted the basis for Adolf Hitler and the National Socialists. Hitler was no more antisemitic than he was anti-Christian, and he considered Christianity a 'Jewish invention'. We cannot blame all Jews for communism and its crimes; but we also cannot close our eyes to the fact that many of them actively helped to create, while even more supported, the communist utopia. This caused protests on the part of their non-Jewish countrymen. This state of affairs was not unique to Germany; it repeated itself many times in different countries. That was why in the 1920s Trotsky was calling for 'continuous revolution'.

The Revd Musiał completely ignores these circumstances. During contacts with the Jewish side they are discussed very rarely and reluctantly. But if we completely neglect them, we arrive at a monstrous lie: that is, portraying National Socialism (with the antisemitism that was a part of it and eventually assumed the form of genocide) as an extension or result of Christianity. To assign to the Church the blame for the destruction of east European Jewry inexcusably misses the true causes, origins, and nature of National Socialism. By the way, even today in our part of the world, and not only here, a tendency exists to avoid this name, for it is unseemly for socialism to be labelled 'national'. Instead, the name Nazism is used, which is somewhat less suggestive; and then Nazism is attributed to the Right. From there, it is only a short path to condemning and impugning all right-wing parties and political movements, and the Church. There are plenty of contenders who derive the racist Nuremberg laws from the writings of the Church Fathers, but they pass in complete silence over the Church's warnings and condemnations of antisemitism, which were not infrequent even before the war. The encyclical of Pius XI, *Mit brennender Sorge* (published in German!), is particularly inconvenient to them, because it contains a stern condemnation of communism as well.

We must not treat anti-Jewishness and anti-Judaism lightly. Expressions of it have occurred, and still occur, among Christians. However, they should not be equated with racist antisemitism. These problems were the focus of attention during the recent Vatican conference on the roots of anti-Judaism (and not 'Christian antisemitism', as the Revd Jan Kracik and the Revd Musiał stubbornly propose in *Tygodnik Powszechny*!) in the Christian context. The Catholic Church made an honest effort 'to cleanse its memory'. But in connection with the centuries-long coexistence of Christians and Jews, we cannot call only *Christians* to give an account of their conscience. Every dialogue, including one with Jews, presumes reciprocity. Does the Revd Musiał believe that the privilege of immaculate conception and a resulting impeccability must be attributed to the Jews?

Most Jews, and their religion, have survived in the Christian world. Their mutual contacts resemble *a rainbow in which one can find all colours*. To present it as all black, as a chain of persecution and loathing, is to falsify history and to offend common sense. And that is where the search for the roots of National Socialism in Christianity comes in. Such mental reduction on the part of the Jews is a symptom of old stereotypes and prejudices; that a Catholic cleric subscribes to this view is surprising and hurtful. Dialogue means not uncritically repeating borrowed accusations, but truthfully representing one's own religious community, giving an honest account of its weaknesses and flaws, but also taking pride in its achievements and successes. The Church cannot 'cleanse its memory' at the price of whitewashing everybody else. In writing and thinking about the Holocaust, one must not pass over another destruction, perpetrated by communists, which cost the lives of more than 100 million human beings. The Church may forget neither Auschwitz nor Kolyma.

IN THE REALM OF NONSENSE

The Revd Musiał thunders at everyone: at the Revd Jankowski for his sermon, which Musiał sees as extremely antisemitic; at the public, that it did not rush into the streets to demonstrate its indignation; at intellectuals for their inertia and for lacking the initiative formerly exemplified by the staff of the *Tygodnik Powszechny* (only there?); at the bodies influencing public opinion, and the moral authorities (is the list of them from the early 1990s still valid?), because he is disappointed with them; at politicians because this matter does not interest them and does not prevent them from sleeping well; at Solidarity, with its roots in Gdańsk, for its lack of action; at residents of Gdańsk for their passivity; and finally at the Church and, above all, the episcopate.

In this last instance Musiał fears 'hurting some of our shepherds'. In this he failed: he has offended everyone (citing the Gospel, by the way), and offended worst those who swiftly and resolutely reacted to the Gdańsk incident. In the Revd Musiał's picture not only is black black; all is black. Gdańsk has become the 'capital of Polish antisemitism' (thus reads his text) 'or even European antisemitism'. Hence his anxiety about Poland's 'joining the family of European nations', which 'have many problems, but the problem of antisemitism does not appear in such acute form'. Is that true? Is it true that we, the Poles, live 'East of Eden'? Or perhaps we need to examine more carefully what takes place in the Western countries. Then it will become clear that similar problems are not only found and solved there, but hushed up and suppressed as well.

The Revd Musiał sorts the bishops' responses into four approaches. The first three of these are: a boundless leniency stemming from not seeing the problem; a circling round things and not calling them by their names; and an outsider's perspective. These attitudes he regards as 'trivializing evil'. This convenient phrase, itself borrowed, allows Musiał to distort the intentions of the bishops, quote their statements selectively, and interpret them according to a preconceived pattern. To clarify all of that, one would have to compile a complete anthology of statements and compare them with the respective accusations. The person probably most surprised was Bishop Pieronek; this was even acknowledged in the comment in *Gazeta Wyborcza*. But I think that the others, the (in Musiał's article) anonymous members of the episcopate, were also appalled by the twisting of their words. Over the fourth attitude—laconically mentioned as 'Great suffering because of the existing situation, prayer, repentance'—the Revd Musiał otherwise passes over in silence. So the role of the Church is apparently to protest, drag people onto the streets, condemn, punish, remove from offices and positions—and when someone says an event requires prayer and repentance, their opinion does not count?

It is hurtful not to acknowledge the Polish bishops reacted immediately and with all seriousness. In this case they presented a broad unanimity, indicating that they are neither treating the matter lightly nor hiding their heads in the sand. The

Revd Jankowski has been suspended for a year from his position as a parish priest, and barred from delivering sermons. Is that a small thing? Doesn't it matter that his bishop feels painfully the punishment he issued? This matter has another side, too. Recently we witnessed several extremely anti-Polish and anti-Catholic statements issued by important representatives of the Jewish side. Some of that provocation caused much wrong. Was anybody punished with a year of silence? Did Musiał and *Tygodnik Powszechny* feel equally hurt and appalled? What happens among ethnic and religious communities must be described and evaluated in a just and impartial way. Shocking events do not occur in a vacuum. A subject may have only one essential element, but a stick always has two ends.

The Revd Musiał's logic is twisted, I am sorry to say. I shall limit myself to two examples, of which one is like a minefield, the other a little easier. The Revd Musiał asks rhetorically: Is there really a 'Jewish minority' in the Polish government? But the prelate he criticizes spoke of a Jewish minority in Polish *society*, whose *representatives* in the Polish government are, in his opinion, 'feared by the nation'. Is there a difference, or isn't there? Can such issues be topics of public debate in the formation of a government, or do they constitute another taboo that, if touched upon, necessarily expresses antisemitism and obscurantism?

A few years ago in neighbouring Belarus a fierce controversy took place over the appointment of that country's ambassador to Israel. One of the candidates faced distrust and open protests because of his Jewish descent. His opponents were immediately blamed with antisemitism, the quarrels were silenced, and in 1992 the candidate began his diplomatic mission. In the spring of 1997 his tenure ended, and Michael Parfal, the first Belarusian ambassador to Israel, submitted his resignation to the Belarusian foreign minister and applied for the status of immigrant, a new *oleh*. Despite his previous high salary, he now lives in Herzliyah on unemployment relief. In one of his numerous interviews the former ambassador stated, 'All these years I lived with a split conscience. Here I represented my country, Belarus, but in my heart I grew more and more attached to Israel.'[1]

Is this a normal thing or not? Were the worries of the opponents of this nomination somehow justified? I shall not refer here to members of the Polish government. I am not evaluating political decisions, even if as a citizen of my country I have a complete right to do so. I am only asking: Must we really distort problems in order to avoid real dilemmas and questions? Must possible reservations about appointments to political posts in the Polish government, if raised openly, necessarily stem from a prejudice against the 'biological' fact of being a Jew, or might they have political grounds and bases? (Let me add that when the Belarusian ex-ambassador applied for a job in the Jewish agency and in the Israeli foreign ministry, he was rejected owing to a lack of trustworthiness.) On the other hand, to compare the forming of a Polish government to a Church conclave is a complete nonsense. It is such a pure fiction I won't even try to discuss it.

---

[1] Parfal's comments are quoted from *Nowiny Kurier*, 15 Oct. 1997.

The second issue also makes one think. Although 'not all [are] convinced of the antisemitic character of the prelate's statement', the Revd Musiał possesses a metaphysical certainty about this matter: it was 'an antisemitic statement of the worst possible, Hitlerian, kind'. Musiał accuses Jankowski of antisemitism that is 'deadly . . . even if often not directly or immediately'. This is a very strong accusation directed against a distinguished Catholic priest. Is it just? (By the way, if anti-Zionism is equal to antisemitism, there are not a few antisemites among the ultra-Orthodox Jews!) One of the main theses of Musiał's article is that Christianity abundantly infused National Socialism, and that 'the quoted statement by the Revd Jankowski comes directly from Nazi antisemitism'. Is it proper to throw around words like this? Haven't they the weight and force of stones?

By the end of his article the Revd Musiał declares that 'the person of the Revd Jankowski is merely the backdrop to this issue' since the Church's 'first concern should be to enlighten the minds of the faithful and properly shape their consciences in regard to the sin of antisemitism'. And then Musiał demands a letter or a longer pastors' admonition on the sin of antisemitism. If he lived in Kamchatka, I would not be surprised if his familiarity with the implementation of Church teaching on the Jews and Judaism in Poland was so poor. No other church in our part of the world attempts to modify the consciousness of the faithful with such intensity. Has the Revd Musiał forgotten about the groundbreaking 1990 letter of the episcopate, containing a strong and clear condemnation of antisemitism? Is it possible to ignore some hundred publications appearing every year, and dozens of conferences, meetings, and symposia organized for clergy, catechists, teachers, and students, all addressing this theme? Is it really true, as the ending of the unfortunate article suggests, that the only feeling our 'elder brethren' hold towards us Christians is fear? It is ironic that the publication of the Revd Musiał's article in *Tygodnik Powszechny* and *Gazeta Wyborcza* coincided with the episcopate's approval for an annual Day of Judaism in the Catholic Church, on the eve of the Week of Common Prayer for the Unity of Christians. The first such day is to take place on 17 January 1998. How can one only inflate the obstacles and difficulties, and ignore what has been achieved?

I do not want to overestimate what has been achieved in Poland in the area of dialogue. But although much more remains to be done, continually beating our breasts is not the way to go. No achievement has been accomplished without the knowledge and approval of the bishops, or without their participation. The former Commission, currently the Council for Religious Dialogue, and, within it, the Commission for Dialogue with Judaism, are among the most active and dynamic agencies in the episcopate. Their reaction to all anti-Jewish events is clear and swift. The Revd Musiał demands a new letter or pastors' admonition. But maybe it is worth learning about and using what already exists. I know of a few important Church initiatives about which *Tygodnik Powszechny* and *Gazeta Wyborcza* have written not a word; and many others they have treated with just small notes.

In regard to the notoriety, so emphasized by the Revd Musiał, that the Revd Jankowski's statement has gained in the world media, I repeat what I recently said in an interview for one mass-circulation weekly:

My impression is that Prelate Henryk Jankowski, with all that he sometimes says, is needed in some Jewish circles. In this area the phenomenon of this cleric would not exist without extensive amplification of his statements. If, however, even a part of that energy were used to publicize what is being done in the Catholic Church to change thinking about the Jews and Judaism, in Poland as elsewhere, the results of our dialogue would be immeasurably greater.

Translated from Polish by Gwido Zlatkes

The Sin of Antisemitism: A Response to Waldemar Chrostowski

STANISŁAW MUSIAŁ

I SHALL not discuss the accusations of a personal nature directed against me by the Revd Waldemar Chrostowski, especially since they bear no relation to the content of my article in *Tygodnik Powszechny*. Also, I shall not discuss his views on subjects I did not address in my article. (It remains a mystery to me how my text could have provided the Revd Chrostowski with the occasion or reference-points for touching on so many different topics.) Finally, I shall not attempt polemics about the core of my article and the Revd Chrostowski's 'response' to it. I shall simply state that in our texts we are speaking of two different matters. I, on the one hand, address the antisemitic character of one of Jankowski's public enunciations, and the lack of reaction, or inadequate reaction, to the antisemitism of this enunciation on the part of the episcopate. Chrostowski, on the other hand, addresses the political character of that enunciation of Jankowski's, and the bishops' reaction to this political character (the reaction undertaken 'immediately and with all seriousness').

I should like to limit my remarks about the Revd Chrostowski's article to making four corrections and to expressing my regret about two clearly antisemitic emphases present in his text.

THE FIRST CORRECTION

The Revd Waldemar Chrostowski, while partially summarizing and partially quoting my text, committed a serious error: he skipped a small but extremely important phrase—'in part'—so as to change completely the meaning of my statement, giving him a chance to accuse me of 'demagoguery' and 'demonizing the Church'.

First let me quote my own text, with a few unimportant omissions:

At the beginning of the 1880s in Berlin the Revd Adolf Stoecker—the emperor's court preacher, an activist in the Christian social movement . . . thundered in one of his sermons: 'We will not rest . . . until our German nation . . . rises up to cast off Jewish rule. My

This article was first published in *Tygodnik Powszechny*, 11 Jan. 1998.

German country, Christian nation, I admonish you, wake up!' . . . Today we know what demons were awakened in Germany and in Europe, *in part because of* Catholic and Protestant preachers such as the Revd Stoecker. This reawakening of hatred was paid for with the lives of 6 million Jews, the number of victims who fell to Nazi antisemitism. (emphasis added)

This thought of mine was rendered by the Revd Chrostowski in the following manner:

The opening thesis of the Revd Musiał's article is clear. In the early 1880s the Revd Adolf Stoecker, the emperor's court preacher in Berlin, called the Germans to 'awake' and 'cast off Jewish rule'. In this way, *because of* preachers, 'demons were awakened' in Germany and Europe, and that 'reawakening of hatred was paid for with the lives of 6 million Jews'. (emphasis added)

The difference between the two texts requires no comment.

My article stated only that antisemitic activity by *some* Catholic and Protestant preachers was *one* of the contributing factors in the Nazi destruction of 6 million Jews. I illustrated this view with the example of the Revd Stoecker; of course, many similar examples could be given. As for Stoecker, we may quote an opinion expressed about him by one of the greatest 'authorities' in Hitlerian and post-Hitlerian Germany on the history of German antisemitism (himself a zealous advocate of the ideas of antisemitism). This is Theodor Fritsch, a man hostile to Christianity, who in his *Antisemitic Catechism* writes of Stoecker: 'In regard to the proliferating antisemitic movement, he deserves more thanks than any other person.'[1] In the last editions of the *Catechism*—which was constantly enlarged and in time was retitled *Handbook on the Jewish Question*—Reverend Stoecker is regarded as 'in a way a father of German antisemitism'.[2]

THE SECOND CORRECTION

The Revd Chrostowski attributes very ill intentions to all who use the word 'Nazism'. This accusation concerns me as well. He writes:

To assign to the Church the blame for the destruction of east European Jewry inexcusably misses the true causes, origins, and nature of National Socialism. By the way, even today in our part of the world, and not only here, a tendency exists to avoid this name, for it is unseemly for socialism to be labelled 'national'. Instead, the name Nazism is used, which is somewhat less suggestive; and then Nazism is attributed to the Right.

This construction falls apart as soon as we open any German dictionary (for example, *Duden*) to the appropriate page. The official name of Hitler's party was very long: Nationalsozialistische Deutsche Arbeiterpartei (National Socialist German

---

[1] Quoted from the 22nd edn. of the *Antisemitic Catechism* (first pub. 1887; Leipzig, 1892), 319.
[2] Quoted from the 49th edn. (Leipzig, 1944), 552.

Workers' Party, or NSDAP). The shorter term used by the Nazis themselves, which merits our recollection, was Nationalsozialismus (National Socialism). Another abbreviated term for Hitler's party, Nazismus (Nazism), is, according to the dictionary, a pejorative, 'derogatory' term (*abwertendes Kurzwort*), and of course the Nazis did not use it. The word 'Nazism' is also in current use in the Polish language. If I use it for Hitler's party, I do so out of respect for the words 'national' and 'socialism'—respect for the reality these words connote. I reserve the base word 'Nazism' for the base reality that was the Hitlerian NSDAP. By the way, there was a time when the Revd Chrostowski, too, had no trouble using the word 'Nazism'. See his articles 'Who is a Heretic?' and 'The Church and the Jews and Judaism'.[3]

THE THIRD CORRECTION

The Revd Chrostowski blames me for stubbornly promoting in *Tygodnik Powszechny* the phrase 'Christian antisemitism' instead of 'Christian anti-Judaism' (the honour of which accusation, incidentally, I share with the Revd Jan Kracik). I ask: how can I 'stubbornly promote' anything in *Tygodnik Powszechny* if my previous article published there (before 'Black is Black') appeared in 1991?

As to the issue itself—that is, of using the phrase 'Christian anti-Judaism' rather than 'Christian antisemitism', as some Church circles have recently recommended—I consider it a deplorable attempt at terminological revisionism for dubious apologetic purposes. I intend to write a separate essay about this subject soon.

THE FOURTH CORRECTION

The author of the polemic accuses me of equating antisemitism and anti-Zionism. In fact, what I wrote was: 'not long ago the subject of antisemitism was taboo, and to be a patriot meant, in the interpretation of the ruling Communist Party, to be anti-Zionist (which in practice equalled being an antisemite)'. The Revd Chrostowski ironizes with unconcealed delight at catching me at an, in his opinion, obvious contradiction. To quote from his text: 'if anti-Zionism is equal to antisemitism, there are not a few antisemites among the ultra-Orthodox Jews!' My opponent forgets about the basic difference. The anti-Zionism of non-Jews is quite different from the anti-Zionism of Jews. Non-Jews' anti-Zionism is always antisemitism, because it does not limit itself to hostility to the idea of a Jewish state in the Holy Land, but is in fact hostility to the Jews as such. On the other hand, the anti-Zionism of some Jews (that is, some ultra-Orthodox Jews) bears no resemblance to antisemitism. These Jews are not hostile to Jewish statehood as such.

[3] *Tygodnik Powszechny*, 24 (1988), and 35 (1989).

They only believe that the Jews are not allowed to reach for this statehood themselves. According to them, the regaining of an independent state can only be the work of special divine intervention. Recall that the Zionist movement was, in its initial stage, a lay and agnostic movement. Its leaders represented the view that, instead of awaiting miraculous intervention by God, Jews should take their fate into their own hands, above all by regaining their independent state, lost in AD 70.

WORDS OF REGRET

Much of the Revd Chrostowski's article is devoted to 'historical' problems, primarily the triangle between Jews, communism, and Nazism. I do not intend to enter a polemic with him about these issues. For how should one respond to such a sequence of cause and effect as the following? 'The overrepresentation of Jews in creating the new "order" [i.e. the communist order] was obvious. In those circumstances the stereotype of Judaeo-communism emerged, followed by a significant increase in anti-Jewish attitudes. It was these factors, and not Christian teachings, that constituted the basis for Adolf Hitler and the National Socialists.' The conclusion is self-evident: without the 'overrepresentation of Jews in the new order', there would have been no destruction of the Jews!

In Chrostowski's text there are, however, two statements that cannot be passed over in silence. Both merit deep regret. The first concerns the story of the first ambassador of Belarus to Israel. From the Revd Chrostowski's text we learn that

> his tenure ended, and Michael Parfal, the first Belarusian ambassador to Israel, submitted his resignation... and applied for the status of immigrant, a new *oleh*. Despite his previous high salary, he now lives in Herzliyah on unemployment relief. In one of his numerous interviews the former ambassador stated, 'All these years I lived with a split conscience. Here I represented my country, Belarus, but in my heart I grew more and more attached to Israel.'

This story is set against the context of the current Polish situation and the staffing of the new Polish cabinet. The message of this passage is unambiguous: namely, one should not fully trust Poles of Jewish extraction, because of their 'split conscience'. However, to know who in particular is not to be trusted, one would have to know which Poles are of Jewish origin; this presumes certain 'investigative' efforts and research in birth records. Only thus could Poland avoid what happened in Belarus.

I feel a profound need to apologize to all Poles of Jewish origin for the insult thrown in their faces by one man's use of a particular story to discredit them all.

The second regrettable passage is at the end of Chrostowski's article: 'My impression is that Prelate Henryk Jankowski, with all that he sometimes says, is needed in some Jewish circles. In this area the phenomenon of this cleric would not exist without extensive amplification of his statements.' This statement is not a proverbial *lapsus calami*, an opinion ventured in the heat of discussion. The author knows what he is writing, for he is quoting himself.

Doesn't the Revd Chrostowski realize that his statement—that 'some Jewish circles' 'need' the Revd Jankowski's antisemitic utterances—indicates a first-degree affinity, obvious even to a non-specialist, with old, worn-out antisemitic prejudices repeated about the Jews since medieval times, i.e. that the Jews are the incarnation of evil, that they desire evil for its own sake, even if that evil turns against them? True, Chrostowski does not blame all Jews with desiring evil for evil's sake. He points out that he charges only 'some Jewish circles' with provoking antisemitic actions. This tactic is now used by almost all antisemites. They, too, have learned something over time, namely, that the best means of self-protection is to hide behind qualifiers such as *some*, *part*, *certain*, etc.

Also, according to the Revd Chrostowski, the publicizing of the Revd Jankowski's statements is the work of the Jews, apparently following the old antisemitic stereotype that the media are the exclusive domain of Jews. Everything falls into one logical pattern, for if 'Prelate Henryk Jankowski, with all that he sometimes says, is needed in some Jewish circles', then keeping these statements hushed would be counterproductive. Of course, it is necessary to publicize these statements maximally and so create 'the phenomenon of this cleric'. And again it is necessary to provoke this 'cleric' from time to time to make the statements. And then they are amplified. It is a curious *perpetuum mobile*. It is strange that the Revd Chrostowski, who has penetrated this 'tactic', has not somehow influenced the Revd Jankowski to act like a man and declare: 'I will not do service to "some Jewish circles"; from now on I'll be silent.' As of now, there is a 'quarantine' of a year-long silence imposed upon the Revd Jankowski in political matters. We should be glad of that.

The Revd Chrostowski's article contains a few more acrimonious remarks 'lined' with antisemitism. Here is one example: 'Does the Revd Musiał believe that the privilege of immaculate conception and a resulting impeccability must be attributed to the Jews?' This is acrimony in bad taste. Let us remind readers unfamiliar with Catholic theology that 'immaculate conception' is the name for the Catholic tenet of faith that Mary was conceived without original sin. This phrase does not appear, and simply makes no sense, in any other case under the sun. Can we begrudge cabaret actors for sometimes over-using religious terminology if we ourselves do not respect this 'reserved' terminology?

The Revd Chrostowski waxes ironic about my proposal that the Polish Church publish a pastor's letter or a longer priestly admonition explaining what the sin of antisemitism is, and why that sin is so hideous in the eyes of God and should be equally hideous in human eyes. For him, I am alienated from the ecumenical reality in Poland, especially concerning initiatives in the area of Jewish–Christian dialogue.

Of course I do know the several statements by the Polish episcopate about anti-Judaism and antisemitism. But what the Revd Chrostowski has written 'justifies' the need for the priestly admonition or pastoral letter I proposed. It 'justifies' it, for recipients of the Catholic Information Agency service received an illustration of the sin of antisemitism (one of these sins), which is the fuelling of distrust and suspicion against our fellow citizens of Jewish extraction (in the passage about the Belarusian ex-ambassador to Israel). They also received an illustration of another sin of antisemitism: demonizing Jews (in the statement that the Revd Jankowski 'is needed in some Jewish circles').

I am truly sorry that the Revd Chrostowski did not just sign his response with his name, but deemed it proper to buttress himself with the authority of the high office he holds by indicating that he is an 'adviser to the Council for Religious Dialogue of the Polish Episcopate'. Our poor common Church in Poland!

Translated from Polish by Gwido Zlatkes

Difficult Remarks to Write

STANISŁAW KRAJEWSKI

I AM stunned. The Revd Musiał attempted to deal with the deepest springs of my anxiety, and the Revd Chrostowski completely ignored this dimension. In the light of historical experience, in listening to the Revd Jankowski I cannot but associate him with the Nazis. Reverend Musiał felt this and expressed it very well.

Were the Revd Jankowski one of thousands of ordinary priests, nobody would care. But he is a powerful figure. He is a friend of Lech Wałęsa. He has been close to many politicians. He has received visits from presidents of the United States. He awards his own medals; recently one was presented to, and accepted by, Marian Krzaklewski [head of the Solidarity trade union]. The Revd Jankowski is a politician. And he could become (or already is?) a leader of the extreme right in Poland.

The fact the Revd Chrostowski mentions, that socialism had developed in Germany at the end of the previous century, illuminates nothing. The socialists of that time had done nothing particularly evil. So how does the fact that they existed explain (excuse) contemporary antisemitism?

The Revd Chrostowski's example of the Belarusian ambassador who defected to Israel generalizes from the concrete in an unacceptable way (while the Revd Chrostowski himself reproaches the Revd Musiał for supposedly too abstract an approach). Today many people are defecting from Belarus. They are seeking opportunities to improve their living conditions. In the case of that ambassador one ought to ask whether his disinclination to return to present-day Belarus was not the main factor. Besides, some politicians escape from there to Poland: so what? Is their Polish descent supposed to disqualify them there? (I think such opinions have already been heard there.) Despite the Revd Chrostowski's claim that he was making no references to the present government, it is hard not to see such a reference in his response. I do not want taboos; but either we look at politicians individually—in terms of their careers, achievements, or failures—or we look only at their nationality, their Jewishness. Bronisław Geremek [the Polish Foreign Minister] was not installed by the Jewish community. The Revd Musiał expressed this in a remarkable way in writing about a commando.

The claim that the bishops reacted 'immediately' is surprising. The Revd

---

This is the text of a letter I wrote to the Revd Chrostowski immediately after reading the article.

Jankowski started his attacks (about the Star of David inscribed in the swastika) more than two years ago! It is evident that even recently some of the bishops (not Bishop Pieronek) wanted to play down the matter. They probably underestimated its importance.

The newspapers do not write enough about what is taking place in the Christian–Jewish dialogue, claims the Revd Chrostowski. This is true, but it has nothing to do with evaluating the accuracy of the Revd Musiał's remarks! No grudge against him or against the press that published his article should prevent our understanding his point. After reading the Revd Musiał's article, I felt relief.

It was hard for me to read the Revd Chrostowski's response. It is hard to write these remarks. But I do not want to be silent. I feel that the Polish Council of Christians and Jews could lose its credibility in the eyes of Jews, and not only theirs. I know that the Revd Musiał's views are shared by many Catholics. In my opinion the differences I am addressing are another reason for deep discussions. We must convince others of this. Otherwise, the council's achievements at meetings and conferences, of which the public knows all too little, will be dubious.

Translated from Polish by Gwido Zlatkes

A Shadow over the Dialogue

MONIKA ADAMCZYK-GARBOWSKA

AFTER reading the article by the Revd Stanisław Musiał, and the letters in support of his stand subsequently published in *Tygodnik Powszechny*, I breathed a sigh of relief and decided the matter was resolved, at least temporarily. My reasoning, I must admit, smacked a bit of élitism: no doubt there is some prejudice against Jews in Poland, but, at least in circles such as the academic community and the Polish episcopate's Commission for Dialogue with Judaism, certain things are understood and require no further explanation, I thought.

But my belief was revealed as an illusion when I read the statement by the Revd Waldemar Chrostowski, which, unlike Musiał's article, depressed me and made me feel even more helpless than I had felt after reading the Revd Henryk Jankowski's comments. Jankowski can be considered an extreme and irresponsible individual (although I cannot agree with Bishop Tadeusz Pieronek's comment that he is a psychiatric case; if that were so, most extreme nationalist authors should be sent to psychiatrists, not to mention the writers of the letters supporting Jankowski's views included in the book *Ksiądz Jankowski nie ma za co przepraszać* ('The Revd Jankowski does not Need to Apologize').[1] But when insensitivity to Polish–Jewish matters comes up in a statement by an official representative of the Polish episcopate's Commission for Religious Dialogue, this is disheartening indeed.

In Chrostowski's statement, instead of openness, an eagerness for dialogue, and admission of transgressions, one finds a somewhat competitive, obstinate attitude. Such an attitude is not rare in this context. Some Poles think that the very fact that they are interested and involved in Jewish culture or Judaism should make all Jews in the world grateful to them; therefore, if they happen to come across criticism or hostility towards Poles or Poland on the part of a Jew, in spite of their own—as they maintain—good will, they start to resent the whole Jewish community. We see this type of attitude in Chrostowski's arguments when he speaks of 'representatives of the Jewish side who are most hostile towards the Church. They participate in no dialogue, nor do they wish to.' Even if such standpoints do exist, why focus on them instead of noticing the positive ones?

This piece was first published as 'Cień na dialogu', *Słowo Żydowskie (Dos yidishe wort)*, 4 (20 Feb. 1998), 4–5.

[1] 2nd edn. (Warsaw, 1996).

This kind of 'dialogue' resembles a marital argument in which one side apparently begs the other for forgiveness but at the same time adds, 'It's all because you always . . .' or 'And don't you remember your mother [twenty years ago] saying that . . .'. In such an approach the dominant concern is not to be open towards the other, but to demonstrate at any cost that one is right.

Chrostowski is mistaken when he says that 'no other church in our part of the world attempts to modify the attitudes of the faithful with similar intensity'. As evidence he cites numerous publications, conferences, and meetings. It is true that various documents have been issued, including the pastoral letter of the Polish episcopate in 1990, but they have entered the public consciousness and taken root to only a very small degree. I have never had occasion to hear an ordinary Sunday sermon in which the priest took a personal stand against antisemitism. (I use the word 'ordinary' because although I have certainly heard a few such sermons, they always took place on some special occasion such as a Jewish culture week.) I am not implying that the rarity of such sermons must be a result of ill will or antisemitic views of the clergy. It may rather result from a lack of preparation, or an inability to realize that such a need exists, or a fear of how the faithful would respond.

Despite appearances, the Church in Poland has not analysed deeply and openly their attitudes towards Jews. For example, the book by American Catholic theologian Ronald Modras *The Catholic Church and Antisemitism: Poland, 1933–1939*[2] has passed unnoticed in Church circles, as far as I know, and I think (I would like to be wrong) there would be no chance of its being published in Poland by any publisher directly or indirectly connected with the Church. In his book Modras analyses, among other things, the attitude of the Polish Church towards the growing antisemitism in the 1930s and the views and attitudes of the Church hierarchy as reflected in the Catholic press. He gives the example of a delegation of rabbis who asked Cardinal Kakowski of Warsaw to take a stand against anti-Jewish violence. The cardinal responded by saying that the Jews themselves were responsible for antisemitic excesses because of the provocations and blasphemies committed by Jewish communists and atheists (p. 402). When the Revd Chrostowski, in his article, seeks the causes of inter-war Europe's increasing antisemitism in the 'overrepresentation' of Jews in communist parties, it is clear that some lines of reasoning previously abandoned by the Catholic Church in other countries still linger in Poland.

Modras's book was the topic of a session at a conference organized by the Polish Institute of Arts and Sciences in New York—an organization that can hardly be suspected of anti-Polish or anti-Catholic sentiments—where it was highly praised by most participants for its reliability and moderation. Modras worked in the secretariat of the American Council of Catholic Bishops for Relations between Catholic and Jews. (One could wish for more such people in the council of the Polish episcopate.)

[2] Harwood Academic Publishers, 1994.

The author points out that in the inter-war period antisemitism was a problem not only in the Polish Church. Nevertheless, he notes, the problem of antisemitism in the Polish Church before the war is not solely a Polish problem if the Catholic Church in this country constitutes part of the universal Church. It seems that in Poland this 'universal' dimension of the local Church is often forgotten.

I do not know how to treat some statements made by Polish Church representatives relating to the Revd Jankowski's sermons. Are they just pretending not to understand certain things, or is it really the case? When Bishop Gocłowski says that Jankowski's statement indirectly referring to Bronisław Geremek's selection to the post of Minister of Foreign Affairs was not antisemitic but merely political in nature, a sober-minded individual will wonder if he has not misheard, for it obviously was an antisemitic statement of a political nature (or vice versa: a political statement of an antisemitic nature). Similarly puzzling is the logic of some of Chrostowski's remarks, especially those on the dual loyalty of the Belarusian politician of Jewish descent (and conclusions therefrom), or the comment that the ones who really need the Revd Jankowski are the Jews themselves. As for the first argument, how does Chrostowski imagine this test of loyalty? Is the probability of a politician's loyalty higher if only one of his grandfathers was Jewish and not two? As for the other argument, it is not far from the reasoning, sometimes encountered in extreme nationalist periodicals, that the Jews are responsible for their own misfortunes—that they themselves brought about the Holocaust, the pogrom in Kielce, etc., in order to achieve their own aims (that is, to speed up the creation of the state of Israel). The Revd Chrostowski will certainly be indignant to hear he is criticized for making antisemitic statements. If he himself does not realize this, it shows how deeply some stereotypes and prejudices are rooted.

I do not like to resort to lofty words, but often in the context of similar controversies Julian Tuwim's words come to my mind. On the first anniversary of the Warsaw ghetto uprising, he wrote from America in his manifesto *We, Polish Jews*:

> Upon the armbands which you wore in the ghetto the star of David was painted. I believe in a future Poland in which that star on your armbands will become the highest order bestowed upon the bravest among Polish officers and soldiers. . . . And there shall be in Warsaw and in every other Polish city some fragment of the ghetto left standing and preserved in its present form in all its horror of ruin and destruction . . . and every day we shall twine fresh live flowers into its iron links, so that the memory of the massacred people shall remain forever fresh in the minds of generations to come, and also as a sign of our undying sorrow for them.[3]

Unfortunately, Tuwim's reasoning was idealistic and naïve. Antoni Słonimski sensed the whole thing more accurately (besides, he had greater experience of the first post-war years) when he wrote in 1947 in the last stanza of his 'Elegy for the *Shtetl*s':

---

[3] Julian Tuwim, *My Żydzi polscy/We, Polish Jews*, ed. Chone Shmeruk (Jerusalem, 1984), 19.

> Gone are the little *shtetl*s, passed into shadow
> And this shadow shall lie between our words,
> Ere two nations fed on centuries of suffering
> Will draw near and unite anew.

Undoubtedly the 'shadow' lasted many more years largely owing to the political system that hindered any free exchange of ideas. But why do the phantoms from the past emerge so often now? Is Krzysztof Kieślowski right when in his book-length interview he says, 'Antisemitism and Polish nationalism are a stain on my country which has remained to this day and I don't think we'll ever be able to get rid of it'?[4]

Sharing Tuwim's naïve faith that the Holocaust should have made antisemitism totally unacceptable to all decent people in Poland, I would like to imagine that somewhere in Poland one can hear sermons in which priests, in response to Jankowski's words, tell the faithful that we should all be happy that, in spite of what befell the Jews during the war, there is still a Jewish community that is trying to make it possible for a small group of religious Jews to live in accordance with the principles of Judaism; also that there are in Polish political and cultural life assimilated Jews who often do a lot of good, just as other Jews, assimilated and not, have done in the country's past. But what parish priest will say such words if even the adviser to the Commission for Religious Dialogue speaks in completely different tones?

[4] Krzysztof Kieślowski, *Kieślowski on Kieślowski*, ed. Danusia Stok (London, 1993), 38.

PART III

An Interview

Marian Małowist on History and Historians

MARIAN MAŁOWIST was a prominent scholar of the history of Europe, Africa, and Asia, and of the long period from the thirteenth to the seventeenth century, and the mentor of many prominent historians in Poland. Among Polish historians, he was one of the best known in the wider scholarly world. Born in 1909, he studied history at the University of Warsaw, where he wrote his doctorate and habilitation thesis. From 1949 he was a full professor at that university and also for a time worked in the Institute of History of the Polish Academy of Sciences.[1]

This exchange with Professor Małowist was conducted by Bronisław Geremek (medieval historian), Michał Tymowski (historian of Africa), Henryk Szlajfer (economist and sociologist), and Ryszard Stemplowski (historian of Latin America, who had initiated the meeting and edited the text of the conversation for the Polish reader). The full record of it, augmented by footnotes and extensive bibliography, has been published in the twelfth volume of *Estudios Latinoamericanos*.

The conversation took place on 7 October 1986. Marian Małowist died on 3 September 1988.

STEMPLOWSKI: Let us start with a few words about your family and early childhood.

Yes. I was born in Łódź. My father was a physician. My family belonged to the intelligentsia and it was no different from many others, except that it was Jewish, although completely assimilated. There was no religious tradition at home

---

[1] He was the first editor (1958–70) of the semi-annual *Acta Poloniae Historica*, published by the institute. Among his most important works are: *Kaffa—kolonia genueńska na Krymie i problem wschodni w latach 1453–1475* ('Kaffa, a Genoese Colony in the Crimea and the Eastern Problem, 1453–1475' (Warsaw, 1947)); *Studia z dziejów rzemiosła w okresie kryzysu feudalizmu w zachodniej Europie w XVI i XVII wieku* ('Studies on the History of the Crafts during the Feudal Crisis in Western Europe in the Sixteenth and Seventeenth Centuries' (Warsaw, 1954)); *Wielkie państwa Sudanu Zachodniego w późnym średniowieczu* ('Great States of the Western Sudan in the Late Middle Ages' (Warsaw, 1964)); *Europa w dobie wczesnej ekspansji kolonialnej* ('Europe in the Time of Early Colonial Expansion' (Warsaw, 1969)); *Croissance et regression en Europe XIV–XVII siècles* (Paris, 1972); *Wschód a Zachód Europy w XIII–XVI wieku* ('The East and the West of Europe in the Thirteenth–Sixteenth Centuries' (Warsaw, 1973)); *Konkwistadorzy portugalscy* ('Portuguese Conquistadors' (Warsaw, 1976)); *Tamerlan i jego czasy* ('Tamerlane and his Time' (Warsaw, 1985)), and, with Iza Bieżuńska-Małowist, *Niewolnictwo* ('Slavery' (Warsaw, 1987)).

whatsoever, but there was a great culture of knowledge, enormous respect for learning. It was cultivated by my parents, who wanted their sons (I had a brother) to become professors. This certainly influenced my life. The second thing was my interest in history, which had already manifested itself when I was 7, as I learned to read and write, and it has dominated my life ever since. You must take into account the fact that I had polio, and my physical skills were somewhat limited, and certain areas of life were for me difficult, if not entirely inaccessible. So history was for me from the beginning a kind of compensation. At first I read Dumas a lot, I stuffed myself blindly with Dumas. Later I found out that for my generation of historians this was typical. My interest in history corresponded well with the way I was brought up, i.e. with a distrust towards religion and an enormous, positivistic respect for learning. But at school I was not a good student; I was quite average; the only things I was good at were history, Latin, and Polish. I was not well liked in school, especially by the history teachers, which was not surprising, since most of the time I knew more than they did, and . . .

STEMPLOWSKI: Did you encounter antisemitism in school?

Of course; it was impossible to live in Poland and, being Jewish, not encounter it. But I went to school in 1918, in the wake of independent Poland, and then it was not yet fashionable and was even considered bad taste. I remember only one instance when something of this kind had happened to me. I was 11, and it came from one stupid teacher. I made a scene to him about it, and so did my parents. But on the streets it was different; for example, one could be jeered at and called names like 'Beilis'. Beilis was a Jew in tsarist Russia who was accused of ritual murder, and there was a great stir about it; the clergy, especially Russian Orthodox, but also Catholic, behaved quite badly, but the intelligentsia in general sided with the accused. He was eventually acquitted, but the whole thing caused great offence, and deepened the antisemitic-Endek sentiments in Poland.

STEMPLOWSKI: How accurate did you find the depiction of your home town in Reymont's novel *The Promised Land*, or in Wajda's film?

I had very little in common with the world of big business in Łódź, but the destitution of the workers there sticks in my memory. My family belonged to the middle-class liberal intelligentsia. My father was, among other things, a factory physician. He himself came from a poor family, and he made his way through school and university completely on his own; so I had some contact with that element. Besides, it was difficult to live at that time in Łódź, a city of chronic poverty, and not encounter it, especially the poverty of the unemployed.

GEREMEK: Was there a relation between poverty and national structure? Was the bourgeoisie German and Jewish, and the poverty, Polish?

There was poverty among both Poles and Jews. There was not that much German poverty. The poverty was very upsetting. It raised protest in me. These were first, still childish thoughts. I remember, I was 10, and it already disturbed me.

GEREMEK: Did the poverty appear as a social problem, or did it reflect a young man's interests?

On the one hand, it was connected with my awareness of my situation; on the other, it stimulated my interest in socialism. Initially, I did not even realize that I was between two stools: it soon became obvious to me that I was not a part of the Jewish community, but it was also becoming more and more apparent that Polish society did not want me. To this I reacted normally, i.e. I regarded this attitude as obscurantist and offensive and I did not want to give in to it. When I was already adult and my father was seriously ill, at a time of great poverty and unemployment, he wanted me to convert to Christianity. I responded that I would somehow manage without baptism. And I noticed a spark of pride in my father's eyes. It was not a nationalistic question either, because I had very little to do with the Jewish community. It was a question of dignity. And then socialism revealed itself to me. I plunged into Kautsky. I started reading him, and I hated everything around me, and this too was connected with observing that poverty. Soon after I was recruited by the illegal at that time Union of Communist Youth.

STEMPLOWSKI: You had already become a communist in Łódź?

It was not that clear at the beginning. I had a friend, Samuel Engel, who was then 20. He shot a police *agent provocateur*. And they put him before a summary tribunal, and then he was executed.[2] This pushed me towards communism. At the same time I became fascinated by revolutionary romanticism, by the Russian literature of the initial period of the revolution. Also, we were related to Fuerstenberg-Hanecki, and this too impressed me greatly. But the decisive factor was that execution. It prompted me to join the community of workers, which scared my parents. At the age of 15–16 I became very active. It was the second half of the 1920s, a very different period in the history of the workers' movement from what came later. It was a period when rank-and-file members were not merely informed about the policy of the leadership; they were actually asked their opinions. And there were discussions, in which some were for and other were against. I supported Kostrzewa and Warski, while Leński and his strategy irritated me. I gave lectures for the workers' cells of the union. It was easy for me to make contacts. In these circles the intelligentsia of Jewish origin made contacts more easily than the young intellectuals of wholly Polish origin,

---

[2] On 24 Apr. 1924 Engel volunteered to carry out a sentence imposed by the Polish Communist Party. He was soon caught, and during the interrogation he was tortured; he was sentenced to death and executed by a killing squad within less than twenty-four hours of being sentenced.

who were often burdened by the tradition of the nobility. And then, the matriculation exams came, and I was arrested, but my father bailed me out. And in 1927 I found myself in Warsaw: of course, studying history.

STEMPLOWSKI: As a student, were you still active in the communist youth organization?

Only at the beginning. I did not like the environment where I was told to work, that is among students; and, above all, I started noticing the general changes. The period of free thinking was about to end, and the rule of the bureaucracy, even though still illegal, was already starting: the party line imposed from above, very dogmatic. And at the same time, I was more and more immersed in my studies.

TYMOWSKI: How were the research and teaching organized at Warsaw University?

There were chairs, individual professors, often fighting between themselves. Among the historians, a real power was Marceli Handelsman, the most prominent among his contemporaries. Also, Stefan Czarnowski drew attention. I was annoyed with the university's very strong traditionalism. It annoyed me even with Handelsman; still, he had an open mind, and if he saw a student was interested in something, he let him pursue his studies in that direction. As for me, initially I thought of becoming a historian of the modern period. I loved the Middle Ages, but they seemed to me too difficult. But Handelsman, who ran the seminar on modern history, allowed me to study the medieval period as well.

STEMPLOWSKI: The role of the master was then great...

Enormous! It was decisive!

STEMPLOWSKI: You worked with Handelsman and Czarnowski.

From Handelsman I learned, first, the craft, and secondly, a broad approach to historical developments. From Czarnowski I took a way of thinking. He used to have these long conversations, sometimes quite tortuous for the student. He cured me of dogmatism, because at that time I was inclined to pseudo-Marxist axioms. Besides, Czarnowski drew my attention to the then strange to me field of the history of religion.

STEMPLOWSKI: What was the situation at the university? You mentioned quarrels among the faculty. How was it among the students?

There was virtually no contact between Jews and non-Jews, especially in social life.

STEMPLOWSKI: Now it is even hard to imagine...

Sadly, that's how it was. Handelsman's and Czarnowski's seminars were different, they were very élitist, but even there people did not have social contact. The university was no exception to the rule. Later, when I was a teacher, I conducted a poll among our students with an 'Aryan' friend. We asked Jews: what Poles do you know, what Polish streets? We asked the same of Poles regarding Jews. It came out that my Jewish students knew no Poles except for the janitor: they knew practically nothing about that society. And the results were the same on the Polish side. It was a perfect ground for nationalistic demagoguery. In the university this division deepened in the 1930s. When I first came to the university, excluding Jews from academic societies was unheard of; in 1931 it became common practice. None of my 'Aryan' colleagues attended my doctoral examination. [Ludwik] Widerszal, who was baptized, could not get his habilitation confirmed until 1939. Previously we had come across antisemitism of the religious type; now it became racist.

TYMOWSKI: What was Polish scholarship like compared to international scholarship?

We had in Poland a few true masters among historians: Franciszek Bujak, Stanisław Kętrzyński, Jan Rutkowski, Handelsman, Czarnowski. Handelsman and Czarnowski were linked to French scholarship. Czarnowski was a follower of Durkheim. But our libraries were poor; we already felt the scarcity of books, for there was no money unless one had a rich father. But I could not take much from my father, who was already sick. I saved money on food and I bought books. Besides, we were provincial; and now we are becoming provincial again. We flourished in the second half of the 1950s and in the 1960s.

STEMPLOWSKI: You wrote your master's thesis on trade in Flanders...

Flanders fascinated me as a developed medieval country. I learned to read and write Flemish. I put a lot of work into that project; it was about trade between the Hanseatic cities and Flanders at the beginning of the fifteenth century. After the exam Handelsman told me that he had sent it to a publisher. It was my first great achievement. The publication of a master's thesis was something exceptional. It came out in 1931 in the *Revue Belge de Philologie et d'Histoire*. As a Jew I had no chance of getting a job at the university. Fortunately, I had very rich relations in Sweden; they invited me there for a year. I learned Swedish and I went. I wanted to research whether there was a link between trade and politics. At that time I already had nothing to do any more with the Communist Party, but my head was still stuffed with various slogans. I was still very young, and the book I wrote was very immature, as it is obvious that there is an unbreakable connection between trade and politics.

STEMPLOWSKI: Did you work in Stockholm?

In Stockholm, in the Central Archive, and a little in Uppsala, where the university was more conservative than in Stockholm. I made contact with Professor Eli Hecksher, who at that time was creating the beginnings of a school of economic history of Sweden. My book was finally published with the financial support of the Ericsson corporation. I converted it into my doctoral dissertation under the guidance of Handelsman. I remember today my exam with Professor Czarnowski, although it was on my subsidiary subject, the Renaissance. After I had submitted my doctorate, I could have got a grant to go to Paris, but Handelsman advised me to accept a position in the Kreczmar's High School. It turned out that I was interested in teaching. But the vice-principal there was an antisemite, and he made my life difficult. Another student of Handelsman's, Franciszek Skibiński, was the school inspector, and when he saw that things were not good for me there, he got me a transfer to Jewish schools. I taught there thirty-six hours a week. They paid me only for ten months. Nevertheless, it was a happy time in my life. I got married. My wife was a psychologist. At that time, through another of Handelsman's students, I met Władysław Pobóg-Malinowski, who got me a grant from the ministry of foreign affairs to go to Italy. I was there for three months. These were years of hard work, but a very interesting period. I went abroad several times.

STEMPLOWSKI: At that time, you worked on . . .

Kaffa. During those years I did teaching, and I studied Levantine problems. I tried to make time for my scholarly work. In 1938 I finished the monograph of Kaffa, a Genoese colony. Later I went with my wife to Crimea to see Kaffa. I went as a regular tourist, not some rich man. We travelled on overcrowded trains. Some passengers would talk a little, but not much.

STEMPLOWSKI: It was 1939, after the trials . . .

They really did not talk much.

STEMPLOWSKI: What did Kaffa look like?

I did not see Kaffa-Theodosia; there was a military base there, and they did not let anybody in. But I saw Crimea, and I saw the Tartars who were still there—even Tartar newspapers. One of them had the title *Kizykl Krim*, Red Crimea. Then we saw Leningrad. There was great democracy within society, and a superhuman patriotism amongst the people, especially in Leningrad. Later I told Tadeusz Manteuffel that should there be a war, they would fight until the last man. But nobody wanted to believe me.

STEMPLOWSKI: Did you meet any foreigners in Crimea?

There was one American, a very intelligent man, and we talked. I also met a Latin American politician who predicted that Poland would give in to Germany without resistance.

GEREMEK: But that trip was at the same time a confrontation with the reality of the vision of a man who in his youth was a communist.

It was not a great disillusionment, because my attitude was already critical. Besides, the remnants of revolutionary winds could be still felt in that specific democratic atmosphere; but there were awful things too: I was not able to even move without somebody following me; I could not get in touch with my family in Moscow, and then it came out that they had been in camps for a long time. I saw great chaos and a very low standard of living, but at the same time that anticipation of fighting until the last man. I returned to Poland three days before the outbreak of the war.

STEMPLOWSKI: In Ringelblum's *Chronicle of the Warsaw Ghetto* we find this entry with the date 21-3 February 1940: 'Completely assimilated Jewish intelligentsia is coming to us: the director of the Public Library Dina Steinberg, Małowist'.[3] I realize that I am touching on a painful nerve, but your testimony as a historian is very important—about the ghetto and after. The experiences of this kind which you lived through cannot fail to influence the way you write history.

Only a great writer can portray the atmosphere of the ghetto, not a historian. The facts are there, but not the atmosphere—a great novelist is necessary for that. It was frightful. And it made me very pessimistic for the rest of my life. I found out that oppression and suffering are not at all a school of heroism, but of debasement. This proved useful for me later, when studying slavery. Furthermore, only very strong personalities can avoid this debasement: there was the very small group around Ringelblum, and that around the socialist Bund. I did not belong to any organization in the ghetto; I got involved in recording clandestine teaching, and that was what I was doing. The disaster came on 13 August 1942. It is for me a horrible date. My wife was taken to Treblinka. Let's not talk about it ... When my wife was no more, I escaped to the 'Aryan' side. There I was caught by a gang of hoodlums; they ripped off my jacket. It was strange that they did not hand me over to the Germans. I found shelter at Mrs Czeczot's, a teacher at the Kreczmar School. Shortly afterwards Stanisław Herbst took me away from there; I spent two weeks at his place. Herbst was of rather right-wing orientation, and a very devout Catholic. Then, all devout Catholics were on the right. He found me shelter so that I could stay with my mother, and later Witold Kula and Helena Brodowska suggested that I should leave Warsaw and go to the countryside to teach clandestinely. Finally, I ended

[3] Emanuel Ringelblum, *The Chronicle of the Warsaw Ghetto, September 1939–January 1943* (Warsaw, 1983). Dina Steinberg was the wife of Tadeusz Kotarbiński.

up in Jabłoń, near Radzyń, in the Podlasie region. After all my experiences I felt there as if I was in Paris—that was literally how I felt. It was a very cultured and friendly village.

The family with whom I lived knew everything about me—in fact, two families knew. After the war it came out that more families knew, and also the chief of the navy-blue police, a Pole, a very decent person. Juliusz Kleiner was hiding in the neighbourhood; in the next village there was a Jewess; in that area many were hiding. But there was also a case of a Jew who, after returning to his village, was robbed and murdered. In the forest the NSZ [Narodowe Siły Zbrojne: National Armed Forces] people hunted the Jews, the Home Army there was taken over by the NSZ. But my village collaborated with the BCh [Bataliony Chłopskie: Peasants' Battalions] which were left-wing-orientated. I was a teacher in the clandestine schools. The whole village discussed politics. In this part of Poland relations between the organizations were bad, and towards the end, hostile. As you read their bulletins, sometimes you got the impression of an insane asylum. I warned the farmers that they should read them the opposite way in order to find some logic. In those bulletins you could read that the Americans and the British would come there, and Russia would go to hell.

STEMPLOWSKI: This kind of thinking is still around . . .

What? Oh, yes, this idiocy has lasted until today. I was scared watching the activity of the government in London. I was in touch with the Peasants' Battalions. They had a press agency *Wieś* ('The Village') and I wrote reports for them. They were very kind to me, and some of them knew who I was. They even brought me my books from Warsaw. This contact with people gave me a sense of being useful. Before I knew the workers, and now I started knowing the peasants.

GEREMEK: This attitude of the peasants to the Jews undermines the stereotype of antisemitism as deeply rooted in the masses.

There was antisemitism there, but there was not that split that I was talking about. The family that hid me had hidden others before me, fully aware of the risk and risking everything—risking their own lives. The antisemitism of the peasantry was inspired by landowners and priests. The landed gentry was not antisemitic of itself, but they did not want land reform and they tried to persuade the peasants that instead of sharing their land the countryside should be saved by throwing out Jewish tradesmen.

On the other hand, I see the sources of antisemitism in the city in the Christian commercial class, above all in Poznań. My blood boils when I see that today some want to make Dmowski a national hero, and I remember him applauding Hitler for burning books. In any case, the village kept us hidden from the Germans. When the Russians came, their security called me; they figured out at once that there was something strange about that Józef Mil. I told them that it was my pseudonym, in the underground, that I was so-and-so—I had escaped from the ghetto and then taught clandestinely. And they asked: How come the Germans didn't know? I answered: Had they known, I wouldn't be standing before you.

STEMPLOWSKI: Was this in the autumn of 1944?

Yes, I learned that there were Polish authorities in Lublin. I went there, and by chance I met a captain who used to be a teacher at the Kreczmar's High School; and he introduced me to the then director of Polish Radio. Billig, I must say that Billig acted very well towards me. First of all, he asked me if I was hungry. I wasn't hungry, but I was all in rags. I got a job in radio, and because I knew foreign languages I was assigned to listen to foreign stations. In a short time I became one of the best-informed people in Lublin.

GEREMEK: Information is power...

First of all, there was destitution. Once I spilled broth on my trousers, and there was no stain, it was so free of fat. Socks were patched together from pieces. At that time I had a car accident, and I became disabled. In the spring of 1945 I was back in Warsaw. I was prostrated, I had nobody left, nothing left. And then Tadeusz Manteuffel suggested that I do a habilitation thesis, because one copy of my monograph of Kaffa had survived among his books. So there was the colloquium.

GEREMEK: I would like to return to the question of your war experience. In the introduction to the book on Kaffa its author wrote that then, after the war, he looked differently at what he had written because he understood cruelty...

Before the war people did not believe in the possibility of such atrocities. I survived the mass murder of the Jews and the deportation of my wife. After she was abducted I went running through that sea of corpses and ruins to the Umschlagplatz to catch up with her, and a German aimed at me (crossing was forbidden at that place), but he changed his mind and did not shoot. I will carry that moment with me for ever. If I later started dealing with Tamerlane, it was partly in order to comprehend cruelty. In the introduction to *Kaffa* I wanted to point out that the book was appearing in a different time than when it was written, and I had a different, changed understanding of history.

GEREMEK: You always studied economic history.

I am a socio-economic historian. I never had a great passion for political history.

STEMPLOWSKI: I heard a joke: 'A student comes to Małowist and says that he would like to work on the nineteenth century; and he answers: It's not history yet, newspapers write about it, just leave it alone!'

I did not say this about the nineteenth century, but about the twentieth; but be comforted that Marian Serejski considered *belles lettres* all historiography after the fall of Rome. I was interested in economic history, and that was the influence of Marxism.

GEREMEK: It is not all that simple—dealing with the economy as a result of Marxism. Marxism has a deep-rooted distrust of commerce and the market, and you are enchanted by commerce.

This attitude of Marxism dates only from Stalinist times. Remember that Pokrovsky was a pure continuation of Pirenne, and Pirenne had such enormous influence that we all yielded to it.[4] I remember that delight of working in Antwerp and Venice, where through the materials on commerce I got an insight into the whole world. I was never a Stalinist, either politically or intellectually. As for my field, there was a moment before the war when I thought that I might study the Manichees and the Albigenses; I was reading Adolph von Harnack. After the war I had a choice, and Herbst advised me, quite reasonably, not to deal with the history of religion—and he was right. If a Jew wrote anything about religion, even intellectually honest, you know what people would say. So I stayed with economic history even if I was not particularly fond of the new trend in it—rigorously quantitative. I stayed with economic history and wrote about the problems of production. Already before the war, influenced by Strieder[5] and other German historians, I had written about mining. After the war I started writing something like a history of European commerce; I had written some 200 pages and then threw it in the rubbish. Why? Because I had encountered a field that I didn't know, artisanship, and without that you couldn't understand commerce. So I had to deal with the problem of production.

TYMOWSKI: What directed you in choosing the geographical areas of your studies?

I will tell you what drove me. I was long bothered by the question of why Poland was backward. And immediately I found the problem of the noble estate and the problem of the serfdom.

SZLAJFER: I am interested in the comparison of serfdom and slavery. In the areas of slave colonization, and in the areas of central eastern Europe—do we encounter a delayed capitalism, or a different form of capitalism altogether?

---

[4] Mikhail N. Pokrovsky (d. 1932), a historian of the medieval Russian economy, and editor-in-chief of the principal journal of Soviet historians, *Istorik-marksist*, publisher of the sources and 'a central figure in the Marxist remodelling of historiography' (J. Topolski). Henri Pirenne, a Belgian historian at the beginning of the 20th c., developed a theory of the medieval origins of capitalism, ideologically linked with the French school of *Annales*.

[5] Jacob Strieder, a researcher on the origins of capitalism. At the beginning of the 20th c. he published a number of works on south German trade and credit in the 16th c.

In central eastern Europe we had a backward capitalism, called by some a dependent capitalism. Our capitalism was backward, among other things, because there was no agricultural reform. That is where we come across the problem of the noble estate. I think that the noble estate with the corvée stopped the progress. The noble estate destroyed the internal market and caused these enormous social distances. This led me to the crisis of the fourteenth and fifteenth centuries, when the roads of the East and the West in Europe parted. I was fascinated by that crisis. I read a lot of Postan's work.[6] I certainly felt that Postan overestimated the demographic factor and I probably underestimated it in my work; at that time I found out about Kosminsky.[7] In short, I took on the noble estate and the export of Polish grain. I looked through archives in the Netherlands and Belgium. Since the Netherlands was not only the principal recipient, but also a transit station, other regions needed to be investigated as well; in this way I started studying England, northern France, and then, during my year lecturing at the École Pratique in Paris, I began to look at the role of Portugal.

STEMPLOWSKI: Through the Portuguese problematics you could have gone to Latin America; instead you took on the issues of Africa.

I read in Portuguese, Spanish, Catalonian...

STEMPLOWSKI: Your students are convinced that there is no language that you don't read.

But I don't speak these Iberian languages; it is important for me to be able to read the literature. I think Spanish scholarship is on a higher level than Portuguese. I have read a lot of that because I am passionate about reading sources. When I arrived at the Portuguese questions, I found there more than just Polish grain. I was fascinated by the question: how does it happen that backward countries can create empires? In that way I reached Africa, especially since it was at the time of its emancipation, the 1960s.

TYMOWSKI: You observe Africa from two sides: from the perspective of Europe, and from inside Africa. Your book on the states of western Sudan...

This separates me from, for example, Verlinden,[8] who sees slavery exclusively from the perspective of the European merchant, whereas I analyse it also from the vantage-point of the people who were carried away. That was why I also studied African and Arab sources. Of course, I had to take into account

---

[6] Michel Postan, a contemporary British historian of medieval commerce and industry, co-editor of *Economic History Review*.

[7] Evgeny A. Kosminsky, a contemporary Soviet historian of agriculture in 13th-c. England.

[8] Charles Verlinden, contemporary author of a synthesis of general economic history, here recalled as the author of a book on medieval slavery in the European countries of the Mediterranean basin.

American issues as well, and I had to read the Latin American literature. I have to say that, in general, I am not impressed with it.

GEREMEK: What interested you so much in these empires?

Their social forms. At once I started thinking that colonial slavery is an equivalent of the east European corvée, and the European core, i.e. north-western Europe, has developed to some extent due to the emergence of these backward social formations...

STEMPLOWSKI: ... At the system's peripheries. Wallerstein[9] quotes you as his inspiration: Fernand Braudel and Małowist.

Yes, but, unlike Wallerstein, I think that these forms emerge not only as a result of the influence of the centre, but also because of the work of local factors.

TYMOWSKI: What do you regard as particularly important among internal factors?

The social structure. I was led to this conclusion by reading the fourteenth-century Arab writer Omari. I found there, for example, the explanation of different forms and methods of the slave-trade, and of the relation of these to the general level of economy. The voluntary trade, if we can call it that, that is a kind of self-selling, had great importance; also selling children and prisoners of war—mainly because of poverty, especially selling the young, sons and daughters.

STEMPLOWSKI: Your analyses of Africa, and even more of Europe, are of great importance for a student of Latin America. In your book *The East and the West of Europe in the Thirteenth–Sixteenth Centuries* you wrote about the genesis of the international division of labour, that is about the structural development of the system of international connections, or even better, inter-regional connections. If a division of labour creates asymmetry in a system of inter-regional connections, does that asymmetry, in the long run, tend to deepen, or the opposite?

An asymmetry may slow down the development of the weaker side in a partnership. I think this was the case with the contacts of the West with the European East. However, nineteenth-century Japan provides an example of something different. Maybe in both cases the decisive factors were in the different political and economic orientations of the dominating social groups.

STEMPLOWSKI: People talk about the 'Małowist school'—many people took you as their adviser for the master's thesis: Rafał Karpiński, Marcin Kula, Tadeusz Lalik, Janusz Potkowski, Ewa Toczek, Stanisław Trawkowski, Jan Szemiński, and

---

[9] Immanuel Wallerstein, working in the United States; contemporary author of widely discussed works about capitalist economy as the world system in the modern era.

others. You also supervised many doctorates: Maria Bogucka, Andrzej Dziubiński, Bronisław Geremek, Jan Kieniewicz, Antoni Mączak, Danuta Molendowa, Michał Tymowski, Henryk Samsonowicz, Andrzej Wyrobisz, Benedykt Zientara, and others. What do all these people have in common?

TYMOWSKI: How did you select your students? How did you know who was good for you?

What united my students at the beginning of their scholarly careers were certain common interests in the area of socio-economic history, particularly the problem of relations between the village and the city. Then each of them grew according to his or her own interests. I closely observed their intellectual and character development, trying to stimulate their positive inclinations. Besides, close contact with them was possible because these were small seminar groups. I always encouraged them to learn foreign languages—so that they would have access to the historiography of other countries. I tried to stimulate discussion about scholarly and other issues, and implant in them the conviction that scholarship obeys no authorities. That was important.

TYMOWSKI: Earlier you were talking about the historical milieu at Warsaw University before the war. What it was like after the war?

At the beginning Manteuffel did a good job. He selected talented people both in research and in teaching. He was very demanding and he was guided only by the general interest. During the first decade the atmosphere was good, and whoever was good could advance. This allowed us to develop good groups. These first dozen or so years of the university Institute of History were decisive to my staying in Poland after 1968.

STEMPLOWSKI: How do you evaluate that period as a Marxist?

I never joined the party but I was a Marxist, and as such I had to wage the struggle on two fronts: on one hand, against the old-style reactionary historians, and on the other, against the Stalinists.

TYMOWSKI: What counts above all is what a historian leaves in his works, and in the minds of the readers.

When I was young, and even long after, I thought that historiography helped to break stereotypes. It was an illusion. For example, my book *The East and the West of Europe* had no resonance in Poland. Do not believe in this kind of impact, I warn you.

STEMPLOWSKI: And what about our conversation? Besides, the reception of great works requires a long time ...

PART IV

New Views

The Day after the Pogrom: A Documentary Account

JÓZEF BEKKER

INTRODUCTION

ANTONY POLONSKY

THE pogrom in Siedlce, which took place in September 1906, was the last outbreak of the wave of violence which began in Kishinev in April 1903. Siedlce lay about 60 miles east of Warsaw and before the First World War had a population of about 25,000 people, of whom perhaps a third were Jews. The main railway line from Warsaw to Terespol and on to Moscow ran through the town and was responsible for its expansion in the last part of the nineteenth century. It also accounted both for its strategic importance and for the presence there of a significant socialist movement. These factors explain the role of the Russian army, and in particular the Libau regiment, as well as the Monarchist League in organizing the pogrom. Estimates of Jewish casualties range from twenty-three dead to 100 dead and 300 wounded.[1]

This account was written in Russian by Józef Bekker, who was a well-known Yiddish journalist. Because of the censorship he was unable to publish this material and incorporated it into his unpublished memoirs. He survived the war in the Soviet Union, where he died in 1956. His daughter Mary gave his writings to the historian Dora Kacnelson of Drohobych, who sent this extract to us. It illustrates many aspects of the problems raised by the wave of pogroms of 1903–6, in particular the vexed question of the degree to which this was orchestrated centrally and the role of the army and local tsarist officials in initiating anti-Jewish violence.

THE POGROM IN SIEDLCE

The town of Siedlce is ruined. The residents are fleeing. There are no young people at all. Some of them are injured, some (sixty-two people) are in gaol and hospitals; others are trying as quickly as possible to leave the town, where their lives are in danger.

Two houses on Piękna and Kalewska Streets leave a terrible impression. One of

---

[1] *The Times*, 11 Sept., 13 Dec. 1906, quoted in John Klier and Shlomo Lambroza (eds.), *Pogroms: Anti-Jewish Violence in Modern Russian History* (Cambridge, 1992), 238.

the houses is completely burned down, and huge holes, breached by mortars, yawn in the walls of the other.

The looted shops are all boarded up, and all the locks are torn off. If one looks inside a store, the emptiness on the shelves is astonishing—everything is looted, gone. The windows of houses are without glass: they were all destroyed by bullets that rained like hail. The ceilings are demolished. Everything is broken, wrecked.

The Polish-owned shops are open here and there. They did not get damaged during the pogrom; they are full of goods, as before. This plenitude, next to the empty and looted neighbouring shops, is depressing.

The remaining residents of the town are wandering the streets aimlessly. Nobody knows what to do, where to go. The wealthy of yesterday have become beggars. There is nothing to eat. The Jewish bakeries are closed and the Jewish butchers have stopped slaughtering livestock. There are no Christian butchers in town, and the entire population, including the local officers, is left without meat. The police requested that the butchers start to slaughter again, but they maintain that they do not have money to buy livestock. They want to be given livestock and to be paid 50 kopecks a day. Only then will they be able to go back to work.

The Jewish stores are closed. The shopkeepers decided not to open them for seven days to express, even if passively, their protest against the pogrom.

The rabbi told me that the local governor had shown him a piece of paper that allegedly had the seal of the Bund on it, in which he was threatened with death. This piece of paper apparently was enough proof for the governor that the Bund was responsible for everything that had happened in town, as well as for the shooting by the officers.

I arrived in Siedlce on Wednesday, at seven o'clock in the evening. All the Jews who travelled with me in the railway carriage wondered throughout their journey whether it would be safe to stop in town or whether it was better to stay on board until the next station. Among the passengers there were some who had just escaped the Siedlce hell and taken their families with them. Now they were returning simply to find out what remained of their apartments and stores. As soon as the shooting erupted, they left everything to fate, grabbed their children, and hurried away in all directions. 'I still can't get my senses back,' said one of them. 'I still hear the whistle of the bullets. It is a miracle that I managed to escape and save myself.'

The train stopped. Everyone, even those afraid to return to town, dared to get out of the train. But it was not possible to return to town. At every door there were soldiers and police who subjected everyone to a search.

I walked through rows of soldiers. Rude hands grabbed me. One policeman had already let me go, but another one felt like displaying his power, and he, too, searched my clothes. At last the search was over. But the soldiers did not let anyone go, waiting for the departure of the train. Time dragged on. At last the train

The Day after the Pogrom 349

jerked and moved away. The soldiers were opening the door. One passenger had the urge to run away, but a shout stopped him: 'Stop or I'll shoot! Stand still!' A new order: all the coachmen gathered at the railway station must leave. No one dared to take a carriage. The soldiers ordered everyone to line up and move, under police protection, only after the coachmen left.

Everyone who arrived in town, regardless of sex or age, was taken to the police. But they obviously had not expected such a massive influx of people and did not want to let anyone in. The soldiers screamed again in blood-curdling voices, 'Stop!' Their voices were those of savages, the soldiers naturally having got used to the idea that human life is worth nothing. Finally, they had checked everyone's passports and discharged us.

It was pitch dark on the streets. With great difficulty I managed to get to the Jewish hotel and immediately found myself in the centre of events that were not so remote. Everyone started to share and tell what had been going on here, what they had lived through in the past dreadful days. Each fact recounted was more horrible than the last. Everyone tried to share their experience, as if this would make it easier to bear.

The local residents greeted the newly arrived strangers, whom they were seeing gladly and almost happily for the first time in their lives. They acted as though this newspaper correspondent was their best friend, their closest relative. Everyone tried to evoke all the details of their experience so that the out-of-town correspondent could have the most vivid impression, the most precise picture of what had happened.

They were under the impression that nowhere had there ever been such a terrifying pogrom as in Siedlce. (And this despite the provocative threats that if the Bund people were not turned in, the entire town would be looted to pieces.) Dismissing the authorities' claims that the revolutionaries were to blame for everything, that they were the ones who had provoked the pogrom, not one of the people I talked to about the pogrom blamed the Bund. Even the old people were shrewd enough to see through the provocative fabrications of the authorities who had tried to blame the revolutionaries for what had happened. No one else, even those who were left virtually naked and barefoot after the pogrom, had tried to blame the pogrom on the Bund and its people.

From all the stories I heard about the events in Siedlce, one may draw the following picture of what happened in this greatly suffering town.

It seems that the local police chief was killed by a bomb, and an excited mood of pogrom immediately arose in the town. The killings and the forceful agitation among the soldiers started immediately after the police chief's assassination. The Ostrolensky regiment had been quartered in Siedlce, and its soldiers were on friendly terms with the local Jewish population. Among the soldiers were heavily propagandized men in a revolutionary mood, and the organizers of the pogrom could not count on such soldiers. Quite the contrary, many soldiers had promised Jews their help in case of a pogrom. This regiment therefore was moved from Siedlce. In place of the Ostrolensky regiment, the Libau regiment arrived in the town. According to the local Jews, it had already managed to participate in five pogroms. Among the soldiers of this regiment incitement grew to retaliate for the assassination of the police chief.

On the roof of the town hall someone placed a long pole with a furled flag. The pole aroused everyone's curiosity, and the police explained that the moment the flag was raised would be the sign to begin the pogrom. Officer T., who had played a major role in the pogrom back on 22 August, after shooting at the house of Mandel Forschpan right across from the town hall, screamed, 'Get the kikes, guilty or not!'

Preparations for the coming pogrom were carried out so conspicuously that the strange mood of the local Polish residents was visible to all. When a Jew requested that a Polish merchant pay back the money he owed him, the merchant screamed, 'You won't need the money pretty soon. We'll get rid of you!'

On Saturday morning the Polish workers, as well as some Polish merchants, were openly discussing the coming pogrom. The Jews simply could not understand it when the Polish merchants found time to display icons in their shop windows, since as soon as the shooting erupted, no one would go out into the streets for fear of being killed; bullets would rain from all directions like hail. Later the Jews remembered that during the course of Saturday all the outposts around town were abundantly supplied with cases of ammunition. And when all the preparations were finished, military patrols showed up in the streets, announcing that this time the shops would be allowed to stay open until ten at night (under normal circumstances they were only open until eight). Therefore, many opened their shops only in the evening, although they otherwise wouldn't do so on a Saturday evening. The soldiers' words were believed, so much so that some old people went to visit their acquaintances or to take a walk.

The overall mood was very peaceful when suddenly the shooting started. No one knew who was shooting or from where. Different people pointed in different directions, but at all outposts they knew that it was the soldiers.

The owner of a printing shop told me that a soldier was placed next to his shop as a guard to make sure that no illegal publication or leaflet left the shop. However, as soon as a shot was heard, the soldier announced at once that another soldier had been shot, and he opened fire himself.

At the town hall the flag was raised. The shooting started immediately in all the streets. Passers-by who happened to be there by accident were shot at. Thus began the pogrom, which continued in this way from Saturday evening until two o'clock on Monday afternoon. All this time the shooting went on without interruption. It paused only when the supply of bullets ran out and resumed when the reserves were again full.

Who actually shot first? This question probably cannot be fully answered, just as, perhaps, no one knows for sure who threw the first firecracker in Białystok. But from one Jew I heard the following account. Lying in his courtyard behind the gate, he saw a police guard approach a military patrol and ask if they had made money today. One of the soldiers answered that they were guarding public property and therefore couldn't get anything out of it. The policeman said that he would step back a couple of steps and shoot; when they heard the shot, they should immediately start shooting as well, and then they would get something. But, he added, don't shoot me. The guard repeated the same scene with another group of soldiers at the other end of the street. And, indeed, soon a shot was heard, following by shooting and looting by the soldiers.

Another one told me that while hiding in the attic in Suchodolski's house, he saw a policeman, along with some official, walk into the garden near the quartermaster corps building (at the Koński market). There he fired a shot and ran to Warszawski Street. The nearby soldiers immediately opened fire.

I could supply many more such eyewitness accounts, but I will limit myself to one that shows how thoroughly and in what detail the entire hellish plan of the pogrom was plotted.

During the shooting a dragoon came to Z.'s house and began to knock on the gates very forcefully. Reluctantly, they had to open the gates, because everybody knew that in case of delay the gates would be knocked down. To the amazement of Z. and other Jews in the house, the dragoon did not demand money but rather announced that he was appalled by the shooting and looting and therefore wanted to hide from his comrades. He was even ready to change clothes and dress up in Jewish clothes and wanted, along with all the Jews, to hide in the attic or cellar. To Z.'s question what he would do should the shooting begin, the dragoon answered that he would return fire. Z. did not like this answer of the self-appointed Jew-defender. He could easily imagine what the consequences would be if this dragoon, dressed in Jewish clothes, started to shoot from the attic. Therefore, he begged the dragoon to leave him in peace. However, the dragoon insisted on his wish to be among Jews and to be hidden along with them. The Jews in the house pooled some money they had, gave it to their pushy would-be defender, and at last he left. After some time went by, an officer approached the house and started to interrogate the soldiers standing nearby about whether someone had shot from the house in question, and was obviously surprised to receive a negative answer. He asked again and again. Repeatedly being told no, he left in discontent. The plan of the soldier in disguise had not worked.

Those participating in the pogrom did not restrict themselves to shooting. Mass searches followed of the houses from which, as it was claimed, the shots had come. And at this stage the most horrible atrocities occurred. The soldiers, breaking into a house, immediately started shouting and brutalizing everyone who happened to be there, regardless of sex or age. They used rifle-butts, sticks, fists, and blows to kill. Simultaneously they demanded that the allegedly used firearms be turned in.

No firearm ever turned up, for the simple reason that there never was one—and this served as the pretext for renewed brutalities. While some soldiers pretended to conduct searches for guns, others struck people and looted. They turned all pockets inside out and collected everything there. Not having enough prey, they opened chests, desks, and dressers, and devastated them. The soldiers took money, clothes, underwear, jewellery, anything—it didn't matter what it was. Anyone who dared object was severely punished. They had no mercy on old people, women, or children. All shared the same fate. After the scrupulous personal search they lined up everyone in the street and sent them to the police station. *En route* to the police, the atrocities continued with a special ferocity, and many were killed. However, not even those who managed to make it alive to the police station were saved from torture.

One elderly Jew told me his story. He endured all the blows that the soldiers rained on him in his home, but on the street, for some miraculous reason, they did not touch him. Having arrived at the police station, he hoped that it would be the end of his sufferings and that he would be safe. There were a lot of officers at the station. 'Now they won't beat me any more,' he thought, only to be proved grievously wrong. One of the officers suddenly shouted, 'Get all the kikes!', and immediately the Jew received such a blow to the head from a rifle-butt that he fell to the ground. An officer ran up and started to kick him in the head. He jumped up and tried to run away, but along the hallway the blows fell on him like hail. All this took place in front of a large group of police officers.

Many people gathered at the police station, another elderly man told me. The floor was covered with blood from wounds inflicted by sabres and rifles. There was not a drop of water to wash the wounds. Some officer came in and separated the men from the women, and young people from everyone else. The latter group was beaten especially severely and sent to gaol. After that an officer stepped forward and in the name of Chief Guard Tihanovich announced that if the revolutionaries were not turned in immediately, all those detained would be executed. He repeated this a few times. The Jews all began to prepare to die. But after the deadline passed, the detainees were not murdered but were also sent to gaol, where they stayed until Monday. During all this time they were not fed, and they had to buy bread from the inmates. There were 1,100 people in the gaol at that time, all of whom were released on Monday. But the gaoled ones were actually the luckiest. They survived and did not have to witness the horror going on in town at the same time.

The people hiding in attics or cellars turned out to be in a much more difficult situation. In one cellar several families were hiding, old and young. They stayed there from Saturday night until Monday without food or water. The children cried and begged for water. The adults feared that the children's cries would be noticed by the soldiers, and in their horror were even ready to strangle the crying children. Fortunately, things did not go that far. In some cellars people gave children urine to drink. One can well imagine in what state of despair the people must have been to do such things.

No one in hiding could be sure of safety. The soldiers knew that Jews were hiding, and they looked for them everywhere. Sorrow was the fate of those discovered. If someone had cash, he still might have a chance to buy his life. But without money there was no mercy at the hands of the soldiers. Sometimes, however, money did not help either. The soldiers would take the money, then mercilessly kill the person. When one soldier left, another would come with the same demand: 'Guns, money'. Then these left but yet others came, and the looting continued before the eyes of sergeants and other superiors.

When one Jewish man who was being mugged screamed that he would report them, a sergeant jumped at him, pointed a gun to his temple, and shouted, 'Shut up or I'll shoot you!' Another Jew was visited by a group of soldiers and officers who were quartered at his home. The officer grabbed the Jew by his beard, lifted him, and then pointed a sabre to his chest and demanded money. They took the 85 roubles they found in the house and started to beat him. After this the soldiers and the officers left. As soon as they had gone, other soldiers showed up, this time without an officer, and again asked for money. But there was no more. Then the soldiers went into the wine cellar of the house and destroyed everything. Four officers and some soldiers came to another Jewish home. After the usual request for money they conducted a search, which, of course, led to nothing. To get rid of them, the Jew who lived there gave 14 roubles to the officers and four loaves of bread to the soldiers. On Sunday, dragoons stopped by and found 240 more roubles carefully concealed. They took the money and beat everyone in the house to death.

One Jewish shopkeeper was asked by a colonel for cigarettes. Leaving without having paid for them, the colonel said that the shopkeeper would get plenty soon. The colonel had not even gone when shooting erupted. Soldiers broke into the shop, wounded the keeper, and looted everything. Another shopkeeper was asked by an officer to change a 10-rouble note. When the shooting started, the shopkeeper wanted to flee, but the officer calmed him down. But as soon as the shopkeeper opened the counter to give the change, the officer grabbed the cash and shouted, 'OK, guys, get him!' The men did not have to be asked twice. They looted the shop and injured the shopkeeper, his wife, and their two children.

The worst incidents involving robbery took place on Saturday and Sunday. As soon as the shooting started, the soldiers broke into one of the shops, looted everything, and raped the saleswoman. That same evening the soldiers took a whole family, father, mother, and daughter, to the police station. On the way they raped the girl right before her parents' eyes and then shot her. The parents were taken on to the police.

The closed shops were subjected to even more devastating ransacking than the open ones. The soldiers and firefighters were led by policemen who would show them the Jewish stores. The firefighters would break down the door and shameless looting would ensue. They would take everything, down to the most insignificant items. Then they would sprinkle kerosene all around and torch the place. The soldiers took so much that they were not able to carry all the loot away; hired carriages came to transport the goods. In their haste, they would even grab things that had no value whatsoever. One soldier, for instance, grabbed ten boots, all of them left-footed. Only the Jewish stores were looted. In one house there were two stores, one owned by a Jew, the other by a Pole, next to each other. The first was looted, the other was not touched. And not only the soldiers and firefighters were looting, but the policemen as well. On Wednesday, when the pogrom ended, on the outskirts of town a policeman was detained who had tried to escape with goods he had looted from the town.

For the perpetrators of the pogrom, robberies and atrocities were not enough: they also took care to inflict on the suffering Jewish population of Siedlce moral offence and humiliation. In one house, while the inhabitants hid in the back rooms, safe from the bullets, soldiers broke into the house, grabbed all the valuables, took the jam out of the kitchen cabinet, and, having settled at the table, devoured it all. After this they broke all the dishes and turned the room into a lavatory. When another house on the outskirts of town was set ablaze, the soldiers would not let anyone out of the burning house, threatening to kill anyone who tried to fight the fire. The residents of another burning house started to jump out of the windows. The soldiers were about to open fire on them when an officer of the Dubensky regiment arrived and saved the poor people from burning to death.

In front of their officers the soldiers would mercilessly beat children who were throwing themselves on the ground trying to escape the bullets. They showed special cruelty towards the injured lying helplessly on the streets. G. was wounded while being escorted to the police station. He fell in the street. The soldiers wanted to make sure that he was dead, so they stuck a lit cigarette up his nose and tried to open his eyes, but G. showed no signs of life. The soldiers then threw him onto the carriage, took him to the hospital, and again tried to find out if he was alive. Finally, they decided that he was dead and they left. But even in the hospital G. tried not to give any indications that he was alive. They even wanted to transfer him to the morgue. Only when he was sure that the soldiers had left did G. reveal that he was not dead. Telling me some days later what he had experienced on his way to the hospital. G. wondered how he had had enough strength of will to endure everything that had befallen him. R. was not so lucky. The dragoons who took him to the hospital kept trampling on him all the way. They decided he must be dead. But he made a movement, and the dragoons threw him to the ground and beat him to death.

A 69-year-old man was searched, mugged, and beaten. Then he and his wife were taken to the police station. In the street the solders hit him with a rifle so hard that he fell. One soldier struck his head with a sabre, and another shot at him. The bullet hit his face and he was left lying in the street. With great difficulty the old man crawled to his house, where he was let in. There his wound was washed, he was taken care of, and he survived. A 70-year-old man was stabbed with a pike and robbed of his 4 roubles. The soldiers, leaving the poor man, warned him that if he ever again fired at soldiers they would kill him.

It is hard to say whether the soldiers truly believed that every Jew was hiding a revolver or a Browning somewhere, or if such talk only served as an excuse for their murders and looting during the horrible days of the Siedlce pogrom. The case of the hunchback is revealing in this regard. When the pogrom started, Z., the hunchback, was not at home. He was unable to rush home, and spent the whole day hiding at another person's place. When he finally decided to return home, he asked the soldiers he met on his way to take him to a safe place. The hunchback's appearance was so miserable that the soldiers took pity on him and went with him. Leaving town was impossible, because it was guarded on every side by military cordons and nobody was let through. The soldiers took the hunchback through quiet streets, but as they passed some mortars in the street, he stumbled and fell. A dragoon rushed over and started to beat him. The soldiers protested, but the dragoon yelled at them, 'Didn't you see that he wanted to steal the mortar?' Also, at the Angel Hotel and the Hungarian Hotel provocateurs were shooting into the streets, but despite this the hotels remained untouched. Moreover, the Jews who were staying there also survived.

There were non-Jews in Siedlce who, even in these terrible days, displayed humanity towards Jews. The woman who managed the 'Monopol' (liquor) shop on Długa Street hid a few Jewish families at her home. When the soldiers demanded vodka, she refused to open the store, for she did not want the Jews to be discovered, but instead served vodka through the window, arguing that she was afraid of random bullets. A woman whose husband was an officer from the Dubensky regiment hid a couple of Jewish families in her home. Someone reported on her, and the soldiers demanded that they be turned in. The orderly who came out of the house to meet the soldiers swore to God that he hated Jews himself and if he had discovered one he would have killed him already. This convinced the soldiers and they left.

The Jews who told me stories of such unusual manifestations of humanity in Siedlce would say, 'There you have the lucky ones who reserved the right to eternal life in Paradise in exchange for just a few minutes.' Unfortunately, such candidates for life in Paradise were very few in Siedlce.

Translated from Russian by Andrej Huszvai

Jewish Theatre in Poland before the Second World War: Its Audiences and its Critics

MAYA PERETZ

IN his book *Jews in Polish Culture* Aleksander Hertz argues that inter-group relations within a culture depend on 'how the image of one group ... is reflected in the minds of the members of another group'; even if the images represent emotional rather than objective conditions, they nevertheless have tremendous social significance.[1] With the importance of images in mind, it seems an interesting project to examine reviews of the Jewish theatre before the Second World War. Reviews allow a glimpse into Polish–Jewish relations as indirectly reflected in the views of Polish drama critics. They can be more revealing than the sources in which emotions are more rigidly controlled. Here I examine the reviews reprinted in the 1992 single-issue volume of *Pamiętnik Teatralny* devoted to the Polish Yiddish theatre.[2]

The paucity of material in itself is an indication of the most striking characteristic of Polish–Jewish relations during the sixty or so years these reviews cover: a gulf that separated the two ethnic groups, and the scant interest in the Polish community in bridging the gap. Among Catholic Poles the lack of information about Jewish culture was almost total. The Jewish critic Jakub Appenszlak grieved that Polish reviewers kept avoiding Jewish theatre even when truly great art could be seen there. The anonymous author reviewing the first Polish performance of Goldfaden's *Shulamis* at the Alhambra theatre in Warsaw in 1887 was taken by surprise when, expecting a vulgar farce, he saw instead a serious drama based on the Talmud. With incredulity, he reported the absence of obscenities, dirty language, or 'indecent cancan'. In the place of 'degrading cynicism' he found a 'healthy' and uplifting story. He admired the earnest simplicity of the romantic plot, and found the oriental music and dancing that accompanied it vivid and original. He was amazed by the crowds of spectators ('our black-coated Jewish intelligentsia'), many of whom hailed from 'a far province' and whom he estimated at nearly 3,000, and by the enthusiasm and profound solemnity with which they viewed the

[1] Aleksander Hertz, *The Jews in Polish Culture* (Evanston, Ill., 1988).
[2] *Pamiętnik Teatralny*, 41 (1992).

moving play. He admits that the seriousness of intent of the moral drama, which he juxtaposes with 'our usual foolishness and clownery', as well as the audience's reaction, prove 'undoubtedly, a certain level of sophistication' among the Jews, and 'a certain sense of aesthetics, naturally unlike ours, and differently understood'. The reviewer suggests that 'our' (i.e. Polish) provincial theatre should follow a similar path in order to attract and 'civilize the Jewish masses'.

Czesław Jankowski, a columnist for the *Tygodnik Ilustrowany*, reflected on a performance of *Hershele Dubrovner* ('God, Man and Devil') by Jacob Gordin which he saw at the Bagatela Theatre in Warsaw in 1909. He was as shocked by the large audience ('What a number of people in such a huge hall!') as by the absence of good manners they exhibited, the 'absolute lack of formality . . . No one apologizes for pushing a neighbour, which happens more than often. . . . You can tell that they all give vent to their tempers, finding themselves *en famille*.' What puzzled the critic as much as the spectators' lack of civility was their fascination with scholarly and theoretical talk, their tolerance for 'lengthy and clever speech', and their interest in philosophical speculation. The Jewish audience, he felt, 'has talmudic studies in its blood'. Among the audience he noticed many well-off people; the majority, however, were of the third estate. The audience included a large number of youths from nationalist parties. Overheard conversation was in Yiddish ('jargon'), but also in Polish, used by educated Jews even among themselves during the intermissions, while walking in the garden, at the buffet, or the ticket office; also not uncommon was Russian, 'adopted as the mother tongue' by 'Jewish intellectuals' from the Russian partition. Jankowski's tone is slightly sarcastic as he explains what brought him to a Yiddish-language theatre, 'one of three summer Jewish theatres that apparently do great business': a guest performance by a celebrated (and well-publicized) American actor, Maurice Moskowitz. The better-educated audience, too, had come not so much for pleasure as out of duty, the reviewer felt: to honour the 'international fame' of one of their own, and to 'demonstrate their respect for the national jargon'. The non-intellectual crowd, on the other hand, listened attentively and expressed its reactions 'loudly and freely'. According to the critic, the play was rather primitive as a work of literature, but excellent as a spectacle for the crowd. The celebrated American's performance struck Jankowski as pretentious, but he found other actors talented and subtle, the staging interesting, and the choir's singing impressive: 'Altogether, quite a good company, worthy of better stage sets than the extremely poor ones displayed at the Bagatela.'

The review by another writer, Lew Kaltenbergh, recollects Gimpel's theatre in Galician L'viv of 1920, and the unusual way it was run by its owner (simultaneously director, cashier, and box-office clerk) with the help of his sometime manager, Moyshe the Moustache (occasionally also an actor, prompter, and usher). Kaltenbergh remembers superb performances there by such guest actors as Granach, Granowski, Tsemach, Baratov, the 'old' Esther Rachel Kaminska, and the unforgettable Vilna Troupe. However, when there was no star visiting, Gimpel's was a true plebeian theatre, with a traditional repertoire of mediocre musical comedies. The theatre building was a dilapidated shed, cold in the autumn and winter, overheated from spring to early October, but almost always full. Kaltenbergh, too, was even more fascinated with the audience than with the stage, but his observations are those of a frequent visitor. The Gimpel's audience, according to him, was quite an exceptional gathering. People went there having fought over the price of tickets, with teenagers trying to sneak in for free; sometimes more serious scuffles broke out between respectable citizens. Those who came expected and demanded 'something different from their everyday reality, and yet true to life'. Kaltenbergh never figured out how that authenticity was to be achieved, he admits:

Through acting, by choosing a special theme—who knows?—but what [the Jews] demanded was not to be deceived. Which suggests some hidden standards, for after all a great lot of nonsense and trash raised more excitement that some plays of literary value.

But literature is literature, and theatre is theatre:

Books are good to read, while theatre has to be seen. Though, wait a minute; it's not just that. For you have to add the sometimes even too lively participation of the audience in creating the action on stage. I recall how during a performance of an Ibsen drama . . . the hero addressed the heroine: 'Zug mir dem emes!' (Tell me the truth!) and just as the lips of the victim of passion covered in bright lipstick were opening to reveal that 'emes', from various seats in the audience spasmodic cries of frank horror were heard: 'Zug nisht, zug nisht, zei nish a kapora!' (Say nothing, say nothing, don't be a martyr!)

'Nowhere outside that theatre could you see such an audience', Kaltenbergh sighs. There, too, the public was mixed: a street porter next to a pharmacist, a rich merchant's wife or a baker's apprentice, 'all excited, anxiously watching the stage. . . . The crowd of spectators listened attentively, but not quietly. Many whispered, repeating the dialogue. Others commented on the plot.' In Gimpel's theatre, the reviewer says, he acquired a rudimentary knowledge of Yiddish, and learned about the autonomy of a stage play: that it is not always, and perhaps should not be, a repetition of a literary work.

In 1925 the great Polish actor Juliusz Osterwa, director of the Teatr Narodowy, admitted he had hardly any acquaintance with Jewish art and was quite unfamiliar with Jewish literature. Four years earlier, however, he had taken the opportunity to see An-ski's *The Dybbuk* put on by the touring Vilna Troupe, had admired its professionalism, considered Herman's stage direction, especially in group scenes, a masterpiece, and was impressed with the 'dance of death'. He was all the more impressed since the resources the actors and director had to operate with were primitive, and the conditions unbearable. He praised the players' clear enunciation, their ability to enter into the spirit of the characters, and their unusual attention to detail. Osterwa perceived similarity between their style and that of

Polish actors and Stanisławski's school; the actor Noah Nachbush, however, struck him as completely original in his work. The Polish director declared his great interest in the Yiddish theatre: according to the poet, critic, and translator Tadeusz Boy-Żeleński, he even discussed with director Mordekhai Mazo the possibility of staging Stanisław Wyspiański's *The Judges* with Jewish actors in the roles of Jews, and Polish ones playing Christians. Yet, in spite of all that, Osterwa admitted, *The Dybbuk* remained the only Jewish theatrical performance he ever saw.

The literary historian and classicist Tadeusz Sinko, familiar with the art of Habima, considered the existence of a Jewish theatre in his native Kraków 'basically undesirable'. Even so, Sinko praised the 1927 staging of *The Judges* in Yiddish: he was greatly impressed with some of the Yiddish actors' musical ability and talent, and with their teamwork. With extremely modest means, he admitted, the Jews achieved a profound effect. Their reverence for Wyspiański's biblical drama, he believed, arose from their interpretation of the Polish prophetic allegory in the spirit of Zionism. According to Sinko, Wyspiański—with his cryptic philosophy —had a special appeal to Jews, always eager to react to the latest fashion, and so skilled in solving puzzles. The Polish poet's ambiguity drew to him a large number of Jewish commentators, and significantly influenced contemporary Polish Jewish playwrights. If some major Hebrew and Yiddish language troupes adopted his 'Jewish' drama into their repertoire, Sinko believed, Wyspiański would circle the globe.

The actor and director Aleksander Zelwerowicz, who read Yiddish books and plays in translation, became familiar with Jewish theatre and regarded highly such directors as Zygmunt Turkow and especially David Herman, whom he considered a personal friend. Zelwerowicz, who kept in close touch with professional colleagues in the Jewish theatre, was disappointed with its level—although it was not lower, in his opinion than the Polish one—because he had trusted that Jews, who were intellectually and musically gifted, could make especially good actors. He knew of many, in particular from Orthodox families, who distinguished themselves on the Polish stage under assumed names. In an 1927 interview with S. L. Schneiderman for *Literarishe bleter* he praised the performance of Shlomo Ettinger's *Serkele* at the Central Theatre in Warsaw. Asked whether he would agree to direct a play in Yiddish, he responded enthusiastically.

So did Leon Schiller, perhaps the best-known Polish director. Unlike Zelwerowicz, who did not appreciate Goldfaden's 'old and primitive theatre', Schiller liked its folk simplicity. He also saw and was awed by Herman's staging of *The Dybbuk*, and agreed with Zelwerowicz that Jews, with their 'deep inner gesture . . . and ability to create characters, could make excellent actors: witness the many well-known ones on European stages'. Schiller gave high praise to the 1933 staging of *Boston*, by Michał Weichert, in the Jung Theatre, and to its talented young actors, daring experimentation, and successful team effort. The distinguished actress Irena Solska called Weichert a creative genius, and praised the whole company. Schiller patronized Yiddish theatre and confessed that, though he did not understand the language, he sensed a certain 'poetic greatness' in it; he expressed an interest in putting on a Jewish drama himself, and was surprised that, with Yiddish literature and art all the rage in other countries, Poland was silent about it. Less than a year before the outbreak of the war, in October 1938, he finally succeeded in staging Shakespeare's *The Tempest* in the Folks un Yugnt-Teater in Łódź: it was an unusual artistic, as well as social and political, event, marked by the presence, among the 1,200 spectators who filled the enormous hall of the Philharmonic on the opening night, of Polish actors and the Łódź theatre director Aleksander Rodziewicz. But the media showed no interest in that event. The Polish-language Jewish *Nasz Przegląd* reported: '*The Tempest* has become the Warsaw theme. The Jewish part of Warsaw, that is. Silence reigns in the Polish press.' Even the Polish literary periodical *Wiadomości Literackie* was silent, without its usual friendly interest in Leon Schiller's work.

Tadeusz Boy-Żeleński likewise expressed wonder at the fantastic poetry of Yiddish drama, having seen the Vilna Troupe perform Y. L. Perets's *Night at the Old Market*, directed by David Herman, at the Warsaw Elizeum in 1928. The Vilna Troupe's technical level was high, he noted, perhaps thanks to its closer contact with Russian theatre. He especially liked the natural way the Jewish players used stylized gesture and combined the musical and visual elements so as not to slow the pace of the action. (The three-act drama lasted only two hours. But even when the performance of *The Dybbuk* went on until one o'clock in the morning because of trouble with the scenery, he found it worth staying until the end.) Boy-Żeleński was deeply moved by excellent acting, the 'lovely voices, and the method by which they shifted from recitation to song'. In reviewing the Perets play, he gently chastised the apparent lack of interest in Jewish drama by Polish directors:

> One thing has struck me. Does it make any sense to have so little knowledge of one another, while we live so closely? Plays from the whole world, often poor and of no consequence, are staged in our theatres, yet we do nothing at all to recognize the soul of the people with whom we have been destined to coexist. Would it not be a good idea to show some representative Jewish works on the Polish stage? . . . Jewish theatre is worth knowing.

However, by 1932 Boy-Żeleński's call for increased interest in Jewish stage art had as yet had no effect, as the writer Zygmunt Tonecki mourned: 'Jewish theatre still remains on the margin of general theatre life in Poland. Our theatre so far has not used its appeal to attract minority drama to Polish culture.' In 1937 *Wiadomości Literackie* published Tonecki's article on Yiddish theatre in Poland, in which he praised the theatre's excellent musical and visual designs, as well as the systematic training of the gifted young actors.

Tonecki considered the Vilna Troupe, with its mainly Russian repertoire, the most interesting expression of Jewish literary drama, and noticed that, after the original triumph of the mystical *Dybbuk*, theatre was drawn to more secular forms and became a powerful tool in the struggle against the domination of hasidic rabbis over the lives of Polish Jews. He saw in Michał Weichert's production of Sholem Asch's *Kidush hashem* a successful attempt to link modern European drama with the traditional Jewish stage. Weichert's German education and his daring treatment of traditional themes, as well as his introduction of modern comedies, Tonecki believed, made the troupe a truly European theatre. As he grew more familiar with the Jewish stage, the Polish reviewer was struck by the young actors' professional competence and the beautiful staging and vigorous direction of plays, which were good enough to be shown on Polish stages.

In 1936 the reviewer Jerzy Stempowski described performances of two plays on similar subjects, and compared the Polish audience with the Jewish one. He notes the difference in values, which he attributes not to any 'biological' traits, nor to differences in temper, but to the groups' respective social positions and levels of prosperity. Whereas in the Polish theatre there was a lack of contact between the stage and the audience, in the Jewish one 'spectators followed the course of the action and the work of their favourite actors with bated breath . . . People were very moved. There was no end to the applause. The author appeared after the last curtain to address the audience.'

The great Polish actor Stefan Jaracz commended the Jewish actors' superb delivery of texts and a 'European' level of stage direction: 'the general impression', he pronounced, was 'most favourable. This may be the way to revitalize contemporary theatre.'

In 1934, as German Jews started arriving in Poland, the popular novelist Maria Kuncewiczowa had a chance to see the Berlin actor Alexander Granach in her first viewing of a Yiddish drama. The play, *The Yellow Patch* by Friedrich Wolf (known in German as *Professor Mamlock*), was at Kamiński's theatre in Warsaw, and its subject was fascist brutality against Jews. Kuncewiczowa's article is a truly amazing document of social psychology, as it shows how difficult it is, even for an artist skilled at probing individual feelings, to distance herself from cultural stereotypes.

Not only was Kuncewiczowa a newcomer to Jewish theatre, but apparently she found herself surrounded by Jews for the first time, and her sense of isolation and discomfort is evident in her review; after all, as she writes,

an ethnic Pole rarely appears among Jews unless on a practical business matter and with a feeling of fateful biological differences. One enters usually not as a private person but as if in the role of a messenger with a specific mission.

At the theatre she felt unprotected,

for after all no Jew will fail to identify an Aryan among even the most uniform pack of Semites. You do not need to have hair the colour of wheat, nor eyes the colour of bluebells, nor a wistfully Slavic brow, to be immediately exposed. I was standing to the side of a group of women, and noticed soon that the Jewesses behind me, having barely glanced at the back of my neck, seized by a sneaking suspicion, started elbowing their way closer to me through the crowd to peek under my hat and make sure that here I, a stranger, had come, for some unfathomable reason.

Kuncewiczowa's text is interesting as much for what it says about the observer as about the observed. She came for the best of reasons: curiosity, a friendly interest; she even feared for the Jews as, upon leaving the theatre, she noticed a group of hoodlums in the street (in describing them, she uses a most uncomplimentary word for Polish youth). And yet both the performance and the audience seemed so exotic to her that the reader cannot help wondering whether she might have been projecting her own sense of fear, vulnerability, and repulsion upon those she was portraying.

Entering the hall of the enormous wooden rotunda, made into a theatre, a stranger is immediately struck by the density of the atmosphere. And Jews—when spotting a goy in their midst—are used to seeing him rather as an agent than a guest. In such circumstances therefore, when a Jewish affair takes place within a private circle, shielded by a foreign tongue, when Jerusalem can speak to a stranger only through the intangible idiom of art, when there is nothing to buy and nothing to sell, and also nothing to hide from an enemy except one's own grief, the presence of a goy—a phenomenon as incomprehensible as the appearance of a comet upon a familiar fragment of the sky—raises uneasiness and disgust.

The stereotype of the Jew as a weakling must also have been present in her mind as she watched the play. Kamiński's theatre was located at Dynasy, a sports park, the site of bicycle races, and the writer observed:

It was hard for me to accept the fact that . . . the Jewish drama would be played on the stage of the celebrated exploits of Aryan brawn. . . . Each time I heard that name, I always imagined the stout calves of master mechanics and apprentices, flitting by with swollen veins among glistening wheels, before the rows of robust Slavic mugs sweating from ardour and heat.

An attempt to challenge the stereotype proved too much to her, and she seems to suspect its constant presence in the minds of the others as well.

The actors, she recalls, were Yiddish-speaking Jews. The Aryan effect was achieved with blond wigs. Unlike the female performers, whom she found moving in their individual tragedy, the actor playing a Hitler dignitary, 'satisfied with his brown shirt and a swastika on his sleeve, completely forgot to mark his character's humanity, and appeared as a propaganda puppet of Germany. . . . He gave full vent to his imagined Aryanism, vigorously stamping his feet, throwing out his chest, and with real contempt and authentic *ḥutspah* mistreated his Israelite brethren.' What shocked the Polish writer above all was the spectators' reaction to this show of ruthlessness. The same intelligent neighbours who expressed embarrassment when some young men started brawls for seats appeared delighted with the crude maleness in the shape of the German officer: 'When . . . the Nazi started yelling and brutalizing the people on stage . . . to my greatest amazement, I noticed exhilaration, tenderness, and pride in their faces . . . A fat, elegant lady [next to me] bent over her thin husband, whispering: "Just like some Cossack or uhlan . . . There is nothing Jewish at all about this boy!" ' That the Jewish actor pretended to be a Nazi with so much zeal offended and embarrassed Kuncewiczowa. What she observed was not a totally unfamiliar phenomenon: the tendency of the minority to identify with and internalize the values of the majority. In the case of the Jewish intelligentsia in Poland it often led to attraction to different values and a desire to abandon tradition, hence assimilation, as well as fascination with radical politics. Some of the viewers at the Jewish theatre observed by the Polish critic Jankowski did support their own art, but were far from admiring it. 'They like Polish theatre better . . . of course, but *hebraïsme oblige*.'[3]

The desire to be viewed as people like everybody else was evident among the audiences in various ways, and Maria Kuncewiczowa made a fair effort not to be prejudiced in her judgement. Sitting among those people, she states, 'I felt by no means frightened or disgusted by the exotic milieu.' On the contrary, 'I enjoyed absorbing that strangeness and regretted finding underneath the common human drama of life, subject to death.'

The audience in the Yiddish theatre, she observed, did not smell of onions, nor were the men all dressed in black gabardines. The spectators looked like merchants, salesmen, salesgirls, from Nalewki, Muranów, the whole hierarchy of small trade: European, because the oriental costumes and scents would adversely affect business, but still Asian enough for haggling about prices to be an everyday occurrence. Many among them, dignified and tolerant, moody or commendably preoccupied with their neighbours' manners, revealed an affiliation with the intelligentsia. (In fact, Polish critics observe that all Jewish political parties were represented in the theatre audiences: Orthodox, as well as Bundists and Zionists.)

Unable to rid herself of the cultural stereotype of 'the Other', Kuncewiczowa was convinced that that collective 'other' viewed her solely as a representative of her race, and much as she denies feeling threatened, her observations reveal a sense of fear—a sense she seems to project on those she observes:

The men—sensitive to sex, as all people destined for warm climes—couldn't pass a woman's coat on a not-too-shapeless frame with indifference but—having recognized the mark of an Aryan—shuddered as if touched by an electric current. Not by the current of sex by any means, but the current of a defence instinct. What surrounded me in a moment,

---

[3] The desire to leave behind traditional attitudes of quiet scholarship, diligence, and passivity sometimes led to Zionism, with its heroic yet judaically based Jewish aspirations. The need to free oneself from the diaspora stereotype of a weakling is still observable in Israel today. When in Amos Oz's *Fima* the protagonist shouts at his father: 'We're the Cossacks now, and the Arabs are the victims of the pogroms,' the old man replies: 'Nu? What of it? So what's wrong with our being the Cossacks for a change?'

however, was not hostility; it was rather a nervous anticipation of a miracle: for the Lord of Israel to wipe me from the surface of the earth, or for me to turn their tired hearts into stone, their doomed hopes into ashes, with the force of my powerful goyish witchcraft.

The discrepancies between the various Polish reviewers' treatment of Jewish theatre reveal as much about the critics as about their subjects. Those familiar with the art and the performers were mainly interested in the way the theatre worked, and did not in any way comment on external matters, unless on the lack of interest by the general Polish public. They were strictly professional in their criticism and rarely given to stereotypical thinking. They reviewed Jewish plays the way they would review any other. The more professional they were, indeed, the more matter-of-fact their opinions. It was the writers less familiar with theatrical form, and even less so with the Jewish community, who could not relate to their topic without revealing all kinds of stereotypical fears and resentments.

In his investigation of Polish–Jewish relations, which he wrote in the United States, Aleksander Hertz often refers to Gunnar Myrdal's study *The American Dilemma: The Negro Problem and Modern Democracy* (1944), and I can see why. After spending a quarter of a century in the United States I have stopped regarding the situation of the Jewish community in Poland as unique to its place and time and now tend to view it more in general terms, as a minority in the context of a larger society that is different from it, and unfamiliar with it. Recently I went to a theatre in the predominantly black area of Washington where I live. The play, dealing with all manner of problems of black urban life, was well written and very well produced, though with obviously meagre resources. The musical variety and the actors' vocal ability were amazing. The audience reacted to the plot with great enthusiasm, applauding loudly, sometimes jumping up and down and dancing in the aisles. I enjoyed watching both stage and audience—while all the time I kept thinking: 'Why is mine one of only three pale faces among the audience of about 500 blacks? With all the complications and conflicts of our urban coexistence, why didn't more whites attend the performance? Aren't they interested in understanding the people so many of them fear? Or is this fear the reason for the apparent lack of interest?' I couldn't help comparing this experience with the Polish reviews of Jewish shows in Poland and what they reveal: a similar isolation in the midst of a larger society, a similar gulf between the two communities, similar resentments and prejudices.

In a situation marked by such a gulf, minority theatre is an expression of more than the need for entertainment and aesthetics; it comes to express all its cultural longing. The reaction to it therefore is equally intense, on the part of both its audiences and critics from the outside. The critics' attitudes seem to reflect their attitude to the 'Jewish question' or 'Black question' in general, and point to the distance that separates them from the minority community. What Jakub Appenszlak said about the Poles' abysmal lack of knowledge of the Jewish theatre can also be said about the awareness of African American drama among the majority of American whites: 'They are less familiar with [it] . . . than with that of distant China.'

The reviews in *Pamiętnik Teatralny* reveal what another Polish writer, the historical novelist Antoni Gołubiew, lamented: the extent to which, in pre-war Poland, 'the two worlds, the Christian and the Jewish one, living next to one another in the same land, united by thousands of links and connections, meeting daily, were really separated by an unsurmountable wall, remote, almost foreign'.[4]

[4] Antoni Gołubiew, *Szaja Ajzensztok* (Kraków, 1984), foreword. The passages from Gołubiew and all the reviews quoted in this article appear in my translation.

Forbidden Fruit: Illicit Love Affairs between Jews and Gentiles in the Novels of Julian Stryjkowski

REGINA GROL

THE historic encounter of Jewish, Polish, and Ukrainian communities in the territories of east-central Europe belongs to an irretrievable past. Gone is one of the communities. Gone are the geopolitical circumstances in the heart of Europe that brought the three nationalities together. The challenge before today's scholars, therefore, is to reconstruct a vanished world, with all its ethnic, linguistic, cultural, religious, and ideological diversity. A primary avenue of access to this past is literature. Not uncommonly, however, social scientists dismiss the value of literary works as sources of historical and social information: after all, their argument goes, a work of fiction may or may not have a basis in fact, and even if it does, it reflects only one person's interpretation of those facts, rendering it scientifically unreliable. Yet there are domains of human experience—matters of the heart, for instance—that can be reflected much more adequately and truly in literary texts than in sociological and historical treatises. Indeed, literature is epistemologically privileged in seeking and expressing human truths. It can convey emotional intensity and reflect moral perplexity, directly and powerfully. And if a literary work happens to be autobiographical, or based on the author's intimate, first-hand knowledge of a subject, the insights it offers can be valuable, even if slanted or stylized. The historical significance of such literary testimonials is inestimable.

A clear case in point is the work of Julian Stryjkowski (1905–96), a Polish Jewish writer born Pesach Stark in Stryi, eastern Galicia. In most of his *œuvre* Stryjkowski exhibits a pronounced loyalty to his Jewish heritage, and several of his novels are dedicated specifically to the reconstruction of the pre-First World War Jewish milieu of the region where he was born and lived. In four of Stryjkowski's novels the lost world of early twentieth-century Galician towns, from Kolomyia to L'viv, that were inhabited largely by Poles and Jews and embedded in a sea of Ukrainian villages, comes vividly to life. This chronologically disjointed tetralogy consists of *Głosy w ciemności* ('Voices in the Darkness', published in 1957, although written in the mid-1940s), *Austeria* ('The Inn', 1966), *Sen Azrila* ('Azril's Dream',

1975), and *Echo* (1988).[1] Stryjkowski's incorporation of eyewitness accounts into his novels and the autobiographical nature of his writing are corroborated in interviews he has granted in recent decades, adding weight to the factual content of his fiction.[2]

Together Stryjkowski's four Galician novels constitute a subtly evoked return to a segment of Europe now vanished, and they focus heavily on the Jewish community. The author reconstructs the reality of Jewish life with such sympathy and meticulousness that one never doubts its authenticity. He is faithful to details of custom and tradition, to nuances of speech; he traces the changes effected in the Jewish community by political movements and explores the characteristics and conflicts of the group with exceptional powers of social observation. Poles and Ukrainians, by contrast, are marginal presences in his works. Indeed, the thrust of his writing appears to be to underscore the *separateness* of the Jews in Galicia, the gulf that existed between them and their Christian neighbours prior to the First World War. (The period is crucial to bear in mind, since in that region interactions between ethnic groups in the realms of politics and love increased significantly only in subsequent years.)

Their own distinctiveness and separateness is deeply ingrained in the consciousness of Stryjkowski's Jewish characters. In all four novels one finds explicit testimonials to that effect. One character in *Austeria* declares: 'The world has been divided ever since Creation into Jews and *goyim*' (p. 150). In *Sen Azrila*, as the church bells begin to chime the hours, the protagonist, Azril, reminisces about his father's early instructions similarly: 'Father taught him that it is better not to count church hours. A Jew shouldn't take advantage of it. Just as one shouldn't mix kosher with *treyf*, one shouldn't mix their time with ours' (pp. 32–3). At times the father's lessons are even more insistent. He admonishes young Azril to maintain his religious distinctiveness in these telling words: 'Remember that you are a Jew, and if you ever have the choice between baptism and death, you'll prefer death' (p. 36). In *Głosy w ciemności* the protagonist, Aronek, though a very curious little boy, instinctively utters a Hebrew charm and turns his head away as he passes the Greek Orthodox church.[3]

The separateness of the communities results in a lack of mutual understanding and in bewilderment about customs and habits. In *Echo*, when the funeral of Bejrish, a Jewish youngster killed by a Hungarian hussar, takes place on market-day, the peasants feel inconvenienced, of course, but they also cannot comprehend the logic of such scheduling. Nor can they fathom the solemnity of the occasion.

---

[1] All were published by Czytelnik (Warsaw). Of them, only *Austeria* has come out in English, as *The Inn*, trans. Celina Wieniewska (New York, 1972).

[2] See e.g. 'Poeta bolszewicki', interview with Julian Stryjkowski by Piotr Szewc, *Zeszyty Literackie*, 28 (Autumn 1989), 106–14.

[3] With the exception of passages from *Austeria*, which are excerpted from Wieniewska's English translation, all citations here are my own translations from the original Polish editions.

As Stryjkowski puts it: 'The peasants were insulted and kept spitting'—and here Stryjkowski introduces a statement in Ukrainian—'The Jews are acting stupidly. As if Emperor Franz himself had come' (*Chłopi byli obrażeni i pluwali. 'Zydy podurily. Mabut Cisar Franc prijichal'*; p. 50).

An even more telling example of misunderstanding is found in *Głosy w ciemności*. The Ukrainian Wasyl Prejmycz is puzzled each and every year when his Jewish neighbours ask him to help them make their houses kosher for Passover by buying their *humets*, that is, flour and beans—with the expectation that he will return the goods when the eight days of Passover are over. Prejmycz cannot understand the logic of the transaction. He is willing to store the food but sees no reason to buy it and then return it to the Jews a few days later. The intricate explanation that disposal of these goods has to be validated by the act of selling is beyond him. He ends up infuriating the woman of the house and makes her suspect that he only pretends not to understand, in order to extricate more money.

Separateness and emotional distance are also underscored through scenes reflecting Jewish bias and contempt towards Poles and Ukrainians. When Aronek, in the same novel, is less than attentive during a Bible lesson, his father, Reb Tojwie, suggests the boy will amount to nothing and grow up to be like their stupid Ukrainian neighbour, the same Prejmycz: 'What are you thinking of? A *goyish* head! Wasyl Prejmycz! You'll end up like him, carrying water for the Jews' (*O czym ty myślisz? Gojowska głowo! Wasylko Prejmycz! Będziesz jak on nosić Żydom wodę*; p. 40). By insulting comparing his son to 'a *goyish* head' (a phrase taken directly from the Yiddish *a goyishe kop*) Reb Tojwie shows his condescension towards Ukrainians.

In another vein Stryjkowski provides statements by self-hating Jews who, while disputing Jewish superiority, by the same token underscore Jewish separateness. In *Echo* Lorka, an advocate of assimilation, makes this public accusation: 'Normal nations are satisfied with one language, but Jews in addition to all their troubles must have two [Hebrew and Yiddish], instead of learning and mastering the speech of the country in which they have lived for hundreds of years. Where is the proverbial Jewish intelligence, if after years of living on this soil they haven't been able to learn the Polish language?' And she adds: 'Jews are an alien body among the populations surrounding them. They themselves have created the ghetto; they are enraged by symptoms of hatred, and yet they themselves have contempt for *goyim*, and consider themselves superior' (p. 101).

Stryjkowski's Galician tetralogy reflects Jewish separateness not only in linguistic and social terms. The author renders it in religious, theological terms as well. The lives of Stryjkowski's Jewish characters are controlled, often to the point of suffocation, by a myriad of religious dictates that distinctly differ from those of their Christian neighbours. The Jews also have a profound sense of the distinctiveness of their God. As the student Selig in *Głosy w ciemności* proclaims: 'A Jew doesn't have to ask God for rain in the spring, nor for good weather during harvest time. For a peasant, God sprouts in his fields and is most intimately connected with him through the soil. For the peasant, God is, like all life, a creation. For Jews, ever since they lost their fatherland, God, like their own life, is suspended in the air, is an abstraction' (p. 348).

These examples amply illustrate Stryjkowski's insistence on reflecting the enormous chasm between Jews and their Polish and Ukrainian neighbours. He shows biases and resentments, as well as cultural, linguistic, and religious barriers. There is an almost hermetic quality to Jewish life in Galicia as depicted by Stryjkowski. And yet a closer look at the novels reveals that the locus of their emotional intensity and the major cause or underpinning of the characters' moral agonies are precisely instances where Jews and non-Jews come together. I refer not to innocent professional or social encounters but to much more intimate ties: illicit love affairs. Though treated briefly and elliptically, these affairs give impetus within the novels to most profound introspection and agonizing self-assessment, on both the personal and the communal level.

In *Głosy w ciemności* Reb Tojwie—a pious and learned man of unshakeable integrity, almost to the point of moral rigidity (his wife refers to him as 'God's policeman')—suffers emotional trauma as a result of his daughter's affair with a Polish official, Kassaraba. Reb Tojwie's address to God is heart-rending: 'You hit me with a thunderbolt. I lie crushed in dust like an earthenware pot. Yes, You did kill me, even though You tell me to continue to shuffle my feet' (p. 447).[4] The Pole, Kassaraba, is said to 'prowl on the Jewish street'. He has attempted other affairs with Jewish women and has previously married—and divorced—a Jewish woman as well. Tojwie's daughter, Chamariem, who adopts the Polish name Maria, abandons her career as a teacher in a Polish school and elopes with Kassaraba to Vienna. The reputation of the whole family is ruined as a consequence. Reb Tojwie's moral authority is undermined and he is forced to leave town. His sons are expelled from the synagogue. The parents are devastated; they declare Maria dead and cut all ties with her.

The most intense sentiments in *Echo*—which although written about forty years later constitutes a sequel to *Głosy w ciemności*—revolve around the same illicit affair. We find out through various allusions and fleeting second- or even third-hand accounts that, because of Maria's refusal to convert to Christianity, Kassaraba has abandoned her. Maria went into shock and ended up paralysed in a Viennese hospital, where she died after much suffering. It is worth noting that the second novel of the tetralogy, *Austeria*, contains a dedication 'to the memory of my sister Maria Stark, who died in Vienna in the year 1922'. This appears to suggest a factual basis to the story of Maria in *Echo*.

An altogether different illicit affair is presented in *Austeria*—one, however, that also results in personal torment and the main character's assumption of responsi-

---

[4] Trans. Ida Pizem-Karczag, 'The Jewish "Trilogy" of Julian Stryjkowski', *Polish Review*, 4 (1983), 91.

bility on behalf of the entire Jewish community. The action takes place during one night, at an inn on the outskirts of an unspecified Galician town. The First World War has just begun; the town is already burning. Facing the menace of an imminent pogrom, various Jews seek refuge in the inn. Old Tag, the innkeeper, takes on the role of their leader and spokesman. This character has been likened to the biblical Noah, and his inn to Noah's Ark amid a sea of calamity.[5] Indeed, he appears a righteous old man, a patriarchal figure, spouting biblical verses and exuding wisdom. And yet just a few pages before the novel's end we come upon a startling revelation. Tag has lived in sin with his Ukrainian maid, Jewdocha; his wife's final words were: 'You could have waited until I was dead.' In Tag's concluding and emotionally dense confrontation with God he accuses God of endowing him with weak flesh, but concedes his sin, admits that individual sins affect the community, and therefore shoulders responsibility and guilt for the outbreak of the entire war. The epigram to the book, significantly, reads: 'Can a man take fire in his bosom and his clothes not be burned?' (Prov. 6: 27). The context in the book of Proverbs suggests a clear admonition against carnal weakness. Only a few lines further we read: 'So he who goes in to his neighbour's wife; whoever touches her shall not be innocent.' The authority of the Bible is brought to bear on Tag's transgression.

In the novel *Azril's Dream* the action also takes place during one long night, suffused with the oppressive atmosphere of a nightmare. Azril, a recently widowed man, returns to his native town after a twenty-year absence. Ostensibly, he comes to visit the graves of his parents. His motives may also include finding a second wife, since he still dreams of a son, or perhaps finding a husband for his choosy and bookish daughter. Primarily, however, he comes haunted by a dream of his father and determined to restore his ties with his Jewish past. He is a tormented man, desperately in need of inner peace. Once more Stryjkowski keeps the secret of the character's turmoil until the very end. Three pages before the conclusion of this short (140-page) novel, we discover the cause of Azril's anxiety and despair. He had married for money, never loved his wife, and worse still, drove her to suicide by having a blatant affair with his Ukrainian maid, Nastka. Though Nastka bore him a child, Azril has never acknowledged her son, Wasyl. Guilt-ridden, confused, and anxious to return to a pious Jewish life, Azril contemplates marrying a young Jewish woman and chasing Nastka and Wasyl away. He vacillates and agonizes. The conflict between his spiritual and carnal needs exhausts him. At one point he confronts God with a poignant self-defence: 'What have I done that's worse than the deeds of King David?' The end of the novel strongly implies Azril's suicide.

Other illicit attractions and affairs are repeatedly alluded to in Stryjkowski's Galician tetralogy. The passionate liaison between the Jewish girl Fancia and Petro, the son of a Ruthenian (Ukrainian) priest, resonates throughout *Głosy w ciemności* as well as in *Echo*. In the latter book there are also brief references to the

---

[5] Z. Bieńkowski, 'Pierwszy dzień potopu', *Kultura*, 47 (1966), 8.

budding love between Matylda, a Jewish carpenter's daughter, and her father's young Polish employee. (Interestingly, the novel ends with two Jewish young men emigrating to Palestine because the Jewish girls they fancy are in love with 'goyim'.) But perhaps the most drastic depiction of an illicit affair concerns Rachmil, the bead-seller of *Głosy w ciemności*, who seduces a Ukrainian girl. The two lovers are struck by lightning and found dead under a tree. The girl is still wearing the damaging evidence: the beads offered her by Rachmil. The incident galvanizes the Jewish and Ukrainian communities and sets them against one another, and the possibility of a pogrom looms large. The transgression is perceived not only as a violation of a social taboo but as a disturbance of the natural order of things. Hence, ominously, the lightning and thunder are interpreted by both communities as evidence of God's wrath.

If I provide no steamy details about the various illicit affairs, that is because none are to be found. Stryjkowski's works are not sensationalist in a vulgar or sordid way, nor are they graphic. All the affairs are treated elliptically. The books are sensationalist only in that the events they describe send shockwaves through the Jewish and non-Jewish communities within the novels and make apparent to both sides the violation of a taboo.

What do all the affairs and secret liaisons in Stryjkowski's novels attest to? In terms of literary archetypes and myths, they are not unusual, of course. In Western culture, at least, there appears to be, as Denis de Rougemont has noted, a secret desire for obstruction in love and an obsession with 'the love that breaks the law'.[6] According to Rougemont, the allure of the forbidden—or taboo—is enormous; in effect it is a powerful aphrodisiac.[7] The exoticism of Jewish women for Polish men, and conversely the allure of Polish and Ukrainian women for Jewish men, thus, is not surprising.

The illicit liaisons and attractions in Stryjkowski's Galician novels reflect the irrational arbitrariness of instincts. They attest to the overwhelming force of Eros. In a related interview Stryjkowski explicitly acknowledges the importance of this domain of life.[8] Freud's *Civilization and its Discontents* and Marcuse's *Eros and Civilization* would certainly support the irrationality of attraction and corroborate the tensions between primal urges and imposed cultural constructs.

Despite the obvious strictures of civilization and religion, one might be tempted to interpret the cross-religious affairs in Stryjkowski's works as optimistic—as indications of positive mutual perceptions of the Galician ethnic groups' common humanity and their capacity to ignore differences. In Stryjkowski's rendition, however, the affairs appear to be exploited primarily to test a Jew's capacity to adhere to Judaism. The illicit liaisons lead to personal and communal reassessments

[6] Denis de Rougemont, *Love in the Western World* (New York, 1956), 17, 52.
[7] Denis de Rougemont, *Love Declared: Essays on the Myths of Love* (New York, 1963).
[8] Szewc, 'Poeta bolszewicki', 107, 111.

within the Jewish community, and enhance the delineation of ethnic, religious, social, and moral boundaries. They represent extreme behaviour that serves to underscore the limits. The affairs constitute a serious threat to the survival of the community as a distinct entity. Although not expressed directly, the need for the maintenance and cohesiveness of the community seems to be a given for the author. Thus, the treatment of the episodes of illicit love may be perceived as implicit moralizing. The affairs are negative object lessons intended to uphold the Jews' psychological and moral integrity, as well as the integrity of the community. That is why all end so tragically. Chamariem–Maria dies paralysed and abandoned; her father is left morally broken; Rachmil and his paramour are struck by lightning; and Azril commits suicide. These affairs are presented as transgressions, with severe repercussions for the individuals, their families, and their communities. They are reminders, in a word, of the limits that should not be overstepped.

At the same time, however, the liaisons seem to have a real basis in fact. If we accept the historical validity of Stryjkowski's novels, the affairs undercut the notion of the hermetic isolation of the Jewish community, its total separateness and impenetrability. His works reflect the powerful centrifugal forces operative in the Jewish communities, and they convey grippingly the moral tensions, and emotional tangles and confusion, engendered by intimate encounters between Jews and non-Jews in the Galicia of the early twentieth century. Stryjkowski's writing is in a very deep sense the artistic product of the culture of the multinational Habsburg empire, of the borderland where Polish, Ukrainian, and Jewish paths and lives intertwined.

Ludwik Rajchman: A Biographical Sketch of a Polish Jew

MARTA ALEKSANDRA BALIŃSKA

LUDWIK RAJCHMAN'S principal claim to fame is his role in the establishment of the United Nations International Children's Emergency Fund (Unicef). Until recently his story has gone largely untold.[1] His contributions to Unicef, and to the World Health Organization, established by the League of Nations, however, deserve acknowledgement and further study, as do the reasons why his role in these institutions has largely been ignored.

Ludwik Rajchman (1881–1965) was not a man who sought renown, and to compound this reticence, the last twenty years of his life were overshadowed by the painful contradictions of the Cold War, amongst which seems to have been the effacement of more than one interesting international figure.[2] In addition, Rajchman's identification with three communities—the Polish, the Jewish, and the international—has meant that none has entirely 'claimed' him for its own. There are perhaps only three milieux where Rajchman's name and deeds are familiar. At the National Institute of Hygiene in Warsaw several photographs and plaques commemorate his role as founder of the institution. Followers of his friend and contemporary Jean Monnet are impressed by the universal vision of one of their mentor's closest friends; finally—and paradoxically—the French antisemitic writer Céline's love–hate portrayal of Rajchman has been explored by all his biographers.[3]

Rajchman was born into an assimilated Jewish family belonging to the Warsaw upper bourgeoisie. On his father's side were several engineers and medical men, while his mother was descended from the prominent Hirszfeld family. Rajchman's

---

[1] Marta A. Balińska, *For the Good of Humanity: Ludwik Rajchman, Medical Statesman* (Budapest, 1998).
[2] The political failure of the League of Nations has led to several exceptional figures being ignored, while the foundations they laid in international co-operation are often attributed to the United Nations or other post-war organizations. Among others: Albert Thomas, Fridtjöf Nansen, and Rachel Crowdy. Even Jean Monnet has only recently been the subject of a biography: Eric Roussel, *Jean Monnet* (Paris, 1996). For Zaleski and Lange see Piotr Wandycz, *Z Piłsudskim i Sikorsim: August Zaleski minister spraw zefrenicznych v latach 1926–1932 i 1939–1941* (Warsaw, 1999), and O. Lange, *Dzieło*, vol. viii, which contains a detailed chronicle of Lange's life.
[3] e.g. Philippe Almeras, *Les Idées de Céline* (Paris, 1992); François Gibault, *Céline: le temps des espérances* (Paris, 1974); Frédéric Vitoux, *La Vie de Céline* (Paris, 1988).

grandfather, Ludwik Hirszfeld, was a well-to-do banker who had supposedly financed the insurrection of 1863, and who encouraged the artistic inclinations of his daughter and son-in-law by supporting their weekly salons. Rajchman's uncle, Bolesław Hirszfeld, a chemist by training, belonged to the progressive Warsaw intelligentsia (he was a close friend of the father of Polish sociology, Ludwik Krzywicki) and was known as an ardent patriot and defender of political prisoners. His brother Stanisław ran the highly fashionable Mineral Waters Institute in the Saxon Gardens and was the father of Ludwik Hirszfeld, one of the first immunologists of this century and author of *Historia jednego życia*.[4]

Rajchman's mother, Melania, was an active member of the Polish movement and the instigator of the first international women's congress, held in Paris in 1909. As a prolific publicist she used various pen-names for her column in Wilhelm Feldman's prestigious *Krytyka* and her contributions to *Echo muzyczne, artystyczne i literackie*, edited by her husband, Aleksander Rajchman. He is best remembered as the creator of the Filharmonia in Warsaw (inaugurated in 1901), whose orchestra was directed by Rubinstein's future father-in-law, Emil Młynarski. The Rajchmans' salon was a cultural event attended by people such as Ignacy Paderewski, Bolesław Prus, Maria Konopnicka, Henryk Sienkiewicz, Eliza Orzeszkowa and, from abroad, Richard Strauss, Edvard Grieg, and Isadora Duncan. This lively environment provided considerable stimulus for the three Rajchman children: Helena Radlińska (1879–1957), Ludwik, and Aleksander (1890–1940), who became, respectively, historian and pedagogue, epidemiologist, and mathematician. Taking after their mother and uncle Bolesław, all three developed deep social and patriotic commitments.

Helena, after escaping from Siberia subsequent to the revolution of 1905 (in which she played a prominent role), collaborated intimately with Piłsudski during the First World War. After Polish independence she left the Polska Partia Socjalistyczna (Polish Socialist Party: PPS) and devoted herself to adult education and historical research. Among other activities, she co-founded and directed the Institute of Social Work, where Janusz Korczak, for example, gave his memorable lectures.[5] Radlińska survived the war in a convent and later held a chair at the University of Łódź until political pressure led to her early retirement.[6]

Aleksander Rajchman taught mathematics between the wars at the Warsaw and Popular Universities, where his students included two of the most brilliant mathematicians of the twentieth century, Antoni Zygmund and Alfred Tarski. Politically, Aleksander was more radical than his siblings, belonging to the

---

[4] L. Hirszfeld, *Historia jednego życia* (Warsaw, 1946).

[5] For an English biography of Korczak, see B. J. Lifton, *The King of the Children: A Biography of Janusz Korczak* (New York, 1988).

[6] For biographical material on Radlińska, see H. Radlińska, *Z dziejów pracy społecznej i oświatowej* (Wrocław, 1961); I. Lepalczyk and B. Wasilewska (eds.), *Helena Radlińska: i wychowawca* (Warsaw, 1994–5).

Trotskyist wing of the Polish Communist Party. With the rise of the far right in the 1930s, he advocated an alliance with the PPS, and in 1936 came out publicly against the antisemitic campaign being waged in Polish universities.[7] Three years later he was caught in one of the first Nazi round-ups of Polish professors and died a few months afterwards, probably at Sachsenhausen.

Ludwik Rajchman completed the Russian gymnasium in 1900. He then acceded to his parents' wish that he train as a physician (he himself had wanted to read law) on condition that he do so at the Jagiellonian University in Kraków, at that time the leading Polish institution in many disciplines. The university's location in Galicia, which held autonomous status within Austria–Hungary, brought numerous political and social advantages.

The chair of bacteriology at the Jagiellonian University was occupied by Odon Bujwid, the father of Polish microbiology, who inspired the young Rajchman with a passion for this relatively new science. In the 1880s Bujwid had travelled to Germany and France to acquaint himself personally with Koch and Pasteur and their work. Bujwid was also prominent in the PPS[8] and quickly introduced Rajchman to the Popular University and related activities. The political philosopher Edward Abramowski was another source of inspiration for Rajchman, who joined his Ethics Circle before entering the official ranks of the PPS, with which he had been collaborating since 1901, overseeing the bureau which fabricated false documents for political refugees. In 1907 Rajchman married a fellow medical student, Maria Bojańczyk, who came from an upper-middle-class Catholic family in Włocławek and was as radical in her political views as her husband.

After the failure of the 1905 uprising the young couple settled in Warsaw, where Rajchman began his internship at the Praga Hospital. This training was cut short by his arrest at a PPS meeting subsequent to the split which had occurred at the Vienna Congress earlier in 1906.[9] He was bailed out of prison by his parents-in-law, on condition that he leave the Congress Kingdom. As a precaution, Rajchman repassed his medical degree in Kazan (his Austro-Hungarian qualifications would not have been recognized in Russia, had he wished to practise in Warsaw), before leaving for the Pasteur Institute in Paris for two years of postdoctoral work.

In Paris Rajchman studied under two leading scientists of Russian origin, Elie Metchnikov and Constantine Levaditi. Although he participated in the activities of the Polish *émigré* community in Paris, his real political support for Polish independence began in London, when in 1911 he took a position at the Royal Institute of Public Health. Rajchman's eight years in England turned out to be

---

[7] A. Rajchman, 'Na wyższych uczelniach', *Oblicze Dnia*, 10 June 1936.
[8] On Bujwid, see J. Chomiczewski, 'Odon Bujwid', *Acta Microbiologica Polonica* (1960), 8–32; and Bolesław Limanowski, *Pamiętniki, 1870–1907* (Warsaw, 1958).
[9] The split came about over the question whether Polish independence would be obtained through violence or social transformation.

decisive for him both scientifically (he also worked at the Medical Research Committee and taught at King's College, London) and politically. He played an active part in the Polish Information Committee, run by Poland's future foreign secretary August Zaleski, and had a number of *entrées* into international socialist circles.[10]

As the First World War drew to an end, Rajchman returned to Poland with his wife and children. The newly established Poland was faced with unprecedented social, political, and economic upheaval. One-third of Polish citizens were believed to be seriously undernourished, and there was an upsurge in contagious diseases such as dysentery and diphtheria, while the largest recorded typhus epidemic was sweeping westward from Russia and Ukraine through Poland. Given the massive movements of population in the three years following the war and the fact that the insecticide DDT had not yet been invented to destroy the louse which carried the disease, the Polish government was vitally concerned with containing the epidemic. In February 1919 the invasion of the Red Army coincided with a new wave of contagion, meaning that typhus was henceforth associated with Bolshevism and viewed as a particularly Russian threat.

In the administrative void which existed in Poland immediately following the war, a man like Rajchman—who had the capacity to see beyond immediate problems as well as a rare organizational talent—was able to prove himself quickly. He wasted no time in setting up several cordons sanitaires along what was still the eastern front and suggested to the government that they create a central agency for epidemic control. The National Epidemiological Institute was established in 1918, and Rajchman was appointed director. Before the year was over, he had installed laboratories concerned with epidemiological intelligence, research, and prevention in Warsaw and eastern regions, albeit in extremely primitive conditions. Later the institution was transformed into the National Institute of Hygiene with subsidiaries throughout the country and a school of public health endowed by the Rockefeller Foundation and the Joint Distribution Committee.[11]

In 1921 Rajchman was chosen by the League of Nations to establish and direct its health section; throughout the existence of the league he would be the only east European member of the secretariat. The choice of Rajchman was based largely on the fact that Poland was seen as having taken the lead in stamping out the Eastern epidemic threat, with which certain Western statesmen such as Lord Balfour were gravely concerned. Conveniently, also, Rajchman's postgraduate training had been in the West (but not in Germany) and he spoke fluent French and English.

The foundations which Rajchman laid in international health through his directorship of the League's Health Organization constitute his greatest contribution to

---

[10] Rajchman also had connections with Ramsay MacDonald and the German socialists, although it has been impossible to determine their nature.

[11] See M. A. Balińska, 'The National Institute of Hygiene and Public Health in Poland, 1918–1939', *Social History of Medicine* (Dec. 1996), 427–45.

the field of health promotion. When he created Unicef after the Second World War, he merely continued along the lines he had drawn in Geneva with the added advantage of funds for relief and development measures. The Health Organization is regarded as one of the greatest achievements of the League and, significantly, to have made the sometimes distant institution 'a reality [in places] where it was little more than a name'.[12] It was revolutionary in many respects. It was the first international body to study all aspects of public health, conduct parallel and comparative medical and public health research programmes in different parts of the world, organize relief and research missions as well as exchange programmes of national health personnel and medical experts (including Germans and Russians at a time when neither country belonged to the league), and raise preventative medicine to the same standard of international importance as therapeutic medicine.

Throughout his directorship (1929–39) Rajchman travelled extensively. He first directed his efforts towards securing the scientific co-operation of Germany and Soviet Russia. His real passion, however, turned out to be for Kuomintang China. He drew up an ambitious plan of 'technical collaboration' between China and the League in the fields of public health, finance, education, and road communications. In the process he became increasingly intimate with Chiang Kai-shek's 'progressive' and Westernized brother-in-law T. V. Soong, who was at various times minister of finance, president of the Bank of China, foreign secretary, and prime minister. When Japan invaded Manchuria in 1931, Rajchman supposedly prevailed on Chiang not to deal directly with the Japanese, but rather to negotiate through the League. From then on his political reputation (he was already 'suspect' because of his dealings with Russia) was made: Rajchman became the *bête noire* of the Japanese and subsequently of all the appeaser regimes. As one of the pioneering idealists of internationalism, Rajchman, like many of his early colleagues, was increasingly disappointed by the successive political failures of the League.

Rajchman's relations with the Polish government ranged from excellent (Paderewski had taken Rajchman with him to the first assembly of the League in January 1920), to good (notably when his friend Zaleski was foreign secretary, 1926–33), to increasingly bad after Józef Beck became Polish foreign minister. In 1937 he was falsely accused of interfering in the nomination of the League's high commissioner for Danzig, a highly controversial affair for which he provided a convenient scapegoat. Soon after it was rumoured that Warsaw was thinking of depriving him of his Polish passport—a step which was never taken, although Tytus Komarnicki's correspondence reveals just how eager Beck's group was to be rid of him.[13] They were spared the job thanks to the actions of the French secretary-general of the League, Joseph Avenol. In January 1939 he dismissed Rajchman as one of the last in a general purge of the institution's 'old guard'.

[12] F. P. Walters, *A History of the League of Nations* (Oxford, 1952), 182.
[13] See Komarnicki's papers, Sikorski Institute, London, KOL 37/7.

On the eve of the Second World War Rajchman decided to devote his energies to helping China and, much as his friend Monnet was doing at the same time for France, sought to build up China's air force by co-ordinating French, British, and American assistance. He was unsuccessful, for the most part (the Westerners were reticent, while Chiang was suspicious, disorganized, or both), and the only highly placed government authority who seems to have supported him was France's Jewish minister of the colonies, Georges Mandel[14] (later imprisoned with Léon Blum and shot by the French police in 1944).[15]

After leaving Geneva, Rajchman bought a house in France. When Sikorski's government was formed, he offered to take over relief measures for Poland and Polish refugees as an independent agent. However, he was seen more as a kind of *éminence grise* of Sikorski, and somewhat resented by the Allies, who were loath to deal with someone whose status could not be clearly defined. Rajchman had no more success in raising humanitarian aid for Poland than he had in acquiring planes for China. Asking for money for victims of an as yet remote but looming war promoted more unease than enthusiasm. The only help forthcoming was from Polish Americans, and that was limited in scope.

When the Germans invaded France, Rajchman (blacklisted by the Gestapo since 1937) fled with his family through Spain to Portugal and then flew by clipper to New York. Although he was sent officially as Sikorski's delegate for humanitarian affairs, he was badly received in Washington. The pre-war Polish ambassador Jerzy Potocki knew that Sikorski wanted to replace him with Jan Ciechanowski, and rightly guessed that Rajchman was encouraging the general in that direction. The dissension which ensued not only compromised relief for Poland and delayed Ciechanowski's arrival, but also deprived Rajchman of his diplomatic passport when those favourable to Potocki in the state department made Ciechanowski's arrival conditional on the termination of all special missions of the government in exile in the United States. The only special mission at this time was Rajchman's. In any case, it soon became apparent that even with the best of Allied will, relief for Poland was little more than an illusion.

Rajchman next turned his attention back to Chinese affairs, officially becoming an adviser to the Bank of China in matters of reconstruction. In fact, he was Foreign Minister Soong's right-hand man for most of his dealings in the United States. Rajchman inspired the China Defence Supplies (a kind of lend-lease for China which preceded the bill), later regarded as the main agency of the famous China Lobby. He became increasingly uncomfortable with his position as Chiang's policy and especially his tactics became less and less defensible, and he resigned

---

[14] See M. A. Balińska, 'Georges Mandel, Ludwik Rajchman et l'aide à la Chine à la vielle de la deuxième guerre mondiale', *Revue d'Histoire Diplomatique* (Jan. 1997), 21–41.

[15] For biographies of Mandel, see J. N. Jeanneney, *Georges Mandel: L'Homme qu'on attendait* (Paris, 1991); B. Favreau, *Georges Mandel, ou la passion de la république* (Paris, 1996); and N. Sarkozy, *Georges Mandel: le moine de la politique* (Paris, 1994).

from his position early in 1944, at the same time as Soong's own demise from the circle of power in Chungking. Rajchman's espousal of the Chinese cause can be explained by his love of the country, his repulsion for Western colonial domination in Asia, and his deep friendship for Soong, who, he believed, would be able to introduce a New Deal for China after the war.

At the same time Rajchman was eager to participate in European reconstruction, particularly in Poland. At the request of Senator Lehmann, director-general of the United Nations Relief and Rehabilitation Administration (UNRRA), he delivered a detailed advisory report on public-health measures for Europe, which resulted in UNRRA setting up its London European bureau. At the time, in early spring 1944, UNRRA already had a Polish representative from the government in exile: Brunon Nowakowski, an epidemiologist whom Rajchman had recruited after the First World War in Warsaw for the National Institute of Hygiene and who had spent the war at the Polish medical faculty of the University of Edinburgh.[16]

When the Allies officially recognized the Lublin government a few months later, there was an urgent need to name a representative to UNRRA. Oskar Lange, who was soon to become the new government's ambassador to the United States, suggested Rajchman, as did the Brain Trust member Oscar Cox. Ciechanowski too considered him the most competent man in the field, but Tadeusz Romer, the ambassador in Moscow, feared that Rajchman would want to use his position to encourage a *rapprochement* between the Lublin and London Polish governments.

The choice of Rajchman was, from the Polish perspective, an obvious one: he was a leading world expert in public health and relief, and, as a former League official he belonged to the cosmopolitan élite and had well-placed connections and friendships throughout the world. In addition, his marked sympathy for the Left made him acceptable to the new communist authorities, while the Allies, who had known him for many years, considered him a viable spokesman. Rajchman was also encouraged to accept the nomination by Zygmunt Szymanowski, the minister of health of the provisional government and a former laboratory colleague from pre-First World War days.

It took Rajchman several weeks to make up his mind, but after much hesitation he accepted, explaining to his Western friends that he wanted to do one last thing for Poland (he was by that time 64 years old). In July 1944 he flew to Poland and went on to participate in the Potsdam Conference, acting as Hilary Minc's interpreter and speaking openly to his American friends there about Soviet domination in Poland. At that time, indeed, he suffered more doubts about whether he should collaborate with the Lublin government, but ultimately put his hesitations aside. From then on he never wavered in his efforts to secure as much relief and assistance for Poland as possible. As far as political issues were concerned, he tried to keep aloof (especially regarding the issue of forced repatriation), advising the

[16] Z. Teleszyński, 'Polski Wydział Lekarski przy Uniwersytecie w Edynburgu', *Archiwum Historii Medycyny* 30 (1967), 45–63.

American government that, in order to favour fair electoral procedures in Poland, full diplomatic and foreign press representation should be ensured.

When serious complications connected with the Cold War inevitably compromised UNRRA's activities, the United States decided to withdraw, effectively ending the relief administration. This step was opposed by Herbert Hoover and Fiorello La Guardia, both of whom were concerned about the poor economic and health conditions existing in many European countries and who feared a return to isolationism on the part of the United States. At the June 1946 UNRRA plenum in Geneva, when La Guardia (who had replaced Lehmann as director-general) was forced to announce the resignation of the United States, Rajchman stood up and, in Polish, made a passionate plea on behalf of children, suggesting that the subsidiary UNRRA funds be used to create a special emergency agency for them.

Although Rajchman was considered one of, if not the, foremost expert in international public health, he had been completely left out of the meetings called to set up a World Health Organization (which had ended up adopting his ideas). This came as a bitter disappointment to him. Through Unicef he saw his chance to remain in the field of international health by carrying out practical measures such as relief and development, which were not part of the WHO mandate. According to Rajchman's friend the journalist Edgar Ansel Mowrer, Rajchman had had the idea of creating a special organization for children before the end of the war, probably thinking that his ideal of international collaboration could best be realized through the common and theoretically apolitical cause of children.

The proposal to create a United Nations fund for children was officially approved by the UN assembly in December 1946. Rajchman was appointed chairman, as well as Polish delegate. Unicef carried out remarkable and invaluable work in the war-devastated countries, bringing short-term relief as well as long-term measures of disease prevention and health promotion. Poland benefited substantially, undoubtedly thanks to Rajchman in part, but also due to the fact that Hoover (who gave inestimable backing to Unicef) and Maurice Pate (the director of Unicef chosen by Rajchman) had a 'soft spot' for Poland dating back to post-First World War days.

Rajchman was the driving force behind all the early Unicef policies which influenced the agency for many years afterwards. He remained chairman until 1950, when the double embarrassment of the Eastern Bloc countries' expulsion of the Unicef missions and protest against the UN's refusal to recognize communist China led him to resign. Both these events were extremely paradoxical for Rajchman: the organization he had set up, and which had brought great aid to Poland, was rudely dismissed from his own homeland, while, as Polish delegate, he was more or less obliged to participate in the Soviet walk-out in support of communist China, although he himself had been one of the closest advisers to and believers in Nationalist China. Not long afterwards a further paradox came when the Polish government took away his diplomatic passport, while the McCarthyites in the

United States accused him of having spied for the Soviets during the war. For one who had naïvely hoped to form a sort of bridge—as he once explained to a friend—between East and West, this came as a great disillusionment.

Until his resignation from Unicef Rajchman was based in the United States, travelling to Poland fairly frequently, where he was anxious to help in a private capacity as well, notably at the National Institute of Hygiene, which he had founded. In 1950 he moved back to the house he had bought in France before the war and worked with his friend Robert Debré, a paediatrician and son of the grand rabbi of France, father of De Gaulle's prime minister and grandfather of a recent minister of the interior, to set up an International Children's Centre (ICC) outside Paris. The centre was devoted primarily to research and specialized education. The more neutral status of the ICC, as a result of its location in Paris, allowed him to keep connections with Poland by bringing out young Polish doctors for periods of study in Paris.

After Gomułka came to power in Poland in 1956, the new ambassador to France, Stanisław Gajewski (whose parents had belonged to the same group of young socialist intellectuals before the First World War as Rajchman), persuaded Rapacki to restore Rajchman's passport. Rajchman returned to Poland a few more times: in 1957, when his sister died, and later in 1963, when the Institute of Hygiene celebrated its forty-fifth anniversary. By the time he was made an honorary member of the Polish Society of Microbiology in 1964, he was too ill to travel. A year later, in July 1965, he died at his home in France. His funeral took place in the village graveyard, attended only by family members, Robert Debré, and Jean Monnet.

A few obituaries recalled Rajchman's role in international health and humanitarian relief, but, all in all, he received shockingly little recognition during his life and even after his death for his contributions to the field. A *New Yorker* article on Unicef in 1961 did not even mention him.[17] The organization was presented as the creation of Hoover and his devoted assistant Maurice Pate (whom Rajchman had nominated as director partly for his exceptional qualifications and partly so as to enlist the support of Hoover and the Republicans for the fledgling agency). Although a 1986 official history of the organization clearly states Rajchman's role as founder of Unicef, there still appears to be a curious reluctance to pay him his deserved tribute,[18] and it was only a few years ago that Unicef headquarters in New York thought of naming a meeting room after him. At the formal commemoration of Unicef's fiftieth anniversary in Paris in April 1996, Rajchman's name was not once mentioned, even though by then his biography, published in France, had received a certain amount of publicity.[19]

---

[17] J. Wechsberg, 'At the Heart of Unicef', *New Yorker*, 2 Dec. 1961.

[18] M. Black, *The Children and the Nations* (New York, 1986).

[19] M. A. Balińska, *Une Vie pour l'humanitaire: Ludwik Rajchman* (Paris, 1995); in 1996 the book was awarded the Grand Prix du MEDEC, France's most prestigious award for medical literature.

How is this forgetting of Rajchman, now that the Cold War is over, to be explained? One answer could be that Unicef and much of the United Nations have always been seen as Western, indeed, primarily American, institutions. Furthermore, in all areas there is a marked 'Western centricity', focusing mainly on France, Great Britain, the United States, and sometimes Germany, which perpetuates the impression that eastern Europe has made little contribution to international life. Finally, in our age of at least superficial cynicism, there is some discomfort with someone like Rajchman who, for all his political mistakes, nevertheless managed—because of his unfailing determination and faith in man's capacity to rise above national and political ambitions—to institutionalize principles of international co-operation and welfare that exist to this day. Indeed, Rajchman could probably most aptly be described as a nineteenth-century idealist with twenty-first-century ideas.

Abraham Joshua Heschel in Poland: Hasidism Enters Modernity

EDWARD K. KAPLAN

ABRAHAM JOSHUA HESCHEL emigrated to the United States in 1940, but his first thirty-three years in Europe made him the religious philosopher, biblical interpreter, and social activist he became as a naturalized American citizen. Born in Warsaw on 11 January 1907, his ancestors were hasidim, continuing the eighteenth-century pietistic movement founded by Rabbi Israel ben Eliezer, the Ba'al Shem Tov. This Jewish consciousness, according to Heschel, assumed a spontaneous awareness of divine presence: 'Miracles no longer startled anyone, and it was no surprise to discover among one's contemporaries men who had attained the holy spirit, men whose ear perceived the voice of heaven.'[1]

As an adolescent in Warsaw, Heschel was expected to inherit the position of *rebbe*—a spiritual and community leader—held by his father and uncles. However, he reconciled his hasidic vision with west European culture and history's demands, making the transition by leaving Warsaw to earn a diploma at the recently established secular, Yiddish-language *Realgymnasium* in Vilna. By 1933 he had completed a doctorate in philosophy at the University of Berlin. From there he went to Frankfurt, and returned for one academic year to Warsaw before finally leaving Poland in July 1939.[2]

Heschel's relationship with Poland was painful and complex. Growing up in hasidic Warsaw, he had little contact with Polish culture, and to prepare for his secular studies he had to learn Polish from tutors. As a child he experienced the common antisemitism of the streets. After 1939 he lost his mother, three sisters, and countless relatives, friends, and colleagues in the Holocaust. The June 1967 war in Israel revived these bitter memories, as he wrote in *Israel: An Echo of Eternity*: 'If I should go to Poland or Germany, every stone, every tree would remind me of

---

The substance of this paper is expanded in Edward K. Kaplan and Samuel H. Dresner, *Abraham Joshua Heschel: Heschel, Prophetic Witness* (New Haven, 1998), vol. i of the first cultural and intellectual biography of Heschel.

[1] A. J. Heschel, *The Earth is the Lord's* (New York, 1951), 91.

[2] For biographical summaries, see Fritz Rothschild, 'Abraham Joshua Heschel, 1907–1972', *American Jewish Yearbook*, 74 (1973), 533–44; Edward Kaplan, *Holiness in Words: A. J. Heschel's Poetics of Piety* (Albany, NY, 1996), ch. 1; and Susannah Heschel, Introduction to A. J. Heschel, *Moral Grandeur and Spiritual Audacity: Essays* (New York, 1996).

contempt, hatred, murder, of children killed, of mothers burned alive, of human beings asphyxiated.'[3]

IMMIGRANTS IN CENTRAL POLAND

Nevertheless, Poland was the soil in which his dynastic tradition flourished. Heschel's parents, indigenous to Poland, eventually settled in Warsaw to escape pogroms, the Russian Revolution, the civil wars—and world war. Heschel described himself as an immigrant from Medzibozh (in Polish, Międzybóż, Ukrainian, Medzhybizh): 'I was born in Warsaw, Poland, but my cradle was in Medzibozh (a small town in the province of Podolia, Ukraine), where the Ba'al Shem Tov, founder of the Hasidic movement, lived during the last twenty years of his life. That is where my father came from, and he continued to regard it as his home.'[4]

Heschel's original namesake and spiritual prototype was Rabbi Abraham Joshua Heschel (1748–1825), the *rebbe* of Apt (in Polish, Opatów), known by the title of his book *Ohev yisra'el* ('Lover of Israel, the Jewish People'). After the death of the Ba'al Shem Tov, the Apter Rebbe became the spokesman for the third hasidic generation. Heschel's grandfather, also named Abraham Joshua Heschel (1832–84), continued the dynasty and established his court in Medzhybizh. Heschel's father, Moses Mordecai (1873–1916), was born there, as were his uncles and aunts.

Heschel absorbed Lithuanian hasidism through his mother, Rivka Reizel Perlow (1874–1942). Her father, Rabbi Jacob Perlow (1847–1902), although born in Poland, was brought up in the home of his maternal grandfather, Solomon Hayim of Koidanov (Keidainiai) (1797–1862), a great Lithuanian *rebbe*.[5] Rivka Reizel and her twin brother were born in Mińsk-Mazowiecki (known by Jews as Novominsk), an industrial town located about 41 kilometres from Warsaw.

Heschel's parents were married around 1890 in Novominsk, where they lived for ten years at the lively hasidic court of the bride's father. Rabbi Perlow had built a large yeshiva, the first such hasidic school of higher Torah learning in Poland, where hundreds of students came to live. Their synagogue was huge, and Novominsk became a place of such popular pilgrimage that the authorities organized special trains to accommodate the large numbers of hasidim who made the journey. Heschel's sisters and brother were all born in Novominsk.

Moving closer to Warsaw, Heschel's parents, four sisters, and brother settled in the Pelcowizna district, a rather poor, predominantly Jewish area on the right bank of the River Vistula. There Moses Mordecai established himself as a *vinkl rebbe* (literally, a 'corner *rebbe*'). Finally, they moved to the centre of Warsaw's Jewish

---

[3] A. J. Heschel, *Israel: An Echo of Eternity* (New York, 1969), 113.

[4] A. J. Heschel, *A Passion for Truth* (New York, 1973), p. xiii; see Samuel H. Dresner, 'Introduction: Heschel as a Hasidic Scholar', in A. J. Heschel, *The Circle of the Baal Shem Tov* (Chicago, 1985).

[5] Harry Rabinowicz, *Hasidism: The Movement and its Masters* (Northvale, NJ, 1988), 269–70.

district, at 40 Muranowska Street. In this large, modern grey stone apartment building[6] the Pelzovizner Rebbe (as Moses Mordecai was still known) established his hasidic court.

Heschel learned the role of *rebbe* in the family apartment. The 'dearest friend of Heschel's youth', Yehiel Hofer, described Moses Mordecai's aristocratic manner of dressing, which reflected his Galician upbringing on the Austrian side of the Pale of Settlement: 'He wore a silk caftan [a long black coat] with velvet button loops. The collar of his shirt was stiffly pressed and tied with a long, colourful cravat. On his white collar was visible a black silk string, on which hung a pair of spectacles with thin horn rims.'[7] 'The *rebbe* wore long trousers and slippers. On his head a plush hat over a tall velvet *yarmulkeh* [skullcap]. He always stuck a white handkerchief into the left sleeve of his silk caftan.' Polish hasidim, on the contrary, preferred the style of Russian peasant clothing.

On 11 January 1907 Abraham Joshua Heschel, their second son and last child, was born. From the Muranowska district several religious and secular Jewish centres were within reach.

CROSSING JEWISH CULTURAL BORDERS

In Warsaw the hasidim made up the largest grouping among observant Jews. There was also a diverse Jewish political life: numerous Zionist organizations (some of them religious), other youth and student circles, and the socialist Bund. There were important Hebrew publishing efforts as well, and a remarkable array of newspapers and periodicals in both Hebrew and Yiddish. After he was prepared by tutors, as was common among children of hasidic nobility, Heschel went on with his studies at a *shtiebl* (literally, a small hall) associated with the hasidic dynasty of Ger, which was located on his street, at 17 Muranowska.[8] *Shtiebl*s, a uniquely hasidic institution found throughout the city, were abundant in the neighbourhood. Two of them thrived on Dzika Street (part of which became Zamenhof), two on Twarda, and two on nearby Nalewki and Franciszkańska Streets.

At the age of 7 Heschel's relatively secure life was upset by the impending war. Hofer describes how Moses Mordecai's 'court on Muranowska Street was filled with Jews drafted for the Russian army and about to be sent to the front. Their pleas and those of their families that he should pray for them and free them from their troubles gave him no rest.'[9]

The calamities of the time were to bring the Heschel family closer geographically. From August 1914 to October 1920 Jewish ancestral towns in Galicia and the

---

[6] Interview with Szulim Rozenberg, Paris.

[7] Yehiel Hofer, 'Milkhome—1914' ('War—1914'), *Tsukunft* (Oct. 1967), 381–7.

[8] The following information from Abraham Zemba, 'Shtieblakh in Warsaw' (Heb.), in S. Mirsky, *Jewish Institutions of Higher Learning in Europe: Their Development and Destruction* (Heb.) (New York, 1956), 355–63.   [9] Hofer, 'Milkhome—1914'.

Russian Pale of Settlement were battered by military action. Two of his father's brothers—Rabbis Meshulam Zusya Heschel and Israel Sholem Joseph Heschel—were hasidic leaders in the Ukrainian town of Medzhybizh. The other, Rabbi Isaac Meir Heschel, presided over his court in Kopitzhinitz (in Ukrainian, Kopychyntse, between Chortkiv and Husyatin), a Galician *shtetl* in Austria–Hungary. The irony was that each rabbi blessed Jewish soldiers compelled by their oppressive governments to slaughter one another on the battlefield.

Heschel's uncle Isaac Meir Heschel arrived in Vienna in September 1914 with his family, including his son, Rabbi Abraham Joshua Heschel (1888–1967), who had married Heschel's eldest sister, Sarah. Heschel was 8 years old in 1915, when his maternal uncle Rabbi Alter Israel Simeon Perlow, the *rebbe* of Novominsk, became their neighbour, establishing his court at 10 Franciszkańska Street, a block away, with his wife and eight children (there would eventually be twelve).[10]

Within a year, in November 1916, Moses Mordecai Heschel died at the age of 43 in a typhus epidemic aggravated by the British blockade of the Central Powers.[11] He was buried in the Jewish cemetery whose entrance on Okopowa Street stood about three blocks away from his home. Six weeks later Heschel turned 10 and came under the tutelage of his uncle the Novominsker Rebbe, who made talmudic study and contemplative prayer the focus of his existence.

THRESHOLDS TO MODERNITY

Young Heschel reached a high level of competence in talmudic study and entered the Mesivta yeshiva—foremost among hasidic Poland's contribution to the revival of traditional learning—which his older brother Jacob (1903–70) had begun to attend.[12] Founded in 1919 by rabbinic authorities and the Agudat Yisrael community, it conceived learning differently from the Lithuanian-style yeshivas, adding hasidic customs to intellectual rigour. Teachers and students wore sidecurls and retained their distinctive clothing. The *rebbe* of Ger, as president of the Agudah, was the unofficial head of the institute.

Paradoxically, this hasidic institution may also have kindled Heschel's drive for secular knowledge. Since the Polish Ministry of Education required all schools, even religious academies, to introduce secular subjects, the Mesivta established a separate programme with its own teachers and principal. Two hours a day it offered courses in Polish, mathematics, history, and other literary or scientific

---

[10] Abraham Bromberg, *Megedolei hatorah vehaḥasidut*, 20 (Jerusalem, 1963), 141–53, for the Novominsker Rebbe; see also Dresner, 'Introduction: Heschel as a Hasidic Scholar'.

[11] Interview with Israel Heschel (1911–1994), Heschel's nephew, eldest son of the Kopitzhintzer *rebbe*.

[12] Abraham Zemba, 'The Mesivta in Warsaw' (Heb.), in Mirsky, *Jewish Institutions of Higher Learning in Europe*, 363–75. The following discussion is taken from this important article.

topics. This minimal modern curriculum gave the candidates rights similar to students in public institutions and so Orthodox young men might qualify to enter a gymnasium required for university matriculation.

Heschel's lifelong desire to publish his writings now began to manifest itself. His first reflections as a nascent talmudic scholar appeared in the Hebrew-language Warsaw monthly *Sha'arei torah: kovets rabani hodeshi* ('Gates of Torah: Monthly Rabbinic Journal'), whose editorial office was located nearby, at 4 Muranowska Street.[13] Contributors included rabbis from Poland and Russia, hasidic and non-hasidic. Heschel was 14 years old when his commentaries, called *hidushei torah* (notes on points of rabbinic law), were published in the special student supplement *Beit midrash*, the first in autumn 1922, followed by two more in the winter and spring of 1923. These short, elliptical pieces are concerned with purely legal issues, with no hint of personal emotion or spirituality.

By now Heschel was experiencing an internal revolution. He was guided towards a secular education by Fishl Schneersohn, a descendant of the Lubavitch hasidic founders, a physician, psychiatrist, writer, and acclaimed public speaker. They probably met in 1923, when Schneersohn was director of a psychological-hygiene clinic in Warsaw. It was probably Fishl Schneersohn who, with remarkable foresight, directed Heschel to study in Berlin. Born in Kam'ianes-Podilskyi, Schneersohn was brought up by his grandfather the Retshitzer Rebbe, learning Talmud and kabbalah.[14] Ordained a rabbi by age 16, Schneersohn earned a medical degree from the University of Berlin and in 1920 became professor of curative pedagogy at the University of Kiev, soon returning to Warsaw to escape the political turmoil in Russia. Heschel's Warsaw mentor anticipated Heschel's future journey from hasidism to modernity. Schneersohn's novel *Khaym gravitser*[15] depicts a Lubavitcher hasid caught between a strictly regulated existence and spontaneous creativity, while his scientific manifesto *Der veg tsum mensh* ('The Path to Humanity'[16] synthesizes psychology, the nascent field of psychoanalysis, art, philosophy, and hasidic piety.

Heschel entered modernity through Yiddish literature. He could learn about reading and publishing opportunities from numerous Yiddish and Hebrew newspapers, and the centre of modern Jewish culture was within walking distance. Leaving his home on Muranowska Street, instead of turning left from Nalewki to reach his uncle's court on Franciszkańska he could continue to the end of Nalewki

---

[13] Founded in 1893, the journal ceased publication during the First World War and was revived in 1919—the year Mesivta began—by the founder's son, Israel Isser Feigenbaum. The *Beit midrash* supplement was started in 1922 and edited by R. Shlomo Altman, head of the *beit din* (rabbinical court) of Kikel, located in Warsaw. See *EJ*.

[14] Zalman Reisen, *Leksikon fun der nayer yidisher literatur* (New York, 1956), 755–7; Y. Hofer, *Mit yenem un mit zich* (Tel Aviv, 1976), 474–82. Schneersohn emigrated to Palestine in 1937. For information on Fishl Schneersohn in English, see Shaul Shimon Deutsch, *Larger than Life: The Life and Times of the Lubavitcher Rebbe Rabbi Menachem Mendel Schneerson*, ii (New York, 1997), 124–33.

[15] Yiddish, 2 vols. (Berlin, 1922–6). [16] Vilna, 1928.

to the headquarters of the Yiddish Writers' and Journalists' Association (later to become the PEN club) at 13 Tłomackie Street.

At home Heschel began to study Polish and Latin in preparation for higher education.[17] With the support of Fishl Schneersohn and other Yiddish writers, he hired tutors. To disguise the subject he was studying from his mother, he would chant declensions as if he were studying Talmud. Later he was tutored in German, the language of advanced Western culture, which he had not yet learned.

Two years later Heschel took the decisive step. A newly established Yiddish weekly, *Literarishe bleter* ('Literary Pages: Illustrated Weekly of Literature, Theatre and Art'), announced that Melekh Ravitch, its literary editor, was preparing a new anthology.[18] Ravitch, also secretary of the Yiddish Writers' Club, received manuscripts at the Tłomackie Street headquarters. As Ravitch's memoirs describe him, Heschel, dressed in hasidic garb, presented several manuscripts to the editor, himself an experimental poet and writer.

Heschel's first personal publication is a short prose piece in Yiddish entitled *Der tsadik fun frayd* ('The *Tsadik* of Joy'). It appeared in the 21 May 1925 issue of the Warsaw weekly *Ilustrirte vokh*, and describes an ailing *tsadik* lying on his deathbed; instead of elaborating a *devar torah* (a homily on the biblical text), he speaks only a word or two, and, Heschel notes, his face inspires fear in everyone. He dies and is buried on Friday before the Sabbath. As the young people, following his command, dance and sing *nigunim*, a fiery beam is seen coming from the grave.[19]

About a year later Heschel's first published poem unveiled his sensual sensibility. It appeared late in 1926 in Ravitch's new anthology *Varshaver shriftn* ('Warsaw Writings') as an untitled *lid* (song or poem), playing the full range from delicate longing, through fierce desire, to shyness and inhibition. It begins:

> The womanly skin
> Silvers so purely
> The silken skin of a woman
> Is so delicate.[20]

Heschel qualified for university by earning a diploma from the Matematyczno-Przyrodnicze Gymnazjum (Mathematics–Natural Science Gymnasium), known as the Realgymnasium of Vilna, where diplomas were printed in both Yiddish and Polish. This secular school fell under the auspices of the progressive Central Yiddish Schools Organization (CYSHO), and was well suited to Heschel's skills and values. CYSHO was established in Warsaw in 1921 as an umbrella organization for several Yiddish-language groups, and its ideals were progressive and

---

[17] See Dresner, 'Introduction: Heschel as a Hasidic Scholar', pp. xxvii–xxix.

[18] Leonard Prager, *Yiddish Literary and Linguistic Periodicals and Miscellanies* (Darby, Penn., 1982). M. Ravitch, *Mayn leksikon*, 2 vols. (Montreal, 1947).

[19] *Ilustrirte vokh*, 3/20, erroneously dated 1924 in the *Leksikon fun der nayer yidisher literatur*. Ravitch was probably responsible for this first literary publication of Heschel's.

[20] *Varshaver shriftn* (Warsaw, 1927); poem trans. Sylvia Fuks Fried.

democratic. Instead of learning from professorial-style lectures, students and teachers would work together, developing co-operative relationships both inside and outside the classroom.

There Heschel absorbed the best of Jewish secularism. Founded in 1918 by the Jewish central education committee (Tsentraler Bildungs-Komitet),[21] the Realgymnasium offered the complete Polish curriculum. Although the sciences were emphasized, its humanities classes were excellent, out of the ordinary. It was especially distinguished by its courses on literature given by Yiddish poets and university-trained professors. But it was much more than a school; it was a community—almost a family network. Teachers and students shared an intimate, imponderable love of being Jewish, while students revered their teachers as nurturing parents who instilled pride and inner strength.

In Vilna Heschel also furthered his political education. He rented a cheap room in the home of a simple, very pious old Jewish man, located on Poplawes Street. (Students of the Realgymnasium either lived at home or boarded in town.) Far from the city centre, this area was sparsely populated by poverty-stricken Jews.[22] In Warsaw Heschel had known poverty, but in Vilna he lived among secular Jews who supported revolution. On the road that led to the Realgymnasium was a large expanse of subsidized housing and the centre of Bund activity, and in that area socialists, some communists, and other leftist groups had celebrations and meetings.

In addition to his academic work at the Realgymnasium, Heschel joined a group of avant-garde Yiddish-language writers and artists, probably recommended by acquaintances in Warsaw. This group of men with left-wing ideals—which later became known as Yung Vilne (Young Vilna)—provided support for the poetry he had begun to develop in Warsaw, although he stood out among these sceptics as a *ben-toyre* (literally, son of the Torah), quiet and somewhat aloof, a thinker steeped in religious learning. At this time Heschel broadened his subject-matter and furthered his publishing ambitions.

Religious observance posed no problems. For public services, near the Strashun Library, there were about thirty small places of worship in the synagogue courtyard, each belonging to a different trade, including a hasidic *shtiebl*.

Graduation from the Realgymnasium took place on 26 June 1927, and, thus prepared for a modern education, Heschel left Poland.

BERLIN AND BEYOND

Heschel's spiritual and intellectual personality matured fully at the University of Berlin, where he became a doctor of philosophy. He was recognizable as an east

---

[21] They produced a remarkable array of pedagogical manuals, Yiddish grammar books, and curricula on literary theory, sciences, geography, history, etc.

[22] Shlomo Beilis, 'Bay di onheybn fun Yung Vilne', *Di goldene keyt*, 101 (1980), 11–65. Interview with Benyamin Pumpiansky (Realgymnasium, 1926).

European Jew by his accent, since he had begun to learn German in Warsaw among speakers of Polish and Yiddish. When he arrived in Berlin in the autumn of 1927, the presence of the Weimar republic's cultural giants was still felt. Heschel formed his own synthesis of Jewish tradition and Western culture, adapting academic disciplines to his hasidic devotion to God. Languages brought these disparate worlds together. Heschel used German to benefit from the broad curriculum of the university and the historically based (or 'scientific') Jewish studies at the Liberal Hochschule für die Wissenschaft des Judentums, where he matriculated. The ancient and rabbinic Hebrew and Aramaic of the Bible, Talmud, and the Zohar and other hasidic texts provided the sources.

Yet in Berlin Heschel found it necessary to go on writing Yiddish poetry to preserve his spiritual integrity. By this time he had accumulated a body of work of which he was proud. He contacted Yiddish periodicals in the United States, and in December 1929, in the middle of his third academic year at Berlin University, four of his Yiddish poems appeared in the progressive journal *Di tsukunft* ('The Future'), the influential Yiddish monthly run by the Forward Association of New York.[23] This confirmed his personal ambition, for almost every significant Yiddish writer appeared in the journal, which reached Poland, Russia, South America, and Palestine, as well as North America.

The first and last poems which frame the sequence—entitled 'God pursues me everywhere . . .' and 'I and Thou'—are emblems of Heschel's characteristic combination of intimacy with God with an intense moral sensitivity. Asserting the unity of the religious and ethical dimensions of human experience, they remain his finest poems. 'God pursues me everywhere' anticipates the intuition at the heart of Heschel's biblical theology, and, more immediately, of the doctoral dissertation on prophetic consciousness he soon began at university. Within the secular city of Berlin the poet senses how the Almighty takes extraordinary initiatives:

> God pursues me everywhere—
> Spinning a web around me . . .
> Blinding my sightless back like a sun . . .

The sequence ends with 'I and Thou', whose Yiddish title evokes Martin Buber's famous book *I and Thou* (*Ich und Du*), first published in 1923 while Heschel was still studying Talmud in Warsaw. Heschel's Yiddish *Ikh un du* expresses his exceptional intermingling of self and God, surpassing Buber's 'dialogue' between separate entities, one human and the other divine.

> My nerves' tendrils are intertwined with Yours . . .
> Your dreams meet in mine . . .
> Are we not one embraced in millions?

---

[23] *Di tsukunft* was founded in 1892 as an organ of the Socialist Labour Party, and acquired in 1912 by the Forward Association. It was not necessary to be a Bundist or even to express leftist sympathies in order to appear in its pages. Its editorial offices were located at 175 East Broadway.

Heschel boldly implies here that God's feelings pulse within him, as he does in his doctoral study of the prophet's sympathy with 'God's pathos', the 'emotions' God experiences in response to human events. These poetic and academic self-expressions both anticipate his theological summa, *God in Search of Man* (1955), in which the righteous person becomes an object of God's awareness, recentring the reader's consciousness from the self to God.[24]

RECONNECTING WITH POLAND

In December 1932 Heschel completed the manuscript of his doctoral dissertation, *Das prophetische Bewusstsein* ('On Prophetic Consciousness'), but could not find a publisher in Germany. Required to submit 200 bound copies in book form to the university in order to receive the diploma, he sought a publisher in Poland. He made an exploratory trip, staying in Warsaw with his mother and sisters during the Passover holidays (15–21 April 1933) at 3 Dzika Street, where they had moved. While there he contacted the Polish Academy of Arts and Sciences in Kraków, in the hope that its oriental studies division might publish his dissertation.[25]

During this stay he also arranged to publish his powerful Yiddish poem 'In tog fun has' ('On the Day of Hate'), inspired in Berlin by the Nazi boycott of April 1933. The Warsaw Yiddish daily *Haynt* published it anonymously on 10 May 1933, the very day the Nazis planned to burn Jewish books in public. A note accompanying the piece informed readers that the pseudonymous author, 'Itzik'—a derogatory nickname for a Jew—was 'a world famous German Jewish writer whose books found "a place of honour" in a bonfire which burned in the German State'. (If the Nazis had discovered such a poem signed by Heschel, the university could well have denied him his doctorate.)

> On the day of Sabbath
> At ten o'clock, a filthy-brown mass of people
> Sat on shoulders, on doorsteps, on thresholds.
> Like snakes, grown dumb and large,
> A guard at every entrance—murderously poisonous, a desecrator
> Of genuine lives, and my throat choking with disgust
> The mob spitting laughter at all who go inside.[26]

After a successful six months in Poland Heschel returned to Berlin. In Kraków he had located a possible publisher for his dissertation and arranged to produce his

---

[24] Kaplan, *Holiness in Words*, chs. 3–5.

[25] Heschel's first letter to the Polish Academy of Sciences was dated 8 Mar. 1934. He then began a long correspondence, in Polish, with Prof. Tadeusz Kowalski, who supervised the acceptance, correction, and printing of his thesis, which appeared two years later. See Henryk Hałkowski, 'A Brand Plucked from the Fire', in Andrzej K. Paluch (ed.), *The Jews of Poland*, i (Kraków, 1992), 223–34.

[26] Trans. Jeffrey Shandler, 'Heschel and Yiddish: A Struggle with Signification', *Journal of Jewish Thought and Philosophy*, 2 (1993), 245–99.

book of Yiddish poems. In the winter of 1933 his collection of sixty-six poems, *Der shem hameforash. Mensh. Lider* ('God's Ineffable Name: Mankind, Poems'), appeared.[27]

Crossing the threshold from hasidism into modernity, at 26 years of age Heschel had defined himself as a Yiddish poet. The collection's epigraph—'I asked for wonder instead of happiness, and you gave it to me'—implies that his creative energy arose from tensions between awe ('wonder'), a closeness to God, and an inescapable loneliness and alienation. This polarity energized his neo-hasidism.

Heschel now had to transform his dissertation into a book. In Poland his sympathetic sponsor was Tadeusz Kowalski, professor at the liberal Jagiellonian University and recently appointed to the chair of the oriental studies committee. With the patient support of Kowalski, a specialist in Muslim languages and cultures, Heschel began painstakingly to revise his thesis.

During his time in Berlin Heschel was perceived as a Polish Jew, an east European who represented 'authentic Jewishness' to those unfamiliar with their roots. Since the 1920s a number of relatively assimilated German-speaking Jews—among them Franz Rosenzweig and Franz Kafka, and earlier Martin Buber—had been attracted to hasidism, and its idealized image (a form of orientalism) still engaged the Germans.[28] Heschel was recognized as a Jewish ideal in the March 1935 issue of *Der Morgen*, in which a reviewer praised his Yiddish book as 'modern poems from a Polish Jew'.[29] The poet's 'scientific training', the reviewer continued, lent credence to his 'innate Jewish force nourished equally by the deepest natural feeling and by a special understanding'. It was hoped that this sampling of Yiddish culture could preserve German Jewry against assimilation and increasing repression.

During this time Heschel corresponded with Professor Kowalski in Polish. As the political crisis intensified the normal pressures of bringing to fruition a complicated scholarly work, his anxiety as a man without a national identity rose to the surface. Negotiations with a possible German distributor fell through and other problems remained. On 21 February he asked Kowalski to correct grammatical and idiomatic errors in his Polish abstract: 'A feeling of uncertainty in the Polish language, caused by years of not using it, produced this very sad delay. I apologize.'[30] Only Yiddish—not Polish or German, which he also mastered—was indigenous to his spirit. Heschel had acknowledged his homelessness, pinpointing his political, cultural, and metaphysical exile.

---

[27] Printed in Yiddish as follows: published by Farlag Indzl, typeset by Hutner, printed by Grafia on Nowolipki, no. 7. The book cost two zlotys, and could be ordered from Al. Welczer, at Miłanów 39, apartment 6, in Warsaw. Printed in English: 'Copyright by Abraham Heszel, Warsaw.' This was Heschel's first published book.

[28] See Paul Mendes-Flohr, 'Fin de siècle Orientalism, the *Ostjuden*, and the Aesthetics of Jewish Self-Affirmation', in *Divided Passions: Jewish Intellectuals and the Experience of Modernity* (Detroit, 1991), 77–132.   [29] *Der Morgen*, 10 (1934–5), 570.

[30] Letters stored at the Jagiellonian University Archives, Kraków. My thanks to Henryk Hałkowski for obtaining copies for me.

(*Left*) Abraham Heschel, 1937/8, Atelier May, Frankfurt-am-Main. (*Right*) Tadeusz Kowalski, chairman of the oriental studies division of the Polish Academy of Arts and Sciences, 1939. Courtesy of the Archives of the Polish Academy of Arts and Sciences, Kraków.

By March 1936 the revisions were virtually complete. Concentrating on final details, Heschel's long letter of 8 March demonstrated unusual astuteness, as he justifies his request that the publisher's name, Polska Akademja Umiejętności, should be translated as Verlag der Polnischen Akademie der Wissenschaften on the cover of copies distributed in Germany. To guarantee that German readers would understand the publisher's name, two separate sets of the book, each with a different cover and title-page, were printed. The volume for general sale was printed in Kraków by the presses of the Jagiellonian University. The cover and title-page state in Polish the name of the academy, followed by 'Publications of the Oriental Commission' in both Polish and French. In the middle, in handsome capital letters, is: ABRAHAM HESCHEL *DIE PROPHETIE*.

It had taken three years and two months to come to publication. On 23 March 1936 Heschel sent Kowalski this succinct letter of appreciation: 'I have received today the first copies of my book about prophecy. I remember very clearly your careful attention to my case. The mere words "thank you" do injustice to my true feelings. Therefore I can only say that I think of you with great respect and that I have always read your words with gratitude and reverence.'

RETURN TO WARSAW

In March 1937 Heschel moved to Frankfurt-am-Main, invited by Martin Buber to help further his pedagogical programme at the Jüdisches Lehrhaus. But he remained in close touch with his mother and sisters by mail, and in April 1938 he returned briefly, hardly able to bear what he saw. In a letter to Buber of 25 April 1938, writing from his mother's apartment, he poured out his anguish: 'In addition to the epidemic of despair, the lack of planning together with spiritual lethargy are too great an evil. It will hardly be possible to undertake anything durable here for the near future.'[31]

On 28 October 1938 disaster struck. Heschel was one of thousands of Jews with Polish passports shipped in trains to the border town of Zbąszyń, between Germany and Poland.[32] Allowed to communicate with the outside, those refugees who could get official invitations could leave, and Heschel did not remain long. Contacts in Warsaw helped him to return home by the first week in November. He found refuge with his mother and sisters, near the neighbourhood where he had grown into adolescence.

The full extent of the danger in Poland was not yet obvious, although members of his family were already attempting to emigrate. Antisemitism was increasing, yet many Jews still perceived no grave danger. Some rabbinical leaders, in fact, hoped that accommodation with Polish nationalism was possible, and some rabbis counselled Jews to remain.[33] 'Abraham Heszel' (as his Polish documents read), seeking a job and a visa, continued to teach, write, ponder, and pray. He was 31 years old.

A week after the mass expulsion of Polish Jews Hitler sent a forthright message to the world. The appalling details of the pogrom of 9–10 November 1938, known at the time as Bloody Thursday, were broadcast immediately. Heschel was fortunate to have been deported from Germany, for he was spared this aggression, subsequently called Kristallnacht (the Night of the Broken Glass).

Now in Warsaw, standing in for the eminent rabbi and historian Moses Schorr, Heschel was hired as a *Docent* (lecturer) to teach the Bible and Jewish philosophy at the Instytut Nauk Judaistycznych (Institute for Jewish Sciences), located at 5

---

[31] Letter from Heschel to Buber, 25 Apr. 1938, MS Var. 290: 13. Heschel's letters to Buber (most of them still unpublished) are preserved at the Martin Buber Archive, National Jewish Library, and Hebrew University, Ramat Gan campus, Jerusalem. The call numbers are MS Var. 290: 1–59.

[32] Among the voluminous literature, see Sybil Milton, 'The Expulsion of Polish Jews from Germany, October 1938 to July 1939', *Leo Baeck International Yearbook*, 29 (1984), 169–99; Trude Maurer, 'The Background of Kristallnacht: The Expulsion of Polish Jews', in Walter H. Pehle (ed.), *November 1938: From Reichskristallnacht to Genocide*, trans. from the German by William Templer (New York, 1991); Shalom Adler-Rudel, *Ostjuden in Deutschland* (Tübingen, 1959), 152–3.

[33] In Nov. 1938 it was reported: 'Union of University Graduate Rabbis issues appeal to Jews for participation in celebration of twentieth anniversary of Poland's independence, expressing hope Poland will respect equality of Jews who aided in her creation and development' (*Contemporary Jewish Record* (Jan. 1939), 116).

Tłomackie Street, behind the Great Synagogue and in the same building as the Jewish Library.[34] This was the neighbourhood of the Yiddish Writers' and Journalists' Club, where as a youth he had submitted his first poems to Melekh Ravitch.

The Warsaw Institute for Jewish Sciences was founded in 1928 by Schorr and the historian Majer Bałaban, among others, combining Wissenschaft des Judentums (the scientific study of Judaism developed in Germany), a broad conception of Judaic studies, and openness to spiritual issues. It had a four-year programme divided into two parts: one preparing teachers of the Hebrew language and Judaic subjects, the other training rabbis in advanced critical methods. Potential teachers concentrated mainly on modern Hebrew literature, while rabbinical students concentrated on Talmud. Most of the lectures and seminars were conducted in Hebrew, with only Majer Bałaban and Ignacy Schiper, the two historians, lecturing in Polish. Students were required to enrol at the University of Warsaw and attain at least a master's degree.

It was something of an accomplishment when Heschel replaced Schorr, who, since 1935, had been a Jewish representative to the Sejm. He had been elected to the Polish Academy of Sciences in 1928, preached as a rabbi at the Great Synagogue and taught Semitic languages and ancient Near Eastern history at the university. Schorr now expended his energies protecting Jewish rights in the political arena.

Heschel began his lectures on the evening of 24 November 1938. In the turbulence of the time he considered his intellectual work—a combination of scholarship and prophetic judgement—to be of acute consequence. Amidst Europe's collapse, his own insecurity and that of his family, he analysed the emergency: German outrages against humanity were an opportunity to repudiate moral relativism; Europe could not survive if every ethical system was deemed, at least partially, valid. As he wrote to Buber: 'Perhaps this affliction will teach us something. The unrest is there, but the direction is missing. Concepts suddenly regain their clarity—for everyone. Maybe we can now take relativism to its grave.'[35]

Anticipating Buber's visit to Poland from Jerusalem, where he had recently emigrated, Heschel invited him to lecture at the institute, asked for a recent

---

[34] Abraham Tartakover, 'The Institute for Jewish Sciences' (Heb.), in Louis Ginzberg and Abraham Weiss (eds.), *Studies in Memory of Moses Schorr, 1874–1941* (New York, 1944). Schorr, a founding faculty member of the institute, rector, and professor of the Bible and Hebrew, had virtually withdrawn from teaching and scholarship since his election in 1935 to the Sejm, where he defended Jewish interests against antisemitic political opponents. See also Shevah Eden, 'The Institute for Jewish Studies and Research in Warsaw' (Heb.), in Mirsky, *Jewish Institutions of Higher Learning in Europe*, 561–84; I. M. Biderman, *Mayer Bałaban: Historian of Polish Jewry* (New York, 1976), esp. 75–83.

[35] Letter from Heschel to Buber, 25 Nov. 1938, in Martin Buber, *Briefwechsel aus sieben Jahrzehnten*, iii: *1938–1965* (Heidelberg, 1975), trans. in Nahum Glatzer and Paul Mendes-Flohr (eds.), *The Letters of Martin Buber: A Life of Dialogue* (New York, 1991), 474–5, letter 521, which I have modified slightly.

reprint, and inquired about volume ii of *The Kingship of God*, a work on Job, and Buber's striking German translations of the Bible. Heschel had attempted to disseminate Buber's thought by publishing a speech of his either in Yiddish translation or in Hebrew, but he failed to do so, he explained, because of a general indifference to spiritual thinking in Poland: 'Here, people still orientate themselves politically, although one senses beneath it all that politics must also be taken seriously.'

By 1938 Heschel was constructing the systematology (a philosophy of Judaism) he elaborated during his first decade in the United States. After studying the prophets, Maimonides, and other ancient and medieval religious thinkers, he was formulating a phenomenology of prayer. He then contributed exploratory essays on the inner life of piety to scholarly volumes. Probably even before he was expelled from Germany, Heschel had been invited to contribute essays to two prestigious journals, each representing his Polish and German Jewish communities. He therefore wrote two reflections on prayer, one in Hebrew, 'Al mahut hatefilah' ('On the Essence of Prayer'), intended for the Majer Bałaban Festschrift in Warsaw; and the other in German, 'Das Gebet als Äusserung und Einfühlung' ('Prayer as Expression and Empathy'), solicited by Leo Baeck for the *Monatsschrift* in Berlin. Both collections, confiscated by the Nazis, proved to be the swansong of his teachers' generation.

A MODERN SPIRITUAL LEGACY

Heschel was at a low point, but he clear-headedly organized his many activities, the most pressing of which was to leave Europe. He also suggested the possibility of a faculty position at the Reform rabbinical seminary, the Hebrew Union College, in Cincinnati, Ohio, whose president, Julian Morgenstern, had for several years dedicated himself, with institutional support, to saving European Jewish scholars, whom he called his 'college in exile'.[36]

Still allowed to travel, Heschel planned to visit Germany for three weeks at the beginning of March 1939, while attempting to co-ordinate his departure with Martin Buber's forthcoming lecture tour in Poland.[37] But they missed one other and the disappointed Heschel left Warsaw for Berlin and Frankfurt, where he was unsuccessful in retrieving his books and papers. Writing to Buber again on 13 March from Berlin, Heschel expressed his regret at missing him and again urged him to lecture at the Warsaw Institute, telling him he should expect calls from Dr Stein or Professor Bałaban, but should not be surprised at the community's lack of spiritual discernment: 'The society whose guest you are encompasses a socially

[36] See Michael Meyer, 'The Refugee Scholars' Project of the Hebrew Union College', in Bertram Korn (ed.), *A Bicentennial Festschrift for Jacob Rader Marcus* (Waltham, Mass., 1976), 359–75.

[37] Maurice Friedman, *Martin Buber: His Life and Work. The Middle Years, 1923–1945* (New York, 1983), 263–4.

one-sided class.' Heschel returned to Warsaw on 2 April and met Buber in L'viv three days later. There he learned that Buber's lectures in flawless Polish were admired by people wherever he spoke.[38]

By this time few if any American quota visas remained, and only some clergy and academics sponsored by institutions might qualify for non-quota visas. Thus an unhealable wound formed which it is impossible to imagine: while seeking support for himself, he knew that exit permits for his mother and sisters in Warsaw could not be obtained. He did not give expression to his feelings, but kept his most intimate anguish private. He finally received official confirmation of his post from the president of the Hebrew Union College (dated 6 April 1939), and so he could apply for his own immigration visa to the United States.[39] He remained unmarried until 1946, years after he settled there.

As Heschel's world was being demolished, his two exploratory essays on prayer combined academic analysis and testimony and laid the foundation for his neo-hasidic philosophy of Judaism. Like all his subsequent writings, they open the modern mind to God's reality. 'The Essence of Prayer', which he wrote in Hebrew for the Warsaw volume, seeks 'to understand the contents of consciousness at the time of prayer itself, and not the facts that preceded it in the life of the mind'.[40] Heschel's theocentric perspective insists upon the priority of God: 'Within the reality of religion, God and man meet. It is there that human consciousness touches God's consciousness; it is there that man has to answer to his purpose, and the matters between a person and his maker take place within its boundaries.' Prayer is a metaphysical 'event' transforming our vision of reality.

In his shattered world Heschel remained confident that prayer could connect man with God and fortify ethical courage. The essay ends by urging us to retrieve the moment at Sinai. The praying person is 'heroic', for, 'intentionally or not, he puts his life in danger. He surrenders himself to the One to whom his being and essence belong; he makes a decision, he accuses God, gives notice, confesses himself, makes a vow, accepts the yoke of His rule, pawns his soul, accepts an acquisition, and seals a covenant.' Prayer is a total commitment, affecting God as it affects the person.

Heschel's theology of divine pathos was thus complete by 1933, and when he left Warsaw in July 1939 he had formulated his philosophy of prayer and piety. His European writings underlie his two foundational books in English, *Man is not Alone* (1951) and *God in Search of Man* (1955): 'We have to press the religious consciousness with questions, compelling man to understand and unravel the

---

[38] Letter from Heschel to Eduard Strauss, 3 May 1939. Conserved at the Leo Baeck Institute, New York.

[39] Preserved in the American Jewish Archives, Cincinnati, HUC, Morgenstern file. See Meyer, 'The Refugee Scholars' Project of the Hebrew Union College', 363 ff.

[40] 'Al mahut hatefilah', prepared for the *Mayer Bałaban Jubilee Volume*, ii (Warsaw, destroyed by the Nazis before publication); published for the first time in the Hebrew monthly *Bitsaron* (1941). See Biderman, *Mayer Bałaban*, bibliography.

meaning of what is taking place in his life as it stands at the divine horizon. By penetrating the consciousness of the pious man, we may conceive the reality behind it.'[41]

The destruction of European Jewry only magnified the urgency of Heschel's mission. Remarkably, what was subsequently called the Holocaust did not compromise his love of God, his fervour for social justice, and his reverence for the divine human image.

---

[41] A. J. Heschel, *God in Search of Man* (New York, 1955), 3; cf. Heschel, *Man is not Alone* (New York, 1951), 60–1, for a more general statement of Heschel's phenomenological goal.

PART V

Reviews

REVIEW ESSAYS

Recent Books on the Catholic Church in Poland

JOHN T. PAWLIKOWSKI

MICHAEL BRON JR. (ed.), *Jews and Christians: Who is your Neighbor after the Holocaust? A Polish–Swedish Colloquium on Jewish–Christian Dialogue*
(Uppsala: Acta Sueco-Polonica, Bokserie 2, 1997); pp. 166

EWA KUREK-LESIK, *Gdy klasztor znaczył życie: Udział żeńskich zgromadzeń zakonnych w akcji ratowania dzieci żydowskich w Polsce w latach 1939–1945*
(Kraków: Wydawnictwo Znak, 1992); pp. 172

RONALD MODRAS, *The Catholic Church and Antisemitism: Poland, 1933–1939*
(Chur, Switzerland: Harwood Academic Publishers, 1994); pp. xvi + 430

MARIAN MUSHKAT, *Philo-Semitic and Anti-Jewish Attitudes in Post-Holocaust Poland*
(Lewiston: Edwin Mellen Press, 1992); pp. vi + 442

ALL four of these books raise issues that are crucial to a continued Polish–Jewish dialogue. The journalist Konstanty Gebert has broken down the complex Polish–Jewish relationship into three main components: cultural and national identity, Christian–Jewish relations, and the 'mythological' function given to Jews and Judaism as representations of all that is problematic in society, a theme especially prevalent among Polish religio-nationalists past and present. All three of these components emerge in a consideration of the four books under review.

Bron's *Jews and Christians* and Kurek-Lesik's *When the Convent Meant Life: The Role of Nuns in Saving Jewish Children in Poland in the Years 1939–1945* raise issues relevant to Christian–Jewish dialogue today—though the latter is primarily historical in its orientation. Modras and Mushkat are also historical in their respective approaches, but their analyses bring the reader face to face with images of a mythical Jew which still make possible today accusations of 'Jewishness' against Polish leaders who are, in fact, without Jewish ancestry; these images are the basis for 'antisemitism' without Jews. The central concern in Mushkat's book, however, is the related issue of cultural and national identity.

CHRISTIAN–JEWISH DIALOGUE

Kurek-Lesik's brief volume is best read in tandem with her work *Your Life is Worth Mine* (New York, 1997) in which she records the reflections of Catholic nuns who rescued Jewish children in Nazi-occupied Poland. Her research into this area of Polish Jewish history, under-explored in the past decade of books and scholarly papers, is a valuable addition to the study of the Holocaust. She has brought to Polish, as well as international, attention stories of genuine heroism by religious women that might otherwise have fallen from memory. One hopes that more will be done in the future to honour these dedicated women in a more lasting way.

It is necessary, however, to point out the clear theological limitations present in the attitude of some of the Catholic rescuers more directly than Kurek-Lesik does. Her materials clearly show a pronounced 'conversionist' mentality within some of the nuns who engaged in rescue. While this does not diminish the nobility of their deeds at the time, and while one must recognize it as part of the mentality of the time, it is important—for the sake of an enhanced understanding between Christians and Jews today—to contextualize her research. While it surely reveals behaviour by Poles towards Jews during the Holocaust that too many people ignore or do not know of, Kurek-Lesik's research should not be used to cloak the antisemitism prevalent in so much of Polish nationalistic thinking during the period she discusses.

While the dialogue between Poles and Swedes from which Michael Bron Jr.'s *Jews and Christians* comes was an important event, the book itself breaks no new ground, especially when viewed in a North American context. Given both the history and the contemporary links between the two nations, the dialogue was no doubt a useful experience in international understanding, with the participation on the Polish side of people such as Stanisław Krajewski, Bishop Stanisław Gądecki, the Revd Waldemar Chrostowski, and Krzysztof Śliwiński, who have been in the forefront of Polish–Jewish reconciliation. Some of the personal comments and observations are interesting, but the volume cannot compare in depth of scholarship with Modras's book nor even with Mushkat's volume. It does not represent an original contribution to the study of the Polish–Jewish relationship. This is not to say it is without value, but rather that it is not a major piece of scholarship.

MYTHS OF JEWS AND JUDAISM

Ronald Modras's book encapsulates several years of research under the auspices of the Vidal Sassoon International Centre for the study of antisemitism at the Hebrew University in Jerusalem. Modras examines in detail the attitudes of *Mały Dziennik* during the critical years leading up to the Nazi invasion of Poland and to the Holocaust. This newspaper, it should be recalled, was published by Fr. Kolbe and had a wide circulation. Thus Modras sees it as reflecting a pervasive attitude in Poland at the time.

Some have criticized Modras's study as too narrow because of the decided focus on *Mały Dziennik* and other like-minded publications of the period. While it is true that any complete picture of Polish society and Polish attitudes towards Jews in the 1930s must draw on a wider variety of sources, Modras certainly identifies a central strain in Polish consciousness at the time, whose implications for the past and present have yet to be fully confronted by Poles or Polish Americans.

Modras sets his investigation of *Mały Dziennik* and the popular religious press within a broader framework of developments in European society. The notion of an alliance between masons and the Jews to subvert Christian culture has its roots in France, but in the 1930s it infiltrated Polish consciousness in a significant way. Following Konstanty Gebert's observations about the three main components of Polish–Jewish relations, we clearly see at work in publications such as *Mały Dziennik* the myth that Jews represent all that is pernicious and corrupting in society and that they are potential agents of secularity. However, Modras does speak in his final chapter (chapter 14) of the Polish opponents of antisemitism, thus giving some balance to his presentation. And in the epilogue he refers to the heroic activities of Żegota.

Much as Kurek-Lesik's research needs to be placed alongside the reality of Polish antisemitism, especially among religio-nationalists, so people reading Modras's book need to remind themselves that the story of Polish rescue is more extensive than is normally portrayed. Like Kurek-Lesik's studies, Modras's account of the Polish rescue of Jews demands some qualification—which, to his credit, Modras provides, unlike some others who write on the subject. While duly praising the leaders of Żegota for their courage under the most trying circumstances found in any region under Nazi control, Modras points out that Zofia Kossak, one of Żegota's founders, while unquestionably not an antisemite, regarded Jews as ultimately alien to Polish nationalistic interests. She herself supported the idea that it would be best if Jews left Poland, even though she strongly opposed the Nazi solution to the 'Jewish problem'.

In raising the issue, neither Modras nor I intend to accuse people such as Kossak. But, as we honour them for their profound commitment to human decency, it is important for our own situation today to confront certain limitations in their perspective. The question of minorities remains one of Poland's most important challenges, as it reconstructs its national life after communism. The integration and protection of minorities is a basic test of the nation's commitment to democracy. Poland can learn from a soul-searching examination of even those who stood out as moral heroes during the darkness of Nazism.

Modras in the end argues that the anti-liberal, anti-masonic, anti-secularist position which coalesced into the myth, so prevalent in the popular religious press, of an international Jewish conspiracy against Catholicism was quite in line with the general policy of the Vatican and of leading Catholic thinkers and theologians, such as Hilaire Belloc, Père Lagrange, Karl Adam, and Michael Schumaus. It was not even so far removed from the perspective of the infamous, and censured, Fr. Charles Coughlin of Detroit.

Again Modras has raised a critical issue with implications well beyond the Polish context, even if one does not fully accept some of the linkages he posits between the articles in certain Polish Catholic publications and concrete antisemitic activities by Polish Catholics. What if the Vatican had chosen to see liberalism as a potential ally rather than the fascist-leaning movements of the time? Would the Vatican's stand against the Nazi invasion of Poland and its consequences—criticized by many Poles at the time and by contemporary historians such as Fr. John Morley and Richard Lukas—have been more decisive if the Vatican had not seen the fascists as necessary allies, whatever their failings? This is a question worth pursuing, not merely for historical reasons, but for a better understanding of the directions we must take in today's world.

Marian Mushkat's volume is partly historical investigation, partly personal recollection. It begins with a brief overview of the history of the Jews in Poland prior to the Holocaust. Mushkat is rather balanced in his treatment of antisemitism as well as of the Jews' positive contributions to Polish society. He particularly stresses the importance of the Frankist movement as a conduit for Jewish influence on the overall national life and culture of Poland. Yet he admits that the picture of the Frankists remains mixed, since some of the members joined antisemitic groups. He also underscores the Jewish influence on Polish cultural icons such as the poet Adam Mickiewicz.

Mushkat's treatment of the new philosemitism in Poland is well balanced on the whole. He stresses that it is limited in scope, though not confined to intellectuals. But he takes issue with those Jewish scholars who suggest it may be only a passing phenomenon. He genuinely believes that the greater interest in Jews and Judaism is ultimately tied to the continuing recapture of Polish history, of which Polish Jewry is a central part.

CULTURAL AND NATIONAL IDENTITY

Most of Mushkat's book focuses on the period of the Second World War and the subsequent communist era. In terms of the latter period Mushkat joins a growing number of historians, both Polish and Jewish, who are gradually turning their attention to Jewish religious and cultural issues in the period after the war. He clearly shows how classical anti-Judaism was utilized by communist leaders for their own political purposes, and he traces the continuation of some antisemitic perspectives among conservative Polish political groups, including Church-related associations, despite the virtual absence of Jewish inhabitants in the country.

His analysis does not quite reach the scholarly standards set by Modras's volume, but his book does have the advantage of including observations rooted in personal experiences, whereas Modras's account is based solely on archival sources. Perhaps the most glaring deficiency in Mushkat's work, as in similar volumes, is the lack of any in-depth treatment of the complexity of the Jewish community in Poland in the decades prior to the Second World War and of how the various Jewish groups interacted with general social movements in the country. Within such an analysis, an objective investigation of the role played by Jews in the Polish Communist Party before and after the Second World War is a necessity. A few scholars have begun such an examination, but thus far we have witnessed mostly silence on the issue from Jewish scholars and some outlandish claims from some Polish and Polish American authors who imply that Polish communism was essentially Jewish and that, as a result, Polish hostility towards Jews in this era was justified.

Polish communism would have emerged as a controlling political force in postwar Poland with or without Jewish involvement. Jewish involvement was not a decisive factor. But the accuracy of the historical record as well as the painful experience of some Poles still alive at the hands of Jewish communists requires the end of both silence and exaggeration regarding the issue. Measured by this standard, Mushkat's volume falls short.

A common feature of all these books is that they represent contributions from a transition period. We can see significant shifts in the scholarly approach to the study of Polish–Jewish relations, compared to a decade ago. Each of the four books, in its own way, contributes to this shift of focus, where issues such as Polish rescue, the persistence of Polish religio-nationalism, and Polish–Jewish relations in the communist and post-communist periods are finally receiving the serious attention they warrant.

'You shall not bear false witness'

JERZY TOMASZEWSKI

STANISŁAW C. NAPIÓRKOWSKI, OFM Conv. (ed.), *A bliźniego swego . . . Materiały z sympozjum 'Św Maksymilian Maria Kolbe—Żydzi—masoni'*
(Lublin: Catholic University of Lublin, 1997); pp. 176

IN the course of 1997 a handful of publications of a distinctly antisemitic character found their way onto the shelves of bookshops in Poland (and, rather more frequently, onto street stalls, since self-respecting bookshops do not, on the whole, stock such literature), and some contain, in all seriousness, the infamous nonsense about 'ritual murder'. We read about a 'Jewish–masonic plot' aimed at world domination (this is based, apparently, on the notorious 'Protocols of the Elders of Zion' forged by the tsarist *Okhrana*, which the curious and naïve passer-by can buy, for example, at the stall by the entrance to Solidarity's headquarters in Warsaw). There are also publications that openly break a law that is binding in more places than Poland (an appeal, for example, to beat up Jews), but the department of public prosecution appears to pay no attention to such 'trifles'. A singular curiosity is a publication denying the Holocaust—the murder of the Jewish nation on Polish soil by the occupier. According to the authors, there were no gas chambers in Auschwitz. Until recently, I had thought that no one would publish such rubbish in our country, though they might find publishers and naïve readers overseas, where information about the barbarity of the German occupation of Poland during the Second World War and the heroism of the resistance are considered incredible. I appear to have been mistaken.

Such publications have, until now, appeared courtesy of a number of hole-and-corner publishers, declaring to the world that they alone are true Polish patriots. Serious publishing houses, and particularly universities, have avoided being compromised, regardless of their own ideological sympathies. It was with some astonishment, therefore, that I read the latest publication from the faculty of theology of the Catholic University of Lublin, which contains the proceedings of the symposium 'Saint Maksymilian Maria Kolbe, the Jews and the Masons'. I was—and remain—convinced that Maksymilian Kolbe deserves respect and admiration for his stand in the face of the Nazi death machine. I understood his canonization as the acknowledgement by the Church of his embodiment of the commandment 'Love your neighbour as yourself'. This does not mean, however, that all the deeds and views of this Franciscan deserve similar respect. The life journey of more than one Christian martyr has been complicated, gaining sanctity precisely through their prodigal actions. Mary Magdalene was not glorified because of her profession before meeting Christ, and Maksymilian Kolbe by no means merits glory because *Rycerz Niepokalanej* ('Knight of the Immaculate Conception'), the paper he established and edited, disseminated belief in 'ritual murder' (no. 7, 1925) and acknowledged as true the forgeries of the tsarist police (no. 4, 1924; no. 9, 1926).

Perusal of a number of the conference papers (excluding the pieces on masonry or freethinking) and the statements of participants in the discussion published in this volume leads one to the conclusion that my point about canonization is not quite so obvious to the contributors. They seek justification for a significant proportion of the anti-Jewish views expressed in the journals published under the editorship, or at least the auspices, of Kolbe. It is possible that the reason for these peculiar opinions was that the authors were theology experts and sometimes media analysts, unfortunately with no elementary knowledge of the social, economic, or political situation of inter-war Poland. As a rule, they also display no understanding of the most elementary historical questions concerning national minorities in Poland. (This emerges, in part, from the notes and bibliographies, in which there is an almost total lack of references to Polish or foreign publications on these questions; the reference to two of my publications is purely formal in character.) As a result—despite the hopes expressed in the foreword—all too frequently one perceives 'intense emotions which successfully eliminate correct thinking' (Celestyn Napiórkowski, p. 8) dictated by a deep belief in the sanctity of Kolbe and a disdainful attitude towards those who try to analyse the past critically.

Let us begin with the most general questions. The premiss accepted, more or less openly, by the authors is that Jewish society in inter-war Poland was distinguished by its wealth, that it obstructed the country's economic development, spread communism, was hostile (or at least indifferent) to Poland, and, finally, that it encouraged immorality. In sum, it was a threat to civilization. (There were noble exceptions, but they were few and far between.) Poles had to defend themselves against the Jews, which resulted in, among other things, the occurrence of sometimes unacceptable excesses, which were, however, condemned by the Church.

Such was the general stance of the inter-war Catholic press and particularly of *Rycerz Niepokalanej* and *Mały Dziennik*, the publications for which Kolbe was responsible. The author of one article, 'Problematyka żydowska w prasie katolickiej okresu międzywojennego' ('The Jewish Question in the Catholic Press in the Inter-War Period'), Kazimierz Malinowski, cites with approval the absurd words of Zofia Kossak-Szczucka (praised for saving Jews during the Nazi occupation) in which he sees the 'de-mythologizing of the Jewish question': 'The Jews are for us a real and terrible danger, growing daily. They have settled on us like mistletoe on a rotting tree. Polish youth embarking on life finds itself in a hopeless situation. Wherever they look, the place has already been occupied by a shrewder, more enterprising, more ruthless Jew' (p. 27).

One of the arguments in favour of such a view is the oft-cited statement of Primate August Hlond, summarized in the following words:

He wrote about the hostility of Jews towards the Catholic Church, about their participation in the propagation of godlessness, bolshevism, and subversive action. He repeated the generally known facts about Jewish fraud, usury, and participation in the white slave-trade, and the propagation of pornography by their publishing concerns. He warned against the negative religious and ethical influence of Jewish youth on Catholic youth. He pointed out, however, that this did not apply to all Jews. Many of them were people of faith—honest, just, merciful, philanthropic; some were ethically outstanding, noble, and worthy of honour. Although one had to defend oneself against the morally harmful influence of Jews, it was not permissible to attack, beat, maim, or defame them, or to destroy their private property. (Waldemar Mackiewicz, 'Obraz Żyda w *Rycerzu Niepokalanej*' ('The Image of the Jew in *Rycerz Niepokalanej*'), 92)

If one reads the original text, one is struck by the preponderance in it of negative evaluations of Jews in general, with the occasional admonishments that not all were like this. In other words, Jews in general deserved condemnation, but exceptional, decent individuals should be respected. A popular expression of such reasoning is illustrated by the outrageous designation: he's a Jew, but honest. This mirrors the view, expressed by some Jewish journalists in the United States, against whom many Polish writers protest, and rightly so: the view that all Poles are antisemites, and only a few are free of this prejudice—or another conventional opinion captured in the vulgar saying 'a Pole, but a sober one'. It is astonishing that neither the author nor the publisher of this book see this.

The method of presenting the views contained in the publications analysed is also often ambiguous. Sometimes it is difficult to tell if we are dealing with a straightforward account of the newspaper under consideration or with an expression of approval for the views it expresses. On more than one occasion the construction of the sentences leads to the conclusion that the contributors accept the sometimes completely absurd judgements of the pre-war journalists. Thus we read:

Employing source materials and critical studies, the authors demonstrate the destructive and ruinous activity of the Jews from the moment of their arrival in Poland. (Ewa Banaś, 'Problematyka żydowska i masońska na łamach *Małego Dziennika*' ('Jewish and Masonic Questions in the Columns of *Mały Dziennik*', 79)

Mały Dziennik stressed and demonstrated that the power and greatness of Poland was closely linked with the national ideal, whereas her fall and ruin was brought about by the international ideal, disseminated by the Jews, through freemasonry and communism. (p. 84)

Throughout its appearance, *Mały Dziennik* exposed and openly fought all alien forces in Poland. (p. 89)

We do come across rather singular formulations which conform to reality superficially but ignore certain basic facts:

A number of fights and riots between Polish and Jewish students were connected with the *numerus clausus*. One such incident took place in December 1932 in L'viv, when a Polish student was killed. (Malinowski, p. 26)

The author of these words omitted to say that the cause of these fights 'between students' (this formulation suggests that in some instances the Jews were the guilty party and in others, the Poles) were attacks by students belonging to some (right-wing) oganizations on Jews or on other Polish students helping them. The chance fatal victim referred to was an attacker, and the sources (and press) list notably more names of Jewish students who were killed, not to mention the numerous wounded and badly beaten who needed hospital treatment. Another author also states as an undoubted fact: 'The Jewish press . . . and its sympathizers propagated pornography and masonic and communist ideas' (Mackiewicz, p. 95).

That means that Mackiewicz accuses all Jewish newspapers, including serious publications with the largest circulations—which suggests strongly that he has never held one in his hand. If he had bothered to pick up such influential and widely read papers as *Haynt*, *Nasz Przegląd* (for which Janusz Korczak worked), *Der moment*, or *Chwila*, he would certainly have hesitated before writing such nonsense. It would be difficult to cite all the more or less erroneous statements or suggestions contained in this book. I shall add just one more quotation: 'In all the texts [of *Rycerz Niepokalanej*] one can perceive a respect for the person of the Jew, praise for those who are honest, just, and sincerely seeking truth, but also efforts to convert those who stray' (Mackiewicz, p. 107).

It is easy to show that this has little to do with reality. In almost every volume from 1930 on the *Rycerz Niepokalanej Almanach* contained crude 'jokes' in which it was difficult to find any trace of respect for 'the person of the Jew'. In *Rycerz Niepokalanej* itself we often read expressions of contempt for Jews and for the whole of Jewish society and culture.

In some of the conference papers we do find careful critical comments directed at inter-war Catholic journalism, particularly where certain theological problems are concerned that are now differently evaluated by the Church authorities in Rome. I also think that none of the contributors would today approve the use of the term 'the synagogue of Satan', for example, which we come across in the *Rycerz Niepokalanej Almanach* of 1936 (p. 62), although no mention of it is made in this book. In one of the papers we meet a critical, albeit extremely pithy and euphemistic, evaluation of the position proclaimed by the Polish Catholic press between the wars concerning certain theological questions:

There are basic doubts as to whether the interpretation of the history of the Jewish nation in inter-war journalism was adequate from the theological point of view and honest in the light of historical facts. One must state, however, in the interests of historical truth, that such was the state of awareness and knowledge at the time and that mutual relations between the Christian world and Jewish society were interpreted in this way. (Malinowski, p. 23).

There is no doubt that the reservations concerning the 'state of awareness' of Catholic authors of the time are pertinent, but they justify nothing. Independently of the author's intention, I perceive in these words a general condemnation of ignorance and the propagation of glaring falsities and antisemitic slogans concerning Jews by all Catholic theologians and journalists throughout the inter-war years. The reality was, however, rather more complicated. In Poland there were also Catholics who did not share this type of interpretation, belief in 'ritual murder', the authenticity of the 'Protocols', and so on (and thus having a different 'state of awareness'), and the generalization seems to me exaggerated.

I do not accuse the authors of ill will because, among other things, at certain points in these papers one can perceive a critical stance towards the Catholic journalism in question. Far too often, however, hackneyed stereotypes hostile to Jews and Judaism are approvingly repeated. These problems have been analysed by Polish and foreign authors in literally hundreds of articles and books, so I do not think it necessary to present yet another analysis of the economic, social, and political relations of the Second Republic and the place and situation of Jewish society within it. I dare say that ignorance of the historical literature can no doubt serve as moral justification for the authors (forgive them, for they know not what they write . . .), but it compromises them as scholars. It is true that, as we read in the introduction, 'It is strange how often honest thinking walks hand in hand with taking a risk' (Napiórkowski, p. 61). But the greatest honesty will not help a thinker if his views are based on ignorance, preventing the critical rejection of false stereotypes. The title of the book alludes to the well-known injunction in the Gospels to love one's neighbour. Juxtaposed with the book's content, this has a mocking ring. It is a pity that the publishers and contributors overlooked a different commandment, inscribed on the tablets brought down from Sinai by Moses: 'You shall not bear false witness against your neighbour'.

I put the book aside with some sadness, since, in spite of some contradictory experiences, I had up to now considered the Catholic University of Lublin a serious academic institution.

Translated from Polish by Anna Zaranko

A Lithuanian Account of Life in the Camps

NERIJUS UDRENAS

BALYS SRUOGA, *Forest of the Gods: Memoirs*
(Vilnius: Vaga, 1996); pp. 340

JEWS, along with many other people, suffered a tragic fate in east central Europe during the Second World War at the hands of Nazis and their allies. Some survived. What was the main difference between death and survival? Death did not visit individually: it selected groups. The Nazis slaughtered Jews for being Jews, no matter how diverse they were; they killed Gypsies, no matter where they came from. Death came *en masse*, while survival always meant singularity. Survivors of the war, of concentration camps, all had individual experiences of luck. They survived by chance and did not believe what was happening to them then, nor do they now. Dehumanization aimed to bar every way to return to life. Those who survived had to adapt to human society again. They were deprived of their name, voice, personality. Freedom forced survivors to create a new language of return.

Marek Edelman has reminded us of a Latin motto, short, plain, and powerful: *Homo homini lupus est*. People are bad, and one needs to fight against them. He personifies a Spartan fighter—tough, laconic in speech, inward-looking, and devoted to his land. A similarly savage picture of life in the camps was painted by the Polish writer Tadeusz Borowski, while Primo Levi's gloomy view of the 'war of all against all', which characterized life in the *Lager*, is tempered by his faith in the redemptive power of understanding and of the importance of the individual act of resistance, no matter how small.

Different languages have specific purposes: adaptive, moralistic, analytic, or didactic. What language has the most powerful effect on contemporary listeners and readers who want to understand what happened in the camps? The language of sarcasm and irony is the strongest and shocks the most. Balys Sruoga (1896–1947) is a Lithuanian intellectual and a survivor of Stutthof concentration camp, whose account of his stay in Stutthof, first published in 1957 in Lithuanian under the title *Miškas*, has now appeared in a well-wrought and readable English translation, as *Forest of the Gods*. Sruoga is a master of the language of irony. The reader reads and laughs and is immediately stunned both consciously and subconsciously at the appalling nature of the sociobiological experimentation carried out by the Nazis. Irony strikes the reader and captures his undivided attention. Such language is painful and hard to create. Balys Sruoga himself could not speak it for long: he died shortly after writing his memoir.

The testimony remains to teach the living. It deserves an exceptional place in Sruoga's work as a poet, dramatist, and novelist. All his other books are products of the writer's fantasy or of scholarly investigation, while *Forest of the Gods* emerged as a product of living pain, of the suffering he experienced from 1943 to 1945 while a prisoner at Stutthof. He wrote the memoirs immediately after being liberated from the camp by the Red Army. The plane which brought him to Vilnius landed in May 1945, and in the autumn the author started to edit his manuscript. The book did not appear in print until 1957 because the censors would not allow publication. They expected socialist realism and a more favourable account of Russian prisoners. Sruoga always distinguished himself with a spontaneous style of writing, full of emotion. In this particular case, however, the author felt a social responsibility to write a testimony, expressing respect for the victims in his own particular style and immortalizing their suffering in Stutthof. While in the concentration camp he urged other prisoners to record—if they survived—everything they experienced. Once in the position to do so himself, he tried to look at his suffering from the point of view of an observer. In this way, he seems to reconcile himself with his memories and return to a normal way of life, for which he had longed so much in Stutthof. As he had hoped, he is not alone in his efforts to preserve the memory of victims. Memoirs formed a huge part of anti-Nazi literature after the war and quite a few were written of 'life' in Stutthof, where 'only' 80,000 victims were worked to death, killed, or gassed.

Forest of the Gods offers vital and precise documentation of all the events—a feature common to memoir literature. Sruoga worked before the liberation in the chancellery of the camp, so he knew very well both its internal and external life. He recorded what he saw with his own eyes or learned through other sources. All but a few names are genuine. The writer reconstructs the mechanics of the camp—its hierarchies, interpersonal relations, and organizational life. The book describes the history of the camp, the everyday life of prisoners, various functional institutions, and their internal workings. Sruoga, a Lithuanian intellectual, devotes much attention to the group of his colleagues who were deported from Lithuanian universities and schools for obstructing SS efforts to recruit Lithuanian youth into the SS. According to German documents, the hostages were accused by the Germans of 'heading the Lithuanian resistance movement and, specifically, agitating against the Reichcommissar's declaration of mobilization of the Lithuanian nation'. Mainly, however, the book depicts how the camp physically and spiritually 'tortured, sucked all energy, all health, all strength, and starved people to death'.

The author gives us more than a hundred portraits in the book. Camp leaders and overseers make up most of them. With deep irony, Sruoga emphasizes certain biographical facts or characteristic features and masterfully depicts the psychological abyss between the normal psyche and the ultimately sadistic nature. His talents as a writer and as an observer of psychology allow the reader to look more deeply into the problem of mass extermination. In this sense *Forest of the Gods* reveals the anti-human nature of Nazism. The book is unique in its impact on the reader. Most other memoirs record direct experiences, suffering, and pain. Sruoga suppresses his own suffering and emotions, and writes as if he is afraid to touch his wounds. Even when writing of the most horrifying episodes—such as a march of prisoners to the crematorium, the burning of corpses, and 'gold fever'—he writes with some restraint. There is little overt protest. He does not write about his own longing for home and family, although his letters record much pain stemming from the enforced separation.

Sruoga employs irony, angry sarcasm, or plain humour when writing on the most tragic events. He laughs at everything—from executioners to 'humiliated and desecrated death', which in the context of mass extermination became an everyday fact. Death marches along with each camp prisoner, shadowing every step. Sruoga's laughter is irony drenched with tears, his only means of expressing the dreadful agony. Ironic narrative shocks the reader and achieves rare levels of artistic exhortation.

Many hostages in Stutthof were placed under the direct command of Heinrich Himmler and officially labelled *Ehrenshäftslinge*—'honorary prisoners'. The camp housed many political prisoners, including members of German political parties, groups of intellectuals from Norway, Lithuania, Latvia, and Poland, and French and Latvian SS members. Towards the end of the war the Germans paid more attention to international opinion and did not dare to treat prisoners as elsewhere. Conditions were harsh in the camp, but they gradually improved so that many prisoners managed to survive. Nevertheless, death was at home in Stutthof. Prisoners starved, were worked to death, or became ill and died. Many were beaten to death, or simply executed. Beating became commonplace everywhere, especially at work. Balys Sruoga has described his first day of work. 'While pushing the trolley, you have to hurry whether the trolley is empty or full. Your clogs sink in the loose sand and don't stay on your feet. A couple of galloping leaps and your feet are already bleeding from the damn clogs! Then while you're loading the trolley with sand, the *Hilfskapo* drums on your ribs with his stick and harangues you for laziness.... He slams down the club and like a broken record repeats over and over: "Die Arbeit macht das Leben süss! Die Arbeit macht ... Work makes life sweet!" ' (p. 75).

Slave work was not productive—that was its aim. Work for a free person is the main creator of sense in life. Work without purpose and a creative goal has the most demoralizing effect. Such work dehumanizes the individual, takes away the soul, and makes one an instrument. The old convicts knew very well that the final products of camp labour were immaterial. All that mattered was to keep you on the move, to tire you out, to torture you—so you'd kick the bucket sooner (p. 76). A living-dead, numbered, and shaved unit of statistics, that was the ideal type of a prisoner. He or she should not talk, think, or feel. There were many prisoners, but they should be divided and separated. Internal official and unofficial hierarchies ensured that prisoners controlled and beat each other just as well or even more than the SS guards did. Old prisoners tortured newcomers, German criminals would have greater status than others, Poles would beat others because they were more numerous, and so on. The old prisoners, hovering to one side, sullenly scowl at you, grind their teeth, and keep pushing their share of the work at you: 'Here, you putrefied toad! Work, if you're so smart! Let him do the work! He'll cuss you out worse than the *kapo*, damn you, and even swing a shovel at you' (p. 76). Germans had no trouble finding professional sadists among the prisoners. They encouraged the killing of fellow prisoners and awarded the prisoners the office of *kapo*—labour leader—or even block chief. Fighting and beating other prisoners were considered a good sign by the authorities. If an old-timer beat a newcomer, the old-timer must have already 'reformed', 'repented' of his crime, 'caught onto the game'. If you wanted to gain the trust of the authorities, if you aspired to make a career in the camp republic, or even if you simply wished to rise in esteem among fellow prisoners, your easiest recourse was to beat up others, especially newcomers (p. 39). Why did convicts even of the same nationality beat each other so brutally? That was a question Balys Sruoga asked himself and others. There were several explanations. Human nature is rotten, and people are animals—the most simplistic explanation. Sadists and murderers hoped to receive better treatment from the Germans themselves. The most interesting rationalization, however, is shocking. Gerwinski, a classic thug, confessed that beating was necessary to a prisoner's survival. The ideologist of corporal punishment laughed over this.

> A person arriving in camp doesn't know the score. He's got to learn it in a way that's really going to sink in, and while he's still got strength. He's got to be toughened up immediately; later it'll be too late. If he gets a beating right off, he'll be more careful later. He'll keep his eyes peeled, he'll be on guard for his life. If you don't beat them while they're healthy, they'll weaken and die while you watch. Later on they're easy prey. You've got to put some meanness into them from the start. Listen, by beating them, I'm doing them a favour. I'm teaching them to survive... (p. 101)

Wacek Kozłowski's portrait, however, does not support such a philosophy. He became block chief, and a virtuoso of brutal beating and killing. He enjoyed it and often volunteered to assist Germans if they needed his services. He was beating not to survive—he was beating to kill. There were times when he transformed prisoners into lizards, commanding them to crawl on their bellies across the yard; sometimes he made them frogs (they had to leap), sometimes fakirs (they had to squat on one leg). In this respect he was inventive. For more solemn occasions, he used another special method of beating, one quite popular among murderers in the camp. With a swift, sharp, unexpected blow to the head he'd knock the prisoner to the ground, hop on his chest, and jump up and down like a billy goat in front of a nanny goat. The results were at least a few pulverized ribs (p. 81).

Overworked and beaten prisoners never had enough food. Authorities and everybody else who could stole products—while transporting, unloading, cooking, serving—all the time food vanished and only meagre remains reached the prisoners' stomachs. Prisoners had to rely on parcels from relatives (if they were not stolen on the way) or on their wits. The Germans encouraged internal struggle for food and hence survival. The quality and quantity of food became the primary denominator of sociobiological hierarchy. Knut Hamsun's *Hunger* could not rival the hunger of camp prisoners:

> Wacek would sometimes pick out bits of food from parcels sent into the camp and divide them among those prisoners in his block who were in the worst shape. Once he gave me a few little pieces of dried black bread—for some reason he was benevolent to me. . . . I picked up these two pieces of dried bread by bending down low and then moving aside—at least I could suck on them! I crawled out of the crowd, squeezed through, and—hey! My breadcrumbs are gone! Some brute already filched them! What a crook! . . . Now I finally understood why my father used to tell me when I was small that after picking up a piece of bread that had fallen on the ground, you must kiss it. (p. 210)

Hungry and weak prisoners, if they survived beating and torture, were easy prey to different infectious diseases: typhus, cholera, typhoid fever, dysentery, pneumonia, and other lesser-known diseases. When the camp first opened, prisoners with a temperature lower than 39°C (102.2°F) could not get admitted to hospital for medical treatment. The hospital itself was an institution not for getting well, but often for dying sooner. People crowded into small rooms with various diseases died like flies.

Death presided over life in the camp. Many died at night in their sleep: they were the lucky ones. Many died at work, or collapsed on the way to barracks. No one really cared why they died. The authorities aimed to destroy all vestiges of personal dignity before they let prisoners die. Balys Sruoga himself came to the conclusion that 'perhaps the most horrifying thing that the camp does to a person is this inexorable erosion of every trace of what people call conscience, humanity, simple respect' (p. 256). SS leaders were concerned, however, to keep the books in order. Nine people had died in the block overnight. The block secretary undressed them, wrote numbers on their chests, lined them up primly in the washroom, and presented a notice to the authorities of the number of dead, with appropriate numbers and the block chief's signature:

> The block chief . . . glances over his shoulder, just in case, at his corpses lying in the corner like a pile of northern pike. . . . 'One, two, three . . . seven, eight . . . Well yes, eight! Of course, eight . . . Franz, Franz!' rants the block chief calling his secretary. 'Franz, I'll drown

you in the latrine!' . . . Franz is visibly distressed. Looks here, looks there—there's no ninth, no matter what! What imbecile could have stolen a corpse? For what? Maybe he was hungry . . . . Then from the washroom emerges some kind of indefinite creature of the shadows, once perhaps something like a man. Perhaps he really once was a man, who knows? . . . 'My stomach hurts so bad, *brzuch boli*, hurts so bad—hurts so bad I can't stand it . . . I went . . . I'm sorry . . .' He lay down naked on the cement next to the eight other naked corpses. A broom's bristles he took for a pillow. He lay down and died. What was there left for him to do? Some have survived both hunger and beating, harsh work and diseases. They adapted to life in the camp and managed to escape the crematorium.

Luck and chance travelled alone, and yet there were factors which could help a prisoner to survive. Carpenters, blacksmiths, shoemakers, and other artisans had more chance of survival than intellectuals. Their skills were in demand, and they were often stronger physically. They usually got jobs indoors, while intellectuals or farmers had to toil in the fields, come rain or snow. Criminals and thieves applied their skills to rise high in the internal camp hierarchy, and also managed to get better places of work, as *kapos*, cooks, and canteen-keepers. Those who knew German had the chance to get work indoors as well, as a registrar in the hospital or in the camp chancellery. The workplace was the single most important factor of survival. Your sex, nationality, and relationship to other groups of prisoners and to the authorities were other important conditions for survival. A majority of the women, for example, worked inside. Only at harvest time did they appear in the open fields. They peeled potatoes in the kitchen. They also peeled potatoes in the SS kitchen—and thus could pick up a nice supplement to their meal. They serviced the SS officers' mess hall, and did all the housekeeping chores in the headquarters. Work in the laundry was hard and unpleasant, but everywhere else, compared to men, the women had it much easier.

Jews, especially poor Jews, fared the worst. They were not allowed to receive parcels from outside the camp and most of them could not find a better job. They were the most hated by the Germans. For Jews living was more painful than dying right away. Those who went to the gas chamber straight away were incomparably better off: an hour or two and all their accounts with life were squared. Nothing hurt them any more. It was quite another story in barrack 30. 'Hard labour, starvation and the cold sapped their strength, while they died slowly of sores caused by starvation. . . . These women had one great interest in common—how to die as quickly as possible; but they weren't all successful in this. . . . And so the corpses lay there alone or in heaps, waiting for the corpse-removers to step in and pick them up for the trip to the crematorium or the tar pit' (p. 268). Latvians, on the other hand, were the only ones hated by both prisoners and German authorities. They were arrogant, and aggressively flaunted their own background. They kept themselves to themselves, and tried to organize all-Latvian work detachments. And they sang their songs, though this caused them many misfortunes. What is peculiar, however, about other nationalities is the importance of national character for their chances of survival. According to Sruoga, Latvians adapted the worst to life in the camp, and especially to various diseases.

The camp's Latvians became notorious for a very peculiar trait, rarely observed elsewhere. They were basically healthy men, well-built and strong, like farmers, but in Stutthof, they, too, got sick. Their response in such cases was strange. 'A Latvian would get a touch of bronchitis or flu, something another person would just brush off—and he'd decide he was going to die from it. This was very different from the typical Russian response, for example. A Russian, even one sick with something as bad as typhus, would take odd pills and recover. He wouldn't care one way or another about the contents of the pill, so long as it was a pill—you could treat a sick Russian with zinc or pomade: the man was just as likely to get well. But the Latvians took their illness more seriously. A Latvian, having worked his influenza up to a fever of 38°C (100.4°F), would sigh deeply and declare: "It's bad. Now I'm going to die. I'd say in about three days . . .". And the snake would be true to his word!' (p. 312).

Prisoners of different nationalities could expect help from their compatriots who were recruited or taken by force into the SS. The sole Lithuanian SS guard, Seselga, helped others a lot, and Latvians after a while became more patriotic towards Latvian intellectuals imprisoned in Stutthof. Frenchmen could rely on the French SS. The Ukrainian and Polish SS, however, were not as supportive as they could have been, even to their compatriots. Since Poles outnumbered all other groups in the camp their attitude was a very important factor for the survival of Lithuanians. As it turned out, Polish attitudes towards Lithuanians were mixed. Many Poles maltreated Lithuanians, but many helped them as well. Polish leaders in the camp thought of the future, and tried to save the Lithuanian intelligentsia from the brutal assaults of other Poles. Much later, certain Poles admitted that there were, in that group, people they thought they might meet in the future, when the circumstances would have changed utterly, and that in such a case it would be intolerable if fools had done away with some of them in camp. 'We've already done enough foolish harm in the past. Now is the time to sober up, not to count how many times who wronged who, where, and when. We have to help one another' (p. 87).

Prisoners in the camp fought with each other and helped one another. In this chaotic relationship of life and death there were no rules. Some survived; many died. Those who survived did not wish the experience upon others. Balys Sruoga's book remains a testimony to those who died.

Analyses of World Antisemitism Published between 1991 and 1997

ALINA CAŁA

RENE COHEN and JENNIFER L. GOLUB, *Attitudes toward Jews in Poland, Hungary, and Czechoslovakia: A Comparative Survey*, Working Papers on Contemporary Antisemitism
(New York: American Jewish Committee, Institute of Human Relations, Aug. 1991); pp. 44

The Skinhead International: A Worldwide Survey of Neo-Nazi Skinheads
(New York: Anti-Defamation League, 1995); pp. 90

Report Drawn up on behalf of the Committee of the Inquiry
(Luxembourg: Office for Official Publications of the European Communities, European Parliament, 1991); pp. 178

Antisemitism: World Report 1992
(London: Institute of Jewish Affairs in association with the World Jewish Congress, 1992); pp. xvi + 128

Antisemitism: World Report 1994
(London: Institute of Jewish Affairs, 1994); pp. xxvi + 254

Antisemitism: World Report 1995
(London: Institute of Jewish Affairs, American Jewish Committee, 1995); pp. xxxiv + 282

Antisemitism Worldwide 1994
(Tel Aviv: Tel Aviv University, Project for the Study of Antisemitism, Anti-Defamation League, World Jewish Congress, 1995); pp. 274

GARY M. GROBMAN, *Holocaust*, 'Virtual Jerusalem' (internet) (1990)

SIMON EPSTEIN, *Cyclical Patterns in Antisemitism: The Dynamics of Anti-Jewish Violence in Western Countries since the 1950s*, Analysis of Current Trends in Antisemitism, Acta no. 2
(Jerusalem: SICSA, Hebrew University of Jerusalem, 1993); pp. 28

LEON VOLOVICI, *Antisemitism in Post-Communist Eastern Europe: A Marginal or Central Issue?*, Analysis of Current Trends in Antisemitism, Acta no. 5
(Jerusalem: SICSA, Hebrew University of Jerusalem, 1994); pp. 28

DANIEL PERDURANT, *Antisemitism in Contemporary Greek Society*,
Analysis of Current Trends in Antisemitism, Acta no. 7
(Jerusalem: SICSA, Hebrew University of Jerusalem, 1995); pp. 22

SIMON EPSTEIN, *Extreme Right Electoral Upsurges in Western Europe: 1984–1995 Wave as Compared with the Previous Ones*, Analysis of Current Trends in Antisemitism, Acta no. 8
(Jerusalem: SICSA, Hebrew University of Jerusalem, 1996); pp. 30

GILAD MARGALIT, *Antigypsism in the Political Culture of the Federal Republic of Germany: A Parallel with Antisemitism?*, Analysis of Current Trends in Antisemitism, Acta no. 9
(Jerusalem: SICSA, Hebrew University of Jerusalem, 1996); pp. 30

EWA NOWICKA and JAN NAWROCKI (eds.), *Inny–obcy–wróg*
(Warsaw: Oficyna Naukowa, 1996); pp. 262

BARBARA FATYGA and MICHAŁ SZYMAŃCZAK (eds.),
Raport o młodzieży—Report on Polish Youth
(Warsaw, Wyd. Interpress, 1992); pp. 374

MIROSŁAWA JASTRZĄB-MROŻICKA, JOLANTA KULPIŃSKA, *et al.*,
Tolerancja i uprzedzenia młodzieży: raport z badań
(Warsaw: Wyd. Instytutu Filozofii i Socjologii Polskiej Akademii Nauk, 1993); pp. 264

MIROSŁAW KOFTA and GRZEGORZ SĘDEK, *Struktura poznawcza stereotypu etnicznego: bliskość wyborów parlamentarnych a przejawy antysemityzmu*,
Kolokwia Psychologiczne no. 1
(Warsaw: Instytut Psychologii, 1992); pp. 69–86

IRENEUSZ KRZEMIŃSKI (ed.), *Czy Polacy są antysemitami?*
(Warsaw: Oficyna Naukowa, 1996); pp. 306

THE fall of the Soviet block, awaited with hope, brought forth manifold and not always positive consequences. One of the negative ones has been the eruption of extreme right and neo-Nazi political ideas. Like the nineteenth-century ideology of antisemitism, they advance from the West towards eastern Europe: from France, through Germany, to the post-communist countries. This phenomenon is observed by concerned journalists, politicians, activists, and scholars who are trying to discern its causes and find a means to counteract it. Strangely, however, besides the public opinion polls, which are mostly superficial (by their nature), relatively little sociological research has attempted to assess and describe this dangerous phenomenon. A survey measuring the scope and influence of antisemitism in different countries has been undertaken only once (the results were published by Rene Cohen and Jennifer L. Golub). Still, numerous publications have appeared dealing with antisemitism and the political movements that spread antisemitic ideology.

Two centres, the London-based Institute of Jewish Affairs, and the Anti-Defamation League–World Jewish Congress in the USA, have published in recent years several annual reports on the influence of antisemitic ideology in different countries of the world. Among them, *The Skinhead International* describes the influence and the forms of activity of the skinhead subculture in particular countries. A report issued in 1991 by the Committee of Inquiry into Racism and Xenophobia at the European Parliament belongs to the same group. It contains information about international legal norms and laws accepted by the European Parliament in order to protect the rights of national and ethnic minorities, and about legal initiatives of governments and local authorities in particular countries; this part is especially valuable and deserves broad distribution. However, its country by country analysis of organized racism and right-wing extremism is very superficial, and there is very little information about post-communist countries. On the other hand, it includes a valuable compilation of instances of discrimination and acts of violence against various minorities, not only against the Jews, and pays particular attention to actions against the Gypsies. Research into antisemitism is permanently conducted by the Vidal Sassoon International Centre for the Study of Antisemitism at the Hebrew University in Jerusalem, the Project for the Study of Antisemitism at the University of Tel Aviv, and the Zentrum für Antisemitismusforschung at the Technische Universität in Berlin. The last organized a survey conference in 1993; the papers presented there were published in *Patterns of Prejudice*, xxvii (London, 1993). The Jewish Historical Institute of Warsaw has undertaken the task of monitoring the phenomenon of antisemitism in Poland.

The reports published annually by the Institute of Jewish Affairs include a country by country analysis. These reports are usually introduced by a brief characterization of the country and its system of government. Then the report gives the names of political parties and organizations advocating antisemitism in their programmes, together with the names of their leaders and the number of followers; their activities and publications are also described. Sometimes the attitude of political élites towards the phenomenon of antisemitism is discussed, as well as the attitudes of governments and legal systems towards the movements and organizations advocating antisemitism. Usually, the report treats separately the motif of 'Holocaust denial' in the local varieties of antisemitism. Finally, the results of public opinion polls are recorded. Necessarily, these overviews are superficial, and it is hard to avoid errors in them (for example, in the translations of the names of organizations). Their basic flaw is that they rely on press reports from particular countries, which are not always prepared by respondents dealing professionally with this problem. Still, they are an important source of information in the field of political science, and especially invaluable for comparative studies.

A similar report was prepared in 1994 by Tel Aviv University in collaboration with the Anti-Defamation League and the World Jewish Congress. *Antisemitism Worldwide 1994* is repetitive compared to the reports of the Institute of Jewish

Affairs. Designed according to a similar pattern, it is more superficial, and contains more errors and stereotypical oversimplifications. These are clearly evident in the chapter about Poland. The authors, though they borrowed the idea and the pattern from the reports of the Institute of Jewish Affairs, did not read them too carefully and did not know how to use the information they derived from them so as to develop and broaden them. Instead, they provide short descriptions of several organizations, quite randomly chosen, and without any particular consideration of their character, scope, or influence. As a result, the once influential Party X (which ceased its activities and was dissolved in 1994–5) has been put together with a virtually unknown organization, the Community of Grey Wolves. The former, even if it employed antisemitism, was not an antisemitic party *per se*, that is, one with a programme of activity limited to advocating antisemitism. The latter is probably some local mutation of a neo-Nazi organization, possibly trying to work among the German minority in Poland, judging by its name, which recalls the Hitlerite conspiracy in the western part of Poland immediately after the war. On active and influential *strictly* antisemitic parties, there is only one sentence, and that is devoted to the Senioral National party.

The part devoted to 'Holocaust denial' is redolent with stereotypes popular in Israel: 'In Poland, where only several tens of thousands of Jews out of 3.3 million survived, and where six extermination camps were located, the Holocaust *per se* cannot be denied. However, antisemitic voices have been raised denying *co-operation with the Germans*, or alternatively, justifying co-operation, with all the differences implied between co-operation in German allied states, such as Slovakia, Hungary, or Romania, as opposed to Poland' (p. 118). In addition to the factual errors in these two sentences, the authors have here 'demonstrated' in a quite superficial manner, that *all* Poles, without exception, are antisemites, since they deny (justly) the claim that during the Second World War they collaborated with the German occupation authorities. (A similar claim appeared in the text of an educational programme on the Internet, 'Virtual Jerusalem' in which its author, Gary M. Grobman, wrote, 'In other countries such as Poland . . . the deportations of Jews to the death camps were facilitated by the cooperation of the government.' The authors of the survey then describe the controversy in *Gazeta Wyborcza*, the most widely read Polish daily, regarding the incident in which a group of Jews in hiding were murdered by a detachment of the Narodowe Siły Zbrojne (National Armed Forces) incorporated into the Armia Krajowa (Home Army) during the Warsaw insurrection of 1944. They move on to polemics about Auschwitz and the ways of commemorating the victims of that camp. According to the authors, these discussions are supposed to be related to 'Holocaust denial', although this relation remains unclear even to themselves. It is hard not to conclude that it was a waste of money to prepare such an inadequate and unprofessional report, covering, moreover, the same material as the much more carefully prepared reports by the

Institute of Jewish Affairs. It would be much better to spend these funds on organizing a sociological survey in one or several countries.

From a scholarly perspective, the most valuable publications are those of the Vidal Sassoon International Centre for the Study of Antisemitism (SICSA) at the Hebrew University in Jerusalem. The series of booklets by single authors published by the centre not only include in-depth analyses of the phenomenon of antisemitism in various countries, but also cover theoretical problems and attempt syntheses. Particularly interesting are two brochures by Simon Epstein: *Cyclical Patterns in Antisemitism: The Dynamics of Anti-Jewish Violence in Western Countries since the 1950s* and *Extreme Right Electoral Upsurges in Western Europe: 1984–1995 Wave as Compared with the Previous Ones*. In both articles the author points to the periodic emergence of right-wing political extremisms and attempts an explanation of their origins and character by analysing various factors determining their growth. These articles are pioneering in many respects. The author is the first scholar who proposes a quantitative synthesis of the phenomenon of antisemitism after the Second World War by indicating its permanent presence in European culture and delineating the factors determining its subsequent eruptions. These interestingly presented analyses just ask to be deepened! Also of interest is a comparison between the fluctuations of left-wing and right-wing extremisms: are these extreme manifestations of political activity complementary, or do they appear alternately? What conditions determine them?

Exceedingly interesting, and in many respects pioneering, is the work by Gilad Margalit, *Antigypsism in the Political Culture of the Federal Republic of Germany: A Parallel with Antisemitism?* As one of the few scholarly works, it undertakes the subject of similarities between anti-Jewish and anti-Gypsy attitudes, the analogies in the traditional images of these groups, and their role in the ideologies of contemporary right-wing extremisms. This subject, often disregarded or minimized by the scholars of antisemitism, provides the opportunity for a new look at the phenomenon of antisemitism and its historical origins. It is even more timely since it is the Gypsies who replaced the Jews at the top of the 'scale of hostility', according to sociological surveys conducted in many countries in the 1980s and 1990s. The Roms are one of a few ethnic groups that in Europe are *physically* threatened in the same way that Jews were in 1930s. They are subject to pogroms and violence occurring more often than is reported in the press. They are the only group in the contemporary world to which, in public view and with the approval of societies and governments, the abuse of expulsion is being applied. They are the only group for whom citizenship in a given state is not accompanied by rights to protection from those states.

In Poland, where the problem of antisemitism is not sufficiently widespread to threaten the young democracy, a few serious works on this subject have appeared in print. However, there is not one popular publication on this social pathology; on the contrary, there are schoolbooks, still in use, that promote antisemitic ways of thinking and repeat anti-Jewish stereotypes. Public discussions of the issue has also waned somewhat in recent years, just as antisemitic groups, like the supporters of Radio Maryja, have strengthened. It seems as if fear of the danger of antisemitism has paralysed the world of the humanities. In this respect, the situation is similar across most post-communist countries. Thus, evidence of a shrinking number of adherents to antisemitic ideology is surprising, and, in addition, it is not clear if this trend is permanent.

Among the publications devoted to studying the nature of xenophobic attitudes, a work by Ewa Nowicka and Jan Nawrocki, *Inny–obcy–wróg* ('Other–Stranger–Enemy'), which discusses research conducted on adolescents and students, should be mentioned. In this excellent work the problem of antisemitic attitudes is not the main thread; however, its presence in such a broad psychosocial context yields plenty of material for further investigation. Similar in character is the collection of essays *Tolerancja i uprzedzenia młodzieży* ('Tolerance and Prejudices amongst Young People'); in it a very interesting article by Barbara Wilska-Duszyńska deserves attention: ' "My" i "Oni": młodzież wobec etnicznie obcych' (' "Us" and "Them": Attitudes amongst Young People towards the Ethnically Alien'). The author measures the ethnic distance, declarations of sentiment or aversion, and the stereotypes professed towards different nationalities, including the Jews. The problem of antisemitism, however, was outside her main interest. *Raport o młodzieży—Report on Polish Youth*, published by Warsaw University's Centre for Research on Youth, includes a chapter on the subculture of skinheads in Poland; in this work, however, the problem of antisemitism also only appears marginally. Very interesting and pioneering research on anti-Jewish attitudes has been conducted by Mirosław Kofta and Grzegorz Sędek; its results are published in their study *Struktura poznawcza stereotypu etnicznego: bliskość wyborów parlamentarnych a przejawy antysemityzmu* ('The Cognitive Structure of Ethnic Stereotype: The Closeness of the Parliamentary Elections and the Manifestations of Antisemitism'). In their survey, conducted amongst high-school students, they discover a relation between pre-election political agitation in Poland and an increase in antisemitic attitudes. They introduce a distinction between the exemplary stereotype (*stereotyp egzemplaryczny*), which relies on images of the Jew as an individual, and the positively anti-Jewish stereotype of the group soul (*stereotyp duszy grupowej*), much more prone to fluctuations, which contains shreds of antisemitic ideology and conspiracy theory. The latter stereotype is especially susceptible to political manipulations. The findings of the authors may bring new input into theoretical reflection about the nature of antisemitism.

A collaborative study edited by Ireneusz Krzemiński, *Czy Polacy są antysemitami?* ('Are the Poles Antisemites?'), published in 1996, is based on a sociological survey conducted by the Jewish Historical Institute in 1991–3. It was the largest survey to date of this question ever conducted in Poland. Although I participated in it, I am not entirely satisfied with the analysis of the results presented in the book, nor with my own input, which is the essay 'Auto-Stereotype and National Stereotype'. The work lacks theoretical premises and consequently exhibits the flaw common to many other studies in which authors research different manifestations of a phenomenon giving them the same name: as a result it is difficult to compare the results of these experiments. But there is more in it that bothers me than imprecise terminology. The wealth of material gathered in the survey has not been adequately used or analysed in depth. Also, it lacks organizational principles, and the title does not reflect the book's content—nor does the book answer its basic question. Moreover, to answer a question put in this way there is no need to conduct elaborate sociological surveys.

There are certainly many more publications about the problem of antisemitism which I have omitted in this cursory and selective review. In particular, I did not have access to American sociological work. Nevertheless, I believe that I have presented the main areas of scholarly interest in antisemitism and xenophobia. There is not enough theoretical work, nor is there adequate discussion of the very definition of this phenomenon and its origins, nor are there enough surveys using the methods of sociology and cultural anthropology. One thing is certain: the phenomenon of antisemitism with its uniqueness, and at the same time its relation to other forms of xenophobia and racism, still remains for us a mysterious and continually frightening problem.

BOOK REVIEWS

JOSEPH PERL
Revealer of Secrets: The First Hebrew Novel

EDITED AND TRANSLATED BY

DOV TAYLOR

Modern Hebrew Classics

(Boulder, Colo.: Westview Press, 1997); pp. lxxvi + 370

The end of the eighteenth and much of the nineteenth centuries have been characterized as the era of the growth and eventual dominance of hasidism in eastern Europe. During this period two small but determined groups of opponents of hasidism fought against the new movement. The first were the traditionalist rabbis, the mitnagedim, who feared hasidism's departure from time-honoured rabbinic values and tried unsuccessfully to stop the movement by excommunicating its leaders. After the active traditionalist hostility to hasidism died out at the beginning of the nineteenth century, hasidism was confronted by a new group of opponents, the modernizing maskilim, who saw the hasidic movement as a severe hindrance to the acculturation and emancipation of the Jewish masses within the Russian and Austro-Hungarian empires.

Joseph Perl (1773–1839) was a leading figure of the Galician Haskalah and one of the foremost activists who struggled against the hasidic movement. The Austrian authorities refused to permit the publication of Perl's first major work about hasidism, his 1816 *Über das Wesen der Sekte Chassidim. Aus ihren eigene Schriften gezogen* ('On the Nature of the Hasidic Sect, Drawn from their own Writings'), either out of reluctance to upset the hasidim themselves, or out of a fear of inciting the gentiles against the Jewish population in general (pp. xxviii–xxix). In 1819, however, Perl did succeed in publishing a second work on hasidism, *Megaleh temirin* ('Revealer of Secrets') and he also wrote a sequel to *Megaleh temirin*, called *Boḥen tsadik* ('The Test of the Righteous'), which appeared in 1838.

The most important of these three works was *Megaleh temirin*, an epistolary novel that parodied the hasidic books and idiom of the early nineteenth century. As the reader gradually becomes aware, the letters of the hasidic protagonists reveal at least two interrelated plots: (1) the effort to locate and destroy the *bukh* (none other than Perl's book, *Über das Wesen der Sekte Chassidim*, as if it had in fact been published), and (2) the quixotic attempts of the followers of two rival hasidic groups (loosely modelled on the courts of Barukh ben Jehiel of Medzibizh and Shneur Zalman of Lyady) to champion one *rebbe* over the other. Accompanying these letters is a commentary by another 'hasid', Obadiah ben Petahiah, who adduces citations from the classic hagiography of the Ba'al Shem Tov, *Shivḥei habesht*, and especially from Nahman of Bratslav's *Midot moharan*, both of which demonstrate how the foolish activities of the hasidim have a basis in hasidic literary classics.

The very richness of *Megaleh temirin* has probably discouraged previous scholars from translating it into English, but on this score Dov Taylor has done an admirable job at making this volume, under the title *Revealer of Secrets*, accessible to the modern reader of English. In order to convey a sense of the faulty written Hebrew of the hasidic protagonists, Taylor has translated their letters into the somewhat ungrammatical English of Jews whose mother tongue is Yiddish or Polish (pp. iv–lvi). Although a literary language like Hebrew and a spoken one like late twentieth-century non-native English are not entirely parallel, Taylor's translation technique works surprisingly well. The only minor exceptions appear when he translates using idioms that are clearly anachronistic or are not culturally appropriate. For example, 'shelo yavo hadavar legedolot' (lit. 'so that the matter will not come to extremes') is transformed into 'shouldn't become a federal case'; (p. 79). Or, 'lema'an hashem' (lit. 'for the sake of the Name [of God]') becomes, 'for cryin' out loud' (p. 93).

In addition to the translation, Taylor has included an introduction, extensive notes on the text, an afterword, and three excursuses. The introduction and notes do a good job of analysing Perl's parody and providing its literary context. On the other hand, Taylor's historical observations, though adequate for a lay audience, are at times weak for a scholarly one. To take one example, his discussion of the origins of *Shivḥei habesht*, a book which plays a major role in *Megaleh temirin*, would have been much stronger had it made use of Moshe Rosman's fascinating chapter on that hagiographic work which appeared in the latter's recent work on the historical Ba'al Shem Tov. While Taylor's third excursus, the prologue to Perl's Yiddish translation, will appeal to those interested in Perl's attitude towards Yiddish, the first and especially the second excursus, which unscrambles many of the names for some of the leading characters and towns, will be of use to all readers.

Taylor concludes *Revealer of Secrets* with an afterword entitled 'Was Perl Fair?' After raising this question, Taylor frustratingly refuses to answer it. Instead, he evades it by arguing that it is unfair to single out Perl's critique from the work of other writers, be they maskilic, scholarly, or even hasidic, since 'Each had his own predilections, preconceptions, prejudices.' This is of course true, but it in no way exempts authors from being critically examined; and Perl should be no exception. The many strengths of Dov Taylor's edition of Joseph Perl's *Megaleh temirin* easily outweigh its shortcomings. *Revealer of Secrets* is a welcome and important contribution to the growing body of English translations of east European Jewish literature.

PAUL RADENSKY
Jewish Theological Seminary

HANNA KOZIŃSKA-WITT
Die Krakauer Jüdische Reformgemeinde, 1864–1874
(Berlin: Peter Lang, 1999); pp. 312

In *The Kraków Reformed Jewish Community, 1864–1874* Hanna Kozińska-Witt has tackled an extremely important episode in the history of the Galician Jews. Attempts to establish an independent Reformed commune (*gmina*) in Kraków coincided with the peak of the development in Galicia of the Haskalah ideology which had emerged from Germany and of great religious, cultural, and social ferment, mobilizing the Jewish élites in their ultimately victorious battle for full civic and political rights. In the Austrian monarchy this campaign continued uninterrupted from the revolutionary year of 1848; however, final success was achieved only with the granting of the new state constitution of December 1867, forced on Franz Joseph by the difficult situation in which the state found itself following defeat in the war against Prussia.

Pressures to improve the legal status of the Jewish population had, in fact, come mainly from Vienna where, by the middle of the century, the powerful Jewish financiers, the *Ringbaronen*, already occupied influential positions in the financial and economic affairs of the state. Provincial centres, including those of Galicia, were not indifferent towards these efforts. In all the larger towns of the monarchy at this time—Pest, Prague, L'viv and Kraków—local Jewish communities manifested significant internal differences. The decisive factor in this development was the improvement of the economic situation; economic development naturally demanded improvements in competence and specialization; growing prosperity allowed the most able to invest in the future of their sons, to prepare them for the universities and academies which were beginning to open their doors to wealthy Jews. With each year increasing numbers of *ḥeder* and yeshiva students discarded traditional dress and sought contacts with their non-Jewish surroundings. The epoch of assimilation had begun, of the widespread and often indiscriminate imitation of the surrounding world by wealthier and more culturally open Jewish circles. Success was no longer guaranteed by money alone; an appropriate education was also necessary.

Progressive circles had to reassess their attitude to their own tradition which, in the case of Jews, was very resistant to all change. One serious problem was the urgent reform of religious ritual, which, in practice, displayed a certain external similarity to the changes which were introduced in Christian models: the introduction of choirs, sometimes with an organ, the appointment of a preacher whose sermons would remind his congregation of the ethical values of Judaism. The synagogue revolution was, however, unacceptable to the Orthodox majority of the local community. The dissolution of the communal organization appeared inevitable. For a number of reasons, this suited neither the political authorities nor some more far-sighted Jewish intellectuals. The authorities feared that, divested of their élites and left to their own devices, the Jewish masses, who were usually poor and rarely familiar with the local language, would prove to be a threat to social order. Furthermore, the Reformed minority might, in time, blend into local society, and this was feared greatly by the majority of Christians, who were convinced of their 'moral' superiority, which had been maintained throughout the ages by the Church. Nor were all the progressives ready to break their family ties. There were more than emotions at work here—less disinterested motives took into account the fact that without support within their native milieu, the progressives would count for nothing. This fundamental, apparently insoluble conflict grew less acute with time, as both sides grew accustomed to each other, and sometimes, apart from extreme zealots, even helped each other in difficult times.

Hanna Kozińska-Witt relates the history of such a violent and bitter conflict, taking the example of Kraków. The example is well chosen, and in Polish historical literature has already been cited often in discussions of the evolution of central European Jewish communities. The history of the Jewish commune in Kraków, at that time comprising over 20,000 believers, allows an almost model analysis of the processes taking place in Polish Jewry. The author has successfully described most of these with great clarity. She begins her dissertation by presenting the most influential Jewish families in Kraków—the Gumplowicz family at their head—who had contributed much to the process of reform. She then describes the work they undertook, taking into account their motives and the influences of German models. She completes her description with an account of the local Christian milieu. In Kraków, unlike Budapest, there was no formal break from the mother commune by the progressive commune—the leaders of the community were able to exercise restraint and come to a reasonable compromise with the dominant Orthodox Jewry, guaranteeing denominational independence and control over the activities of the traditionalists. They continued to lead the local commune, and thanks to the votes of their brothers in faith, gained mandates to civic and national political bodies. At the same time they prayed and married in their own Tempel synagogue with their own preacher.

The model outlined here by the author appears to correspond faithfully to the truth. However, a careful reading of the work reveals many statements with which one cannot wholly concur. From what does this arise? In my opinion, it arises above all from a sense that the author has placed too great a faith in the sources she has consulted. These are almost entirely journalistic, the work, in the main, of progressive German and Austrian Jews, with the co-operation, of course, of local correspondents, but we do not know the degree to which the reports of these correspondents were rewritten. The commune records are referred to very selectively, as are memoirs of the period. One should not, therefore, be surprised at the one-sidedness of the accounts, in spite of facts favouring the Orthodox. Against this background, the figure of their leader, Rabbi Szymon Schreiber, appears rather vague and one-dimensional, though we know from other sources that this was no commonplace individual but a clever politician, respected in some Polish political circles. This is evidenced by his somewhat later political career as leader of the influential group Mahazikei Hadat and as a deputy to the Viennese parliament. A characterization of him in complete contrast to that of the Kraków correspondents of *Die Neuzeit* was that produced at the beginning of the 1880s by a journalist from the L'viv *Gazeta Narodowa*. The Orthodox were, then, a 'silent' majority, admittedly irritating progressive circles with their resistance to change. Nevertheless, historical honesty does not permit their fears and anxieties to be trivialized.

Another misgiving concerns the method of presenting the progressive circles themselves and, in particular, the evaluation of arguments concerning the direction of assimilation—pro-Polish or pro-German. The most radical agents in the drive for reform, though not necessarily the most influential, were those supporting German culture as a model for the assimilating Jews. As a politician, however, Artur Eibenshütz did not equal Szymon Samelson, Jonatan Warschauer, or Józef Oettinger—the advocates of accelerated Polonization. This trio began their political careers in the revolutionary 1840s, and for better or worse linked themselves with the Polish national cause. Thanks to the friendships they struck up then, in the 1850s and 1870s they were able to work successfully in the political arena. It was they who successfully placed a Polish preacher disliked by *Die Neuzeit* and its readers, Szymon Dankowicz, in the Progressive Synagogue. They also Polonized the Kazimierz school and the commune council itself. The author barely mentions these worthy persons. Therefore, it is perhaps worth remembering that even in those stormy years one did not live in Kraków and Kazimierz by politics alone. A closer reading of the local press and any kind of communal or civic records and also antisemitic brochures shows that Jewish society had to answer daily a variety of provocations from the Christian majority reproaching the Jews with their low level of culture and civilization, intrusiveness and bad manners in business interests, numerous bankruptcies, and no less frequent common frauds. In 1873, during the cholera epidemic, the whole town was gripped by an obsessive fear of 'dirty' Kazimierz and its inhabitants. The situation was pacified by the moderate leaders of the community, and the worthy doctors Warschauer and Oettinger gained great respect for their dedication in fighting the epidemic. The former later made over his entire fortune to the neglected Jewish lending library, which was very positively acknowledged by Polish Kraków.

Another problem is that the author displays a poor knowledge of the real influence exercised in the town by particular leaders of the Jewish community. In my opinion, this was not due to more or less successful journalism (Ludwig Gumplowicz and Artur Eibenschütz) but to the position one held in the economic–financial milieu of Kraków. It is worth pointing out that all presidents of the Jewish commune or deputies elected in Kraków to the L'viv Sejm and Viennese parliament—Szymon Samelson, Albert Mendelsburg, Leon Horowitz, Samuel Tilles, Hirsz Landau, Arnold Rappoport, Adolf Gross, and Józef Sare—were heads of the largest solicitors' practices and/or influential financiers. The institution in which these careers were decided was the Chamber of Trade and Industry. It was directed for many years by Mendelsburg and later Tadeusz Epstein and Maurycy Dattner. It is interesting that the deputy elected to the Viennese parliament, Arnold Rappoport, was accused by the omnipotent *Czas* of only one thing, namely of writing for *Die Neue Freie Presse* in his youth.

Certain simplifications in the political mosaic of Galicia in which the leaders of Jewish communities moved are clearly evident in the second part of the study devoted to the L'viv commune. Omissions of source material are to blame also on this occasion, for without archives and a careful perusal of the Polish press published in L'viv, particularly *Gazeta Narodowa*, the picture of the disputes and encounters of the time must appear tendentious. The reader insufficiently familiar with Polish history will not grasp why the L'viv Polish democrats were so hostile towards their Jewish neighbours that they did not wish to permit them access to civic property and an appropriate level of participation in local institutions. But it was something concrete—the daily economic rivalry—that stood behind this conflict. Similarly unclear is the nature of the problem between Poles and Jews in the turbulent year of 1873 and why, when deputies to the Viennese parliament were being elected for the first time in Galicia, the Jews should make an electoral alliance with the Ukrainians and did not later join the Koło Polskie (Polish Parliamentary Club). What were the real concerns of the leaders of Shomer Yisrael? Of course, they resented the Polish landowners after their reluctance to grant Jews full public rights in the L'viv of 1868. However, the arguments of the landowners, who feared that the Jews would buy out their ancestral properties following a wave of bankruptcies, should have been set out. Six years later these fears gave rise to the anti-*kehilla* campaign of Teofil Merunowicz which ended in a great debate in the provincial Sejm.

There are, then, many omissions in the work; happily, they do not outweigh its more valuable aspects—the honest presentation of the struggles throughout several years of Galician progressive Jews with the Orthodox majority, bound by the fetters of medieval tradition, superstition, and hostility towards the outside world.

ANDRZEJ ŻBIKOWSKI
Jewish Historical Institute

EMANUEL MELZER
No Way Out: The Politics of Polish Jewry, 1935–1939
Monographs of the Hebrew Union College, no. 19
(Cincinnati: Hebrew Union College Press, 1997); pp. xii + 236

The first edition of this book, written as a doctoral dissertation, was published in 1982 in Hebrew. The present edition was condensed but also updated, now that political changes have made it possible to study documents from Polish archives (notably Archiwum Akt Nowych in Warsaw). The author presents the basic political and economic problems of Jewish society in Poland; the attitudes of the government, political parties, and Polish society towards Jews; and the responses of the Jewish leaders, political parties, and ordinary people. Several of these topics have been treated in books and articles published by both Polish and Jewish historians and covering specific areas of Polish and Jewish history. This book's merit is that it analyses a complex of issues and takes into consideration different elements of the changes going on not only in Poland, but in the whole of Europe as well. Such analysis can help readers to understand the situation of Jews in Poland and indicate the main directions for future studies.

In his treatment of economic problems suffered by Jews between 1935 and 1939 (chapter 3) Melzer discusses the economic policy of the government and the attitudes of local authorities and of several Polish professional associations. Problematically, however, the sources on government policy are the polemics in parliament and the press—Jewish and Polish. To escape the exaggerations of both the government and the opposition, one must turn to the files of the government offices, but they are often lacking owing to the war losses in the Polish archives. Analysis of government policy has to be based, therefore, on second-rate sources.

My own knowledge of the files that are preserved in Polish archives suggests that these do not allow for definite conclusions about the government's economic policy towards Jews after 1935. My sense has been that there was a general change in favour of radical nationalism, and I am not sure whether the Jews were particularly adversely affected. Though it is true that the political phraseology indicates special bias against the Jews, the documents reveal similar trends of bias against all the national minorities in Poland and reveal, at the same time, differences between individual politicians and departments in government. There remains, however, the large question of the effectiveness of the apparently important actions and decrees. Fragmentary evidence suggests, for example, that endeavours to settle the Polish shopkeepers and artisans from the west in the eastern provinces of Poland were mostly a failure. Much more significant, in my view, was the modernization of the Polish economy. This trend influenced negatively the sectors of the economy most important for the Jews. And this was independent of any government intentions, good or bad.

Even more difficult to obtain has been evidence of the attitudes of the local administration. Melzer mentions their growing anti-Jewish sentiments and probably, in many cases, is right. As yet there has been no thorough analysis of these questions and it would be impossible to present a full picture. Yet one of the merits of the book is that the author indicates not only general trends and problems but individual cases and exceptions as well.

In his analysis of political developments, Melzer is critical not only of government policy but of the attitudes and activity of the Jewish political parties as well. He stresses inability to co-operate against antisemitism, conflicts concerning secondary issues, and a lack of well-defined aims and strategies. Even individual Zionist factions could not unite. The stereotype of Jewish unity, often promulgated in antisemitic political pamphlets, appears to be a legend. This is, generally speaking, in accordance with the opinion of Ezra Mendelsohn. At the same time the author indicates a significant trend towards co-operation among the followers of the different Jewish ideological camps at the local level. The growing difficulties of everyday life were a strong incentive to look for common practical solutions.

Another interesting question is the influence of the anti-Jewish programmes on Polish society and the other national minorities (Ukrainians and Germans). Adolf Hitler's victory in Germany influenced, no doubt, the situation in Poland. The author is right in stressing this fact (mentioning that the Polish National Democrats, traditional enemies of Germans, experienced some ambivalence in this respect). Poland was, however, not an exception, and the influence of radical nationalism was growing in the whole of Europe. There was at the same time another trend, a slow consolidation of the Polish democratic camp, and many people understood that antisemitism was helping to strengthen authoritarian rule.

A similar conviction may have been growing among the governing group of politicians and, in turn, may have been a source of anti-Jewish agendas. Anti-Judaism played a role in the internal feuds among the politicians from the same camp. The Jewish politician Fiszel Rottenstreich, for example, supposed that this was the reason for introducing anti-Jewish legislation in parliament (p. 56).

Despite some minor inaccuracies, this book ought to be widely appreciated for its original interpretation of sources and its detailed information that increases understanding of the historical events; for example, Melzer's data on the Polish–German controversies concerning the fate of the Polish Jews in Germany, notably

Gestapo demands for their expulsion as early as 21 April 1938 (p. 122). The flow of time has little mercy for scholars of recent history. In this case, however, the scholarly merits of Melzer's book are unquestionable: it is a welcome addition to the Hebrew Union College series.

JERZY TOMASZEWSKI
University of Warsaw

EZRA MENDELSOHN (ED.)
Essential Papers on Jews and the Left
(New York: New York University Press, 1997); pp. viii + 552 (paperback)

Ezra Mendelsohn's book appeared in the series Essential Papers on Jewish Studies and is an excellent continuation of the previous volume, *Essential Papers on Zionism*. Both books present a complicated picture of the two most significant currents in contemporary Jewish political and ideological life. I would be glad to see a third volume on the traditional, conservative movements (with Agudat Yisrael as the most important) and perhaps another containing the other currents which cannot be represented in the previous books.

One can observe, however, that there was—and still is—no distinct borderline between these main Jewish political camps. It is true that the majority of socialists and conservatives fought against Zionism, but at the same time there were socialist and conservative factions among the Zionists. A symbol of these intersections is the article 'Social and Intellectual Origins of the Hashomer Hatzair Youth Movement, 1913–1920', by Elkana Margalit, included in both volumes.

Essential Papers on Jews and the Left is composed of three parts. The first, 'The Jewish Left', contains nine chapters, ranging from an essay on the life and opinions of Moses Hess, by Isaiah Berlin, to one on attitudes of the Palestinian labour movement facing the Russian revolution, by Anita Shapira. Other authors of the studies in this part are: Jonathan Frankel, Moshe Mishkinsky, Henry Tobias, Matityahu Mintz, Elkana Margalit, Antony Polonsky, Dan Horowitz and Moshe Lissak. The second part, 'Jews in the Left', contains three chapters, two on the participation of Jews in the Russian revolutionary movement, by Israel Getzler and Leonard Shapiro, and one on US left-wing movements, by Arthur Liebman. The third and last part, 'The Left and the Jews', presents five chapters: two concerning the attitude of Karl Marx towards the Jews, by Edmund Silberner and Shlomo Avineri, one on Soviet policy against Zionism, by Jonathan Frankel—and others by Moshe Mishkinsky, on socialist attitudes to the 1881–2 pogroms, and Jack Jacobs on Karl Kautsky.

The editor opens the volume with a short but well-written introduction, important for understanding the role of the left-wing movements in the Jewish tradition. From Mendelsohn's perspective it is inevitable that

> the horrendous crimes committed in socialism's name have cast considerable doubt on the claims traditionally made by socialists that they and they alone understand the workings of history and that in the struggle against their adversaries they invariably occupy the high moral ground. Nevertheless, it would be premature to raise a memorial to movements of social protest and to bury socialism in the graveyard reserved for once important but now bankrupt and discredited ideologies.

The volume, which also includes a short (too short!) bibliography in English and an index, is very useful for every student of Jewish contemporary political history. A volume that contains 'essential papers' invites criticism of its selections from the wide range of available literature, but I have only one quarrel of importance. The chapters included in this volume—with rare exceptions—are devoted to the era ending with the beginning of the Second World War. Mendelsohn omits the authors from east central Europe and the hotly discussed topic of Jewish participation in the communist parties and administration, including their responsibility for 'the horrendous crimes committed in socialism's name'. To have included a paper by Krystyna Kersten, for instance, would have enriched this volume significantly.

JERZY TOMASZEWSKI
University of Warsaw

DAVID WEINFELD (ED.)
Hebrew Poetry in Poland between the Two World Wars
(Jerusalem: Mossad Bialik, 1997); pp. 496

The Hebrew Nobel Laureate S. Y. Agnon describes in his semi-autobiographical novel *A Guest for the Night* (1939) a Hebrew writer's return in about 1930 to the Galician town of his birth. What was once a thriving centre of Jewish culture is now virtually a ghost town, its population depleted and traumatized by war and privation. The writer tries to renew his ties with the past but fails, and in the end returns to Jerusalem, his only true home.

Agnon's novel reflects in somewhat exaggerated form the fateful shift in the inter-war period of the Hebrew cultural centre from eastern Europe to Palestine. By 1933 most of the important Hebrew writers had moved to Palestine. (Agnon had gone in 1924.) While Polish and Yiddish culture thrived in Poland, Hebrew declined. Poland, once a major centre of Hebrew literature, and birthplace of some of the greatest modern Hebrew writers, including Agnon and Uri Tsevi Greenberg, was left with a shrinking group of Hebrew writers and readers. Though Polish Jewry reached 3 million between the wars and there were hundreds of Jewish schools where Hebrew was taught, its Hebrew culture could not compete with Yiddish and Polish and with the dynamism of the Palestinian *yishuv*, whose Jewish population was ten times smaller than Poland's. After the closure of *Hatekufah* in Warsaw in 1924 there were no major Hebrew journals in Poland, and the number of Polish Jewish subscribers to Hebrew journals—even to the best of them, such as *Hashiloaḥ*—was pitiful. Eliezer Steinman, who left for Palestine in 1924, wrote in the previous year of the anguish and isolation of being a Hebrew writer in Poland.

Yet Hebrew poetry survived in Poland between the wars. David Weinfeld's anthology includes two dozen Hebrew poets and is valuable if only from a historical viewpoint as most of these poets are forgotten and their works are mostly unavailable. These poets are: Yitshak Katznelson, Meir Tshudner, Władysław Chrapusta, Ya'akov Netaneli-Rotman, Matityahu Moshe Shoham, Natan Neta Shtokhammer, Aaron Zeitlin, Moshe Basok, Shmuel Nadler, Avraham Iser Yoskovitz, Avraham Dov Verbner, Malkiel Lusternik, Gabriel Joseph Talpir, Shmuel David Bunin, Berl Pomerantz, Yitzhak Arieh Berger, Tuviah Levin, Shlomo Shtein, Moshe Wiener, Ya'akov Chopai, Moshe Teitelman, Noah Palnetovsky, Dov Chomsky, and Azriel Hachaimi.

Weinfeld includes biographical details on each writer and a ninety-two-page introduction to the social and historical background, with sections on the most important of the poets, Yitzhak Katznelson (better known as a Yiddish poet), Matityahu Shoham, and especially Berl Pomerantz. However, most of the poems, Weinfeld concedes, are of limited artistic interest.

This poetry is inadvertently a tombstone for Polish Hebrew literature and, indeed, for Polish Jewry (though Chrapusta was exceptional in being Christian). About half the poets—Katznelson, Tshudner, Shtokhammer, Pomerantz, Berger, Nadler, Yoskovitz, Verbner, Lusternik, Levin, and Wiener—died in the Holocaust. Their poetry is, to borrow an image from Bialik, a guttering flame of culture about to die. In comparison with the Hebrew centre in Palestine, it suggests that writers can rarely achieve originality and individuality unless they are part of a strong, living culture. Yet there is also something heroic in their struggle against the current in what was clearly, in retrospect, a lost cause.

DAVID ABERBACH
McGill University

WŁODZIMIERZ MICH

Obcy w polskim domu: nacjonalistyczne koncepcje rozwiązania problemu mniejszości narodowych 1918–1939

(Lublin: Wydawnictwo Uniwersytetu Marii Curie-Skłodowskiej, 1994); pp. 144

The question of how to ensure the rights of ethnic minorities constituted one of the most controversial and troublesome aspects of the Paris peace settlement at the end of the First World War. As early as spring 1919 ongoing peace negotiations revealed a reluctance and even open opposition on the part of the new nation-states of east central Europe towards the implementation of provisions for ethnic minorities. Under pressure from the Allied powers, the new nation-states eventually signed their respective minority treaties, but opposition towards ethnic minorities rights not only remained, but actually increased in many of these states during the course of the next twenty years.

Poland, the largest resurrected nation-state of east central Europe, is a good example of how the issue of ethnic minorities, especially the Jewish community, became one of the most contentious issues in political culture throughout the entire inter-war period. Not only was this question continually addressed in various political programmes and in the press on both national and local levels, but it also served as a potent catalyst for the social and political mobilization of the masses.

It is generally recognized that the primary cause of this development was the spread of integral exclusivist nationalism among the Polish political élites. Nationalism of this kind posits the state as the representative of a singular, integral people and, as a rule, is characterized by a low tolerance of internal diversity. Integral nationalists tend to define ethnic minorities as aliens—who could hope to obtain at best the status of 'guest' in a territory only truly belonging to the host nation—and, furthermore, perceive ethnic minorities as an element that could divide or weaken the nation-state, that is to say, its 'core' people, and lead to the destruction of national culture. Therefore, in their political programmes integral nationalists postulate strategies of expulsion or segregation of ethnic minorities or their complete cultural assimilation. Needless to say, integral nationalists interpret rights of ethnic minorities as a potential or existing threat against the 'core' nation and thus aim at the curtailment or even abolition of these rights at any price.

Because of the wide application of the traditional 'continental' (as opposed to the Anglo-Saxon) definition of nationalism, historians of inter-war Poland tend to ascribe integral nationalism to only one major political movement, the Endecja (National Democrats) and their offshoot radical organizations, and therefore neglect manifestations of such nationalism in other political parties. Indeed, this narrow ascription of integral nationalism constitutes the major trend in studies on Polish politics and nationalism. The application of such a methodology leads to a situation where, on the one hand, there is a substantial body of works on the origin and development of the Endecja, the Falanga, and the Obóz Narodowo-Radylcalny (National Radical Camp: ONR), while on the other hand, there is a glaring lack of works dealing with the broader impact of integral exclusivist nationalism on political culture and the society as a whole. And scholars are still left with crucial and challenging questions: to what extent was the ideology of integral exclusivist nationalism endorsed by different Polish political parties, movements, and social groupings? What major effect did the imprint of this nationalism have on the Polish ethnic community and on its perception of ethnic minorities?

Włodzimierz Mich's book should definitely be welcomed as an original attempt to provide some answers to the above questions. As is the case with works of a pioneering approach, it raises important issues rather than giving a comprehensive study of the subject. Its main aim is to present some general theses on the impact of the Endecja's thought on the broader political spectrum, with respect to the question of ethnic minorities. This is Mich's second published work. The first was an in-depth historical analysis of the question of ethnic minorities in Polish conservative thought of the inter-war period (*Problem mniejszości narodowych w myśli politycznej polskiego ruchu konserwatywnego* (Lublin, 1992)).

Throughout this short and well-written volume the author compares the positions of the Endecja and the ONR to those of the Chrześcijańska Demokracja (Christian Democrats), the Polskie Stronnictwo Ludowe—Piast (Polish Peasant Party 'Piast'), and sections of the monarchist and conservative movements. Though less frequently, he also refers to the stance within the ruling political camp of the Sanacja after the death of Marshal Józef Piłsudski and to that of the Stronnictwo Pracy (Party of Labour). Furthermore, in this challenging examination Mich discusses each of the ethnic minorities separately, dividing them into three main groups: the Jews, the Ukrainians and Belarusians (the Slavic minorities), and the Germans.

The comparative analytical approach employed by Mich enables him to make an important summary of integral nationalist tendencies in inter-war Poland. He has two main theses: (1) Polish nationalist thought, as defined by the Endecja camp, shaped to a greater extent than previously allowed the ideologies and programmes of different political groupings, including those that did not identify themselves as primarily national or nationalistic. And, furthermore, the only significant difference among the various political camps was that of tactics rather than ideology, as far as the treatment of ethnic minorities was concerned. (2) The predominant policies towards ethnic minorities were threefold: assimilation into the Polish nation, advocated in the case of Slavic minorities; marginalization, in the case of the German ethnic group; emigration, as was chiefly favoured in the case of the Polish Jewish community.

Interestingly, Roger Brubaker came to similar conclusions in his article 'Nationalizing States in the Old "New Europe"—and the New' (*Ethnic and Racial Studies*, 2 (1996)). In a sense these two works could be interpreted as complementary. Brubaker's sociological analysis of integral nationalism is much more lucid and theoretical, whereas Mich's strength lies in his presentation of historical detail. He makes substantial reference to primary sources, including state documents, the press, political programmes, and memoirs—and his assertions are supported by a far greater number of secondary sources.

A Stranger in the Polish Home is divided into three sections: the first discusses the general problematics of nationalism and also antisemitism; the second examines political programmes on the subject of solving the problem of the Jewish minority; the third investigates political programmes on the matter of solving the problem of the Slavic and German minorities. Least explored in the book is the German community, with only seven pages dedicated to it by the author. Instead, the Jewish ethnic minority is Mich's main concern, taking up half of the first and the entire second section.

The first section is very dense and contains some contradictory statements and approaches. Nationalism clearly poses a theoretical problem for Mich as he struggles to combine the Gellnerian definition of it with the traditional 'continental' interpretation to which he himself adheres. Yet his discussion of antisemitism, although not free of flaws such as his equating antisemitism with nationalism, raises many salient aspects that have been neglected in previous writing on the subject. In this section Mich shows a good understanding of the ethno-nationalist political, economic, and cultural argumentation that served as a justification for anti-Jewish postulates and actions. He briefly describes a variety of definitions of antisemitism prominent in the Endecja's and the Church's writings, as well as in the Polish historiography of that period. Furthermore, he presents his own definition of antisemitism as an intellectual concept claiming the incompatibility of Polish and Jewish interest and therefore advocating inevitable conflict between the two ethnic groups. According to him, such an idea was present to some degree in the programmes of all political parties in inter-war Poland. The section concludes with an important assertion that the main characteristic of Polish antisemitic thought was its irrationality and its 'paranoid obsession' with the Jews. In fact, the Endecja created an image of every Polish Jew as the 'objective' enemy of the Polish nation-state and the nation, and that image had an impact on the broader political culture. Therefore, the issue of the Jews generated a different type of political debate than did that of other ethnic minorities.

The second section looks closely at the political postulates and programmes directed at the Jews in their perceived role as an alien, hostile minority. It covers a great range of issues such as the evolution of the concepts of emigration and isolation of the Jewish minority; the postulates of 'de-Judaization' of Polish politics, economy, and culture; the problem of the relations between the call for emigration and anti-Jewish violence; and the radicalization of the 'Jewish question' in the 1930s.

The most problematic concept put forward by Mich is the influence of German racist theories on the Polish political élites. Except for those on the Falanga and the ONR, his judgements are definitely questionable. In the case of the concept of isolation and emigration, however, Mich succeeds in demonstrating the impact of the Endecja's thought on the conservative, Christian-democratic, monarchist, and peasant parties, as well as on the post-1935 Sanacja.

His short paragraph on the 'de-Judaization' of Polish culture is worth mentioning as this crucial subject has been almost completely neglected by historians. Here Mich manages to indicate many issues that need further separate historical analysis, such as the support for the de-Judaization of culture by different political parties, sections of the Church, and the student movement, the emergence of exclusive ethnically Polish cultural associations, the attitudes towards Poles of Jewish origin and Polonized Jewish writers and artists, and the use of the Polish language by the Jews.

The last, much shorter, part of Mich's book discusses the ethno-nationalist programmes directed at the Slavic and German minorities. In the case of the Slavic groups, most convincingly examined is the connection between the growing popularity of the Endecja's programme of the Polonization of the Kresy and the postulates related to the Ukrainian and Belarusian minorities. According to the Endecja, the solution to the problem of the Slavic minorities lay in the rapid process of national and cultural assimilation. In fact, both ethnic groups were simply seen as 'raw material' for becoming a part of the Polish nation. After the death of Marshal Piłsudski this postulate was endorsed by the Sanacja's government. At the same time, the Endecja, Christian Democrats, the Poznań conservatives, and the PSL—Piast, among others, all supported the programme of colonization of the Kresy by ethnic Poles.

Mich also observes that the promise of improved economic life for the Ukrainians and Belarusians had the purely propagandist character of gaining support for the Polish nation-state. Another interesting point raised by the author is that the Polish ethno-nationalists manipulated relations between the Slavic groups and the Jewish minority that inhabited the Kresy in order to achieve two goals: integration of the Slavs into the Polish nation and the 'voluntary' emigration of the Jews. This issue needs further exploration.

In the case of the German minority, Mich has two major contentions: first, that the Polish ethno-nationalists treated the German ethnic minority through the perspective of relations between Poland and Germany (as the Weimar Republic and then as the Third Reich); and secondly, that, on the grounds of this perspective, the principle of marginalization of the German minority and the principle of tit-for-tat were generally advocated in the political programmes. The author also suggests that political thought on the subject of the German minority was much more static than that on the Jewish minority.

Overall, despite the difficulty with theoretical problems of nationalism, antisemitism, and assimilation, and despite uneven coverage of various issues, this volume constitutes an important contribution to the understanding of the ethnic nationalization of Polish political culture in the inter-war period. Mich's investigation reveals a substantial level of support for integral exclusivist nationalism among the Polish political élites. It also points out both differences and similarities in the perceptions and treatment of the main ethnic minorities by the ethno-nationalists. Above all, the volume sheds more light on one of the most difficult and emotive problems of Polish–Jewish relations, that of the Polish Jews being singled out as the Malign Other, for whom there was no place on Polish soil.

JOANNA MICHLIC-COREN
University of London

NATAN GROSS
Toledot hakolnoa hayehudi befolin, 1901–1950
(Jerusalem: Magnes Press, Hebrew University, Jerusalem, 1990); pp. 160

A recent documentary on the United States Public Broadcasting Network called *Hollywoodism* examined the influence of Jews on the fledgling film industry in America. The documentary did not try to prove that influence. It examined, rather, a well-established fact. Surprisingly, Natan Gross's *The History of Jewish Cinema in Poland* is able to begin with the same assumption about the Jewish involvement in Polish cinema during the 1920s and 1930s. The vibrant Jewish community in the urban centres of Poland, first under the tsarist regime and then as part of independent Poland, supplied not only most of the film-makers and many of the writers and actors, but a large part of moviegoers as well. One of the most remarkable results of that phenomenon was that during the twenty years of independent Poland (1918–39), a country known for its widespread and deep-seated antisemitism, not even one overtly anti-Jewish film was produced.

This is not to say that most of the films that were produced in Poland were Jewish. But the commercial success enjoyed by many Yiddish films influenced non-Jewish film-makers, who included Jewish themes in many of the early films they produced for the general Polish public. Indeed, it seems as if the Polish film industry between the two world wars provided an unprecedented and rare opportunity for Poles and Jews to come together, not only as close collaborators, but as two communities who, through the new and accessible mass medium of film, finally had the chance to get to know each other after a thousand years of estrangement.

Natan Gross's short account of Jewish cinema in Poland reads like a cross between a production list and an annotated anthology of all the Jewish films that were ever produced in Poland. This may not sound like a resounding recommendation, but these are notable features for two reasons. First, Gross has valuable firsthand knowledge of the subject-matter because he was a Jewish film-maker who worked on various Jewish films in Poland after the Second World War. Secondly, the tragic demise of that old and remarkable community lends a transcendent value to this—as well as any other—account of it.

This is especially true of film, which can provide a historical document of the life and times of an era in a uniquely vivid way. The cultural understanding that may be gleaned from the medium of film is certainly different from that of historical or literary texts. The fleeting images of temporal existence which make up human culture, such as manners, gestures, attitudes, dress, and language, are usually much better captured on film than through any other medium. The content of commercial films should clearly not be confused with history in the usual sense. After all, they are a subjective impression of events and their possible impact on fictional characters. But precisely because they are subjective, films can convey the spirit of an age, of a group of people, or in this case of a now extinct ethnic community with unparalleled power and immediacy.

After defining what constitutes a 'Jewish film', Gross proceeds chronologically, surveying all the films that were ever produced in Poland in either Yiddish, Hebrew, or Polish. He identifies three periods of Jewish film-making: silent films before and after the First World War, talking films between the two World Wars, and documentary films after the Second World War.

One of the interesting things about the films Gross mentions is not so much what distinguishes them from one another but the things they share. Despite the Jewish community in Poland's unprecedented degree of cultural and political development during the inter-war period, most Jewish films tend towards melodramatic ethnography and do not show great artistic sophistication. In part, this phenomenon may be due to the relative crudeness of cinema as a young art form. Another reason may be the rapid changes that occurred in Polish Jewish life during those years of transformation from a rural, or small-town, traditional society to an urban, modern one. Such changes are often attended by sentimentalism and nostalgia. But, as Gross points out, these changes did not affect the burst of original Jewish culture which flourished in Poland in the 1920s and 1930s, especially Yiddish literature and Yiddish theatre. Jewish films had to contend with these challenges, and many early movies were indeed either films of actual theatre shows, or cinematic adaptations of them, such as Gordin's popular plays *Mirele*

Efros and *Khasie di yesome* ('Khasie the Orphan'). Jewish folklore and mysticism were also recurrent elements in many films, such as *A Hand-Shake*, whose plot was similar to that of An-Ski's *The Dybbuk*, and *Lamed Vav*, an adaptation of the hasidic legend of the thirty-six holy men who roam the world performing good deeds. Jewish, as well as many Polish, viewers loved these films, and most of them enjoyed commercial success.

Polish Jews who emigrated to America also played an important part in the production of Jewish films in Poland, both as potential viewers and as film-makers. Joseph Green, the famous Yiddish film producer who was born in Łódź and moved to America in 1924, made many of his films in Poland specifically for the Jewish *émigrés* in the United States who longed for a glimpse of the 'old country'. His film *A brivele der mamen* ('A Letter from Mother') and his most famous *Yidl mitn fidl* ('A Jew with a Violin') try to connect the two communities through sentimental stories that are designed to ease the various gaps between them, the geographic, the generational, and the religious–traditional.

The last period of Jewish film-making in Poland includes, fittingly, mostly documentary films. The few film-makers who survived the war and came back to Poland started documenting the destruction soon after their return in 1945. The Goskind brothers, for instance, who were among the most prolific Jewish film producers in Poland before the war, were convinced that American Jews would be keenly interested to see accounts in Yiddish from the graveyards of Poland. But their efforts were ultimately unsuccessful and epitomized the problems that plagued Polish Jewish cinema from the start: the lack of financial and human resources, the lack of professional expertise, and an unhealthy reliance on foreign markets—America and Israel—for its products. In 1950, with the completion of the last and only feature film that was produced in Poland after the war, *Unzere kinder* ('Our Children'), and with the emigration of its creators to Israel, Jewish film-making in Poland came to an end.

Gross's book is written with the enthusiasm and knowledge of an eyewitness of, and active participant in, the history he describes. And while the book is not a carefully studied history of Jewish film in Poland, the author's obvious fondness and dedication to the subject represents in a way the very cinema he describes—a cinema which never broke new ground or reached artistic heights, but which always reflected the traditions, vitality, and spirit of Polish Jews. Many of the production stories in the book are enlivened with quotations from contemporary critiques, interviews with film-makers, and citations from more scholarly works. Of special value are many of the footnotes. These are biographical notes on the different people who took part in the various film productions and who are mentioned only in passing in the text itself. The result is a sort of concise encyclopaedia about many of the film-makers, actors, script writers, and musicians who made Jewish films in Poland from 1911 to 1950. Another important part is the detailed list of films that appears at the end of the volume, with complete technical and artistic information, including all participants, and the film's current holding, as well as the date of its première, when applicable.

YARON PELEG
Brandeis University

ROBERT LIBERLES
Salo Wittmayer Baron: Architect of Jewish History
(New York: New York University Press, 1995); pp. xiii + 426

Salo Baron (1895–1989), born in Tarnów, Galicia, became one of the foremost Jewish historians of the twentieth century and one of the pioneers of academic Jewish studies in the United States. Liberles attempts to interweave two stories in this first full-length study of Baron and his *œuvre*. First, we are presented with Baron's life, in so far as the author was able to reconstruct it from the documents available to him. This means, essentially, that his sojourn in the United States, beginning in the 1920s, is well recorded and that his life in Tarnów and, later, in Vienna, before his emigration to North America, is relatively sparse. It is to be hoped that the eventual publication of Baron's memoirs, alluded to by Liberles, will help fill in this chapter.

Baron's life was that of a scholar, and included in Liberles's work is a fine attempt to sort out the academic politics which served as a background to his appointments and sojourn at the Jewish Institute of Religion and, later, in the Miller chair of Jewish history and institutions at Columbia University. Liberles places this story properly in the context of the transfer of Judaic scholars and their scholarship from Europe to the United States in the early part of the twentieth century. He also places proper emphasis on the novelty of Jewish history studied in the context of a non-Jewish institution of higher education. And, further, the author chronicles and analyses Baron's ambitions to be heard and respected by the Jewish community beyond the academy and to influence that community through his more popular writings as well as his leadership of such organizations as the Conference on Jewish Social Studies and the American Jewish Historical Society.

Ultimately, though, Baron's strength was his scholarly vision of Jewish history, and the strength of this book is in Liberles's analysis of Baron's role as Jewish historian. He subjects Baron's works to a close and sensitive reading and situates Baron's historiography both in terms of his relationship to his predecessors, notably Heinrich Graetz and Simon Dubnow, and his reaction to the current Jewish scene.

Liberles gives us a full appreciation of Baron's contribution to our understanding of Jewish history. He also carefully delineates the reasons why, even in Baron's own lifetime, his magisterial style of historiography, whereby one person could be said to control the multiple languages, civilizations, and cultures required to write a history of the Jews from ancient to modern times, progressively yielded to a tendency towards an ever narrowing specialization within the field of Jewish studies, which reflects trends within the academy as a whole.

Ultimately, Salo Baron will have a key place in any analysis of the development of Jewish studies in the twentieth century. We are therefore indebted to Liberles for his masterful evocation of a critical chapter of that history.

IRA ROBINSON
Concordia University

MICHAEL C. STEINLAUF
Bondage to the Dead: Poland and the Memory of the Holocaust
(Syracuse, NY: Syracuse University Press, 1997); pp. xiv + 190 + 28 illus.

The author of this book is well known among Polish historians. Since 1983 he has visited Poland several times and studied Polish–Jewish relations on site. In his new book he undertakes the difficult task of analysing the changing attitudes of Polish society towards the Holocaust, until 1995. He is probably the best person to write such a book. The Polish and Jewish historians who spent the Second World War in Poland or who are living now in Poland seem the best situated for gathering sources. They are, however, significantly affected by past and contemporary debates over the problems discussed in this book, and it would be difficult for them to free themselves from their own personal experiences. Yet most of the scholars living abroad are too far from the primary sources. Michael Steinlauf, who was born in France, speaks all the necessary languages (Polish and Yiddish, notably), has spent a long time in Poland, and has many Polish friends. He is free from the most significant personal biases and, at the same time, has the necessary knowledge of Polish literature, the press, and the people. He can, therefore, understand the problems and has sufficient distance from Poland and her current hot quarrels to view them with a properly critical eye.

One of the most significant difficulties he met was inadequate sources. In a country with censorship—as under the previous regime—only opinions approved or (more or less) tolerated by the ruling party were published. The opportunities to take opinion polls were very limited—a situation that has changed only in the last decade. During the last years of communist rule, however, there was illegal publishing (books—and journals, as well). In turn, Michael Steinlauf bases his book primarily on printed sources (daily press, journals, literary works, published opinion polls from the last decade, etc.) and secondary literature. It appears, none the less, that this material was sufficient for an excellent analysis of changes in views of the Holocaust expressed in Poland (though he was also aided, in part, by discussions with many people in Poland).

The book is divided into seven chapters. The first and second chapters present a brilliant view of Polish Jewish history before the Holocaust and in the years 1939–44. The chapters that follow present the Polish memory of the Holocaust in the periods 1944–8, 1948–68, 1968–70, 1970–89, and 1989–95. This structure is based on general Polish political history, though, in addition, it helps one understand changes in the dominant opinions. It would be useful, perhaps, to take separately the years 1956–1967. The first half of the 1950s is, however, relatively poorly represented in the sources. One can expect that in the future some additional information will be found in the files of the security service and, to some extent, in those of the Polish United Workers' Party, that is, in reports presenting the attitudes of common people. Critical analysis of these sources, however, would be a difficult task.

The two opening chapters are a useful introduction, necessary for an American reader, to the ten centuries of Jewish presence in Poland: the author stresses the most important facts that influenced the coexistence of two nations—the positive sides as well as the negative. At the same time, Steinlauf's contexts—ranging from the changing Polish–Jewish relations in the nineteenth century (p. 12) to consequences of the 'national unity' of Poles against German invaders during the Second World War (p. 33)—are all relevant to an understanding of attitudes towards the Holocaust today.

An important merit of the book is its analysis of the changing memories of the Holocaust in light of contemporary Polish history. Steinlauf shows how the past was interpreted according to the nation's changing conditions and how current problems of the country influenced the way in which the past was evaluated. Behind these changes traditional stereotypes were often hidden and evolving, however slowly.

A historian will find topics in this book which deserve additional investigation; these tend, however, to be on the margins of the book's main subject. Such topics include: the rapid growth of the number of Jews in Poland in the nineteenth century; Jews and 'revisionism' in the communist movement in post-war Poland; and the scope and importance of the traditional (mostly religious) stereotypes pertaining to Jews in Poland. I personally would have liked to see deeper analysis of the growing interest in Jewish history and culture in Poland after 1980—a topic interesting in itself, which cannot be fully presented in a book on memory of the Holocaust. It would be useful to indicate, however, that the new Polish memory of Jews (and other national minorities) began before 1980 and had its roots in previous years, when serious articles and letters to the editor concerning national minorities in Poland began to appear in the weeklies (especially *Polityka* and *Tygodnik Powszechny*) and monthlies (*Więź* and *Znak*).

The book was destined for an American readership. It would be useful for Polish readers as well.

JERZY TOMASZEWSKI
University of Warsaw

AGATA TUSZYŃSKA
Lost Landscapes: In Search of the Jews of Poland,
TRANSLATED BY
MADELINE LEVINE
(New York: William Morrow, 1998); pp. viii + 184

In *Lost Landscapes* Agata Tuszyńska pulls together diverse threads: a literary and historical contextualization of the work of Isaac Bashevis Singer, contemporary Poles' current views on Jews, and Polish Jewish survivors' perspectives on Poland and on Singer's writing. The essays are not connected as a single narrative, but hang together as a book through the implication of the continuing connection between Jews and Poles. For Poles, the old Jewish communities' absence in most of Poland has left a shadow. For Polish Jews, memories of Poland, its land and language, persist like an echo. The landscapes of the title unite both groups, as surviving expatriate Polish Jews of Singer's generation remember Poland, and Poles remember their absent and murdered Jewish neighbours.

Tuszyńska decided to write this book when she realized that Isaac Bashevis Singer was born and had grown up in the town where she spent every summer vacation. Having never read Singer until he won the Nobel Prize in 1978, Tuszyńska had never known anything about Jews or Judaism. After she began to read Singer, she began to perceive the absence in Poland of the Jewish community that had lived there for six centuries, and to feel the loss of not knowing Jews. She reflects, 'We can assume that were it not for the war and Hitler's madness, it would have been possible to visit his [Singer's] grave in the Jewish cemetery on Gęsia Street in Warsaw, not far from the places where he spent his childhood and youth. That he wound up across the ocean and his literary maturation occurred in America is a matter of historical accident' (p. 5). Tuszyńska hopes to recapture her own lost past, a past that should have included Jews, by probing the wound of Jewish absence from Polish life.

If this were a work of history, Tuszyńska might have compared the testimonies of surviving Jews and Poles with archival documents to create a single, coherent narrative. But it is not a work of history; instead of a single story, the author creates a polyphony of varied recollections. In one section of the book Tuszyńska transmits her interviews with non-Jewish Poles who lived through the Second World

War in small towns in central Poland, many of the towns that Singer wrote about in his stories and novels. The pre-war Jewish Poland that Tuszyńska uncovered in the memories of these Poles was neither a paradise of integration nor a hell of antisemitism. Her interviewees freely admitted to some acts of antisemitism, and some of the same people described Jewish friends they had loved and admired. Some of them have kept souvenirs of the Jewish presence in their towns, and some have retained stereotypes about Jews that they believed before the war.

Even more discomfiting than the memories of adult Poles are the opinions of Polish children. In the spring of 1990 Tuszyńska administered a questionnaire to measure attitudes about Jews among students in Warsaw schools. In addition to some analysis of her data, she passes on quotes from the students' responses. These quotes reflect both antisemitism and also a sense that tolerance should be encouraged. Tuszyńska seems most disturbed by how inaccurate are Polish perceptions of how many Jews remain in Poland. The Joint Distribution Committee estimates that there are around 10,000 Jews, but Tuszyńska has found sociological studies that show that one in four Poles believe that 350,000 to 3.5 million Jews live in Poland. The reader has a sense of Tuszyńska's isolation in her search for absent Jews. Her images—silence, the traces left behind by *mezuzot*, the orchard growing in a Jewish cemetery—reveal her own feelings of loss. In the midst of finding a missing culture, she learns that a large number of Poles don't even know that anything is gone. In fact their antisemitic stereotypes of powerful Jews, combined with a lack of knowledge of real Jews, allow them to see Jews where there are none.

In the last section of the book Tuszyńska relates her attempts to recapture Singer's experience as a writer by meeting the Yiddish-speaking Polish Jews who were his literary audience. In the United States she discovered Yiddish writers who deplored Singer's representation of Polish Jewish culture. In Israel she discovered a Polish Jewry that seemed to reflect back the culture that Singer first showed her. 'Over there in Poland people always told them, "You are foreign," but they felt at home. Here they say, "You are at home" but they often feel foreign' (p. 120). Again and again the people she interviews tell her that they can never return to Poland, in familiar words; 'For me, Poland is a cemetery' (p. 127). 'I don't want to go to Poland. It means nothing to me. Nothing' (p. 133). At the same time she was taken into the confidence of Polish immigrants in cafés and on promenades. The baker of the Ghetto Fighter's Kibbutz fed Tuszyńska the best poppyseed cake she had ever eaten. In Miami Beach she was offered jobs cleaning houses, because the survivors could not imagine why else a Pole would approach them. Everywhere she hears painful memories of the Holocaust, memories of betrayal. Every Jew remembers Poles who betrayed Jews, and Poles who betrayed other Poles for helping Jews. Everywhere Tuszyńska was met with a combination of kindness and distrust, pain, anger, and longing.

When this book was first published in Polish, one of the great scholars of Yiddish literature, the late Chone Shmeruk, reviewed it for this publication.[1] He disliked it and found it 'inaccurate'. As a monograph about Singer the book was a failure. Shmeruk also noted that only a few of the Polish Jews who knew Singer agreed to be interviewed for the book and that those interviewed expressed envy and bitterness towards Singer. (I wonder whether they accepted the invitation to be interviewed precisely in order to express these opinions?)

I have to question why this book made such a positive impression on me. Perhaps it has something to do with my expectations of the book and something to do with my generation. Shmeruk said the book contributed nothing to our knowledge of Singer. Perhaps this is true, but I think Singer is only the beginning of the book; perhaps the English translation makes this clearer than the original. Tuszyńska essentially reported what she found, even when she found antisemitism among her fellow Poles. In Shmeruk's review he expressed his concern that Polish readers would take as truth the overtly antisemitic comments and the recollections tinged with bias. I saw in Tuszyńska's decision not to comment on these obvious stereotypes a sort of intellectual honesty. She seemed confident that the majority of her Polish readers were not antisemites. In performing this study, Tuszyńska made herself very vulnerable. In her book she shows how every uncovering of Polish antisemitism hurt her as a Pole. Every time she interviewed a Polish Jew, she put herself in an equally difficult position of representing Poland and Polish to people with painful memories. This wasn't research designed to reveal historical truth, but instead to show the marks that history has left on Polish and Jewish lives. Though the material itself is inherently subjective, Tuszyńska does not hesitate to quote people who said things with which she disagreed, even those who had criticisms of Singer. Her editorial decisions frame an essential question about inheritance. Who has a claim to the writings of the Singer family as a cultural legacy? Do I, as an American Jew, have a greater claim than Tuszyńska, as a Pole? Or is this something she and I share across cultural boundaries?

I grew up in a North American Jewish community in the 1970s with the assumption that Poles were antisemitic. In my home town Poles and other non-Jewish east European immigrants lived on the other side of the river from the close-knit Jewish community. I was taught, not explicitly but through hints and jokes, that these people hated me. During my adolescence an east European car-worker was brought to trial in my city as a war criminal in the Holocaust. The lines between the children of non-Jewish east Europeans and the children of east European Jews were clearly drawn. We Jews in the United States were the inheritors of the culture of the murdered Jews of Europe. This was the simple picture I had, growing up.

Today that picture is a little more complicated. It was only in adulthood, when I met Poles my own age, that I realized that the assumption that all Poles were

[1] *Polin*, 10 (London, 1997), 332–6.

biased against Jews was itself a bias. Now that Tuszyńska and her generation know that Polish Jewry is missing from their landscapes, they feel a sense of loss. We have read how Jewish culture has become chic in Poland among non-Jewish Poles. Tuszyńska's book shows us that this loss isn't only expressed through trivialization and commercialism. It impressed me as an attempt to draw together disparate present voices, speaking about a recent past. Shmeruk reviewed this book negatively because the world that Tuszyńska and her Polish peers lost was a world he knew well. It is a world that was lost to me, too. The subjectivity of this scholarship speaks to me, another claimant on a rich inheritance.

RUTH ABRAMS
University of Massachusetts at Amherst

OBITUARY

Teresa Prekerowa
1922–1998

On 19 May 1998 Teresa Prekerowa, one of the most prominent and well respected contributors to these pages, passed away quietly after a long illness. As the 18-year-old Teresa Dobrska she entered the Warsaw ghetto illegally numerous times to bring aid to the family of her friend Alina Wolman; later she helped to smuggle the whole family out of the ghetto and found hiding-places for them on the 'Aryan side' near Warsaw. In 1941 she rescued a 4-year-old Jewish girl whom she found crying in the street in 'Aryan' Warsaw, taking her into her own home and later placing her in a convent. In 1943 she and her new husband hid a Jew for nine months in their own flat.

Official recognition of her heroism and devotion was long delayed. The Polish Union of Fighters for Freedom and Democracy (Związek Bojowników za Wolność i Demokrację; ZBoWiD) refused her membership, as they had refused it to others, on the grounds that they did not consider rescuing Jews to be a valid form of participation in the Polish underground struggle. It was only in 1985, after she had gained prominence through the publication of her first book, that she was awarded the title 'Righteous among the Nations' by Yad Vashem.

Mrs Prekerowa turned to the historian's trade later in life, and although she never gained formal academic qualifications or held a formal post, she had a great deal more influence on students and colleagues alike than many an academic with an impressive list of diplomas. She wrote two books and numerous articles of the highest standard, and was an energetic and knowledgeable participant in all the debates and discussions that have animated the question of Polish–Jewish relations over the past few decades. As she recounted it, she was a puzzle to Israel Gurman, who told her that he could never work out whether she was on the 'Polish' or the 'Jewish' side in these debates.

She first became involved in historical research by helping Władysław Bartoszewski and Zofia Lewin gather material for their book, *Ten jest z ojczyzny mojej* (1967), published in English as *Righteous among Nations* (1969). Her own career as a published author began in 1979, with a valuable study of the 'Felicja' cell of the Council for Aid to the Jews, based on remarkable archival materials. This study later formed the foundation of her best-known work, her history of the Council to Aid Jews in Warsaw (*Konspiracyjna Rada Pomocy Żydom w Warszawie,*

1942–1945 (Warsaw, 1982)). Turning her attention to education, she wrote her *Zarys dziejów Żydów w Polsce, 1939–1945* ('Outline of the History of the Jews in Poland, 1939– 1945') as a textbook for the use of students at the University of Warsaw. Published independently in 1992, this work was later incorporated into the volume *Najnowsze dzieje Żydów w Polsce*, edited by Jerzy Tomaszewski and published in 1996. This is today considered to be the authoritative Polish work on the modern history of the Jews of Poland. English-speaking readers will perhaps best remember her article 'The "Just" and the "Passive" ', first published in *Tygodnik Powszechny* in 1987 and in translation in the volume *'My Brother's Keeper?' Recent Polish Debates about the Holocaust* (London, 1990).

A linguistic virtuoso, Mrs Prekerowa was fluent in English and German and mastered Yiddish as well. Armed with her command of the *mame-loshn* and a decent knowledge of Hebrew, she next undertook a study of the underground press in the Warsaw ghetto, presenting a controversial paper on the subject to the conference on the fiftieth anniversary of the Warsaw ghetto uprising held in Warsaw in April 1993. A version of this paper was published in *Polin*, volume 9, in 1996 under the title 'The Jewish Underground and the Polish Underground'. In the following year a still sharper controversy broke out in connection with the fiftieth anniversary of the 1944 Warsaw uprising. At the focus of the storm was Michał Cichy's article in *Gazeta Wyborcza* on atrocities committed by members of the Polish underground during the uprising, with Mrs Prekerowa emerging as one of Cichy's strongest defenders. Subsequently she presented an article on Jewish participation in the uprising, the most comprehensive study of the subject to date, to the fiftieth anniversary conference in Warsaw. Despite her illness, she continued working until the end.

Those of us who knew Teresa Prekerowa remember her as tough, sympathetic, cheerful, and always full of energy. She never withheld her opinions, even when they were displeasing to her audience, but had the knack of presenting them in a way that disarmed dissent. She will be missed by all as a scholar with an uncompromising devotion to truth, by some as a worthy adversary, but by far more as a warm, inspiring presence, and a friend.

GUNNAR S. PAULSSON

CORRESPONDENCE

Exchange between Rafał Żebrowski and Hanna Kozińska-Witt

The Editors
Polin: Studies in Polish Jewry

Dear Sir,

In volume 11 of *Polin* there appeared a review written by Hanna Kozińska-Witt of my book *Mojżesz Schorr i jego listy do Ludwika Gumplowicza*. A few years ago Dr Kozińska-Witt published an article about the Gumplowicz family entitled 'Asymilacja "po krakowsku": przypadek Ludwika Gumplowicza' (*Teksty Drugie*, 5 (1992), 92–101), which I cited in my work purely pro forma, since it did not add anything significant to our knowledge of the subject. Dr Kozińska-Witt is clearly very attached to the personality of Ludwik Gumplowicz, as was demonstrated by a paper on the Gumplowicz family which she presented at the recent conference entitled Jews and Judaism in Contemporary Scholarship, held in Kraków on 26–8 November 1998. With great regret, I have to state that her review has the character of a personal attack on me. Its basic scholarly character has been submerged by a series of insulting observations. Naturally, anyone can make mistakes. One such mistake is the identification in a note of the socialist periodical *Neue Zeit* with *Neuzeit*, which was linked with the Reform movement in Judaism. However, in her zealous search for mistakes committed by the author in the course of putting together this volume, the reviewer does not perceive what was made very clear in both the text and the notes. In the first place the translation of German texts was checked with specialists in the field. Secondly, the translation of Latin tags was taken from the standard Polish edition of Latin sayings. I did not think it necessary to document in the notes the fact that I followed Czesław Jeraszko's *Łacina na co dzień* in the version of the Latin sentences I cited. Jeraszko's may not be a scholarly book, but it was published in its eighth edition in 1990. Even if a very superficial reading of my book did not allow the reviewer to notice this, she should have known that this is standard scholarly procedure.

Dr Kozińska-Witt does not seem to perceive that the book she was reviewing is composed of two parts. One part consists of extended sketches describing Mojżesz Schorr and a number of the members of the Gumplowicz family, while the other is made up of documents (letters and annexes). The two parts of the book are fundamentally different in character. In publishing the letters of Mojżesz Schorr, I was obliged to include in the notes all the information that was necessary for them to be understood. I was not under a similar obligation in the biographical essays. I also cannot understand why the reviewer claims that the information about Baron Maurice de Hirsch was difficult to find.

What saddens me most is the fact that in the review the main threads of my book are not described. Its main 'hero' is indeed Mojżesz Schorr, who was one of the leading figures of Polish Jewry in the inter-war period. His letters certainly do shed a certain light on the last phase in the life of the great sociologist Ludwik Gumplowicz. But the most important matter is the presentation of the genealogy of Schorr—a man who played an important role before the tragic end of Polish Jewry in the Holocaust. Dr Kozińska-Witt does report in literally the final sentence of her review my opinion that these two individuals must be seen as embodying a sort of thesis and antithesis. However, she is completely unable to grasp the significance of this point. In his time Ludwik Gumplowicz was recognized as a leading figure in the intellectual life of Europe. Yet his significance from a historical perspective is solely linked with the history of sociology, in which his theories rapidly lost their relevance. For his part, Schorr, who obtained a university position with great difficulty, played an unusually important role in the history of Polish Jewry (for this reason I attached less weight to his achievements in the field of Assyriology). His role in the history of Polish Jewry has been to a considerable degree forgotten because of the mass murder of the community and his own death in a Soviet camp: in the history of the Jewish people it was Mojżesz Schorr who left a permanent mark. This thesis could form the basis for an interesting discussion and it is a pity that this was not undertaken by the reviewer. It could have borne fertile intellectual fruit—something which cannot be said, unfortunately, of the review by Dr Kozińska-Witt.

 Yours faithfully,
  Rafał Żebrowski   *December 1998*

The Editor
Polin: Studies in Polish Jewry

Dear Sir,

The fact that I like Dr Żebrowski as a person does not mean that I do not continue to regard his book *Mojżesz Schorr i jego listy do Ludwika Gumplowicza* as having been written too swiftly and carelessly.

It may be that some of its defects can be attributed to inadequate proof-reading and editing by the publishers. Other defects, in my opinion, are the result of inadequate consultation with other scholars. Dr Żebrowski limited his contacts to the descendants of the Schorr family and did not attempt to reach anyone who could have widened his knowledge about the scholarly achievements of Mojżesz Schorr. One consequence of this method of writing a biography is the very inadequate treatment of Baron Maurice de Hirsch.

I wrote my review, not because my own work is without faults, but because I read the book with interest and very carefully (as I am sure Dr Żebrowski will admit). The achievement of the author, as I see it, is that he has located some remarkable material, has found the Schorr family, and has written a most useful book. At the same time the work is marred by carelessness. And it is against this that I wanted to warn a potential reader.

Yours faithfully,
Hanna Kozińska-Witt *February 1999*

Notes on the Contributors

MONIKA ADAMCZYK-GARBOWSKA is professor of American and comparative literature at the Department of English, Maria Curie-Skłodowska University, in Lublin. She is the author of *Polskie tlumaczenia angielskiej literatury dziecięcej: Problemy krytyki przekładu* ('Polish Translations of English Children's Classics: Problems of Translation Critique') (Wrocław, 1988) and *Polska Isaaca Bashevisa Singera: rozstanie i powrót* ('Isaac Bashevis Singer's Poland: Exile and Return') (Lublin, 1994), as well as a translator from English and Yiddish into Polish. She is co-editor, with Antony Polonsky, of an English-language anthology of post-war Polish Jewish writing to be published by the University of Nebraska Press.

MARTA ALEKSANDRA BALIŃSKA is a historian specializing in the origins of international health and relief structures. She is currently pursuing research into the development of health care in twentieth-century Poland, and is undertaking additional training in epidemiology with a view to further research into public health in eastern Europe.

ALINA CAŁA is a researcher at the Jewish Historical Institute in Warsaw. She is the author of *Wizerunek Żyda w polskiej kulturze ludowej* (Warsaw, 1987), translated into English as *The Image of the Jew in Polish Folk Culture* (Jerusalem, 1995), and of *Asymilacja Żydów w królestwie Polskim (1864–1897): postawy, konflikty, stereotypy* ('The Assimilation of the Jews in the Kingdom of Poland (1864–1897): Attitudes, Conflicts, Stereotypes') (Warsaw, 1989), which will shortly appear in English. Her main field of interest is the history of Polish–Jewish relations.

WALDEMAR CHROSTOWSKI studied at the Higher Metropolitan Theological Seminary in Warsaw, the Papal Biblical Institute in Rome, and the Hebrew University of Jerusalem. He became a priest in 1976 and holds the degree of Doctor of Theology. He holds the position of director of the Institute for Catholic–Jewish Dialogue and is the principal editor of Collectanea Theologica. He edited *Żydzi i judaizm w dokumentach Kościoła a i nauczaniu Jana Pawła II (1965–89)* ('Jews and Judaism in the Documents of the Church and the Teachings of John Paul II') (Warsaw, 1990). He is also vice-president of the Commission of the Polish Episcopate for Dialogue with Judaism. One of the founders and formerly co-chairman of the Polish Council of Christians and Jews, he resigned from this position as a consequence of the controversy reprinted in this volume of *Polin*. Explaining his decision in *Gazeta Wyborcza*, he stated, 'I resign my position with pain, but Christian–Jewish dialogue must be based on partnership and not on the stressing of one's own complexes.'

MARIA EINHORN-SUSUŁOWSKA was born in Gorlice and studied at the Jagiellonian University, where from 1969 she was professor of psychology. From 1945 to 1972 she was the editor of Zeszyty Naukowe UJ, Seria Prace Psychologicno-Pedagogiczne (Scholarly Publications of the Jagiellonian University, Psychological and Pedagogical Series) and from 1961 to 1966 pro-dean of the philosophical and historical faculty. She published widely on psychological problems. Her last work was *Psychologia starzenia się i starości* ('The Psychological Problems of Ageing and of Old Age') (Warsaw, 1989). She died in December 1998.

ELŻBIETA FICOWSKA is one of the founders of the association Children of the Holocaust in Poland, whose members number between 200 and 250 people still living in Poland. She gave a fuller account of how she survived the war in *The Last Eyewitness: Children of the Holocaust Speak*, edited by Wiktoria Śliwowska (Evanston, Ill., 1998). She is married to the Polish poet Jerzy Ficowski, author of an important cycle of Holocaust poetry, *Odczytanie popiołów* ('A Reading of Ashes') (Warsaw, 1988).

REGINA GROL is professor of comparative literature at Empire State College, State University of New York. She is a graduate of Warsaw University and holds a Ph.D. (with distinction) from the State University of New York at Binghampton. An author of numerous studies in east European literature, she is also a translator of several plays and three volumes of Polish poetry, including *Ambers Aglow: An Anthology of Contemporary Polish Women's Poetry* (Austin, Tex., 1996).

JAN GROSS is professor of politics and European studies at New York University and the author of *Polish Society under German Occupation: The Generalgouvernement, 1939–1944* (Princeton, 1977), *Revolution from Abroad: The Soviet Conquest of Poland's Western Ukraine and Western Belorussia* (Princeton, 1988), and *Upiorna dekada: trzy eseje o stereotypach na temat Żydów, Polaków i komunistów, 1939–1948* ('An Appalling Decade: Three Essays on the Stereotypes Connected with Poles, Jews, and Communists') (Kraków, 1998). He is the co-editor of *War through Children's Eyes: The Soviet Occupation of Poland and the Deportations, 1939–1941* (Stanford, Calif., 1981), published in Polish as *W czterdziestym nas Matko na Sybir zesłali* (London, 1983).

EDWARD KAPLAN is professor of French and comparative literature and research associate of the Tauber Institute for the Study of European Jewry at Brandeis University. In addition to books on Jules Michelet and Charles Baudelaire, he has published *Holiness in Words* (Albany, NY, 1996), translated into French as *La Sainteté en paroles: Abraham Heschel, piété, poétique, action* (Paris, 1999), and the first intellectual and cultural biography of Heschel, written with Samuel Dresner, *Abraham Joshua Heschel: Prophetic Witness*, a 1988 finalist of the National Jewish Book Award, Jewish Scholarship.

Notes on the Contributors

PADRAIC KENNEY is associate professor of history at the University of Colorado. He is the author of *Rebuilding Poland: Workers and Communists, 1945–1950* (Ithaca, NY, 1997), which received the 1998 American Association for the Advancement of Slavic Studies Orbis prize for the best English-language book in any area of Polish studies. He is currently writing a book on social movements in the east European revolutions of 1989.

STANISŁAW KRAJEWSKI has a Ph.D. in mathematics and now teaches in the philosophy department of the University of Warsaw. Born into an assimilated family, he found his way back to Judaism and became active first in underground circles and in the 1990s in Jewish organizations in Poland as well as in Christian–Jewish dialogue. He is the author of *Jews, Judaism, Poland* (Warsaw, 1997), a member of the board of the Union of Jewish Communities in Poland, co-chair of the Polish Council of Christians and Jews, president of the Jewish Forum Foundation, and Polish consultant to the American Jewish Committee.

DIANA KUPREL has a Ph.D. in comparative literature from the University of Toronto. She is currently postdoctoral fellow at the Literary History Project, University of Toronto, and editor-in-chief of *Books in Canada: The Canadian Review of Books*.

JÓZEF LEWANDOWSKI is a historian specializing in the area of central and eastern Europe. His most important books are *Federalizm: Litwa i Białorus w polityce obozu belwederskiego* ('Federalism: Lithuania and Belarus in the Politics of the Pilsudskiite Camp') (Warsaw, 1962), *Imperializm słabości* ('The Imperialism of Weakness') (Warsaw, 1967), *The Swedish Contribution to the Polish Resistance Movement* (Uppsala, 1979), and a memoir, *Cztery dni w Atlantydzie* ('Four Days in Atlantis') (Uppsala, 1991). He has also written numerous articles on political and historical topics. Since 1969 he has been a political refugee in Sweden, where, until his retirement, he was professor of history at Uppsala University.

JOANNA MICHLIC-COREN is completing a doctorate at University College London on the image of the Jew as the Threatening Other in modern Polish society. Her scholarly interests lie in Polish Jewish history and culture, the Holocaust, Polish nationalism and its attitude to ethnic minorities, and the problems of nationalism and ethnicity. She was a historical consultant and researcher for the BBC Radio 4 programme 'Number Seven Planty Street', which was awarded the 1995 Silver Sony Ward.

STANISŁAW MUSIAŁ is an essayist and a former editor of *Tygodnik Powszechny*. He studied philosophy and theology in Kraków and Warsaw, as well as in Italy, Germany, and France. From 1986 to 1995 he was secretary of the Commission of the Polish Episcopate for Dialogue with Judaism. He participated in the Geneva meetings in 1986 and 1987 on the Carmelite convent at Auschwitz.

GUNNAR S. PAULSSON was born in Sweden to a Swedish father and a Polish Jewish mother whom the Swedish Red Cross had rescued from the camps. After a lengthy career as a computer software developer he turned to historical studies, gaining his MA from the University of Toronto in 1992 and his D.Phil. from the University of Oxford in 1998. His D.Phil. thesis won the 1998 Fraenkel prize for contemporary history. He was lecturer in Jewish studies and Holocaust studies and director of the Stanley Burton Centre for Holocaust Studies at Leicester University from 1994 to 1998, and is presently the senior historian of the Holocaust Exhibition Project at the Imperial War Museum, London, and an honorary research fellow at the University of Warwick.

JOHN T. PAWLIKOWSKI is professor of social ethics at the Catholic Theological Union in Chicago. He has co-chaired the National Polish American–Jewish American Council and currently serves on the executive committee of the United States Holocaust Memorial Museum in Washington.

ADAM PENKALLA is a lecturer at the Institute of History of the College of Education in Kielce. He is interested in the social history of the Jews in the Radom and Kielce regions in the nineteenth and twentieth centuries. He is also working on the compilation of an inventory for conservation purposes of Jewish cemeteries and synagogues in the area. His works include *Żydzi na terenie guberni radomskiej w latach 1815–1862* ('The Jewish Population of the Province of Radom, 1815–1862') (Radom, 1991), *Żydowskie ślady w województwie kieleckim i radomskim* ('Jewish Traces in the Provinces of Kielce and Radom') (Radom, 1992), and *Akta dotyczące Żydów w radomskim Archiwum Państwowym* ('Documents concerning Jews in the Radom State Archives') (Radom, 1998).

MAYA PERETZ is an independent translator living in Washington. She received her Ph.D. in comparative literature in 1979. She recently published *indeed I love/właśnie kocham*, a bilingual volume of Polish poetry in translation. She has published translations, articles, and reviews in the *Jewish Spectator*, *Modern Judaism*, and several Polish and American literary periodicals.

ANTONY POLONSKY is Albert Abramson professor at Brandeis University and the United States Holocaust Memorial Museum. Until 1991 he was professor of international history at the London School of Economics and Political Science. He is chair of the editorial board of *Polin*, author of *Politics in Independent Poland* (Oxford, 1972), *The Little Dictators* (London, 1975), and *The Great Powers and the Polish Question* (London, 1976), and co-author of *A History of Modern Poland* (Cambridge, 1980) and *The Beginnings of Communist Rule in Poland* (London, 1981). He is co-editor, with Monika Garbowska, of an English-language anthology of post-war Polish Jewish writing to be published by the University of Nebraska Press.

JOANNA ROSTROPOWICZ CLARK is a graduate of Warsaw University and received her Ph.D. in comparative literature from the University of Pennsylvania. A literary critic and teacher at Rutgers University, she is currently working on a book entitled *Poetry after Auschwitz: The Holocaust in Polish Literature*.

M. M. RUBEL is an independent scholar with a particular interest in the Bełżec murder camp, where part of her family from Lemberg perished. In 1995–6 she organized and financed an exhibition commemorating the life and death of the Jews of Galicia in a seventeenth-century synagogue in Lesko, a small county town in the south-eastern corner of Poland. She has also arranged for the first monument to be put up at the Jewish cemetery in Lesko to the memory of the Jews murdered in Bełżec. Margaret Rubel is currently preparing for publication an introduction to a selection of documents relating to Bełżec.

SIMON SCHOCHET is a historian and writer. His research to identify the Polish Jewish officers who were killed in Katyn is ongoing, and his work has been published by the Yeshiva University in New York and by the Piłsudski Institute. He is a member of the Katyn Institute in Kraków and was awarded its commemorative medal in 1994. His essay 'The Postcard from Starobielsk' was included in Jerzy Krzyżanowski (ed.), *Katyń w literaturze: Międzynarodowa antologia poezji, dramatu i prozy* ('Katyń in Literature: An International Anthology of Poetry, Drama, and Prose') (Lublin, 1995).

BOŻENA SZAYNOK is a lecturer in the history department at the University of Wrocław. She has published a monograph on the Kielce pogrom of July 1946, as well as articles on the history of the Jews in Poland after the Second World War. She has been a visiting professor at the University of Illinois at Chicago and has received grants from the Joram Schnitzer Foundation, the Kościuszko Foundation, the Stefan Batory Foundation, and the Polish Scholarly Foundation.

TERESA ŚWIEBOCKA is a historian and museologist. She is the editor-in-chief of *Zeszyty Oświęcimskie* and head of the Auschwitz-Birkenau State Museum Publishing House. She is the author of albums, articles, scenarios, and exhibitions presented in Poland and abroad describing the establishment and history of the Auschwitz camp and the activities of the Auschwitz Museum.

JERZY TOMASZEWSKI is professor at the Historical Institute and head of the Mordekhai Anielewicz Research Centre on the History of Jews in Poland at Warsaw University. He is a member of the council and board of the Jewish Historical Institute in Poland. Among his publications are *Z dziejów Polesia, 1921–1939: zarys stosunków społeczno-ekonomicznych* ('On the History of Polesie, 1921–1939: An Outline of Social and Economic Conditions') (Warsaw, 1963); *Rzeczpospolita wielu narodów* ('A Republic of Many Nations') (Warsaw, 1985), and *Preludium Zagłady: Wygnanie Żydów polskich z Niemiec w 1938r.* (Warsaw, 1998).

NERIJUS UDRENAS is a lecturer in the department of history at Vilnius University. He completed his doctorate in the comparative history programme at Brandeis University on the development of the Lithuanian national idea and the emergence of an independent Lithuanian state.

JONATHAN WEBBER is fellow in Jewish social studies at the Oxford Centre for Hebrew and Jewish Studies and Hebrew Centre lecturer in social anthropology, University of Oxford. He is a founder member of the International Auschwitz Council and co-author of *Auschwitz: A History in Photographs* (Bloomington, Ind., 1993).

ANDRZEJ ŻBIKOWSKI was born in Warsaw and since 1985 has worked at the Jewish Historical Institute. He defended his doctoral dissertation in the department of history at the University of Warsaw. His thesis was published in 1994 under the title *Żydzi krakowscy i ich gmina, 1869–1919* ('The Jews of Kraków and their Communal Organization, 1869–1919'). In 1996 he published an illustrated history entitled *Żydzi* ('Jews') in the series A to Polska właśnie (And this is Truly Poland).

Glossary

Anders' Army   The army established in the Soviet Union in 1941 by General Władysław Anders under the auspices of the Polish government in exile in London. This army left the Soviet Union for Persia and the Middle East in mid-1942.

Dror   A Zionist youth movement which developed in Poland and other countries of eastern Europe between the two world wars. Dror combined maximalist Zionism with radical socialism and appealed for the most part to the poorer sections of Jewish society.

Endecja   Popular name for the Polish National Democratic Party, a right-wing party which had its origins in the 1890s. Its principal ideologue was Roman Dmowski, who advocated a Polish version of the integral nationalism which became popular in Europe at the turn of the nineteenth century. The Endecja advanced the slogan 'Poland for the Poles' and called for the exclusion of the Jews from Polish political and economic life. Its adherents were called Endeks. *See also* Obóz Wielkiej Polski.

General Government   An administrative-territorial unit created in Poland during the Nazi occupation from some of the territory seized by Germany after the Polish defeat. The GG was established on 26 October 1939 and first comprised four districts: Kraków, Lublin, Warsaw, and Radom. Its capital was the city of Kraków and its administration was headed by Hans Frank. After the Nazi invasion of the Soviet Union an additional province, Galicia, made up of parts of the pre-war Polish provinces of Lwów, Stanisławów, and Tarnopol, was added to the GG. Within the GG the Germans came to pursue a policy of mass murder of the Jews and, denying the Christian Poles all civil rights, made them a reservoir of labour for the Third Reich.

government in exile   After the German defeat of Poland in 1939 a Polish government in exile was established in France by General Sikorski. Based in Angers, it was made up of the less compromised elements of the Sanacja (q.v.) regime and representatives of the democratic opposition. After the fall of France it moved to London. It attempted to represent the Polish cause, but was abandoned by the Western powers at the Yalta Conference in February 1945, when it was decided that the pro-communist government established in Poland by Stalin be recognized on condition that it broaden its ranks by the addition of democratic politicians from Poland and the West and hold free elections. In practice, neither condition was fulfilled in any meaningful way.

Judenrat   The Jewish administrative councils established by the German authorities in the Jewish communities of occupied Europe. Judenräte were first established in occupied Poland according to the guide-lines laid down by Reinhard Heydrich on 21 September 1939 and through an order promulgated by Hans Frank, head of the General Government (q.v.) on 18 November 1939. They were subsequently created in many other countries occupied by the Germans. They did not have a uniform structure: some held authority in one town only, while others administered all the Jewish communities in a district or even in a country. Their role has been bitterly disputed. Some, such as Raul Hilberg and Hannah Arendt, have argued that they considerably facilitated the anti-Jewish genocide; others, such as Isaiah Trunk, that their role was much more positive and that they were able on many occasions to mitigate the harsh effects of Nazi rule and to strengthen the Jews' ability to withstand the deadly onslaught to which they were being subjected.

kahal, kehilah, kehile (Yiddish)   Although both terms mean 'community', *kahal* is used to denote the institution of Jewish autonomy in a particular locality, while *kehilah* denotes the community of Jews who live in the town. The *kahal* was the lowest level of the Jewish autonomous institutions in the Polish–Lithuanian Commonwealth. Above the local *kehilot* were regional bodies, and above these a central body, the Va'ad Arba Aratsot (Council of Four Lands) for the Kingdom of Poland and the Va'ad Lita (Council of Lithuania). The Va'ad Arba Aratsot was abolished by the Polish authorities in 1764, but autonomous institutions continued to operate legally until 1844 and in practice for many years after this date in those parts of the Polish–Lithuanian Commonwealth directly annexed by the tsarist empire and until the emergence of the Polish state in the kingdom of Poland and Galicia. Here the reorganized communal body, which no longer had the power to punish religious heterodoxy, but administered synagogues, schools, cemeteries, and *mikva'ot* was often called the *gmina* (commune). In inter-war Poland the legal status of the *kehilot* was regulated by statute in October 1927 and March 1930. The legislation gave them control over many aspects of Jewish communal life with both religious and social functions. All adherents of the 'Mosaic faith' were required to belong to a *kehilah*, and one could not withdraw except through baptism or by declaring oneself an atheist.

Małopolska (Polish: lit. 'lesser Poland' or 'little Poland')   Southern Poland, the area around Kraków. Also referred to under the Habsburgs as (western) Galicia.

Obóz Wielkiej Polski (Polish: 'The Camp for a Greater Poland').   Extreme right-wing and pro-fascist organization founded in December 1926 by Roman Dmowski because of his dissatisfaction over the weak reaction of the National Democratic Party (Endecja, q.v.) to the coup of May 1926 which brought Józef Piłsudski back to power.

Sanacja (From Latin *sanatio*: 'healing', 'restoration')   The popular name taken by the regime established by Józef Piłsudski after the coup of May 1926. It referred to Piłsudki's aim of restoring health to the political, social, and moral life of Poland.

Sejm   The central parliamentary institution of the Polish–Lithuanian Commonwealth, composed of a senate and a chamber of deputies; after 1501 both of these had a voice in the introduction of new legislation. The Sejm met regularly for six weeks every two years, but could be called for sessions of two weeks in an emergency. When it was not in session, an appointed commission of sixteen senators, in rotation four at a time, resided with the king both to advise and to keep watch over his activities. Until the middle of the seventeenth century the Sejm functioned reasonably well; after that the use of the *liberum veto* began to paralyse its effectiveness. Also used for the Lower House of the Parliament in independent Poland.

Wielkopolska (Polish: lit. 'Great Poland' or 'Greater Poland')   Western Poland, the area around Poznań.

Yishuv (Heb., lit. 'settlement')   The Jewish settlement in Palestine before the establishment of the state of Israel, particularly its Zionist aspects.

Index

A
Abarinov, Vladimir 73
Aberbach, David 435
Abramowski, Edward 375
Abrams, Ruth 449
Adamczyk-Garbowska, Monika 325–8, 457
Adiv, Gershon 66
Agnon, S. Y. 434
Agudas Yisroel 80, 84
Akademicka Młodzież Państwowa 51
Akiba 80
Aktion Reinhard 268, 272 n. 4, 279 n. 17, 280 n. 18, 281 n. 19
All-Polish Youth, *see* Młodzież Wszechpolska
Alpert, Jechiel 257 n. 13, 263 n. 24
Alter, Mendele 140
Altman, Shlomo 387 n. 13
Anders, Gen. Władysław 10, 11, 191
Anders' Army 463
Andrzejewski, Jerzy 7, 171, 173
Anielewicz, Mordekhai 19
An-Ski, Shloyme Zanvil Rapoport 358, 442
Antczak, Jan 43
anti-Gypsism 422
anti-Jewish violence 9, 11–13, 34–61
    inter-war 35–8
    post-war 196–205
    1945–7 38–40
    in Kielce in 1945 237
    as national self-defence 44–50
    in Radom region in 1945 241–2, 249–52
    in universities 50–2
    see also Kielce pogrom
anti-Judaism 312, 319, 404, 432
antisemitism in Poland 191–2, 335
    in early 20th c. 332
    1919–39 438
    1935–9 432
    post-war 31–2
    in contemporary Poland 447–8
    anti-Jewish boycotts 40
    and anti-Jewish violence 254–67
    and the Catholic Church 46, 303–28
    effect on Jews in hiding 99
    historiography of 418–24
    in the inter-war Catholic press 406–10
    among peasantry 338
    Polish denunciation of 7
    prohibited under Soviet occupation of the Kresy 63
    without Jews 401
    and working-class nationalism, 1945–7 224–35
    see also anti-Jewish violence
Appelfeld, Aharon 105, 107
Appenszlak, Jakub 356, 364
Arczyński, Marek 83
Armia Krajowa (Home Army: AK) 26–8, 181
Armia Ludowa (People's Army) 27
Aryan identification papers, use of 104–11
Asch, Sholem 361
Asserodobraj, Nina 82 n. 4
assimilation 429
Auschwitz 138, 142, 288
    Carmelite convent in 311
    destruction of 292
    history of the camp 290–1
    Jewish rituals in 139
    post-war 198
    as symbol of Holocaust 129
    symbolic meaning of 291–2
Auschwitz-Birkenau Memorial and Museum 290–9
Avenol, Joseph 377
Avigdor, Jacob 137
Avineri, Shlomo 433

B
Ba'al Shem Tov, Israel 384, 426
Bachner, Lesser 198
Baczyńska, Stefania 169
Baczyński, Krzysztof Kamil 3, 166–78
Baczyński, Stanisław 166
Baeck, Leo 396
Bałaban, Majer 395
Balicki, Dr 261 n. 21
Balińska, Marta Aleksandra 373–82, 457
Banach, Comr. 263, 266
Banaś, Ewa 408
Baratov, Pavil (actor) 357
Barbel (SS man at Bełżec) 281 n. 20
Baron, Salo Wittmayer 443–4
Bartoszewski, Władysław 25–6, 75, 450
Barukh ben Jehiel of Medzibizh 426
Basok, Moshe 435
Bataliony Chłopskie (Peasants' Battalions) 338
Bauman, Zygmunt 8, 32

Beck, Józef 377
Bednarz, Capt. 258
Beilis case 332
Beit Lohamei Hagetaot (BLHG) 78, 100
Bejlin, Idalia 92
Bekker, Józef 347–55
Bełżec 130, 461
  eyewitness account of camp 268–89
Berger, Yitzhak Arieh 435
Berihah 213
Berlin, Isaiah 433
Berlinski, Hersch 81 n. 3
Berman, Adolf 78–9, 81–5, 99–101, 215
Berman, Basia Temkin- 78, 81, 82 n. 4, 83, 86, 92, 100–1
Berman Archive 78–103
Bernadotte, Folke 126
Białobrzegi, Jewish population in 1945 246
Bienik, Bishop 57
Bierut, Bolesław 31, 261
Birenbaum, Halina, memoirs 38
Biskupska, Antonina 60
Bitter, Marek 209
Biuletyn Informacyjny 19
blackmail 97–8, 107, 110, 192
Blasbalgowa, J. 243
Błaszczyk, Henryk 57–8
Bloc of Democratic Parties, *see* Blok Demokratyczny
Bloch, Felicja 92
Blok Demokratyczny (Bloc of Democratic Parties) 214
Błoński, Jan 7–8, 19–20, 33
Bochnia 201
Bodzentyn, Jewish population in 1945 244
Bogucka, Maria 343
Boheman, Eric 125
Bojańczyk, Maria 375
Bojm, Mojżesz 238, 243, 247
Bolshevism 11
Bonhöffer, Dietrich 126
Borejsza, Jerzy 260
Borowski, Tadeusz 182, 411
Borwicz, Michał 105
Borysov, murder of Jews at 124
Boy-Żeleński, Tadeusz 359–60
Bratnia Pomoc 35, 54
Brodowska, Helena 337
Bron, Michael, Jr. 401–2
Brubaker, Rogers 438
Bruner, Ignacy 92
Buber, Martin 394–7
Bugajska, Pola 82 n. 4
Bujak, Franciszek 335
Bujak, Jan 55

Bujwid, Odon 375
Bund (Ogólno-Żydowski Związek Robotniczy) 79, 80–1, 85, 100, 102, 201, 389
  blamed for Siedlce pogrom 348–9
  opposition to Zionism 220
  in post-war Poland 206–23
Bunin, Shmuel David 435
Bychowski, Gustaw 188
Bychowski, Jan Ryszard 188–93

C
Cała, Alina 418–24, 457
Camp for a Greater Poland, *see* Ruch Młodych Obozu Wielkiej Polski
Caritas 80
Catholic Church:
  and anti-Jewish violence 46–8
  and antisemitism 303–28, 401–5
  and the Jews 28
  anti-Judaic tradition 29
  attitude towards Jews, 1939–41 17
  religious orders and the rescue of Jews 402
  and ritual murder accusations 57–8
Catholic Front for the Rebirth of Poland, *see* Front Odrodzenia Polski
Catholic Press Agency, *see* Katolicka Agencja Prasowa
Cavendish-Bentinck, Victor 29, 57
Céline 373
CENTOS 79
Central Committee of Jews in Poland, *see* Centralny Komitet Żydów w Polsce
Central Yiddish Schools Organization (CYSHO) 388
Centralny Komitet Żydów w Polsce (Central Committee of Jews in Poland: CKŻP) 4, 28, 38, 46, 58
  Centralna Komisja Specjalna (Central Special Commission) 194–5, 202–5
Chaskielewicz, Judka Lejb 55
Chaskielewicz, Stefan 107
Chełkowski, Hilary 255, 257, 265–6
Chiang Kai-shek 377–8
Chmielnik-Busko, Jewish population in 1945 245–6
Chomsky, Dov 435
Chopai, Ya'akov 435
Chrapusta, Władysław 435
Chrostowski, Waldemar 310–26, 402, 457
Chrzanów, antisemitism in 198–9
Chrześcijańska Demokracja (Christian Democrats) 437
Chudy, Władysław 69
Cichy, Michał 451

Ciechanowski, Jan 378–9
cinema, Jewish, in Poland 440–3
Citizens' Militia, antisemitism in 198–9
Cohen, Rene 418–19
collaboration with Germans 98–9
Commission for the Investigation of Nazi War Crimes 181–2
communism 333
  and antisemitism 256
  identification of Jews with 43–9
  and increase in antisemitism 311–12
  in post-war Poland 224–35
concentration camps, see Stutthof; see also death camps
Council for Aid to the Jews, see Rada Pomocy Żydom
Cox, Oscar 379
Cukier, Mojżesz 58
culture, Polish, de-Judaization of 439
Czarnowski, Stefan 334–6
Czeczot, Mrs 337
Czerniakow, Adam 169
Częstochowa:
  anti-Jewish violence in 60
  Jewish emigration from in 1946 201–2

D
Dachsel (SS man at Bełżec) 281 n. 20
Dankowicz, Szymon 429
Daszyński, Ignacy 44
Dattner, Maurycy 430
Davies, Norman 30
death camps, see Auschwitz; Bełżec; Sobibór; Treblinka; see also Stutthof
Debré, Robert 381
Dmowski, Roman 338, 463, 464
Doboszyński, Adam 45
Dobroszycki, Lucjan 196
Dotkiewicz, S. 55
Drapczyńska, Barbara 171, 173
Dreszer, Knecht 222
Dror Hehaluts 80, 84, 463
Drożdżeński, Andrzej 60
Dubois (SS man at Bełżec) 281 n. 20
Duncan, Isadora 374
Duschinsky, Eugene 208
Dutch Nazi Party (Nationaalsocialistise Beweging: NSB) 98
Działoszyce, Jewish population in 1945 245
Dziubiński, Andrzej 343

E
Edelman, Marek 195, 207, 219, 411
education, Jewish:
  and the Bund 215–16
  in Hebrew 215
  during the Nazi occupation 147–62
  yeshiva 386–7
  in Yiddish 215, 388–9
Ehrenpreis, Rabbi 125
Eibenschütz, Artur 429–30
Eidem, Archbishop 126
Einhorn-Susułowska, Maria 104–11, 458
Eisner, Jack 106
Ellbogen (inmate at Bełżec) 282
Elster, Bela 82 n. 4
Elster, Pola 81 n. 3
emigration of Jews from Poland:
  after 1945 205
  opposition to 208–23
Endecja, see Stronnictwo Narodowe
Engel, David 16, 254
Engel, Samuel 333
Epstein, Krystyna 104–5
Epstein, Simon 418–19, 422
Epstein, Tadeusz 430
Ettinger, Shlomo 359
Etzdorf, Hasso von 122

F
Fajgenbaum, Mrs 92
Falk, Ignacy 211, 216, 220
Fatyga, Barbara 419
Feigenbaum, Israel Isser 387 n. 13
Fein, Helen 9
Feiner, Leon 79, 83, 207
Feix, Reinhold 281 n. 20, 286
Feldman, Wilhelm 374
Ferber, Sanio 279 n. 15
Fichtner (SS man at Bełżec) 281 n. 20
Ficowska, Elżbieta 112, 458
Fiszgrunt, Salomon 207–8, 213–14, 219–20
Folman, Mark, mother of 82 n. 4
Forschpan, Mandel 350
Frank, Hans 12
Frankel, Jonathan 433
Frankist movement 404
Freedom and Independence, see Wolność i Niepodległość
Freedom, Equality, Independence, see Wolność, Równość, Niepodległość
freemasonry, linked with Jewish international conspiracy theory 406
Friedental, citizen 243, 247
Fritsch, Theodor 318
Fromm, Erich 107
Front Odrodzenia Polski (Catholic Front for the Rebirth of Poland) 19, 80
Fuswerk, Klima 82 n. 4

G

Gądecki, Stanisław 402
Gajcy, Tadeusz 173
Gajewski, Stanisław 381
gas chambers, *see* Bełżec
Gazeta Wyborcza 421
Gdańsk 305, 313
Gebert, Konstanty 401
Gelblum, Irena 82 n. 4
General Government 116, 463
General Zionists 80, 84
genocide, Nazi, report of 1942 117–18
Geremek, Bronisław 327, 331–3, 337–40, 342–3
Gerstein, Kurt 119, 268 n. 1, 285 n. 25
Gertner, Halina 82 n. 4
Gerwinski (Stutthof guard) 414
Getzler, Israel 433
ghetto benches 36
Girtzig (SS man at Bełżec) 281 n. 20
Glemp, Cardinal Józef 305 n. 1
Gley, Heinrich 273 n. 7, 281 n. 20
Glikman, Anya 222
Globocnik, Odilo 279 n. 17
Gloss (SS man at Bełżec) 281 n. 20
Głuchowski, Lech 30–1
Gniewoszów, Jewish population in 1945 246
Göckel, Rudolf 272 n. 5
Gocłowski, Archbishop Tadeusz 305 n. 1, 327
Goldberg, Mordka 243, 247
Goldfaden, Avrom (dramatist) 356
Goldschmidt (inmate at Bełżec) 282
Golfarb, Hersh 222
Golub, Jennifer L. 418–19
Gołubiew, Antoni 365
Gombrowicz, Witold 180
Gomułka, Władysław 232, 255
Gordin, Jacob 357
Gordon, Comr. 266
Gordonia 80
Gościński, Comr. 263, 266
Goskind brothers 442
Gotesman, Anna 82 n. 4
Gottesmann, Szymon 81 n. 3
government in exile 84, 258, 463
  policy towards Jews 16
Grafström, Sven 126
Grajek, Stefan 81 n. 3
Granach, Alexander 357, 361
Granowski, Alexander (actor) 357
Green, Joseph 442
Greenberg, Tsevi 435
Grieg, Edvard 374
Grobman, Gary M. 418, 421
Groh (Groth) (SS man at Bełżec) 281 n. 20
Grol, Regina 366–72, 458

Grom-Potyka, Capt. 100
Gross, Adolf 430
Gross, Jan T. 62–4, 194–205, 254, 458
Gross, Natan 166–7, 440–3
Grotkowski, Jan 54–5
Grot-Rowecki, Gen. Stefan 10, 15, 26–7, 70
Grupa Szańca (Rampart Group) 27
Grynbaum, Albert 261 n. 21, 263 n. 24
Gumplowicz, Ludwig 430, 453–4
Gumplowicz family 428
Gutman, Israel 450
Gwardia Ludowa (People's Guard) 27
Gwiazdowicz, Kazimierz 257 n. 13, 259 n. 17

H

Hachaimi, Azriel 435
Hackenholt, Lorenz 277 n. 13
Hafets Hayim 145
Haggberg, Sigge 125
Haller, Józef, army 37, 44
Handelsman, Marceli 98, 334–6
Hanson, Per Albin 125
Hashiloah 435
Hashomer Hatsa'ir 66, 80–1
hasidism 392
  opponents of 425
  in Warsaw 385
Haskalah 425, 427
Hatekufah 435
Hausner, Leopold 92
Haynt 391
Hebrew literature and culture in Poland 434–5
Hebrew Union College 396–7
Hecksher, Eli 336
Herbst, Stanisław 337
Hering, Gottlieb 281 n. 20, 285 n. 24
Herman, David 359–60
Herslow, Carl Wilhelm 125
Herszenhorn, Szlomo 242, 247
Hertz, Aleksander 356, 364
Heschel, Abraham Joshua (1748–1825) 384
Heschel, Abraham Joshua (1832–84) 384
Heschel, Abraham Joshua (1888–1967) 386
Heschel, Abraham Joshua (b. 1907) 383–98
Heschel, Isaac Meir 386
Heschel, Israel 386
Heschel, Jacob 386
Heschel, Meshulam Zusya 386
Heschel, Moses Mordecai 384–6
Heschel, Sholem Joseph 386
Hess, Moses 433
Himmler, Heinrich 123
  and Bełżec death camp 268 n. 1, 279, 281, 284–5, 287
  order to incarcerate Poles 13

settlement policy in the east 115–17
  and Stutthof concentration camp 413
Hirsch, Maurice de 454–5
Hirshaut, Julien 93–4
Hirszenhorn, Szlomo 206–8, 211
Hirszfeld, Bolesław 374
Hirszfeld, Ludwik (immunologist) 374
Hirszfeld, Stanisław 374
Hirszman, Chaim 268
Hitler, July plot against 121–4
Hiż, Henryk 167
Hlond, Cardinal Augustus 17, 47–8, 408
Hochfeld, Julian 213
Hofer, Yehiel 385
Holocaust:
  AK strategy during 26
  denial of 406, 421
  Polish memoirs of 444–6
  Polish response to 5–33
  rabbinic responses to persecution 135–41
  representations of 130, 182
  rescue of Jews: by Poles 25–6; religious orders and 28, 402–3
  term 133 n. 8
  victims as martyrs 128–46
Hoover, Herbert 380–1
Horowitz, Dan 433
Horowitz, Leon 430
Höss, Rudolf 142
Huberband, Shimon 143

I
Ilustrirte vokh 388
Instytut Nauk Judaistycznych (Institute for Jewish Sciences) 394–5
intelligence gathering by Sweden in Nazi Germany 113–27
Irrmann, Franz (Fritz) 273, 278, 281 n. 20, 284–8
Iwaszkiewicz, Jarosław 173, 183
Izrael, Igiel 222

J
Jacobs, Jack 433
Jakubowicz (doctor at Bełżec) 282
Jakubowski, Antoni 44
Jankowski, Czesław 357, 363
Jankowski, Henryk 303–10, 313–17, 320–5, 327–8
Jaracz, Stefan 361
Jastrzą B-Mrożicka, Mirosława 419
Jaszuński, Grzegorz 207
Jaworski, Michał 178
Jedlińsk 238, 249
Jędrzejów, Jewish population in 1945 244

Jeleński, Konstanty A. 188
Jewish Combat Organization, *see* Żydowska Organizacja Bojowa
Jewish Co-ordinating Committee, *see* Żydowski Komitet Koordynacyjny
Jewish Expert Library (Biblioteka Żydoznawcza) 42
Jewish Military Union, *see* Żydowski Związek Wojskowy
Jewish National Committee, *see* Żydowski Komitet Narodowy
Jews, Polish memory of 446–9
Johansson, Sven 120, 122
Joint Distribution Committee (JDC) 80, 447
Judaeo-communism, *see* Żydokomuna
Judenrat 463

K
Kacnelson, Dora 347
Kaftor, Daniel (David Guzik) 81 n. 3
kahal 464
Kahane, Seweryn 237, 242–3, 247, 258 n. 14
Kakowski, Cardinal Aleksander 47, 326
Kalinowski, Comr. 257, 266
Kalisz, anti-Jewish violence in 59, 259–60
Kaltenbergh, Lew 357–8
Kaminska, Esther Rachel 357
Kamiński, Aleksander 19
Kamm (SS man at Bełżec) 281 n. 20
Kaplan, Edward K. 383–98, 458
Kaplan, Harold 187
Karpiński, Rafał 342
Karski, Jan 118, 123
  report of Feb. 1940 14–15, 70–1
Karubin, Comr. 262, 266
Katolicka Agencja Prasowa (Catholic Press Agency) 47
Katyn massacre 73–7, 461
Katzman, Generalmajor 270, 287
Katznelson, Yitshak 435
Kaunas ghetto 135–7
Kautsky, Karl 433
Kenney, Padraic 224–35, 459
Kętrzyński, Stanisław 335
kidush hashem, interpretations of 132–46
Kielce, Jewish population in 1945 245–6
Kielce pogrom 46–50, 52–3, 58–60, 232, 253–67, 461
  aftermath of 195, 202, 213, 232–4
Kielce region, Polish–Jewish relations before the pogrom 236–52
Kieniewicz, Jan 343
Kieślowski, Krzysztof 328
Kimelman, Zofia 82 n. 4

Kleinbaum, Moshe 66, 72
Kleiner, Juliusz 338
Kliszko, Zenon 266
Knoll, Roman 13
Koblik, Steven 119–20, 125–6
Kobzdej, Edward 271 n. 3
Kobzdej, Marjan 271 n. 3
Kofta, Mirosław 419, 423
Kolbe, Maksymilian 402, 406–7
Koło Polskie (Polish Parliamentary Club) 430
Komarnicki, Tytus 377
Komitet Organizacyjny Żydów Polskich (Organizing Committee of Polish Jews: KOŻP) 236
Komunistyczna Partia Polski 375
Kon, Lejb 222
Konopnicka, Maria 374
Kopitzhinitz (Kopychyntse) 386
Korczak, Janusz 163–5, 374
Kosior, Józef 265
Kosminsky, Evgeny A. 341
Kossak-Szczucka, Zofia 19–21, 24, 79–80, 403, 407
Kossower, Emilka 82 n. 4
Koszucki, Dr 260
Kot, Stanisław 71, 191
Kowalczyk, Jan 199
Kowalski, Tadeusz 391 n. 25, 392–3
Kozienice, Jewish population in 1945 245–6
Kozińska-Witt, Hanna 427–31, 453–5
Kozłowski, Comr. 262, 266
Kozłowski, Wacek 414–15
Kracik, Jan 312, 319
Krajewski, Stanisław 323–4, 402, 459
Krajowa Rada Narodowa (National Council: KRN) 181, 206, 209–20, 236
Kraków:
  anti-Jewish violence in 58, 60
  antisemitism in, post-war 199
  pogrom (Aug. 1945) 200–1
  Progressive Synagogue 429
  Reformed commune (*gmina*) 427–31
  Yiddish theatre in 359
Kresy, Jewish reaction to Soviet occupation of 62–72
Kristallnacht 394
Krych, Comr. 261
Krzaklewski, Marian 323
Krzemiński, Ireneusz 419, 423
Krzywicki, Ludwik 374
Kubina, Teodor 57
Kula, Marcin 342
Kula, Witold 337
Kulpińska, Jolanta 419
Kuncewiczowa, Maria 361–3

Kunz (*asker* at Bełżec) 281 n. 20
Kuprel, Diana 459
Kurek-Lesik, Ewa 401–2
Kuźnica (the Forge, group of writers) 29–30
Kuźnica (literary weekly) 181
Kuźnicki, Wiktor 46, 257 n. 13, 259 n. 17
Kwapiński, Jan 191
Kwiecień, Comr. 266

L
La Guardia, Fiorello 380
Lalik, Tadeusz 342
Landau, Hirsz 430
Landau, Ludwik 98
Lange, Oskar 379
Lauder, Ronald 293–4
League for Fighting Youth, *see* Związek Walk Młodych
League of Nations 376–7
Left, Jews and the 433–4
Left Labour Zionists 80, 84
Łęga, Aron 250
Legomski, Comr. 262
Lehndorff, Count Heinrich von 120–3, 126
Lehrer, Shlomo Zalman 139 n. 17
Lemberg, *see* L'viv
Lepek, Helcze 204
Lepek, Icek 204
Lerman, Mrs Miles 139 n. 16
Lesko 461
Lesko, Szolem 55
Leszcz, Chil 243, 246–7
Levaditi, Constantine 375
Levi, Primo 411
Levin, Tuviah 435
Lewandowski, Józef 113–27, 459
Lewental, Mr 250
Lewin, Abraham 33
Lewin, Lejzer 81 n. 3
Lewin, Zofia 450
Lewkowicz, citizen 243
Liberal Hochschule für die Wissenschaft des Judentums 390
Liberfreund, Henryk 196
Liberles, Robert 443–4
Liberman, Gecel 222
Liebman, Arthur 433
Lipszyc, Janina 92
Lissak, Moshe 433
literature, Polish, on the Holocaust 182–7
Łódź 239
  anti-Jewish violence in 53, 261–2
  antisemitism in 230
  demography in 19th c. 225
  poverty in 332–3

strike of 1946 231–2
theatre in 360
Lubetkin, Zivia 81 n. 3
Lusternik, Malkiel 435
L'viv 268–9, 288, 430
　anti-Jewish violence in 54–5
　Jewish quarter 270
　Yiddish theatre in 357–8

M

Mackiewicz, Waldemar 408–9
Mączak, Antoni 343
Mahazikei Hadat 429
Maimonides 143
Main Welfare Council, *see* Rada Główna Opiekuńcza
Majdrowicz, Comr. 259–60
Majzel, Kazimierz 92
Malinowski, Kazimierz 407, 410
Małopolska 464
Małowist, Marian 331–43
　memoirs 147–62
Mały Dziennik 402–3, 407–8
Mandel, Bronisław 243, 247
Mandel, Georges 378
Manteuffel, Tadeusz 339, 343
Margalit, Elkana 433
Margalit, Gilad 419, 422
Mariańska, Miriam 109
Martuzalski, Revd 260
martyrdom as a representative category 128–46
Marx, Karl, attitude towards the Jews 433
Marxism 340
maskilim 425
Mastalerz, Comr. 263, 266
Matywiecki, Anatol 82 n. 4
Mazo, Mordekhai 359
Medzibozh (Medzhybizh) 384, 386
Meisels, Zvi Hirsch 138–9
Mellenthin, Col. von 122
Melzer, Emanuel 431–3
memoirs and diaries 412
　credibility of 65
　demographic evidence of 91, 93
　of the Holocaust 130, 132, 133 n. 8
　Orthodox 135
　see also Birenbaum, Halina; Małowist, Marian; Nałkowska, Zofia; Polisiuk, Leon; Sruoga, Balys; Warm, Ber; Zalewski, Jan
Mendelsburg, Albert 430
Mendelsohn, Ezra 432–4
Merenholc, Helena 82 n. 4, 83 n. 5, 100
Merunowicz, Teofil 430
Mesivta yeshiva 386
Metchnikov, Elie 375

Mich, Włodzimierz 436–40
Michlic-Coren, Joanna 9, 11, 34–61, 253–67, 440, 459
Mickiewicz, Adam 404
Mielnik, Chaja 222
Mijał, Kazimierz 262
Minc, Hilary 232, 260, 379
minorities, ethnic 436–40
　non-Jewish 439–40
Mińsk Mazowiecki, anti-Jewish violence in 55
Mintz, Matityahu 433
Mishkinsky, Moshe 433
mitnagedim 425
Młoda Polska (Young Poland) 179
Młodzież Wszechpolska (All-Polish Youth) 35, 50
Młynarski, Emil 374
Moczar, Mieczysław 262
Modras, Ronald 326, 401–3
Molendowa, Danuta 343
Moniek (engine operator in Bełżec) 277 n. 13
Monnet, Jean 373, 381
Morgenstern, Julian 396
Moskowitz, Maurice 357
Moszkowicz, Riva 82 n. 4
Mowrer, Edgar Ansel 380
Mushkat, Marian 401, 404–5
Musiał, Stanisław 303–9, 310, 313–15, 317–25, 459
Myrdal, Gunnar 364
Myśl Mocarstwowa 51
myths:
　of Jew as enemy of Polish nation 40–4, 49
　of Polish victimhood 49–50
　see also ritual murder

N

Nachbush, Noah 359
Nadler, Shmuel 435
Nahman of Bratslav 426
Nałkowska, Zofia 179–87
Nałkowski, Wacław 179
Napiórkowski, Celestyn 407, 410
Narodowe Siły Zbrojne (National Armed Forces) 27, 39, 98, 204, 258, 261, 267, 338, 421
National Armed Forces, *see* Narodowe Siły Zbrojne
National Council, *see* Krajowa Rada Narodowa
National Democrats, *see* Stronnictwo Narodowe
National Minorities Treaty 436
National Radical Camp, *see* Obóz Narodowo-Radykalny
nationalism and ethnic minorities 438
Nawrocki, Jan 419, 423

Nazism:
　Final Solution 113–27
　term 312, 318–19
neo-Nazism 419
Netaneli-Rotman, Ya'akov 435
Niemcewicz, Julian Ursyn 11
Nissenbaum, Yitzhak 136–7
Norrman, Sven 125
Novominsk (Mińsk-Mazowiecki) 384
Nowakowski, Brunon 379
Nowicka, Ewa 419, 423
numerus clausus 35, 72, 409
numerus nullus 36 n. 11

O

Oberhauser (SS man at Bełżec) 281 n. 20
Obornicki, Andrzej (Stanisław Marczak) 173
Obóz Narodowe-Radykalny (National Radical
　Camp: ONR) 36–7, 52, 437
Obóz Wielkiej Polski 464
Ochotnicze Rezerwy Milicji Obywatelskiej
　(Voluntary Reserve of the Civic Militia:
　ORMO) 258
Oettinger, Józef 429
Ogólno-Żydowski Związek Robotniczy, *see*
　Bund
Olejniczak, Czesław 260
Olkusz district, Jewish population in 1945
　245
Organizing Committee of Polish Jews, *see*
　Komitet Organizacyjny Żydów Polskich
Orsenigo, Archbishop 120 n. 10
Orzeszkowa, Eliza 374
Oshry, Ephraim 135, 137
Osóbka-Morawski, Edward 52, 210
Oster, Gen. Hans 122
Osterwa, Juliusz 358–9
Ostrowiec, Jewish population in 1945 245
Ostrowiec Świętokrzyski 56 n. 83
Ostrowski, Dezydery 44, 45
Oz, Amos 363 n. 3

P

Paczkowski, Andrzej 30–1, 254
Paderewski, Ignacy 374, 377
Palestine, immigration to 211–14
Palnetovsky, Noah 435
Pamiętnik Teatralny 356
Parasol, citizen 243, 247
Parfal, Michael 314, 320
Passenstein, Marek 100
Pate, Maurice 380–1
Paulsson, Gunnar S. 78–103, 451, 460
Pawlikowski, John T. 401, 460
Peleg, Mordecai 109

Peleg, Yaron 443
Penkalla, Adam 236–52, 460
People's Army, *see* Armia Ludowa
People's Guard, *see* Gwardia Ludowa
Perdurant, Daniel 419
Perets, Y. L. 360
Peretz, Maya 356–65, 460
Perko, Lt. 260
Perl, Joseph 425–7
Perlow, Alter Israel Simeon 386
Perlow, Jacob 384
Pfannenstiel, Wilhelm 268 n. 1, 285 n. 25
Pfefferberg, Marta 92
philosemitism in Poland 404
Piątek, Brunon 59
Pieńkowska, Ewa 183
Pieronek, Bishop Tadeusz 313, 324–5
Piłsudski, Józef 374
Pirenne, Henri 340
Pirotte, Julia 59
Piszczakowski, Michał 92
Po'alei Zion-Left 215
Pobóg-Malinowski, Władysław 22, 336
poetry, Hebrew 434–5
poetry, Yiddish 388, 390–2
pogroms:
　of 1881–2 433
　see also Kielce; Przytyk; Siedlce
Pokrovsky, Mikhail N. 340
Polish army, Jews in 74–5
Polish Committee of National Liberation,
　see Polski Komitet Wyzwolenia
　Narodowego
Polish Peasant Party, *see* Polskie Stronnictwo
　Ludowe
Polish Red Cross 80
Polish Scouts 81
Polish Socialist Party, *see* Polska Partia
　Socjalistyczna
Polish Socialists, *see* Polscy Socjaliści
Polish Union of Fighters for Freedom and
　Democracy, *see* Związek Bojowników za
　Wolność i Demokrację
Polish United Workers' Party, *see* Polska
　Zjednoczona Partia Robotnicza
Polish Workers' Party, *see* Polska Partia
　Robotnicza
Polish–Jewish relations:
　1935–9 431–3
　after 1945 194–205
　in Kielce and Radom, 1945–6 236–52
Polish–Soviet relations in 1943 190
Polisiuk, Leon, ghetto memoirs 100
Polonsky, Antony 3–33, 347, 433, 460
Polscy Socjaliści (Polish Socialists) 81

Polska Partia Robotnicza (Polish Workers' Party: PPR) 18, 32, 38, 80, 86, 207, 226, 231–4, 254–6, 261–2, 264, 266
 Jewish fraction and the Bund 208–23
Polska Partia Socjalistyczna (Polish Socialist Party: PPS) 44, 81, 86
Polska Zjednoczona Partia Robotnicza 222–3, 254–5
Polski Komitet Wyzwolenia Narodowego (Polish Committee of National Liberation: PKWN) 206
Polskie Stronnictwo Ludowe (Polish Peasant Party: PSL) 232
Polskie Stronnictwo Ludowe—Piast 437
Pomerantz, Berl 435
Post, Erik von 115, 122, 124–5
Postan, Michel 341
Potocki, Jerzy 378
prayer, Heschel on 397–8
Prekerowa, Teresa 25–6, 85, 450–1
press, Catholic:
 responses to anti-Jewish violence 47
 and ritual murder accusations 56
press, Jewish 409
press, Polish, antisemitism in 42–3
prisoners of war, Polish, in 1939 73–7
Prus, Bolesław 374
Przytyk pogrom 45, 47, 55
Ptaszek, Kazimierz 100
Putowski, Lejb 207

R

Rada Główna Opiekuńcza (Main Welfare Council: RGO) 79–80, 86
Rada Pomocy Żydom (Council for Aid to the Jews; Żegota) 24–5, 79–81, 83–5, 91, 94, 97, 99, 100, 102, 104–5, 113, 403, 450
Radensky, Paul 427
Radkiewicz, Stanisław 31
Radlińska, Helena 374
Radom:
 Jewish cemetery 240, 249
 Jewish population in 1945 246
 synagogue 240
Radom region:
 Polish–Jewish relations in 1945–6 237–42
 situation of Jews in 1945 248–52
Rajchman, Alexander (father of Ludwik) 374
Rajchman, Alexander (son of Ludwik) 374
Rajchman, Ludwik 373–82
Rajchman, Ludwik (son of Ludwik) 374
Rajchman, Melania 374
Rampart Group, see Grupa Szańca
Rappoport, Arnold 430

Rathajzer, Symcha (Simcha Rotem, 'Kazik') 82 n. 4
Ravitch, Melekh 388
Reale, Eugenio 210
Reder, Bronisław 269
Reder, Rudolf 268–89
Reder, Sophia 269
Referat Pomocy Ludności Żydowskiej (Department of Assistance to the Jewish Population) 206
Reizel Perlow, Rivka 384
Rek, Tadeusz 83
resistance, Polish 28
Revisionist Zionists 80
Revolutionary Party of Polish Socialists, see Rewolucyjna Partia Polskich Socjalistów
Rewolucyjna Partia Polskich Socjalistów (Revolutionary Party of Polish Socialists) 81
Reymont, Władysław Stanisław 332
Ribbentrop, Joachim von 115, 118
Richert, Arvid 118, 124–5
Right Labour Zionists 80, 84
Ringelblum, Emanuel 6, 25, 26, 81 n. 3, 91, 93, 99, 168, 337
Ringelblum, Judyta 100
Ringelblum Archive 67–8, 141, 147
ritual murder accusations 56–61, 197, 200–2, 233, 256, 258–9, 262, 332, 406–7
Robak, Roman 269
Robinson, Ira 444
Rodziewicz, Aleksander 360
Rolle, Hieronim 272 n. 5
Romer, Tadeusz 379
Rosman, Moshe 426
Rost, Nella 268–9
Rostropowicz Clark, Joanna 166–78, 461
Roth, Jakub 82 n. 4
Rottenstreich, Fiszel 432
Rougemont, Denis de 371
Rozenberg, Szulim 385 n. 6
Rubel, M. M. 268–9, 461
Ruch Młodych Obozu Wielkiej Polski (Camp for a Greater Poland: OWP) 35, 39, 51, 54
Rutkowski, Jan 335
Rycerz Niepokalanej 407, 409
Ryncarz, Władysław 201

S

Sacks, John 30
Salaj, Antoni 59
Samelson, Szymon 429–30
Samsonowicz, Henryk 343
Sanacja 437, 464
Sandauer, Artur 30

Sandomierz, Jewish population in 1945 244, 246
Sapieha, Bishop 47
Sare, Józef 430
Schenker, Amalia 196
Schiller, Leon 359–60
Schiper, Ignacy 395
Schlabrendorff, Fabian von 121–2
Schluch (SS man at Bełżec) 281 n. 20
Schlüssel (inmate at Bełżec) 282
Schmidt, Christian (Heni) 279–82, 284, 286, 288
Schneersohn, Fishl 387–8
Schneider (*asker* at Bełżec) 281 n. 20
Schneiderman, S. L. 359
Schneur Zalman of Lyady 426
Schnitzer, Gusta 198
Schochet, Simon 73–7, 461
Schorr, Mojżesz (Moses) 394–5, 453–5
Schreiber (Jewish worker at Bełżec) 278
Schreiber, Szymon 429
Schulz, Bruno 179
Schwarz, Gottfried 281 n. 20, 284, 286
scouting organizations 216
Security Office (UB) 251, 257–8, 262
    Jews in 30–1, 230
Sędek, Grzegorz 419, 423
Sehn, Jan 269, 277 n. 13, 281 n. 20
Sejm 464
Sejm PRL 181
Sejm Ustawodawczy 181
separateness, Jewish, in Stryjkowski's novels 366–72
Serejski, Marian 340
Seselga (Stutthof guard) 417
Sha'arei torah: kovets rabani ḥodeshi 387
Shakespeare, William 360
Shapira, Anita 433
Shapiro, Leonard 433
Shelley, Lore 184
Shmeruk, Chone 448–9
Shoham, Matityahu Moshe 435
Shomer Yisrael 430
Shpilevoy, Col. 257 n. 13
Shtein, Shlomo 435
Shtokhammer, Natan Neta 435
Siberia, deportation of Jews to in 1940 64
Siedlce, pogrom in 347–55
Sienkiewicz, Henryk 374
Sikorski, Gen. Władysław 15, 23, 378
Siła-Nowicki, Władysław 6–8
Silberner, Edmund 433
Singer, Isaac Bashevis 446–8
Sinko, Tadeusz 359
Skarżysko, Jewish population in 1945 244
Skibiński, Franciszek 336

Skif 216
skinhead culture 420, 423
Sliwiński, Krzysztof 402
Słonimski, Antoni 327
Slowes, Salomon W. 75–6
Słuszny, S. 47
Smolar, Grzegorz 217–18
Sobczyński, Władysław 46, 257, 266
Sobibór 277 n. 14, 287 n. 30, 288 n. 34
Social Self-Help Organization, *see* Społeczna Organizacja Samopomocy
socialism 333, 433–4
Söderblom, Staffan 125
Solomon Hayim of Koidanov 384
Sołowicz, Helena 92
Solska, Irena 360
Sołtan, Tadeusz 169–70, 173
Sommerstein, Emil 209–10
Soong, T. V. 377–9
Soprunienko, Major 74, 76
Sowiński, Comr. 262
Spilke (inmate of Bełżec) 289
Społeczna Organizacja Samopomocy (Social Self-Help Organization: SOS) 80, 86
Sruoga, Balys, concentration camp memoirs 411–17
Stachacz, Comr. 263, 266
Starachowice, Jewish population in 1945 246
Stauffenberg, Count Claus von 121
Steinberg, Baruch 75
Steinberg, Dina 337
Steinlauf, Michael C. 444–6
Steinman, Eliezer 435
Stemplowski, Ryszard 331–9, 341–3
Stempowski, Jerzy 361
stereotypes of the pro-Soviet and anti-Polish Jew 11
Stoecker, Adolf 303, 310–11, 317–18
Strauss, Richard 374
Strieder, Jacob 340
Stronnictwo Ludowe 201
Stronnictwo Narodowe (National Democrats; Endecja; SN) 21, 35, 437, 439, 463
    and anti-Jewish boycott 40
    attitudes to Jews 40–2
    encouragement of anti-Jewish violence 37
Stronnictwo Pracy (Party of Labour) 437
Stryjkowski, Julian 366–72
Strzyżów 56 n. 83
Stutthof concentration camp 411–17
suicide:
    rabbinic opinions on 136–7
    as sacrifice 133
survivors of Holocaust, psychological problems of 104–11

Index

Swianiewicz, Stanisław 76
Świebocka, Teresa 290–9, 461
Święch, Jerzy 170
Swoleń, Jewish population in 1945 245
synagogue, changes in ritual of 428
Szare Szeregi 81, 177
Szaynok, Bożena 206–23, 254, 461
Szemiński, Jan 342
Szenwic, Leokadia 92
Szlajfer, Henryk 331, 340
Szmulak, Chaim 222
Sztajer, Jakub 222
Szuldenfrei, Michał 207–10, 215, 217, 219–20
Szydłowiec 239, 245
Szylkdraut, M. 47
Szymańczak, Michał 419
Szymanowski, Zygmunt 379

T
Tajtelbaum, Wolf 222
Talpir, Gabriel Joseph 435
Tarski, Alfred 374
Taylor, Dov 425–7
Teitelman, Moshe 435
Temporary Committee to Aid Jews, *see* Tymczasowy Komitet Pomocy Żydom
Tenenbaum, Judka 244
Tenenbaum, Mordekhai 5
theatre, Jewish, in Poland before the Second World War 356–65
Threatening Other, myth of 40–4, 49–50
Tilles, Samuel 430
Tobias, Henry 433
Toczek, Ewa 342
Tomaszewski, Jerzy 406, 433–4, 446, 461
Tomaszewski, Stefan 43, 260–1
Tonecki, Zygmunt 360–1
Trawkowski, Stanisław 342
Trawniki labour camp 91, 280 n. 18
Treblinka 140, 277 n. 14, 287 n. 30
Tresckow, Gen. Henning von 121–4, 126
Trottwein (*asker* at Bełżec) 281 n. 20
Trunk, Isaiah 141
Trzeciak, Stanisław 43
Tschudner, Meir 435
Tsentraler Bildungs-Komitet 389
Tsukunft (Bund's youth organization) 208, 216, 221
tsukunft, Di (Yiddish monthly) 390
Turkow, Zygmunt 359
Turowicz, Jerzy 311
Tuszyńska, Agata 446–9
Tuwim, Julian 327–8
Tykocinska, Joanna 82 n. 4

Tymczasowy Komitet Pomocy Żydom (Temporary Committee to Aid Jews) 79
Tymowski, Michał 331, 334–5, 340–3

U
Udrenas, Nerijus 411–17, 462
underground, Polish 167–8, 175–7, 190, 451
aid to Jews 97
Unicef 373, 377, 380–2
Union of Rabbis of the Polish Republic, *see* Związek Rabinów Rzeczypospolitej
UNRRA 379–80
Upfal, Kajta 222

V
Varshaver shriftn 388
Vendel, Karl Yngve, report on Poland in 1942 114–27
Verbner, Avraham Dov 435
Verlinden, Charles 341
victimhood, Jewish 128–46
Vilna 388–9
Soviet arrival in 66
Vogler, Henryk 186
Volksdeutsch 225–6, 228–9
Volovici, Leon 418
Voluntary Reserve of the Civic Militia, *see* Ochotnicze Rezerwy Milicji Obywatelskiej

W
Wacławki, Stanisław 50–2
Wajda, Andrzej 332
Wajnsztok, citizen 247
Wałbrzych 215
Wallenberg, Raoul 125–6
Wallerstein, Immanuel 342
Warm, Ber, ghetto memoirs 100
Warman, Avram 81 n. 3
Warsaw:
  demography of Jews in hiding 78–103
  Pawiak prison 93–5, 100
  Yiddish theatre in 356–7, 360
Warsaw ghetto 141, 143, 337
  uprising 176
Warsaw Housing Co-operative, *see* Warszawska Spółdzielnia Mieszkaniowa
Warschauer, Jonatan 429–30
Warszawska Spółdzielnia Mieszkaniowa (Warsaw Housing Co-operative: WSM) 81, 86
Wasersztrum, Jakub 215, 218
Wasilewski, Zbigniew 177
Wasser, Hirsch 81, 83, 87, 101–2
Ważyk, Adam 30
Webber, Jonathan 128–46, 462

Wegmajster, Lota 82 n. 4
Weichert, Michał 359–61
Weinfeld, David 434–5
Weintraub, Jerzy Kamil 169
Weintraub, Joanna 169–70, 175
Widerszal, Ludwik 335
Wielkopolska 464
Wielkopolska army 37, 44
Wiener, Moshe 435
Wiernik, Jakub 82 n. 4
Wieśniak, Stanisław 55
Wilska-Duszyńska, Barbara 423
Wirth, Christian 274 n. 9, 279 n. 17, 285 n. 24
Wiślicz, Comr. 257–8, 266
Witaszewski, Kazimierz 232
Włocławek 204
Włoszczowa, Jewish population in 1945 246
Wójcik, Włodzimierz 182
Wolf, Friedrich 361
Woliński, Henryk 100
Wolman, Alina 450
Wolność i Niepodległość (Freedom and Independence: WiN) 204
Wolność, Równość, Niepodległość (Freedom, Equality, Independence) 81
Woźnicki, Comr. 263, 265–6
Wrona, Zenon 254
Wyka, Kazimierz 31, 167, 169–70, 173, 175
Wyleżyńska, Aurelia 21
Wyrobisz, Andrzej 343
Wyspiański, Stanisław 359
Wyszyński, Cardinal Stefan 29, 47–8

Y

Yiddish language 211, 426
Yishuv 464
Yoskovitz, Avraham Iser 435
Young Poland, see Młoda Polska
youth organizations, post-war 215–16
Yung Vilne 389

Z

Zachariasz, Szymon 211, 217–20
Zajdenszir, Jakub 240 n. 22
Zak, Józef 81 n. 3
Załek, Wiktor 168
Zaleski, August 376
Zalewski, Jan, memoirs of Soviet occupation 69
Zambrowski, Roman 217
Zarecki, Pres. 265
Zawadzki, Major 261 n. 21
Zawodny, Janusz 75
Zbąszyń 394
Żbikowski, Andrzej 62–72, 431, 462
Żebrowski, Rafał 453–5
Żegota, see Rada Pomocy Żydom
Zeitlin, Aaron 435
Zelcer, Ludwika 92
Zelek, R. 48–9
Zeliwski, H. 242
Zelwerowicz, Aleksander 359
Zerubavel, Yaacov 208
Zespół Literacki Przedmieście 179
Zhukov, Gen. 191
Zieleńczyk, Adam 166
Ziemba, Menahem 137
Ziemian, Janina 76
Zientara, Benedykt 343
Zionism 320
  and the Bund 220
  Soviet policy against 433
Zionist Revisionists 84
Zirke (Zierke) (SS man at Bełżec) 281 n. 20
Zucker (dentist at Bełżec) 279
Zuckerman, 'Antek' 100, 102
Zuckerman, Yitzhak 195, 207, 210
Związek Bojowników za Wolność i Demokrację (Polish Union of Fighters for Freedom and Democracy: ZBoWiD) 450
Związek Rabinów Rzeczypospolitej (Union of Rabbis of the Polish Republic) 47
Związek Walk Młodych (League for Fighting Youth) 209
Żydokomuna (Judaeo-communism) 11, 47, 71, 194, 234, 311, 405
Żydowska Organizacja Bojowa (Jewish Combat Organization: ŻOB) 27, 79–80
Żydowski Komitet Koordynacyjny (Jewish Co-ordinating Committee: ŻKK) 79–80
Żydowski Komitet Narodowy (Jewish National Committee: ŻKN) 78–81, 83–5, 91, 94, 99–100
Żydowski Związek Wojskowy (Jewish Military Union) 27
Zygmund, Antoni 374
Zysman, Joseph 82 n. 4

www.ingramcontent.com/pod-product-compliance
Ingram Content Group UK Ltd.
Pitfield, Milton Keynes, MK11 3LW, UK
UKHW021316180426
11947UKWH00015B/1253